WORLD TOURISM ORGANIZATION
ORGANISATION MONDIALE DU TOURISME
ORGANIZACION MUNDIAL DEL TURISMO
ВСЕМИРНАЯ ТУРИСТСКАЯ ОРГАНИЗАЦИЯ

Compendium of Tourism Statistics

(2001 - 2005)

2007 Edition

Compendium of Tourism Statistics, 2007 Edition – Data 2001–2005
ISBN 13: 978-92-844-1227-3

Published and printed by the World Tourism Organization, Madrid, Spain
First printing: 2007

World Tourism Organization
Calle Capitán Haya, 42
28020 Madrid, Spain
Tel.: (+34) 915 678 100
Fax: (+34) 915 713 733
Website: www.unwto.org
Email: omt@unwto.org

Disclaimer

The World Tourism Organization gives no warranty that the information or data supplied contains no errors. However, all care and diligence has been used in processing, analysing and extracting the information.

Compendium of Tourism Statistics

Data 2001-2005

2007 Edition

TABLE OF CONTENTS

TABLE OF CONTENTS

INTRODUCTION

The Compendium of Tourism Statistics has been prepared by the UNWTO Department of Statistics and Economic Measurement of Tourism. It provides statistical information on tourism in 208 countries and territories around the world. This is the twenty-seventh in a series that began in 1975 as a biennial publication; it has been issued annually since 1986.

The present edition of the Compendium of Tourism Statistics is edited in English only, with countries classified according to English alphabetical order. For easy reference in Arabic, French, German, Russian and Spanish, the text of the basic indicators and the basic references has been printed in a separate pasteboard.

The statistical data published are those officially received from national tourism administrations, national statistical offices and international organizations (International Monetary Fund and World Bank).

All the data received are subject to different kind of controls:

- Comparison with the data provided at a previous moment, but referred to the same period;
- Comparison of the total figures with the corresponding breakdown;
- Comparison of the same figures with the corresponding breakdown by concepts;
- Control for logic consistency between data;
- Control for percentage variation to remain acceptable.

Any discrepancies observed are consulted with the informing unit that confirms or rectifies, if necessary, the data previously sent.

Due to the rounding in the partial figures, the totals shown in the different tables of the Yearbook of Tourism Statistics may not coincide with the totals shown in the basic indicators of the Compendium of Tourism Statistics.

Statistical data on individual countries are grouped under:

- Inbound tourism
- Domestic tourism
- Outbound tourism
- Tourism industries
- Related indicators

Consequently, **the data included in this Compendium have an official character and have been entered in the UNWTO database as of 31 March 2007**. Therefore, any corrections or changes received after this date will be included in the next edition of the Compendium.

The Compendium is designed to provide a condensed and quick-reference guide on the major tourism statistical indicators in each country. Users who wish to obtain more detailed statistics than those presented here are invited to consult other statistical publications of UNWTO, or visit the UNWTO website: *http://www.unwto.org*.

The World Tourism Organization wishes to express its gratitude to the national tourism administrations, national statistical offices of the various countries and territories and the above-mentioned international organizations for their valuable co-operation.

Madrid, April 2007

INTRODUCTION

La Section Statistiques et mesure économique du tourisme de l'OMT est chargée d'élaborer le Compendium des statistiques du tourisme. Ce dernier fournit des informations statistiques sur le tourisme dans 208 pays et territoires du monde entier. Il s'agit de la vingt-septième édition d'une publication bisannuelle lancée en 1975, qui est devenue annuelle à partir de 1986.

Cette édition du Compendium des statistiques du tourisme n'est publiée qu'en anglais, avec les pays classés dans l'ordre alphabétique anglais. Pour l'allemand, l'arabe, l'espagnol, le français et le russe, le texte des indicateurs de base et des références de base figure à part dans un fascicule.

Les données publiées sont celles officiellement reçues des administrations nationales du tourisme, des instituts nationaux de la statistique et d'autres organisations internationales (Fonds monétaire international et Banque mondiale).

Toutes les données reçues sont soumises à différents types de contrôle:

- comparaison avec les données fournies précédemment pour la même période,
- comparaison des totaux et de leur ventilation,
- comparaison des mêmes chiffres avec la ventilation correspondante par concepts,
- contrôle de la cohérence logique des données,
- contrôle de l'acceptabilité, compte tenu du pourcentage de variation.

Les anomalies éventuellement relevées sont consultées avec l'unité chargée de l'information qui confirme ou, au besoin, rectifie les données envoyées.

Etant donné l'arrondissement des données partielles, les totaux qui apparaissent dans les différents tableaux de l'Annuaire des statistiques du tourisme peuvent ne pas correspondre aux totaux des Indicateurs de base du Compendium des statistiques du tourisme.

Les données statistiques des divers pays sont regroupées sous les rubriques suivantes :

- Tourisme récepteur
- Tourisme interne
- Tourisme émetteur
- Filières touristiques
- Indicateurs apparentés

En conséquence, **les données figurant dans le présent Compendium ont un caractère officiel et ont été introduites dans la base de données de l'OMT jusqu'à la date limite du 31 mars 2007.** Toute correction ou modification reçue après cette date sera incorporée à la prochaine édition du Compendium.

De par sa conception, le Compendium est un condensé rapidement consultable des principaux indicateurs statistiques du tourisme de chaque pays. Les utilisateurs souhaitant obtenir des statistiques plus détaillées que celles présentées ici sont invités à consulter les autres publications de l'OMT dans le domaine des statistiques ou à visiter le site Internet de l'OMT (*http://www.unwto.org*).

L'Organisation mondiale du tourisme tient à exprimer sa gratitude aux administrations nationales du tourisme, aux instituts nationaux de la statistique des divers pays et territoires et aux organisations internationales mentionnées plus haut pour leur précieuse coopération.

Madrid, avril 2007

INTRODUCCION

La Sección de Estadísticas y Evaluación Económica del Turismo de la OMT es la encargada de elaborar el Compendio de Estadísticas de Turismo. Esta publicación ofrece información estadística sobre el turismo en 208 países y territorios de todo el mundo. Este número es el vigésimo séptimo de una serie que comenzó en 1975 como publicación bienal y siguió publicándose desde 1986 anualmente.

La presente edición del Compendio de Estadísticas de Turismo sólo se edita en inglés, con clasificación de los países en el orden alfabético correspondiente a este idioma. Para una fácil referencia en alemán, árabe, español, francés y ruso, el texto de los indicadores básicos y las referencias básicas han sido impresas sobre cartulina por separado.

Los datos publicados son los remitidos oficialmente por las administraciones nacionales de turismo, los institutos nacionales de estadística y las organizaciones internacionales (Fondo Monetario Internacional y Banco Mundial).

Todos los datos recibidos están sujetos a diversos controles:

- comparación con los datos facilitados con anterioridad y referidos al mismo periodo;
- comparación de los totales con el desglose correspondiente;
- comparación de las mismas cifras con el desglose correspondiente por conceptos;
- control de coherencia lógica entre diferentes datos;
- control de mantenimiento de aceptabilidad, cuenta habida del porcentaje de variación.

Se consultan todas las discrepancias con la unidad informante, la cual confirma o rectifica, si es necesario, los datos remitidos.

Debido al redondeo de las cifras parciales, los totales que aparecen en los distintos cuadros del Anuario de Estadísticas del Turismo, pueden no coincidir con los totales que aparecen en los Indicadores Básicos del Compendio de Estadísticas del Turismo.

Los datos estadísticos correspondientes a cada país se agrupan de la siguiente forma:

- Turismo receptor
- Turismo interno
- Turismo emisor
- Actividades turísticas
- Indicadores relacionados

Así pues, **las cifras incluidas en este Compendio tienen carácter oficial y han sido introducidas en la base de datos de la OMT al 31 de marzo de 2007**. Por consiguiente, cualquier corrección o cambio recibido después de esta fecha aparecerá en la próxima edición del Compendio.

El Compendio está concebido como guía resumida y de referencia rápida sobre los principales indicadores estadísticos de turismo de cada país. Los usuarios que deseen obtener estadísticas más detalladas pueden consultar otras publicaciones estadísticas de la OMT o visitar el sitio de Internet: *http://www.unwto.org*.

La Organización Mundial del Turismo quiere expresar su gratitud a las administraciones nacionales de turismo, a los institutos nacionales de estadística de los diversos países y territorios y a las organizaciones internacionales mencionadas anteriormente por su valiosa colaboración.

Madrid, abril de 2007

Country tables
2001-2005

Basic Indicators		Units	2001	2002	2003	2004	2005
	INBOUND TOURISM						
	Arrivals						
1.1	Visitors	('000)	354	470	557	645	748
1.2	Tourists (overnight visitors)	('000)	34	36	41	42	46
1.3	Same-day visitors	('000)	..	..	..	..	..
1.4	Cruise passengers	('000)	..	..	..	..	..
	Arrivals by region						
2.1	Africa	('000)	..	..	..	..	..
2.2	Americas	('000)	14	16	19	26	35
2.3	Europe	('000)	320	439	532	610	703
2.4	East Asia and the Pacific	('000)	2	3	4	4	5
2.5	South Asia	('000)	..	..	..	..	..
2.6	Middle East	('000)	1	1	1	1	1
	Arrivals by means of transport used						
3.1	Air	('000)	91	80	87	103	128
3.2	Rail	('000)	..	..	..	..	..
3.3	Road	('000)	160	279	351	404	490
3.4	Sea	('000)	103	111	120	139	130
	Arrivals by purpose of visit						
4.1	Leisure, recreation and holidays	('000)	150	262	310	415	430
4.2	Business and professional	('000)	97	100	88	63	68
4.3	Other	('000)	93	108	160	167	250
	Accommodation						
5.1	Overnight stays in hotels and similar establishments	('000)	91	143	137	140	176
5.2	Guests in hotels and similar establishments	('000)	34	36	41	42	46
5.3	Overnight stays in all types of accommodation establishments	('000)	..	..	..	..	..
5.4	Average length of stay of non-resident tourists in all accommodation establishments	Nights	2.70	3.97	3.34	3.57	3.60
6.1	**Tourism expenditure in the country**	US$ Mn	451	492	537	756	880
6.2	"Travel" (*)	US$ Mn	446	487	522	735	854
6.3	"Passenger transport" (*)	US$ Mn	5	5	15	21	26
	DOMESTIC TOURISM						
	Accommodation						
7.1	Overnight stays in hotels and similar establishments	('000)	303	390	410	442	480
7.2	Guests in hotels and similar establishments	('000)	136	135	137	146	164
7.3	Overnight stays in all types of accommodation establishments	('000)	..	..	..	..	..
7.4	Average length of stay of resident tourists in all accommodation establishments	Nights	2.20	2.90	3.00	3.20	2.90
	OUTBOUND TOURISM						
8.1	**Departures**	('000)	955	1,303	1,350	1,694	2,097
8.2	**Tourism expenditure in other countries**	US$ Mn	269	387	507	668	808
8.3	"Travel" (*)	US$ Mn	257	366	489	641	786
8.4	"Passenger transport" (*)	US$ Mn	12	21	18	27	22
	TOURISM INDUSTRIES						
	Hotels and similar establishments						
9.1	Number of rooms	Units	3,881	4,107	4,161	4,200	4,226
9.2	Number of bed-places	Units	7,677	7,996	8,420	8,500	8,670
9.3	Occupancy rate	Percent	29.00	41.00	42.00	45.00	45.00
9.4	Average length of stay	Nights	2.20	2.10	2.10	2.20	2.30
	RELATED INDICATORS						
	Share of tourism expenditure (6.1) in:						
10.1	Gross Domestic Product (GDP)	Percent	11.0	11.0	9.6	10.1	10.5
10.2	Exports of goods	Percent	147.9	149.1	120.1	125.4	134.1
10.3	Exports of services	Percent	84.5	84.1	74.6	75.4	75.5

(*) Balance of Payments items: 6.1 to 6.3 correspond to the "Credit" side (and are receipts for the country) while 8.2 to 8.4 correspond to the "Debit" side (and are expenditures in other countries).

ALGERIA

	Basic Indicators		Units	2001	2002	2003	2004	2005
	INBOUND TOURISM							
	Arrivals							
1.1	Visitors		('000)	901	988	1,166	1,234	1,443
1.2	Tourists (overnight visitors)		('000)	..	..	..	..	..
1.3	Same-day visitors		('000)	..	..	..	..	..
1.4	Cruise passengers		('000)	..	..	..	..	..
	Arrivals by region							
2.1	Africa		('000)	63	72	112	131	161
2.2	Americas		('000)	3	5	5	7	8
2.3	Europe		('000)	107	140	157	198	228
2.4	East Asia and the Pacific		('000)	5	9	8	9	15
2.5	South Asia		('000)	..	..	..	..	..
2.6	Middle East		('000)	18	24	23	23	29
	Arrivals by means of transport used							
3.1	Air		('000)	403	456	..	..	..
3.2	Rail		('000)	..	..	..	..	..
3.3	Road		('000)	295	210	..	..	..
3.4	Sea		('000)	203	322	..	..	..
	Arrivals by purpose of visit							
4.1	Leisure, recreation and holidays		('000)	..	..	240	267	323
4.2	Business and professional		('000)	..	..	65	101	118
4.3	Other		('000)	..	..	..	..	..
	Accommodation							
5.1	Overnight stays in hotels and similar establishments		('000)	226	292	371	394	483
5.2	Guests in hotels and similar establishments		('000)	..	..	..	..	..
5.3	Overnight stays in all types of accommodation establishments		('000)	..	..	..	..	..
5.4	Average length of stay of non-resident tourists in all accommodation establishments		Nights	..	..	..	..	..
6.1	**Tourism expenditure in the country**	(**)	US$ Mn	100	110	112	178	184
6.2	"Travel" (*)		US$ Mn	..	..	..	..	..
6.3	"Passenger transport" (*)		US$ Mn	..	..	..	..	..
	DOMESTIC TOURISM							
	Accommodation							
7.1	Overnight stays in hotels and similar establishments		('000)	4,028	2,959	3,948	4,149	4,222
7.2	Guests in hotels and similar establishments		('000)	..	..	..	..	..
7.3	Overnight stays in all types of accommodation establishments		('000)	..	..	..	..	..
7.4	Average length of stay of resident tourists in all accommodation establishments		Nights	..	..	..	..	..
	OUTBOUND TOURISM							
8.1	**Departures**		('000)	1,190	1,257	1,254	1,417	1,513
8.2	**Tourism expenditure in other countries**	(**)	US$ Mn	194	248	255	394	370
8.3	"Travel" (*)		US$ Mn	..	..	..	..	..
8.4	"Passenger transport" (*)		US$ Mn	..	..	..	..	..
	TOURISM INDUSTRIES							
	Hotels and similar establishments							
9.1	Number of rooms		Units	..	..	..	..	..
9.2	Number of bed-places		Units	66,523	72,567	77,473	82,034	83,895
9.3	Occupancy rate		Percent	..	..	..	..	..
9.4	Average length of stay		Nights	3.39	4.02	4.79	3.13	4.00
	RELATED INDICATORS							
	Share of tourism expenditure (6.1) in:							
10.1	Gross Domestic Product (GDP)		Percent	..	..	..	..	..
10.2	Exports of goods		Percent	..	..	..	..	..
10.3	Exports of services		Percent	..	..	..	..	..

(*) Balance of Payments items: 6.1 to 6.3 correspond to the "Credit" side (and are receipts for the country) while 8.2 to 8.4 correspond to the "Debit" side (and are expenditures in other countries).

(**) See Annex "Country notes".

Basic Indicators		Units	2001	2002	2003	2004	2005
	INBOUND TOURISM						
	Arrivals						
1.1	Visitors	('000)	..	..	..	..	..
1.2	Tourists (overnight visitors)	('000)	36.0	..	..	..	24.5
1.3	Same-day visitors	('000)	..	..	..	..	..
1.4	Cruise passengers	('000)	4.9	2.8	8.2	3.5	6.1
	Arrivals by region						
2.1	Africa	('000)	..	..	..	..	..
2.2	Americas	('000)	7.3	..	..	..	6.9
2.3	Europe	('000)	0.5	..	..	..	0.4
2.4	East Asia and the Pacific	('000)	28.1	..	..	..	16.9
2.5	South Asia	('000)	..	..	..	..	..
2.6	Middle East	('000)	..	..	..	..	..
	Arrivals by means of transport used						
3.1	Air	('000)	..	..	..	..	..
3.2	Rail	('000)	..	..	..	..	..
3.3	Road	('000)	..	..	..	..	..
3.4	Sea	('000)	..	..	..	..	..
	Arrivals by purpose of visit						
4.1	Leisure, recreation and holidays	('000)	6.5	..	..	..	7.0
4.2	Business and professional	('000)	7.7	..	..	..	4.4
4.3	Other	('000)	21.8	..	..	..	13.1
	Accommodation						
5.1	Overnight stays in hotels and similar establishments	('000)	..	..	..	..	..
5.2	Guests in hotels and similar establishments	('000)	..	..	..	..	..
5.3	Overnight stays in all types of accommodation establishments	('000)	..	..	..	..	..
5.4	Average length of stay of non-resident tourists in all accommodation establishments	Nights	..	..	..	..	..
6.1	**Tourism expenditure in the country**	US$ Mn	..	..	..	..	..
6.2	"Travel" (*)	US$ Mn	..	..	..	..	..
6.3	"Passenger transport" (*)	US$ Mn	..	..	..	..	..
	DOMESTIC TOURISM						
	Accommodation						
7.1	Overnight stays in hotels and similar establishments	('000)	..	..	..	..	..
7.2	Guests in hotels and similar establishments	('000)	..	..	..	..	..
7.3	Overnight stays in all types of accommodation establishments	('000)	..	..	..	..	..
7.4	Average length of stay of resident tourists in all accommodation establishments	Nights	..	..	..	..	..
	OUTBOUND TOURISM						
8.1	**Departures**	('000)	44	..	..	..	35
8.2	**Tourism expenditure in other countries**	US$ Mn	..	..	..	..	..
8.3	"Travel" (*)	US$ Mn	..	..	..	..	..
8.4	"Passenger transport" (*)	US$ Mn	..	..	..	..	..
	TOURISM INDUSTRIES						
	Hotels and similar establishments						
9.1	Number of rooms	Units	143	143	243	243	..
9.2	Number of bed-places	Units	222	222	341	341	..
9.3	Occupancy rate	Percent	..	..	..	..	..
9.4	Average length of stay	Nights	..	..	..	..	..
	RELATED INDICATORS						
	Share of tourism expenditure (6.1) in:						
10.1	Gross Domestic Product (GDP)	Percent	..	..	..	..	..
10.2	Exports of goods	Percent	..	..	..	..	..
10.3	Exports of services	Percent	..	..	..	..	..

(*) Balance of Payments items: 6.1 to 6.3 correspond to the "Credit" side (and are receipts for the country) while 8.2 to 8.4 correspond to the "Debit" side (and are expenditures in other countries).

ANDORRA

	Basic Indicators	Units	2001	2002	2003	2004	2005
	INBOUND TOURISM						
	Arrivals						
1.1	Visitors	('000)	11,351	11,507	11,601	11,668	11,049
1.2	Tourists (overnight visitors)	('000)	3,516	3,387	3,138	2,791	2,418
1.3	Same-day visitors	('000)	7,835	8,120	8,463	8,877	8,631
1.4	Cruise passengers	('000)	..	..	..	..	..
	Arrivals by region						
2.1	Africa	('000)	..	..	..	..	..
2.2	Americas	('000)	..	..	..	..	..
2.3	Europe	('000)	..	..	..	..	..
2.4	East Asia and the Pacific	('000)	..	..	..	..	..
2.5	South Asia	('000)	..	..	..	..	..
2.6	Middle East	('000)	..	..	..	..	..
	Arrivals by means of transport used						
3.1	Air	('000)	..	..	..	..	..
3.2	Rail	('000)	..	..	..	..	..
3.3	Road	('000)	11,351	11,507	11,601	11,668	11,049
3.4	Sea	('000)	..	..	..	..	..
	Arrivals by purpose of visit						
4.1	Leisure, recreation and holidays	('000)	10,364	10,439	10,253	10,156	9,522
4.2	Business and professional	('000)	664	601	626	691	645
4.3	Other	('000)	323	467	722	821	882
	Accommodation						
5.1	Overnight stays in hotels and similar establishments	('000)	..	6,765	5,581	5,525	5,199
5.2	Guests in hotels and similar establishments	('000)	..	..	..	..	..
5.3	Overnight stays in all types of accommodation establishments	('000)	9,809	9,336	7,745	7,322	6,762
5.4	Average length of stay of non-resident tourists in all accommodation establishments	Nights	2.85	2.87	2.68	2.62	2.80
6.1	**Tourism expenditure in the country**	US$ Mn	..	..	..	..	..
6.2	"Travel" (*)	US$ Mn	..	..	..	..	..
6.3	"Passenger transport" (*)	US$ Mn	..	..	..	..	..
	DOMESTIC TOURISM						
	Accommodation						
7.1	Overnight stays in hotels and similar establishments	('000)	..	..	..	..	..
7.2	Guests in hotels and similar establishments	('000)	..	..	..	..	..
7.3	Overnight stays in all types of accommodation establishments	('000)	..	..	..	..	..
7.4	Average length of stay of resident tourists in all accommodation establishments	Nights	..	..	..	..	..
	OUTBOUND TOURISM						
8.1	**Departures**	('000)	..	..	..	..	..
8.2	**Tourism expenditure in other countries**	US$ Mn	..	..	..	..	..
8.3	"Travel" (*)	US$ Mn	..	..	..	..	..
8.4	"Passenger transport" (*)	US$ Mn	..	..	..	..	..
	TOURISM INDUSTRIES						
	Hotels and similar establishments						
9.1	Number of rooms	Units	..	..	..	..	..
9.2	Number of bed-places	Units	..	..	34,522	38,310	38,957
9.3	Occupancy rate	Percent	..	..	..	..	..
9.4	Average length of stay	Nights	2.85	2.87	2.68	2.62	2.80
	RELATED INDICATORS						
	Share of tourism expenditure (6.1) in:						
10.1	Gross Domestic Product (GDP)	Percent	..	..	..	..	..
10.2	Exports of goods	Percent	..	..	..	..	..
10.3	Exports of services	Percent	..	..	..	..	..

(*) Balance of Payments items: 6.1 to 6.3 correspond to the "Credit" side (and are receipts for the country) while 8.2 to 8.4 correspond to the "Debit" side (and are expenditures in other countries).

Basic Indicators		Units	2001	2002	2003	2004	2005
	INBOUND TOURISM						
	Arrivals						
1.1	Visitors	('000)	..	..	..	..	..
1.2	Tourists (overnight visitors)	('000)	67	91	107	194	210
1.3	Same-day visitors	('000)	..	..	..	..	..
1.4	Cruise passengers	('000)	..	..	..	..	..
	Arrivals by region						
2.1	Africa	('000)	15	17	31	42	43
2.2	Americas	('000)	9	15	15	34	36
2.3	Europe	('000)	38	52	55	101	110
2.4	East Asia and the Pacific	('000)	4	5	5	16	15
2.5	South Asia	('000)	1	1	..	..	2
2.6	Middle East	('000)	..	1	..	1	3
	Arrivals by means of transport used						
3.1	Air	('000)	58	61	83	144	153
3.2	Rail	('000)	..	..	..	..	..
3.3	Road	('000)	8	27	21	46	52
3.4	Sea	('000)	1	3	3	4	5
	Arrivals by purpose of visit						
4.1	Leisure, recreation and holidays	('000)	6	6	13	12	13
4.2	Business and professional	('000)	11	29	19	21	23
4.3	Other	('000)	50	56	75	161	174
	Accommodation						
5.1	Overnight stays in hotels and similar establishments	('000)	..	183	212	143	176
5.2	Guests in hotels and similar establishments	('000)	..	..	..	92	120
5.3	Overnight stays in all types of accommodation establishments	('000)	112	207	217	149	182
5.4	Average length of stay of non-resident tourists in all accommodation establishments	Nights	..	..	..	..	..
6.1	**Tourism expenditure in the country**	US$ Mn	36	51	63	82	103
6.2	"Travel" (*)	US$ Mn	22	37	49	66	88
6.3	"Passenger transport" (*)	US$ Mn	14	14	14	16	15
	DOMESTIC TOURISM						
	Accommodation						
7.1	Overnight stays in hotels and similar establishments	('000)	..	34	78	61	72
7.2	Guests in hotels and similar establishments	('000)	..	..	..	48	47
7.3	Overnight stays in all types of accommodation establishments	('000)	11	133	124	87	124
7.4	Average length of stay of resident tourists in all accommodation establishments	Nights	..	..	..	..	..
	OUTBOUND TOURISM						
8.1	**Departures**	('000)	..	..	..	..	..
8.2	**Tourism expenditure in other countries**	US$ Mn	80	53	49	86	135
8.3	"Travel" (*)	US$ Mn	66	19	12	39	74
8.4	"Passenger transport" (*)	US$ Mn	14	34	37	47	61
	TOURISM INDUSTRIES						
	Hotels and similar establishments						
9.1	Number of rooms	Units	7,897	8,262	9,244	9,358	9,593
9.2	Number of bed-places	Units	14,060	14,893	10,612	10,736	10,723
9.3	Occupancy rate	Percent	71.00	79.00	82.00	96.00	97.60
9.4	Average length of stay	Nights	..	4.00	4.00	..	..
	RELATED INDICATORS						
	Share of tourism expenditure (6.1) in:						
10.1	Gross Domestic Product (GDP)	Percent	0.4	0.5	0.5	0.4	0.4
10.2	Exports of goods	Percent	0.6	0.6	0.7	0.6	0.4
10.3	Exports of services	Percent	17.7	24.6	31.3	25.4	58.2

(*) Balance of Payments items: 6.1 to 6.3 correspond to the "Credit" side (and are receipts for the country) while 8.2 to 8.4 correspond to the "Debit" side (and are expenditures in other countries).

ANGUILLA

	Basic Indicators	Units	2001	2002	2003	2004	2005
	INBOUND TOURISM						
	Arrivals						
1.1	Visitors	('000)	105	111	109	121	143
1.2	Tourists (overnight visitors)	('000)	48	44	47	54	62
1.3	Same-day visitors	('000)	57	67	62	67	81
1.4	Cruise passengers	('000)	..	..	..	..	..
	Arrivals by region						
2.1	Africa	('000)	..	..	..	..	..
2.2	Americas	('000)	39	37	39	45	52
2.3	Europe	('000)	8	5	6	8	8
2.4	East Asia and the Pacific	('000)	..	..	..	..	..
2.5	South Asia	('000)	..	..	..	..	..
2.6	Middle East	('000)	..	..	..	..	..
	Arrivals by means of transport used						
3.1	Air	('000)	32	30	28	24	32
3.2	Rail	('000)	..	..	..	..	..
3.3	Road	('000)	..	..	..	..	..
3.4	Sea	('000)	73	81	81	97	111
	Arrivals by purpose of visit						
4.1	Leisure, recreation and holidays	('000)	101	107	105	117	138
4.2	Business and professional	('000)	4	4	4	4	5
4.3	Other	('000)	..	..	..	..	..
	Accommodation						
5.1	Overnight stays in hotels and similar establishments	('000)	..	..	..	..	..
5.2	Guests in hotels and similar establishments	('000)	..	..	..	..	..
5.3	Overnight stays in all types of accommodation establishments	('000)	411	369	399	410	502
5.4	Average length of stay of non-resident tourists in all accommodation establishments	Nights	8.50	8.40	8.50	7.60	8.10
6.1	**Tourism expenditure in the country**	US$ Mn	..	..	..	..	..
6.2	"Travel" (*)	US$ Mn	62	57	60	69	86
6.3	"Passenger transport" (*)	US$ Mn	..	..	..	..	..
	DOMESTIC TOURISM						
	Accommodation						
7.1	Overnight stays in hotels and similar establishments	('000)	..	..	..	..	..
7.2	Guests in hotels and similar establishments	('000)	..	..	..	..	..
7.3	Overnight stays in all types of accommodation establishments	('000)	..	..	..	..	..
7.4	Average length of stay of resident tourists in all accommodation establishments	Nights	..	..	..	..	..
	OUTBOUND TOURISM						
8.1	**Departures**	('000)	..	..	..	..	..
8.2	**Tourism expenditure in other countries**	US$ Mn	..	..	..	..	..
8.3	"Travel" (*)	US$ Mn	9	8	9	9	10
8.4	"Passenger transport" (*)	US$ Mn	..	..	..	..	..
	TOURISM INDUSTRIES						
	Hotels and similar establishments						
9.1	Number of rooms	Units	1,069	1,037	759	756	746
9.2	Number of bed-places	Units	..	..	..	..	..
9.3	Occupancy rate	Percent	48.80	43.95	45.50	52.00	..
9.4	Average length of stay	Nights	8.50	8.40	8.50	7.60	8.10
	RELATED INDICATORS						
	Share of tourism expenditure (6.1) in: (**)						
10.1	Gross Domestic Product (GDP)	Percent	..	..	..	..	..
10.2	Exports of goods	Percent	1550.0	1425.0	1500.0	1150.0	573.3
10.3	Exports of services	Percent	88.6	86.4	87.0	88.5	90.5

(*) Balance of Payments items: 6.1 to 6.3 correspond to the "Credit" side (and are receipts for the country) while 8.2 to 8.4 correspond to the "Debit" side (and are expenditures in other countries).

(**) See Annex "Country notes".

	Basic Indicators	Units	2001	2002	2003	2004	2005
	INBOUND TOURISM						
	Arrivals						
1.1	Visitors	('000)	624	530	623	791	728
1.2	Tourists (overnight visitors)	('000)	215	218	239	268	261
1.3	Same-day visitors	('000)	..	..	..	..	..
1.4	Cruise passengers	('000)	409	312	384	523	467
	Arrivals by region						
2.1	Africa	('000)	..	..	..	..	..
2.2	Americas	('000)	107	108	113	129	124
2.3	Europe	('000)	78	82	99	113	106
2.4	East Asia and the Pacific	('000)	..	..	..	..	..
2.5	South Asia	('000)	..	..	..	..	..
2.6	Middle East	('000)	..	..	..	..	..
	Arrivals by means of transport used						
3.1	Air	('000)	193	198	224	245	239
3.2	Rail	('000)	..	..	..	..	..
3.3	Road	('000)	..	..	..	..	..
3.4	Sea	('000)	..	..	..	..	..
	Arrivals by purpose of visit						
4.1	Leisure, recreation and holidays	('000)	..	..	..	..	..
4.2	Business and professional	('000)	..	..	..	..	..
4.3	Other	('000)	..	..	..	..	..
	Accommodation						
5.1	Overnight stays in hotels and similar establishments	('000)	..	..	..	..	..
5.2	Guests in hotels and similar establishments	('000)	..	..	..	..	..
5.3	Overnight stays in all types of accommodation establishments	('000)	..	..	..	..	..
5.4	Average length of stay of non-resident tourists in all accommodation establishments	Nights	..	..	..	..	..
6.1	**Tourism expenditure in the country**	US$ Mn	..	..	..	..	..
6.2	"Travel" (*)	US$ Mn	272	274	300	338	327
6.3	"Passenger transport" (*)	US$ Mn	..	..	..	..	..
	DOMESTIC TOURISM						
	Accommodation						
7.1	Overnight stays in hotels and similar establishments	('000)	..	..	..	..	..
7.2	Guests in hotels and similar establishments	('000)	..	..	..	..	..
7.3	Overnight stays in all types of accommodation establishments	('000)	..	..	..	..	..
7.4	Average length of stay of resident tourists in all accommodation establishments	Nights	..	..	..	..	..
	OUTBOUND TOURISM						
8.1	**Departures**	('000)	..	..	..	..	..
8.2	**Tourism expenditure in other countries**	US$ Mn	..	..	..	..	..
8.3	"Travel" (*)	US$ Mn	32	33	35	37	40
8.4	"Passenger transport" (*)	US$ Mn	..	..	..	..	..
	TOURISM INDUSTRIES						
	Hotels and similar establishments						
9.1	Number of rooms	Units	..	..	..	..	..
9.2	Number of bed-places	Units	..	..	..	..	..
9.3	Occupancy rate	Percent	..	..	..	..	..
9.4	Average length of stay	Nights	..	..	..	..	..
	RELATED INDICATORS						
	Share of tourism expenditure (6.1) in: (**)						
10.1	Gross Domestic Product (GDP)	Percent	38.3	38.1	39.5	39.1	36.1
10.2	Exports of goods	Percent	663.4	685.0	666.7	614.5	563.8
10.3	Exports of services	Percent	67.8	69.5	72.6	72.2	70.9

(*) Balance of Payments items: 6.1 to 6.3 correspond to the "Credit" side (and are receipts for the country) while 8.2 to 8.4 correspond to the "Debit" side (and are expenditures in other countries).

(**) See Annex "Country notes".

ARGENTINA

	Basic Indicators	Units	2001	2002	2003	2004	2005
	INBOUND TOURISM						
	Arrivals						
1.1	Visitors	('000)	..	..	..	..	..
1.2	Tourists (overnight visitors)	('000)	2,620	2,820	2,995	3,457	3,895
1.3	Same-day visitors	('000)	..	..	..	..	..
1.4	Cruise passengers	('000)	..	..	..	..	..
	Arrivals by region						
2.1	Africa	('000)	..	..	..	..	..
2.2	Americas	('000)	2,157	2,420	2,425	2,722	3,052
2.3	Europe	('000)	371	324	456	546	634
2.4	East Asia and the Pacific	('000)	..	..	..	..	..
2.5	South Asia	('000)	..	..	..	..	..
2.6	Middle East	('000)	..	..	..	..	..
	Arrivals by means of transport used						
3.1	Air	('000)	998	928	1,227	..	2,069
3.2	Rail	('000)	..	..	..	..	..
3.3	Road	('000)	1,322	1,617	1,430	..	1,509
3.4	Sea	('000)	300	275	339	..	318
	Arrivals by purpose of visit						
4.1	Leisure, recreation and holidays	('000)	1,954	2,117	2,223	2,889	3,264
4.2	Business and professional	('000)	666	703	773	568	632
4.3	Other	('000)	..	..	..	..	..
	Accommodation						
5.1	Overnight stays in hotels and similar establishments	('000)	..	..	..	..	9,283
5.2	Guests in hotels and similar establishments	('000)	..	..	..	..	3,988
5.3	Overnight stays in all types of accommodation establishments	('000)	26,986	27,636	31,148	36,576	40,664
5.4	Average length of stay of non-resident tourists in all accommodation establishments	Nights	10.30	9.80	10.40	10.58	10.44
6.1	**Tourism expenditure in the country**	US$ Mn	2,756	1,716	2,306	2,662	3,241
6.2	"Travel" (*)	US$ Mn	2,642	1,535	2,006	2,235	2,753
6.3	"Passenger transport" (*)	US$ Mn	114	181	300	427	488
	DOMESTIC TOURISM						
	Accommodation						
7.1	Overnight stays in hotels and similar establishments	('000)	..	..	..	..	28,767
7.2	Guests in hotels and similar establishments	('000)	..	..	..	..	11,890
7.3	Overnight stays in all types of accommodation establishments	('000)	..	..	..	..	..
7.4	Average length of stay of resident tourists in all accommodation establishments	Nights	..	..	..	..	..
	OUTBOUND TOURISM						
8.1	**Departures**	('000)	4,762	3,008	3,088	3,904	4,002
8.2	**Tourism expenditure in other countries**	US$ Mn	4,888	2,744	2,997	3,204	3,572
8.3	"Travel" (*)	US$ Mn	3,893	2,328	2,511	2,604	2,817
8.4	"Passenger transport" (*)	US$ Mn	995	416	486	600	755
	TOURISM INDUSTRIES						
	Hotels and similar establishments						
9.1	Number of rooms	Units	167,828	170,746	176,685	182,444	190,257
9.2	Number of bed-places	Units	407,084	413,690	428,217	452,565	469,802
9.3	Occupancy rate	Percent	..	..	..	..	41.92
9.4	Average length of stay	Nights	..	..	..	..	..
	RELATED INDICATORS						
	Share of tourism expenditure (6.1) in:						
10.1	Gross Domestic Product (GDP)	Percent	1.0	1.7	1.8	1.7	1.8
10.2	Exports of goods	Percent	10.4	6.7	7.7	7.7	8.1
10.3	Exports of services	Percent	59.6	49.9	52.3	52.2	53.1

(*) Balance of Payments items: 6.1 to 6.3 correspond to the "Credit" side (and are receipts for the country) while 8.2 to 8.4 correspond to the "Debit" side (and are expenditures in other countries).

	Basic Indicators	Units	2001	2002	2003	2004	2005
	INBOUND TOURISM						
	Arrivals						
1.1	Visitors	('000)	..	..	..	..	..
1.2	Tourists (overnight visitors)	('000)	123	162	206	263	319
1.3	Same-day visitors	('000)	..	..	..	..	..
1.4	Cruise passengers	('000)	..	..	..	..	..
	Arrivals by region						
2.1	Africa	('000)	..	..	..	..	..
2.2	Americas	('000)	41	46	58	75	86
2.3	Europe	('000)	48	80	99	127	160
2.4	East Asia and the Pacific	('000)	3	3	6	9	14
2.5	South Asia	('000)	18	19	24	28	30
2.6	Middle East	('000)	13	14	19	23	28
	Arrivals by means of transport used						
3.1	Air	('000)	107	135	173	196	225
3.2	Rail	('000)	5	2	3	14	19
3.3	Road	('000)	12	25	30	52	74
3.4	Sea	('000)	..	..	..	..	..
	Arrivals by purpose of visit						
4.1	Leisure, recreation and holidays	('000)	97	126	160	204	235
4.2	Business and professional	('000)	25	31	39	46	67
4.3	Other	('000)	2	5	7	13	16
	Accommodation						
5.1	Overnight stays in hotels and similar establishments	('000)	..	..	..	..	..
5.2	Guests in hotels and similar establishments	('000)	..	..	..	..	..
5.3	Overnight stays in all types of accommodation establishments	('000)	200	202	343	385	420
5.4	Average length of stay of non-resident tourists in all accommodation establishments	Nights	6.50	7.00	10.00	10.00	10.00
6.1	**Tourism expenditure in the country**	US$ Mn	81	82	90	103	161
6.2	"Travel" (*)	US$ Mn	65	63	73	86	141
6.3	"Passenger transport" (*)	US$ Mn	16	19	17	17	20
	DOMESTIC TOURISM						
	Accommodation						
7.1	Overnight stays in hotels and similar establishments	('000)	..	..	..	..	..
7.2	Guests in hotels and similar establishments	('000)	..	..	..	..	..
7.3	Overnight stays in all types of accommodation establishments	('000)	468	726	975	1,200	1,350
7.4	Average length of stay of resident tourists in all accommodation establishments	Nights	..	..	..	..	..
	OUTBOUND TOURISM						
8.1	**Departures**	('000)	110	131	169	221	269
8.2	**Tourism expenditure in other countries**	US$ Mn	59	85	97	102	146
8.3	"Travel" (*)	US$ Mn	40	54	67	65	117
8.4	"Passenger transport" (*)	US$ Mn	19	31	30	37	29
	TOURISM INDUSTRIES						
	Hotels and similar establishments						
9.1	Number of rooms	Units	..	..	..	..	..
9.2	Number of bed-places	Units	12,132	12,578	13,774	14,964	17,387
9.3	Occupancy rate	Percent	24.00	25.00	50.00	58.00	59.00
9.4	Average length of stay	Nights	6.50	7.00	10.00	10.00	10.00
	RELATED INDICATORS						
	Share of tourism expenditure (6.1) in:						
10.1	Gross Domestic Product (GDP)	Percent	3.8	3.5	3.2	2.9	3.3
10.2	Exports of goods	Percent	22.9	16.0	12.9	14.0	16.0
10.3	Exports of services	Percent	43.3	44.6	43.5	41.7	48.5

(*) Balance of Payments items: 6.1 to 6.3 correspond to the "Credit" side (and are receipts for the country) while 8.2 to 8.4 correspond to the "Debit" side (and are expenditures in other countries).

ARUBA

	Basic Indicators	Units	2001	2002	2003	2004	2005
	INBOUND TOURISM						
	Arrivals						
1.1	Visitors	('000)	1,178	1,225	1,184	1,304	1,286
1.2	Tourists (overnight visitors)	('000)	691	643	642	728	733
1.3	Same-day visitors	('000)	..	..	..	..	..
1.4	Cruise passengers	('000)	487	582	542	576	553
	Arrivals by region						
2.1	Africa	('000)	..	..	..	..	..
2.2	Americas	('000)	643	595	585	665	666
2.3	Europe	('000)	45	44	55	60	63
2.4	East Asia and the Pacific	('000)	..	..	..	..	..
2.5	South Asia	('000)	..	..	..	..	..
2.6	Middle East	('000)	..	..	..	..	..
	Arrivals by means of transport used						
3.1	Air	('000)	691	643	642	728	733
3.2	Rail	('000)	..	..	..	..	..
3.3	Road	('000)	..	..	..	..	..
3.4	Sea	('000)	..	..	..	..	..
	Arrivals by purpose of visit						
4.1	Leisure, recreation and holidays	('000)	634	591	583	669	681
4.2	Business and professional	('000)	40	31	33	33	34
4.3	Other	('000)	17	21	26	26	18
	Accommodation						
5.1	Overnight stays in hotels and similar establishments	('000)	4,177	3,945	4,059	4,615	4,735
5.2	Guests in hotels and similar establishments	('000)	611	567	568	647	653
5.3	Overnight stays in all types of accommodation establishments	('000)	5,145	4,863	5,098	5,640	5,695
5.4	Average length of stay of non-resident tourists in all accommodation establishments	Nights	8.00	7.57	7.90	7.80	7.77
6.1	**Tourism expenditure in the country**	US$ Mn	825	831	858.2	..	..
6.2	"Travel" (*)	US$ Mn	821	830	858	1,052	1,096
6.3	"Passenger transport" (*)	US$ Mn	4	1	0.2	..	..
	DOMESTIC TOURISM						
	Accommodation						
7.1	Overnight stays in hotels and similar establishments	('000)	..	..	..	..	..
7.2	Guests in hotels and similar establishments	('000)	..	..	..	..	..
7.3	Overnight stays in all types of accommodation establishments	('000)	..	..	..	..	..
7.4	Average length of stay of resident tourists in all accommodation establishments	Nights	..	..	..	..	..
	OUTBOUND TOURISM						
8.1	**Departures**	('000)	..	..	..	..	..
8.2	**Tourism expenditure in other countries**	US$ Mn	156	173	213	253	268
8.3	"Travel" (*)	US$ Mn	135	160	189	223	241
8.4	"Passenger transport" (*)	US$ Mn	21	13	24	30	27
	TOURISM INDUSTRIES						
	Hotels and similar establishments						
9.1	Number of rooms	Units	7,783	7,040	7,731	7,206	7,966
9.2	Number of bed-places	Units	15,566	14,080	15,462	14,412	15,932
9.3	Occupancy rate	Percent	74.27	69.80	74.40	80.70	81.70
9.4	Average length of stay	Nights	..	..	..	..	..
	RELATED INDICATORS						
	Share of tourism expenditure (6.1) in:						
10.1	Gross Domestic Product (GDP)	Percent	43.4	43.5	..	..	..
10.2	Exports of goods	Percent	34.0	55.8	41.8	..	..
10.3	Exports of services	Percent	83.5	83.4	81.9	..	..

(*) Balance of Payments items: 6.1 to 6.3 correspond to the "Credit" side (and are receipts for the country) while 8.2 to 8.4 correspond to the "Debit" side (and are expenditures in other countries).

	Basic Indicators	Units	2001	2002	2003	2004	2005
	INBOUND TOURISM						
	Arrivals						
1.1	Visitors	('000)	4,856	4,841	4,746	5,215	5,497
1.2	Tourists (overnight visitors)	('000)	4,435	4,420	4,354	4,774	5,020
1.3	Same-day visitors	('000)	41	43	30	23	26
1.4	Cruise passengers	('000)	..	..	..	..	..
	Arrivals by region						
2.1	Africa	('000)	73	68	69	68	71
2.2	Americas	('000)	577	556	537	561	584
2.3	Europe	('000)	1,197	1,198	1,228	1,261	1,329
2.4	East Asia and the Pacific	('000)	2,893	2,924	2,812	3,205	3,374
2.5	South Asia	('000)	66	61	63	75	89
2.6	Middle East	('000)	35	31	34	43	49
	Arrivals by means of transport used						
3.1	Air	('000)	4,832	4,819	4,730	5,201	5,484
3.2	Rail	('000)	..	..	..	..	..
3.3	Road	('000)	..	..	..	..	..
3.4	Sea	('000)	24	22	16	14	13
	Arrivals by purpose of visit						
4.1	Leisure, recreation and holidays	('000)	2,484	2,401	2,441	2,685	2,951
4.2	Business and professional	('000)	837	873	900	999	1,104
4.3	Other	('000)	1,535	1,567	1,406	1,531	1,442
	Accommodation						
5.1	Overnight stays in hotels and similar establishments	('000)	31,950	31,546	31,596	34,111	36,768
5.2	Guests in hotels and similar establishments	('000)	3,011	3,034	2,936	3,252	3,441
5.3	Overnight stays in all types of accommodation establishments	('000)	69,849	73,532	69,842	75,403	77,703
5.4	Average length of stay of non-resident tourists in all accommodation establishments	Nights	18.30	19.80	20.90	21.50	21.30
6.1	**Tourism expenditure in the country**	US$ Mn	12,376	13,030	15,510	18,908	20,637
6.2	"Travel" (*)	US$ Mn	8,796	9,377	11,301	13,669	14,940
6.3	"Passenger transport" (*)	US$ Mn	3,580	3,653	4,209	5,239	5,697
	DOMESTIC TOURISM						
	Accommodation						
7.1	Overnight stays in hotels and similar establishments	('000)	75,395	75,190	77,417	80,395	78,591
7.2	Guests in hotels and similar establishments	('000)	25,814	26,085	26,137	27,181	26,386
7.3	Overnight stays in all types of accommodation establishments	('000)	132,454	136,393	138,450	134,741	128,488
7.4	Average length of stay of resident tourists in all accommodation establishments	Nights	3.70	3.70	3.80	3.70	3.60
	OUTBOUND TOURISM						
8.1	**Departures**	('000)	3,443	3,461	3,388	4,369	4,754
8.2	**Tourism expenditure in other countries**	US$ Mn	8,070	8,513	10,085	13,884	15,076
8.3	"Travel" (*)	US$ Mn	5,877	6,091	7,295	10,290	11,282
8.4	"Passenger transport" (*)	US$ Mn	2,193	2,422	2,790	3,594	3,794
	TOURISM INDUSTRIES						
	Hotels and similar establishments						
9.1	Number of rooms	Units	198,133	196,431	204,461	205,495	212,784
9.2	Number of bed-places	Units	571,560	563,779	580,252	586,217	603,192
9.3	Occupancy rate	Percent	57.30	58.70	63.50	63.70	64.50
9.4	Average length of stay	Nights	2.30	2.30	2.30	2.30	2.30
	RELATED INDICATORS						
	Share of tourism expenditure (6.1) in:						
10.1	Gross Domestic Product (GDP)	Percent	3.4	3.2	2.9	3.0	2.9
10.2	Exports of goods	Percent	19.5	20.0	22.0	21.7	19.3
10.3	Exports of services	Percent	70.9	69.8	70.1	71.7	72.6

(*) Balance of Payments items: 6.1 to 6.3 correspond to the "Credit" side (and are receipts for the country) while 8.2 to 8.4 correspond to the "Debit" side (and are expenditures in other countries).

AUSTRIA

	Basic Indicators	Units	2001	2002	2003	2004	2005
	INBOUND TOURISM						
	Arrivals						
1.1	Visitors	('000)	..	..	..	..	..
1.2	Tourists (overnight visitors)	('000)	18,180	18,611	19,078	19,373	19,952
1.3	Same-day visitors	('000)	..	..	..	..	..
1.4	Cruise passengers	('000)	..	..	..	..	..
	Arrivals by region						
2.1	Africa	('000)	36	26	27	32	42
2.2	Americas	('000)	788	647	599	674	692
2.3	Europe	('000)	16,474	16,984	17,387	17,446	18,031
2.4	East Asia and the Pacific	('000)	576	594	619	755	792
2.5	South Asia	('000)	32	39	30	40	39
2.6	Middle East	('000)	33	29	38	43	68
	Arrivals by means of transport used						
3.1	Air	('000)	..	..	..	..	..
3.2	Rail	('000)	..	..	..	..	..
3.3	Road	('000)	..	..	..	..	..
3.4	Sea	('000)	..	..	..	..	..
	Arrivals by purpose of visit						
4.1	Leisure, recreation and holidays	('000)	..	..	..	..	..
4.2	Business and professional	('000)	..	..	..	..	..
4.3	Other	('000)	..	..	..	..	..
	Accommodation						
5.1	Overnight stays in hotels and similar establishments	('000)	58,737	60,249	60,622	60,746	62,396
5.2	Guests in hotels and similar establishments	('000)	13,886	14,165	14,489	14,853	15,363
5.3	Overnight stays in all types of accommodation establishments	('000)	65,523	67,346	68,217	68,270	69,733
5.4	Average length of stay of non-resident tourists in all accommodation establishments	Nights	4.60	4.60	4.53	4.40	4.40
6.1	**Tourism expenditure in the country**	US$ Mn	12,033	13,046	16,342	18,385	19,310
6.2	"Travel" (*)	US$ Mn	10,291	11,136	13,842	15,290	15,589
6.3	"Passenger transport" (*)	US$ Mn	1,742	1,910	2,500	3,095	3,721
	DOMESTIC TOURISM						
	Accommodation						
7.1	Overnight stays in hotels and similar establishments	('000)	19,329	19,302	19,634	19,800	20,329
7.2	Guests in hotels and similar establishments	('000)	6,408	6,444	6,603	6,766	7,072
7.3	Overnight stays in all types of accommodation establishments	('000)	26,615	26,424	27,023	26,980	27,298
7.4	Average length of stay of resident tourists in all accommodation establishments	Nights	..	3.50	3.50	3.40	3.40
	OUTBOUND TOURISM						
8.1	**Departures**	('000)	4,207	3,907	6,620	6,798	6,564
8.2	**Tourism expenditure in other countries**	US$ Mn	9,787	10,301	12,894	13,411	12,755
8.3	"Travel" (*)	US$ Mn	8,956	9,460	11,757	11,834	10,994
8.4	"Passenger transport" (*)	US$ Mn	831	841	1,137	1,577	1,761
	TOURISM INDUSTRIES						
	Hotels and similar establishments						
9.1	Number of rooms	Units	288,346	282,735	282,614	290,491	289,879
9.2	Number of bed-places	Units	642,753	628,730	631,085	637,095	639,369
9.3	Occupancy rate	Percent	34.90	35.90	36.10	34.60	..
9.4	Average length of stay	Nights	3.80	3.86	3.81	3.72	3.69
	RELATED INDICATORS						
	Share of tourism expenditure (6.1) in:						
10.1	Gross Domestic Product (GDP)	Percent	6.2	6.3	6.4	6.3	6.3
10.2	Exports of goods	Percent	18.0	17.7	18.2	16.4	16.5
10.3	Exports of services	Percent	36.1	36.9	38.0	37.4	35.8

(*) Balance of Payments items: 6.1 to 6.3 correspond to the "Credit" side (and are receipts for the country) while 8.2 to 8.4 correspond to the "Debit" side (and are expenditures in other countries).

	Basic Indicators	Units	2001	2002	2003	2004	2005
	INBOUND TOURISM						
	Arrivals						
1.1	Visitors	('000)	..	..	..	..	..
1.2	Tourists (overnight visitors)	('000)	767	834	1,014	1,349	1,177
1.3	Same-day visitors	('000)	..	..	..	..	..
1.4	Cruise passengers	('000)	..	..	..	..	..
	Arrivals by region						
2.1	Africa	('000)	..	..	..	1	1
2.2	Americas	('000)	..	6	8	12	11
2.3	Europe	('000)	272	582	747	1,051	946
2.4	East Asia and the Pacific	('000)	..	3	4	6	7
2.5	South Asia	('000)	322	241	253	275	211
2.6	Middle East	('000)	..	2	2	2	2
	Arrivals by means of transport used						
3.1	Air	('000)	739	798	950	1,260	1,100
3.2	Rail	('000)	5	5	8	12	11
3.3	Road	('000)	21	28	49	68	61
3.4	Sea	('000)	2	2	5	7	5
	Arrivals by purpose of visit						
4.1	Leisure, recreation and holidays	('000)	7	8	16	23	21
4.2	Business and professional	('000)	718	775	915	1,230	1,065
4.3	Other	('000)	42	51	82	95	91
	Accommodation						
5.1	Overnight stays in hotels and similar establishments	('000)	161	350	439	929	1,064
5.2	Guests in hotels and similar establishments	('000)	69	118	146	213	264
5.3	Overnight stays in all types of accommodation establishments	('000)	..	..	..	..	..
5.4	Average length of stay of non-resident tourists in all accommodation establishments	Nights	..	..	..	..	..
6.1	**Tourism expenditure in the country**	US$ Mn	57	63	70	79	100
6.2	"Travel" (*)	US$ Mn	43	51	58	65	78
6.3	"Passenger transport" (*)	US$ Mn	14	12	12	14	22
	DOMESTIC TOURISM						
	Accommodation						
7.1	Overnight stays in hotels and similar establishments	('000)	51	86	142	414	524
7.2	Guests in hotels and similar establishments	('000)	44	56	68	113	133
7.3	Overnight stays in all types of accommodation establishments	('000)	..	..	..	..	..
7.4	Average length of stay of resident tourists in all accommodation establishments	Nights	..	..	..	..	..
	OUTBOUND TOURISM						
8.1	**Departures**	('000)	1,130	1,141	1,376	1,473	1,830
8.2	**Tourism expenditure in other countries**	US$ Mn	119	111	120	140	188
8.3	"Travel" (*)	US$ Mn	109	106	111	126	164
8.4	"Passenger transport" (*)	US$ Mn	10	5	9	14	24
	TOURISM INDUSTRIES						
	Hotels and similar establishments						
9.1	Number of rooms	Units	5,259	5,300	5,034	9,827	10,661
9.2	Number of bed-places	Units	9,403	9,591	9,569	21,144	22,492
9.3	Occupancy rate	Percent	..	..	..	..	..
9.4	Average length of stay	Nights	..	..	..	..	..
	RELATED INDICATORS						
	Share of tourism expenditure (6.1) in:						
10.1	Gross Domestic Product (GDP)	Percent	1.0	1.0	1.0	0.9	0.8
10.2	Exports of goods	Percent	2.7	2.7	2.7	2.1	1.3
10.3	Exports of services	Percent	19.7	17.4	16.2	16.1	14.6

(*) Balance of Payments items: 6.1 to 6.3 correspond to the "Credit" side (and are receipts for the country) while 8.2 to 8.4 correspond to the "Debit" side (and are expenditures in other countries).

BAHAMAS

	Basic Indicators	Units	2001	2002	2003	2004	2005
	INBOUND TOURISM						
	Arrivals						
1.1	Visitors	('000)	4,183	4,406	4,594	5,004	5,036
1.2	Tourists (overnight visitors)	('000)	1,538	1,513	1,510	1,561	1,608
1.3	Same-day visitors	('000)	93	91	114	83	93
1.4	Cruise passengers	('000)	2,552	2,802	2,970	3,360	3,335
	Arrivals by region						
2.1	Africa	('000)	1	1	1	1	1
2.2	Americas	('000)	1,418	1,406	1,393	1,455	1,485
2.3	Europe	('000)	94	79	92	83	84
2.4	East Asia and the Pacific	('000)	11	8	6	7	7
2.5	South Asia	('000)	..	..	..	..	..
2.6	Middle East	('000)	1	..	..	1	..
	Arrivals by means of transport used						
3.1	Air	('000)	1,428	1,403	1,429	1,450	1,515
3.2	Rail	('000)	..	..	..	..	..
3.3	Road	('000)	..	..	..	..	..
3.4	Sea	('000)	2,755	3,003	3,165	3,554	3,521
	Arrivals by purpose of visit						
4.1	Leisure, recreation and holidays	('000)	1,324	1,290	1,306	1,306	..
4.2	Business and professional	('000)	162	156	127	148	..
4.3	Other	('000)	52	67	77	107	..
	Accommodation						
5.1	Overnight stays in hotels and similar establishments	('000)	..	..	..	..	..
5.2	Guests in hotels and similar establishments	('000)	..	1,086	1,098	1,152	1,188
5.3	Overnight stays in all types of accommodation establishments	('000)	8,973	8,704	8,957	9,898	10,297
5.4	Average length of stay of non-resident tourists in all accommodation establishments	Nights	5.80	5.75	5.90	6.30	6.40
6.1	**Tourism expenditure in the country**	US$ Mn	1,665	1,773	1,770	1,897	2,079
6.2	"Travel" (*)	US$ Mn	1,648	1,760	1,757	1,884	2,069
6.3	"Passenger transport" (*)	US$ Mn	17	13	13	13	10
	DOMESTIC TOURISM						
	Accommodation						
7.1	Overnight stays in hotels and similar establishments	('000)	..	..	..	..	..
7.2	Guests in hotels and similar establishments	('000)	..	..	..	..	..
7.3	Overnight stays in all types of accommodation establishments	('000)	..	..	..	..	..
7.4	Average length of stay of resident tourists in all accommodation establishments	Nights	..	..	..	..	..
	OUTBOUND TOURISM						
8.1	**Departures**	('000)	..	..	..	..	..
8.2	**Tourism expenditure in other countries**	US$ Mn	342	338	404	469	528
8.3	"Travel" (*)	US$ Mn	256	244	305	316	344
8.4	"Passenger transport" (*)	US$ Mn	86	94	99	153	184
	TOURISM INDUSTRIES						
	Hotels and similar establishments						
9.1	Number of rooms	Units	15,195	15,145	15,393	15,508	14,800
9.2	Number of bed-places	Units	30,390	30,290	30,786	31,016	29,600
9.3	Occupancy rate	Percent	60.50	62.00	59.20	66.40	70.40
9.4	Average length of stay	Nights	4.41	4.43	4.47	4.88	..
	RELATED INDICATORS						
	Share of tourism expenditure (6.1) in:						
10.1	Gross Domestic Product (GDP)	Percent	32.4	32.8	32.2	..	..
10.2	Exports of goods	Percent	399.3	420.1	414.5	397.7	378.7
10.3	Exports of services	Percent	92.3	86.0	86.1	84.5	83.8

(*) Balance of Payments items: 6.1 to 6.3 correspond to the "Credit" side (and are receipts for the country) while 8.2 to 8.4 correspond to the "Debit" side (and are expenditures in other countries).

Basic Indicators		Units	2001	2002	2003	2004	2005
	INBOUND TOURISM						
	Arrivals						
1.1	Visitors	('000)	4,388	4,831	4,844	5,667	6,313
1.2	Tourists (overnight visitors)	('000)	2,789	3,167	2,955	3,514	3,914
1.3	Same-day visitors	('000)	1,599	1,664	1,889	2,153	2,399
1.4	Cruise passengers	('000)	..	..	..	..	..
	Arrivals by region						
2.1	Africa	('000)	39	47	60	76	82
2.2	Americas	('000)	139	177	192	200	190
2.3	Europe	('000)	235	256	260	334	358
2.4	East Asia and the Pacific	('000)	135	187	212	268	287
2.5	South Asia	('000)	392	522	561	648	720
2.6	Middle East	('000)	3,447	3,642	3,559	4,141	4,676
	Arrivals by means of transport used						
3.1	Air	('000)	791	920	974	1,176	1,301
3.2	Rail	('000)	..	..	..	..	..
3.3	Road	('000)	3,588	3,897	3,862	4,484	5,007
3.4	Sea	('000)	9	13	8	7	5
	Arrivals by purpose of visit						
4.1	Leisure, recreation and holidays	('000)	3,462	3,642	3,769	4,005	4,187
4.2	Business and professional	('000)	330	419	542	647	627
4.3	Other	('000)	596	770	533	1,015	1,500
	Accommodation						
5.1	Overnight stays in hotels and similar establishments	('000)	1,571	1,386	1,290	2,290	2,224
5.2	Guests in hotels and similar establishments	('000)	787	686	695	1,132	1,237
5.3	Overnight stays in all types of accommodation establishments	('000)	..	..	..	..	..
5.4	Average length of stay of non-resident tourists in all accommodation establishments	Nights	2.01	2.06	1.89	2.02	2.00
6.1	**Tourism expenditure in the country**	US$ Mn	886	986	1,206	1,504	1,603
6.2	"Travel" (*)	US$ Mn	630	741	720	864	920
6.3	"Passenger transport" (*)	US$ Mn	256	245	486	640	683
	DOMESTIC TOURISM						
	Accommodation						
7.1	Overnight stays in hotels and similar establishments	('000)	..	..	..	..	..
7.2	Guests in hotels and similar establishments	('000)	..	..	..	..	..
7.3	Overnight stays in all types of accommodation establishments	('000)	..	..	..	..	..
7.4	Average length of stay of resident tourists in all accommodation establishments	Nights	..	..	..	..	..
	OUTBOUND TOURISM						
8.1	**Departures**	('000)	..	..	..	..	..
8.2	**Tourism expenditure in other countries**	US$ Mn	423	550	492	528	574
8.3	"Travel" (*)	US$ Mn	250	380	372	387	414
8.4	"Passenger transport" (*)	US$ Mn	173	170	120	141	160
	TOURISM INDUSTRIES						
	Hotels and similar establishments						
9.1	Number of rooms	Units	7,368	7,368	7,880	..	..
9.2	Number of bed-places	Units	10,314	10,314	10,759	..	..
9.3	Occupancy rate	Percent	55.79	53.72	44.68	54.78	56.30
9.4	Average length of stay	Nights	..	..	..	..	..
	RELATED INDICATORS						
	Share of tourism expenditure (6.1) in:						
10.1	Gross Domestic Product (GDP)	Percent	11.2	11.7	12.4	13.7	12.3
10.2	Exports of goods	Percent	15.7	16.7	17.9	19.7	15.8
10.3	Exports of services	Percent	93.3	92.3	95.7	96.5	96.5

(*) Balance of Payments items: 6.1 to 6.3 correspond to the "Credit" side (and are receipts for the country) while 8.2 to 8.4 correspond to the "Debit" side (and are expenditures in other countries).

BANGLADESH

	Basic Indicators	Units	2001	2002	2003	2004	2005
	INBOUND TOURISM						
	Arrivals						
1.1	Visitors	('000)	..	..	..	..	..
1.2	Tourists (overnight visitors)	('000)	207	207	245	271	208
1.3	Same-day visitors	('000)	..	..	..	..	..
1.4	Cruise passengers	('000)	..	..	..	..	..
	Arrivals by region						
2.1	Africa	('000)	2	1	2	2	2
2.2	Americas	('000)	19	18	31	37	19
2.3	Europe	('000)	50	47	64	77	49
2.4	East Asia and the Pacific	('000)	38	41	43	51	36
2.5	South Asia	('000)	94	97	102	100	99
2.6	Middle East	('000)	4	3	3	3	3
	Arrivals by means of transport used						
3.1	Air	('000)	158	151	187	218	140
3.2	Rail	('000)	..	..	..	..	..
3.3	Road	('000)	49	56	58	53	68
3.4	Sea	('000)	..	..	..	..	..
	Arrivals by purpose of visit						
4.1	Leisure, recreation and holidays	('000)	38	41	43	40	68
4.2	Business and professional	('000)	34	30	34	55	103
4.3	Other	('000)	135	136	168	176	37
	Accommodation						
5.1	Overnight stays in hotels and similar establishments	('000)	..	..	..	..	..
5.2	Guests in hotels and similar establishments	('000)	..	..	..	..	..
5.3	Overnight stays in all types of accommodation establishments	('000)	..	..	..	..	..
5.4	Average length of stay of non-resident tourists in all accommodation establishments	Nights	6.00	5.50	4.50	4.50	4.50
6.1	**Tourism expenditure in the country**	US$ Mn	..	59	59	76	78
6.2	"Travel" (*)	US$ Mn	48	57	57	67	70
6.3	"Passenger transport" (*)	US$ Mn	..	2	2	9	8
	DOMESTIC TOURISM						
	Accommodation						
7.1	Overnight stays in hotels and similar establishments	('000)	..	..	..	..	..
7.2	Guests in hotels and similar establishments	('000)	..	..	..	..	..
7.3	Overnight stays in all types of accommodation establishments	('000)	..	..	..	..	..
7.4	Average length of stay of resident tourists in all accommodation establishments	Nights	..	..	..	..	..
	OUTBOUND TOURISM						
8.1	**Departures**	('000)	1,075	1,158	1,414	1,565	1,767
8.2	**Tourism expenditure in other countries**	US$ Mn	341	309	389	442	371
8.3	"Travel" (*)	US$ Mn	165	113	165	161	132
8.4	"Passenger transport" (*)	US$ Mn	176	196	224	281	239
	TOURISM INDUSTRIES						
	Hotels and similar establishments						
9.1	Number of rooms	Units	4,550	4,550	4,565	4,575	4,590
9.2	Number of bed-places	Units	9,789	9,789	10,165	10,435	10,557
9.3	Occupancy rate	Percent	41.61	39.00	38.00	32.00	38.63
9.4	Average length of stay	Nights	..	..	..	..	..
	RELATED INDICATORS						
	Share of tourism expenditure (6.1) in:						
10.1	Gross Domestic Product (GDP)	Percent	..	0.1	0.1	0.1	0.1
10.2	Exports of goods	Percent	..	1.0	0.8	0.9	0.8
10.3	Exports of services	Percent	..	6.9	5.8	7.0	6.3

(*) Balance of Payments items: 6.1 to 6.3 correspond to the "Credit" side (and are receipts for the country) while 8.2 to 8.4 correspond to the "Debit" side (and are expenditures in other countries).

	Basic Indicators	Units	2001	2002	2003	2004	2005
	INBOUND TOURISM						
	Arrivals						
1.1	Visitors	('000)	1,035	1,021	1,090	1,273	1,111
1.2	Tourists (overnight visitors)	('000)	507	498	531	552	548
1.3	Same-day visitors	('000)	..	..	..	..	..
1.4	Cruise passengers	('000)	528	523	559	721	563
	Arrivals by region						
2.1	Africa	('000)	1	1	1	1	1
2.2	Americas	('000)	256	275	292	301	311
2.3	Europe	('000)	247	219	234	246	230
2.4	East Asia and the Pacific	('000)	2	2	4	3	3
2.5	South Asia	('000)	..	1	..	1	1
2.6	Middle East	('000)	..	..	..	..	..
	Arrivals by means of transport used						
3.1	Air	('000)	498	492	526	546	544
3.2	Rail	('000)	..	..	..	..	..
3.3	Road	('000)	..	..	..	..	..
3.4	Sea	('000)	537	529	564	727	567
	Arrivals by purpose of visit						
4.1	Leisure, recreation and holidays	('000)	428	417	436	445	432
4.2	Business and professional	('000)	57	58	65	70	72
4.3	Other	('000)	22	22	30	36	44
	Accommodation						
5.1	Overnight stays in hotels and similar establishments	('000)	..	..	..	..	..
5.2	Guests in hotels and similar establishments	('000)	..	..	..	..	..
5.3	Overnight stays in all types of accommodation establishments	('000)	2,460	2,031	2,459	2,463	..
5.4	Average length of stay of non-resident tourists in all accommodation establishments	Nights	10.20	11.00	10.00	9.90	9.80
6.1	**Tourism expenditure in the country**	US$ Mn	706	666	767	785	905
6.2	"Travel" (*)	US$ Mn	697	658	758	776	897
6.3	"Passenger transport" (*)	US$ Mn	9	8	9	9	8
	DOMESTIC TOURISM						
	Accommodation						
7.1	Overnight stays in hotels and similar establishments	('000)	..	..	..	..	..
7.2	Guests in hotels and similar establishments	('000)	..	..	..	..	..
7.3	Overnight stays in all types of accommodation establishments	('000)	..	..	..	..	..
7.4	Average length of stay of resident tourists in all accommodation establishments	Nights	..	..	..	..	..
	OUTBOUND TOURISM						
8.1	**Departures**	('000)	..	..	..	..	..
8.2	**Tourism expenditure in other countries**	US$ Mn	149	146	154	163	153
8.3	"Travel" (*)	US$ Mn	101	99	105	108	96
8.4	"Passenger transport" (*)	US$ Mn	48	47	49	55	57
	TOURISM INDUSTRIES						
	Hotels and similar establishments						
9.1	Number of rooms	Units	6,781	6,742	6,210	5,945	6,353
9.2	Number of bed-places	Units	13,176	13,050	10,770	11,237	12,417
9.3	Occupancy rate	Percent	51.10	42.50	49.90	49.70	53.80
9.4	Average length of stay	Nights	7.30	7.20	6.80	6.80	7.40
	RELATED INDICATORS						
	Share of tourism expenditure (6.1) in:						
10.1	Gross Domestic Product (GDP)	Percent	27.6	25.8	28.6	28.1	30.4
10.2	Exports of goods	Percent	260.5	263.2	290.5	267.9	238.8
10.3	Exports of services	Percent	66.0	64.0	65.8	64.1	62.1

(*) Balance of Payments items: 6.1 to 6.3 correspond to the "Credit" side (and are receipts for the country) while 8.2 to 8.4 correspond to the "Debit" side (and are expenditures in other countries).

BELARUS

Basic Indicators		Units	2001	2002	2003	2004	2005
	INBOUND TOURISM						
	Arrivals						
1.1	Visitors	('000)	..	..	..	..	..
1.2	Tourists (overnight visitors)	('000)	61	63	64	67	91
1.3	Same-day visitors	('000)	..	..	..	..	..
1.4	Cruise passengers	('000)	..	..	..	..	..
	Arrivals by region						
2.1	Africa	('000)	..	..	..	..	..
2.2	Americas	('000)	5	3	4	6	5
2.3	Europe	('000)	55	57	58	59	82
2.4	East Asia and the Pacific	('000)	1	3	2	2	2
2.5	South Asia	('000)	..	..	..	..	1
2.6	Middle East	('000)	..	..	..	..	1
	Arrivals by means of transport used						
3.1	Air	('000)	..	..	..	..	..
3.2	Rail	('000)	..	..	..	..	..
3.3	Road	('000)	..	..	..	..	..
3.4	Sea	('000)	..	..	..	..	..
	Arrivals by purpose of visit						
4.1	Leisure, recreation and holidays	('000)	..	..	..	..	..
4.2	Business and professional	('000)	..	..	..	..	..
4.3	Other	('000)	..	..	..	..	..
	Accommodation						
5.1	Overnight stays in hotels and similar establishments	('000)	..	..	..	..	..
5.2	Guests in hotels and similar establishments	('000)	..	..	..	..	..
5.3	Overnight stays in all types of accommodation establishments	('000)	..	..	..	..	..
5.4	Average length of stay of non-resident tourists in all accommodation establishments	Nights	..	..	..	..	..
6.1	**Tourism expenditure in the country**	US$ Mn	273	295	339	362	346
6.2	"Travel" (*)	US$ Mn	212	234	267	270	253
6.3	"Passenger transport" (*)	US$ Mn	61	61	72	92	93
	DOMESTIC TOURISM						
	Accommodation						
7.1	Overnight stays in hotels and similar establishments	('000)	..	..	..	..	..
7.2	Guests in hotels and similar establishments	('000)	..	..	..	..	..
7.3	Overnight stays in all types of accommodation establishments	('000)	..	..	..	..	..
7.4	Average length of stay of resident tourists in all accommodation establishments	Nights	..	..	..	..	..
	OUTBOUND TOURISM						
8.1	**Departures**	('000)	1,387	1,436	1,108	514	572
8.2	**Tourism expenditure in other countries**	US$ Mn	533	593	510	588	672
8.3	"Travel" (*)	US$ Mn	501	559	473	538	604
8.4	"Passenger transport" (*)	US$ Mn	32	34	37	50	68
	TOURISM INDUSTRIES						
	Hotels and similar establishments						
9.1	Number of rooms	Units	..	..	..	..	..
9.2	Number of bed-places	Units	..	..	..	..	..
9.3	Occupancy rate	Percent	..	..	..	..	..
9.4	Average length of stay	Nights	..	..	..	..	..
	RELATED INDICATORS						
	Share of tourism expenditure (6.1) in:						
10.1	Gross Domestic Product (GDP)	Percent	2.2	2.0	1.9	1.6	1.2
10.2	Exports of goods	Percent	3.7	3.7	3.4	2.6	2.1
10.3	Exports of services	Percent	23.9	22.0	22.6	20.7	17.7

(*) Balance of Payments items: 6.1 to 6.3 correspond to the "Credit" side (and are receipts for the country) while 8.2 to 8.4 correspond to the "Debit" side (and are expenditures in other countries).

	Basic Indicators	Units	2001	2002	2003	2004	2005
	INBOUND TOURISM						
	Arrivals						
1.1	Visitors	('000)	..	..	..	..	..
1.2	Tourists (overnight visitors)	('000)	6,452	6,720	6,690	6,710	6,747
1.3	Same-day visitors	('000)	..	..	..	..	..
1.4	Cruise passengers	('000)	..	..	..	..	..
	Arrivals by region						
2.1	Africa	('000)	64	60	63	61	62
2.2	Americas	('000)	428	400	369	382	390
2.3	Europe	('000)	5,592	5,798	5,847	5,800	5,836
2.4	East Asia and the Pacific	('000)	268	348	294	318	298
2.5	South Asia	('000)	27	39	32	33	35
2.6	Middle East	('000)	19	18	18	18	20
	Arrivals by means of transport used						
3.1	Air	('000)	9,786	7,102	7,505	7,709	8,027
3.2	Rail	('000)	..	..	..	..	..
3.3	Road	('000)	..	..	..	..	..
3.4	Sea	('000)	..	..	..	..	..
	Arrivals by purpose of visit						
4.1	Leisure, recreation and holidays	('000)	3,913	4,183	4,330	4,352	4,381
4.2	Business and professional	('000)	2,398	2,400	2,284	2,333	2,366
4.3	Other	('000)	141	136	76	25	..
	Accommodation						
5.1	Overnight stays in hotels and similar establishments	('000)	10,011	10,410	10,280	10,315	10,297
5.2	Guests in hotels and similar establishments	('000)	5,117	5,323	5,261	5,385	5,409
5.3	Overnight stays in all types of accommodation establishments	('000)	15,373	15,895	15,929	15,545	15,553
5.4	Average length of stay of non-resident tourists in all accommodation establishments	Nights	..	..	..	..	..
6.1	**Tourism expenditure in the country**	US$ Mn	8,304	7,598	8,848	10,091	10,879
6.2	"Travel" (*)	US$ Mn	6,887	6,935	8,193	9,209	9,842
6.3	"Passenger transport" (*)	US$ Mn	1,417	663	655	882	1,037
	DOMESTIC TOURISM						
	Accommodation						
7.1	Overnight stays in hotels and similar establishments	('000)	4,057	4,091	4,061	4,090	4,313
7.2	Guests in hotels and similar establishments	('000)	2,093	2,103	2,119	2,208	2,364
7.3	Overnight stays in all types of accommodation establishments	('000)	13,321	13,177	13,089	12,950	12,827
7.4	Average length of stay of resident tourists in all accommodation establishments	Nights	..	..	..	..	..
	OUTBOUND TOURISM						
8.1	**Departures**	('000)	6,570	6,773	7,268	8,783	9,318
8.2	**Tourism expenditure in other countries**	US$ Mn	10,878	11,270	13,402	15,456	16,636
8.3	"Travel" (*)	US$ Mn	9,776	10,185	12,210	13,956	14,814
8.4	"Passenger transport" (*)	US$ Mn	1,102	1,085	1,192	1,500	1,822
	TOURISM INDUSTRIES						
	Hotels and similar establishments						
9.1	Number of rooms	Units	61,769	62,686	63,220	64,004	66,568
9.2	Number of bed-places	Units	158,676	161,510	163,688	169,613	168,443
9.3	Occupancy rate	Percent	..	..	..	..	..
9.4	Average length of stay	Nights	..	..	..	..	..
	RELATED INDICATORS						
	Share of tourism expenditure (6.1) in:						
10.1	Gross Domestic Product (GDP)	Percent	3.7	3.1	2.9	2.9	3.0
10.2	Exports of goods	Percent	..	4.5	4.3	4.1	4.1
10.3	Exports of services	Percent	..	20.1	19.8	19.1	19.5

(*) Balance of Payments items: 6.1 to 6.3 correspond to the "Credit" side (and are receipts for the country) while 8.2 to 8.4 correspond to the "Debit" side (and are expenditures in other countries).

BELIZE

	Basic Indicators	Units	2001	2002	2003	2004	2005
	INBOUND TOURISM						
	Arrivals						
1.1	Visitors	('000)	385	694	999	1,329	..
1.2	Tourists (overnight visitors)	('000)	196	200	221	231	237
1.3	Same-day visitors	('000)	134	174	203	247	..
1.4	Cruise passengers	('000)	48	320	575	851	800
	Arrivals by region						
2.1	Africa	('000)	..	..	..	..	..
2.2	Americas	('000)	149	154	175	185	..
2.3	Europe	('000)	30	29	34	33	33
2.4	East Asia and the Pacific	('000)	4	3	4	4	..
2.5	South Asia	('000)	..	..	..	..	..
2.6	Middle East	('000)	..	..	..	..	..
	Arrivals by means of transport used						
3.1	Air	('000)	134	130	152	163	175
3.2	Rail	('000)	..	..	..	..	..
3.3	Road	('000)	53	62	60	60	54
3.4	Sea	('000)	9	8	8	8	8
	Arrivals by purpose of visit						
4.1	Leisure, recreation and holidays	('000)	186	186	208	219	225
4.2	Business and professional	('000)	10	13	13	12	12
4.3	Other	('000)	..	..	..	..	..
	Accommodation						
5.1	Overnight stays in hotels and similar establishments	('000)	533	536	..	..	..
5.2	Guests in hotels and similar establishments	('000)	..	..	..	..	..
5.3	Overnight stays in all types of accommodation establishments	('000)	..	..	..	..	..
5.4	Average length of stay of non-resident tourists in all accommodation establishments	Nights	7.60	7.60	6.80	6.80	..
6.1	**Tourism expenditure in the country**	US$ Mn	..	..	..	..	..
6.2	"Travel" (*)	US$ Mn	111	122	150	168	204
6.3	"Passenger transport" (*)	US$ Mn	..	..	..	..	..
	DOMESTIC TOURISM						
	Accommodation						
7.1	Overnight stays in hotels and similar establishments	('000)	..	..	..	..	..
7.2	Guests in hotels and similar establishments	('000)	..	..	..	..	..
7.3	Overnight stays in all types of accommodation establishments	('000)	56	80	..	..	..
7.4	Average length of stay of resident tourists in all accommodation establishments	Nights	..	..	..	..	..
	OUTBOUND TOURISM						
8.1	**Departures**	('000)	..	..	..	..	..
8.2	**Tourism expenditure in other countries**	US$ Mn	45	48	50	47	45
8.3	"Travel" (*)	US$ Mn	42	44	46	43	42
8.4	"Passenger transport" (*)	US$ Mn	3	4	4	4	3
	TOURISM INDUSTRIES						
	Hotels and similar establishments						
9.1	Number of rooms	Units	4,463	4,705	5,050	5,139	5,593
9.2	Number of bed-places	Units	7,187	7,902	8,166	8,722	9,327
9.3	Occupancy rate	Percent	44.80	40.10	41.30	40.70	40.60
9.4	Average length of stay	Nights	7.60	7.60	6.80	6.80	..
	RELATED INDICATORS						
	Share of tourism expenditure (6.1) in: (**)						
10.1	Gross Domestic Product (GDP)	Percent	12.4	13.2	15.3	16.2	18.5
10.2	Exports of goods	Percent	41.3	39.4	47.5	54.7	63.4
10.3	Exports of services	Percent	66.9	69.3	70.8	71.5	69.6

(*) Balance of Payments items: 6.1 to 6.3 correspond to the "Credit" side (and are receipts for the country) while 8.2 to 8.4 correspond to the "Debit" side (and are expenditures in other countries).

(**) See Annex "Country notes".

	Basic Indicators	Units	2001	2002	2003	2004	2005
	INBOUND TOURISM						
	Arrivals						
1.1	Visitors	('000)	1,155	853	850	845	960
1.2	Tourists (overnight visitors)	('000)	88	72	175	174	176
1.3	Same-day visitors	('000)	..	..	..	..	..
1.4	Cruise passengers	('000)	2	..	..	..	..
	Arrivals by region						
2.1	Africa	('000)	50.2	49.4	148.6	147.5	140.2
2.2	Americas	('000)	0.6	1.3	0.5	0.4	0.5
2.3	Europe	('000)	36.2	21.1	25.4	25.2	31.5
2.4	East Asia and the Pacific	('000)	0.5	0.2	0.2	0.3	0.3
2.5	South Asia	('000)	0.3	0.1	0.1	0.1	3.0
2.6	Middle East	('000)	0.2	0.2	0.1	0.1	0.5
	Arrivals by means of transport used						
3.1	Air	('000)	..	..	..	..	..
3.2	Rail	('000)	..	..	..	..	..
3.3	Road	('000)	..	..	..	..	..
3.4	Sea	('000)	..	..	..	..	..
	Arrivals by purpose of visit						
4.1	Leisure, recreation and holidays	('000)	..	..	..	..	..
4.2	Business and professional	('000)	..	..	..	..	..
4.3	Other	('000)	..	..	..	..	..
	Accommodation						
5.1	Overnight stays in hotels and similar establishments	('000)	..	..	..	..	..
5.2	Guests in hotels and similar establishments	('000)	..	..	..	..	..
5.3	Overnight stays in all types of accommodation establishments	('000)	190	144	219	215	348
5.4	Average length of stay of non-resident tourists in all accommodation establishments	Nights	..	..	..	..	..
6.1	**Tourism expenditure in the country**	US$ Mn	85.5	94.5	107.9	121.9	..
6.2	"Travel" (*)	US$ Mn	85	93	106	119	..
6.3	"Passenger transport" (*)	US$ Mn	0.5	1.5	1.9	2.9	..
	DOMESTIC TOURISM						
	Accommodation						
7.1	Overnight stays in hotels and similar establishments	('000)	20	17	..	..	..
7.2	Guests in hotels and similar establishments	('000)	..	..	..	..	..
7.3	Overnight stays in all types of accommodation establishments	('000)	..	..	..	..	..
7.4	Average length of stay of resident tourists in all accommodation establishments	Nights	..	..	..	..	..
	OUTBOUND TOURISM						
8.1	**Departures**	('000)	..	..	..	..	..
8.2	**Tourism expenditure in other countries**	US$ Mn	48	49	53	59	..
8.3	"Travel" (*)	US$ Mn	17	20	21	29	..
8.4	"Passenger transport" (*)	US$ Mn	31	29	32	30	..
	TOURISM INDUSTRIES						
	Hotels and similar establishments						
9.1	Number of rooms	Units	..	..	..	..	..
9.2	Number of bed-places	Units	..	..	..	..	..
9.3	Occupancy rate	Percent	..	..	..	..	..
9.4	Average length of stay	Nights	..	..	..	..	..
	RELATED INDICATORS						
	Share of tourism expenditure (6.1) in:						
10.1	Gross Domestic Product (GDP)	Percent	3.6	3.4	3.0	3.0	..
10.2	Exports of goods	Percent	22.9	21.1	19.9	21.4	..
10.3	Exports of services	Percent	58.2	62.2	62.7	56.4	..

(*) Balance of Payments items: 6.1 to 6.3 correspond to the "Credit" side (and are receipts for the country) while 8.2 to 8.4 correspond to the "Debit" side (and are expenditures in other countries).

BERMUDA

	Basic Indicators		Units	2001	2002	2003	2004	2005
	INBOUND TOURISM							
	Arrivals							
1.1	Visitors		('000)	458	484	483	478	521
1.2	Tourists (overnight visitors)		('000)	278	284	257	272	270
1.3	Same-day visitors		('000)	..	..	..	..	..
1.4	Cruise passengers		('000)	180	200	226	206	251
	Arrivals by region							
2.1	Africa		('000)	..	..	..	..	..
2.2	Americas		('000)	241	244	222	236	233
2.3	Europe		('000)	29	31	26	26	27
2.4	East Asia and the Pacific		('000)	1	1	1	1	1
2.5	South Asia		('000)	..	..	..	..	..
2.6	Middle East		('000)	..	..	..	..	..
	Arrivals by means of transport used							
3.1	Air		('000)	278	284	257	272	270
3.2	Rail		('000)	..	..	..	..	..
3.3	Road		('000)	..	..	..	..	..
3.4	Sea		('000)	180	200	226	206	251
	Arrivals by purpose of visit							
4.1	Leisure, recreation and holidays		('000)	219	218	167	172	170
4.2	Business and professional		('000)	34	39	51	55	59
4.3	Other		('000)	25	26	39	44	41
	Accommodation							
5.1	Overnight stays in hotels and similar establishments		('000)	..	..	..	..	..
5.2	Guests in hotels and similar establishments		('000)	..	220	196	206	207
5.3	Overnight stays in all types of accommodation establishments		('000)	1,775	1,822	1,598	1,733	1,729
5.4	Average length of stay of non-resident tourists in all accommodation establishments		Nights	6.38	6.42	6.43	6.38	6.40
6.1	**Tourism expenditure in the country**	(**)	US$ Mn	351	378	342	354	393
6.2	"Travel" (*)		US$ Mn	..	..	..	..	..
6.3	"Passenger transport" (*)		US$ Mn	..	..	..	..	..
	DOMESTIC TOURISM							
	Accommodation							
7.1	Overnight stays in hotels and similar establishments		('000)	..	..	..	..	..
7.2	Guests in hotels and similar establishments		('000)	..	..	..	..	..
7.3	Overnight stays in all types of accommodation establishments		('000)	..	..	..	..	..
7.4	Average length of stay of resident tourists in all accommodation establishments		Nights	..	..	..	..	..
	OUTBOUND TOURISM							
8.1	**Departures**		('000)	140	145	141	156	161
8.2	**Tourism expenditure in other countries**	(**)	US$ Mn	..	243	248	276	294
8.3	"Travel" (*)		US$ Mn	..	..	..	..	..
8.4	"Passenger transport" (*)		US$ Mn	..	..	..	..	..
	TOURISM INDUSTRIES							
	Hotels and similar establishments							
9.1	Number of rooms		Units	3,337	3,251	3,100	2,921	3,067
9.2	Number of bed-places		Units	7,915	6,523	6,293	5,888	6,167
9.3	Occupancy rate		Percent	51.90	55.01	54.50	62.40	56.90
9.4	Average length of stay		Nights	6.00	6.50	6.20	6.40	6.40
	RELATED INDICATORS							
	Share of tourism expenditure (6.1) in:							
10.1	Gross Domestic Product (GDP)		Percent	..	..	..	..	..
10.2	Exports of goods		Percent	..	..	..	..	..
10.3	Exports of services		Percent	..	..	..	..	..

(*) Balance of Payments items: 6.1 to 6.3 correspond to the "Credit" side (and are receipts for the country) while 8.2 to 8.4 correspond to the "Debit" side (and are expenditures in other countries).

(**) See Annex "Country notes".

	Basic Indicators		Units	2001	2002	2003	2004	2005
	INBOUND TOURISM							
	Arrivals							
1.1	Visitors		('000)	..	..	..	..	..
1.2	Tourists (overnight visitors)		('000)	6.4	5.6	6.3	9.2	13.6
1.3	Same-day visitors		('000)	..	..	..	..	..
1.4	Cruise passengers		('000)	..	..	..	..	..
	Arrivals by region							
2.1	Africa		('000)	..	..	..	..	..
2.2	Americas		('000)	2.4	2.1	2.0	3.6	5.1
2.3	Europe		('000)	2.5	2.0	2.8	3.9	5.4
2.4	East Asia and the Pacific		('000)	1.4	1.3	1.4	1.7	2.8
2.5	South Asia		('000)	..	..	..	..	..
2.6	Middle East		('000)	..	..	..	..	..
	Arrivals by means of transport used							
3.1	Air		('000)	6.4	4.1	5.1	5.9	13.0
3.2	Rail		('000)	..	..	..	..	..
3.3	Road		('000)	..	1.5	1.1	3.4	0.6
3.4	Sea		('000)	..	..	..	..	..
	Arrivals by purpose of visit							
4.1	Leisure, recreation and holidays		('000)	6.4	5.3	6.3	9.2	13.6
4.2	Business and professional		('000)	..	..	..	..	..
4.3	Other		('000)	..	0.3	..	..	..
	Accommodation							
5.1	Overnight stays in hotels and similar establishments		('000)	53	47	49	74	74
5.2	Guests in hotels and similar establishments		('000)	..	..	..	..	..
5.3	Overnight stays in all types of accommodation establishments		('000)	..	..	..	..	..
5.4	Average length of stay of non-resident tourists in all accommodation establishments		Nights	7.00	7.00	7.00	8.00	8.00
6.1	**Tourism expenditure in the country**	(**)	US$ Mn	9	8	8	13	19
6.2	"Travel" (*)		US$ Mn	..	..	..	..	..
6.3	"Passenger transport" (*)		US$ Mn	..	..	..	..	..
	DOMESTIC TOURISM							
	Accommodation							
7.1	Overnight stays in hotels and similar establishments		('000)	..	..	..	..	..
7.2	Guests in hotels and similar establishments		('000)	..	..	..	..	..
7.3	Overnight stays in all types of accommodation establishments		('000)	..	..	..	..	..
7.4	Average length of stay of resident tourists in all accommodation establishments		Nights	..	..	..	..	..
	OUTBOUND TOURISM							
8.1	**Departures**		('000)	..	..	..	..	..
8.2	**Tourism expenditure in other countries**		US$ Mn	..	..	..	..	..
8.3	"Travel" (*)		US$ Mn	..	..	..	..	..
8.4	"Passenger transport" (*)		US$ Mn	..	..	..	..	..
	TOURISM INDUSTRIES							
	Hotels and similar establishments							
9.1	Number of rooms		Units	1,215	1,239	1,239	1,239	1,436
9.2	Number of bed-places		Units	2,153	2,366	2,366	2,366	2,636
9.3	Occupancy rate		Percent	..	25.00	25.00	25.00	25.00
9.4	Average length of stay		Nights	..	8.00	8.00	8.00	8.50
	RELATED INDICATORS							
	Share of tourism expenditure (6.1) in:							
10.1	Gross Domestic Product (GDP)		Percent	..	..	..	..	..
10.2	Exports of goods		Percent	..	..	..	..	..
10.3	Exports of services		Percent	..	..	..	..	..

(*) Balance of Payments Items: 6.1 to 6.3 correspond to the "Credit" side (and are receipts for the country) while 8.2 to 8.4 correspond to the "Debit" side (and are expenditures in other countries).

(**) See Annex "Country notes".

BOLIVIA

	Basic Indicators	Units	2001	2002	2003	2004	2005
	INBOUND TOURISM						
	Arrivals						
1.1	Visitors	('000)	..	..	..	..	..
1.2	Tourists (overnight visitors)	('000)	316	334	420	478	504
1.3	Same-day visitors	('000)	..	..	..	..	..
1.4	Cruise passengers	('000)	..	..	..	..	..
	Arrivals by region						
2.1	Africa	('000)	1	1	1	1	2
2.2	Americas	('000)	215	217	210	227	250
2.3	Europe	('000)	146	146	141	143	142
2.4	East Asia and the Pacific	('000)	17	16	15	19	20
2.5	South Asia	('000)	..	..	..	..	..
2.6	Middle East	('000)	..	..	..	..	..
	Arrivals by means of transport used						
3.1	Air	('000)	208	199	220	247	271
3.2	Rail	('000)	9	10	7	6	6
3.3	Road	('000)	95	123	192	223	225
3.4	Sea	('000)	4	2	1	2	1
	Arrivals by purpose of visit						
4.1	Leisure, recreation and holidays	('000)	177	187	236	268	283
4.2	Business and professional	('000)	56	59	45	51	54
4.3	Other	('000)	83	88	139	158	167
	Accommodation						
5.1	Overnight stays in hotels and similar establishments	('000)	960	969	1,006	1,030	1,099
5.2	Guests in hotels and similar establishments	('000)	379	380	367	391	413
5.3	Overnight stays in all types of accommodation establishments	('000)	..	..	..	..	..
5.4	Average length of stay of non-resident tourists in all accommodation establishments	Nights	2.54	2.55	2.74	2.64	2.66
6.1	**Tourism expenditure in the country**	US$ Mn	119	144	244	283	346
6.2	"Travel" (*)	US$ Mn	76	101	167	192	239
6.3	"Passenger transport" (*)	US$ Mn	43	43	77	91	107
	DOMESTIC TOURISM						
	Accommodation						
7.1	Overnight stays in hotels and similar establishments	('000)	1,263	1,322	1,404	1,523	1,644
7.2	Guests in hotels and similar establishments	('000)	673	742	775	871	933
7.3	Overnight stays in all types of accommodation establishments	('000)	..	..	..	..	..
7.4	Average length of stay of resident tourists in all accommodation establishments	Nights	1.88	1.78	1.81	1.75	1.76
	OUTBOUND TOURISM						
8.1	**Departures**	('000)	222	217	305	331	312
8.2	**Tourism expenditure in other countries**	US$ Mn	114	114	198	232	258
8.3	"Travel" (*)	US$ Mn	83	80	139	164	186
8.4	"Passenger transport" (*)	US$ Mn	31	34	59	68	72
	TOURISM INDUSTRIES						
	Hotels and similar establishments						
9.1	Number of rooms	Units	16,810	18,463	19,800	20,862	20,949
9.2	Number of bed-places	Units	28,707	30,171	32,087	33,388	33,490
9.3	Occupancy rate	Percent	23.10	20.60	20.80	21.30	21.04
9.4	Average length of stay	Nights	2.11	2.04	2.11	2.02	2.04
	RELATED INDICATORS						
	Share of tourism expenditure (6.1) in:						
10.1	Gross Domestic Product (GDP)	Percent	1.5	1.8	3.0	3.2	3.7
10.2	Exports of goods	Percent	9.3	11.1	15.3	13.2	13.0
10.3	Exports of services	Percent	50.4	56.0	67.0	68.0	70.8

(*) Balance of Payments items: 6.1 to 6.3 correspond to the "Credit" side (and are receipts for the country) while 8.2 to 8.4 correspond to the "Debit" side (and are expenditures in other countries).

	Basic Indicators	Units	2001	2002	2003	2004	2005
	INBOUND TOURISM						
	Arrivals						
1.1	Visitors	('000)	94	94	107	116	103
1.2	Tourists (overnight visitors)	('000)	50	52	62	63	63
1.3	Same-day visitors	('000)	1	..	..	..	..
1.4	Cruise passengers	('000)	43	42	45	53	40
	Arrivals by region						
2.1	Africa	('000)	..	..	..	..	..
2.2	Americas	('000)	34	34	33	34	32
2.3	Europe	('000)	16	18	29	28	30
2.4	East Asia and the Pacific	('000)	..	..	..	..	..
2.5	South Asia	('000)	..	..	..	..	..
2.6	Middle East	('000)	..	..	..	..	..
	Arrivals by means of transport used						
3.1	Air	('000)	50	52	62	63	63
3.2	Rail	('000)	..	..	..	..	..
3.3	Road	('000)	..	..	..	..	..
3.4	Sea	('000)	43	42	45	53	40
	Arrivals by purpose of visit						
4.1	Leisure, recreation and holidays	('000)	30	34	60	48	..
4.2	Business and professional	('000)	4	1	2	1	..
4.3	Other	('000)	16	16	3	13	..
	Accommodation						
5.1	Overnight stays in hotels and similar establishments	('000)	374	340	415	419	..
5.2	Guests in hotels and similar establishments	('000)	..	..	..	..	..
5.3	Overnight stays in all types of accommodation establishments	('000)	484	486	574	578	587
5.4	Average length of stay of non-resident tourists in all accommodation establishments	Nights	9.60	9.30	9.23	9.15	9.38
6.1	**Tourism expenditure in the country**	US$ Mn	..	..	..	..	..
6.2	"Travel" (*)	US$ Mn	64	65	84	84	85
6.3	"Passenger transport" (*)	US$ Mn	..	..	..	..	..
	DOMESTIC TOURISM						
	Accommodation						
7.1	Overnight stays in hotels and similar establishments	('000)	..	..	..	..	..
7.2	Guests in hotels and similar establishments	('000)	..	..	..	..	..
7.3	Overnight stays in all types of accommodation establishments	('000)	..	..	..	..	..
7.4	Average length of stay of resident tourists in all accommodation establishments	Nights	..	..	..	..	..
	OUTBOUND TOURISM						
8.1	**Departures**	('000)	..	..	..	..	..
8.2	**Tourism expenditure in other countries**	US$ Mn	..	..	..	..	..
8.3	"Travel" (*)	US$ Mn	2	2	3	6	5
8.4	"Passenger transport" (*)	US$ Mn	..	..	..	..	..
	TOURISM INDUSTRIES						
	Hotels and similar establishments						
9.1	Number of rooms	Units	1,001	1,070	1,699	1,175	..
9.2	Number of bed-places	Units	2,907	3,069	3,337	3,258	..
9.3	Occupancy rate	Percent	46.00	60.00	42.00	61.00	..
9.4	Average length of stay	Nights	8.80	9.33	9.23	9.15	..
	RELATED INDICATORS						
	Share of tourism expenditure (6.1) in:						
10.1	Gross Domestic Product (GDP)	Percent	..	..	..	..	..
10.2	Exports of goods	Percent	..	..	..	..	..
10.3	Exports of services	Percent	..	..	..	..	..

(*) Balance of Payments items: 6.1 to 6.3 correspond to the "Credit" side (and are receipts for the country) while 8.2 to 8.4 correspond to the "Debit" side (and are expenditures in other countries).

BOSNIA AND HERZEGOVINA

	Basic Indicators	Units	2001	2002	2003	2004	2005
	INBOUND TOURISM						
	Arrivals						
1.1	Visitors	('000)	..	..	..	..	..
1.2	Tourists (overnight visitors)	('000)	139	160	165	190	217
1.3	Same-day visitors	('000)	..	..	..	..	..
1.4	Cruise passengers	('000)	..	..	..	..	..
	Arrivals by region						
2.1	Africa	('000)	..	..	..	..	..
2.2	Americas	('000)	8	8	7	8	8
2.3	Europe	('000)	125	146	152	177	204
2.4	East Asia and the Pacific	('000)	1	1	2	2	2
2.5	South Asia	('000)	..	..	..	..	..
2.6	Middle East	('000)	..	..	..	..	..
	Arrivals by means of transport used						
3.1	Air	('000)	..	..	..	..	..
3.2	Rail	('000)	..	..	..	..	..
3.3	Road	('000)	..	..	..	..	..
3.4	Sea	('000)	..	..	..	..	..
	Arrivals by purpose of visit						
4.1	Leisure, recreation and holidays	('000)	..	..	..	..	..
4.2	Business and professional	('000)	..	..	..	..	..
4.3	Other	('000)	..	..	..	..	..
	Accommodation						
5.1	Overnight stays in hotels and similar establishments	('000)	..	..	..	..	..
5.2	Guests in hotels and similar establishments	('000)	..	..	..	..	..
5.3	Overnight stays in all types of accommodation establishments	('000)	330	392	419	460	485
5.4	Average length of stay of non-resident tourists in all accommodation establishments	Nights	..	..	..	..	..
6.1	**Tourism expenditure in the country**	US$ Mn	279	307	404	543	604
6.2	"Travel" (*)	US$ Mn	265	288	377	517	565
6.3	"Passenger transport" (*)	US$ Mn	14	19	27	26	39
	DOMESTIC TOURISM						
	Accommodation						
7.1	Overnight stays in hotels and similar establishments	('000)	..	..	..	..	..
7.2	Guests in hotels and similar establishments	('000)	..	..	..	..	..
7.3	Overnight stays in all types of accommodation establishments	('000)	452	496	494	511	533
7.4	Average length of stay of resident tourists in all accommodation establishments	Nights	..	..	..	..	..
	OUTBOUND TOURISM						
8.1	**Departures**	('000)	..	..	..	..	..
8.2	**Tourism expenditure in other countries**	US$ Mn	96	112	145	162	160
8.3	"Travel" (*)	US$ Mn	74	85	106	117	123
8.4	"Passenger transport" (*)	US$ Mn	22	27	39	45	37
	TOURISM INDUSTRIES						
	Hotels and similar establishments						
9.1	Number of rooms	Units	6,956	7,280	7,731	8,353	8,687
9.2	Number of bed-places	Units	14,074	14,662	15,872	17,294	18,164
9.3	Occupancy rate	Percent	..	..	..	..	..
9.4	Average length of stay	Nights	..	..	..	..	..
	RELATED INDICATORS						
	Share of tourism expenditure (6.1) in:						
10.1	Gross Domestic Product (GDP)	Percent	5.8	5.5	5.7	6.3	6.4
10.2	Exports of goods	Percent	24.6	27.7	27.4	26.0	23.4
10.3	Exports of services	Percent	56.1	58.6	56.4	60.7	59.6

(*) Balance of Payments items: 6.1 to 6.3 correspond to the "Credit" side (and are receipts for the country) while 8.2 to 8.4 correspond to the "Debit" side (and are expenditures in other countries).

	Basic Indicators	Units	2001	2002	2003	2004	2005
	INBOUND TOURISM						
	Arrivals						
1.1	Visitors	('000)	1,451	1,485	1,592	1,727	1,885
1.2	Tourists (overnight visitors)	('000)	1,193	1,274	1,406	1,523	1,675
1.3	Same-day visitors	('000)	257	211	187	204	210
1.4	Cruise passengers	('000)	..	..	..	..	..
	Arrivals by region						
2.1	Africa	('000)	1,019	1,096	1,235	1,353	..
2.2	Americas	('000)	25	19	18	21	..
2.3	Europe	('000)	55	57	55	58	..
2.4	East Asia and the Pacific	('000)	12	12	12	12	..
2.5	South Asia	('000)	3	5	2	2	..
2.6	Middle East	('000)	..	..	..	..	..
	Arrivals by means of transport used						
3.1	Air	('000)	77	95	71	66	..
3.2	Rail	('000)	..	1	1	1	..
3.3	Road	('000)	1,106	1,176	1,332	1,455	..
3.4	Sea	('000)	..	..	..	..	..
	Arrivals by purpose of visit						
4.1	Leisure, recreation and holidays	('000)	275	178	231	248	..
4.2	Business and professional	('000)	98	123	106	80	..
4.3	Other	('000)	820	973	1,069	1,195	..
	Accommodation						
5.1	Overnight stays in hotels and similar establishments	('000)	..	..	..	..	..
5.2	Guests in hotels and similar establishments	('000)	84	100	211	232	271
5.3	Overnight stays in all types of accommodation establishments	('000)	..	..	..	..	..
5.4	Average length of stay of non-resident tourists in all accommodation establishments	Nights	..	..	..	..	..
6.1	**Tourism expenditure in the country**	US$ Mn	235	324	459	550	563
6.2	"Travel" (*)	US$ Mn	230	319	457	549	562
6.3	"Passenger transport" (*)	US$ Mn	5	5	2	1	1
	DOMESTIC TOURISM						
	Accommodation						
7.1	Overnight stays in hotels and similar establishments	('000)	..	..	..	..	..
7.2	Guests in hotels and similar establishments	('000)	74	149	119	89	145
7.3	Overnight stays in all types of accommodation establishments	('000)	..	..	..	..	..
7.4	Average length of stay of resident tourists in all accommodation establishments	Nights	..	..	..	..	..
	OUTBOUND TOURISM						
8.1	**Departures**	('000)	..	..	..	..	..
8.2	**Tourism expenditure in other countries**	US$ Mn	215	197	235	280	301
8.3	"Travel" (*)	US$ Mn	204	184	230	276	282
8.4	"Passenger transport" (*)	US$ Mn	11	13	5	4	19
	TOURISM INDUSTRIES						
	Hotels and similar establishments						
9.1	Number of rooms	Units	2,800	3,100	3,589	4,050	..
9.2	Number of bed-places	Units	5,400	6,200	6,646	7,800	..
9.3	Occupancy rate	Percent	24.60	24.10	30.50	35.50	41.50
9.4	Average length of stay	Nights	10.30	8.20	6.00	9.60	11.90
	RELATED INDICATORS						
	Share of tourism expenditure (6.1) in:						
10.1	Gross Domestic Product (GDP)	Percent	4.5	6.0	5.9	6.1	6.0
10.2	Exports of goods	Percent	10.2	14.0	15.2	14.9	12.7
10.3	Exports of services	Percent	69.1	66.1	71.4	73.5	65.8

(*) Balance of Payments items: 6.1 to 6.3 correspond to the "Credit" side (and are receipts for the country) while 8.2 to 8.4 correspond to the "Debit" side (and are expenditures in other countries).

BRAZIL

	Basic Indicators		Units	2001	2002	2003	2004	2005
	INBOUND TOURISM							
	Arrivals							
1.1	Visitors		('000)	..	..	..	..	..
1.2	Tourists (overnight visitors)		('000)	4,773	3,785	4,133	4,794	5,358
1.3	Same-day visitors		('000)	..	..	..	..	..
1.4	Cruise passengers		('000)	..	..	..	..	..
	Arrivals by region							
2.1	Africa		('000)	36	40	52	65	76
2.2	Americas		('000)	3,132	2,206	2,397	2,703	2,998
2.3	Europe		('000)	1,446	1,415	1,544	1,860	2,097
2.4	East Asia and the Pacific		('000)	127	108	129	156	177
2.5	South Asia		('000)	..	..	..	..	..
2.6	Middle East		('000)	11	7	6	6	7
	Arrivals by means of transport used							
3.1	Air		('000)	2,960	2,815	3,083	3,569	3,938
3.2	Rail		('000)	..	..	..	..	..
3.3	Road		('000)	1,678	891	993	1,151	1,314
3.4	Sea		('000)	134	79	57	74	106
	Arrivals by purpose of visit							
4.1	Leisure, recreation and holidays		('000)	2,649	1,938	2,228	2,325	2,379
4.2	Business and professional		('000)	1,443	1,070	1,075	1,376	1,559
4.3	Other		('000)	681	776	831	1,093	1,420
	Accommodation							
5.1	Overnight stays in hotels and similar establishments		('000)	..	..	..	..	..
5.2	Guests in hotels and similar establishments		('000)	..	..	..	..	..
5.3	Overnight stays in all types of accommodation establishments		('000)	..	..	..	..	..
5.4	Average length of stay of non-resident tourists in all accommodation establishments		Nights	12.20	14.00	13.50	12.70	12.70
6.1	**Tourism expenditure in the country**	(**)	US$ Mn	1,845	2,142	2,673	3,389	4,169
6.2	"Travel" (*)		US$ Mn	1,731	1,998	2,479	3,222	3,861
6.3	"Passenger transport" (*)		US$ Mn	114	144	194	167	308
	DOMESTIC TOURISM							
	Accommodation							
7.1	Overnight stays in hotels and similar establishments		('000)	..	..	..	..	..
7.2	Guests in hotels and similar establishments		('000)	..	..	..	..	..
7.3	Overnight stays in all types of accommodation establishments		('000)	..	..	..	..	..
7.4	Average length of stay of resident tourists in all accommodation establishments		Nights	..	..	..	..	..
	OUTBOUND TOURISM							
8.1	**Departures**		('000)	2,674	2,364	3,225	3,738	4,696
8.2	**Tourism expenditure in other countries**		US$ Mn	3,765	2,929	2,874	3,752	5,905
8.3	"Travel" (*)		US$ Mn	3,199	2,396	2,261	2,871	4,720
8.4	"Passenger transport" (*)		US$ Mn	566	533	613	881	1,185
	TOURISM INDUSTRIES							
	Hotels and similar establishments							
9.1	Number of rooms		Units	..	..	..	..	..
9.2	Number of bed-places		Units	..	..	..	..	..
9.3	Occupancy rate		Percent	..	..	..	..	..
9.4	Average length of stay		Nights	..	..	..	..	..
	RELATED INDICATORS							
	Share of tourism expenditure (6.1) in:							
10.1	Gross Domestic Product (GDP)		Percent	0.4	0.5	0.5	0.6	0.5
10.2	Exports of goods		Percent	3.2	3.5	3.7	3.5	3.5
10.3	Exports of services		Percent	19.8	22.4	25.6	26.9	25.9

(*) Balance of Payments items: 6.1 to 6.3 correspond to the "Credit" side (and are receipts for the country) while 8.2 to 8.4 correspond to the "Debit" side (and are expenditures in other countries).

(**) See Annex "Country notes".

	Basic Indicators		Units	2001	2002	2003	2004	2005
	INBOUND TOURISM							
	Arrivals							
1.1	Visitors		('000)	535	544	658	813	821
1.2	Tourists (overnight visitors)		('000)	296	282	318	304	337
1.3	Same-day visitors		('000)	37	32	40	42	34
1.4	Cruise passengers		('000)	202	230	300	467	449
	Arrivals by region							
2.1	Africa		('000)	..	..	..	..	..
2.2	Americas		('000)	259	250	261	..	..
2.3	Europe		('000)	33	29	50	..	..
2.4	East Asia and the Pacific		('000)	..	..	..	..	..
2.5	South Asia		('000)	..	..	..	..	..
2.6	Middle East		('000)	..	..	..	..	..
	Arrivals by means of transport used							
3.1	Air		('000)	144	135	153	220	205
3.2	Rail		('000)	..	..	..	..	..
3.3	Road		('000)	..	..	..	..	..
3.4	Sea		('000)	391	409	504	593	616
	Arrivals by purpose of visit							
4.1	Leisure, recreation and holidays		('000)	282	271	287	293	..
4.2	Business and professional		('000)	7	6	6	5	..
4.3	Other		('000)	7	5	25	7	..
	Accommodation							
5.1	Overnight stays in hotels and similar establishments		('000)	86	80	..	..	..
5.2	Guests in hotels and similar establishments		('000)	74	58	60	85	94
5.3	Overnight stays in all types of accommodation establishments		('000)	106	105	..	..	..
5.4	Average length of stay of non-resident tourists in all accommodation establishments		Nights	9.90	9.30	..	..	..
6.1	**Tourism expenditure in the country**	(**)	US$ Mn	401	345	342	393	437
6.2	"Travel" (*)		US$ Mn	..	..	..	..	..
6.3	"Passenger transport" (*)		US$ Mn	..	..	..	..	..
	DOMESTIC TOURISM							
	Accommodation							
7.1	Overnight stays in hotels and similar establishments		('000)	..	..	..	..	..
7.2	Guests in hotels and similar establishments		('000)	..	..	..	..	..
7.3	Overnight stays in all types of accommodation establishments		('000)	..	..	..	..	..
7.4	Average length of stay of resident tourists in all accommodation establishments		Nights	..	..	..	..	..
	OUTBOUND TOURISM							
8.1	**Departures**		('000)	..	..	..	..	..
8.2	**Tourism expenditure in other countries**		US$ Mn	..	..	..	..	..
8.3	"Travel" (*)		US$ Mn	..	..	..	..	..
8.4	"Passenger transport" (*)		US$ Mn	..	..	..	..	..
	TOURISM INDUSTRIES							
	Hotels and similar establishments							
9.1	Number of rooms		Units	2,645	2,661	2,661	2,760	2,722
9.2	Number of bed-places		Units	..	..	..	..	..
9.3	Occupancy rate		Percent	59.90	61.40	66.80	67.10	68.60
9.4	Average length of stay		Nights	12.00	9.00	10.00	11.00	9.00
	RELATED INDICATORS							
	Share of tourism expenditure (6.1) in:							
10.1	Gross Domestic Product (GDP)		Percent	..	..	..	..	..
10.2	Exports of goods		Percent	..	..	..	..	..
10.3	Exports of services		Percent	..	..	..	..	..

(*) Balance of Payments items: 6.1 to 6.3 correspond to the "Credit" side (and are receipts for the country) while 8.2 to 8.4 correspond to the "Debit" side (and are expenditures in other countries).

(**) See Annex "Country notes".

BRUNEI DARUSSALAM

	Basic Indicators	Units	2001	2002	2003	2004	2005
	INBOUND TOURISM						
	Arrivals						
1.1	Visitors	('000)	840	..	..	..	815
1.2	Tourists (overnight visitors)	('000)	..	..	..	..	..
1.3	Same-day visitors	('000)	..	..	..	..	..
1.4	Cruise passengers	('000)	..	..	..	..	..
	Arrivals by region						
2.1	Africa	('000)	..	..	..	..	..
2.2	Americas	('000)	6	..	..	..	4
2.3	Europe	('000)	30	..	..	..	14
2.4	East Asia and the Pacific	('000)	786	..	..	..	791
2.5	South Asia	('000)	15	..	..	..	5
2.6	Middle East	('000)	2	..	..	..	1
	Arrivals by means of transport used						
3.1	Air	('000)	..	..	..	..	..
3.2	Rail	('000)	..	..	..	..	..
3.3	Road	('000)	..	..	..	..	..
3.4	Sea	('000)	..	..	..	..	..
	Arrivals by purpose of visit						
4.1	Leisure, recreation and holidays	('000)	29	..	..	..	27
4.2	Business and professional	('000)	17	..	..	..	4
4.3	Other	('000)	794	..	..	..	784
	Accommodation						
5.1	Overnight stays in hotels and similar establishments	('000)	..	..	..	..	..
5.2	Guests in hotels and similar establishments	('000)	118	141	151	197	300
5.3	Overnight stays in all types of accommodation establishments	('000)	..	..	..	..	..
5.4	Average length of stay of non-resident tourists in all accommodation establishments	Nights	..	..	..	..	..
6.1	**Tourism expenditure in the country**	US$ Mn	..	..	..	..	..
6.2	"Travel" (*)	US$ Mn	..	..	..	..	..
6.3	"Passenger transport" (*)	US$ Mn	..	..	..	..	..
	DOMESTIC TOURISM						
	Accommodation						
7.1	Overnight stays in hotels and similar establishments	('000)	..	..	..	..	..
7.2	Guests in hotels and similar establishments	('000)	..	..	..	..	..
7.3	Overnight stays in all types of accommodation establishments	('000)	..	..	..	..	..
7.4	Average length of stay of resident tourists in all accommodation establishments	Nights	..	..	..	..	..
	OUTBOUND TOURISM						
8.1	**Departures**	('000)	..	..	..	..	..
8.2	**Tourism expenditure in other countries**	US$ Mn	..	..	..	..	..
8.3	"Travel" (*)	US$ Mn	..	..	..	..	..
8.4	"Passenger transport" (*)	US$ Mn	..	..	..	..	..
	TOURISM INDUSTRIES						
	Hotels and similar establishments						
9.1	Number of rooms	Units	2,111	2,142	2,311	2,311	2,371
9.2	Number of bed-places	Units	3,115	3,157	3,405	3,405	3,501
9.3	Occupancy rate	Percent	31.50	35.80	33.20	35.40	39.30
9.4	Average length of stay	Nights	..	..	..	..	..
	RELATED INDICATORS						
	Share of tourism expenditure (6.1) in:						
10.1	Gross Domestic Product (GDP)	Percent	..	..	..	..	..
10.2	Exports of goods	Percent	..	..	..	..	..
10.3	Exports of services	Percent	..	..	..	..	..

(*) Balance of Payments items: 6.1 to 6.3 correspond to the "Credit" side (and are receipts for the country) while 8.2 to 8.4 correspond to the "Debit" side (and are expenditures in other countries).

BULGARIA

	Basic Indicators	Units	2001	2002	2003	2004	2005
	INBOUND TOURISM						
	Arrivals						
1.1	Visitors	('000)	5,104	5,563	6,241	6,982	7,282
1.2	Tourists (overnight visitors)	('000)	3,186	3,433	4,048	4,630	4,837
1.3	Same-day visitors	('000)	1,918	2,130	2,193	2,352	2,445
1.4	Cruise passengers	('000)	..	..	..	..	..
	Arrivals by region						
2.1	Africa	('000)	3	4	4	3	3
2.2	Americas	('000)	52	47	55	68	77
2.3	Europe	('000)	4,951	5,426	6,088	6,807	7,088
2.4	East Asia and the Pacific	('000)	24	22	27	32	35
2.5	South Asia	('000)	13	9	12	12	11
2.6	Middle East	('000)	15	14	15	16	18
	Arrivals by means of transport used						
3.1	Air	('000)	1,008	1,185	1,409	1,715	2,007
3.2	Rail	('000)	205	192	170	148	157
3.3	Road	('000)	3,774	4,082	4,542	4,963	4,940
3.4	Sea	('000)	117	104	120	156	178
	Arrivals by purpose of visit						
4.1	Leisure, recreation and holidays	('000)	2,756	2,993	3,532	4,010	4,090
4.2	Business and professional	('000)	184	180	216	272	340
4.3	Other	('000)	2,164	2,390	2,493	2,699	2,852
	Accommodation						
5.1	Overnight stays in hotels and similar establishments	('000)	6,118	6,985	8,987	10,139	11,471
5.2	Guests in hotels and similar establishments	('000)	864	1,030	1,376	1,668	1,909
5.3	Overnight stays in all types of accommodation establishments	('000)	6,190	7,055	9,142	10,304	11,624
5.4	Average length of stay of non-resident tourists in all accommodation establishments	Nights	8.35	8.50	8.60	4.20	4.20
6.1	**Tourism expenditure in the country**	US$ Mn	1,262	1,392	2,051	2,797	3,026
6.2	"Travel" (*)	US$ Mn	994	1,096	1,621	2,202	2,383
6.3	"Passenger transport" (*)	US$ Mn	268	296	430	595	643
	DOMESTIC TOURISM						
	Accommodation						
7.1	Overnight stays in hotels and similar establishments	('000)	2,842	2,982	3,058	3,423	3,957
7.2	Guests in hotels and similar establishments	('000)	1,207	1,355	1,431	1,503	1,721
7.3	Overnight stays in all types of accommodation establishments	('000)	3,194	3,231	3,379	3,857	4,447
7.4	Average length of stay of resident tourists in all accommodation establishments	Nights	..	..	..	..	..
	OUTBOUND TOURISM						
8.1	**Departures**	('000)	2,730	3,188	3,403	3,882	4,235
8.2	**Tourism expenditure in other countries**	US$ Mn	836	1,018	1,467	1,893	1,836
8.3	"Travel" (*)	US$ Mn	589	717	1,033	1,333	1,293
8.4	"Passenger transport" (*)	US$ Mn	247	301	434	560	543
	TOURISM INDUSTRIES						
	Hotels and similar establishments						
9.1	Number of rooms	Units	..	..	..	..	..
9.2	Number of bed-places	Units	116,044	132,024	143,960	171,000	221,144
9.3	Occupancy rate	Percent	29.00	30.70	34.80	35.90	37.60
9.4	Average length of stay	Nights	4.30	4.20	4.30	4.30	4.30
	RELATED INDICATORS						
	Share of tourism expenditure (6.1) in:						
10.1	Gross Domestic Product (GDP)	Percent	9.3	8.9	10.3	11.5	11.4
10.2	Exports of goods	Percent	24.7	26.0	29.0	28.2	25.8
10.3	Exports of services	Percent	58.3	63.2	69.3	69.4	71.1

(*) Balance of Payments items: 6.1 to 6.3 correspond to the "Credit" side (and are receipts for the country) while 8.2 to 8.4 correspond to the "Debit" side (and are expenditures in other countries).

BURKINA FASO

	Basic Indicators		Units	2001	2002	2003	2004	2005
	INBOUND TOURISM							
	Arrivals							
1.1	Visitors		('000)	..	..	..	..	..
1.2	Tourists (overnight visitors)		('000)	128	150	163	222	245
1.3	Same-day visitors		('000)	..	..	..	..	..
1.4	Cruise passengers		('000)	..	..	..	..	..
	Arrivals by region							
2.1	Africa		('000)	50	55	65	96	101
2.2	Americas		('000)	8	10	10	13	15
2.3	Europe		('000)	63	73	77	100	113
2.4	East Asia and the Pacific		('000)	3	4	3	5	7
2.5	South Asia		('000)	..	..	..	..	..
2.6	Middle East		('000)	1	1	1	2	2
	Arrivals by means of transport used							
3.1	Air		('000)	..	..	..	..	..
3.2	Rail		('000)	..	..	..	..	..
3.3	Road		('000)	..	..	..	..	..
3.4	Sea		('000)	..	..	..	..	..
	Arrivals by purpose of visit							
4.1	Leisure, recreation and holidays		('000)	55	54	63	71	50
4.2	Business and professional		('000)	53	111	115	165	225
4.3	Other		('000)	76	34	38	53	49
	Accommodation							
5.1	Overnight stays in hotels and similar establishments		('000)	442	527	554	632	789
5.2	Guests in hotels and similar establishments		('000)	128	150	163	222	245
5.3	Overnight stays in all types of accommodation establishments		('000)	..	..	..	..	..
5.4	Average length of stay of non-resident tourists in all accommodation establishments		Nights	2.77	3.22	3.05	2.50	2.90
6.1	**Tourism expenditure in the country**	(**)	US$ Mn	25	..	..	..	..
6.2	"Travel" (*)		US$ Mn	20	..	..	..	..
6.3	"Passenger transport" (*)		US$ Mn	5	..	..	..	..
	DOMESTIC TOURISM							
	Accommodation							
7.1	Overnight stays in hotels and similar establishments		('000)	93	112	119	135	173
7.2	Guests in hotels and similar establishments		('000)	56	49	54	68	80
7.3	Overnight stays in all types of accommodation establishments		('000)	..	..	..	..	..
7.4	Average length of stay of resident tourists in all accommodation establishments		Nights	..	..	..	..	..
	OUTBOUND TOURISM							
8.1	**Departures**		('000)	..	..	..	..	..
8.2	**Tourism expenditure in other countries**		US$ Mn	35	..	..	..	..
8.3	"Travel" (*)		US$ Mn	22	..	..	..	..
8.4	"Passenger transport" (*)		US$ Mn	13	..	..	..	..
	TOURISM INDUSTRIES							
	Hotels and similar establishments							
9.1	Number of rooms		Units	..	..	..	..	..
9.2	Number of bed-places		Units	..	..	..	..	..
9.3	Occupancy rate		Percent	59.96	59.93	59.10	63.95	69.00
9.4	Average length of stay		Nights	..	..	..	..	..
	RELATED INDICATORS							
	Share of tourism expenditure (6.1) in:							
10.1	Gross Domestic Product (GDP)		Percent	0.9	..	..	..	..
10.2	Exports of goods		Percent	11.2	..	..	..	..
10.3	Exports of services		Percent	67.6	..	..	..	..

(*) Balance of Payments items: 6.1 to 6.3 correspond to the "Credit" side (and are receipts for the country) while 8.2 to 8.4 correspond to the "Debit" side (and are expenditures in other countries).

(**) See Annex "Country notes".

	Basic Indicators	Units	2001	2002	2003	2004	2005
	INBOUND TOURISM						
	Arrivals						
1.1	Visitors	('000)	..	..	..	..	..
1.2	Tourists (overnight visitors)	('000)	36	74	74	133	148
1.3	Same-day visitors	('000)	..	..	..	..	..
1.4	Cruise passengers	('000)	..	..	..	..	..
	Arrivals by region						
2.1	Africa	('000)	17	25	25	1	49
2.2	Americas	('000)	2	2	2	6	10
2.3	Europe	('000)	14	6	8	29	29
2.4	East Asia and the Pacific	('000)	3	1	1	5	4
2.5	South Asia	('000)	..	..	..	..	..
2.6	Middle East	('000)	..	..	..	..	..
	Arrivals by means of transport used						
3.1	Air	('000)	14	18	17	39	49
3.2	Rail	('000)	..	..	..	..	..
3.3	Road	('000)	19	35	36	48	50
3.4	Sea	('000)	3	21	21	46	49
	Arrivals by purpose of visit						
4.1	Leisure, recreation and holidays	('000)	10	17	18	38	49
4.2	Business and professional	('000)	12	22	22	45	49
4.3	Other	('000)	14	35	34	50	51
	Accommodation						
5.1	Overnight stays in hotels and similar establishments	('000)	115	..	..	..	..
5.2	Guests in hotels and similar establishments	('000)	..	..	..	..	..
5.3	Overnight stays in all types of accommodation establishments	('000)	..	..	..	..	..
5.4	Average length of stay of non-resident tourists in all accommodation establishments	Nights	..	..	..	..	..
6.1	**Tourism expenditure in the country**	US$ Mn	0.9	1.6	1.2	1.8	1.9
6.2	"Travel" (*)	US$ Mn	0.5	1.1	0.7	1.2	1.5
6.3	"Passenger transport" (*)	US$ Mn	0.4	0.5	0.5	0.6	0.4
	DOMESTIC TOURISM						
	Accommodation						
7.1	Overnight stays in hotels and similar establishments	('000)	..	..	..	..	..
7.2	Guests in hotels and similar establishments	('000)	..	..	..	..	..
7.3	Overnight stays in all types of accommodation establishments	('000)	..	..	..	..	..
7.4	Average length of stay of resident tourists in all accommodation establishments	Nights	..	..	..	..	..
	OUTBOUND TOURISM						
8.1	**Departures**	('000)	35	..	..	..	..
8.2	**Tourism expenditure in other countries**	US$ Mn	..	..	..	30	62
8.3	"Travel" (*)	US$ Mn	12	14	15	24	60
8.4	"Passenger transport" (*)	US$ Mn	..	..	..	6	2
	TOURISM INDUSTRIES						
	Hotels and similar establishments						
9.1	Number of rooms	Units	110	115	130	130	130
9.2	Number of bed-places	Units	1,220	1,270	1,420	1,420	1,420
9.3	Occupancy rate	Percent	..	..	..	..	..
9.4	Average length of stay	Nights	..	..	..	..	..
	RELATED INDICATORS						
	Share of tourism expenditure (6.1) in:						
10.1	Gross Domestic Product (GDP)	Percent	0.1	0.3	0.2	0.3	0.2
10.2	Exports of goods	Percent	2.3	5.2	3.2	3.8	3.3
10.3	Exports of services	Percent	18.0	20.0	17.1	11.3	5.4

(*) Balance of Payments items: 6.1 to 6.3 correspond to the "Credit" side (and are receipts for the country) while 8.2 to 8.4 correspond to the "Debit" side (and are expenditures in other countries).

CAMBODIA

	Basic Indicators	Units	2001	2002	2003	2004	2005
	INBOUND TOURISM						
	Arrivals						
1.1	Visitors	('000)	..	..	..	..	..
1.2	Tourists (overnight visitors)	('000)	605	787	701	1,055	1,422
1.3	Same-day visitors	('000)	..	..	..	..	..
1.4	Cruise passengers	('000)	..	..	..	..	..
	Arrivals by region						
2.1	Africa	('000)	..	..	..	..	..
2.2	Americas	('000)	44	113	89	122	152
2.3	Europe	('000)	66	219	183	243	310
2.4	East Asia and the Pacific	('000)	158	409	412	589	787
2.5	South Asia	('000)	5	4	5	7	8
2.6	Middle East	('000)	..	..	..	..	..
	Arrivals by means of transport used						
3.1	Air	('000)	408	523	456	626	857
3.2	Rail	('000)	..	..	..	..	..
3.3	Road	('000)	197	264	226	336	445
3.4	Sea	('000)	..	..	19	25	32
	Arrivals by purpose of visit						
4.1	Leisure, recreation and holidays	('000)	335	448	609	954	1,197
4.2	Business and professional	('000)	62	58	71	68	87
4.3	Other	('000)	11	17	21	33	49
	Accommodation						
5.1	Overnight stays in hotels and similar establishments	('000)	..	..	..	..	..
5.2	Guests in hotels and similar establishments	('000)	..	..	..	..	..
5.3	Overnight stays in all types of accommodation establishments	('000)	..	..	..	..	..
5.4	Average length of stay of non-resident tourists in all accommodation establishments	Nights	5.50	5.80	5.50	6.30	6.30
6.1	**Tourism expenditure in the country**	US$ Mn	429	509	441	674	927
6.2	"Travel" (*)	US$ Mn	380	454	389	604	840
6.3	"Passenger transport" (*)	US$ Mn	49	55	52	70	87
	DOMESTIC TOURISM						
	Accommodation						
7.1	Overnight stays in hotels and similar establishments	('000)	..	..	..	..	..
7.2	Guests in hotels and similar establishments	('000)	..	..	..	..	..
7.3	Overnight stays in all types of accommodation establishments	('000)	..	..	..	..	..
7.4	Average length of stay of resident tourists in all accommodation establishments	Nights	..	..	..	..	..
	OUTBOUND TOURISM						
8.1	**Departures**	('000)	37	45	60	239	427
8.2	**Tourism expenditure in other countries**	US$ Mn	59	64	60	80	138
8.3	"Travel" (*)	US$ Mn	37	38	36	48	97
8.4	"Passenger transport" (*)	US$ Mn	22	26	24	32	41
	TOURISM INDUSTRIES						
	Hotels and similar establishments						
9.1	Number of rooms	Units	10,804	11,426	19,698	21,955	24,471
9.2	Number of bed-places	Units	18,277	19,398	29,547	32,932	36,706
9.3	Occupancy rate	Percent	48.00	50.00	50.00	52.00	52.00
9.4	Average length of stay	Nights	..	..	..	..	..
	RELATED INDICATORS						
	Share of tourism expenditure (6.1) in:						
10.1	Gross Domestic Product (GDP)	Percent	11.3	12.5	10.1	13.8	17.2
10.2	Exports of goods	Percent	27.3	28.8	21.1	26.0	31.9
10.3	Exports of services	Percent	81.7	84.3	80.9	84.1	83.7

(*) Balance of Payments items: 6.1 to 6.3 correspond to the "Credit" side (and are receipts for the country) while 8.2 to 8.4 correspond to the "Debit" side (and are expenditures in other countries).

	Basic Indicators	Units	2001	2002	2003	2004	2005
	INBOUND TOURISM						
	Arrivals						
1.1	Visitors	('000)	..	..	..	..	..
1.2	Tourists (overnight visitors)	('000)	221	226	..	190	176
1.3	Same-day visitors	('000)	..	..	..	..	..
1.4	Cruise passengers	('000)	..	..	..	..	..
	Arrivals by region						
2.1	Africa	('000)	100	105	..	80	89
2.2	Americas	('000)	13	14	..	12	10
2.3	Europe	('000)	100	99	..	83	68
2.4	East Asia and the Pacific	('000)	4	5	..	4	5
2.5	South Asia	('000)	..	..	..	..	..
2.6	Middle East	('000)	1	1	..	5	2
	Arrivals by means of transport used						
3.1	Air	('000)	..	..	..	..	..
3.2	Rail	('000)	..	..	..	..	..
3.3	Road	('000)	..	..	..	..	..
3.4	Sea	('000)	..	..	..	..	..
	Arrivals by purpose of visit						
4.1	Leisure, recreation and holidays	('000)	..	..	..	..	..
4.2	Business and professional	('000)	..	..	..	..	..
4.3	Other	('000)	..	..	..	..	..
	Accommodation						
5.1	Overnight stays in hotels and similar establishments	('000)	420	458	..	414	355
5.2	Guests in hotels and similar establishments	('000)	221	226	..	190	176
5.3	Overnight stays in all types of accommodation establishments	('000)	..	..	..	..	..
5.4	Average length of stay of non-resident tourists in all accommodation establishments	Nights	..	..	..	..	..
6.1	**Tourism expenditure in the country**	US$ Mn	182	124	162	..	..
6.2	"Travel" (*)	US$ Mn	73	62	114	..	..
6.3	"Passenger transport" (*)	US$ Mn	109	62	48	..	..
	DOMESTIC TOURISM						
	Accommodation						
7.1	Overnight stays in hotels and similar establishments	('000)	1,108	..	..	1,393	1,399
7.2	Guests in hotels and similar establishments	('000)	..	..	..	886	977
7.3	Overnight stays in all types of accommodation establishments	('000)	..	..	..	..	..
7.4	Average length of stay of resident tourists in all accommodation establishments	Nights	..	..	..	..	..
	OUTBOUND TOURISM						
8.1	**Departures**	('000)	..	..	..	..	..
8.2	**Tourism expenditure in other countries**	US$ Mn	199	205	294	..	..
8.3	"Travel" (*)	US$ Mn	160	171	212	..	..
8.4	"Passenger transport" (*)	US$ Mn	39	34	82	..	..
	TOURISM INDUSTRIES						
	Hotels and similar establishments						
9.1	Number of rooms	Units	..	..	..	..	22,112
9.2	Number of bed-places	Units	..	..	..	..	24,598
9.3	Occupancy rate	Percent	..	..	..	..	..
9.4	Average length of stay	Nights	..	..	..	..	..
	RELATED INDICATORS						
	Share of tourism expenditure (6.1) in:						
10.1	Gross Domestic Product (GDP)	Percent	1.9	1.1	1.2	..	..
10.2	Exports of goods	Percent	9.6	6.3	6.6	..	..
10.3	Exports of services	Percent	21.2	13.2	36.4	..	..

(*) Balance of Payments items: 6.1 to 6.3 correspond to the "Credit" side (and are receipts for the country) while 8.2 to 8.4 correspond to the "Debit" side (and are expenditures in other countries).

CANADA

	Basic Indicators	Units	2001	2002	2003	2004	2005
	INBOUND TOURISM						
	Arrivals						
1.1	Visitors	('000)	47,147	44,896	38,903	38,845	36,160
1.2	Tourists (overnight visitors)	('000)	19,679	20,057	17,534	19,095	18,770
1.3	Same-day visitors	('000)	27,468	24,839	21,369	19,750	17,390
1.4	Cruise passengers	('000)	..	..	..	..	..
	Arrivals by region						
2.1	Africa	('000)	61	54	52	58	62
2.2	Americas	('000)	15,974	16,576	14,589	15,469	14,867
2.3	Europe	('000)	2,324	2,095	1,873	2,202	2,397
2.4	East Asia and the Pacific	('000)	1,195	1,210	900	1,222	1,282
2.5	South Asia	('000)	78	79	80	96	110
2.6	Middle East	('000)	47	42	40	48	52
	Arrivals by means of transport used						
3.1	Air	('000)	7,348	7,193	6,408	7,497	7,746
3.2	Rail	('000)	117	108	102	97	97
3.3	Road	('000)	11,684	12,226	10,398	10,837	10,221
3.4	Sea	('000)	530	531	626	714	706
	Arrivals by purpose of visit						
4.1	Leisure, recreation and holidays	('000)	11,244	11,503	9,669	9,386	9,951
4.2	Business and professional	('000)	2,519	2,560	2,231	3,780	2,622
4.3	Other	('000)	5,817	5,901	5,519	5,866	6,039
	Accommodation						
5.1	Overnight stays in hotels and similar establishments	('000)	..	..	..	..	..
5.2	Guests in hotels and similar establishments	('000)	..	..	..	..	..
5.3	Overnight stays in all types of accommodation establishments	('000)	125,022	122,150	107,698	123,426	125,656
5.4	Average length of stay of non-resident tourists in all accommodation establishments	Nights	..	..	..	..	..
6.1	**Tourism expenditure in the country**	US$ Mn	12,680	12,744	12,236	14,953	15,830
6.2	"Travel" (*)	US$ Mn	10,623	10,687	10,602	12,847	13,590
6.3	"Passenger transport" (*)	US$ Mn	2,057	2,057	1,634	2,106	2,240
	DOMESTIC TOURISM						
	Accommodation						
7.1	Overnight stays in hotels and similar establishments	('000)	48,980	59,217	53,882	55,312	..
7.2	Guests in hotels and similar establishments	('000)	..	..	..	..	..
7.3	Overnight stays in all types of accommodation establishments	('000)	244,608	308,046	278,468	284,093	..
7.4	Average length of stay of resident tourists in all accommodation establishments	Nights	..	..	..	..	..
	OUTBOUND TOURISM						
8.1	**Departures**	('000)	18,359	17,705	17,739	19,545	21,101
8.2	**Tourism expenditure in other countries**	US$ Mn	14,635	14,257	16,309	19,657	23,061
8.3	"Travel" (*)	US$ Mn	11,961	11,722	13,337	15,914	18,341
8.4	"Passenger transport" (*)	US$ Mn	2,674	2,535	2,972	3,743	4,720
	TOURISM INDUSTRIES						
	Hotels and similar establishments						
9.1	Number of rooms	Units	367,271	..	363,628	377,771	..
9.2	Number of bed-places	Units	..	..	..	..	..
9.3	Occupancy rate	Percent	62.10	61.90	58.70	62.10	..
9.4	Average length of stay	Nights	..	..	..	..	..
	RELATED INDICATORS						
	Share of tourism expenditure (6.1) in:						
10.1	Gross Domestic Product (GDP)	Percent	1.8	1.8	1.4	1.5	1.4
10.2	Exports of goods	Percent	4.7	4.8	4.3	4.5	4.2
10.3	Exports of services	Percent	32.7	31.5	28.0	30.4	29.5

(*) Balance of Payments items: 6.1 to 6.3 correspond to the "Credit" side (and are receipts for the country) while 8.2 to 8.4 correspond to the "Debit" side (and are expenditures in other countries).

Basic Indicators		Units	2001	2002	2003	2004	2005
	INBOUND TOURISM						
	Arrivals						
1.1	Visitors	('000)	..	..	..	..	..
1.2	Tourists (overnight visitors)	('000)	134	126	150	157	198
1.3	Same-day visitors	('000)	..	..	..	..	..
1.4	Cruise passengers	('000)	..	..	..	..	..
	Arrivals by region						
2.1	Africa	('000)	3	10	5	10	9
2.2	Americas	('000)	2	2	2	1	2
2.3	Europe	('000)	122	106	135	136	173
2.4	East Asia and the Pacific	('000)	..	..	..	..	..
2.5	South Asia	('000)	..	..	..	..	..
2.6	Middle East	('000)	..	..	..	..	..
	Arrivals by means of transport used						
3.1	Air	('000)	115	..	..	..	..
3.2	Rail	('000)	..	..	..	..	..
3.3	Road	('000)	..	..	..	..	..
3.4	Sea	('000)	..	..	..	..	..
	Arrivals by purpose of visit						
4.1	Leisure, recreation and holidays	('000)	..	..	..	..	..
4.2	Business and professional	('000)	..	..	..	..	..
4.3	Other	('000)	..	..	..	..	..
	Accommodation						
5.1	Overnight stays in hotels and similar establishments	('000)	725	624	820	787	850
5.2	Guests in hotels and similar establishments	('000)	134	126	150	157	198
5.3	Overnight stays in all types of accommodation establishments	('000)	..	..	..	..	..
5.4	Average length of stay of non-resident tourists in all accommodation establishments	Nights	..	..	..	..	..
6.1	**Tourism expenditure in the country**	US$ Mn	77	101	137	164	177
6.2	"Travel" (*)	US$ Mn	54	66	85	110	122
6.3	"Passenger transport" (*)	US$ Mn	23	35	52	54	55
	DOMESTIC TOURISM						
	Accommodation						
7.1	Overnight stays in hotels and similar establishments	('000)	81	70	83	78	85
7.2	Guests in hotels and similar establishments	('000)	28	26	28	28	36
7.3	Overnight stays in all types of accommodation establishments	('000)	..	..	..	..	..
7.4	Average length of stay of resident tourists in all accommodation establishments	Nights	..	..	..	..	..
	OUTBOUND TOURISM						
8.1	**Departures**	('000)	..	..	..	..	..
8.2	**Tourism expenditure in other countries**	US$ Mn	55	63	89	91	82
8.3	"Travel" (*)	US$ Mn	47	56	71	78	67
8.4	"Passenger transport" (*)	US$ Mn	8	7	18	13	15
	TOURISM INDUSTRIES						
	Hotels and similar establishments						
9.1	Number of rooms	Units	2,489	2,820	3,146	3,150	4,406
9.2	Number of bed-places	Units	4,628	5,159	5,715	5,804	8,278
9.3	Occupancy rate	Percent	49.10	41.20	44.20	40.90	..
9.4	Average length of stay	Nights	4.60	4.20	4.70	4.60	..
	RELATED INDICATORS						
	Share of tourism expenditure (6.1) in:						
10.1	Gross Domestic Product (GDP)	Percent	14.0	16.4	17.2	17.3	17.3
10.2	Exports of goods	Percent	208.1	240.5	258.5	282.8	198.9
10.3	Exports of services	Percent	59.2	66.0	61.2	67.8	63.9

(*) Balance of Payments items: 6.1 to 6.3 correspond to the "Credit" side (and are receipts for the country) while 8.2 to 8.4 correspond to the "Debit" side (and are expenditures in other countries).

CAYMAN ISLANDS

	Basic Indicators		Units	2001	2002	2003	2004	2005
	INBOUND TOURISM							
	Arrivals							
1.1	Visitors		('000)	1,549	1,878	2,113	1,953	1,967
1.2	Tourists (overnight visitors)		('000)	334	303	294	260	168
1.3	Same-day visitors		('000)	..	..	..	..	..
1.4	Cruise passengers		('000)	1,215	1,575	1,819	1,693	1,799
	Arrivals by region							
2.1	Africa		('000)	..	..	..	..	..
2.2	Americas		('000)	310	282	272	242	153
2.3	Europe		('000)	21	19	19	16	13
2.4	East Asia and the Pacific		('000)	2	1	1	1	1
2.5	South Asia		('000)	..	..	..	..	..
2.6	Middle East		('000)	..	..	..	..	..
	Arrivals by means of transport used							
3.1	Air		('000)	334	303	294	260	168
3.2	Rail		('000)	..	..	..	..	..
3.3	Road		('000)	..	..	..	..	..
3.4	Sea		('000)	1,215	1,575	1,819	1,693	1,799
	Arrivals by purpose of visit							
4.1	Leisure, recreation and holidays		('000)	252	243	227	196	100
4.2	Business and professional		('000)	10	13	15	14	12
4.3	Other		('000)	72	47	52	50	56
	Accommodation							
5.1	Overnight stays in hotels and similar establishments		('000)	..	..	..	..	..
5.2	Guests in hotels and similar establishments		('000)	..	..	..	..	..
5.3	Overnight stays in all types of accommodation establishments		('000)	..	..	..	..	..
5.4	Average length of stay of non-resident tourists in all accommodation establishments		Nights	6.40	5.80	6.90	6.30	6.80
6.1	**Tourism expenditure in the country**	(**)	US$ Mn	585	607	518	519	353
6.2	"Travel" (*)		US$ Mn	..	..	..	..	..
6.3	"Passenger transport" (*)		US$ Mn	..	..	..	..	..
	DOMESTIC TOURISM							
	Accommodation							
7.1	Overnight stays in hotels and similar establishments		('000)	..	..	..	..	..
7.2	Guests in hotels and similar establishments		('000)	..	..	..	..	..
7.3	Overnight stays in all types of accommodation establishments		('000)	..	..	..	..	..
7.4	Average length of stay of resident tourists in all accommodation establishments		Nights	..	..	..	..	..
	OUTBOUND TOURISM							
8.1	**Departures**		('000)	..	..	..	..	..
8.2	**Tourism expenditure in other countries**		US$ Mn	..	..	..	..	..
8.3	"Travel" (*)		US$ Mn	..	..	..	..	..
8.4	"Passenger transport" (*)		US$ Mn	..	..	..	..	..
	TOURISM INDUSTRIES							
	Hotels and similar establishments							
9.1	Number of rooms		Units	5,428	5,238	5,108	..	2,954
9.2	Number of bed-places		Units	17,445	16,565	15,186	..	..
9.3	Occupancy rate		Percent	55.30	50.60	51.20	61.70	55.80
9.4	Average length of stay		Nights	4.50	4.80	4.70	4.90	4.90
	RELATED INDICATORS							
	Share of tourism expenditure (6.1) in:							
10.1	Gross Domestic Product (GDP)		Percent	..	..	..	..	..
10.2	Exports of goods		Percent	..	..	..	..	..
10.3	Exports of services		Percent	..	..	..	..	..

(*) Balance of Payments items: 6.1 to 6.3 correspond to the "Credit" side (and are receipts for the country) while 8.2 to 8.4 correspond to the "Debit" side (and are expenditures in other countries).

(**) See Annex "Country notes".

	Basic Indicators	Units	2001	2002	2003	2004	2005
	INBOUND TOURISM						
	Arrivals						
1.1	Visitors	('000)	..	..	..	..	..
1.2	Tourists (overnight visitors)	('000)	9.9	2.9	5.7	8.2	12.0
1.3	Same-day visitors	('000)	..	..	..	..	..
1.4	Cruise passengers	('000)	..	..	..	..	..
	Arrivals by region						
2.1	Africa	('000)	5.0	1.5	3.1	3.5	6.2
2.2	Americas	('000)	0.7	0.2	0.4	0.4	0.6
2.3	Europe	('000)	3.5	1.0	1.9	3.7	4.3
2.4	East Asia and the Pacific	('000)	0.4	0.2	0.3	0.3	0.4
2.5	South Asia	('000)	..	..	..	..	..
2.6	Middle East	('000)	0.1	..	..	0.2	0.4
	Arrivals by means of transport used						
3.1	Air	('000)	9.9	2.9	5.7	8.2	12.0
3.2	Rail	('000)	..	..	..	..	..
3.3	Road	('000)	..	..	..	..	..
3.4	Sea	('000)	..	..	..	..	..
	Arrivals by purpose of visit						
4.1	Leisure, recreation and holidays	('000)	1	..	1	2	..
4.2	Business and professional	('000)	4	1	2	2	..
4.3	Other	('000)	5	2	3	4	..
	Accommodation						
5.1	Overnight stays in hotels and similar establishments	('000)	35	42	42	23	33
5.2	Guests in hotels and similar establishments	('000)	10	13	13	6	8
5.3	Overnight stays in all types of accommodation establishments	('000)	..	..	..	..	..
5.4	Average length of stay of non-resident tourists in all accommodation establishments	Nights	5.67	4.01	4.00	3.31	4.16
6.1	**Tourism expenditure in the country**	US$ Mn	5	3	4	4	..
6.2	"Travel" (*)	US$ Mn	..	..	..	..	..
6.3	"Passenger transport" (*)	US$ Mn	..	..	..	..	..
	DOMESTIC TOURISM						
	Accommodation						
7.1	Overnight stays in hotels and similar establishments	('000)	1	3	3	3	..
7.2	Guests in hotels and similar establishments	('000)	..	..	1	1	..
7.3	Overnight stays in all types of accommodation establishments	('000)	..	..	..	..	..
7.4	Average length of stay of resident tourists in all accommodation establishments	Nights	1.41	2.66	2.91	2.48	..
	OUTBOUND TOURISM						
8.1	**Departures**	('000)	..	5	6	7	..
8.2	**Tourism expenditure in other countries**	US$ Mn	29	29	31	32	..
8.3	"Travel" (*)	US$ Mn	..	..	..	..	..
8.4	"Passenger transport" (*)	US$ Mn	..	..	..	..	..
	TOURISM INDUSTRIES						
	Hotels and similar establishments						
9.1	Number of rooms	Units	201	201	201	235	241
9.2	Number of bed-places	Units	..	..	..	..	355
9.3	Occupancy rate	Percent	35.77	42.78	40.27	34.03	41.00
9.4	Average length of stay	Nights	4.77	4.11	5.61	3.01	4.22
	RELATED INDICATORS						
	Share of tourism expenditure (6.1) in:						
10.1	Gross Domestic Product (GDP)	Percent	..	..	..	..	..
10.2	Exports of goods	Percent	..	..	..	..	..
10.3	Exports of services	Percent	..	..	..	..	..

(*) Balance of Payments items: 6.1 to 6.3 correspond to the "Credit" side (and are receipts for the country) while 8.2 to 8.4 correspond to the "Debit" side (and are expenditures in other countries).

CHAD

	Basic Indicators	Units	2001	2002	2003	2004	2005
	INBOUND TOURISM						
	Arrivals						
1.1	Visitors	('000)	175	149	101	106	59
1.2	Tourists (overnight visitors)	('000)	57	32	21	26	29
1.3	Same-day visitors	('000)	..	..	..	..	..
1.4	Cruise passengers	('000)	..	..	..	..	..
	Arrivals by region						
2.1	Africa	('000)	17	8	5	6	7
2.2	Americas	('000)	5	6	4	6	6
2.3	Europe	('000)	32	15	10	13	15
2.4	East Asia and the Pacific	('000)	2	1	..	..	1
2.5	South Asia	('000)	..	..	..	..	..
2.6	Middle East	('000)	1	2	1	1	1
	Arrivals by means of transport used						
3.1	Air	('000)	79	80	54	48	21
3.2	Rail	('000)	..	..	..	..	..
3.3	Road	('000)	39	40	27	21	9
3.4	Sea	('000)	..	..	..	..	..
	Arrivals by purpose of visit						
4.1	Leisure, recreation and holidays	('000)	..	..	..	..	..
4.2	Business and professional	('000)	..	..	..	..	..
4.3	Other	('000)	..	..	..	..	..
	Accommodation						
5.1	Overnight stays in hotels and similar establishments	('000)	197	107	60	76	64
5.2	Guests in hotels and similar establishments	('000)	57	32	21	26	29
5.3	Overnight stays in all types of accommodation establishments	('000)	..	..	..	..	..
5.4	Average length of stay of non-resident tourists in all accommodation establishments	Nights	3.50	3.00	3.00	3.00	3.00
6.1	**Tourism expenditure in the country**	US$ Mn	23	25	..	..	..
6.2	"Travel" (*)	US$ Mn	..	..	..	..	..
6.3	"Passenger transport" (*)	US$ Mn	..	..	..	..	..
	DOMESTIC TOURISM						
	Accommodation						
7.1	Overnight stays in hotels and similar establishments	('000)	9	5	4	5	4
7.2	Guests in hotels and similar establishments	('000)	..	..	..	..	..
7.3	Overnight stays in all types of accommodation establishments	('000)	..	..	..	..	..
7.4	Average length of stay of resident tourists in all accommodation establishments	Nights	..	..	..	..	..
	OUTBOUND TOURISM						
8.1	**Departures**	('000)	40	23	..	..	..
8.2	**Tourism expenditure in other countries**	US$ Mn	56	80	..	..	..
8.3	"Travel" (*)	US$ Mn	..	..	..	..	..
8.4	"Passenger transport" (*)	US$ Mn	..	..	..	..	..
	TOURISM INDUSTRIES						
	Hotels and similar establishments						
9.1	Number of rooms	Units	719	904	835	835	922
9.2	Number of bed-places	Units	1,308	1,274	1,320	1,320	1,434
9.3	Occupancy rate	Percent	92.00	49.00	28.00	..	..
9.4	Average length of stay	Nights	3.90	..	3.00	3.00	3.00
	RELATED INDICATORS						
	Share of tourism expenditure (6.1) in:						
10.1	Gross Domestic Product (GDP)	Percent	..	..	..	..	..
10.2	Exports of goods	Percent	..	..	..	..	..
10.3	Exports of services	Percent	..	..	..	..	..

(*) Balance of Payments items: 6.1 to 6.3 correspond to the "Credit" side (and are receipts for the country) while 8.2 to 8.4 correspond to the "Debit" side (and are expenditures in other countries).

CHILE

	Basic Indicators	Units	2001	2002	2003	2004	2005
	INBOUND TOURISM						
	Arrivals						
1.1	Visitors	('000)	..	..	..	..	..
1.2	Tourists (overnight visitors)	('000)	1,723	1,412	1,614	1,785	2,027
1.3	Same-day visitors	('000)	..	..	448	856	901
1.4	Cruise passengers	('000)	..	..	..	..	..
	Arrivals by region						
2.1	Africa	('000)	2	2	3	4	4
2.2	Americas	('000)	1,429	1,119	1,243	1,360	1,553
2.3	Europe	('000)	250	245	309	345	385
2.4	East Asia and the Pacific	('000)	37	41	54	70	75
2.5	South Asia	('000)	2	2	2	4	4
2.6	Middle East	('000)	1	1	1	1	1
	Arrivals by means of transport used						
3.1	Air	('000)	649	606	708	760	855
3.2	Rail	('000)	8	1	2	3	3
3.3	Road	('000)	1,032	777	867	955	1,094
3.4	Sea	('000)	34	28	37	67	75
	Arrivals by purpose of visit						
4.1	Leisure, recreation and holidays	('000)	1,088	886	1,054	1,109	1,193
4.2	Business and professional	('000)	213	250	229	272	322
4.3	Other	('000)	422	276	331	404	512
	Accommodation						
5.1	Overnight stays in hotels and similar establishments	('000)	1,912	1,709	1,947	2,086	2,877
5.2	Guests in hotels and similar establishments	('000)	883	779	850	951	1,397
5.3	Overnight stays in all types of accommodation establishments	('000)	..	..	..	..	..
5.4	Average length of stay of non-resident tourists in all accommodation establishments	Nights	10.30	13.10	12.30	12.80	12.90
6.1	**Tourism expenditure in the country**	US$ Mn	1,184	1,221	1,310	1,626	1,779
6.2	"Travel" (*)	US$ Mn	799	898	883	1,149	1,256
6.3	"Passenger transport" (*)	US$ Mn	385	323	427	477	523
	DOMESTIC TOURISM						
	Accommodation						
7.1	Overnight stays in hotels and similar establishments	('000)	3,872	4,308	4,879	4,751	5,799
7.2	Guests in hotels and similar establishments	('000)	1,900	2,124	2,199	2,287	2,888
7.3	Overnight stays in all types of accommodation establishments	('000)	..	..	..	..	..
7.4	Average length of stay of resident tourists in all accommodation establishments	Nights	..	..	..	..	..
	OUTBOUND TOURISM						
8.1	**Departures**	('000)	1,608	1,938	2,100	2,343	2,651
8.2	**Tourism expenditure in other countries**	US$ Mn	939	932	1,109	1,250	1,381
8.3	"Travel" (*)	US$ Mn	708	673	850	977	1,057
8.4	"Passenger transport" (*)	US$ Mn	231	259	259	273	324
	TOURISM INDUSTRIES						
	Hotels and similar establishments						
9.1	Number of rooms	Units	49,895	51,793	52,362	53,794	53,335
9.2	Number of bed-places	Units	113,010	117,315	117,905	127,085	131,634
9.3	Occupancy rate	Percent	32.50	31.00	32.50	32.20	34.10
9.4	Average length of stay	Nights	2.10	2.10	2.20	2.10	2.00
	RELATED INDICATORS						
	Share of tourism expenditure (6.1) in:						
10.1	Gross Domestic Product (GDP)	Percent	1.7	1.8	1.8	1.7	1.5
10.2	Exports of goods	Percent	6.5	6.7	6.0	5.0	4.4
10.3	Exports of services	Percent	28.6	27.8	26.3	26.8	24.8

(*) Balance of Payments items: 6.1 to 6.3 correspond to the "Credit" side (and are receipts for the country) while 8.2 to 8.4 correspond to the "Debit" side (and are expenditures in other countries).

CHINA

	Basic Indicators	Units	2001	2002	2003	2004	2005
	INBOUND TOURISM						
	Arrivals						
1.1	Visitors	('000)	89,013	97,908	91,662	109,038	120,292
1.2	Tourists (overnight visitors)	('000)	33,167	36,803	32,970	41,761	46,809
1.3	Same-day visitors	('000)	..	..	..	..	..
1.4	Cruise passengers	('000)	..	..	..	..	..
	Arrivals by region						
2.1	Africa	('000)	63	85	92	154	211
2.2	Americas	('000)	1,278	1,510	1,133	1,790	2,146
2.3	Europe	('000)	2,732	3,007	2,790	4,097	5,166
2.4	East Asia and the Pacific	('000)	84,610	92,866	87,214	102,394	112,053
2.5	South Asia	('000)	277	381	383	514	599
2.6	Middle East	('000)	37	52	47	84	111
	Arrivals by means of transport used						
3.1	Air	('000)	8,617	10,343	8,080	12,617	14,736
3.2	Rail	('000)	1,188	1,252	1,110	1,470	1,610
3.3	Road	('000)	75,092	81,936	78,684	90,224	98,735
3.4	Sea	('000)	4,115	4,377	3,787	4,727	5,212
	Arrivals by purpose of visit						
4.1	Leisure, recreation and holidays	('000)	..	5,560	4,307	7,412	9,345
4.2	Business and professional	('000)	..	3,220	2,902	3,861	4,598
4.3	Other	('000)	..	4,659	4,194	5,659	6,312
	Accommodation						
5.1	Overnight stays in hotels and similar establishments	('000)	86,765	99,360	80,121	114,231	138,411
5.2	Guests in hotels and similar establishments	('000)	..	39,142	30,169	43,937	53,258
5.3	Overnight stays in all types of accommodation establishments	('000)	..	..	..	..	..
5.4	Average length of stay of non-resident tourists in all accommodation establishments	Nights	..	2.54	2.66	2.60	2.60
6.1	**Tourism expenditure in the country**	US$ Mn	19,006	21,742	18,708	27,755	31,842
6.2	"Travel" (*)	US$ Mn	17,792	20,385	17,406	25,739	29,296
6.3	"Passenger transport" (*)	US$ Mn	1,214	1,357	1,302	2,016	2,546
	DOMESTIC TOURISM						
	Accommodation						
7.1	Overnight stays in hotels and similar establishments	('000)	201,045	246,325	236,341	296,764	289,073
7.2	Guests in hotels and similar establishments	('000)	..	..	..	..	..
7.3	Overnight stays in all types of accommodation establishments	('000)	..	..	..	..	..
7.4	Average length of stay of resident tourists in all accommodation establishments	Nights	..	..	..	..	..
	OUTBOUND TOURISM						
8.1	**Departures**	('000)	12,133	16,602	20,222	28,853	31,026
8.2	**Tourism expenditure in other countries**	US$ Mn	14,992	16,759	16,716	21,360	24,715
8.3	"Travel" (*)	US$ Mn	13,909	15,398	15,187	19,149	21,759
8.4	"Passenger transport" (*)	US$ Mn	1,083	1,361	1,529	2,211	2,956
	TOURISM INDUSTRIES						
	Hotels and similar establishments						
9.1	Number of rooms	Units	816,260	897,206	992,804	1,237,851	1,332,083
9.2	Number of bed-places	Units	1,533,053	1,729,460	1,887,740	2,366,638	2,571,664
9.3	Occupancy rate	Percent	58.45	60.15	56.14	60.62	60.96
9.4	Average length of stay	Nights	2.54	2.54	2.66	2.60	2.60
	RELATED INDICATORS						
	Share of tourism expenditure (6.1) in:						
10.1	Gross Domestic Product (GDP)	Percent	1.4	1.5	1.1	1.4	1.4
10.2	Exports of goods	Percent	7.1	6.7	4.3	4.7	4.2
10.3	Exports of services	Percent	57.0	54.7	40.0	44.5	42.8

(*) Balance of Payments items: 6.1 to 6.3 correspond to the "Credit" side (and are receipts for the country) while 8.2 to 8.4 correspond to the "Debit" side (and are expenditures in other countries).

	Basic Indicators	Units	2001	2002	2003	2004	2005
	INBOUND TOURISM						
	Arrivals						
1.1	Visitors	('000)	616	567	625	791	933
1.2	Tourists (overnight visitors)	('000)	..	..	..	..	..
1.3	Same-day visitors	('000)	..	..	..	..	..
1.4	Cruise passengers	('000)	172	94	43	49	48
	Arrivals by region						
2.1	Africa	('000)	1	1	1	1	1
2.2	Americas	('000)	469	428	485	618	731
2.3	Europe	('000)	129	118	125	156	183
2.4	East Asia and the Pacific	('000)	12	12	11	13	15
2.5	South Asia	('000)	1	1	1	1	2
2.6	Middle East	('000)	2	1	1	1	1
	Arrivals by means of transport used						
3.1	Air	('000)	549	507	551	701	834
3.2	Rail	('000)	..	..	..	..	..
3.3	Road	('000)	64	58	72	88	97
3.4	Sea	('000)	3	2	2	2	2
	Arrivals by purpose of visit						
4.1	Leisure, recreation and holidays	('000)	421	366	399	493	581
4.2	Business and professional	('000)	56	135	165	217	266
4.3	Other	('000)	138	66	61	81	86
	Accommodation						
5.1	Overnight stays in hotels and similar establishments	('000)	..	..	..	..	..
5.2	Guests in hotels and similar establishments	('000)	..	..	..	..	..
5.3	Overnight stays in all types of accommodation establishments	('000)	..	..	..	..	..
5.4	Average length of stay of non-resident tourists in all accommodation establishments	Nights	..	..	..	..	..
6.1	**Tourism expenditure in the country**	US$ Mn	1,483	1,237	1,191	1,366	1,570
6.2	"Travel" (*)	US$ Mn	1,217	967	893	1,058	1,218
6.3	"Passenger transport" (*)	US$ Mn	266	270	298	308	352
	DOMESTIC TOURISM						
	Accommodation						
7.1	Overnight stays in hotels and similar establishments	('000)	..	..	..	..	..
7.2	Guests in hotels and similar establishments	('000)	..	..	..	..	..
7.3	Overnight stays in all types of accommodation establishments	('000)	..	..	..	..	..
7.4	Average length of stay of resident tourists in all accommodation establishments	Nights	..	..	..	..	..
	OUTBOUND TOURISM						
8.1	**Departures**	('000)	1,381	1,277	1,177	1,405	1,553
8.2	**Tourism expenditure in other countries**	US$ Mn	1,556	1,355	1,349	1,466	1,562
8.3	"Travel" (*)	US$ Mn	1,164	1,075	1,062	1,108	1,127
8.4	"Passenger transport" (*)	US$ Mn	392	280	287	358	435
	TOURISM INDUSTRIES						
	Hotels and similar establishments						
9.1	Number of rooms	Units	52,635	55,755	60,005	66,576	71,247
9.2	Number of bed-places	Units	103,200	108,965	117,455	131,086	141,151
9.3	Occupancy rate	Percent	44.60	42.40	48.40	49.30	49.00
9.4	Average length of stay	Nights	..	..	..	..	..
	RELATED INDICATORS						
	Share of tourism expenditure (6.1) in:						
10.1	Gross Domestic Product (GDP)	Percent	1.8	1.5	1.5	1.4	1.3
10.2	Exports of goods	Percent	11.5	10.0	8.6	7.9	7.2
10.3	Exports of services	Percent	67.7	66.3	62.0	60.6	58.9

(*) Balance of Payments items: 6.1 to 6.3 correspond to the "Credit" side (and are receipts for the country) while 8.2 to 8.4 correspond to the "Debit" side (and are expenditures in other countries).

COMOROS

Basic Indicators			Units	2001	2002	2003	2004	2005
	INBOUND TOURISM							
	Arrivals							
1.1	Visitors		('000)	..	..	..	..	..
1.2	Tourists (overnight visitors)		('000)	19.4	18.9	14.2	17.6	19.6
1.3	Same-day visitors		('000)	..	..	..	..	..
1.4	Cruise passengers		('000)	..	..	..	..	..
	Arrivals by region							
2.1	Africa		('000)	11.8	8.7	5.6	6.3	..
2.2	Americas		('000)	..	..	..	..	..
2.3	Europe		('000)	6.9	9.5	8.0	10.6	..
2.4	East Asia and the Pacific		('000)	..	..	..	..	..
2.5	South Asia		('000)	..	..	..	..	..
2.6	Middle East		('000)	..	..	..	..	..
	Arrivals by means of transport used							
3.1	Air		('000)	19.4	18.9	14.2	17.6	19.6
3.2	Rail		('000)	..	..	..	..	..
3.3	Road		('000)	..	..	..	..	..
3.4	Sea		('000)	..	..	..	..	..
	Arrivals by purpose of visit							
4.1	Leisure, recreation and holidays		('000)	7.7	3.5	1.3	2.4	..
4.2	Business and professional		('000)	3.0	4.3	1.4	3.0	..
4.3	Other		('000)	8.6	10.9	11.5	12.2	..
	Accommodation							
5.1	Overnight stays in hotels and similar establishments		('000)	..	..	..	..	..
5.2	Guests in hotels and similar establishments		('000)	..	..	..	7	..
5.3	Overnight stays in all types of accommodation establishments		('000)	135	133	123	123	137
5.4	Average length of stay of non-resident tourists in all accommodation establishments		Nights	..	..	..	..	..
6.1	**Tourism expenditure in the country**	(**)	US$ Mn	9.0	10.2	10.7	12.5	14.1
6.2	"Travel" (*)		US$ Mn	..	..	..	..	..
6.3	"Passenger transport" (*)		US$ Mn	..	..	..	..	..
	DOMESTIC TOURISM							
	Accommodation							
7.1	Overnight stays in hotels and similar establishments		('000)	..	..	..	..	..
7.2	Guests in hotels and similar establishments		('000)	..	..	..	..	..
7.3	Overnight stays in all types of accommodation establishments		('000)	..	..	..	..	..
7.4	Average length of stay of resident tourists in all accommodation establishments		Nights	..	..	..	..	..
	OUTBOUND TOURISM							
8.1	**Departures**		('000)	..	..	..	..	..
8.2	**Tourism expenditure in other countries**		US$ Mn	..	..	..	..	..
8.3	"Travel" (*)		US$ Mn	..	..	..	..	..
8.4	"Passenger transport" (*)		US$ Mn	..	..	..	..	..
	TOURISM INDUSTRIES							
	Hotels and similar establishments							
9.1	Number of rooms		Units	410	410	375	418	418
9.2	Number of bed-places		Units	820	820	750	836	836
9.3	Occupancy rate		Percent	17.00	19.00	14.00	16.00	..
9.4	Average length of stay		Nights	7.00	7.00	7.00	7.00	7.00
	RELATED INDICATORS							
	Share of tourism expenditure (6.1) in:							
10.1	Gross Domestic Product (GDP)		Percent	..	..	..	..	..
10.2	Exports of goods		Percent	..	..	..	..	..
10.3	Exports of services		Percent	..	..	..	..	..

(*) Balance of Payments items: 6.1 to 6.3 correspond to the "Credit" side (and are receipts for the country) while 8.2 to 8.4 correspond to the "Debit" side (and are expenditures in other countries).

(**) See Annex "Country notes".

Basic Indicators		Units	2001	2002	2003	2004	2005
	INBOUND TOURISM						
	Arrivals						
1.1	Visitors	('000)	..	..	..	..	..
1.2	Tourists (overnight visitors)	('000)	27	22	..	..	..
1.3	Same-day visitors	('000)	..	..	..	..	..
1.4	Cruise passengers	('000)	..	..	..	..	..
	Arrivals by region						
2.1	Africa	('000)	12	11	..	..	..
2.2	Americas	('000)	1	1	..	..	..
2.3	Europe	('000)	12	9	..	..	..
2.4	East Asia and the Pacific	('000)	..	..	..	..	..
2.5	South Asia	('000)	..	..	..	..	..
2.6	Middle East	('000)	..	..	..	..	..
	Arrivals by means of transport used						
3.1	Air	('000)	..	..	..	..	..
3.2	Rail	('000)	..	..	..	..	..
3.3	Road	('000)	..	..	..	..	..
3.4	Sea	('000)	..	..	..	..	..
	Arrivals by purpose of visit						
4.1	Leisure, recreation and holidays	('000)	..	..	..	..	..
4.2	Business and professional	('000)	..	..	..	..	..
4.3	Other	('000)	..	..	..	..	..
	Accommodation						
5.1	Overnight stays in hotels and similar establishments	('000)	100	88	..	..	..
5.2	Guests in hotels and similar establishments	('000)	27	22	..	..	..
5.3	Overnight stays in all types of accommodation establishments	('000)	..	..	..	..	..
5.4	Average length of stay of non-resident tourists in all accommodation establishments	Nights	..	..	..	..	..
6.1	**Tourism expenditure in the country**	US$ Mn	22.6	25.6	30.0	23.1	..
6.2	"Travel" (*)	US$ Mn	22	25	29	22	34
6.3	"Passenger transport" (*)	US$ Mn	0.6	0.6	1.0	1.1	..
	DOMESTIC TOURISM						
	Accommodation						
7.1	Overnight stays in hotels and similar establishments	('000)	50	46	..	..	..
7.2	Guests in hotels and similar establishments	('000)	15	12	..	..	..
7.3	Overnight stays in all types of accommodation establishments	('000)	..	..	..	..	..
7.4	Average length of stay of resident tourists in all accommodation establishments	Nights	..	..	..	..	..
	OUTBOUND TOURISM						
8.1	**Departures**	('000)	..	..	..	..	..
8.2	**Tourism expenditure in other countries**	US$ Mn	82	85	118	176	..
8.3	"Travel" (*)	US$ Mn	65	70	78	103	103
8.4	"Passenger transport" (*)	US$ Mn	17	15	40	73	..
	TOURISM INDUSTRIES						
	Hotels and similar establishments						
9.1	Number of rooms	Units	3,041	2,986	..	..	..
9.2	Number of bed-places	Units	..	..	..	..	..
9.3	Occupancy rate	Percent	42.60	..	..	..	..
9.4	Average length of stay	Nights	3.50	..	..	..	..
	RELATED INDICATORS						
	Share of tourism expenditure (6.1) in:						
10.1	Gross Domestic Product (GDP)	Percent	0.8	0.8	0.8	0.5	..
10.2	Exports of goods	Percent	1.1	1.1	1.1	0.7	..
10.3	Exports of services	Percent	15.7	15.5	15.5	11.7	..

(*) Balance of Payments items: 6.1 to 6.3 correspond to the "Credit" side (and are receipts for the country) while 8.2 to 8.4 correspond to the "Debit" side (and are expenditures in other countries).

COOK ISLANDS

	Basic Indicators		Units	2001	2002	2003	2004	2005
	INBOUND TOURISM							
	Arrivals							
1.1	Visitors		('000)	..	..	..	..	..
1.2	Tourists (overnight visitors)		('000)	75	73	78	83	88
1.3	Same-day visitors		('000)	..	..	..	..	..
1.4	Cruise passengers		('000)	..	..	..	..	..
	Arrivals by region							
2.1	Africa		('000)	..	..	..	..	..
2.2	Americas		('000)	13	11	11	8	6
2.3	Europe		('000)	23	20	22	20	18
2.4	East Asia and the Pacific		('000)	38	41	45	54	63
2.5	South Asia		('000)	..	..	..	..	..
2.6	Middle East		('000)	..	..	..	..	..
	Arrivals by means of transport used							
3.1	Air		('000)	..	..	..	..	..
3.2	Rail		('000)	..	..	..	..	..
3.3	Road		('000)	..	..	..	..	..
3.4	Sea		('000)	..	..	..	..	..
	Arrivals by purpose of visit							
4.1	Leisure, recreation and holidays		('000)	65	62	67	69	73
4.2	Business and professional		('000)	3	4	4	4	3
4.3	Other		('000)	7	7	7	10	12
	Accommodation							
5.1	Overnight stays in hotels and similar establishments		('000)	225	209	205	208	230
5.2	Guests in hotels and similar establishments		('000)	..	..	..	..	..
5.3	Overnight stays in all types of accommodation establishments		('000)	..	..	..	..	..
5.4	Average length of stay of non-resident tourists in all accommodation establishments		Nights	10.67	10.56	10.53	10.41	10.15
6.1	**Tourism expenditure in the country**	(**)	US$ Mn	38	46	69	72	92
6.2	"Travel" (*)		US$ Mn	..	..	..	..	..
6.3	"Passenger transport" (*)		US$ Mn	..	..	..	..	..
	DOMESTIC TOURISM							
	Accommodation							
7.1	Overnight stays in hotels and similar establishments		('000)	..	..	..	..	..
7.2	Guests in hotels and similar establishments		('000)	..	..	..	..	..
7.3	Overnight stays in all types of accommodation establishments		('000)	..	..	..	..	..
7.4	Average length of stay of resident tourists in all accommodation establishments		Nights	..	..	..	..	..
	OUTBOUND TOURISM							
8.1	**Departures**		('000)	9	9	10	12	13
8.2	**Tourism expenditure in other countries**		US$ Mn	..	..	..	..	..
8.3	"Travel" (*)		US$ Mn	..	..	..	..	..
8.4	"Passenger transport" (*)		US$ Mn	..	..	..	..	..
	TOURISM INDUSTRIES							
	Hotels and similar establishments							
9.1	Number of rooms		Units	..	..	1,152	..	1,408
9.2	Number of bed-places		Units	..	..	..	..	..
9.3	Occupancy rate		Percent	71.10	63.10	60.50	55.40	61.40
9.4	Average length of stay		Nights	..	..	..	..	..
	RELATED INDICATORS							
	Share of tourism expenditure (6.1) in:							
10.1	Gross Domestic Product (GDP)		Percent	..	..	..	..	..
10.2	Exports of goods		Percent	..	..	..	..	..
10.3	Exports of services		Percent	..	..	..	..	..

(*) Balance of Payments items: 6.1 to 6.3 correspond to the "Credit" side (and are receipts for the country) while 8.2 to 8.4 correspond to the "Debit" side (and are expenditures in other countries).

(**) See Annex "Country notes".

	Basic Indicators	Units	2001	2002	2003	2004	2005
	INBOUND TOURISM						
	Arrivals						
1.1	Visitors	('000)	1,320	1,335	1,514	1,771	1,959
1.2	Tourists (overnight visitors)	('000)	1,131	1,113	1,239	1,453	1,679
1.3	Same-day visitors	('000)	..	..	..	..	..
1.4	Cruise passengers	('000)	189	222	275	318	280
	Arrivals by region						
2.1	Africa	('000)	1	1	1	1	1
2.2	Americas	('000)	952	928	1,018	1,214	1,412
2.3	Europe	('000)	157	164	198	215	242
2.4	East Asia and the Pacific	('000)	15	16	16	16	24
2.5	South Asia	('000)	..	..	..	..	..
2.6	Middle East	('000)	..	..	..	..	..
	Arrivals by means of transport used						
3.1	Air	('000)	812	798	928	1,088	1,244
3.2	Rail	('000)	..	..	..	..	..
3.3	Road	('000)	308	309	299	355	427
3.4	Sea	('000)	11	6	12	10	9
	Arrivals by purpose of visit						
4.1	Leisure, recreation and holidays	('000)	830	798	908	1,149	1,357
4.2	Business and professional	('000)	210	264	272	250	272
4.3	Other	('000)	91	51	58	54	50
	Accommodation						
5.1	Overnight stays in hotels and similar establishments	('000)	..	..	..	..	..
5.2	Guests in hotels and similar establishments	('000)	..	..	..	..	..
5.3	Overnight stays in all types of accommodation establishments	('000)	..	..	..	..	..
5.4	Average length of stay of non-resident tourists in all accommodation establishments	Nights	12.80	11.00	11.10	11.30	10.50
6.1	**Tourism expenditure in the country**	US$ Mn	1,339	1,292	1,424	1,586	1,804
6.2	"Travel" (*)	US$ Mn	1,173	1,161	1,293	1,459	1,666
6.3	"Passenger transport" (*)	US$ Mn	166	131	131	127	138
	DOMESTIC TOURISM						
	Accommodation						
7.1	Overnight stays in hotels and similar establishments	('000)	..	..	..	..	..
7.2	Guests in hotels and similar establishments	('000)	..	..	..	..	..
7.3	Overnight stays in all types of accommodation establishments	('000)	..	..	..	..	..
7.4	Average length of stay of resident tourists in all accommodation establishments	Nights	..	..	..	..	..
	OUTBOUND TOURISM						
8.1	**Departures**	('000)	361	364	373	425	487
8.2	**Tourism expenditure in other countries**	US$ Mn	434	430	434	481	556
8.3	"Travel" (*)	US$ Mn	364	345	353	406	470
8.4	"Passenger transport" (*)	US$ Mn	70	85	81	75	86
	TOURISM INDUSTRIES						
	Hotels and similar establishments						
9.1	Number of rooms	Units	31,706	33,126	35,003	36,299	38,737
9.2	Number of bed-places	Units	..	..	..	..	..
9.3	Occupancy rate	Percent	59.30	45.10	47.90	55.00	..
9.4	Average length of stay	Nights	..	..	..	..	..
	RELATED INDICATORS						
	Share of tourism expenditure (6.1) in:						
10.1	Gross Domestic Product (GDP)	Percent	8.2	7.7	8.1	8.6	9.3
10.2	Exports of goods	Percent	27.2	24.5	23.1	24.9	25.4
10.3	Exports of services	Percent	69.6	69.2	70.5	70.7	69.0

(*) Balance of Payments items: 6.1 to 6.3 correspond to the "Credit" side (and are receipts for the country) while 8.2 to 8.4 correspond to the "Debit" side (and are expenditures in other countries).

CROATIA

	Basic Indicators	Units	2001	2002	2003	2004	2005
	INBOUND TOURISM						
	Arrivals						
1.1	Visitors	('000)	40,129	41,737	42,857	44,974	45,762
1.2	Tourists (overnight visitors)	('000)	6,544	6,944	7,409	7,912	8,467
1.3	Same-day visitors	('000)	..	..	..	..	..
1.4	Cruise passengers	('000)	..	..	..	..	..
	Arrivals by region						
2.1	Africa	('000)	..	..	..	..	..
2.2	Americas	('000)	67	75	84	119	140
2.3	Europe	('000)	6,429	6,807	7,244	7,693	8,192
2.4	East Asia and the Pacific	('000)	27	36	43	58	83
2.5	South Asia	('000)	..	..	..	..	..
2.6	Middle East	('000)	..	..	..	..	..
	Arrivals by means of transport used						
3.1	Air	('000)	813	887	1,006	1,202	1,566
3.2	Rail	('000)	318	312	335	327	302
3.3	Road	('000)	38,754	40,231	41,132	42,524	42,910
3.4	Sea	('000)	244	306	384	921	984
	Arrivals by purpose of visit						
4.1	Leisure, recreation and holidays	('000)	..	..	..	..	..
4.2	Business and professional	('000)	..	..	..	..	..
4.3	Other	('000)	..	..	..	..	..
	Accommodation						
5.1	Overnight stays in hotels and similar establishments	('000)	16,989	16,905	16,830	17,072	18,415
5.2	Guests in hotels and similar establishments	('000)	2,928	2,988	3,087	3,362	3,744
5.3	Overnight stays in all types of accommodation establishments	('000)	38,384	39,711	41,323	42,516	45,987
5.4	Average length of stay of non-resident tourists in all accommodation establishments	Nights	5.87	5.71	5.58	5.39	5.43
6.1	**Tourism expenditure in the country**	US$ Mn	3,463	3,953	6,514	6,945	7,625
6.2	"Travel" (*)	US$ Mn	3,335	3,812	6,310	6,727	7,370
6.3	"Passenger transport" (*)	US$ Mn	128	141	204	218	255
	DOMESTIC TOURISM						
	Accommodation						
7.1	Overnight stays in hotels and similar establishments	('000)	2,919	2,691	2,839	2,900	2,862
7.2	Guests in hotels and similar establishments	('000)	927	886	960	979	1,002
7.3	Overnight stays in all types of accommodation establishments	('000)	5,021	4,981	5,312	5,281	5,434
7.4	Average length of stay of resident tourists in all accommodation establishments	Nights	3.82	3.62	3.62	3.59	3.56
	OUTBOUND TOURISM						
8.1	**Departures**	('000)	..	..	..	..	..
8.2	**Tourism expenditure in other countries**	US$ Mn	677	852	709	881	786
8.3	"Travel" (*)	US$ Mn	606	781	672	848	754
8.4	"Passenger transport" (*)	US$ Mn	71	71	37	33	32
	TOURISM INDUSTRIES						
	Hotels and similar establishments						
9.1	Number of rooms	Units	74,107	77,347	77,113	79,174	80,743
9.2	Number of bed-places	Units	181,983	187,947	193,538	199,033	203,464
9.3	Occupancy rate	Percent	30.32	25.49	27.84	27.49	28.65
9.4	Average length of stay	Nights	5.50	5.06	5.25	5.08	4.48
	RELATED INDICATORS						
	Share of tourism expenditure (6.1) in:						
10.1	Gross Domestic Product (GDP)	Percent	17.4	17.3	22.6	20.2	20.4
10.2	Exports of goods	Percent	72.8	79.0	103.3	84.6	84.8
10.3	Exports of services	Percent	70.9	70.8	76.0	74.1	76.9

(*) Balance of Payments items: 6.1 to 6.3 correspond to the "Credit" side (and are receipts for the country) while 8.2 to 8.4 correspond to the "Debit" side (and are expenditures in other countries).

CUBA

Basic Indicators		Units	2001	2002	2003	2004	2005
	INBOUND TOURISM						
	Arrivals						
1.1	Visitors	('000)	1,775	1,686	1,906	2,049	2,319
1.2	Tourists (overnight visitors)	('000)	1,736	1,656	1,847	2,017	2,261
1.3	Same-day visitors	('000)	39	30	59	32	58
1.4	Cruise passengers	('000)	14	6	20	5	17
	Arrivals by region						
2.1	Africa	('000)	7	6	7	6	7
2.2	Americas	('000)	835	788	917	1,026	1,216
2.3	Europe	('000)	898	859	942	977	1,048
2.4	East Asia and the Pacific	('000)	29	27	32	34	42
2.5	South Asia	('000)	4	4	6	4	5
2.6	Middle East	('000)	2	2	2	2	2
	Arrivals by means of transport used						
3.1	Air	('000)	1,736	1,656	1,847	2,017	2,261
3.2	Rail	('000)	..	..	..	..	..
3.3	Road	('000)	..	..	..	..	..
3.4	Sea	('000)	..	..	..	..	..
	Arrivals by purpose of visit						
4.1	Leisure, recreation and holidays	('000)	1,628	1,560	1,736	1,830	1,982
4.2	Business and professional	('000)	13	13	12	11	12
4.3	Other	('000)	95	83	99	176	267
	Accommodation						
5.1	Overnight stays in hotels and similar establishments	('000)	10,176	9,755	11,951	13,358	14,572
5.2	Guests in hotels and similar establishments	('000)	2,044	2,029	2,401	2,732	2,911
5.3	Overnight stays in all types of accommodation establishments	('000)	11,250	10,486	12,684	14,190	15,404
5.4	Average length of stay of non-resident tourists in all accommodation establishments	Nights	10.50	10.50	10.50	10.50	10.50
6.1	**Tourism expenditure in the country** (**)	US$ Mn	1,692	1,633	1,846	1,915	1,920
6.2	"Travel" (*)	US$ Mn	..	..	..	..	..
6.3	"Passenger transport" (*)	US$ Mn	..	..	..	..	..
	DOMESTIC TOURISM						
	Accommodation						
7.1	Overnight stays in hotels and similar establishments	('000)	3,361	3,263	3,142	2,529	2,548
7.2	Guests in hotels and similar establishments	('000)	..	..	..	..	..
7.3	Overnight stays in all types of accommodation establishments	('000)	7,573	7,046	6,988	6,421	6,931
7.4	Average length of stay of resident tourists in all accommodation establishments	Nights	..	..	..	..	..
	OUTBOUND TOURISM						
8.1	**Departures**	('000)	121	111	113	115	..
8.2	**Tourism expenditure in other countries**	US$ Mn	..	..	..	..	..
8.3	"Travel" (*)	US$ Mn	..	..	..	..	..
8.4	"Passenger transport" (*)	US$ Mn	..	..	..	..	..
	TOURISM INDUSTRIES						
	Hotels and similar establishments						
9.1	Number of rooms	Units	40,158	41,323	43,696	45,270	45,644
9.2	Number of bed-places	Units	79,178	81,086	84,200	86,494	87,363
9.3	Occupancy rate	Percent	64.70	59.70	61.80	63.50	63.60
9.4	Average length of stay	Nights	..	..	..	..	..
	RELATED INDICATORS						
	Share of tourism expenditure (6.1) in:						
10.1	Gross Domestic Product (GDP)	Percent	..	..	..	..	..
10.2	Exports of goods	Percent	..	..	..	..	..
10.3	Exports of services	Percent	..	..	..	..	..

(*) Balance of Payments items: 6.1 to 6.3 correspond to the "Credit" side (and are receipts for the country) while 8.2 to 8.4 correspond to the "Debit" side (and are expenditures in other countries).

(**) See Annex "Country notes".

CURAÇAO

	Basic Indicators		Units	2001	2002	2003	2004	2005
	INBOUND TOURISM							
	Arrivals							
1.1	Visitors		('000)	519	545	508	452	510
1.2	Tourists (overnight visitors)		('000)	205	218	221	223	222
1.3	Same-day visitors		('000)	14	8	7	10	12
1.4	Cruise passengers		('000)	300	319	279	219	276
	Arrivals by region							
2.1	Africa		('000)	..	..	..	..	..
2.2	Americas		('000)	125	141	126	129	123
2.3	Europe		('000)	73	70	91	90	95
2.4	East Asia and the Pacific		('000)	..	..	..	..	..
2.5	South Asia		('000)	..	..	..	..	..
2.6	Middle East		('000)	..	..	..	..	..
	Arrivals by means of transport used							
3.1	Air		('000)	219	226	228	233	234
3.2	Rail		('000)	..	..	..	..	..
3.3	Road		('000)	..	..	..	..	..
3.4	Sea		('000)	300	319	279	219	276
	Arrivals by purpose of visit							
4.1	Leisure, recreation and holidays		('000)	144	170	183	191	198
4.2	Business and professional		('000)	39	31	24	21	15
4.3	Other		('000)	19	14	12	11	9
	Accommodation							
5.1	Overnight stays in hotels and similar establishments		('000)	680	677	754	782	842
5.2	Guests in hotels and similar establishments		('000)	121	119	127	129	135
5.3	Overnight stays in all types of accommodation establishments		('000)	1,710	1,815	1,919	1,920	1,960
5.4	Average length of stay of non-resident tourists in all accommodation establishments		Nights	8.32	8.35	8.63	8.59	8.82
6.1	**Tourism expenditure in the country**	(**)	US$ Mn	271	290	286	296	284
6.2	"Travel" (*)		US$ Mn	..	..	..	..	..
6.3	"Passenger transport" (*)		US$ Mn	..	..	..	..	..
	DOMESTIC TOURISM							
	Accommodation							
7.1	Overnight stays in hotels and similar establishments		('000)	..	..	..	..	..
7.2	Guests in hotels and similar establishments		('000)	..	..	..	..	..
7.3	Overnight stays in all types of accommodation establishments		('000)	..	..	..	..	..
7.4	Average length of stay of resident tourists in all accommodation establishments		Nights	..	..	..	..	..
	OUTBOUND TOURISM							
8.1	**Departures**		('000)	..	..	..	..	..
8.2	**Tourism expenditure in other countries**		US$ Mn	..	..	..	..	..
8.3	"Travel" (*)		US$ Mn	..	..	..	..	..
8.4	"Passenger transport" (*)		US$ Mn	..	..	..	..	..
	TOURISM INDUSTRIES							
	Hotels and similar establishments							
9.1	Number of rooms		Units	3,203	3,422	3,474	3,557	3,647
9.2	Number of bed-places		Units	..	..	..	..	..
9.3	Occupancy rate		Percent	65.77	57.32	62.10	69.70	81.74
9.4	Average length of stay		Nights	8.39	8.38	8.56	8.59	8.82
	RELATED INDICATORS							
	Share of tourism expenditure (6.1) in:							
10.1	Gross Domestic Product (GDP)		Percent	..	..	..	..	..
10.2	Exports of goods		Percent	..	..	..	..	..
10.3	Exports of services		Percent	..	..	..	..	..

(*) Balance of Payments items: 6.1 to 6.3 correspond to the "Credit" side (and are receipts for the country) while 8.2 to 8.4 correspond to the "Debit" side (and are expenditures in other countries).

(**) See Annex "Country notes".

	Basic Indicators	Units	2001	2002	2003	2004	2005
	INBOUND TOURISM						
	Arrivals						
1.1	Visitors	('000)	2,841	2,495	2,416	2,478	2,657
1.2	Tourists (overnight visitors)	('000)	2,697	2,418	2,303	2,349	2,470
1.3	Same-day visitors	('000)	144	77	113	129	187
1.4	Cruise passengers	('000)	106	59	93	119	176
	Arrivals by region						
2.1	Africa	('000)	8	7	7	5	8
2.2	Americas	('000)	30	27	23	23	29
2.3	Europe	('000)	2,592	2,324	2,207	2,263	2,375
2.4	East Asia and the Pacific	('000)	14	12	12	13	15
2.5	South Asia	('000)	8	3	3	2	3
2.6	Middle East	('000)	45	45	49	41	40
	Arrivals by means of transport used						
3.1	Air	('000)	2,717	2,431	2,320	2,357	2,479
3.2	Rail	('000)	..	..	..	..	..
3.3	Road	('000)	..	..	..	..	..
3.4	Sea	('000)	124	64	96	121	178
	Arrivals by purpose of visit						
4.1	Leisure, recreation and holidays	('000)	2,457	2,172	2,052	2,099	2,194
4.2	Business and professional	('000)	129	131	127	139	143
4.3	Other	('000)	111	115	124	111	133
	Accommodation						
5.1	Overnight stays in hotels and similar establishments	('000)	18,070	15,235	13,424	13,554	13,899
5.2	Guests in hotels and similar establishments	('000)	2,284	2,034	1,818	1,725	1,750
5.3	Overnight stays in all types of accommodation establishments	('000)	18,093	15,289	13,490	13,637	14,006
5.4	Average length of stay of non-resident tourists in all accommodation establishments	Nights	7.75	7.52	7.42	7.91	7.94
6.1	**Tourism expenditure in the country**	US$ Mn	2,203	2,146	2,325	2,550	2,644
6.2	"Travel" (*)	US$ Mn	1,993	1,927	2,097	2,239	2,318
6.3	"Passenger transport" (*)	US$ Mn	210	219	228	311	326
	DOMESTIC TOURISM						
	Accommodation						
7.1	Overnight stays in hotels and similar establishments	('000)	729	868	957	1,069	1,040
7.2	Guests in hotels and similar establishments	('000)	331	376	400	446	449
7.3	Overnight stays in all types of accommodation establishments	('000)	739	870	968	1,081	1,052
7.4	Average length of stay of resident tourists in all accommodation establishments	Nights	2.19	2.31	2.38	2.42	2.31
	OUTBOUND TOURISM						
8.1	**Departures**	('000)	589	645	629	743	781
8.2	**Tourism expenditure in other countries**	US$ Mn	568	588	700	906	1,001
8.3	"Travel" (*)	US$ Mn	428	516	611	810	932
8.4	"Passenger transport" (*)	US$ Mn	140	72	89	96	69
	TOURISM INDUSTRIES						
	Hotels and similar establishments						
9.1	Number of rooms	Units	43,338	44,523	44,892	45,535	45,202
9.2	Number of bed-places	Units	87,834	90,112	91,139	92,239	91,264
9.3	Occupancy rate	Percent	73.92	63.04	57.48	57.61	61.59
9.4	Average length of stay	Nights	6.80	6.70	6.48	6.73	6.79
	RELATED INDICATORS						
	Share of tourism expenditure (6.1) in:						
10.1	Gross Domestic Product (GDP)	Percent	23.2	20.5	17.7	16.5	15.8
10.2	Exports of goods	Percent	225.9	251.0	243.5	220.4	181.8
10.3	Exports of services	Percent	50.8	47.6	43.2	41.0	40.8

(*) Balance of Payments items: 6.1 to 6.3 correspond to the "Credit" side (and are receipts for the country) while 8.2 to 8.4 correspond to the "Debit" side (and are expenditures in other countries).

CZECH REPUBLIC

	Basic Indicators	Units	2001	2002	2003	2004	2005
	INBOUND TOURISM						
	Arrivals						
1.1	Visitors	('000)	..	..	..	..	..
1.2	Tourists (overnight visitors)	('000)	5,405	4,743	5,076	6,061	6,336
1.3	Same-day visitors	('000)	..	..	..	..	..
1.4	Cruise passengers	('000)	..	..	..	..	..
	Arrivals by region						
2.1	Africa	('000)	16	13	14	15	18
2.2	Americas	('000)	297	239	282	380	401
2.3	Europe	('000)	4,849	4,249	4,528	5,314	5,496
2.4	East Asia and the Pacific	('000)	243	242	251	352	421
2.5	South Asia	('000)	..	..	..	..	..
2.6	Middle East	('000)	..	..	..	..	..
	Arrivals by means of transport used						
3.1	Air	('000)	..	..	..	..	..
3.2	Rail	('000)	..	..	..	..	..
3.3	Road	('000)	..	..	..	..	..
3.4	Sea	('000)	..	..	..	..	..
	Arrivals by purpose of visit						
4.1	Leisure, recreation and holidays	('000)	..	..	..	..	..
4.2	Business and professional	('000)	..	..	..	..	..
4.3	Other	('000)	..	..	..	..	..
	Accommodation						
5.1	Overnight stays in hotels and similar establishments	('000)	14,703	13,327	13,688	15,881	16,607
5.2	Guests in hotels and similar establishments	('000)	4,862	4,314	4,485	5,346	5,686
5.3	Overnight stays in all types of accommodation establishments	('000)	17,255	15,569	16,511	18,980	19,595
5.4	Average length of stay of non-resident tourists in all accommodation establishments	Nights	3.20	3.30	3.30	3.10	3.10
6.1	**Tourism expenditure in the country**	US$ Mn	..	3,376	4,069	4,960	5,580
6.2	"Travel" (*)	US$ Mn	3,106	2,964	3,566	4,187	4,623
6.3	"Passenger transport" (*)	US$ Mn	..	412	503	773	957
	DOMESTIC TOURISM						
	Accommodation						
7.1	Overnight stays in hotels and similar establishments	('000)	9,071	10,476	9,779	9,051	8,601
7.2	Guests in hotels and similar establishments	('000)	3,293	3,438	3,462	3,346	3,388
7.3	Overnight stays in all types of accommodation establishments	('000)	21,867	21,541	22,833	21,800	20,725
7.4	Average length of stay of resident tourists in all accommodation establishments	Nights	3.70	3.80	3.60	3.50	3.40
	OUTBOUND TOURISM						
8.1	**Departures**	('000)	..	..	..	..	..
8.2	**Tourism expenditure in other countries**	US$ Mn	..	1,797	2,177	2,660	2,605
8.3	"Travel" (*)	US$ Mn	1,386	1,597	1,934	2,280	2,405
8.4	"Passenger transport" (*)	US$ Mn	..	200	243	380	200
	TOURISM INDUSTRIES						
	Hotels and similar establishments						
9.1	Number of rooms	Units	95,460	96,650	98,086	98,764	99,966
9.2	Number of bed-places	Units	218,645	223,392	226,770	229,689	232,295
9.3	Occupancy rate	Percent	45.10	39.70	35.40	37.00	35.80
9.4	Average length of stay	Nights	3.60	3.80	3.70	3.40	2.80
	RELATED INDICATORS						
	Share of tourism expenditure (6.1) in:						
10.1	Gross Domestic Product (GDP)	Percent	..	4.6	4.5	4.6	4.6
10.2	Exports of goods	Percent	..	8.8	8.4	7.4	7.1
10.3	Exports of services	Percent	..	47.7	52.2	51.1	51.8

(*) Balance of Payments items: 6.1 to 6.3 correspond to the "Credit" side (and are receipts for the country) while 8.2 to 8.4 correspond to the "Debit" side (and are expenditures in other countries).

DEMOCRATIC REPUBLIC OF THE CONGO

	Basic Indicators	Units	2001	2002	2003	2004	2005
	INBOUND TOURISM						
	Arrivals						
1.1	Visitors	('000)	..	..	..	..	..
1.2	Tourists (overnight visitors)	('000)	55	28	35	36	61
1.3	Same-day visitors	('000)	20	20	20	..	..
1.4	Cruise passengers	('000)	..	..	..	..	..
	Arrivals by region						
2.1	Africa	('000)	38	9	20	15	36
2.2	Americas	('000)	3	4	3	5	4
2.3	Europe	('000)	11	11	9	13	15
2.4	East Asia and the Pacific	('000)	3	4	3	4	6
2.5	South Asia	('000)	..	..	..	..	..
2.6	Middle East	('000)	..	..	..	..	..
	Arrivals by means of transport used						
3.1	Air	('000)	26	28	35	36	39
3.2	Rail	('000)	..	..	..	..	..
3.3	Road	('000)	..	..	..	..	22
3.4	Sea	('000)	28	..	..	..	..
	Arrivals by purpose of visit						
4.1	Leisure, recreation and holidays	('000)	3	2	2	7	8
4.2	Business and professional	('000)	5	3	21	22	42
4.3	Other	('000)	46	23	12	7	11
	Accommodation						
5.1	Overnight stays in hotels and similar establishments	('000)	..	..	..	..	..
5.2	Guests in hotels and similar establishments	('000)	17	16	17	26	48
5.3	Overnight stays in all types of accommodation establishments	('000)	175	163	150	99	165
5.4	Average length of stay of non-resident tourists in all accommodation establishments	Nights	7.00	8.00	7.00	5.00	5.00
6.1	**Tourism expenditure in the country**	US$ Mn	..	..	..	..	..
6.2	"Travel" (*)	US$ Mn	..	..	..	..	..
6.3	"Passenger transport" (*)	US$ Mn	..	..	..	..	..
	DOMESTIC TOURISM						
	Accommodation						
7.1	Overnight stays in hotels and similar establishments	('000)	..	..	..	..	..
7.2	Guests in hotels and similar establishments	('000)	5	5	11	16	13
7.3	Overnight stays in all types of accommodation establishments	('000)	68	67	40	85	156
7.4	Average length of stay of resident tourists in all accommodation establishments	Nights	14.00	14.00	14.00	14.00	7.00
	OUTBOUND TOURISM						
8.1	**Departures**	('000)	..	..	..	..	..
8.2	**Tourism expenditure in other countries**	US$ Mn	..	..	..	..	..
8.3	"Travel" (*)	US$ Mn	..	..	..	..	..
8.4	"Passenger transport" (*)	US$ Mn	..	..	..	..	..
	TOURISM INDUSTRIES						
	Hotels and similar establishments						
9.1	Number of rooms	Units	5,829	5,829	5,829	..	..
9.2	Number of bed-places	Units	10,000	10,000	10,000	..	..
9.3	Occupancy rate	Percent	50.00	50.00	50.00	..	..
9.4	Average length of stay	Nights	7.00	8.00	7.00	..	..
	RELATED INDICATORS						
	Share of tourism expenditure (6.1) in:						
10.1	Gross Domestic Product (GDP)	Percent	..	..	..	..	..
10.2	Exports of goods	Percent	..	..	..	..	..
10.3	Exports of services	Percent	..	..	..	..	..

(*) Balance of Payments items: 6.1 to 6.3 correspond to the "Credit" side (and are receipts for the country) while 8.2 to 8.4 correspond to the "Debit" side (and are expenditures in other countries).

DENMARK

	Basic Indicators	Units	2001	2002	2003	2004	2005
	INBOUND TOURISM						
	Arrivals						
1.1	Visitors	('000)	..	..	21,119	22,054	22,448
1.2	Tourists (overnight visitors)	('000)	3,684	3,436	3,474	4,421	4,699
1.3	Same-day visitors	('000)	..	..	17,340	17,340	17,340
1.4	Cruise passengers	('000)	404	193	305	293	409
	Arrivals by region						
2.1	Africa	('000)	..	..	..	..	..
2.2	Americas	('000)	89	80	78	126	147
2.3	Europe	('000)	3,455	3,221	3,253	4,065	4,357
2.4	East Asia and the Pacific	('000)	46	49	47	83	110
2.5	South Asia	('000)	..	..	..	..	..
2.6	Middle East	('000)	..	..	..	..	..
	Arrivals by means of transport used						
3.1	Air	('000)	..	..	..	..	..
3.2	Rail	('000)	..	..	..	..	..
3.3	Road	('000)	..	..	..	..	..
3.4	Sea	('000)	..	..	..	..	..
	Arrivals by purpose of visit						
4.1	Leisure, recreation and holidays	('000)	..	..	..	21,070	21,213
4.2	Business and professional	('000)	..	..	..	984	1,235
4.3	Other	('000)	..	..	..	..	..
	Accommodation						
5.1	Overnight stays in hotels and similar establishments	('000)	4,810	4,735	4,730	4,984	5,015
5.2	Guests in hotels and similar establishments	('000)	1,397	1,379	1,385	1,970	2,230
5.3	Overnight stays in all types of accommodation establishments	('000)	25,456	25,663	26,152	24,925	23,012
5.4	Average length of stay of non-resident tourists in all accommodation establishments	Nights	..	..	..	..	5.00
6.1	**Tourism expenditure in the country**	US$ Mn	..	..	..	..	..
6.2	"Travel" (*)	US$ Mn	4,003	4,750	5,258	5,671	4,493
6.3	"Passenger transport" (*)	US$ Mn	..	..	..	..	..
	DOMESTIC TOURISM						
	Accommodation						
7.1	Overnight stays in hotels and similar establishments	('000)	5,072	5,250	5,104	5,404	5,806
7.2	Guests in hotels and similar establishments	('000)	2,096	2,172	2,112	2,805	3,348
7.3	Overnight stays in all types of accommodation establishments	('000)	20,103	20,953	21,678	21,534	22,273
7.4	Average length of stay of resident tourists in all accommodation establishments	Nights	..	..	..	3.00	3.00
	OUTBOUND TOURISM						
8.1	**Departures**	('000)	4,946	4,935	5,564	4,630	5,469
8.2	**Tourism expenditure in other countries**	US$ Mn	..	..	..	..	..
8.3	"Travel" (*)	US$ Mn	4,861	5,828	6,658	7,269	5,690
8.4	"Passenger transport" (*)	US$ Mn	..	..	..	..	..
	TOURISM INDUSTRIES						
	Hotels and similar establishments						
9.1	Number of rooms	Units	40,181	41,194	41,729	43,163	42,834
9.2	Number of bed-places	Units	103,063	105,185	106,080	109,108	108,095
9.3	Occupancy rate	Percent	36.60	36.40	35.70	35.60	36.20
9.4	Average length of stay	Nights	..	..	..	..	..
	RELATED INDICATORS						
	Share of tourism expenditure (6.1) in: (**)						
10.1	Gross Domestic Product (GDP)	Percent	2.5	2.8	2.5	2.3	1.8
10.2	Exports of goods	Percent	7.9	8.6	8.1	7.6	5.4
10.3	Exports of services	Percent	15.9	17.8	16.6	15.6	10.6

(*) Balance of Payments items: 6.1 to 6.3 correspond to the "Credit" side (and are receipts for the country) while 8.2 to 8.4 correspond to the "Debit" side (and are expenditures in other countries).

(**) See Annex "Country notes".

Basic Indicators		Units	2001	2002	2003	2004	2005
	INBOUND TOURISM						
	Arrivals						
1.1	Visitors	('000)	..	..	..	..	..
1.2	Tourists (overnight visitors)	('000)	21.6	22.5	23.2	26.3	30.2
1.3	Same-day visitors	('000)	..	..	..	..	..
1.4	Cruise passengers	('000)	..	..	..	..	..
	Arrivals by region						
2.1	Africa	('000)	..	..	..	..	..
2.2	Americas	('000)	..	..	..	..	..
2.3	Europe	('000)	..	..	..	..	..
2.4	East Asia and the Pacific	('000)	..	..	..	..	..
2.5	South Asia	('000)	..	..	..	..	..
2.6	Middle East	('000)	..	..	..	..	..
	Arrivals by means of transport used						
3.1	Air	('000)	..	..	..	..	..
3.2	Rail	('000)	..	..	..	..	..
3.3	Road	('000)	..	..	..	..	..
3.4	Sea	('000)	..	..	..	..	..
	Arrivals by purpose of visit						
4.1	Leisure, recreation and holidays	('000)	..	..	..	..	..
4.2	Business and professional	('000)	..	..	..	..	..
4.3	Other	('000)	..	..	..	..	..
	Accommodation						
5.1	Overnight stays in hotels and similar establishments	('000)	53.6	63.4	63.7	66.9	59.0
5.2	Guests in hotels and similar establishments	('000)	21.6	22.5	23.2	26.3	30.2
5.3	Overnight stays in all types of accommodation establishments	('000)	..	..	..	..	..
5.4	Average length of stay of non-resident tourists in all accommodation establishments	Nights	..	..	..	..	..
6.1	**Tourism expenditure in the country**	US$ Mn	..	..	..	..	..
6.2	"Travel" (*)	US$ Mn	..	..	6.9	6.8	7.1
6.3	"Passenger transport" (*)	US$ Mn	..	..	..	..	..
	DOMESTIC TOURISM						
	Accommodation						
7.1	Overnight stays in hotels and similar establishments	('000)	..	..	..	..	..
7.2	Guests in hotels and similar establishments	('000)	..	..	..	..	..
7.3	Overnight stays in all types of accommodation establishments	('000)	..	..	..	..	..
7.4	Average length of stay of resident tourists in all accommodation establishments	Nights	..	..	..	..	..
	OUTBOUND TOURISM						
8.1	**Departures**	('000)	..	..	..	..	..
8.2	**Tourism expenditure in other countries**	US$ Mn	..	..	..	..	..
8.3	"Travel" (*)	US$ Mn	..	..	2.8	2.8	2.8
8.4	"Passenger transport" (*)	US$ Mn	..	..	..	..	..
	TOURISM INDUSTRIES						
	Hotels and similar establishments						
9.1	Number of rooms	Units	450	450	450	450	450
9.2	Number of bed-places	Units	675	675	675	675	675
9.3	Occupancy rate	Percent	31.10	47.20	38.70	39.90	35.90
9.4	Average length of stay	Nights	..	..	..	..	..
	RELATED INDICATORS						
	Share of tourism expenditure (6.1) in:						
10.1	Gross Domestic Product (GDP)	Percent	..	..	..	..	..
10.2	Exports of goods	Percent	..	..	..	..	..
10.3	Exports of services	Percent	..	..	..	..	..

(*) Balance of Payments items: 6.1 to 6.3 correspond to the "Credit" side (and are receipts for the country) while 8.2 to 8.4 correspond to the "Debit" side (and are expenditures in other countries).

DOMINICA

	Basic Indicators	Units	2001	2002	2003	2004	2005
	INBOUND TOURISM						
	Arrivals						
1.1	Visitors	('000)	276	208	254	466	381
1.2	Tourists (overnight visitors)	('000)	66	69	73	80	79
1.3	Same-day visitors	('000)	2.0	1.7	3.9	2.6	0.7
1.4	Cruise passengers	('000)	208	137	177	384	301
	Arrivals by region						
2.1	Africa	('000)	..	..	..	..	..
2.2	Americas	('000)	54	58	61	69	68
2.3	Europe	('000)	11	10	11	10	10
2.4	East Asia and the Pacific	('000)	0.5	0.5	0.5	0.4	0.5
2.5	South Asia	('000)	..	..	..	..	..
2.6	Middle East	('000)	..	..	..	..	..
	Arrivals by means of transport used						
3.1	Air	('000)	47	49	52	56	59
3.2	Rail	('000)	..	..	..	..	..
3.3	Road	('000)	..	..	..	..	..
3.4	Sea	('000)	21	22	25	26	21
	Arrivals by purpose of visit						
4.1	Leisure, recreation and holidays	('000)	54	56	60	66	66
4.2	Business and professional	('000)	12	13	13	14	13
4.3	Other	('000)	0.3	0.3	0.3	0.5	0.5
	Accommodation						
5.1	Overnight stays in hotels and similar establishments	('000)	..	..	..	..	..
5.2	Guests in hotels and similar establishments	('000)	26	26	26	29	27
5.3	Overnight stays in all types of accommodation establishments	('000)	..	..	..	..	..
5.4	Average length of stay of non-resident tourists in all accommodation establishments	Nights	7.80	8.60	9.70	9.50	8.70
6.1	**Tourism expenditure in the country**	US$ Mn	..	..	..	..	..
6.2	"Travel" (*)	US$ Mn	45	44	54	60	56
6.3	"Passenger transport" (*)	US$ Mn	..	..	..	..	..
	DOMESTIC TOURISM						
	Accommodation						
7.1	Overnight stays in hotels and similar establishments	('000)	..	..	..	..	..
7.2	Guests in hotels and similar establishments	('000)	..	..	..	..	..
7.3	Overnight stays in all types of accommodation establishments	('000)	..	..	..	..	..
7.4	Average length of stay of resident tourists in all accommodation establishments	Nights	..	..	..	..	..
	OUTBOUND TOURISM						
8.1	**Departures**	('000)	..	..	..	..	..
8.2	**Tourism expenditure in other countries**	US$ Mn	..	..	..	..	..
8.3	"Travel" (*)	US$ Mn	9	9	9	9	10
8.4	"Passenger transport" (*)	US$ Mn	..	..	..	..	..
	TOURISM INDUSTRIES						
	Hotels and similar establishments						
9.1	Number of rooms	Units	889	931	931	791	787
9.2	Number of bed-places	Units	..	..	..	..	..
9.3	Occupancy rate	Percent	..	..	..	..	..
9.4	Average length of stay	Nights	..	..	..	..	..
	RELATED INDICATORS						
	Share of tourism expenditure (6.1) in: (**)						
10.1	Gross Domestic Product (GDP)	Percent	17.2	17.5	20.9	22.1	20.1
10.2	Exports of goods	Percent	102.3	100.0	131.7	139.5	133.3
10.3	Exports of services	Percent	58.4	55.0	70.1	68.2	66.7

(*) Balance of Payments items: 6.1 to 6.3 correspond to the "Credit" side (and are receipts for the country) while 8.2 to 8.4 correspond to the "Debit" side (and are expenditures in other countries).

(**) See Annex "Country notes".

	Basic Indicators	Units	2001	2002	2003	2004	2005
	INBOUND TOURISM						
	Arrivals						
1.1	Visitors	('000)	3,090	3,058	3,680	3,906	3,981
1.2	Tourists (overnight visitors)	('000)	2,882	2,811	3,282	3,450	3,691
1.3	Same-day visitors	('000)	..	..	..	..	..
1.4	Cruise passengers	('000)	208	247	398	456	290
	Arrivals by region						
2.1	Africa	('000)	..	..	..	..	..
2.2	Americas	('000)	1,239	1,261	1,494	1,592	1,711
2.3	Europe	('000)	1,142	1,031	1,249	1,270	1,370
2.4	East Asia and the Pacific	('000)	2	1	2	2	2
2.5	South Asia	('000)	..	..	..	..	..
2.6	Middle East	('000)	..	..	..	..	..
	Arrivals by means of transport used						
3.1	Air	('000)	2,882	2,811	3,282	3,450	3,691
3.2	Rail	('000)	..	..	..	..	..
3.3	Road	('000)	..	..	..	..	..
3.4	Sea	('000)	208	247	398	456	290
	Arrivals by purpose of visit						
4.1	Leisure, recreation and holidays	('000)	2,724	2,637	3,122	3,294	3,475
4.2	Business and professional	('000)	85	87	96	94	128
4.3	Other	('000)	60	69	64	62	88
	Accommodation						
5.1	Overnight stays in hotels and similar establishments	('000)	26,187	22,318	23,920	23,795	28,411
5.2	Guests in hotels and similar establishments	('000)	..	..	..	..	..
5.3	Overnight stays in all types of accommodation establishments	('000)	..	..	..	..	..
5.4	Average length of stay of non-resident tourists in all accommodation establishments	Nights	9.82	9.65	9.32	8.97	9.20
6.1	**Tourism expenditure in the country**	US$ Mn	..	..	..	..	..
6.2	"Travel" (*)	US$ Mn	2,798	2,730	3,128	3,152	3,508
6.3	"Passenger transport" (*)	US$ Mn	..	..	..	..	..
	DOMESTIC TOURISM						
	Accommodation						
7.1	Overnight stays in hotels and similar establishments	('000)	..	..	..	..	..
7.2	Guests in hotels and similar establishments	('000)	..	..	..	..	..
7.3	Overnight stays in all types of accommodation establishments	('000)	..	..	..	..	..
7.4	Average length of stay of resident tourists in all accommodation establishments	Nights	..	..	..	..	..
	OUTBOUND TOURISM						
8.1	**Departures**	('000)	331	332	321	368	419
8.2	**Tourism expenditure in other countries**	US$ Mn	425	429	408	448	494
8.3	"Travel" (*)	US$ Mn	291	295	272	310	352
8.4	"Passenger transport" (*)	US$ Mn	134	134	136	138	142
	TOURISM INDUSTRIES						
	Hotels and similar establishments						
9.1	Number of rooms	Units	54,034	54,730	56,378	58,932	59,870
9.2	Number of bed-places	Units	135,085	136,825	140,945	147,330	149,675
9.3	Occupancy rate	Percent	66.30	62.80	72.70	74.20	73.90
9.4	Average length of stay	Nights	9.82	9.65	9.32	8.97	9.20
	RELATED INDICATORS						
	Share of tourism expenditure (6.1) in: (**)						
10.1	Gross Domestic Product (GDP)	Percent	13.0	12.6	19.2	17.1	12.4
10.2	Exports of goods	Percent	53.0	52.9	57.2	53.1	57.1
10.3	Exports of services	Percent	90.0	88.9	90.2	90.0	89.7

(*) Balance of Payments items: 6.1 to 6.3 correspond to the "Credit" side (and are receipts for the country) while 8.2 to 8.4 correspond to the "Debit" side (and are expenditures in other countries).

(**) See Annex "Country notes".

ECUADOR

	Basic Indicators	Units	2001	2002	2003	2004	2005
	INBOUND TOURISM						
	Arrivals						
1.1	Visitors	('000)	641	683	761	819	861
1.2	Tourists (overnight visitors)	('000)	..	..	..	..	..
1.3	Same-day visitors	('000)	..	..	..	..	..
1.4	Cruise passengers	('000)	..	..	..	..	..
	Arrivals by region						
2.1	Africa	('000)	1	2	2	2	2
2.2	Americas	('000)	511	550	617	662	683
2.3	Europe	('000)	112	113	124	133	152
2.4	East Asia and the Pacific	('000)	16	17	18	21	24
2.5	South Asia	('000)	..	..	..	..	..
2.6	Middle East	('000)	..	..	..	..	..
	Arrivals by means of transport used						
3.1	Air	('000)	422	432	450	496	532
3.2	Rail	('000)	..	..	..	..	..
3.3	Road	('000)	214	245	306	315	321
3.4	Sea	('000)	5	6	5	8	8
	Arrivals by purpose of visit						
4.1	Leisure, recreation and holidays	('000)	..	..	..	..	..
4.2	Business and professional	('000)	..	..	..	..	..
4.3	Other	('000)	..	..	..	..	..
	Accommodation						
5.1	Overnight stays in hotels and similar establishments	('000)	..	..	..	..	..
5.2	Guests in hotels and similar establishments	('000)	..	..	..	..	..
5.3	Overnight stays in all types of accommodation establishments	('000)	..	..	..	..	..
5.4	Average length of stay of non-resident tourists in all accommodation establishments	Nights	..	..	..	..	..
6.1	**Tourism expenditure in the country**	US$ Mn	438	449	408	464	488
6.2	"Travel" (*)	US$ Mn	430	447	406	462	486
6.3	"Passenger transport" (*)	US$ Mn	8	2	2	2	2
	DOMESTIC TOURISM						
	Accommodation						
7.1	Overnight stays in hotels and similar establishments	('000)	..	..	..	..	..
7.2	Guests in hotels and similar establishments	('000)	..	..	..	..	..
7.3	Overnight stays in all types of accommodation establishments	('000)	..	..	..	..	..
7.4	Average length of stay of resident tourists in all accommodation establishments	Nights	..	..	..	..	..
	OUTBOUND TOURISM						
8.1	**Departures**	('000)	562	627	613	603	661
8.2	**Tourism expenditure in other countries**	US$ Mn	465	507	500	577	616
8.3	"Travel" (*)	US$ Mn	340	364	354	391	401
8.4	"Passenger transport" (*)	US$ Mn	125	143	146	186	215
	TOURISM INDUSTRIES						
	Hotels and similar establishments						
9.1	Number of rooms	Units	36,620	36,766	38,237	38,029	41,342
9.2	Number of bed-places	Units	79,100	81,307	86,466	85,213	93,215
9.3	Occupancy rate	Percent	..	..	..	..	..
9.4	Average length of stay	Nights	..	..	..	..	..
	RELATED INDICATORS						
	Share of tourism expenditure (6.1) in:						
10.1	Gross Domestic Product (GDP)	Percent	2.1	1.8	1.4	1.4	1.3
10.2	Exports of goods	Percent	9.1	8.5	6.3	5.8	4.7
10.3	Exports of services	Percent	50.8	50.8	46.3	45.8	48.2

(*) Balance of Payments items: 6.1 to 6.3 correspond to the "Credit" side (and are receipts for the country) while 8.2 to 8.4 correspond to the "Debit" side (and are expenditures in other countries).

Basic Indicators		Units	2001	2002	2003	2004	2005
	INBOUND TOURISM						
	Arrivals						
1.1	Visitors	('000)	4,648	5,192	6,044	8,104	8,608
1.2	Tourists (overnight visitors)	('000)	4,357	4,906	5,746	7,795	8,244
1.3	Same-day visitors	('000)	291	286	298	309	363
1.4	Cruise passengers	('000)	..	..	..	..	..
	Arrivals by region						
2.1	Africa	('000)	146	161	183	245	264
2.2	Americas	('000)	251	171	188	257	298
2.3	Europe	('000)	3,132	3,584	4,204	5,920	6,047
2.4	East Asia and the Pacific	('000)	210	214	227	296	411
2.5	South Asia	('000)	40	46	51	63	73
2.6	Middle East	('000)	868	1,013	1,189	1,318	1,511
	Arrivals by means of transport used						
3.1	Air	('000)	3,800	4,280	4,841	6,577	6,713
3.2	Rail	('000)	..	..	..	..	..
3.3	Road	('000)	397	475	749	881	800
3.4	Sea	('000)	451	437	454	646	1,094
	Arrivals by purpose of visit						
4.1	Leisure, recreation and holidays	('000)	4,198	4,737	5,529	7,533	7,993
4.2	Business and professional	('000)	86	95	139	182	182
4.3	Other	('000)	73	74	78	80	69
	Accommodation						
5.1	Overnight stays in hotels and similar establishments	('000)	29,813	32,664	53,130	81,668	85,172
5.2	Guests in hotels and similar establishments	('000)	6,147	6,229	6,731	..	..
5.3	Overnight stays in all types of accommodation establishments	('000)	..	..	..	..	..
5.4	Average length of stay of non-resident tourists in all accommodation establishments	Nights	6.40	6.30	8.80	9.90	10.40
6.1	**Tourism expenditure in the country**	US$ Mn	4,119	4,133	4,704	6,328	7,206
6.2	"Travel" (*)	US$ Mn	3,800	3,764	4,584	6,125	6,851
6.3	"Passenger transport" (*)	US$ Mn	319	369	120	203	355
	DOMESTIC TOURISM						
	Accommodation						
7.1	Overnight stays in hotels and similar establishments	('000)	4,331	4,791	4,782	..	..
7.2	Guests in hotels and similar establishments	('000)	1,140	1,397	2,212	..	..
7.3	Overnight stays in all types of accommodation establishments	('000)	..	..	..	..	..
7.4	Average length of stay of resident tourists in all accommodation establishments	Nights	3.80	3.40	2.30	..	..
	OUTBOUND TOURISM						
8.1	**Departures**	('000)	3,074	3,330	3,644	5,210	5,307
8.2	**Tourism expenditure in other countries**	US$ Mn	1,248	1,309	1,465	1,543	1,932
8.3	"Travel" (*)	US$ Mn	1,132	1,266	1,321	1,257	1,629
8.4	"Passenger transport" (*)	US$ Mn	116	43	144	286	303
	TOURISM INDUSTRIES						
	Hotels and similar establishments						
9.1	Number of rooms	Units	120,720	132,109	136,510	148,039	170,776
9.2	Number of bed-places	Units	241,440	264,218	273,020	296,078	341,552
9.3	Occupancy rate	Percent	61.00	56.00	59.00	68.90	64.00
9.4	Average length of stay	Nights	6.40	6.30	8.80	10.70	10.40
	RELATED INDICATORS						
	Share of tourism expenditure (6.1) in:						
10.1	Gross Domestic Product (GDP)	Percent	4.2	4.7	5.7	8.0	8.1
10.2	Exports of goods	Percent	58.6	58.1	52.3	51.4	44.8
10.3	Exports of services	Percent	45.6	44.3	42.5	44.6	49.2

(*) Balance of Payments items: 6.1 to 6.3 correspond to the "Credit" side (and are receipts for the country) while 8.2 to 8.4 correspond to the "Debit" side (and are expenditures in other countries).

EL SALVADOR

	Basic Indicators	Units	2001	2002	2003	2004	2005
	INBOUND TOURISM						
	Arrivals						
1.1	Visitors	('000)	804	1,038	935	1,045	1,333
1.2	Tourists (overnight visitors)	('000)	735	951	857	966	1,154
1.3	Same-day visitors	('000)	69	87	78	79	179
1.4	Cruise passengers	('000)	..	..	..	..	..
	Arrivals by region						
2.1	Africa	('000)	..	..	..	1	1
2.2	Americas	('000)	660	873	812	923	1,112
2.3	Europe	('000)	22	27	35	33	31
2.4	East Asia and the Pacific	('000)	3	4	9	10	10
2.5	South Asia	('000)	..	..	..	..	..
2.6	Middle East	('000)	..	..	..	..	..
	Arrivals by means of transport used						
3.1	Air	('000)	224	253	262	310	341
3.2	Rail	('000)	..	..	..	..	..
3.3	Road	('000)	505	693	594	655	812
3.4	Sea	('000)	6	5	1	1	1
	Arrivals by purpose of visit						
4.1	Leisure, recreation and holidays	('000)	209	197	216	243	382
4.2	Business and professional	('000)	241	344	185	209	187
4.3	Other	('000)	285	410	456	514	585
	Accommodation						
5.1	Overnight stays in hotels and similar establishments	('000)	2,938	3,802	3,430	4,832	6,926
5.2	Guests in hotels and similar establishments	('000)	367	485	436	503	681
5.3	Overnight stays in all types of accommodation establishments	('000)	..	..	..	..	..
5.4	Average length of stay of non-resident tourists in all accommodation establishments	Nights	4.00	4.00	5.00	5.00	6.00
6.1	**Tourism expenditure in the country** (**)	US$ Mn	452	521	664	736	838
6.2	"Travel" (*)	US$ Mn	201	245	383	441	543
6.3	"Passenger transport" (*)	US$ Mn	251	276	281	295	295
	DOMESTIC TOURISM						
	Accommodation						
7.1	Overnight stays in hotels and similar establishments	('000)	..	..	..	..	..
7.2	Guests in hotels and similar establishments	('000)	..	..	..	..	..
7.3	Overnight stays in all types of accommodation establishments	('000)	..	..	..	..	..
7.4	Average length of stay of resident tourists in all accommodation establishments	Nights	..	..	..	..	..
	OUTBOUND TOURISM						
8.1	**Departures**	('000)	933	1,001	940	1,218	1,397
8.2	**Tourism expenditure in other countries**	US$ Mn	247	266	311	383	430
8.3	"Travel" (*)	US$ Mn	195	191	230	302	347
8.4	"Passenger transport" (*)	US$ Mn	52	75	81	81	83
	TOURISM INDUSTRIES						
	Hotels and similar establishments						
9.1	Number of rooms	Units	4,996	5,152	4,501	4,766	5,757
9.2	Number of bed-places	Units	..	..	7,252	8,120	10,113
9.3	Occupancy rate	Percent	50.00	51.00	52.90	52.50	59.50
9.4	Average length of stay	Nights	4.00	4.00	5.00	5.00	6.00
	RELATED INDICATORS						
	Share of tourism expenditure (6.1) in:						
10.1	Gross Domestic Product (GDP)	Percent	3.3	3.6	4.4	4.7	4.9
10.2	Exports of goods	Percent	15.6	17.3	21.1	22.1	24.4
10.3	Exports of services	Percent	64.2	66.5	70.0	68.5	73.4

(*) Balance of Payments items: 6.1 to 6.3 correspond to the "Credit" side (and are receipts for the country) while 8.2 to 8.4 correspond to the "Debit" side (and are expenditures in other countries).

(**) See Annex "Country notes".

	Basic Indicators		Units	2001	2002	2003	2004	2005
	INBOUND TOURISM							
	Arrivals							
1.1	Visitors		('000)	113	101	80	87	83
1.2	Tourists (overnight visitors)		('000)	..	..	..	..	..
1.3	Same-day visitors		('000)	..	..	..	..	..
1.4	Cruise passengers		('000)	..	..	..	..	..
	Arrivals by region							
2.1	Africa		('000)	7	8	3	5	3
2.2	Americas		('000)	3	2	2	3	2
2.3	Europe		('000)	10	8	8	10	8
2.4	East Asia and the Pacific		('000)	3	2	2	2	2
2.5	South Asia		('000)	2	3	3	2	3
2.6	Middle East		('000)	4	4	3	4	4
	Arrivals by means of transport used							
3.1	Air		('000)	59	51	49	51	45
3.2	Rail		('000)	..	..	..	..	..
3.3	Road		('000)	52	48	29	34	37
3.4	Sea		('000)	2	2	2	2	1
	Arrivals by purpose of visit							
4.1	Leisure, recreation and holidays		('000)	6	6	5	3	6
4.2	Business and professional		('000)	22	21	16	13	13
4.3	Other		('000)	85	74	59	71	65
	Accommodation							
5.1	Overnight stays in hotels and similar establishments		('000)	..	..	..	..	176
5.2	Guests in hotels and similar establishments		('000)	..	..	..	..	..
5.3	Overnight stays in all types of accommodation establishments		('000)	..	..	..	..	..
5.4	Average length of stay of non-resident tourists in all accommodation establishments		Nights	24.00	28.00	..	..	3.10
6.1	**Tourism expenditure in the country**	(**)	US$ Mn	74	73	74	73	66
6.2	"Travel" (*)		US$ Mn	..	..	..	..	..
6.3	"Passenger transport" (*)		US$ Mn	..	..	..	..	..
	DOMESTIC TOURISM							
	Accommodation							
7.1	Overnight stays in hotels and similar establishments		('000)	..	..	..	..	669
7.2	Guests in hotels and similar establishments		('000)	..	..	..	..	..
7.3	Overnight stays in all types of accommodation establishments		('000)	..	..	..	..	..
7.4	Average length of stay of resident tourists in all accommodation establishments		Nights	..	..	..	..	1.40
	OUTBOUND TOURISM							
8.1	**Departures**		('000)	..	..	..	..	..
8.2	**Tourism expenditure in other countries**		US$ Mn	..	..	..	..	..
8.3	"Travel" (*)		US$ Mn	..	..	..	..	..
8.4	"Passenger transport" (*)		US$ Mn	..	..	..	..	..
	TOURISM INDUSTRIES							
	Hotels and similar establishments							
9.1	Number of rooms		Units	4,509	4,189	4,139	4,712	5,447
9.2	Number of bed-places		Units	9,312	8,912	8,794	9,445	10,720
9.3	Occupancy rate		Percent	48.00	56.00	52.12	54.37	43.00
9.4	Average length of stay		Nights	..	..	..	..	3.00
	RELATED INDICATORS							
	Share of tourism expenditure (6.1) in:	(**)						
10.1	Gross Domestic Product (GDP)		Percent	..	..	..	..	..
10.2	Exports of goods		Percent	..	..	..	..	..
10.3	Exports of services		Percent	..	..	..	..	..

(*) Balance of Payments items: 6.1 to 6.3 correspond to the "Credit" side (and are receipts for the country) while 8.2 to 8.4 correspond to the "Debit" side (and are expenditures in other countries).

(**) See Annex "Country notes".

ESTONIA

	Basic Indicators	Units	2001	2002	2003	2004	2005
	INBOUND TOURISM						
	Arrivals						
1.1	Visitors	('000)	3,230	3,253	3,378	..	..
1.2	Tourists (overnight visitors)	('000)	1,320	1,362	1,462	1,750	1,900
1.3	Same-day visitors	('000)	1,778	1,773	1,741	..	..
1.4	Cruise passengers	('000)	132	118	175	206	295
	Arrivals by region						
2.1	Africa	('000)	..	..	1	1	1
2.2	Americas	('000)	17	16	15	23	24
2.3	Europe	('000)	949	967	1,081	1,334	1,411
2.4	East Asia and the Pacific	('000)	7	7	11	13	15
2.5	South Asia	('000)	..	..	..	..	..
2.6	Middle East	('000)	..	..	..	..	..
	Arrivals by means of transport used						
3.1	Air	('000)	152	161	185	..	..
3.2	Rail	('000)	36	35	37	..	..
3.3	Road	('000)	899	845	962	..	..
3.4	Sea	('000)	2,143	2,212	2,193	..	..
	Arrivals by purpose of visit						
4.1	Leisure, recreation and holidays	('000)	1,610	..	..	..	..
4.2	Business and professional	('000)	760	..	..	..	..
4.3	Other	('000)	860	..	..	..	..
	Accommodation						
5.1	Overnight stays in hotels and similar establishments	('000)	1,341	1,887	2,086	2,602	2,791
5.2	Guests in hotels and similar establishments	('000)	848	937	1,009	1,300	1,358
5.3	Overnight stays in all types of accommodation establishments	('000)	1,911	1,998	2,268	2,747	2,982
5.4	Average length of stay of non-resident tourists in all accommodation establishments	Nights	1.94	1.99	2.04	2.00	2.05
6.1	**Tourism expenditure in the country**	US$ Mn	661	737	883	1,111	1,207
6.2	"Travel" (*)	US$ Mn	507	555	671	887	948
6.3	"Passenger transport" (*)	US$ Mn	154	182	212	224	259
	DOMESTIC TOURISM						
	Accommodation						
7.1	Overnight stays in hotels and similar establishments	('000)	489	450	558	691	751
7.2	Guests in hotels and similar establishments	('000)	306	250	306	385	428
7.3	Overnight stays in all types of accommodation establishments	('000)	626	698	817	1,011	1,129
7.4	Average length of stay of resident tourists in all accommodation establishments	Nights	1.82	1.75	1.82	1.85	1.82
	OUTBOUND TOURISM						
8.1	**Departures**	('000)	1,658	1,849	2,075	..	..
8.2	**Tourism expenditure in other countries**	US$ Mn	253	305	404	481	538
8.3	"Travel" (*)	US$ Mn	192	231	319	400	448
8.4	"Passenger transport" (*)	US$ Mn	61	74	85	81	90
	TOURISM INDUSTRIES						
	Hotels and similar establishments						
9.1	Number of rooms	Units	8,452	10,845	12,445	14,953	16,610
9.2	Number of bed-places	Units	20,335	22,849	27,487	32,899	38,088
9.3	Occupancy rate	Percent	49.00	45.00	47.00	47.00	47.00
9.4	Average length of stay	Nights	1.59	1.99	2.04	1.95	1.98
	RELATED INDICATORS						
	Share of tourism expenditure (6.1) in:						
10.1	Gross Domestic Product (GDP)	Percent	11.1	10.5	9.6	9.9	9.2
10.2	Exports of goods	Percent	19.6	21.0	19.2	18.6	15.5
10.3	Exports of services	Percent	41.1	43.2	39.7	39.3	38.2

(*) Balance of Payments items: 6.1 to 6.3 correspond to the "Credit" side (and are receipts for the country) while 8.2 to 8.4 correspond to the "Debit" side (and are expenditures in other countries).

	Basic Indicators	Units	2001	2002	2003	2004	2005
	INBOUND TOURISM						
	Arrivals						
1.1	Visitors	('000)	..	..	..	..	..
1.2	Tourists (overnight visitors)	('000)	148	156	180	184	227
1.3	Same-day visitors	('000)	..	..	..	..	..
1.4	Cruise passengers	('000)	..	..	..	..	..
	Arrivals by region						
2.1	Africa	('000)	61	60	82	66	86
2.2	Americas	('000)	15	19	27	34	41
2.3	Europe	('000)	33	34	44	48	57
2.4	East Asia and the Pacific	('000)	7	8	8	10	12
2.5	South Asia	('000)	3	4	4	5	7
2.6	Middle East	('000)	10	9	14	21	22
	Arrivals by means of transport used						
3.1	Air	('000)	123	132	163	173	193
3.2	Rail	('000)	2	18	17	..	..
3.3	Road	('000)	23	6	..	11	34
3.4	Sea	('000)	..	..	..	..	..
	Arrivals by purpose of visit						
4.1	Leisure, recreation and holidays	('000)	41	49	53	57	63
4.2	Business and professional	('000)	32	43	37	35	46
4.3	Other	('000)	43	64	90	92	118
	Accommodation						
5.1	Overnight stays in hotels and similar establishments	('000)	356	391	..	..	..
5.2	Guests in hotels and similar establishments	('000)	..	..	..	..	..
5.3	Overnight stays in all types of accommodation establishments	('000)	..	..	..	..	..
5.4	Average length of stay of non-resident tourists in all accommodation establishments	Nights	4.50	..	..	..	..
6.1	**Tourism expenditure in the country**	US$ Mn	218	261	336	458	533
6.2	"Travel" (*)	US$ Mn	51	72	114	174	168
6.3	"Passenger transport" (*)	US$ Mn	167	189	222	284	365
	DOMESTIC TOURISM						
	Accommodation						
7.1	Overnight stays in hotels and similar establishments	('000)	..	..	..	..	..
7.2	Guests in hotels and similar establishments	('000)	..	..	..	..	..
7.3	Overnight stays in all types of accommodation establishments	('000)	..	..	..	..	..
7.4	Average length of stay of resident tourists in all accommodation establishments	Nights	..	..	..	..	..
	OUTBOUND TOURISM						
8.1	**Departures**	('000)	..	..	..	..	..
8.2	**Tourism expenditure in other countries**	US$ Mn	50	56	63	59	..
8.3	"Travel" (*)	US$ Mn	44	45	50	58	77
8.4	"Passenger transport" (*)	US$ Mn	6	11	13	1	..
	TOURISM INDUSTRIES						
	Hotels and similar establishments						
9.1	Number of rooms	Units	9,676	2,979	3,497	..	3,387
9.2	Number of bed-places	Units	12,570	4,494	5,419	..	5,170
9.3	Occupancy rate	Percent	45.20	..	60.00	..	..
9.4	Average length of stay	Nights	2.40	..	3.00	..	..
	RELATED INDICATORS						
	Share of tourism expenditure (6.1) in:						
10.1	Gross Domestic Product (GDP)	Percent	2.8	3.6	4.2	4.7	4.8
10.2	Exports of goods	Percent	47.8	54.4	67.7	67.6	58.1
10.3	Exports of services	Percent	41.7	44.6	44.1	45.6	52.7

(*) Balance of Payments items: 6.1 to 6.3 correspond to the "Credit" side (and are receipts for the country) while 8.2 to 8.4 correspond to the "Debit" side (and are expenditures in other countries).

FIJI

	Basic Indicators		Units	2001	2002	2003	2004	2005
	INBOUND TOURISM							
	Arrivals							
1.1	Visitors		('000)	446	461	496	..	..
1.2	Tourists (overnight visitors)		('000)	348	398	431	503	550
1.3	Same-day visitors		('000)	91	57	45	..	..
1.4	Cruise passengers		('000)	7	6	13	8	..
	Arrivals by region							
2.1	Africa		('000)	..	..	..	..	..
2.2	Americas		('000)	68	69	69	78	86
2.3	Europe		('000)	51	65	72	71	79
2.4	East Asia and the Pacific		('000)	226	262	288	352	384
2.5	South Asia		('000)	..	..	..	..	..
2.6	Middle East		('000)	..	..	..	..	..
	Arrivals by means of transport used							
3.1	Air		('000)	342	390	422	..	..
3.2	Rail		('000)	..	..	..	..	..
3.3	Road		('000)	..	..	..	..	..
3.4	Sea		('000)	6	8	8	..	..
	Arrivals by purpose of visit							
4.1	Leisure, recreation and holidays		('000)	261	306	332	388	..
4.2	Business and professional		('000)	24	31	33	39	..
4.3	Other		('000)	62	61	66	76	..
	Accommodation							
5.1	Overnight stays in hotels and similar establishments		('000)	1,466	1,914	2,015	2,489	2,760
5.2	Guests in hotels and similar establishments		('000)	..	..	..	..	..
5.3	Overnight stays in all types of accommodation establishments		('000)	..	..	..	..	..
5.4	Average length of stay of non-resident tourists in all accommodation establishments		Nights	8.60	8.70	8.70	8.90	8.90
6.1	**Tourism expenditure in the country**	(**)	US$ Mn	..	..	487	581	670
6.2	"Travel" (*)		US$ Mn	197	254	340	420	436
6.3	"Passenger transport" (*)		US$ Mn	..	..	147	161	234
	DOMESTIC TOURISM							
	Accommodation							
7.1	Overnight stays in hotels and similar establishments		('000)	319	392	412	453	479
7.2	Guests in hotels and similar establishments		('000)	..	..	..	..	..
7.3	Overnight stays in all types of accommodation establishments		('000)	..	..	..	..	..
7.4	Average length of stay of resident tourists in all accommodation establishments		Nights	..	..	..	..	..
	OUTBOUND TOURISM							
8.1	**Departures**		('000)	85	99	104	..	..
8.2	**Tourism expenditure in other countries**	(**)	US$ Mn	..	..	87	118	131
8.3	"Travel" (*)		US$ Mn	65	55	69	94	106
8.4	"Passenger transport" (*)		US$ Mn	..	..	18	24	25
	TOURISM INDUSTRIES							
	Hotels and similar establishments							
9.1	Number of rooms		Units	5,520	5,899	6,116	6,677	6,713
9.2	Number of bed-places		Units	13,075	14,559	14,206	15,680	16,536
9.3	Occupancy rate		Percent	46.50	55.60	55.90	61.30	64.40
9.4	Average length of stay		Nights	..	..	..	..	..
	RELATED INDICATORS							
	Share of tourism expenditure (6.1) in:							
10.1	Gross Domestic Product (GDP)		Percent	..	..	21.8	22.2	23.8
10.2	Exports of goods		Percent	..	..	..	..	..
10.3	Exports of services		Percent	..	..	..	..	..

(*) Balance of Payments items: 6.1 to 6.3 correspond to the "Credit" side (and are receipts for the country) while 8.2 to 8.4 correspond to the "Debit" side (and are expenditures in other countries).

(**) See Annex "Country notes".

	Basic Indicators	Units	2001	2002	2003	2004	2005
	INBOUND TOURISM						
	Arrivals						
1.1	Visitors	('000)	4,252	4,687	4,527	4,854	5,038
1.2	Tourists (overnight visitors)	('000)	2,826	2,875	2,601	2,840	3,140
1.3	Same-day visitors	('000)	1,426	1,812	1,926	2,014	1,898
1.4	Cruise passengers	('000)	..	..	..	..	..
	Arrivals by region						
2.1	Africa	('000)	8	7	9	6	12
2.2	Americas	('000)	161	182	151	159	160
2.3	Europe	('000)	3,916	4,245	4,157	4,417	4,581
2.4	East Asia and the Pacific	('000)	158	244	210	268	273
2.5	South Asia	('000)	6	5	..	4	8
2.6	Middle East	('000)	3	4	..	..	4
	Arrivals by means of transport used						
3.1	Air	('000)	1,558	1,603	1,577	1,640	1,734
3.2	Rail	('000)	83	84	67	71	80
3.3	Road	('000)	1,370	1,638	1,596	1,694	1,686
3.4	Sea	('000)	1,241	1,362	1,287	1,449	1,538
	Arrivals by purpose of visit						
4.1	Leisure, recreation and holidays	('000)	1,718	2,105	2,020	2,077	2,107
4.2	Business and professional	('000)	1,321	1,273	1,257	1,314	1,480
4.3	Other	('000)	1,213	1,309	1,250	1,463	1,451
	Accommodation						
5.1	Overnight stays in hotels and similar establishments	('000)	3,675	3,721	3,758	3,758	3,887
5.2	Guests in hotels and similar establishments	('000)	1,774	1,796	1,814	1,820	1,828
5.3	Overnight stays in all types of accommodation establishments	('000)	4,183	4,290	4,331	4,383	4,499
5.4	Average length of stay of non-resident tourists in all accommodation establishments	Nights	2.09	2.10	2.12	2.10	2.16
6.1	**Tourism expenditure in the country**	US$ Mn	2,066	2,242	2,677	2,976	3,055
6.2	"Travel" (*)	US$ Mn	1,438	1,578	1,870	2,067	2,147
6.3	"Passenger transport" (*)	US$ Mn	628	664	807	909	908
	DOMESTIC TOURISM						
	Accommodation						
7.1	Overnight stays in hotels and similar establishments	('000)	9,882	9,552	9,671	10,032	10,388
7.2	Guests in hotels and similar establishments	('000)	5,442	5,327	5,415	5,736	5,948
7.3	Overnight stays in all types of accommodation establishments	('000)	12,029	11,703	11,751	12,243	12,760
7.4	Average length of stay of resident tourists in all accommodation establishments	Nights	1.85	1.83	1.82	1.79	1.82
	OUTBOUND TOURISM						
8.1	**Departures**	('000)	5,824	5,857	5,585	5,798	6,035
8.2	**Tourism expenditure in other countries**	US$ Mn	2,442	2,437	2,956	3,381	3,529
8.3	"Travel" (*)	US$ Mn	1,852	2,006	2,435	2,820	2,968
8.4	"Passenger transport" (*)	US$ Mn	590	431	521	561	561
	TOURISM INDUSTRIES						
	Hotels and similar establishments						
9.1	Number of rooms	Units	55,268	54,916	55,767	53,537	53,335
9.2	Number of bed-places	Units	118,473	117,870	120,051	120,086	115,202
9.3	Occupancy rate	Percent	48.00	47.00	46.80	46.30	47.80
9.4	Average length of stay	Nights	1.88	1.90	1.89	1.83	1.84
	RELATED INDICATORS						
	Share of tourism expenditure (6.1) in:						
10.1	Gross Domestic Product (GDP)	Percent	1.7	1.7	1.7	1.6	1.6
10.2	Exports of goods	Percent	4.8	5.0	5.1	4.9	4.7
10.3	Exports of services	Percent	35.4	34.5	33.9	30.1	29.9

(*) Balance of Payments items: 6.1 to 6.3 correspond to the "Credit" side (and are receipts for the country) while 8.2 to 8.4 correspond to the "Debit" side (and are expenditures in other countries).

FRANCE

	Basic Indicators	Units	2001	2002	2003	2004	2005
	INBOUND TOURISM						
	Arrivals						
1.1	Visitors	('000)	..	..	..	..	..
1.2	Tourists (overnight visitors)	('000)	75,202	77,012	75,048	75,121	76,001
1.3	Same-day visitors	('000)	..	..	..	..	..
1.4	Cruise passengers	('000)	..	..	..	..	..
	Arrivals by region						
2.1	Africa	('000)	921	924	889	895	910
2.2	Americas	('000)	5,291	4,639	3,954	4,206	4,651
2.3	Europe	('000)	66,491	69,078	68,073	67,711	67,629
2.4	East Asia and the Pacific	('000)	2,114	2,080	1,890	2,058	2,501
2.5	South Asia	('000)	..	..	..	..	..
2.6	Middle East	('000)	325	249	210	237	268
	Arrivals by means of transport used						
3.1	Air	('000)	11,574	..	..	..	15,656
3.2	Rail	('000)	4,708	..	..	..	4,180
3.3	Road	('000)	54,450	..	..	..	50,085
3.4	Sea	('000)	4,470	..	..	..	6,080
	Arrivals by purpose of visit						
4.1	Leisure, recreation and holidays	('000)	49,536	..	..	..	..
4.2	Business and professional	('000)	9,866	..	..	..	..
4.3	Other	('000)	15,800	..	..	..	..
	Accommodation						
5.1	Overnight stays in hotels and similar establishments	('000)	75,652	77,602	69,323	70,391	72,054
5.2	Guests in hotels and similar establishments	('000)	35,097	36,093	32,520	33,988	34,806
5.3	Overnight stays in all types of accommodation establishments	('000)	581,037	588,430	567,006	561,294	566,927
5.4	Average length of stay of non-resident tourists in all accommodation establishments	Nights	7.31	7.64	7.56	7.47	7.46
6.1	**Tourism expenditure in the country**	US$ Mn	..	..	..	..	..
6.2	"Travel" (*)	US$ Mn	30,363	32,437	36,617	40,693	42,167
6.3	"Passenger transport" (*)	US$ Mn	..	..	..	..	..
	DOMESTIC TOURISM						
	Accommodation						
7.1	Overnight stays in hotels and similar establishments	('000)	115,576	114,454	115,536	118,134	120,326
7.2	Guests in hotels and similar establishments	('000)	66,111	65,253	66,365	69,705	71,594
7.3	Overnight stays in all types of accommodation establishments	('000)	969,744	1,004,767	1,002,025	1,016,534	..
7.4	Average length of stay of resident tourists in all accommodation establishments	Nights	5.28	5.24	5.21	4.93	..
	OUTBOUND TOURISM						
8.1	**Departures**	('000)	19,265	18,315	18,576	21,131	22,270
8.2	**Tourism expenditure in other countries**	US$ Mn	..	..	..	..	..
8.3	"Travel" (*)	US$ Mn	18,109	19,518	23,396	28,544	31,180
8.4	"Passenger transport" (*)	US$ Mn	..	..	..	..	..
	TOURISM INDUSTRIES						
	Hotels and similar establishments						
9.1	Number of rooms	Units	600,492	603,619	603,279	615,402	613,798
9.2	Number of bed-places	Units	1,200,984	1,207,238	1,206,558	1,230,804	1,227,596
9.3	Occupancy rate	Percent	60.50	60.30	58.40	58.60	59.10
9.4	Average length of stay	Nights	1.89	1.90	1.87	1.82	1.81
	RELATED INDICATORS						
	Share of tourism expenditure (6.1) in: (**)						
10.1	Gross Domestic Product (GDP)	Percent	2.3	2.2	2.0	2.0	2.0
10.2	Exports of goods	Percent	10.3	10.6	10.1	9.7	9.6
10.3	Exports of services	Percent	36.9	37.7	37.1	37.2	36.4

(*) Balance of Payments items: 6.1 to 6.3 correspond to the "Credit" side (and are receipts for the country) while 8.2 to 8.4 correspond to the "Debit" side (and are expenditures in other countries).

(**) See Annex "Country notes".

	Basic Indicators	Units	2001	2002	2003	2004	2005
	INBOUND TOURISM						
	Arrivals						
1.1	Visitors	('000)	..	..	..	..	..
1.2	Tourists (overnight visitors)	('000)	65	65	..	..	95
1.3	Same-day visitors	('000)	..	..	..	..	1.7
1.4	Cruise passengers	('000)	..	..	..	..	..
	Arrivals by region						
2.1	Africa	('000)	..	..	..	..	..
2.2	Americas	('000)	..	18	..	..	..
2.3	Europe	('000)	..	45	..	..	..
2.4	East Asia and the Pacific	('000)	..	..	..	..	..
2.5	South Asia	('000)	..	..	..	..	..
2.6	Middle East	('000)	..	..	..	..	..
	Arrivals by means of transport used						
3.1	Air	('000)	65	65	..	..	..
3.2	Rail	('000)	..	..	..	..	..
3.3	Road	('000)	..	..	..	..	..
3.4	Sea	('000)	..	..	..	..	..
	Arrivals by purpose of visit						
4.1	Leisure, recreation and holidays	('000)	15	24	..	..	..
4.2	Business and professional	('000)	30	24	..	..	..
4.3	Other	('000)	20	17	..	..	..
	Accommodation						
5.1	Overnight stays in hotels and similar establishments	('000)	..	..	..	..	..
5.2	Guests in hotels and similar establishments	('000)	..	..	..	..	..
5.3	Overnight stays in all types of accommodation establishments	('000)	..	..	..	302	391
5.4	Average length of stay of non-resident tourists in all accommodation establishments	Nights	..	..	..	2.10	2.70
6.1	**Tourism expenditure in the country**	US$ Mn	42	45	..	..	45
6.2	"Travel" (*)	US$ Mn	..	..	..	..	..
6.3	"Passenger transport" (*)	US$ Mn	..	..	..	..	..
	DOMESTIC TOURISM						
	Accommodation						
7.1	Overnight stays in hotels and similar establishments	('000)	..	..	..	..	..
7.2	Guests in hotels and similar establishments	('000)	..	..	..	..	..
7.3	Overnight stays in all types of accommodation establishments	('000)	..	..	..	..	..
7.4	Average length of stay of resident tourists in all accommodation establishments	Nights	..	..	..	..	..
	OUTBOUND TOURISM						
8.1	**Departures**	('000)	..	..	..	..	..
8.2	**Tourism expenditure in other countries**	US$ Mn	..	..	..	..	..
8.3	"Travel" (*)	US$ Mn	..	..	..	..	..
8.4	"Passenger transport" (*)	US$ Mn	..	..	..	..	..
	TOURISM INDUSTRIES						
	Hotels and similar establishments						
9.1	Number of rooms	Units	1,255	..	..	..	1,184
9.2	Number of bed-places	Units	..	..	..	..	..
9.3	Occupancy rate	Percent	50.10	..	..	..	..
9.4	Average length of stay	Nights	..	..	..	..	..
	RELATED INDICATORS						
	Share of tourism expenditure (6.1) in:						
10.1	Gross Domestic Product (GDP)	Percent	..	..	..	..	..
10.2	Exports of goods	Percent	..	..	..	..	..
10.3	Exports of services	Percent	..	..	..	..	..

(*) Balance of Payments items: 6.1 to 6.3 correspond to the "Credit" side (and are receipts for the country) while 8.2 to 8.4 correspond to the "Debit" side (and are expenditures in other countries).

FRENCH POLYNESIA

	Basic Indicators	Units	2001	2002	2003	2004	2005
	INBOUND TOURISM						
	Arrivals						
1.1	Visitors	('000)	..	..	..	..	..
1.2	Tourists (overnight visitors)	('000)	228	189	213	212	208
1.3	Same-day visitors	('000)	..	..	..	..	..
1.4	Cruise passengers	('000)	..	..	..	..	..
	Arrivals by region						
2.1	Africa	('000)	..	..	..	..	..
2.2	Americas	('000)	107	72	89	86	80
2.3	Europe	('000)	84	76	80	80	82
2.4	East Asia and the Pacific	('000)	36	40	42	45	46
2.5	South Asia	('000)	..	..	..	..	..
2.6	Middle East	('000)	..	..	..	..	..
	Arrivals by means of transport used						
3.1	Air	('000)	228	189	213	212	208
3.2	Rail	('000)	..	..	..	..	..
3.3	Road	('000)	..	..	..	..	..
3.4	Sea	('000)	..	..	..	..	..
	Arrivals by purpose of visit						
4.1	Leisure, recreation and holidays	('000)	208	166	187	191	..
4.2	Business and professional	('000)	10	12	14	13	..
4.3	Other	('000)	10	11	12	8	..
	Accommodation						
5.1	Overnight stays in hotels and similar establishments	('000)	2,042	1,666	1,950	1,917	1,897
5.2	Guests in hotels and similar establishments	('000)	193	155	180	178	176
5.3	Overnight stays in all types of accommodation establishments	('000)	2,875	2,592	2,888	2,861	2,787
5.4	Average length of stay of non-resident tourists in all accommodation establishments	Nights	12.63	13.72	13.57	13.50	13.39
6.1	**Tourism expenditure in the country**	US$ Mn	..	471	651	737	779
6.2	"Travel" (*)	US$ Mn	..	372	480	523	550
6.3	"Passenger transport" (*)	US$ Mn	..	99	171	214	229
	DOMESTIC TOURISM						
	Accommodation						
7.1	Overnight stays in hotels and similar establishments	('000)	..	..	..	..	..
7.2	Guests in hotels and similar establishments	('000)	..	..	..	..	..
7.3	Overnight stays in all types of accommodation establishments	('000)	..	..	..	..	..
7.4	Average length of stay of resident tourists in all accommodation establishments	Nights	..	..	..	..	..
	OUTBOUND TOURISM						
8.1	**Departures**	('000)	..	..	..	..	..
8.2	**Tourism expenditure in other countries**	US$ Mn	..	264	335	425	421
8.3	"Travel" (*)	US$ Mn	..	180	236	311	303
8.4	"Passenger transport" (*)	US$ Mn	..	84	99	114	118
	TOURISM INDUSTRIES						
	Hotels and similar establishments						
9.1	Number of rooms	Units	2,943	3,221	3,108	3,326	2,963
9.2	Number of bed-places	Units	..	..	..	..	..
9.3	Occupancy rate	Percent	58.76	59.12	58.50	57.90	..
9.4	Average length of stay	Nights	10.46	10.74	10.84	10.44	..
	RELATED INDICATORS						
	Share of tourism expenditure (6.1) in:						
10.1	Gross Domestic Product (GDP)	Percent	..	..	..	..	..
10.2	Exports of goods	Percent	..	285.5	436.9	411.7	367.5
10.3	Exports of services	Percent	..	61.6	68.2	71.7	70.8

(*) Balance of Payments items: 6.1 to 6.3 correspond to the "Credit" side (and are receipts for the country) while 8.2 to 8.4 correspond to the "Debit" side (and are expenditures in other countries).

	Basic Indicators	Units	2001	2002	2003	2004	2005
	INBOUND TOURISM						
	Arrivals						
1.1	Visitors	('000)	236	269	234	..	..
1.2	Tourists (overnight visitors)	('000)	169	208	222	..	..
1.3	Same-day visitors	('000)	65	60	12	..	..
1.4	Cruise passengers	('000)	2	1	..	..	..
	Arrivals by region						
2.1	Africa	('000)	42	52	55	..	..
2.2	Americas	('000)	3	..	..	..	..
2.3	Europe	('000)	119	..	..	..	..
2.4	East Asia and the Pacific	('000)	1	..	..	..	..
2.5	South Asia	('000)	..	..	..	..	..
2.6	Middle East	('000)	3	..	..	..	..
	Arrivals by means of transport used						
3.1	Air	('000)	169	208	222	..	..
3.2	Rail	('000)	..	..	..	..	..
3.3	Road	('000)	..	..	..	..	..
3.4	Sea	('000)	..	..	..	..	..
	Arrivals by purpose of visit						
4.1	Leisure, recreation and holidays	('000)	..	..	..	..	..
4.2	Business and professional	('000)	..	..	..	..	..
4.3	Other	('000)	..	..	..	..	..
	Accommodation						
5.1	Overnight stays in hotels and similar establishments	('000)	250	250	..	..	..
5.2	Guests in hotels and similar establishments	('000)	..	..	..	..	..
5.3	Overnight stays in all types of accommodation establishments	('000)	..	..	..	..	..
5.4	Average length of stay of non-resident tourists in all accommodation establishments	Nights	..	..	..	..	..
6.1	**Tourism expenditure in the country**	US$ Mn	46	77	84	74	..
6.2	"Travel" (*)	US$ Mn	15	18	15	10	..
6.3	"Passenger transport" (*)	US$ Mn	31	59	69	64	..
	DOMESTIC TOURISM						
	Accommodation						
7.1	Overnight stays in hotels and similar establishments	('000)	..	..	..	..	..
7.2	Guests in hotels and similar establishments	('000)	..	..	..	..	..
7.3	Overnight stays in all types of accommodation establishments	('000)	..	..	..	..	..
7.4	Average length of stay of resident tourists in all accommodation establishments	Nights	..	..	..	..	..
	OUTBOUND TOURISM						
8.1	**Departures**	('000)	189	219	236	..	..
8.2	**Tourism expenditure in other countries**	US$ Mn	256	234	239	275	..
8.3	"Travel" (*)	US$ Mn	225	194	194	214	..
8.4	"Passenger transport" (*)	US$ Mn	31	40	45	61	..
	TOURISM INDUSTRIES						
	Hotels and similar establishments						
9.1	Number of rooms	Units	2,450	2,450	..	..	..
9.2	Number of bed-places	Units	..	..	..	..	..
9.3	Occupancy rate	Percent	70.00	70.00	..	..	..
9.4	Average length of stay	Nights	..	..	..	..	..
	RELATED INDICATORS						
	Share of tourism expenditure (6.1) in:						
10.1	Gross Domestic Product (GDP)	Percent	1.1	1.5	1.4	1.0	..
10.2	Exports of goods	Percent	1.8	3.0	2.6	1.8	..
10.3	Exports of services	Percent	27.4	89.5	48.8	47.4	..

(*) Balance of Payments items: 6.1 to 6.3 correspond to the "Credit" side (and are receipts for the country) while 8.2 to 8.4 correspond to the "Debit" side (and are expenditures in other countries).

GAMBIA

	Basic Indicators	Units	2001	2002	2003	2004	2005
	INBOUND TOURISM						
	Arrivals						
1.1	Visitors	('000)	..	..	..	..	463
1.2	Tourists (overnight visitors)	('000)	57	81	73	90	111
1.3	Same-day visitors	('000)	..	..	..	..	..
1.4	Cruise passengers	('000)	..	..	..	..	..
	Arrivals by region						
2.1	Africa	('000)	..	1	5	1	..
2.2	Americas	('000)	1	1	1	3	..
2.3	Europe	('000)	54	77	64	82	..
2.4	East Asia and the Pacific	('000)	..	..	..	..	..
2.5	South Asia	('000)	..	..	..	..	..
2.6	Middle East	('000)	..	..	..	..	..
	Arrivals by means of transport used						
3.1	Air	('000)	57	81	73	90	111
3.2	Rail	('000)	..	..	..	..	..
3.3	Road	('000)	..	..	..	..	347
3.4	Sea	('000)	..	..	..	..	5
	Arrivals by purpose of visit						
4.1	Leisure, recreation and holidays	('000)	57	81	73	90	111
4.2	Business and professional	('000)	..	..	..	..	..
4.3	Other	('000)	..	..	..	..	..
	Accommodation						
5.1	Overnight stays in hotels and similar establishments	('000)	..	..	..	..	..
5.2	Guests in hotels and similar establishments	('000)	..	..	..	..	..
5.3	Overnight stays in all types of accommodation establishments	('000)	..	..	..	..	..
5.4	Average length of stay of non-resident tourists in all accommodation establishments	Nights	..	..	..	..	..
6.1	**Tourism expenditure in the country**	US$ Mn	..	..	58	51	57
6.2	"Travel" (*)	US$ Mn	..	..	56	47	56
6.3	"Passenger transport" (*)	US$ Mn	..	..	2	4	1
	DOMESTIC TOURISM						
	Accommodation						
7.1	Overnight stays in hotels and similar establishments	('000)	..	..	..	..	..
7.2	Guests in hotels and similar establishments	('000)	..	..	..	..	..
7.3	Overnight stays in all types of accommodation establishments	('000)	..	..	..	..	..
7.4	Average length of stay of resident tourists in all accommodation establishments	Nights	..	..	..	..	..
	OUTBOUND TOURISM						
8.1	**Departures**	('000)	..	..	..	..	387
8.2	**Tourism expenditure in other countries**	US$ Mn	..	..	8	6	7
8.3	"Travel" (*)	US$ Mn	..	..	4	4	5
8.4	"Passenger transport" (*)	US$ Mn	..	..	4	2	2
	TOURISM INDUSTRIES						
	Hotels and similar establishments						
9.1	Number of rooms	Units	..	..	..	..	3,066
9.2	Number of bed-places	Units	..	..	..	..	..
9.3	Occupancy rate	Percent	..	..	..	..	..
9.4	Average length of stay	Nights	12.90	12.90	12.90	..	..
	RELATED INDICATORS						
	Share of tourism expenditure (6.1) in:						
10.1	Gross Domestic Product (GDP)	Percent	..	..	15.8	12.7	12.4
10.2	Exports of goods	Percent	..	..	74.4	46.8	56.4
10.3	Exports of services	Percent	..	..	69.0	69.9	71.3

(*) Balance of Payments items: 6.1 to 6.3 correspond to the "Credit" side (and are receipts for the country) while 8.2 to 8.4 correspond to the "Debit" side (and are expenditures in other countries).

	Basic Indicators	Units	2001	2002	2003	2004	2005
	INBOUND TOURISM						
	Arrivals						
1.1	Visitors	('000)	..	..	..	..	..
1.2	Tourists (overnight visitors)	('000)	302	298	313	368	560
1.3	Same-day visitors	('000)	..	..	..	..	..
1.4	Cruise passengers	('000)	..	..	..	3	..
	Arrivals by region						
2.1	Africa	('000)	1	1	..	1	..
2.2	Americas	('000)	8	7	9	11	15
2.3	Europe	('000)	282	275	289	343	533
2.4	East Asia and the Pacific	('000)	5	7	7	5	3
2.5	South Asia	('000)	5	6	7	7	7
2.6	Middle East	('000)	1	1	2	2	1
	Arrivals by means of transport used						
3.1	Air	('000)	58	67	73	96	131
3.2	Rail	('000)	44	41	40	53	7
3.3	Road	('000)	166	150	155	184	422
3.4	Sea	('000)	34	40	45	34	..
	Arrivals by purpose of visit						
4.1	Leisure, recreation and holidays	('000)	2	2	4	3	..
4.2	Business and professional	('000)	23	25	31	54	..
4.3	Other	('000)	2	2	4	3	..
	Accommodation						
5.1	Overnight stays in hotels and similar establishments	('000)	..	..	..	..	..
5.2	Guests in hotels and similar establishments	('000)	27	29	39	61	..
5.3	Overnight stays in all types of accommodation establishments	('000)	..	..	..	..	..
5.4	Average length of stay of non-resident tourists in all accommodation establishments	Nights	7.80	7.80	..	..	..
6.1	**Tourism expenditure in the country**	US$ Mn	136	144	172	209	288
6.2	"Travel" (*)	US$ Mn	117	126	147	177	242
6.3	"Passenger transport" (*)	US$ Mn	19	18	25	32	46
	DOMESTIC TOURISM						
	Accommodation						
7.1	Overnight stays in hotels and similar establishments	('000)	..	..	..	..	..
7.2	Guests in hotels and similar establishments	('000)	43	41	44	56	..
7.3	Overnight stays in all types of accommodation establishments	('000)	..	..	..	..	..
7.4	Average length of stay of resident tourists in all accommodation establishments	Nights	..	..	..	..	..
	OUTBOUND TOURISM						
8.1	**Departures**	('000)	306	317	..	..	..
8.2	**Tourism expenditure in other countries**	US$ Mn	136	189	170	196	238
8.3	"Travel" (*)	US$ Mn	107	149	130	147	169
8.4	"Passenger transport" (*)	US$ Mn	29	40	40	49	69
	TOURISM INDUSTRIES						
	Hotels and similar establishments						
9.1	Number of rooms	Units	9,381	9,550	9,614	9,680	6,757
9.2	Number of bed-places	Units	18,296	17,550	17,715	18,084	13,978
9.3	Occupancy rate	Percent	71.00	71.00	..	..	..
9.4	Average length of stay	Nights	..	..	..	..	..
	RELATED INDICATORS						
	Share of tourism expenditure (6.1) in:						
10.1	Gross Domestic Product (GDP)	Percent	4.2	4.2	4.3	4.1	4.5
10.2	Exports of goods	Percent	27.4	23.9	20.7	19.1	19.6
10.3	Exports of services	Percent	43.3	36.7	38.8	38.7	41.3

(*) Balance of Payments items: 6.1 to 6.3 correspond to the "Credit" side (and are receipts for the country) while 8.2 to 8.4 correspond to the "Debit" side (and are expenditures in other countries).

GERMANY

	Basic Indicators	Units	2001	2002	2003	2004	2005
	INBOUND TOURISM						
	Arrivals						
1.1	Visitors	('000)	..	..	..	..	..
1.2	Tourists (overnight visitors)	('000)	17,861	17,969	18,399	20,137	21,500
1.3	Same-day visitors	('000)	..	..	..	..	..
1.4	Cruise passengers	('000)	..	..	..	..	..
	Arrivals by region						
2.1	Africa	('000)	147	144	143	146	144
2.2	Americas	('000)	2,334	2,151	2,049	2,337	2,398
2.3	Europe	('000)	13,093	13,289	13,878	14,918	16,100
2.4	East Asia and the Pacific	('000)	1,651	1,716	1,605	1,931	2,001
2.5	South Asia	('000)	..	..	..	..	..
2.6	Middle East	('000)	117	128	143	160	185
	Arrivals by means of transport used						
3.1	Air	('000)	48,667	46,906	49,866	57,194	61,997
3.2	Rail	('000)	..	..	..	..	..
3.3	Road	('000)	..	..	..	..	..
3.4	Sea	('000)	..	..	..	..	..
	Arrivals by purpose of visit						
4.1	Leisure, recreation and holidays	('000)	..	..	..	..	..
4.2	Business and professional	('000)	..	..	..	..	..
4.3	Other	('000)	..	..	..	..	..
	Accommodation						
5.1	Overnight stays in hotels and similar establishments	('000)	34,660	34,553	35,172	38,491	40,839
5.2	Guests in hotels and similar establishments	('000)	16,003	16,093	16,357	17,983	19,171
5.3	Overnight stays in all types of accommodation establishments	('000)	40,798	40,655	41,746	45,374	48,246
5.4	Average length of stay of non-resident tourists in all accommodation establishments	Nights	2.30	2.30	2.30	2.30	2.20
6.1	**Tourism expenditure in the country**	US$ Mn	24,175	26,690	30,154	35,616	38,381
6.2	"Travel" (*)	US$ Mn	18,031	19,278	23,125	27,613	29,151
6.3	"Passenger transport" (*)	US$ Mn	6,144	7,412	7,029	8,003	9,230
	DOMESTIC TOURISM						
	Accommodation						
7.1	Overnight stays in hotels and similar establishments	('000)	171,674	164,383	163,554	165,655	168,843
7.2	Guests in hotels and similar establishments	('000)	72,387	70,023	70,316	72,857	75,363
7.3	Overnight stays in all types of accommodation establishments	('000)	307,143	298,041	296,842	293,395	295,735
7.4	Average length of stay of resident tourists in all accommodation establishments	Nights	3.20	3.20	3.20	3.00	3.00
	OUTBOUND TOURISM						
8.1	**Departures**	('000)	76,400	73,300	74,600	72,300	77,400
8.2	**Tourism expenditure in other countries**	US$ Mn	56,709	59,486	72,597	79,216	80,276
8.3	"Travel" (*)	US$ Mn	51,810	52,660	64,628	70,614	72,488
8.4	"Passenger transport" (*)	US$ Mn	4,899	6,826	7,969	8,602	7,788
	TOURISM INDUSTRIES						
	Hotels and similar establishments						
9.1	Number of rooms	Units	884,534	891,879	892,302	889,297	890,153
9.2	Number of bed-places	Units	1,659,695	1,671,117	1,672,151	1,667,919	1,678,284
9.3	Occupancy rate	Percent	34.70	33.20	33.50	34.20	35.00
9.4	Average length of stay	Nights	2.33	2.31	2.29	2.25	2.22
	RELATED INDICATORS						
	Share of tourism expenditure (6.1) in:						
10.1	Gross Domestic Product (GDP)	Percent	1.3	1.3	1.2	1.3	1.4
10.2	Exports of goods	Percent	4.3	4.4	4.0	4.0	3.9
10.3	Exports of services	Percent	27.3	25.9	24.5	24.9	24.8

(*) Balance of Payments items: 6.1 to 6.3 correspond to the "Credit" side (and are receipts for the country) while 8.2 to 8.4 correspond to the "Debit" side (and are expenditures in other countries).

	Basic Indicators	Units	2001	2002	2003	2004	2005
	INBOUND TOURISM						
	Arrivals						
1.1	Visitors	('000)	..	..	..	..	..
1.2	Tourists (overnight visitors)	('000)	439	483	531	584	429
1.3	Same-day visitors	('000)	..	..	..	..	..
1.4	Cruise passengers	('000)	..	..	..	..	..
	Arrivals by region						
2.1	Africa	('000)	149	164	181	199	173
2.2	Americas	('000)	37	41	45	49	63
2.3	Europe	('000)	109	120	132	145	101
2.4	East Asia and the Pacific	('000)	21	23	26	28	17
2.5	South Asia	('000)	..	..	..	..	..
2.6	Middle East	('000)	3	4	4	4	11
	Arrivals by means of transport used						
3.1	Air	('000)	..	..	..	..	..
3.2	Rail	('000)	..	..	..	..	..
3.3	Road	('000)	..	..	..	..	..
3.4	Sea	('000)	..	..	..	..	..
	Arrivals by purpose of visit						
4.1	Leisure, recreation and holidays	('000)	139	153	168	185	83
4.2	Business and professional	('000)	160	176	193	213	142
4.3	Other	('000)	140	154	170	186	203
	Accommodation						
5.1	Overnight stays in hotels and similar establishments	('000)	..	..	..	..	..
5.2	Guests in hotels and similar establishments	('000)	..	..	..	..	..
5.3	Overnight stays in all types of accommodation establishments	('000)	..	..	..	..	..
5.4	Average length of stay of non-resident tourists in all accommodation establishments	Nights	..	..	..	..	..
6.1	**Tourism expenditure in the country**	US$ Mn	374	383	441	495	827
6.2	"Travel" (*)	US$ Mn	351	358	414	466	796
6.3	"Passenger transport" (*)	US$ Mn	23	25	27	29	31
	DOMESTIC TOURISM						
	Accommodation						
7.1	Overnight stays in hotels and similar establishments	('000)	..	..	..	..	..
7.2	Guests in hotels and similar establishments	('000)	..	..	..	..	..
7.3	Overnight stays in all types of accommodation establishments	('000)	..	..	..	..	..
7.4	Average length of stay of resident tourists in all accommodation establishments	Nights	..	..	..	..	..
	OUTBOUND TOURISM						
8.1	**Departures**	('000)	..	..	..	..	..
8.2	**Tourism expenditure in other countries**	US$ Mn	165	184	216	270	472
8.3	"Travel" (*)	US$ Mn	105	119	138	186	303
8.4	"Passenger transport" (*)	US$ Mn	60	65	78	84	169
	TOURISM INDUSTRIES						
	Hotels and similar establishments						
9.1	Number of rooms	Units	15,453	16,180	17,352	18,079	18,632
9.2	Number of bed-places	Units	19,648	21,442	22,909	23,538	23,915
9.3	Occupancy rate	Percent	..	..	..	..	75.00
9.4	Average length of stay	Nights	..	..	..	..	..
	RELATED INDICATORS						
	Share of tourism expenditure (6.1) in:						
10.1	Gross Domestic Product (GDP)	Percent	7.0	6.2	5.8	5.6	7.7
10.2	Exports of goods	Percent	20.0	19.0	17.2	18.3	29.5
10.3	Exports of services	Percent	70.3	69.0	70.0	70.5	77.6

(*) Balance of Payments items: 6.1 to 6.3 correspond to the "Credit" side (and are receipts for the country) while 8.2 to 8.4 correspond to the "Debit" side (and are expenditures in other countries).

GREECE

	Basic Indicators	Units	2001	2002	2003	2004	2005
	INBOUND TOURISM						
	Arrivals						
1.1	Visitors	('000)	14,678	14,918	14,785	14,268	15,449
1.2	Tourists (overnight visitors)	('000)	14,057	14,180	13,969	13,313	14,276
1.3	Same-day visitors	('000)	..	..	..	..	..
1.4	Cruise passengers	('000)	621	738	815	955	1,173
	Arrivals by region						
2.1	Africa	('000)	24	22	19	23	23
2.2	Americas	('000)	232	217	219	236	297
2.3	Europe	('000)	13,483	13,630	13,459	12,766	13,593
2.4	East Asia and the Pacific	('000)	243	242	213	227	287
2.5	South Asia	('000)	4	4	4	5	4
2.6	Middle East	('000)	71	64	55	55	72
	Arrivals by means of transport used						
3.1	Air	('000)	10,841	10,438	10,417	9,974	10,426
3.2	Rail	('000)	86	89	95	92	104
3.3	Road	('000)	2,322	2,856	2,828	2,692	2,986
3.4	Sea	('000)	1,430	1,535	1,445	1,510	1,932
	Arrivals by purpose of visit						
4.1	Leisure, recreation and holidays	('000)	..	..	..	..	..
4.2	Business and professional	('000)	..	..	..	..	..
4.3	Other	('000)	..	..	..	..	..
	Accommodation						
5.1	Overnight stays in hotels and similar establishments	('000)	41,815	40,350	39,760	38,310	40,075
5.2	Guests in hotels and similar establishments	('000)	6,997	6,654	6,574	6,313	7,143
5.3	Overnight stays in all types of accommodation establishments	('000)	42,494	40,953	40,407	38,796	40,734
5.4	Average length of stay of non-resident tourists in all accommodation establishments	Nights	5.90	5.98	5.97	6.00	5.54
6.1	**Tourism expenditure in the country**	US$ Mn	9,216	10,005	10,842	12,809	13,697
6.2	"Travel" (*)	US$ Mn	9,155	9,909	10,766	12,715	13,578
6.3	"Passenger transport" (*)	US$ Mn	61	96	76	94	119
	DOMESTIC TOURISM						
	Accommodation						
7.1	Overnight stays in hotels and similar establishments	('000)	13,290	13,128	13,716	13,280	13,942
7.2	Guests in hotels and similar establishments	('000)	5,528	5,465	5,650	5,567	5,933
7.3	Overnight stays in all types of accommodation establishments	('000)	13,774	13,513	14,095	13,758	14,530
7.4	Average length of stay of resident tourists in all accommodation establishments	Nights	2.44	2.43	2.46	2.43	2.40
	OUTBOUND TOURISM						
8.1	**Departures**	('000)	..	..	..	..	..
8.2	**Tourism expenditure in other countries**	US$ Mn	4,189	2,453	2,439	2,880	3,046
8.3	"Travel" (*)	US$ Mn	4,177	2,436	2,431	2,872	3,039
8.4	"Passenger transport" (*)	US$ Mn	12	17	8	8	7
	TOURISM INDUSTRIES						
	Hotels and similar establishments						
9.1	Number of rooms	Units	320,467	330,348	339,540	351,891	358,721
9.2	Number of bed-places	Units	608,104	626,914	644,898	668,271	682,050
9.3	Occupancy rate	Percent	63.40	61.80	60.70	55.60	58.60
9.4	Average length of stay	Nights	..	..	..	..	..
	RELATED INDICATORS						
	Share of tourism expenditure (6.1) in:						
10.1	Gross Domestic Product (GDP)	Percent	7.8	7.5	6.3	6.2	6.4
10.2	Exports of goods	Percent	86.8	101.4	86.2	81.4	77.7
10.3	Exports of services	Percent	47.4	49.7	44.6	38.7	40.1

(*) Balance of Payments items: 6.1 to 6.3 correspond to the "Credit" side (and are receipts for the country) while 8.2 to 8.4 correspond to the "Debit" side (and are expenditures in other countries).

GRENADA

Basic Indicators		Units	2001	2002	2003	2004	2005
	INBOUND TOURISM						
	Arrivals						
1.1	Visitors	('000)	277	271	294	370	380
1.2	Tourists (overnight visitors)	('000)	123	132	142	134	99
1.3	Same-day visitors	('000)	7	4	5	6	6
1.4	Cruise passengers	('000)	147	135	147	230	275
	Arrivals by region						
2.1	Africa	('000)	..	..	1	1	..
2.2	Americas	('000)	66	77	80	77	59
2.3	Europe	('000)	40	39	43	36	22
2.4	East Asia and the Pacific	('000)	1	1	1	1	1
2.5	South Asia	('000)	..	..	..	..	..
2.6	Middle East	('000)	..	..	..	..	..
	Arrivals by means of transport used						
3.1	Air	('000)	112	121	134	128	94
3.2	Rail	('000)	..	..	..	..	..
3.3	Road	('000)	..	..	..	..	..
3.4	Sea	('000)	11	11	8	6	5
	Arrivals by purpose of visit						
4.1	Leisure, recreation and holidays	('000)	68	85	90	71	49
4.2	Business and professional	('000)	12	19	22	31	19
4.3	Other	('000)	36	28	31	32	30
	Accommodation						
5.1	Overnight stays in hotels and similar establishments	('000)	..	..	..	..	..
5.2	Guests in hotels and similar establishments	('000)	60	63	72	72	36
5.3	Overnight stays in all types of accommodation establishments	('000)	..	..	..	..	..
5.4	Average length of stay of non-resident tourists in all accommodation establishments	Nights	7.23	7.32	7.65	7.53	7.42
6.1	**Tourism expenditure in the country**	US$ Mn	..	..	..	..	..
6.2	"Travel" (*)	US$ Mn	83	91	104	83	71
6.3	"Passenger transport" (*)	US$ Mn	..	..	..	..	..
	DOMESTIC TOURISM						
	Accommodation						
7.1	Overnight stays in hotels and similar establishments	('000)	..	..	..	..	..
7.2	Guests in hotels and similar establishments	('000)	..	..	..	..	..
7.3	Overnight stays in all types of accommodation establishments	('000)	..	..	..	..	..
7.4	Average length of stay of resident tourists in all accommodation establishments	Nights	..	..	..	..	..
	OUTBOUND TOURISM						
8.1	**Departures**	('000)	..	..	..	..	..
8.2	**Tourism expenditure in other countries**	US$ Mn	..	..	..	..	..
8.3	"Travel" (*)	US$ Mn	8	8	8	9	11
8.4	"Passenger transport" (*)	US$ Mn	..	..	..	..	..
	TOURISM INDUSTRIES						
	Hotels and similar establishments						
9.1	Number of rooms	Units	1,734	1,777	1,758	1,738	1,470
9.2	Number of bed-places	Units	3,142	3,590	3,844	3,892	..
9.3	Occupancy rate	Percent	38.18	71.00	..	..	..
9.4	Average length of stay	Nights	7.23	7.32	7.65	7.53	7.42
	RELATED INDICATORS						
	Share of tourism expenditure (6.1) in: (**)						
10.1	Gross Domestic Product (GDP)	Percent	21.0	22.3	23.4	19.0	15.6
10.2	Exports of goods	Percent	3126.6	4882.9	4354.3	6072.7	5141.0
10.3	Exports of services	Percent	62.4	69.5	77.6	52.9	55.5

(*) Balance of Payments items: 6.1 to 6.3 correspond to the "Credit" side (and are receipts for the country) while 8.2 to 8.4 correspond to the "Debit" side (and are expenditures in other countries).

(**) See Annex "Country notes".

GUADELOUPE

Basic Indicators		Units	2001	2002	2003	2004	2005
	INBOUND TOURISM						
	Arrivals						
1.1	Visitors	('000)	759	..	569	560	445
1.2	Tourists (overnight visitors)	('000)	521	..	439	456	372
1.3	Same-day visitors	('000)	..	..	..	..	..
1.4	Cruise passengers	('000)	238	148	130	104	73
	Arrivals by region						
2.1	Africa	('000)	..	..	..	..	..
2.2	Americas	('000)	13	..	..	..	..
2.3	Europe	('000)	361	..	..	..	370
2.4	East Asia and the Pacific	('000)	..	..	..	..	..
2.5	South Asia	('000)	..	..	..	..	..
2.6	Middle East	('000)	..	..	..	..	..
	Arrivals by means of transport used						
3.1	Air	('000)	521	..	439	456	372
3.2	Rail	('000)	..	..	..	..	..
3.3	Road	('000)	..	..	..	..	..
3.4	Sea	('000)	238	148	130	104	73
	Arrivals by purpose of visit						
4.1	Leisure, recreation and holidays	('000)	..	..	..	..	..
4.2	Business and professional	('000)	..	..	..	..	..
4.3	Other	('000)	..	..	..	..	..
	Accommodation						
5.1	Overnight stays in hotels and similar establishments	('000)	..	..	1,534	1,736	..
5.2	Guests in hotels and similar establishments	('000)	379	..	439	456	..
5.3	Overnight stays in all types of accommodation establishments	('000)	..	..	..	..	..
5.4	Average length of stay of non-resident tourists in all accommodation establishments	Nights	..	..	..	..	..
6.1	**Tourism expenditure in the country**	US$ Mn	..	..	..	..	246
6.2	"Travel" (*)	US$ Mn	..	..	..	..	..
6.3	"Passenger transport" (*)	US$ Mn	..	..	..	..	..
	DOMESTIC TOURISM						
	Accommodation						
7.1	Overnight stays in hotels and similar establishments	('000)	..	..	..	..	..
7.2	Guests in hotels and similar establishments	('000)	..	..	..	..	..
7.3	Overnight stays in all types of accommodation establishments	('000)	..	..	..	..	..
7.4	Average length of stay of resident tourists in all accommodation establishments	Nights	..	..	..	..	..
	OUTBOUND TOURISM						
8.1	**Departures**	('000)	..	..	..	..	..
8.2	**Tourism expenditure in other countries**	US$ Mn	..	..	..	..	..
8.3	"Travel" (*)	US$ Mn	..	..	..	..	..
8.4	"Passenger transport" (*)	US$ Mn	..	..	..	..	..
	TOURISM INDUSTRIES						
	Hotels and similar establishments						
9.1	Number of rooms	Units	8,019	7,433	7,603	4,416	3,506
9.2	Number of bed-places	Units	..	..	..	..	7,012
9.3	Occupancy rate	Percent	60.07	54.80	49.20	53.00	..
9.4	Average length of stay	Nights	5.30	..	3.50	3.90	3.50
	RELATED INDICATORS						
	Share of tourism expenditure (6.1) in:						
10.1	Gross Domestic Product (GDP)	Percent	..	..	..	..	..
10.2	Exports of goods	Percent	..	..	..	..	..
10.3	Exports of services	Percent	..	..	..	..	..

(*) Balance of Payments items: 6.1 to 6.3 correspond to the "Credit" side (and are receipts for the country) while 8.2 to 8.4 correspond to the "Debit" side (and are expenditures in other countries).

	Basic Indicators	Units	2001	2002	2003	2004	2005
	INBOUND TOURISM						
	Arrivals						
1.1	Visitors	('000)	..	..	..	..	..
1.2	Tourists (overnight visitors)	('000)	1,159	1,059	910	1,160	1,228
1.3	Same-day visitors	('000)	..	..	..	..	..
1.4	Cruise passengers	('000)	..	..	..	..	..
	Arrivals by region						
2.1	Africa	('000)	..	..	..	..	..
2.2	Americas	('000)	43	43	..	47	46
2.3	Europe	('000)	1	1	..	2	2
2.4	East Asia and the Pacific	('000)	1,077	984	..	1,069	1,134
2.5	South Asia	('000)	..	..	..	..	..
2.6	Middle East	('000)	..	..	..	..	..
	Arrivals by means of transport used						
3.1	Air	('000)	1,124	1,031	857	1,121	1,185
3.2	Rail	('000)	..	..	..	..	..
3.3	Road	('000)	..	..	..	..	..
3.4	Sea	('000)	35	28	52	39	43
	Arrivals by purpose of visit						
4.1	Leisure, recreation and holidays	('000)	1,112	810	672	895	938
4.2	Business and professional	('000)	18	17	17	31	37
4.3	Other	('000)	202	196	162	195	210
	Accommodation						
5.1	Overnight stays in hotels and similar establishments	('000)	..	..	..	..	..
5.2	Guests in hotels and similar establishments	('000)	..	..	..	..	..
5.3	Overnight stays in all types of accommodation establishments	('000)	..	..	..	..	..
5.4	Average length of stay of non-resident tourists in all accommodation establishments	Nights	..	..	..	..	..
6.1	**Tourism expenditure in the country**	US$ Mn	..	..	..	..	..
6.2	"Travel" (*)	US$ Mn	..	..	..	..	..
6.3	"Passenger transport" (*)	US$ Mn	..	..	..	..	..
	DOMESTIC TOURISM						
	Accommodation						
7.1	Overnight stays in hotels and similar establishments	('000)	..	..	..	..	..
7.2	Guests in hotels and similar establishments	('000)	..	..	..	..	..
7.3	Overnight stays in all types of accommodation establishments	('000)	..	..	..	..	..
7.4	Average length of stay of resident tourists in all accommodation establishments	Nights	..	..	..	..	..
	OUTBOUND TOURISM						
8.1	**Departures**	('000)	..	..	..	..	..
8.2	**Tourism expenditure in other countries**	US$ Mn	..	..	..	..	..
8.3	"Travel" (*)	US$ Mn	..	..	..	..	..
8.4	"Passenger transport" (*)	US$ Mn	..	..	..	..	..
	TOURISM INDUSTRIES						
	Hotels and similar establishments						
9.1	Number of rooms	Units	9,002	8,451	8,915	8,555	9,236
9.2	Number of bed-places	Units	..	..	..	..	..
9.3	Occupancy rate	Percent	58.00	57.00	54.00	58.00	63.00
9.4	Average length of stay	Nights	..	..	..	..	..
	RELATED INDICATORS						
	Share of tourism expenditure (6.1) in:						
10.1	Gross Domestic Product (GDP)	Percent	..	..	..	..	..
10.2	Exports of goods	Percent	..	..	..	..	..
10.3	Exports of services	Percent	..	..	..	..	..

(*) Balance of Payments items: 6.1 to 6.3 correspond to the "Credit" side (and are receipts for the country) while 8.2 to 8.4 correspond to the "Debit" side (and are expenditures in other countries).

GUATEMALA

	Basic Indicators		Units	2001	2002	2003	2004	2005
	INBOUND TOURISM							
	Arrivals							
1.1	Visitors		('000)	..	..	..	..	..
1.2	Tourists (overnight visitors)		('000)	835	884	880	1,182	1,316
1.3	Same-day visitors		('000)	..	..	..	..	..
1.4	Cruise passengers		('000)	..	..	..	..	..
	Arrivals by region							
2.1	Africa		('000)	..	..	..	..	..
2.2	Americas		('000)	676	712	704	1,007	1,148
2.3	Europe		('000)	135	145	151	150	140
2.4	East Asia and the Pacific		('000)	22	24	22	23	25
2.5	South Asia		('000)	..	..	..	..	..
2.6	Middle East		('000)	..	1	1	..	1
	Arrivals by means of transport used							
3.1	Air		('000)	408	403	402	434	480
3.2	Rail		('000)	..	..	..	..	..
3.3	Road		('000)	417	466	452	714	805
3.4	Sea		('000)	11	15	26	34	31
	Arrivals by purpose of visit							
4.1	Leisure, recreation and holidays		('000)	..	..	..	..	..
4.2	Business and professional		('000)	..	..	..	..	..
4.3	Other		('000)	..	..	..	..	..
	Accommodation							
5.1	Overnight stays in hotels and similar establishments		('000)	..	..	..	..	..
5.2	Guests in hotels and similar establishments		('000)	..	..	..	..	..
5.3	Overnight stays in all types of accommodation establishments		('000)	..	..	..	..	..
5.4	Average length of stay of non-resident tourists in all accommodation establishments		Nights	..	..	..	..	..
6.1	**Tourism expenditure in the country**		US$ Mn	588	647	646	806	883
6.2	"Travel" (*)		US$ Mn	562	620	621	776	846
6.3	"Passenger transport" (*)		US$ Mn	26	27	25	30	37
	DOMESTIC TOURISM							
	Accommodation							
7.1	Overnight stays in hotels and similar establishments		('000)	..	..	..	..	..
7.2	Guests in hotels and similar establishments		('000)	..	..	..	..	..
7.3	Overnight stays in all types of accommodation establishments		('000)	..	..	..	..	..
7.4	Average length of stay of resident tourists in all accommodation establishments		Nights	..	..	..	..	..
	OUTBOUND TOURISM							
8.1	**Departures**		('000)	580	629	658	854	982
8.2	**Tourism expenditure in other countries**	(**)	US$ Mn	267	329	373	456	500
8.3	"Travel" (*)		US$ Mn	226	276	312	391	444
8.4	"Passenger transport" (*)		US$ Mn	41	53	61	65	56
	TOURISM INDUSTRIES							
	Hotels and similar establishments							
9.1	Number of rooms		Units	16,595	17,313	17,519	17,570	19,357
9.2	Number of bed-places		Units	43,357	44,421	44,579	44,883	51,955
9.3	Occupancy rate		Percent	..	..	47.04	..	..
9.4	Average length of stay		Nights	..	..	..	..	..
	RELATED INDICATORS							
	Share of tourism expenditure (6.1) in:							
10.1	Gross Domestic Product (GDP)		Percent	2.8	2.8	2.6	2.9	2.8
10.2	Exports of goods		Percent	20.6	23.0	21.1	23.2	23.9
10.3	Exports of services		Percent	56.3	56.5	61.0	68.4	71.3

(*) Balance of Payments items: 6.1 to 6.3 correspond to the "Credit" side (and are receipts for the country) while 8.2 to 8.4 correspond to the "Debit" side (and are expenditures in other countries).

(**) See Annex "Country notes".

Basic Indicators		Units	2001	2002	2003	2004	2005
	INBOUND TOURISM						
	Arrivals						
1.1	Visitors	('000)	..	..	..	..	..
1.2	Tourists (overnight visitors)	('000)	38	43	44	45	45
1.3	Same-day visitors	('000)	..	..	..	..	..
1.4	Cruise passengers	('000)	..	..	..	..	..
	Arrivals by region						
2.1	Africa	('000)	18	22	19	18	17
2.2	Americas	('000)	4	3	4	4	5
2.3	Europe	('000)	13	12	17	16	18
2.4	East Asia and the Pacific	('000)	2	2	2	2	3
2.5	South Asia	('000)	1	1	1	1	1
2.6	Middle East	('000)	1	2	1	1	1
	Arrivals by means of transport used						
3.1	Air	('000)	36.4	40.6	44	42.0	45
3.2	Rail	('000)	..	..	..	..	..
3.3	Road	('000)	0.8	1.6	..	2.5	..
3.4	Sea	('000)	0.5	0.3	..	0.1	..
	Arrivals by purpose of visit						
4.1	Leisure, recreation and holidays	('000)	5	5	5	7	5
4.2	Business and professional	('000)	18	20	20	19	20
4.3	Other	('000)	14	17	19	19	20
	Accommodation						
5.1	Overnight stays in hotels and similar establishments	('000)	115	175	122	152	195
5.2	Guests in hotels and similar establishments	('000)	9	..	16	14	15
5.3	Overnight stays in all types of accommodation establishments	('000)	526	600	928	1,233	1,318
5.4	Average length of stay of non-resident tourists in all accommodation establishments	Nights	3.13	3.10	..	..	4.85
6.1	**Tourism expenditure in the country**	US$ Mn	22	..	32	..	..
6.2	"Travel" (*) **(**)**	US$ Mn	14	43	31	30	..
6.3	"Passenger transport" (*)	US$ Mn	8	..	1	..	..
	DOMESTIC TOURISM						
	Accommodation						
7.1	Overnight stays in hotels and similar establishments	('000)	..	..	..	..	..
7.2	Guests in hotels and similar establishments	('000)	..	..	..	..	..
7.3	Overnight stays in all types of accommodation establishments	('000)	..	..	..	..	..
7.4	Average length of stay of resident tourists in all accommodation establishments	Nights	..	..	..	..	..
	OUTBOUND TOURISM						
8.1	**Departures**	('000)	..	..	..	..	..
8.2	**Tourism expenditure in other countries**	US$ Mn	26	38	36	29	..
8.3	"Travel" (*)	US$ Mn	18	31	26	25	..
8.4	"Passenger transport" (*)	US$ Mn	8	7	10	4	..
	TOURISM INDUSTRIES						
	Hotels and similar establishments						
9.1	Number of rooms	Units	3,594	3,533	3,747	3,886	..
9.2	Number of bed-places	Units	..	..	4,518	4,658	..
9.3	Occupancy rate	Percent	70.00	70.00	..	..	..
9.4	Average length of stay	Nights	3.00	3.00	..	..	..
	RELATED INDICATORS						
	Share of tourism expenditure (6.1) in:						
10.1	Gross Domestic Product (GDP)	Percent	0.7	..	0.9	..	..
10.2	Exports of goods	Percent	3.0	..	5.3	..	..
10.3	Exports of services	Percent	21.4	..	23.9	..	..

(*) Balance of Payments items: 6.1 to 6.3 correspond to the "Credit" side (and are receipts for the country) while 8.2 to 8.4 correspond to the "Debit" side (and are expenditures in other countries).

(**) See Annex "Country notes".

GUINEA-BISSAU

	Basic Indicators	Units	2001	2002	2003	2004	2005
	INBOUND TOURISM						
	Arrivals						
1.1	Visitors	('000)	..	..	..	..	..
1.2	Tourists (overnight visitors)	('000)	7.8	..	..	..	5.4
1.3	Same-day visitors	('000)	..	..	..	..	..
1.4	Cruise passengers	('000)	..	..	..	..	..
	Arrivals by region						
2.1	Africa	('000)	2.1	..	..	..	1.2
2.2	Americas	('000)	0.4	..	..	..	0.5
2.3	Europe	('000)	3.8	..	..	..	3.1
2.4	East Asia and the Pacific	('000)	0.2	..	..	..	0.1
2.5	South Asia	('000)	0.1	..	..	..	0.1
2.6	Middle East	('000)	0.2	..	..	..	..
	Arrivals by means of transport used						
3.1	Air	('000)	7.8	..	..	..	5.2
3.2	Rail	('000)	..	..	..	..	..
3.3	Road	('000)	..	..	..	..	..
3.4	Sea	('000)	..	..	..	..	0.2
	Arrivals by purpose of visit						
4.1	Leisure, recreation and holidays	('000)	1.7	..	..	..	1.2
4.2	Business and professional	('000)	3.2	..	..	..	1.8
4.3	Other	('000)	2.8	..	..	..	2.0
	Accommodation						
5.1	Overnight stays in hotels and similar establishments	('000)	..	..	..	..	..
5.2	Guests in hotels and similar establishments	('000)	..	..	..	..	..
5.3	Overnight stays in all types of accommodation establishments	('000)	..	..	..	..	..
5.4	Average length of stay of non-resident tourists in all accommodation establishments	Nights	..	..	..	..	..
6.1	**Tourism expenditure in the country**	US$ Mn	..	..	3	2	..
6.2	"Travel" (*)	US$ Mn	3	2	2	1	..
6.3	"Passenger transport" (*)	US$ Mn	..	..	1	1	..
	DOMESTIC TOURISM						
	Accommodation						
7.1	Overnight stays in hotels and similar establishments	('000)	..	..	..	..	..
7.2	Guests in hotels and similar establishments	('000)	..	..	..	..	..
7.3	Overnight stays in all types of accommodation establishments	('000)	..	..	..	..	..
7.4	Average length of stay of resident tourists in all accommodation establishments	Nights	..	..	..	..	..
	OUTBOUND TOURISM						
8.1	**Departures**	('000)	..	..	..	..	..
8.2	**Tourism expenditure in other countries**	US$ Mn	6	10	21	22	..
8.3	"Travel" (*)	US$ Mn	3	5	13	13	..
8.4	"Passenger transport" (*)	US$ Mn	3	5	8	9	..
	TOURISM INDUSTRIES						
	Hotels and similar establishments						
9.1	Number of rooms	Units	..	..	..	3,533	..
9.2	Number of bed-places	Units	..	..	..	4,240	..
9.3	Occupancy rate	Percent	..	..	..	..	..
9.4	Average length of stay	Nights	..	..	..	..	..
	RELATED INDICATORS						
	Share of tourism expenditure (6.1) in:						
10.1	Gross Domestic Product (GDP)	Percent	..	..	1.3	0.7	..
10.2	Exports of goods	Percent	..	..	4.6	2.6	..
10.3	Exports of services	Percent	..	..	50.0	25.0	..

(*) Balance of Payments items: 6.1 to 6.3 correspond to the "Credit" side (and are receipts for the country) while 8.2 to 8.4 correspond to the "Debit" side (and are expenditures in other countries).

GUYANA

	Basic Indicators	Units	2001	2002	2003	2004	2005
	INBOUND TOURISM						
	Arrivals						
1.1	Visitors	('000)	..	..	..	..	..
1.2	Tourists (overnight visitors)	('000)	99	104	101	122	117
1.3	Same-day visitors	('000)	..	..	..	..	..
1.4	Cruise passengers	('000)	..	..	..	..	..
	Arrivals by region						
2.1	Africa	('000)	..	..	..	..	..
2.2	Americas	('000)	89	95	91	111	105
2.3	Europe	('000)	9	8	8	9	9
2.4	East Asia and the Pacific	('000)	..	..	..	..	..
2.5	South Asia	('000)	..	..	..	..	..
2.6	Middle East	('000)	..	..	..	..	..
	Arrivals by means of transport used						
3.1	Air	('000)	..	104	101	122	117
3.2	Rail	('000)	..	..	..	..	..
3.3	Road	('000)	..	..	..	..	..
3.4	Sea	('000)	..	..	..	..	..
	Arrivals by purpose of visit						
4.1	Leisure, recreation and holidays	('000)	..	..	..	..	..
4.2	Business and professional	('000)	..	..	..	..	..
4.3	Other	('000)	..	..	..	..	..
	Accommodation						
5.1	Overnight stays in hotels and similar establishments	('000)	..	..	..	..	..
5.2	Guests in hotels and similar establishments	('000)	..	..	..	..	..
5.3	Overnight stays in all types of accommodation establishments	('000)	..	..	..	..	..
5.4	Average length of stay of non-resident tourists in all accommodation establishments	Nights	..	..	..	..	..
6.1	**Tourism expenditure in the country**	US$ Mn	65	53	28	29	37
6.2	"Travel" (*)	US$ Mn	61	49	26	27	35
6.3	"Passenger transport" (*)	US$ Mn	4	4	2	2	2
	DOMESTIC TOURISM						
	Accommodation						
7.1	Overnight stays in hotels and similar establishments	('000)	..	..	..	..	..
7.2	Guests in hotels and similar establishments	('000)	..	..	..	..	..
7.3	Overnight stays in all types of accommodation establishments	('000)	..	..	..	..	..
7.4	Average length of stay of resident tourists in all accommodation establishments	Nights	..	..	..	..	..
	OUTBOUND TOURISM						
8.1	**Departures**	('000)	..	..	..	..	..
8.2	**Tourism expenditure in other countries**	US$ Mn	62	44	30	35	45
8.3	"Travel" (*)	US$ Mn	55	38	26	30	40
8.4	"Passenger transport" (*)	US$ Mn	7	6	4	5	5
	TOURISM INDUSTRIES						
	Hotels and similar establishments						
9.1	Number of rooms	Units	..	..	..	..	..
9.2	Number of bed-places	Units	..	..	..	..	..
9.3	Occupancy rate	Percent	..	..	..	..	..
9.4	Average length of stay	Nights	..	..	..	..	..
	RELATED INDICATORS						
	Share of tourism expenditure (6.1) in:						
10.1	Gross Domestic Product (GDP)	Percent	9.3	7.3	3.8	3.7	4.7
10.2	Exports of goods	Percent	13.4	10.8	5.5	5.0	6.8
10.3	Exports of services	Percent	37.8	30.8	17.8	18.0	25.2

(*) Balance of Payments items: 6.1 to 6.3 correspond to the "Credit" side (and are receipts for the country) while 8.2 to 8.4 correspond to the "Debit" side (and are expenditures in other countries).

HAITI

Basic Indicators		Units	2001	2002	2003	2004	2005
	INBOUND TOURISM						
	Arrivals						
1.1	Visitors	('000)	499	482	518	385	480
1.2	Tourists (overnight visitors)	('000)	142	140	136	96	112
1.3	Same-day visitors	('000)	..	..	..	..	..
1.4	Cruise passengers	('000)	357	342	382	289	368
	Arrivals by region						
2.1	Africa	('000)	..	..	..	..	..
2.2	Americas	('000)	129	127	125	91	104
2.3	Europe	('000)	11	11	8	4	7
2.4	East Asia and the Pacific	('000)	..	..	..	..	..
2.5	South Asia	('000)	..	..	..	..	..
2.6	Middle East	('000)	..	..	..	..	..
	Arrivals by means of transport used						
3.1	Air	('000)	142	140	136	96	112
3.2	Rail	('000)	..	..	..	..	..
3.3	Road	('000)	..	..	..	..	..
3.4	Sea	('000)	357	342	382	289	368
	Arrivals by purpose of visit						
4.1	Leisure, recreation and holidays	('000)	..	..	..	..	..
4.2	Business and professional	('000)	..	..	..	..	..
4.3	Other	('000)	..	..	..	..	..
	Accommodation						
5.1	Overnight stays in hotels and similar establishments	('000)	..	..	..	..	..
5.2	Guests in hotels and similar establishments	('000)	..	..	..	..	..
5.3	Overnight stays in all types of accommodation establishments	('000)	..	..	..	..	..
5.4	Average length of stay of non-resident tourists in all accommodation establishments	Nights	..	..	..	..	..
6.1	**Tourism expenditure in the country**	US$ Mn	..	..	..	..	..
6.2	"Travel" (*)	US$ Mn	105	112	93	87	110
6.3	"Passenger transport" (*)	US$ Mn	..	..	..	..	..
	DOMESTIC TOURISM						
	Accommodation						
7.1	Overnight stays in hotels and similar establishments	('000)	..	..	..	..	..
7.2	Guests in hotels and similar establishments	('000)	..	..	..	..	..
7.3	Overnight stays in all types of accommodation establishments	('000)	..	..	..	..	..
7.4	Average length of stay of resident tourists in all accommodation establishments	Nights	..	..	..	..	..
	OUTBOUND TOURISM						
8.1	**Departures**	('000)	..	..	..	..	..
8.2	**Tourism expenditure in other countries**	US$ Mn	168	174	196	206	173
8.3	"Travel" (*)	US$ Mn	18	18	42	72	54
8.4	"Passenger transport" (*)	US$ Mn	150	156	154	134	119
	TOURISM INDUSTRIES						
	Hotels and similar establishments						
9.1	Number of rooms	Units	..	..	..	..	..
9.2	Number of bed-places	Units	..	..	..	..	..
9.3	Occupancy rate	Percent	..	..	..	..	..
9.4	Average length of stay	Nights	..	..	..	..	..
	RELATED INDICATORS						
	Share of tourism expenditure (6.1) in: (**)						
10.1	Gross Domestic Product (GDP)	Percent	2.9	3.3	3.2	2.3	2.6
10.2	Exports of goods	Percent	34.4	40.9	27.9	23.0	24.0
10.3	Exports of services	Percent	75.5	75.7	68.4	77.0	82.1

(*) Balance of Payments items: 6.1 to 6.3 correspond to the "Credit" side (and are receipts for the country) while 8.2 to 8.4 correspond to the "Debit" side (and are expenditures in other countries).

(**) See Annex "Country notes".

	Basic Indicators	Units	2001	2002	2003	2004	2005
	INBOUND TOURISM						
	Arrivals						
1.1	Visitors	('000)	672	788	887	1,026	1,118
1.2	Tourists (overnight visitors)	('000)	518	550	611	641	673
1.3	Same-day visitors	('000)	..	239	276	118	168
1.4	Cruise passengers	('000)	154	125	162	267	277
	Arrivals by region						
2.1	Africa	('000)	0.2	0.3	0.2	0.3	0.2
2.2	Americas	('000)	460	493	557	585	610
2.3	Europe	('000)	50	49	45	48	53
2.4	East Asia and the Pacific	('000)	7	7	7	8	8
2.5	South Asia	('000)	0.2	0.2	0.3	0.3	0.3
2.6	Middle East	('000)	0.1	0.1	0.1	0.1	0.1
	Arrivals by means of transport used						
3.1	Air	('000)	230	210	248	259	301
3.2	Rail	('000)	..	..	..	..	..
3.3	Road	('000)	271	320	344	362	348
3.4	Sea	('000)	17	20	19	20	23
	Arrivals by purpose of visit						
4.1	Leisure, recreation and holidays	('000)	256	252	280	294	309
4.2	Business and professional	('000)	69	83	93	97	102
4.3	Other	('000)	193	214	238	250	262
	Accommodation						
5.1	Overnight stays in hotels and similar establishments	('000)	..	..	..	..	..
5.2	Guests in hotels and similar establishments	('000)	..	..	..	..	..
5.3	Overnight stays in all types of accommodation establishments	('000)	..	..	..	..	..
5.4	Average length of stay of non-resident tourists in all accommodation establishments	Nights	10.80	10.60	9.70	12.50	10.80
6.1	**Tourism expenditure in the country**	US$ Mn	260	305	358	435	476
6.2	"Travel" (*)	US$ Mn	256	301	350	429	472
6.3	"Passenger transport" (*)	US$ Mn	4	4	8	6	4
	DOMESTIC TOURISM						
	Accommodation						
7.1	Overnight stays in hotels and similar establishments	('000)	..	..	..	..	..
7.2	Guests in hotels and similar establishments	('000)	..	..	..	..	..
7.3	Overnight stays in all types of accommodation establishments	('000)	..	..	..	..	..
7.4	Average length of stay of resident tourists in all accommodation establishments	Nights	..	..	..	..	..
	OUTBOUND TOURISM						
8.1	**Departures**	('000)	279	285	277	295	300
8.2	**Tourism expenditure in other countries**	US$ Mn	203	215	258	291	315
8.3	"Travel" (*)	US$ Mn	128	149	200	228	248
8.4	"Passenger transport" (*)	US$ Mn	75	66	58	63	67
	TOURISM INDUSTRIES						
	Hotels and similar establishments						
9.1	Number of rooms	Units	15,906	17,178	18,590	19,519	20,453
9.2	Number of bed-places	Units	24,841	27,574	26,897	27,703	29,032
9.3	Occupancy rate	Percent	..	..	..	47.00	47.00
9.4	Average length of stay	Nights	10.80	10.60	9.70	12.50	10.80
	RELATED INDICATORS						
	Share of tourism expenditure (6.1) in:						
10.1	Gross Domestic Product (GDP)	Percent	4.1	4.7	5.2	5.9	6.0
10.2	Exports of goods	Percent	13.4	15.4	17.1	18.2	18.0
10.3	Exports of services	Percent	53.4	57.5	59.9	60.5	61.1

(*) Balance of Payments items: 6.1 to 6.3 correspond to the "Credit" side (and are receipts for the country) while 8.2 to 8.4 correspond to the "Debit" side (and are expenditures in other countries).

HONG KONG, CHINA

	Basic Indicators		Units	2001	2002	2003	2004	2005
	INBOUND TOURISM							
	Arrivals							
1.1	Visitors		('000)	13,725	16,566	15,537	21,811	23,359
1.2	Tourists (overnight visitors)		('000)	8,878	10,689	9,676	13,655	14,773
1.3	Same-day visitors		('000)	4,838	5,865	5,857	8,147	8,567
1.4	Cruise passengers		('000)	9	13	4	9	19
	Arrivals by region							
2.1	Africa		('000)	77	92	99	146	206
2.2	Americas		('000)	1,259	1,347	926	1,400	1,565
2.3	Europe		('000)	1,064	1,135	822	1,202	1,472
2.4	East Asia and the Pacific		('000)	11,047	13,654	13,410	18,706	19,707
2.5	South Asia		('000)	249	303	255	326	363
2.6	Middle East		('000)	30	35	25	31	46
	Arrivals by means of transport used							
3.1	Air		('000)	6,530	6,891	4,981	7,015	7,803
3.2	Rail		('000)	..	..	..	..	..
3.3	Road		('000)	5,047	7,166	8,350	11,969	12,768
3.4	Sea		('000)	2,149	2,509	2,206	2,827	2,788
	Arrivals by purpose of visit							
4.1	Leisure, recreation and holidays		('000)	..	..	..	..	..
4.2	Business and professional		('000)	..	..	..	..	..
4.3	Other		('000)	..	..	..	..	..
	Accommodation							
5.1	Overnight stays in hotels and similar establishments		('000)	..	..	..	..	..
5.2	Guests in hotels and similar establishments		('000)	..	..	..	..	..
5.3	Overnight stays in all types of accommodation establishments		('000)	..	..	..	..	..
5.4	Average length of stay of non-resident tourists in all accommodation establishments		Nights	3.08	3.62	4.06	3.73	3.66
6.1	**Tourism expenditure in the country**	(**)	US$ Mn	7,923	9,849	9,004	11,874	13,546
6.2	"Travel" (*)		US$ Mn	5,904	7,410	7,072	8,918	10,179
6.3	"Passenger transport" (*)		US$ Mn	2,019	2,439	1,932	2,956	3,367
	DOMESTIC TOURISM							
	Accommodation							
7.1	Overnight stays in hotels and similar establishments		('000)	..	..	..	..	..
7.2	Guests in hotels and similar establishments		('000)	..	..	..	..	..
7.3	Overnight stays in all types of accommodation establishments		('000)	..	..	..	..	..
7.4	Average length of stay of resident tourists in all accommodation establishments		Nights	..	..	..	..	..
	OUTBOUND TOURISM							
8.1	**Departures**		('000)	4,799	4,709	4,428	5,004	5,786
8.2	**Tourism expenditure in other countries**		US$ Mn	..	..	..	..	..
8.3	"Travel" (*)		US$ Mn	12,317	12,418	11,447	13,270	13,307
8.4	"Passenger transport" (*)		US$ Mn	..	..	..	..	..
	TOURISM INDUSTRIES							
	Hotels and similar establishments							
9.1	Number of rooms		Units	41,842	43,624	42,936	44,362	48,891
9.2	Number of bed-places		Units	..	..	..	..	..
9.3	Occupancy rate		Percent	79.00	84.00	70.00	88.00	86.00
9.4	Average length of stay		Nights	..	..	..	..	..
	RELATED INDICATORS							
	Share of tourism expenditure (6.1) in:							
10.1	Gross Domestic Product (GDP)		Percent	4.8	6.0	5.7	7.2	7.6
10.2	Exports of goods		Percent	4.1	4.9	4.0	4.6	..
10.3	Exports of services		Percent	19.3	22.1	19.3	21.9	..

(*) Balance of Payments items: 6.1 to 6.3 correspond to the "Credit" side (and are receipts for the country) while 8.2 to 8.4 correspond to the "Debit" side (and are expenditures in other countries).

(**) See Annex "Country notes".

	Basic Indicators	Units	2001	2002	2003	2004	2005
	INBOUND TOURISM						
	Arrivals						
1.1	Visitors	('000)	30,679	31,739	31,412	33,934	36,172
1.2	Tourists (overnight visitors)	('000)	..	..	..	12,212	10,048
1.3	Same-day visitors	('000)	..	..	..	21,722	26,125
1.4	Cruise passengers	('000)	..	..	..	518	427
	Arrivals by region						
2.1	Africa	('000)	7	6	6	12	10
2.2	Americas	('000)	181	170	174	202	218
2.3	Europe	('000)	2,730	2,689	2,627	2,861	2,986
2.4	East Asia and the Pacific	('000)	93	83	77	105	133
2.5	South Asia	('000)	..	..	..	..	..
2.6	Middle East	('000)	..	..	..	..	..
	Arrivals by means of transport used						
3.1	Air	('000)	1,391	1,302	1,353	2,282	2,084
3.2	Rail	('000)	1,821	1,746	1,611	1,549	1,516
3.3	Road	('000)	27,315	28,524	28,256	32,548	34,665
3.4	Sea	('000)	153	168	191	256	290
	Arrivals by purpose of visit						
4.1	Leisure, recreation and holidays	('000)	..	..	..	11,128	11,013
4.2	Business and professional	('000)	..	..	..	1,569	1,751
4.3	Other	('000)	..	..	..	21,237	23,409
	Accommodation						
5.1	Overnight stays in hotels and similar establishments	('000)	8,405	8,260	8,046	8,729	9,127
5.2	Guests in hotels and similar establishments	('000)	2,669	2,659	2,599	2,951	3,410
5.3	Overnight stays in all types of accommodation establishments	('000)	10,894	10,361	10,040	10,508	10,779
5.4	Average length of stay of non-resident tourists in all accommodation establishments	Nights	3.55	3.44	3.41	3.21	3.13
6.1	**Tourism expenditure in the country**	US$ Mn	4,191	3,774	4,119	4,129	4,581
6.2	"Travel" (*)	US$ Mn	4,154	3,728	4,061	4,034	4,279
6.3	"Passenger transport" (*)	US$ Mn	37	46	58	95	302
	DOMESTIC TOURISM						
	Accommodation						
7.1	Overnight stays in hotels and similar establishments	('000)	5,321	5,574	5,824	5,933	6,622
7.2	Guests in hotels and similar establishments	('000)	2,148	2,273	2,380	2,452	2,778
7.3	Overnight stays in all types of accommodation establishments	('000)	7,754	8,089	8,571	8,391	8,958
7.4	Average length of stay of resident tourists in all accommodation establishments	Nights	2.58	2.56	2.55	2.51	2.48
	OUTBOUND TOURISM						
8.1	**Departures**	('000)	11,167	12,966	14,283	17,558	18,622
8.2	**Tourism expenditure in other countries**	US$ Mn	1,887	2,209	2,700	2,909	3,037
8.3	"Travel" (*)	US$ Mn	1,808	2,133	2,594	2,848	2,925
8.4	"Passenger transport" (*)	US$ Mn	79	76	106	61	112
	TOURISM INDUSTRIES						
	Hotels and similar establishments						
9.1	Number of rooms	Units	59,897	62,415	64,091	64,263	66,066
9.2	Number of bed-places	Units	148,225	154,643	158,634	157,970	162,235
9.3	Occupancy rate	Percent	41.50	40.00	38.60	41.00	42.10
9.4	Average length of stay	Nights	2.85	2.81	2.79	2.71	2.66
	RELATED INDICATORS						
	Share of tourism expenditure (6.1) in:						
10.1	Gross Domestic Product (GDP)	Percent	8.0	5.8	5.0	4.1	4.2
10.2	Exports of goods	Percent	13.5	10.8	9.5	7.4	7.4
10.3	Exports of services	Percent	59.6	50.9	47.3	38.4	37.2

(*) Balance of Payments items: 6.1 to 6.3 correspond to the "Credit" side (and are receipts for the country) while 8.2 to 8.4 correspond to the "Debit" side (and are expenditures in other countries).

ICELAND

	Basic Indicators	Units	2001	2002	2003	2004	2005
	INBOUND TOURISM						
	Arrivals						
1.1	Visitors	('000)	..	..	..	..	..
1.2	Tourists (overnight visitors)	('000)	672	705	771	836	871
1.3	Same-day visitors	('000)	..	..	..	..	..
1.4	Cruise passengers	('000)	28	30	31	45	55
	Arrivals by region						
2.1	Africa	('000)	..	..	..	..	1
2.2	Americas	('000)	74	69	72	75	85
2.3	Europe	('000)	553	593	643	707	715
2.4	East Asia and the Pacific	('000)	7	7	9	11	30
2.5	South Asia	('000)	..	..	..	..	..
2.6	Middle East	('000)	..	..	..	..	..
	Arrivals by means of transport used						
3.1	Air	('000)	296	278	309	349	356
3.2	Rail	('000)	..	..	..	..	..
3.3	Road	('000)	..	..	..	..	..
3.4	Sea	('000)	33	37	39	54	63
	Arrivals by purpose of visit						
4.1	Leisure, recreation and holidays	('000)	..	..	..	..	..
4.2	Business and professional	('000)	..	..	..	..	..
4.3	Other	('000)	..	..	..	..	..
	Accommodation						
5.1	Overnight stays in hotels and similar establishments	('000)	908	970	1,070	1,146	1,208
5.2	Guests in hotels and similar establishments	('000)	465	513	569	615	643
5.3	Overnight stays in all types of accommodation establishments	('000)	1,184	1,257	1,377	1,479	1,550
5.4	Average length of stay of non-resident tourists in all accommodation establishments	Nights	1.80	1.80	1.80	1.80	1.80
6.1	**Tourism expenditure in the country**	US$ Mn	383	415	486	558	631
6.2	"Travel" (*)	US$ Mn	232	256	319	370	409
6.3	"Passenger transport" (*)	US$ Mn	151	159	167	188	222
	DOMESTIC TOURISM						
	Accommodation						
7.1	Overnight stays in hotels and similar establishments	('000)	275	290	299	323	361
7.2	Guests in hotels and similar establishments	('000)	176	187	194	205	229
7.3	Overnight stays in all types of accommodation establishments	('000)	560	604	608	651	683
7.4	Average length of stay of resident tourists in all accommodation establishments	Nights	1.50	1.60	1.50	1.60	1.60
	OUTBOUND TOURISM						
8.1	**Departures**	('000)	..	..	..	..	..
8.2	**Tourism expenditure in other countries**	US$ Mn	..	372	522	695	986
8.3	"Travel" (*)	US$ Mn	372	370	521	693	975
8.4	"Passenger transport" (*)	US$ Mn	..	2	1	2	11
	TOURISM INDUSTRIES						
	Hotels and similar establishments						
9.1	Number of rooms	Units	6,174	6,807	7,330	7,502	8,005
9.2	Number of bed-places	Units	12,632	14,009	14,948	15,517	16,639
9.3	Occupancy rate	Percent	45.20	44.30	42.30	43.30	45.00
9.4	Average length of stay	Nights	1.85	1.80	1.80	1.80	1.80
	RELATED INDICATORS						
	Share of tourism expenditure (6.1) in:						
10.1	Gross Domestic Product (GDP)	Percent	5.0	5.0	4.7	4.6	4.2
10.2	Exports of goods	Percent	19.0	18.5	20.4	19.3	20.3
10.3	Exports of services	Percent	35.3	37.1	35.3	34.4	31.6

(*) Balance of Payments items: 6.1 to 6.3 correspond to the "Credit" side (and are receipts for the country) while 8.2 to 8.4 correspond to the "Debit" side (and are expenditures in other countries).

	Basic Indicators	Units	2001	2002	2003	2004	2005
	INBOUND TOURISM						
	Arrivals						
1.1	Visitors	('000)	2,591	2,428	2,774	3,512	..
1.2	Tourists (overnight visitors)	('000)	2,537	2,384	2,726	3,457	3,919
1.3	Same-day visitors	('000)	..	..	..	..	..
1.4	Cruise passengers	('000)	54	44	48	55	..
	Arrivals by region						
2.1	Africa	('000)	87	80	89	112	131
2.2	Americas	('000)	440	459	540	690	804
2.3	Europe	('000)	890	797	942	1,257	1,435
2.4	East Asia and the Pacific	('000)	337	328	393	512	585
2.5	South Asia	('000)	672	631	667	791	842
2.6	Middle East	('000)	67	66	69	80	86
	Arrivals by means of transport used						
3.1	Air	('000)	2,210	1,953	2,265	2,960	..
3.2	Rail	('000)	..	..	..	..	..
3.3	Road	('000)	304	417	447	480	..
3.4	Sea	('000)	23	14	14	17	..
	Arrivals by purpose of visit						
4.1	Leisure, recreation and holidays	('000)	2,459	2,272	2,538	3,357	..
4.2	Business and professional	('000)	78	112	188	100	..
4.3	Other	('000)	..	..	..	..	..
	Accommodation						
5.1	Overnight stays in hotels and similar establishments	('000)	..	..	..	..	..
5.2	Guests in hotels and similar establishments	('000)	..	..	..	..	..
5.3	Overnight stays in all types of accommodation establishments	('000)	..	..	..	..	..
5.4	Average length of stay of non-resident tourists in all accommodation establishments	Nights	..	..	..	..	..
6.1	**Tourism expenditure in the country**	US$ Mn	3,497	3,476	4,128	..	..
6.2	"Travel" (*)	US$ Mn	3,198	3,102	3,887	..	..
6.3	"Passenger transport" (*)	US$ Mn	299	374	241	..	..
	DOMESTIC TOURISM						
	Accommodation						
7.1	Overnight stays in hotels and similar establishments	('000)	..	..	..	..	..
7.2	Guests in hotels and similar establishments	('000)	..	..	..	..	..
7.3	Overnight stays in all types of accommodation establishments	('000)	..	..	..	..	..
7.4	Average length of stay of resident tourists in all accommodation establishments	Nights	..	..	..	..	..
	OUTBOUND TOURISM						
8.1	**Departures**	('000)	4,564	4,940	5,351	6,213	7,180
8.2	**Tourism expenditure in other countries**	US$ Mn	5,099	4,990	4,758	..	..
8.3	"Travel" (*)	US$ Mn	3,006	2,988	3,510	..	..
8.4	"Passenger transport" (*)	US$ Mn	2,093	2,002	1,248	..	..
	TOURISM INDUSTRIES						
	Hotels and similar establishments						
9.1	Number of rooms	Units	82,181	85,481	91,720	97,770	..
9.2	Number of bed-places	Units	164,362	170,962	183,440	195,540	..
9.3	Occupancy rate	Percent	50.40	55.40	60.70	65.10	..
9.4	Average length of stay	Nights	..	..	..	..	..
	RELATED INDICATORS						
	Share of tourism expenditure (6.1) in:						
10.1	Gross Domestic Product (GDP)	Percent	0.7	0.7	0.7	..	..
10.2	Exports of goods	Percent	7.8	6.8	7.0	..	..
10.3	Exports of services	Percent	20.2	17.8	17.6	..	..

(*) Balance of Payments items: 6.1 to 6.3 correspond to the "Credit" side (and are receipts for the country) while 8.2 to 8.4 correspond to the "Debit" side (and are expenditures in other countries).

INDONESIA

	Basic Indicators	Units	2001	2002	2003	2004	2005
	INBOUND TOURISM						
	Arrivals						
1.1	Visitors	('000)	..	..	..	..	..
1.2	Tourists (overnight visitors)	('000)	5,153	5,033	4,467	5,321	5,002
1.3	Same-day visitors	('000)	..	..	..	..	..
1.4	Cruise passengers	('000)	..	..	..	..	..
	Arrivals by region						
2.1	Africa	('000)	40	37	30	36	27
2.2	Americas	('000)	243	222	176	210	210
2.3	Europe	('000)	862	808	606	721	798
2.4	East Asia and the Pacific	('000)	3,920	3,877	3,576	4,266	3,837
2.5	South Asia	('000)	51	52	48	54	69
2.6	Middle East	('000)	37	38	31	36	61
	Arrivals by means of transport used						
3.1	Air	('000)	2,766	2,745	2,178	2,790	2,889
3.2	Rail	('000)	..	..	..	..	..
3.3	Road	('000)	33	32	27	22	31
3.4	Sea	('000)	2,355	2,256	2,262	2,509	2,082
	Arrivals by purpose of visit						
4.1	Leisure, recreation and holidays	('000)	2,873	2,903	2,316	2,827	2,835
4.2	Business and professional	('000)	2,196	2,056	1,914	2,191	2,063
4.3	Other	('000)	85	74	237	303	104
	Accommodation						
5.1	Overnight stays in hotels and similar establishments	('000)	7,406	6,996	5,887	7,042	7,109
5.2	Guests in hotels and similar establishments	('000)	4,101	3,947	3,380	4,248	3,883
5.3	Overnight stays in all types of accommodation establishments	('000)	9,394	8,117	7,501	8,487	8,652
5.4	Average length of stay of non-resident tourists in all accommodation establishments	Nights	1.27	1.16	1.27	1.21	1.22
6.1	**Tourism expenditure in the country**	US$ Mn	..	5,797	4,461	5,226	5,092
6.2	"Travel" (*)	US$ Mn	5,277	5,285	4,037	4,798	4,522
6.3	"Passenger transport" (*)	US$ Mn	..	512	424	428	570
	DOMESTIC TOURISM						
	Accommodation						
7.1	Overnight stays in hotels and similar establishments	('000)	19,583	20,439	21,082	23,325	23,052
7.2	Guests in hotels and similar establishments	('000)	8,903	9,861	10,582	11,682	11,599
7.3	Overnight stays in all types of accommodation establishments	('000)	53,740	51,451	56,904	55,105	52,485
7.4	Average length of stay of resident tourists in all accommodation establishments	Nights	2.44	2.58	2.23	2.36	2.67
	OUTBOUND TOURISM						
8.1	**Departures**	('000)	..	..	3,491	3,941	4,106
8.2	**Tourism expenditure in other countries**	US$ Mn	..	5,042	4,427	4,569	4,741
8.3	"Travel" (*)	US$ Mn	3,406	3,289	3,082	3,507	3,584
8.4	"Passenger transport" (*)	US$ Mn	..	1,753	1,345	1,062	1,157
	TOURISM INDUSTRIES						
	Hotels and similar establishments						
9.1	Number of rooms	Units	259,450	259,741	263,014	272,939	280,433
9.2	Number of bed-places	Units	423,519	423,908	428,813	441,032	449,622
9.3	Occupancy rate	Percent	44.79	44.28	45.03	43.30	45.49
9.4	Average length of stay	Nights	..	..	..	..	..
	RELATED INDICATORS						
	Share of tourism expenditure (6.1) in:						
10.1	Gross Domestic Product (GDP)	Percent	..	2.9	1.9	2.1	1.8
10.2	Exports of goods	Percent	..	9.8	7.0	7.4	5.9
10.3	Exports of services	Percent	..	87.0	84.3	43.4	39.4

(*) Balance of Payments items: 6.1 to 6.3 correspond to the "Credit" side (and are receipts for the country) while 8.2 to 8.4 correspond to the "Debit" side (and are expenditures in other countries).

	Basic Indicators	Units	2001	2002	2003	2004	2005
	INBOUND TOURISM						
	Arrivals						
1.1	Visitors	('000)	..	..	..	..	..
1.2	Tourists (overnight visitors)	('000)	1,402	1,585	1,546	1,659	..
1.3	Same-day visitors	('000)	..	..	..	..	..
1.4	Cruise passengers	('000)	..	..	..	..	..
	Arrivals by region						
2.1	Africa	('000)	..	..	..	..	..
2.2	Americas	('000)	..	..	..	..	..
2.3	Europe	('000)	..	..	..	..	..
2.4	East Asia and the Pacific	('000)	..	..	..	..	..
2.5	South Asia	('000)	..	..	..	..	..
2.6	Middle East	('000)	..	..	..	..	..
	Arrivals by means of transport used						
3.1	Air	('000)	395	429	..	545	..
3.2	Rail	('000)	..	..	..	..	..
3.3	Road	('000)	992	1,144	..	1,080	..
3.4	Sea	('000)	15	11	..	33	..
	Arrivals by purpose of visit						
4.1	Leisure, recreation and holidays	('000)	..	..	..	..	..
4.2	Business and professional	('000)	..	..	..	..	..
4.3	Other	('000)	..	..	..	..	..
	Accommodation						
5.1	Overnight stays in hotels and similar establishments	('000)	854	830	854	..	..
5.2	Guests in hotels and similar establishments	('000)	346	323	313	..	..
5.3	Overnight stays in all types of accommodation establishments	('000)	..	..	..	..	..
5.4	Average length of stay of non-resident tourists in all accommodation establishments	Nights	5.00	2.25	2.73	..	..
6.1	**Tourism expenditure in the country**	US$ Mn	1,122	1,607	1,266	1,305	1,329
6.2	"Travel" (*)	US$ Mn	891	1,357	1,033	1,044	992
6.3	"Passenger transport" (*)	US$ Mn	231	250	233	261	337
	DOMESTIC TOURISM						
	Accommodation						
7.1	Overnight stays in hotels and similar establishments	('000)	4,172	4,874	4,910	..	..
7.2	Guests in hotels and similar establishments	('000)	1,987	2,330	2,516	..	..
7.3	Overnight stays in all types of accommodation establishments	('000)	..	..	..	..	..
7.4	Average length of stay of resident tourists in all accommodation establishments	Nights	..	2.04	1.95	..	..
	OUTBOUND TOURISM						
8.1	**Departures**	('000)	2,400	2,921	..	..	..
8.2	**Tourism expenditure in other countries**	US$ Mn	714	3,990	4,120	4,402	4,810
8.3	"Travel" (*)	US$ Mn	708	3,750	3,842	4,093	4,380
8.4	"Passenger transport" (*)	US$ Mn	6	240	278	309	430
	TOURISM INDUSTRIES						
	Hotels and similar establishments						
9.1	Number of rooms	Units	27,889	24,199	27,148	32,360	..
9.2	Number of bed-places	Units	57,661	53,908	56,618	66,289	..
9.3	Occupancy rate	Percent	28.00	37.00	36.00	..	..
9.4	Average length of stay	Nights	1.15	2.16	2.04	..	..
	RELATED INDICATORS						
	Share of tourism expenditure (6.1) in:						
10.1	Gross Domestic Product (GDP)	Percent	1.0	1.4	0.9	0.8	..
10.2	Exports of goods	Percent	4.7	5.7	3.7	..	..
10.3	Exports of services	Percent	..	..	..	..	..

(*) Balance of Payments items: 6.1 to 6.3 correspond to the "Credit" side (and are receipts for the country) while 8.2 to 8.4 correspond to the "Debit" side (and are expenditures in other countries).

IRELAND

Basic Indicators		Units	2001	2002	2003	2004	2005
	INBOUND TOURISM						
	Arrivals						
1.1	Visitors	('000)	..	..	..	..	..
1.2	Tourists (overnight visitors)	('000)	6,353	6,476	6,764	6,953	7,333
1.3	Same-day visitors	('000)	344	305	334	349	367
1.4	Cruise passengers	('000)	..	..	..	..	..
	Arrivals by region						
2.1	Africa	('000)	32	29	32	42	39
2.2	Americas	('000)	915	860	913	975	956
2.3	Europe	('000)	5,189	5,387	5,623	5,677	6,113
2.4	East Asia and the Pacific	('000)	217	201	196	259	226
2.5	South Asia	('000)	..	..	..	..	..
2.6	Middle East	('000)	..	..	..	..	..
	Arrivals by means of transport used						
3.1	Air	('000)	4,322	4,439	4,819	4,980	5,546
3.2	Rail	('000)	..	..	..	..	..
3.3	Road	('000)	688	735	710	761	705
3.4	Sea	('000)	1,343	1,302	1,236	1,213	1,082
	Arrivals by purpose of visit						
4.1	Leisure, recreation and holidays	('000)	3,566	3,665	3,726	3,803	3,832
4.2	Business and professional	('000)	878	838	815	890	910
4.3	Other	('000)	1,909	1,973	2,223	2,260	2,591
	Accommodation						
5.1	Overnight stays in hotels and similar establishments	('000)	17,982	17,714	18,039	17,934	17,446
5.2	Guests in hotels and similar establishments	('000)	..	..	..	..	..
5.3	Overnight stays in all types of accommodation establishments	('000)	45,846	45,346	47,613	47,375	50,678
5.4	Average length of stay of non-resident tourists in all accommodation establishments	Nights	7.85	7.66	7.71	7.42	7.49
6.1	**Tourism expenditure in the country**	US$ Mn	3,789	4,229	5,206	6,075	6,722
6.2	"Travel" (*)	US$ Mn	2,791	3,098	3,862	4,375	4,723
6.3	"Passenger transport" (*)	US$ Mn	998	1,131	1,344	1,700	1,999
	DOMESTIC TOURISM						
	Accommodation						
7.1	Overnight stays in hotels and similar establishments	('000)	7,533	7,395	7,829	7,799	8,174
7.2	Guests in hotels and similar establishments	('000)	..	..	..	..	..
7.3	Overnight stays in all types of accommodation establishments	('000)	23,207	22,222	23,616	24,189	24,607
7.4	Average length of stay of resident tourists in all accommodation establishments	Nights	3.70	3.40	3.50	3.50	3.40
	OUTBOUND TOURISM						
8.1	**Departures**	('000)	4,216	4,634	4,929	5,409	6,113
8.2	**Tourism expenditure in other countries**	US$ Mn	2,956	3,835	4,832	5,291	6,168
8.3	"Travel" (*)	US$ Mn	2,858	3,755	4,736	5,177	6,056
8.4	"Passenger transport" (*)	US$ Mn	98	80	96	114	112
	TOURISM INDUSTRIES						
	Hotels and similar establishments						
9.1	Number of rooms	Units	61,230	62,807	63,077	62,402	64,163
9.2	Number of bed-places	Units	141,435	145,641	146,920	145,299	149,617
9.3	Occupancy rate	Percent	61.00	59.00	60.00	60.00	62.00
9.4	Average length of stay	Nights	..	..	..	..	..
	RELATED INDICATORS						
	Share of tourism expenditure (6.1) in:						
10.1	Gross Domestic Product (GDP)	Percent	3.7	3.5	3.4	3.3	3.4
10.2	Exports of goods	Percent	4.9	5.0	5.9	6.1	6.5
10.3	Exports of services	Percent	16.1	14.1	12.4	11.5	11.7

(*) Balance of Payments items: 6.1 to 6.3 correspond to the "Credit" side (and are receipts for the country) while 8.2 to 8.4 correspond to the "Debit" side (and are expenditures in other countries).

	Basic Indicators		Units	2001	2002	2003	2004	2005
	INBOUND TOURISM							
	Arrivals							
1.1	Visitors		('000)	1,219	862.1	..	1,505.8	1,916
1.2	Tourists (overnight visitors)		('000)	1,196	861.9	1,063	1,505.6	1,903
1.3	Same-day visitors		('000)	..	..	..	..	..
1.4	Cruise passengers		('000)	23	0.3	..	0.2	13
	Arrivals by region							
2.1	Africa		('000)	36	29	30	40	41
2.2	Americas		('000)	350	261	348	487	603
2.3	Europe		('000)	704	484	598	857	1,107
2.4	East Asia and the Pacific		('000)	53	36	42	66	88
2.5	South Asia		('000)	14	11	10	15	23
2.6	Middle East		('000)	31	28	23	29	30
	Arrivals by means of transport used							
3.1	Air		('000)	1,060	778	972	1,339	1,653
3.2	Rail		('000)	..	..	..	..	..
3.3	Road		('000)	130	80	88	162	245
3.4	Sea		('000)	6	3	4	5	5
	Arrivals by purpose of visit							
4.1	Leisure, recreation and holidays		('000)	395	194	255	361	478
4.2	Business and professional		('000)	227	164	213	286	312
4.3	Other		('000)	586	504	595	858	1,113
	Accommodation							
5.1	Overnight stays in hotels and similar establishments		('000)	3,826	2,628	3,285	4,771	6,783
5.2	Guests in hotels and similar establishments		('000)	1,077	694	900	1,374	2,005
5.3	Overnight stays in all types of accommodation establishments		('000)	4,637	2,745	3,438	5,040	7,133
5.4	Average length of stay of non-resident tourists in all accommodation establishments		Nights	22.00	22.00	20.00	22.00	18.00
6.1	**Tourism expenditure in the country**		US$ Mn	2,769	2,325	2,401	2,813	3,414
6.2	"Travel" (*)	(**)	US$ Mn	2,475	2,044	2,060	2,380	2,853
6.3	"Passenger transport" (*)		US$ Mn	294	281	341	433	561
	DOMESTIC TOURISM							
	Accommodation							
7.1	Overnight stays in hotels and similar establishments		('000)	11,288	11,978	11,810	12,202	12,304
7.2	Guests in hotels and similar establishments		('000)	4,963	5,134	5,060	5,180	5,154
7.3	Overnight stays in all types of accommodation establishments		('000)	13,668	14,025	13,855	14,230	14,952
7.4	Average length of stay of resident tourists in all accommodation establishments		Nights	..	..	..	..	..
	OUTBOUND TOURISM							
8.1	**Departures**		('000)	3,561	3,273	3,299	3,614	3,687
8.2	**Tourism expenditure in other countries**		US$ Mn	3,887	3,323	3,342	3,663	3,780
8.3	"Travel" (*)		US$ Mn	2,945	2,543	2,550	2,796	2,895
8.4	"Passenger transport" (*)		US$ Mn	942	780	792	867	885
	TOURISM INDUSTRIES							
	Hotels and similar establishments							
9.1	Number of rooms		Units	46,143	46,935	46,324	46,333	46,701
9.2	Number of bed-places		Units	111,248	114,737	114,042	114,792	114,766
9.3	Occupancy rate		Percent	40.30	38.80	39.70	44.20	49.90
9.4	Average length of stay		Nights	3.60	3.79	2.53	2.59	3.50
	RELATED INDICATORS							
	Share of tourism expenditure (6.1) in:							
10.1	Gross Domestic Product (GDP)		Percent	2.4	2.2	2.2	2.4	2.8
10.2	Exports of goods		Percent	9.9	8.4	8.0	7.7	8.5
10.3	Exports of services		Percent	23.1	19.4	17.8	17.5	19.2

(*) Balance of Payments items: 6.1 to 6.3 correspond to the "Credit" side (and are receipts for the country) while 8.2 to 8.4 correspond to the "Debit" side (and are expenditures in other countries).

(**) See Annex "Country notes".

ITALY

	Basic Indicators	Units	2001	2002	2003	2004	2005
	INBOUND TOURISM						
	Arrivals						
1.1	Visitors	('000)	60,960	63,561	63,026	58,480	59,230
1.2	Tourists (overnight visitors)	('000)	39,563	39,799	39,604	37,071	36,513
1.3	Same-day visitors	('000)	21,397	23,762	23,422	21,409	22,717
1.4	Cruise passengers	('000)	..	..	..	..	..
	Arrivals by region						
2.1	Africa	('000)	193	179	122	206	251
2.2	Americas	('000)	2,158	2,065	1,680	2,988	3,250
2.3	Europe	('000)	35,839	36,001	36,584	32,522	31,571
2.4	East Asia and the Pacific	('000)	1,200	1,383	1,075	1,088	1,112
2.5	South Asia	('000)	75	89	67	135	115
2.6	Middle East	('000)	97	82	76	130	213
	Arrivals by means of transport used						
3.1	Air	('000)	10,926	11,567	12,062	16,927	18,592
3.2	Rail	('000)	2,908	2,727	2,574	2,027	1,935
3.3	Road	('000)	44,396	46,354	45,457	37,504	36,577
3.4	Sea	('000)	2,729	2,913	2,932	2,022	2,126
	Arrivals by purpose of visit						
4.1	Leisure, recreation and holidays	('000)	26,977	27,548	27,350	26,629	25,991
4.2	Business and professional	('000)	9,801	10,630	9,754	8,597	9,190
4.3	Other	('000)	24,182	25,383	25,922	23,253	24,048
	Accommodation						
5.1	Overnight stays in hotels and similar establishments	('000)	100,322	97,837	93,935	97,175	102,312
5.2	Guests in hotels and similar establishments	('000)	29,138	29,340	28,174	29,916	30,943
5.3	Overnight stays in all types of accommodation establishments	('000)	146,672	145,560	139,653	141,169	148,501
5.4	Average length of stay of non-resident tourists in all accommodation establishments	Nights	..	..	3.99	3.84	3.89
6.1	**Tourism expenditure in the country**	US$ Mn	26,916	28,192	32,592	37,872	38,264
6.2	"Travel" (*)	US$ Mn	25,822	26,873	31,247	35,378	35,319
6.3	"Passenger transport" (*)	US$ Mn	1,094	1,319	1,345	2,494	2,945
	DOMESTIC TOURISM						
	Accommodation						
7.1	Overnight stays in hotels and similar establishments	('000)	138,559	133,295	135,217	136,845	138,123
7.2	Guests in hotels and similar establishments	('000)	38,648	38,011	39,155	40,767	41,276
7.3	Overnight stays in all types of accommodation establishments	('000)	203,651	199,687	204,760	204,447	206,754
7.4	Average length of stay of resident tourists in all accommodation establishments	Nights	..	..	4.29	4.15	4.12
	OUTBOUND TOURISM						
8.1	**Departures**	('000)	22,421	25,126	26,817	23,349	24,796
8.2	**Tourism expenditure in other countries**	US$ Mn	16,997	19,636	23,731	24,062	26,459
8.3	"Travel" (*)	US$ Mn	14,795	16,924	20,589	20,460	22,371
8.4	"Passenger transport" (*)	US$ Mn	2,202	2,712	3,142	3,602	4,088
	TOURISM INDUSTRIES						
	Hotels and similar establishments						
9.1	Number of rooms	Units	975,601	986,326	999,722	1,011,773	1,020,478
9.2	Number of bed-places	Units	1,891,281	1,929,544	1,969,495	1,999,729	2,028,452
9.3	Occupancy rate	Percent	43.20	39.60	39.63	39.80	40.10
9.4	Average length of stay	Nights	4.28	4.21	4.16	4.02	4.02
	RELATED INDICATORS						
	Share of tourism expenditure (6.1) in:						
10.1	Gross Domestic Product (GDP)	Percent	2.5	2.4	2.2	2.3	2.2
10.2	Exports of goods	Percent	11.0	11.2	10.9	10.8	10.3
10.3	Exports of services	Percent	46.7	46.6	45.4	44.8	42.5

(*) Balance of Payments items: 6.1 to 6.3 correspond to the "Credit" side (and are receipts for the country) while 8.2 to 8.4 correspond to the "Debit" side (and are expenditures in other countries).

	Basic Indicators	Units	2001	2002	2003	2004	2005
	INBOUND TOURISM						
	Arrivals						
1.1	Visitors	('000)	2,117	2,131	2,483	2,515	2,615
1.2	Tourists (overnight visitors)	('000)	1,277	1,266	1,350	1,415	1,479
1.3	Same-day visitors	('000)	..	..	..	..	..
1.4	Cruise passengers	('000)	840	865	1,133	1,100	1,136
	Arrivals by region						
2.1	Africa	('000)	1	1	1	1	1
2.2	Americas	('000)	1,083	1,076	1,120	1,162	1,234
2.3	Europe	('000)	182	180	219	243	235
2.4	East Asia and the Pacific	('000)	9	8	9	8	8
2.5	South Asia	('000)	1	1	1	1	..
2.6	Middle East	('000)	..	..	..	..	..
	Arrivals by means of transport used						
3.1	Air	('000)	1,277	1,266	1,350	1,415	1,479
3.2	Rail	('000)	..	..	..	..	..
3.3	Road	('000)	..	..	..	..	..
3.4	Sea	('000)	..	..	..	..	..
	Arrivals by purpose of visit						
4.1	Leisure, recreation and holidays	('000)	998	962	1,064	1,132	1,166
4.2	Business and professional	('000)	68	73	71	78	84
4.3	Other	('000)	210	231	215	205	228
	Accommodation						
5.1	Overnight stays in hotels and similar establishments	('000)	5,756	5,544	5,687	6,076	6,967
5.2	Guests in hotels and similar establishments	('000)	856	852	887	932	995
5.3	Overnight stays in all types of accommodation establishments	('000)	12,109	12,038	12,844	13,134	13,608
5.4	Average length of stay of non-resident tourists in all accommodation establishments	Nights	10.20	10.20	10.20	9.90	9.80
6.1	**Tourism expenditure in the country**	US$ Mn	1,494	1,482	1,621	1,733	1,783
6.2	"Travel" (*)	US$ Mn	1,232	1,209	1,355	1,438	1,545
6.3	"Passenger transport" (*)	US$ Mn	262	273	266	295	238
	DOMESTIC TOURISM						
	Accommodation						
7.1	Overnight stays in hotels and similar establishments	('000)	..	..	..	..	..
7.2	Guests in hotels and similar establishments	('000)	..	..	..	..	..
7.3	Overnight stays in all types of accommodation establishments	('000)	..	..	..	..	..
7.4	Average length of stay of resident tourists in all accommodation establishments	Nights	..	..	..	..	..
	OUTBOUND TOURISM						
8.1	**Departures**	('000)	..	..	..	..	..
8.2	**Tourism expenditure in other countries**	US$ Mn	227	274	269	318	291
8.3	"Travel" (*)	US$ Mn	206	258	252	286	250
8.4	"Passenger transport" (*)	US$ Mn	21	16	17	32	41
	TOURISM INDUSTRIES						
	Hotels and similar establishments						
9.1	Number of rooms	Units	20,220	20,425	20,827	21,322	22,528
9.2	Number of bed-places	Units	42,709	43,132	43,909	44,355	46,905
9.3	Occupancy rate	Percent	56.30	55.50	57.90	61.40	61.90
9.4	Average length of stay	Nights	6.60	6.40	6.40	6.50	6.90
	RELATED INDICATORS						
	Share of tourism expenditure (6.1) in:						
10.1	Gross Domestic Product (GDP)	Percent	18.2	17.2	19.7	19.5	18.4
10.2	Exports of goods	Percent	102.8	113.2	117.0	108.2	107.2
10.3	Exports of services	Percent	78.8	77.5	75.8	75.4	76.5

(*) Balance of Payments items: 6.1 to 6.3 correspond to the "Credit" side (and are receipts for the country) while 8.2 to 8.4 correspond to the "Debit" side (and are expenditures in other countries).

JAPAN

	Basic Indicators	Units	2001	2002	2003	2004	2005
	INBOUND TOURISM						
	Arrivals						
1.1	Visitors	('000)	..	..	..	..	..
1.2	Tourists (overnight visitors)	('000)	4,772	5,239	5,212	6,138	6,728
1.3	Same-day visitors	('000)	..	..	..	..	..
1.4	Cruise passengers	('000)	..	..	..	..	..
	Arrivals by region						
2.1	Africa	('000)	15	17	16	17	21
2.2	Americas	('000)	866	928	824	951	1,032
2.3	Europe	('000)	630	688	665	744	817
2.4	East Asia and the Pacific	('000)	3,189	3,528	3,625	4,338	4,761
2.5	South Asia	('000)	66	73	76	84	93
2.6	Middle East	('000)	3	3	3	3	3
	Arrivals by means of transport used						
3.1	Air	('000)	5,061	5,496	5,428	6,399	7,022
3.2	Rail	('000)	..	..	..	..	..
3.3	Road	('000)	..	..	..	..	..
3.4	Sea	('000)	225	276	299	357	428
	Arrivals by purpose of visit						
4.1	Leisure, recreation and holidays	('000)	2,717	3,095	3,055	3,840	4,369
4.2	Business and professional	('000)	1,236	1,287	1,281	1,383	1,477
4.3	Other	('000)	818	857	875	915	882
	Accommodation						
5.1	Overnight stays in hotels and similar establishments	('000)	..	..	..	..	..
5.2	Guests in hotels and similar establishments	('000)	..	..	..	..	..
5.3	Overnight stays in all types of accommodation establishments	('000)	..	..	..	..	..
5.4	Average length of stay of non-resident tourists in all accommodation establishments	Nights	8.50	8.30	8.50	8.10	8.00
6.1	**Tourism expenditure in the country**	US$ Mn	5,750	6,069	11,475	14,343	15,555
6.2	"Travel" (*)	US$ Mn	3,306	3,497	8,848	11,265	12,430
6.3	"Passenger transport" (*)	US$ Mn	2,444	2,572	2,627	3,078	3,125
	DOMESTIC TOURISM						
	Accommodation						
7.1	Overnight stays in hotels and similar establishments	('000)	284,000	286,000	269,000	255,000	..
7.2	Guests in hotels and similar establishments	('000)	..	..	..	..	..
7.3	Overnight stays in all types of accommodation establishments	('000)	..	..	..	..	..
7.4	Average length of stay of resident tourists in all accommodation establishments	Nights	..	..	..	..	..
	OUTBOUND TOURISM						
8.1	**Departures**	('000)	16,216	16,523	13,296	16,831	17,404
8.2	**Tourism expenditure in other countries**	US$ Mn	35,526	34,977	36,505	48,175	48,102
8.3	"Travel" (*)	US$ Mn	26,531	26,656	28,958	38,252	37,565
8.4	"Passenger transport" (*)	US$ Mn	8,995	8,321	7,547	9,923	10,537
	TOURISM INDUSTRIES						
	Hotels and similar establishments						
9.1	Number of rooms	Units	1,572,227	1,564,689	1,562,867	1,551,876	..
9.2	Number of bed-places	Units	..	..	..	..	..
9.3	Occupancy rate	Percent	70.20	70.70	70.90	71.80	73.10
9.4	Average length of stay	Nights	..	..	..	..	..
	RELATED INDICATORS						
	Share of tourism expenditure (6.1) in:						
10.1	Gross Domestic Product (GDP)	Percent	0.1	0.2	0.3	0.3	0.3
10.2	Exports of goods	Percent	1.5	1.5	2.6	2.7	2.7
10.3	Exports of services	Percent	8.9	9.2	14.8	14.7	14.1

(*) Balance of Payments items: 6.1 to 6.3 correspond to the "Credit" side (and are receipts for the country) while 8.2 to 8.4 correspond to the "Debit" side (and are expenditures in other countries).

	Basic Indicators	Units	2001	2002	2003	2004	2005
	INBOUND TOURISM						
	Arrivals						
1.1	Visitors	('000)	3,034	4,677	4,600	5,587	5,817
1.2	Tourists (overnight visitors)	('000)	1,672	2,384	2,353	2,853	2,987
1.3	Same-day visitors	('000)	1,362	2,293	2,247	2,734	2,831
1.4	Cruise passengers	('000)	11	4	3	9	26
	Arrivals by region						
2.1	Africa	('000)	17	20	18	20	30
2.2	Americas	('000)	52	52	65	93	112
2.3	Europe	('000)	285	313	315	374	392
2.4	East Asia and the Pacific	('000)	29	43	44	60	64
2.5	South Asia	('000)	17	36	27	38	43
2.6	Middle East	('000)	897	1,498	1,465	1,781	1,829
	Arrivals by means of transport used						
3.1	Air	('000)	818	948	1,028	1,407	1,449
3.2	Rail	('000)	2	2	2	2	1
3.3	Road	('000)	3,422	5,572	5,338	6,220	6,572
3.4	Sea	('000)	298	221	288	370	356
	Arrivals by purpose of visit						
4.1	Leisure, recreation and holidays	('000)	..	..	..	..	..
4.2	Business and professional	('000)	..	..	..	..	..
4.3	Other	('000)	..	..	..	..	..
	Accommodation						
5.1	Overnight stays in hotels and similar establishments	('000)	2,686	2,726	2,842	3,980	4,488
5.2	Guests in hotels and similar establishments	('000)	..	..	1,037	1,529	1,795
5.3	Overnight stays in all types of accommodation establishments	('000)	..	..	..	..	..
5.4	Average length of stay of non-resident tourists in all accommodation establishments	Nights	4.63	4.35	4.45	5.00	5.00
6.1	**Tourism expenditure in the country**	US$ Mn	884	1,254	1,266	1,621	1,759
6.2	"Travel" (*)	US$ Mn	700	1,048	1,062	1,330	1,441
6.3	"Passenger transport" (*)	US$ Mn	184	206	204	291	318
	DOMESTIC TOURISM						
	Accommodation						
7.1	Overnight stays in hotels and similar establishments	('000)	597	772	974	1,052	1,064
7.2	Guests in hotels and similar establishments	('000)	..	..	452	522	505
7.3	Overnight stays in all types of accommodation establishments	('000)	..	..	..	..	..
7.4	Average length of stay of resident tourists in all accommodation establishments	Nights	..	..	2.20	2.00	2.11
	OUTBOUND TOURISM						
8.1	**Departures**	('000)	1,755	1,276	1,229	1,420	1,523
8.2	**Tourism expenditure in other countries**	US$ Mn	421	505	503	585	653
8.3	"Travel" (*)	US$ Mn	378	453	452	524	585
8.4	"Passenger transport" (*)	US$ Mn	43	52	51	61	68
	TOURISM INDUSTRIES						
	Hotels and similar establishments						
9.1	Number of rooms	Units	19,247	19,389	19,698	19,945	20,827
9.2	Number of bed-places	Units	37,385	37,289	37,859	38,658	40,480
9.3	Occupancy rate	Percent	30.50	32.00	34.20	45.20	48.00
9.4	Average length of stay	Nights	..	..	2.60	2.50	2.40
	RELATED INDICATORS						
	Share of tourism expenditure (6.1) in:						
10.1	Gross Domestic Product (GDP)	Percent	9.8	13.1	12.5	14.1	13.7
10.2	Exports of goods	Percent	38.5	45.3	41.1	41.7	40.9
10.3	Exports of services	Percent	59.6	70.6	72.8	78.8	77.0

(*) Balance of Payments items: 6.1 to 6.3 correspond to the "Credit" side (and are receipts for the country) while 8.2 to 8.4 correspond to the "Debit" side (and are expenditures in other countries).

KAZAKHSTAN

	Basic Indicators	Units	2001	2002	2003	2004	2005
	INBOUND TOURISM						
	Arrivals						
1.1	Visitors	('000)	2,693	3,678	3,237	4,291	4,365
1.2	Tourists (overnight visitors)	('000)	1,845	2,832	2,410	3,073	3,143
1.3	Same-day visitors	('000)	848	846	827	1,218	1,222
1.4	Cruise passengers	('000)	..	..	..	..	..
	Arrivals by region						
2.1	Africa	('000)	2	1	1	2	2
2.2	Americas	('000)	19	25	23	32	31
2.3	Europe	('000)	2,585	3,569	3,114	4,126	4,194
2.4	East Asia and the Pacific	('000)	69	66	72	97	114
2.5	South Asia	('000)	10	12	18	21	19
2.6	Middle East	('000)	2	3	3	2	2
	Arrivals by means of transport used						
3.1	Air	('000)	..	..	767	274	298
3.2	Rail	('000)	..	..	482	1,221	1,242
3.3	Road	('000)	..	..	1,988	2,766	2,813
3.4	Sea	('000)	..	..	..	30	12
	Arrivals by purpose of visit						
4.1	Leisure, recreation and holidays	('000)	..	48	47	57	80
4.2	Business and professional	('000)	..	646	634	825	893
4.3	Other	('000)	..	2,984	2,556	3,409	3,392
	Accommodation						
5.1	Overnight stays in hotels and similar establishments	('000)	122	173	198	220	261
5.2	Guests in hotels and similar establishments	('000)	..	..	..	..	..
5.3	Overnight stays in all types of accommodation establishments	('000)	..	..	..	..	..
5.4	Average length of stay of non-resident tourists in all accommodation establishments	Nights	..	..	3.00	3.00	3.00
6.1	**Tourism expenditure in the country**	US$ Mn	502	680	638	803	809
6.2	"Travel" (*)	US$ Mn	452	622	564	718	701
6.3	"Passenger transport" (*)	US$ Mn	50	58	74	85	108
	DOMESTIC TOURISM						
	Accommodation						
7.1	Overnight stays in hotels and similar establishments	('000)	476	601	689	815	963
7.2	Guests in hotels and similar establishments	('000)	..	..	..	..	..
7.3	Overnight stays in all types of accommodation establishments	('000)	..	..	..	..	..
7.4	Average length of stay of resident tourists in all accommodation establishments	Nights	..	..	..	..	..
	OUTBOUND TOURISM						
8.1	**Departures**	('000)	2,294	2,274	2,374	3,915	3,004
8.2	**Tourism expenditure in other countries**	US$ Mn	761	863	783	997	940
8.3	"Travel" (*)	US$ Mn	673	757	669	844	753
8.4	"Passenger transport" (*)	US$ Mn	88	106	114	153	187
	TOURISM INDUSTRIES						
	Hotels and similar establishments						
9.1	Number of rooms	Units	8,821	9,838	11,104	12,196	15,515
9.2	Number of bed-places	Units	16,296	19,179	22,172	24,257	33,399
9.3	Occupancy rate	Percent	..	..	..	25.30	24.90
9.4	Average length of stay	Nights	..	..	..	..	..
	RELATED INDICATORS						
	Share of tourism expenditure (6.1) in:						
10.1	Gross Domestic Product (GDP)	Percent	2.3	2.8	2.1	1.9	1.4
10.2	Exports of goods	Percent	5.6	6.8	4.8	3.9	2.9
10.3	Exports of services	Percent	39.8	44.2	37.3	40.2	35.9

(*) Balance of Payments items: 6.1 to 6.3 correspond to the "Credit" side (and are receipts for the country) while 8.2 to 8.4 correspond to the "Debit" side (and are expenditures in other countries).

	Basic Indicators	Units	2001	2002	2003	2004	2005
	INBOUND TOURISM						
	Arrivals						
1.1	Visitors	('000)	994	1,001	1,146	1,359	1,675
1.2	Tourists (overnight visitors)	('000)	828	825	927	1,193	1,536
1.3	Same-day visitors	('000)	153	163	216	162	135
1.4	Cruise passengers	('000)	13	13	3	4	5
	Arrivals by region						
2.1	Africa	('000)	556	549	632	827	999
2.2	Americas	('000)	47	49	57	70	94
2.3	Europe	('000)	321	324	367	381	474
2.4	East Asia and the Pacific	('000)	38	44	51	47	65
2.5	South Asia	('000)	24	24	27	19	21
2.6	Middle East	('000)	7	10	12	16	22
	Arrivals by means of transport used						
3.1	Air	('000)	493	496	547	668	832
3.2	Rail	('000)	6	3	2	0.2	0.2
3.3	Road	('000)	482	489	594	686	838
3.4	Sea	('000)	13	13	3	4	5
	Arrivals by purpose of visit						
4.1	Leisure, recreation and holidays	('000)	605	579	577	706	928
4.2	Business and professional	('000)	266	273	343	411	482
4.3	Other	('000)	123	149	226	242	266
	Accommodation						
5.1	Overnight stays in hotels and similar establishments	('000)	2,594	2,766	1,890	5,060	6,832
5.2	Guests in hotels and similar establishments	('000)	..	..	..	..	..
5.3	Overnight stays in all types of accommodation establishments	('000)	..	..	..	..	..
5.4	Average length of stay of non-resident tourists in all accommodation establishments	Nights	10.00	10.00	14.00	14.00	14.00
6.1	**Tourism expenditure in the country**	US$ Mn	536	513	619	799	969
6.2	"Travel" (*)	US$ Mn	309	276	347	486	579
6.3	"Passenger transport" (*)	US$ Mn	227	237	272	313	390
	DOMESTIC TOURISM						
	Accommodation						
7.1	Overnight stays in hotels and similar establishments	('000)	740	656	771	780	840
7.2	Guests in hotels and similar establishments	('000)	..	..	..	..	..
7.3	Overnight stays in all types of accommodation establishments	('000)	..	..	..	..	..
7.4	Average length of stay of resident tourists in all accommodation establishments	Nights	5.00	5.00	5.00	5.00	5.00
	OUTBOUND TOURISM						
8.1	**Departures**	('000)	..	..	..	..	..
8.2	**Tourism expenditure in other countries**	US$ Mn	183	..	..	..	..
8.3	"Travel" (*)	US$ Mn	143	126	127	108	124
8.4	"Passenger transport" (*)	US$ Mn	40	..	..	..	..
	TOURISM INDUSTRIES						
	Hotels and similar establishments						
9.1	Number of rooms	Units	11,209	10,638	15,320	19,660	20,037
9.2	Number of bed-places	Units	22,418	21,276	30,640	39,320	40,074
9.3	Occupancy rate	Percent	40.30	42.00	33.60	72.30	85.00
9.4	Average length of stay	Nights	8.40	8.50	8.40	14.00	14.00
	RELATED INDICATORS						
	Share of tourism expenditure (6.1) in:						
10.1	Gross Domestic Product (GDP)	Percent	4.1	3.9	4.1	5.0	5.4
10.2	Exports of goods	Percent	28.3	23.7	25.7	29.4	29.9
10.3	Exports of services	Percent	47.9	48.7	51.7	51.3	51.4

(*) Balance of Payments items: 6.1 to 6.3 correspond to the "Credit" side (and are receipts for the country) while 8.2 to 8.4 correspond to the "Debit" side (and are expenditures in other countries).

KIRIBATI

Basic Indicators		Units	2001	2002	2003	2004	2005
	INBOUND TOURISM						
	Arrivals						
1.1	Visitors	('000)	14.5	119.5	130.1	63.0	..
1.2	Tourists (overnight visitors)	('000)	4.6	4.9	4.9	3.6	3.0
1.3	Same-day visitors	('000)	..	..	..	..	..
1.4	Cruise passengers	('000)	9.9	114.6	125.2	59.4	..
	Arrivals by region						
2.1	Africa	('000)	..	..	..	..	..
2.2	Americas	('000)	0.9	1.1	0.8	0.1	0.3
2.3	Europe	('000)	0.5	0.5	0.4	0.4	0.1
2.4	East Asia and the Pacific	('000)	2.5	2.7	2.9	2.5	2.2
2.5	South Asia	('000)	..	..	..	..	..
2.6	Middle East	('000)	..	..	..	..	..
	Arrivals by means of transport used						
3.1	Air	('000)	4.6	4.9	4.9	3.6	3.0
3.2	Rail	('000)	..	..	..	..	..
3.3	Road	('000)	..	..	..	..	..
3.4	Sea	('000)	9.9	114.6	125.2	59.4	..
	Arrivals by purpose of visit						
4.1	Leisure, recreation and holidays	('000)	1.0	0.2	0.2	0.1	0.3
4.2	Business and professional	('000)	1.9	1.6	1.6	1.6	1.7
4.3	Other	('000)	1.7	1.5	2.1	1.9	1.0
	Accommodation						
5.1	Overnight stays in hotels and similar establishments	('000)	..	..	..	..	..
5.2	Guests in hotels and similar establishments	('000)	..	..	..	..	..
5.3	Overnight stays in all types of accommodation establishments	('000)	..	..	..	..	..
5.4	Average length of stay of non-resident tourists in all accommodation establishments	Nights	..	..	..	..	..
6.1	**Tourism expenditure in the country** (**)	US$ Mn	3.2	..	..	..	..
6.2	"Travel" (*)	US$ Mn	..	..	..	..	..
6.3	"Passenger transport" (*)	US$ Mn	..	..	..	..	..
	DOMESTIC TOURISM						
	Accommodation						
7.1	Overnight stays in hotels and similar establishments	('000)	..	..	..	..	..
7.2	Guests in hotels and similar establishments	('000)	..	..	..	..	..
7.3	Overnight stays in all types of accommodation establishments	('000)	..	..	..	..	..
7.4	Average length of stay of resident tourists in all accommodation establishments	Nights	..	..	..	..	..
	OUTBOUND TOURISM						
8.1	**Departures**	('000)	..	..	..	..	..
8.2	**Tourism expenditure in other countries**	US$ Mn	..	..	..	..	..
8.3	"Travel" (*)	US$ Mn	..	..	..	..	..
8.4	"Passenger transport" (*)	US$ Mn	..	..	..	..	..
	TOURISM INDUSTRIES						
	Hotels and similar establishments						
9.1	Number of rooms	Units	158	162	162	162	..
9.2	Number of bed-places	Units	309	..	..	..	..
9.3	Occupancy rate	Percent	..	..	..	..	..
9.4	Average length of stay	Nights	7.00	..	..	..	..
	RELATED INDICATORS						
	Share of tourism expenditure (6.1) in:						
10.1	Gross Domestic Product (GDP)	Percent	..	..	..	..	..
10.2	Exports of goods	Percent	..	..	..	..	..
10.3	Exports of services	Percent	..	..	..	..	..

(*) Balance of Payments items: 6.1 to 6.3 correspond to the "Credit" side (and are receipts for the country) while 8.2 to 8.4 correspond to the "Debit" side (and are expenditures in other countries).

(**) See Annex "Country notes".

	Basic Indicators		Units	2001	2002	2003	2004	2005
	INBOUND TOURISM							
	Arrivals							
1.1	Visitors		('000)	5,147	5,347	4,753	5,818	6,023
1.2	Tourists (overnight visitors)		('000)	..	..	..	..	..
1.3	Same-day visitors		('000)	..	..	..	..	..
1.4	Cruise passengers		('000)	..	..	..	..	..
	Arrivals by region							
2.1	Africa		('000)	16	16	15	15	14
2.2	Americas		('000)	507	556	505	611	640
2.3	Europe		('000)	455	536	514	531	541
2.4	East Asia and the Pacific		('000)	3,787	3,829	3,335	4,253	4,442
2.5	South Asia		('000)	88	82	86	95	92
2.6	Middle East		('000)	8	11	8	11	13
	Arrivals by means of transport used							
3.1	Air		('000)	3,948	4,067	3,536	4,529	4,776
3.2	Rail		('000)	..	..	..	..	..
3.3	Road		('000)	..	..	..	..	..
3.4	Sea		('000)	327	326	314	400	404
	Arrivals by purpose of visit							
4.1	Leisure, recreation and holidays		('000)	3,769	3,844	3,217	4,185	4,347
4.2	Business and professional		('000)	213	225	231	267	304
4.3	Other		('000)	1,165	1,279	1,304	1,366	1,371
	Accommodation							
5.1	Overnight stays in hotels and similar establishments		('000)	..	..	..	..	..
5.2	Guests in hotels and similar establishments		('000)	..	..	..	..	..
5.3	Overnight stays in all types of accommodation establishments		('000)	..	..	..	..	..
5.4	Average length of stay of non-resident tourists in all accommodation establishments		Nights	5.20	5.40	6.20	5.60	6.80
6.1	**Tourism expenditure in the country**		US$ Mn	7,919	7,621	7,005	8,226	8,148
6.2	"Travel" (*)		US$ Mn	6,384	5,936	5,358	6,069	5,660
6.3	"Passenger transport" (*)		US$ Mn	1,535	1,685	1,647	2,157	2,488
	DOMESTIC TOURISM							
	Accommodation							
7.1	Overnight stays in hotels and similar establishments		('000)	..	..	..	..	..
7.2	Guests in hotels and similar establishments		('000)	..	..	..	..	..
7.3	Overnight stays in all types of accommodation establishments		('000)	..	..	..	..	..
7.4	Average length of stay of resident tourists in all accommodation establishments		Nights	..	..	..	..	..
	OUTBOUND TOURISM							
8.1	**Departures**		('000)	6,084	7,123	7,086	8,826	10,080
8.2	**Tourism expenditure in other countries**	(**)	US$ Mn	8,349	11,440	11,063	13,507	16,831
8.3	"Travel" (*)		US$ Mn	7,617	10,465	10,103	12,350	15,314
8.4	"Passenger transport" (*)		US$ Mn	732	975	960	1,157	1,517
	TOURISM INDUSTRIES							
	Hotels and similar establishments							
9.1	Number of rooms		Units	53,478	54,086	56,196	59,135	58,950
9.2	Number of bed-places		Units	..	..	..	..	..
9.3	Occupancy rate		Percent	61.60	60.10	51.80	55.10	57.10
9.4	Average length of stay		Nights	..	..	..	..	..
	RELATED INDICATORS							
	Share of tourism expenditure (6.1) in:							
10.1	Gross Domestic Product (GDP)		Percent	1.6	1.4	1.2	1.2	1.0
10.2	Exports of goods		Percent	5.2	4.7	3.6	3.2	2.8
10.3	Exports of services		Percent	27.3	26.8	21.3	19.6	18.0

(*) Balance of Payments items: 6.1 to 6.3 correspond to the "Credit" side (and are receipts for the country) while 8.2 to 8.4 correspond to the "Debit" side (and are expenditures in other countries).

(**) See Annex "Country notes".

KUWAIT

	Basic Indicators	Units	2001	2002	2003	2004	2005
	INBOUND TOURISM						
	Arrivals						
1.1	Visitors	('000)	2,072	2,316	2,602	3,056	..
1.2	Tourists (overnight visitors)	('000)	73	96	94	91	..
1.3	Same-day visitors	('000)	..	..	..	..	..
1.4	Cruise passengers	('000)	..	..	..	..	..
	Arrivals by region						
2.1	Africa	('000)	18	24	26	29	..
2.2	Americas	('000)	39	50	103	115	..
2.3	Europe	('000)	69	81	94	126	..
2.4	East Asia and the Pacific	('000)	99	118	125	158	..
2.5	South Asia	('000)	578	648	746	856	..
2.6	Middle East	('000)	1,264	1,391	1,506	1,769	..
	Arrivals by means of transport used						
3.1	Air	('000)	994	1,139	1,272	1,525	..
3.2	Rail	('000)	..	..	..	..	..
3.3	Road	('000)	1,021	1,120	1,278	1,482	..
3.4	Sea	('000)	57	56	52	48	..
	Arrivals by purpose of visit						
4.1	Leisure, recreation and holidays	('000)	0.2	7.6	7.1	1.2	..
4.2	Business and professional	('000)	46.6	33.7	17.9	2.3	..
4.3	Other	('000)	26.0	54.8	69.2	87.2	..
	Accommodation						
5.1	Overnight stays in hotels and similar establishments	('000)	216	292	315	281	..
5.2	Guests in hotels and similar establishments	('000)	73	96	94	91	..
5.3	Overnight stays in all types of accommodation establishments	('000)	..	..	..	..	..
5.4	Average length of stay of non-resident tourists in all accommodation establishments	Nights	..	3.00	3.30	3.10	..
6.1	**Tourism expenditure in the country**	US$ Mn	285	322	330	413	408
6.2	"Travel" (*)	US$ Mn	106	118	119	179	165
6.3	"Passenger transport" (*)	US$ Mn	179	204	211	234	243
	DOMESTIC TOURISM						
	Accommodation						
7.1	Overnight stays in hotels and similar establishments	('000)	..	..	..	..	..
7.2	Guests in hotels and similar establishments	('000)	..	..	..	..	..
7.3	Overnight stays in all types of accommodation establishments	('000)	..	..	..	..	..
7.4	Average length of stay of resident tourists in all accommodation establishments	Nights	..	..	..	..	..
	OUTBOUND TOURISM						
8.1	**Departures**	('000)	1,666	1,725	1,774	1,928	..
8.2	**Tourism expenditure in other countries**	US$ Mn	3,207	3,413	3,751	4,149	4,743
8.3	"Travel" (*)	US$ Mn	2,842	3,021	3,348	3,701	4,277
8.4	"Passenger transport" (*)	US$ Mn	365	392	403	448	466
	TOURISM INDUSTRIES						
	Hotels and similar establishments						
9.1	Number of rooms	Units	2,646	3,407	3,980	4,281	4,267
9.2	Number of bed-places	Units	2,987	3,870	5,063	5,064	5,024
9.3	Occupancy rate	Percent	..	..	..	..	..
9.4	Average length of stay	Nights	..	..	..	..	..
	RELATED INDICATORS						
	Share of tourism expenditure (6.1) in:						
10.1	Gross Domestic Product (GDP)	Percent	0.8	0.8	0.7	0.7	0.5
10.2	Exports of goods	Percent	1.8	2.1	1.5	1.4	0.9
10.3	Exports of services	Percent	17.2	19.6	10.5	11.0	8.7

(*) Balance of Payments items: 6.1 to 6.3 correspond to the "Credit" side (and are receipts for the country) while 8.2 to 8.4 correspond to the "Debit" side (and are expenditures in other countries).

	Basic Indicators	Units	2001	2002	2003	2004	2005
	INBOUND TOURISM						
	Arrivals						
1.1	Visitors	('000)	199	183	..	..	..
1.2	Tourists (overnight visitors)	('000)	99	140	342	398	315
1.3	Same-day visitors	('000)	..	..	..	..	..
1.4	Cruise passengers	('000)	..	..	..	..	..
	Arrivals by region						
2.1	Africa	('000)	..	..	..	..	..
2.2	Americas	('000)	4	12	13	12	13
2.3	Europe	('000)	45	88	270	357	274
2.4	East Asia and the Pacific	('000)	8	11	14	17	22
2.5	South Asia	('000)	2	3	5	6	6
2.6	Middle East	('000)	..	..	..	..	..
	Arrivals by means of transport used						
3.1	Air	('000)	46	40	47	59	..
3.2	Rail	('000)	61	73	71	86	..
3.3	Road	('000)	91	70	61	140	..
3.4	Sea	('000)	..	..	..	..	..
	Arrivals by purpose of visit						
4.1	Leisure, recreation and holidays	('000)	63	..	..	..	..
4.2	Business and professional	('000)	28	..	..	..	..
4.3	Other	('000)	7	..	..	..	..
	Accommodation						
5.1	Overnight stays in hotels and similar establishments	('000)	80	144	117	119	94
5.2	Guests in hotels and similar establishments	('000)	32	44	46	49	34
5.3	Overnight stays in all types of accommodation establishments	('000)	..	..	..	..	..
5.4	Average length of stay of non-resident tourists in all accommodation establishments	Nights	..	..	..	..	..
6.1	**Tourism expenditure in the country**	US$ Mn	32	53	65	97	94
6.2	"Travel" (*)	US$ Mn	24	36	48	76	73
6.3	"Passenger transport" (*)	US$ Mn	8	17	17	21	21
	DOMESTIC TOURISM						
	Accommodation						
7.1	Overnight stays in hotels and similar establishments	('000)	130	134	131	136	128
7.2	Guests in hotels and similar establishments	('000)	72	80	82	101	92
7.3	Overnight stays in all types of accommodation establishments	('000)	..	..	..	..	..
7.4	Average length of stay of resident tourists in all accommodation establishments	Nights	..	..	..	..	..
	OUTBOUND TOURISM						
8.1	**Departures**	('000)	46	59	116	239	..
8.2	**Tourism expenditure in other countries**	US$ Mn	21	18	25	60	71
8.3	"Travel" (*)	US$ Mn	12	10	17	50	58
8.4	"Passenger transport" (*)	US$ Mn	9	8	8	10	13
	TOURISM INDUSTRIES						
	Hotels and similar establishments						
9.1	Number of rooms	Units	2,172	1,974	1,925	2,248	2,244
9.2	Number of bed-places	Units	3,505	3,498	3,409	4,022	4,472
9.3	Occupancy rate	Percent	..	..	..	..	..
9.4	Average length of stay	Nights	..	..	..	..	..
	RELATED INDICATORS						
	Share of tourism expenditure (6.1) in:						
10.1	Gross Domestic Product (GDP)	Percent	2.1	3.3	3.4	4.4	3.9
10.2	Exports of goods	Percent	6.7	10.6	11.0	13.2	13.7
10.3	Exports of services	Percent	38.6	37.3	41.1	46.2	36.7

(*) Balance of Payments items: 6.1 to 6.3 correspond to the "Credit" side (and are receipts for the country) while 8.2 to 8.4 correspond to the "Debit" side (and are expenditures in other countries).

LAO PEOPLE´S DEMOCRATIC REPUBLIC

	Basic Indicators	Units	2001	2002	2003	2004	2005
	INBOUND TOURISM						
	Arrivals						
1.1	Visitors	('000)	674	736	636	895	1,095
1.2	Tourists (overnight visitors)	('000)	173	215	196	407	672
1.3	Same-day visitors	('000)	501	521	440	488	423
1.4	Cruise passengers	('000)	..	..	..	..	..
	Arrivals by region						
2.1	Africa	('000)	..	..	..	..	..
2.2	Americas	('000)	34	47	39	47	60
2.3	Europe	('000)	84	107	97	116	134
2.4	East Asia and the Pacific	('000)	549	575	495	728	897
2.5	South Asia	('000)	4	4	3	2	2
2.6	Middle East	('000)	..	..	..	..	..
	Arrivals by means of transport used						
3.1	Air	('000)	95	147	159	242	438
3.2	Rail	('000)	..	..	..	..	..
3.3	Road	('000)	579	589	477	653	657
3.4	Sea	('000)	..	..	..	..	..
	Arrivals by purpose of visit						
4.1	Leisure, recreation and holidays	('000)	525	..	503	770	964
4.2	Business and professional	('000)	80	..	89	54	66
4.3	Other	('000)	69	..	44	71	65
	Accommodation						
5.1	Overnight stays in hotels and similar establishments	('000)	..	..	..	..	..
5.2	Guests in hotels and similar establishments	('000)	..	..	..	..	..
5.3	Overnight stays in all types of accommodation establishments	('000)	..	..	..	..	..
5.4	Average length of stay of non-resident tourists in all accommodation establishments	Nights	5.20	4.30	4.00	4.30	4.50
6.1	**Tourism expenditure in the country**	US$ Mn	..	..	..	..	..
6.2	"Travel" (*)	US$ Mn	104	113	87	119	146
6.3	"Passenger transport" (*)	US$ Mn	..	..	..	..	..
	DOMESTIC TOURISM						
	Accommodation						
7.1	Overnight stays in hotels and similar establishments	('000)	..	..	..	..	..
7.2	Guests in hotels and similar establishments	('000)	..	..	..	..	..
7.3	Overnight stays in all types of accommodation establishments	('000)	..	..	..	..	..
7.4	Average length of stay of resident tourists in all accommodation establishments	Nights	..	..	..	..	..
	OUTBOUND TOURISM						
8.1	**Departures**	('000)	..	..	..	..	..
8.2	**Tourism expenditure in other countries**	US$ Mn	..	..	..	..	..
8.3	"Travel" (*)	US$ Mn	0.1	..	..	..	..
8.4	"Passenger transport" (*)	US$ Mn	..	..	..	..	..
	TOURISM INDUSTRIES						
	Hotels and similar establishments						
9.1	Number of rooms	Units	8,797	8,625	12,289	13,666	15,828
9.2	Number of bed-places	Units	14,257	14,222	18,877	20,480	22,142
9.3	Occupancy rate	Percent	51.00	..	45.00	44.00	50.00
9.4	Average length of stay	Nights	..	..	..	..	..
	RELATED INDICATORS						
	Share of tourism expenditure (6.1) in: (**)						
10.1	Gross Domestic Product (GDP)	Percent	5.9	6.2	4.1	4.8	5.1
10.2	Exports of goods	Percent	33.4	..	..	..	..
10.3	Exports of services	Percent	62.7	..	..	..	..

(*) Balance of Payments items: 6.1 to 6.3 correspond to the "Credit" side (and are receipts for the country) while 8.2 to 8.4 correspond to the "Debit" side (and are expenditures in other countries).

(**) See Annex "Country notes".

	Basic Indicators	Units	2001	2002	2003	2004	2005
	INBOUND TOURISM						
	Arrivals						
1.1	Visitors	('000)	2,061	2,297	2,524	3,127	3,791
1.2	Tourists (overnight visitors)	('000)	591	848	971	1,079	1,116
1.3	Same-day visitors	('000)	1,448	1,425	1,499	1,954	2,658
1.4	Cruise passengers	('000)	26	76	79	69	92
	Arrivals by region						
2.1	Africa	('000)	..	..	..	1	..
2.2	Americas	('000)	21	24	22	32	22
2.3	Europe	('000)	1,999	2,218	2,429	2,985	3,739
2.4	East Asia and the Pacific	('000)	16	18	17	13	8
2.5	South Asia	('000)	2	1	1	1	2
2.6	Middle East	('000)	..	..	..	..	..
	Arrivals by means of transport used						
3.1	Air	('000)	156	155	188	299	494
3.2	Rail	('000)	105	128	144	139	147
3.3	Road	('000)	1,676	1,840	2,004	2,481	2,939
3.4	Sea	('000)	124	174	188	208	210
	Arrivals by purpose of visit						
4.1	Leisure, recreation and holidays	('000)	303	480	586	857	1,227
4.2	Business and professional	('000)	434	458	409	466	441
4.3	Other	('000)	1,302	1,335	1,475	1,710	2,106
	Accommodation						
5.1	Overnight stays in hotels and similar establishments	('000)	837	853	963	1,158	1,507
5.2	Guests in hotels and similar establishments	('000)	319	352	402	520	680
5.3	Overnight stays in all types of accommodation establishments	('000)	847	871	983	1,201	1,613
5.4	Average length of stay of non-resident tourists in all accommodation establishments	Nights	2.62	2.41	2.37	2.20	2.21
6.1	**Tourism expenditure in the country**	US$ Mn	154	200	271	343	446
6.2	"Travel" (*)	US$ Mn	120	161	222	267	341
6.3	"Passenger transport" (*)	US$ Mn	34	39	49	76	105
	DOMESTIC TOURISM						
	Accommodation						
7.1	Overnight stays in hotels and similar establishments	('000)	638	674	669	717	796
7.2	Guests in hotels and similar establishments	('000)	210	225	257	287	354
7.3	Overnight stays in all types of accommodation establishments	('000)	769	821	825	865	1,022
7.4	Average length of stay of resident tourists in all accommodation establishments	Nights	2.93	2.69	2.39	2.43	2.41
	OUTBOUND TOURISM						
8.1	**Departures**	('000)	2,697	2,306	2,286	2,457	2,959
8.2	**Tourism expenditure in other countries**	US$ Mn	255	267	365	429	655
8.3	"Travel" (*)	US$ Mn	223	230	328	378	584
8.4	"Passenger transport" (*)	US$ Mn	32	37	37	51	71
	TOURISM INDUSTRIES						
	Hotels and similar establishments						
9.1	Number of rooms	Units	7,034	7,198	7,618	8,826	9,219
9.2	Number of bed-places	Units	13,139	13,744	14,983	17,933	19,229
9.3	Occupancy rate	Percent	32.00	31.10	31.70	31.49	36.38
9.4	Average length of stay	Nights	2.80	2.50	2.48	2.32	2.23
	RELATED INDICATORS						
	Share of tourism expenditure (6.1) in:						
10.1	Gross Domestic Product (GDP)	Percent	1.9	2.1	2.4	2.5	2.8
10.2	Exports of goods	Percent	6.9	7.9	8.5	8.1	8.4
10.3	Exports of services	Percent	13.1	16.1	18.0	19.3	20.7

(*) Balance of Payments items: 6.1 to 6.3 correspond to the "Credit" side (and are receipts for the country) while 8.2 to 8.4 correspond to the "Debit" side (and are expenditures in other countries).

LEBANON

	Basic Indicators		Units	2001	2002	2003	2004	2005
	INBOUND TOURISM							
	Arrivals							
1.1	Visitors		('000)	..	..	..	..	..
1.2	Tourists (overnight visitors)		('000)	837	956	1,016	1,278	1,140
1.3	Same-day visitors		('000)	..	..	..	..	..
1.4	Cruise passengers		('000)	..	..	..	..	..
	Arrivals by region							
2.1	Africa		('000)	30	37	39	45	31
2.2	Americas		('000)	101	108	120	152	137
2.3	Europe		('000)	237	251	267	337	317
2.4	East Asia and the Pacific		('000)	54	61	66	92	88
2.5	South Asia		('000)	84	96	102	131	130
2.6	Middle East		('000)	330	403	421	520	437
	Arrivals by means of transport used							
3.1	Air		('000)	515	582	..	..	..
3.2	Rail		('000)	..	..	..	..	..
3.3	Road		('000)	321	374	..	..	..
3.4	Sea		('000)	1	1	..	..	..
	Arrivals by purpose of visit							
4.1	Leisure, recreation and holidays		('000)	..	..	..	..	..
4.2	Business and professional		('000)	..	..	..	..	..
4.3	Other		('000)	..	..	..	..	..
	Accommodation							
5.1	Overnight stays in hotels and similar establishments		('000)	610	653	1,180	1,484	1,133
5.2	Guests in hotels and similar establishments		('000)	..	..	..	..	..
5.3	Overnight stays in all types of accommodation establishments		('000)	..	..	..	..	..
5.4	Average length of stay of non-resident tourists in all accommodation establishments		Nights	2.93	2.63	2.58	2.65	2.49
6.1	**Tourism expenditure in the country**	(**)	US$ Mn	837	..	6,782	5,931	5,869
6.2	"Travel" (*)		US$ Mn	..	4,284	6,374	5,411	5,432
6.3	"Passenger transport" (*)		US$ Mn	..	..	408	520	437
	DOMESTIC TOURISM							
	Accommodation							
7.1	Overnight stays in hotels and similar establishments		('000)	..	..	..	..	..
7.2	Guests in hotels and similar establishments		('000)	..	..	..	..	..
7.3	Overnight stays in all types of accommodation establishments		('000)	..	..	..	..	..
7.4	Average length of stay of resident tourists in all accommodation establishments		Nights	..	..	..	..	..
	OUTBOUND TOURISM							
8.1	**Departures**		('000)	..	..	..	..	..
8.2	**Tourism expenditure in other countries**		US$ Mn	..	..	3,319	3,719	3,535
8.3	"Travel" (*)		US$ Mn	..	2,683	2,943	3,170	2,878
8.4	"Passenger transport" (*)		US$ Mn	..	..	376	549	657
	TOURISM INDUSTRIES							
	Hotels and similar establishments							
9.1	Number of rooms		Units	15,687	17,601	16,202	16,171	16,735
9.2	Number of bed-places		Units	27,366	30,444	28,246	26,992	28,953
9.3	Occupancy rate		Percent	30.00	35.00	..	..	..
9.4	Average length of stay		Nights	..	..	..	..	..
	RELATED INDICATORS							
	Share of tourism expenditure (6.1) in:							
10.1	Gross Domestic Product (GDP)		Percent	..	..	33.9	27.1	26.4
10.2	Exports of goods		Percent	..	..	391.3	289.3	257.6
10.3	Exports of services		Percent	..	..	71.7	61.1	54.6

(*) Balance of Payments items: 6.1 to 6.3 correspond to the "Credit" side (and are receipts for the country) while 8.2 to 8.4 correspond to the "Debit" side (and are expenditures in other countries).

(**) See Annex "Country notes".

LESOTHO

Basic Indicators		Units	2001	2002	2003	2004	2005
	INBOUND TOURISM						
	Arrivals						
1.1	Visitors	('000)	295	287	329	304	304
1.2	Tourists (overnight visitors)	('000)	..	..	..	..	..
1.3	Same-day visitors	('000)	..	..	..	..	..
1.4	Cruise passengers	('000)	..	..	..	..	..
	Arrivals by region						
2.1	Africa	('000)	286	278	303	290	289
2.2	Americas	('000)	1	1	3	1	1
2.3	Europe	('000)	6	6	13	8	8
2.4	East Asia and the Pacific	('000)	2	2	4	3	3
2.5	South Asia	('000)	..	..	..	..	..
2.6	Middle East	('000)	..	..	..	..	..
	Arrivals by means of transport used						
3.1	Air	('000)	9	9	11	10	11
3.2	Rail	('000)	..	..	..	..	..
3.3	Road	('000)	286	279	318	294	293
3.4	Sea	('000)	..	..	..	..	..
	Arrivals by purpose of visit						
4.1	Leisure, recreation and holidays	('000)	47	46	58	63	67
4.2	Business and professional	('000)	44	43	54	57	60
4.3	Other	('000)	203	198	217	183	177
	Accommodation						
5.1	Overnight stays in hotels and similar establishments	('000)	..	..	..	..	..
5.2	Guests in hotels and similar establishments	('000)	..	..	..	..	..
5.3	Overnight stays in all types of accommodation establishments	('000)	..	..	..	..	..
5.4	Average length of stay of non-resident tourists in all accommodation establishments	Nights	..	..	..	..	..
6.1	**Tourism expenditure in the country**	US$ Mn	..	..	..	..	..
6.2	"Travel" (*)	US$ Mn	23	20	28	34	30
6.3	"Passenger transport" (*)	US$ Mn	..	..	..	..	..
	DOMESTIC TOURISM						
	Accommodation						
7.1	Overnight stays in hotels and similar establishments	('000)	..	..	..	..	..
7.2	Guests in hotels and similar establishments	('000)	..	..	..	..	..
7.3	Overnight stays in all types of accommodation establishments	('000)	..	..	..	..	..
7.4	Average length of stay of resident tourists in all accommodation establishments	Nights	..	..	..	..	..
	OUTBOUND TOURISM						
8.1	**Departures**	('000)	..	..	..	..	..
8.2	**Tourism expenditure in other countries**	US$ Mn	12	16	30	37	36
8.3	"Travel" (*)	US$ Mn	9	14	26	30	27
8.4	"Passenger transport" (*)	US$ Mn	3	2	4	7	9
	TOURISM INDUSTRIES						
	Hotels and similar establishments						
9.1	Number of rooms	Units	..	..	..	1,492	..
9.2	Number of bed-places	Units	..	..	..	..	..
9.3	Occupancy rate	Percent	..	..	..	17.70	..
9.4	Average length of stay	Nights	..	..	..	..	..
	RELATED INDICATORS						
	Share of tourism expenditure (6.1) in: (**)						
10.1	Gross Domestic Product (GDP)	Percent	3.0	2.9	2.6	2.5	2.1
10.2	Exports of goods	Percent	8.2	5.6	5.9	4.8	4.6
10.3	Exports of services	Percent	57.5	57.1	56.0	53.1	54.5

(*) Balance of Payments items: 6.1 to 6.3 correspond to the "Credit" side (and are receipts for the country) while 8.2 to 8.4 correspond to the "Debit" side (and are expenditures in other countries).

(**) See Annex "Country notes".

LIBYAN ARAB JAMAHIRIYA

	Basic Indicators	Units	2001	2002	2003	2004	2005
	INBOUND TOURISM						
	Arrivals						
1.1	Visitors	('000)	953	858	958	999	..
1.2	Tourists (overnight visitors)	('000)	169	135	142	149	..
1.3	Same-day visitors	('000)	784	723	816	850	..
1.4	Cruise passengers	('000)	..	..	..	..	..
	Arrivals by region						
2.1	Africa	('000)	515	439	458	483	..
2.2	Americas	('000)	1	2	2	2	..
2.3	Europe	('000)	40	36	42	46	..
2.4	East Asia and the Pacific	('000)	6	7	7	7	..
2.5	South Asia	('000)	4	4	4	4	..
2.6	Middle East	('000)	388	370	445	458	..
	Arrivals by means of transport used						
3.1	Air	('000)	343	309	342	379	..
3.2	Rail	('000)	..	..	..	..	..
3.3	Road	('000)	590	531	591	658	..
3.4	Sea	('000)	20	18	19	20	..
	Arrivals by purpose of visit						
4.1	Leisure, recreation and holidays	('000)	49	47	45	43	..
4.2	Business and professional	('000)	58	38	40	42	..
4.3	Other	('000)	62	50	57	64	..
	Accommodation						
5.1	Overnight stays in hotels and similar establishments	('000)	571	453	477	502	..
5.2	Guests in hotels and similar establishments	('000)	..	..	..	..	..
5.3	Overnight stays in all types of accommodation establishments	('000)	..	..	..	..	..
5.4	Average length of stay of non-resident tourists in all accommodation establishments	Nights	7.00	7.00	7.00	7.00	..
6.1	**Tourism expenditure in the country**	US$ Mn	90	202	243	261	301
6.2	"Travel" (*)	US$ Mn	78	181	205	218	250
6.3	"Passenger transport" (*)	US$ Mn	12	21	38	43	51
	DOMESTIC TOURISM						
	Accommodation						
7.1	Overnight stays in hotels and similar establishments	('000)	..	..	..	..	..
7.2	Guests in hotels and similar establishments	('000)	..	..	..	..	..
7.3	Overnight stays in all types of accommodation establishments	('000)	970	972	968	964	..
7.4	Average length of stay of resident tourists in all accommodation establishments	Nights	..	..	..	..	..
	OUTBOUND TOURISM						
8.1	**Departures**	('000)	..	..	..	..	..
8.2	**Tourism expenditure in other countries**	US$ Mn	572	654	689	789	920
8.3	"Travel" (*)	US$ Mn	445	586	557	603	680
8.4	"Passenger transport" (*)	US$ Mn	127	68	132	186	240
	TOURISM INDUSTRIES						
	Hotels and similar establishments						
9.1	Number of rooms	Units	12,405	12,405	12,405	12,704	..
9.2	Number of bed-places	Units	20,967	20,967	20,967	21,404	..
9.3	Occupancy rate	Percent	53.00	42.00	45.00	44.00	..
9.4	Average length of stay	Nights	..	..	..	..	..
	RELATED INDICATORS						
	Share of tourism expenditure (6.1) in:						
10.1	Gross Domestic Product (GDP)	Percent	0.3	1.0	1.0	0.9	0.8
10.2	Exports of goods	Percent	0.8	2.1	1.7	1.5	1.0
10.3	Exports of services	Percent	48.9	50.4	55.0	59.7	56.4

(*) Balance of Payments items: 6.1 to 6.3 correspond to the "Credit" side (and are receipts for the country) while 8.2 to 8.4 correspond to the "Debit" side (and are expenditures in other countries).

	Basic Indicators	Units	2001	2002	2003	2004	2005
	INBOUND TOURISM						
	Arrivals						
1.1	Visitors	('000)	..	..	..	..	..
1.2	Tourists (overnight visitors)	('000)	56.5	48.7	49.0	48.5	49.8
1.3	Same-day visitors	('000)	..	..	..	..	..
1.4	Cruise passengers	('000)	..	..	..	..	..
	Arrivals by region						
2.1	Africa	('000)	0.2	0.2	0.2	0.2	0.2
2.2	Americas	('000)	3.7	2.9	2.4	2.7	2.9
2.3	Europe	('000)	51.0	44.0	44.7	43.8	44.9
2.4	East Asia and the Pacific	('000)	1.6	1.7	1.6	1.7	1.6
2.5	South Asia	('000)	..	..	..	..	..
2.6	Middle East	('000)	..	..	..	..	..
	Arrivals by means of transport used						
3.1	Air	('000)	..	..	..	..	..
3.2	Rail	('000)	..	..	..	..	..
3.3	Road	('000)	..	..	..	..	..
3.4	Sea	('000)	..	..	..	..	..
	Arrivals by purpose of visit						
4.1	Leisure, recreation and holidays	('000)	..	..	..	..	..
4.2	Business and professional	('000)	..	..	..	..	..
4.3	Other	('000)	..	..	..	..	..
	Accommodation						
5.1	Overnight stays in hotels and similar establishments	('000)	120.4	105.9	104.6	101.1	108.4
5.2	Guests in hotels and similar establishments	('000)	56.5	48.7	49.0	48.5	49.8
5.3	Overnight stays in all types of accommodation establishments	('000)	..	..	..	..	..
5.4	Average length of stay of non-resident tourists in all accommodation establishments	Nights	2.13	2.17	2.10	2.10	2.20
6.1	**Tourism expenditure in the country**	US$ Mn	..	..	..	..	..
6.2	"Travel" (*)	US$ Mn	..	..	..	..	..
6.3	"Passenger transport" (*)	US$ Mn	..	..	..	..	..
	DOMESTIC TOURISM						
	Accommodation						
7.1	Overnight stays in hotels and similar establishments	('000)	2.8	2.5	2.6	3.1	2.9
7.2	Guests in hotels and similar establishments	('000)	1.3	1.0	1.2	1.6	1.3
7.3	Overnight stays in all types of accommodation establishments	('000)	..	..	..	..	..
7.4	Average length of stay of resident tourists in all accommodation establishments	Nights	..	..	..	..	..
	OUTBOUND TOURISM						
8.1	**Departures**	('000)	..	..	..	..	..
8.2	**Tourism expenditure in other countries**	US$ Mn	..	..	..	..	..
8.3	"Travel" (*)	US$ Mn	..	..	..	..	..
8.4	"Passenger transport" (*)	US$ Mn	..	..	..	..	..
	TOURISM INDUSTRIES						
	Hotels and similar establishments						
9.1	Number of rooms	Units	609	581	591	572	608
9.2	Number of bed-places	Units	1,155	1,112	1,160	1,176	1,188
9.3	Occupancy rate	Percent	29.20	26.70	25.30	24.20	25.60
9.4	Average length of stay	Nights	2.13	2.18	2.10	2.10	2.20
	RELATED INDICATORS						
	Share of tourism expenditure (6.1) in:						
10.1	Gross Domestic Product (GDP)	Percent	..	..	..	..	..
10.2	Exports of goods	Percent	..	..	..	..	..
10.3	Exports of services	Percent	..	..	..	..	..

(*) Balance of Payments items: 6.1 to 6.3 correspond to the "Credit" side (and are receipts for the country) while 8.2 to 8.4 correspond to the "Debit" side (and are expenditures in other countries).

LITHUANIA

	Basic Indicators	Units	2001	2002	2003	2004	2005
	INBOUND TOURISM						
	Arrivals						
1.1	Visitors	('000)	4,195	3,999	3,635	..	..
1.2	Tourists (overnight visitors)	('000)	1,271	1,428	1,491	1,800	2,000
1.3	Same-day visitors	('000)	2,924	2,571	2,144	..	..
1.4	Cruise passengers	('000)	6	8	9	14	24
	Arrivals by region						
2.1	Africa	('000)	..	..	..	1	1
2.2	Americas	('000)	15	16	16	22	24
2.3	Europe	('000)	322	358	400	538	622
2.4	East Asia and the Pacific	('000)	11	10	11	15	15
2.5	South Asia	('000)	..	..	..	..	..
2.6	Middle East	('000)	..	..	..	..	..
	Arrivals by means of transport used						
3.1	Air	('000)	148	161	185	199	320
3.2	Rail	('000)	576	530	443	504	625
3.3	Road	('000)	506	699	808	1,032	960
3.4	Sea	('000)	40	38	55	66	95
	Arrivals by purpose of visit						
4.1	Leisure, recreation and holidays	('000)	459	482	523	682	555
4.2	Business and professional	('000)	272	326	335	408	500
4.3	Other	('000)	540	620	632	710	945
	Accommodation						
5.1	Overnight stays in hotels and similar establishments	('000)	656	708	747	1,113	1,299
5.2	Guests in hotels and similar establishments	('000)	297	335	369	516	603
5.3	Overnight stays in all types of accommodation establishments	('000)	1,073	1,145	1,170	1,526	1,762
5.4	Average length of stay of non-resident tourists in all accommodation establishments	Nights	3.00	2.90	2.70	2.59	2.59
6.1	**Tourism expenditure in the country**	US$ Mn	425	556	700	834	975
6.2	"Travel" (*)	US$ Mn	383	505	638	776	921
6.3	"Passenger transport" (*)	US$ Mn	42	51	62	58	54
	DOMESTIC TOURISM						
	Accommodation						
7.1	Overnight stays in hotels and similar establishments	('000)	281	321	324	486	692
7.2	Guests in hotels and similar establishments	('000)	132	148	165	240	324
7.3	Overnight stays in all types of accommodation establishments	('000)	2,004	1,886	1,845	2,169	2,489
7.4	Average length of stay of resident tourists in all accommodation establishments	Nights	5.70	5.30	4.50	4.10	3.86
	OUTBOUND TOURISM						
8.1	**Departures**	('000)	3,390	3,584	3,502	..	..
8.2	**Tourism expenditure in other countries**	US$ Mn	227	334	476	643	757
8.3	"Travel" (*)	US$ Mn	219	326	471	636	744
8.4	"Passenger transport" (*)	US$ Mn	8	8	5	7	13
	TOURISM INDUSTRIES						
	Hotels and similar establishments						
9.1	Number of rooms	Units	5,649	5,963	7,100	9,090	9,722
9.2	Number of bed-places	Units	10,674	11,518	13,744	17,854	19,075
9.3	Occupancy rate	Percent	31.70	35.20	32.50	36.70	40.80
9.4	Average length of stay	Nights	2.18	2.13	1.98	2.10	2.15
	RELATED INDICATORS						
	Share of tourism expenditure (6.1) in:						
10.1	Gross Domestic Product (GDP)	Percent	3.5	3.9	3.8	3.7	3.8
10.2	Exports of goods	Percent	8.7	9.2	9.1	9.0	8.3
10.3	Exports of services	Percent	36.7	38.0	37.3	34.1	31.4

(*) Balance of Payments items: 6.1 to 6.3 correspond to the "Credit" side (and are receipts for the country) while 8.2 to 8.4 correspond to the "Debit" side (and are expenditures in other countries).

	Basic Indicators	Units	2001	2002	2003	2004	2005
	INBOUND TOURISM						
	Arrivals						
1.1	Visitors	('000)	..	..	..	..	..
1.2	Tourists (overnight visitors)	('000)	836	885	867	878	913
1.3	Same-day visitors	('000)	..	..	..	..	..
1.4	Cruise passengers	('000)	..	..	..	..	..
	Arrivals by region						
2.1	Africa	('000)	..	..	..	..	..
2.2	Americas	('000)	36	33	29	30	32
2.3	Europe	('000)	769	809	801	807	840
2.4	East Asia and the Pacific	('000)	..	..	..	..	..
2.5	South Asia	('000)	..	..	..	..	..
2.6	Middle East	('000)	..	..	..	..	..
	Arrivals by means of transport used						
3.1	Air	('000)	..	..	..	..	..
3.2	Rail	('000)	..	..	..	..	..
3.3	Road	('000)	..	..	..	..	..
3.4	Sea	('000)	..	..	..	..	..
	Arrivals by purpose of visit						
4.1	Leisure, recreation and holidays	('000)	..	..	..	..	..
4.2	Business and professional	('000)	..	..	..	..	..
4.3	Other	('000)	..	..	..	..	..
	Accommodation						
5.1	Overnight stays in hotels and similar establishments	('000)	1,174	1,167	1,144	1,195	1,273
5.2	Guests in hotels and similar establishments	('000)	577	599	581	613	667
5.3	Overnight stays in all types of accommodation establishments	('000)	2,422	2,469	2,541	2,514	2,468
5.4	Average length of stay of non-resident tourists in all accommodation establishments	Nights	2.90	2.80	2.90	2.90	2.70
6.1	**Tourism expenditure in the country**	US$ Mn	..	2,547	3,149	3,883	..
6.2	"Travel" (*)	US$ Mn	1,780	2,406	2,994	3,653	3,614
6.3	"Passenger transport" (*)	US$ Mn	..	141	155	230	..
	DOMESTIC TOURISM						
	Accommodation						
7.1	Overnight stays in hotels and similar establishments	('000)	72	78	80	85	85
7.2	Guests in hotels and similar establishments	('000)	20	22	24	24	29
7.3	Overnight stays in all types of accommodation establishments	('000)	274	281	269	279	275
7.4	Average length of stay of resident tourists in all accommodation establishments	Nights	5.80	5.20	4.80	4.70	4.20
	OUTBOUND TOURISM						
8.1	**Departures**	('000)	261	..	..	..	..
8.2	**Tourism expenditure in other countries**	US$ Mn	..	1,963	2,445	2,950	..
8.3	"Travel" (*)	US$ Mn	1,464	1,942	2,423	2,911	2,976
8.4	"Passenger transport" (*)	US$ Mn	..	21	22	39	..
	TOURISM INDUSTRIES						
	Hotels and similar establishments						
9.1	Number of rooms	Units	7,660	7,640	7,547	7,424	7,508
9.2	Number of bed-places	Units	14,609	14,545	14,620	14,237	..
9.3	Occupancy rate	Percent	25.90	25.60	25.10	28.20	29.50
9.4	Average length of stay	Nights	2.10	2.00	2.00	2.00	2.00
	RELATED INDICATORS						
	Share of tourism expenditure (6.1) in:						
10.1	Gross Domestic Product (GDP)	Percent	..	11.9	11.6	12.2	..
10.2	Exports of goods	Percent	..	26.7	28.6	28.6	..
10.3	Exports of services	Percent	..	12.6	12.4	11.6	..

(*) Balance of Payments items: 6.1 to 6.3 correspond to the "Credit" side (and are receipts for the country) while 8.2 to 8.4 correspond to the "Debit" side (and are expenditures in other countries).

MACAO, CHINA

Basic Indicators			Units	2001	2002	2003	2004	2005
	INBOUND TOURISM							
	Arrivals							
1.1	Visitors		('000)	10,279	11,531	11,888	16,673	18,711
1.2	Tourists (overnight visitors)		('000)	5,842	6,565	6,309	8,324	9,014
1.3	Same-day visitors		('000)	4,437	4,966	5,579	8,349	9,697
1.4	Cruise passengers		('000)	..	..	..	..	..
	Arrivals by region							
2.1	Africa		('000)	4	4	5	6	8
2.2	Americas		('000)	119	128	96	148	183
2.3	Europe		('000)	130	128	94	129	161
2.4	East Asia and the Pacific		('000)	10,005	11,250	11,673	16,362	18,321
2.5	South Asia		('000)	18	18	17	24	32
2.6	Middle East		('000)	1	1	1	2	3
	Arrivals by means of transport used							
3.1	Air		('000)	862	905	655	862	1,040
3.2	Rail		('000)	..	..	..	..	..
3.3	Road		('000)	4,149	4,925	6,059	9,506	10,951
3.4	Sea		('000)	5,268	5,701	5,174	6,305	6,720
	Arrivals by purpose of visit							
4.1	Leisure, recreation and holidays		('000)	7,092	8,533	9,035	12,671	13,098
4.2	Business and professional		('000)	1,336	1,268	1,427	2,001	2,994
4.3	Other		('000)	1,850	1,730	1,426	2,001	2,619
	Accommodation							
5.1	Overnight stays in hotels and similar establishments		('000)	3,344	3,656	3,456	4,426	4,563
5.2	Guests in hotels and similar establishments		('000)	2,625	2,996	2,870	3,790	3,903
5.3	Overnight stays in all types of accommodation establishments		('000)	..	..	..	..	..
5.4	Average length of stay of non-resident tourists in all accommodation establishments		Nights	..	..	..	..	..
6.1	**Tourism expenditure in the country**	(**)	US$ Mn	3,745	4,440	5,303	7,344	7,757
6.2	"Travel" (*)		US$ Mn	..	..	..	..	..
6.3	"Passenger transport" (*)		US$ Mn	..	..	..	..	..
	DOMESTIC TOURISM							
	Accommodation							
7.1	Overnight stays in hotels and similar establishments		('000)	228	218	240	226	281
7.2	Guests in hotels and similar establishments		('000)	142	159	173	166	218
7.3	Overnight stays in all types of accommodation establishments		('000)	..	..	..	..	..
7.4	Average length of stay of resident tourists in all accommodation establishments		Nights	..	..	..	1.44	1.30
	OUTBOUND TOURISM							
8.1	**Departures**		('000)	192	200	156	212	295
8.2	**Tourism expenditure in other countries**		US$ Mn	..	..	..	..	..
8.3	"Travel" (*)		US$ Mn	..	..	..	..	..
8.4	"Passenger transport" (*)		US$ Mn	..	..	..	..	..
	TOURISM INDUSTRIES							
	Hotels and similar establishments							
9.1	Number of rooms		Units	9,030	8,954	9,185	9,168	10,832
9.2	Number of bed-places		Units	18,777	18,628	19,117	18,591	21,460
9.3	Occupancy rate		Percent	60.66	67.13	64.27	75.55	70.93
9.4	Average length of stay		Nights	1.35	1.28	1.26	1.22	1.22
	RELATED INDICATORS							
	Share of tourism expenditure (6.1) in:	(**)						
10.1	Gross Domestic Product (GDP)		Percent	..	..	..	..	..
10.2	Exports of goods		Percent	..	..	..	..	..
10.3	Exports of services		Percent	..	..	..	..	..

(*) Balance of Payments items: 6.1 to 6.3 correspond to the "Credit" side (and are receipts for the country) while 8.2 to 8.4 correspond to the "Debit" side (and are expenditures in other countries).

(**) See Annex "Country notes".

	Basic Indicators	Units	2001	2002	2003	2004	2005
	INBOUND TOURISM						
	Arrivals						
1.1	Visitors	('000)	..	..	..	..	..
1.2	Tourists (overnight visitors)	('000)	170	62	139	229	277
1.3	Same-day visitors	('000)	..	..	..	..	..
1.4	Cruise passengers	('000)	..	..	..	..	..
	Arrivals by region						
2.1	Africa	('000)	31	6	17	39	52
2.2	Americas	('000)	7	2	4	9	14
2.3	Europe	('000)	119	43	100	176	203
2.4	East Asia and the Pacific	('000)	3	1	2	3	6
2.5	South Asia	('000)	..	..	..	..	..
2.6	Middle East	('000)	..	..	..	..	..
	Arrivals by means of transport used						
3.1	Air	('000)	170	62	139	229	277
3.2	Rail	('000)	..	..	..	..	..
3.3	Road	('000)	..	..	..	..	..
3.4	Sea	('000)	..	..	..	..	..
	Arrivals by purpose of visit						
4.1	Leisure, recreation and holidays	('000)	107	39	88	144	172
4.2	Business and professional	('000)	41	15	51	71	80
4.3	Other	('000)	22	8	..	14	25
	Accommodation						
5.1	Overnight stays in hotels and similar establishments	('000)	3,234	555	1,970	3,536	5,221
5.2	Guests in hotels and similar establishments	('000)	..	..	..	..	..
5.3	Overnight stays in all types of accommodation establishments	('000)	..	..	..	..	..
5.4	Average length of stay of non-resident tourists in all accommodation establishments	Nights	20.00	9.00	15.00	16.00	20.00
6.1	**Tourism expenditure in the country**	US$ Mn	149	62	69	84	98
6.2	"Travel" (*)	US$ Mn	115	36	44	56	62
6.3	"Passenger transport" (*)	US$ Mn	34	26	25	28	36
	DOMESTIC TOURISM						
	Accommodation						
7.1	Overnight stays in hotels and similar establishments	('000)	..	..	..	..	..
7.2	Guests in hotels and similar establishments	('000)	..	..	..	..	..
7.3	Overnight stays in all types of accommodation establishments	('000)	..	..	..	..	..
7.4	Average length of stay of resident tourists in all accommodation establishments	Nights	..	..	..	..	..
	OUTBOUND TOURISM						
8.1	**Departures**	('000)	..	..	..	67	41
8.2	**Tourism expenditure in other countries**	US$ Mn	179	109	39	41	27
8.3	"Travel" (*)	US$ Mn	130	91	37	35	25
8.4	"Passenger transport" (*)	US$ Mn	49	18	2	6	2
	TOURISM INDUSTRIES						
	Hotels and similar establishments						
9.1	Number of rooms	Units	8,435	8,780	9,325	10,230	10,879
9.2	Number of bed-places	Units	15,100	15,800	16,700	17,390	18,494
9.3	Occupancy rate	Percent	66.00	22.00	40.00	55.00	57.00
9.4	Average length of stay	Nights	4.00	2.00	4.00	4.00	4.00
	RELATED INDICATORS						
	Share of tourism expenditure (6.1) in:						
10.1	Gross Domestic Product (GDP)	Percent	3.3	1.4	1.3	1.9	1.9
10.2	Exports of goods	Percent	16.1	12.8	14.0	23.3	34.8
10.3	Exports of services	Percent	42.5	27.7	37.1	54.5	58.3

(*) Balance of Payments items: 6.1 to 6.3 correspond to the "Credit" side (and are receipts for the country) while 8.2 to 8.4 correspond to the "Debit" side (and are expenditures in other countries).

MALAWI

	Basic Indicators	Units	2001	2002	2003	2004	2005
	INBOUND TOURISM						
	Arrivals						
1.1	Visitors	('000)	..	..	..	..	..
1.2	Tourists (overnight visitors)	('000)	266	383	424	427	438
1.3	Same-day visitors	('000)	..	..	..	..	..
1.4	Cruise passengers	('000)	..	..	..	..	..
	Arrivals by region						
2.1	Africa	('000)	203	300	320	336	337
2.2	Americas	('000)	12	15	18	21	19
2.3	Europe	('000)	43	55	68	49	60
2.4	East Asia and the Pacific	('000)	..	6	10	11	9
2.5	South Asia	('000)	..	2	4	7	10
2.6	Middle East	('000)	..	..	..	..	..
	Arrivals by means of transport used						
3.1	Air	('000)	84	94	114	114	106
3.2	Rail	('000)	..	12	9	4	8
3.3	Road	('000)	182	277	301	306	317
3.4	Sea	('000)	..	..	..	3	7
	Arrivals by purpose of visit						
4.1	Leisure, recreation and holidays	('000)	71	101	112	95	114
4.2	Business and professional	('000)	144	206	209	208	227
4.3	Other	('000)	51	76	103	124	96
	Accommodation						
5.1	Overnight stays in hotels and similar establishments	('000)	..	..	..	..	..
5.2	Guests in hotels and similar establishments	('000)	..	..	..	95	105
5.3	Overnight stays in all types of accommodation establishments	('000)	2,029	2,893	3,259	3,617	..
5.4	Average length of stay of non-resident tourists in all accommodation establishments	Nights	9.30	8.00	7.90	8.00	8.00
6.1	**Tourism expenditure in the country**	US$ Mn	40	39	35	36	36
6.2	"Travel" (*)	US$ Mn	25	29	23	24	23
6.3	"Passenger transport" (*)	US$ Mn	15	10	12	12	13
	DOMESTIC TOURISM						
	Accommodation						
7.1	Overnight stays in hotels and similar establishments	('000)	..	..	..	..	..
7.2	Guests in hotels and similar establishments	('000)	..	..	..	..	..
7.3	Overnight stays in all types of accommodation establishments	('000)	..	..	..	..	..
7.4	Average length of stay of resident tourists in all accommodation establishments	Nights	..	..	..	..	..
	OUTBOUND TOURISM						
8.1	**Departures**	('000)	..	..	..	..	..
8.2	**Tourism expenditure in other countries**	US$ Mn	53	76	61	62	58
8.3	"Travel" (*)	US$ Mn	41	69	48	50	47
8.4	"Passenger transport" (*)	US$ Mn	12	7	13	12	11
	TOURISM INDUSTRIES						
	Hotels and similar establishments						
9.1	Number of rooms	Units	39,600	59,396	20,871	20,871	..
9.2	Number of bed-places	Units	44,251	63,585	113,874	113,874	..
9.3	Occupancy rate	Percent	41.00	27.00	33.00	40.00	54.00
9.4	Average length of stay	Nights	8.10	7.60	8.10	8.00	8.00
	RELATED INDICATORS						
	Share of tourism expenditure (6.1) in:						
10.1	Gross Domestic Product (GDP)	Percent	2.3	2.0	2.0	1.9	1.7
10.2	Exports of goods	Percent	9.3	9.2	..	..	..
10.3	Exports of services	Percent	90.9	79.6	..	..	..

(*) Balance of Payments items: 6.1 to 6.3 correspond to the "Credit" side (and are receipts for the country) while 8.2 to 8.4 correspond to the "Debit" side (and are expenditures in other countries).

	Basic Indicators	Units	2001	2002	2003	2004	2005
	INBOUND TOURISM						
	Arrivals						
1.1	Visitors	('000)	22,995	20,756	16,293	24,432	24,209
1.2	Tourists (overnight visitors)	('000)	12,775	13,292	10,577	15,703	16,431
1.3	Same-day visitors	('000)	10,219	7,464	5,716	8,729	7,778
1.4	Cruise passengers	('000)	..	..	..	..	..
	Arrivals by region						
2.1	Africa	('000)	162	148	134	137	128
2.2	Americas	('000)	322	283	270	272	275
2.3	Europe	('000)	704	637	456	540	618
2.4	East Asia and the Pacific	('000)	10,833	11,456	9,074	13,983	14,686
2.5	South Asia	('000)	212	244	209	249	321
2.6	Middle East	('000)	108	126	78	124	146
	Arrivals by means of transport used						
3.1	Air	('000)	2,827	2,434	1,810	1,988	2,846
3.2	Rail	('000)	169	96	21	34	247
3.3	Road	('000)	8,646	9,869	7,989	12,299	11,878
3.4	Sea	('000)	420	245	265	330	449
	Arrivals by purpose of visit						
4.1	Leisure, recreation and holidays	('000)	4,240	5,572	4,018	5,477	5,427
4.2	Business and professional	('000)	1,532	2,160	1,629	2,168	3,053
4.3	Other	('000)	6,290	4,912	4,438	7,006	7,951
	Accommodation						
5.1	Overnight stays in hotels and similar establishments	('000)	..	..	..	..	..
5.2	Guests in hotels and similar establishments	('000)	13,115	15,615	13,239	20,009	21,448
5.3	Overnight stays in all types of accommodation establishments	('000)	..	..	..	..	..
5.4	Average length of stay of non-resident tourists in all accommodation establishments	Nights	..	..	..	..	..
6.1	**Tourism expenditure in the country**	US$ Mn	7,627	8,084	6,799	9,181	10,389
6.2	"Travel" (*)	US$ Mn	6,863	7,118	5,901	8,198	8,846
6.3	"Passenger transport" (*)	US$ Mn	764	966	898	983	1,543
	DOMESTIC TOURISM						
	Accommodation						
7.1	Overnight stays in hotels and similar establishments	('000)	..	..	..	..	..
7.2	Guests in hotels and similar establishments	('000)	15,564	16,458	18,335	27,885	29,926
7.3	Overnight stays in all types of accommodation establishments	('000)	..	..	..	..	..
7.4	Average length of stay of resident tourists in all accommodation establishments	Nights	..	..	..	..	..
	OUTBOUND TOURISM						
8.1	**Departures**	('000)	36,248	29,866	32,201	30,761	..
8.2	**Tourism expenditure in other countries**	US$ Mn	3,391	3,330	3,401	3,737	4,339
8.3	"Travel" (*)	US$ Mn	2,614	2,618	2,846	3,093	3,711
8.4	"Passenger transport" (*)	US$ Mn	777	712	555	644	628
	TOURISM INDUSTRIES						
	Hotels and similar establishments						
9.1	Number of rooms	Units	130,757	137,196	144,380	151,135	155,356
9.2	Number of bed-places	Units	..	..	..	..	..
9.3	Occupancy rate	Percent	58.60	57.90	53.30	60.80	63.60
9.4	Average length of stay	Nights	..	..	..	..	..
	RELATED INDICATORS						
	Share of tourism expenditure (6.1) in:						
10.1	Gross Domestic Product (GDP)	Percent	8.7	8.5	6.5	7.8	8.0
10.2	Exports of goods	Percent	8.7	8.7	6.5	7.2	7.3
10.3	Exports of services	Percent	52.8	54.3	50.1	54.8	53.1

(*) Balance of Payments items: 6.1 to 6.3 correspond to the "Credit" side (and are receipts for the country) while 8.2 to 8.4 correspond to the "Debit" side (and are expenditures in other countries).

MALDIVES

	Basic Indicators	Units	2001	2002	2003	2004	2005
	INBOUND TOURISM						
	Arrivals						
1.1	Visitors	('000)	..	..	..	..	..
1.2	Tourists (overnight visitors)	('000)	461	485	564	617	395
1.3	Same-day visitors	('000)	..	..	..	..	..
1.4	Cruise passengers	('000)	5	3	4	4	4
	Arrivals by region						
2.1	Africa	('000)	2	3	4	5	3
2.2	Americas	('000)	7	7	8	9	7
2.3	Europe	('000)	364	373	443	476	307
2.4	East Asia and the Pacific	('000)	69	77	84	100	56
2.5	South Asia	('000)	17	20	21	22	19
2.6	Middle East	('000)	2	3	4	5	2
	Arrivals by means of transport used						
3.1	Air	('000)	461	485	564	617	395
3.2	Rail	('000)	..	..	..	..	..
3.3	Road	('000)	..	..	..	..	..
3.4	Sea	('000)	..	..	..	..	..
	Arrivals by purpose of visit						
4.1	Leisure, recreation and holidays	('000)	461	485	564	617	395
4.2	Business and professional	('000)	..	..	..	..	..
4.3	Other	('000)	..	..	..	..	..
	Accommodation						
5.1	Overnight stays in hotels and similar establishments	('000)	3,933	4,067	4,705	5,110	3,300
5.2	Guests in hotels and similar establishments	('000)	..	..	..	..	..
5.3	Overnight stays in all types of accommodation establishments	('000)	..	..	..	..	..
5.4	Average length of stay of non-resident tourists in all accommodation establishments	Nights	..	..	..	..	..
6.1	**Tourism expenditure in the country**	US$ Mn	..	..	..	..	..
6.2	"Travel" (*)	US$ Mn	327	337	402	471	287
6.3	"Passenger transport" (*)	US$ Mn	..	..	..	..	..
	DOMESTIC TOURISM						
	Accommodation						
7.1	Overnight stays in hotels and similar establishments	('000)	..	..	..	..	..
7.2	Guests in hotels and similar establishments	('000)	..	..	..	..	..
7.3	Overnight stays in all types of accommodation establishments	('000)	..	..	..	..	..
7.4	Average length of stay of resident tourists in all accommodation establishments	Nights	..	..	..	..	..
	OUTBOUND TOURISM						
8.1	**Departures**	('000)	41	43	44	61	77
8.2	**Tourism expenditure in other countries**	US$ Mn	59	60	60	75	94
8.3	"Travel" (*)	US$ Mn	45	46	46	56	70
8.4	"Passenger transport" (*)	US$ Mn	14	14	14	19	24
	TOURISM INDUSTRIES						
	Hotels and similar establishments						
9.1	Number of rooms	Units	8,503	8,535	8,557	8,747	8,992
9.2	Number of bed-places	Units	17,006	17,070	17,114	17,494	17,984
9.3	Occupancy rate	Percent	65.61	68.98	77.23	83.93	64.39
9.4	Average length of stay	Nights	8.53	8.40	8.35	8.29	8.35
	RELATED INDICATORS						
	Share of tourism expenditure (6.1) in: (**)						
10.1	Gross Domestic Product (GDP)	Percent	52.3	52.6	58.2	58.9	35.1
10.2	Exports of goods	Percent	297.3	255.3	264.5	260.2	177.2
10.3	Exports of services	Percent	92.4	92.8	93.1	92.9	90.5

(*) Balance of Payments items: 6.1 to 6.3 correspond to the "Credit" side (and are receipts for the country) while 8.2 to 8.4 correspond to the "Debit" side (and are expenditures in other countries).

(**) See Annex "Country notes".

	Basic Indicators	Units	2001	2002	2003	2004	2005
	INBOUND TOURISM						
	Arrivals						
1.1	Visitors	('000)	..	..	..	..	..
1.2	Tourists (overnight visitors)	('000)	89	96	110	113	143
1.3	Same-day visitors	('000)	..	..	..	..	..
1.4	Cruise passengers	('000)	..	..	..	..	..
	Arrivals by region						
2.1	Africa	('000)	19	21	28	29	36
2.2	Americas	('000)	8	9	9	12	13
2.3	Europe	('000)	51	56	63	64	81
2.4	East Asia and the Pacific	('000)	1	1	1	3	2
2.5	South Asia	('000)	..	..	..	..	..
2.6	Middle East	('000)	2	3	3	2	1
	Arrivals by means of transport used						
3.1	Air	('000)	89	96	110	113	143
3.2	Rail	('000)	..	..	..	..	..
3.3	Road	('000)	..	..	..	..	..
3.4	Sea	('000)	..	..	..	..	..
	Arrivals by purpose of visit						
4.1	Leisure, recreation and holidays	('000)	..	..	..	..	..
4.2	Business and professional	('000)	..	..	..	..	..
4.3	Other	('000)	..	..	..	..	..
	Accommodation						
5.1	Overnight stays in hotels and similar establishments	('000)	178	193	229	291	310
5.2	Guests in hotels and similar establishments	('000)	89	96	110	113	143
5.3	Overnight stays in all types of accommodation establishments	('000)	..	..	..	..	..
5.4	Average length of stay of non-resident tourists in all accommodation establishments	Nights	2.00	2.00	2.30	2.80	2.20
6.1	**Tourism expenditure in the country**	US$ Mn	91	105	136	142	149
6.2	"Travel" (*)	US$ Mn	88	104	128	140	148
6.3	"Passenger transport" (*)	US$ Mn	3	1	8	2	1
	DOMESTIC TOURISM						
	Accommodation						
7.1	Overnight stays in hotels and similar establishments	('000)	7	9	54	64	71
7.2	Guests in hotels and similar establishments	('000)	..	..	38	36	44
7.3	Overnight stays in all types of accommodation establishments	('000)	..	..	..	..	..
7.4	Average length of stay of resident tourists in all accommodation establishments	Nights	..	..	..	..	2.00
	OUTBOUND TOURISM						
8.1	**Departures**	('000)	..	..	..	..	..
8.2	**Tourism expenditure in other countries**	US$ Mn	65	62	94	125	133
8.3	"Travel" (*)	US$ Mn	36	36	48	66	77
8.4	"Passenger transport" (*)	US$ Mn	29	26	46	59	56
	TOURISM INDUSTRIES						
	Hotels and similar establishments						
9.1	Number of rooms	Units	2,816	3,492	3,907	4,659	5,311
9.2	Number of bed-places	Units	3,146	5,349	5,066	5,546	7,521
9.3	Occupancy rate	Percent	34.00	36.50	38.00	40.00	40.00
9.4	Average length of stay	Nights	2.00	2.00	2.00	2.80	2.20
	RELATED INDICATORS						
	Share of tourism expenditure (6.1) in:						
10.1	Gross Domestic Product (GDP)	Percent	3.5	3.1	3.1	2.9	2.9
10.2	Exports of goods	Percent	12.6	12.0	14.7	14.5	13.5
10.3	Exports of services	Percent	60.3	62.1	60.7	58.9	54.4

(*) Balance of Payments items: 6.1 to 6.3 correspond to the "Credit" side (and are receipts for the country) while 8.2 to 8.4 correspond to the "Debit" side (and are expenditures in other countries).

MALTA

	Basic Indicators	Units	2001	2002	2003	2004	2005
	INBOUND TOURISM						
	Arrivals						
1.1	Visitors	('000)	1,439	1,483	1,516	1,448	1,491
1.2	Tourists (overnight visitors)	('000)	1,180	1,134	1,127	1,156	1,171
1.3	Same-day visitors	('000)	..	..	..	..	..
1.4	Cruise passengers	('000)	259	349	389	292	320
	Arrivals by region						
2.1	Africa	('000)	9	9	..	..	..
2.2	Americas	('000)	28	27	21	19	18
2.3	Europe	('000)	1,080	1,040	940	983	990
2.4	East Asia and the Pacific	('000)	22	25	..	..	..
2.5	South Asia	('000)	2	2	..	..	..
2.6	Middle East	('000)	34	25	20	13	11
	Arrivals by means of transport used						
3.1	Air	('000)	1,145	1,098	1,097	1,127	1,151
3.2	Rail	('000)	..	..	..	..	..
3.3	Road	('000)	..	..	..	..	..
3.4	Sea	('000)	35	35	29	29	20
	Arrivals by purpose of visit						
4.1	Leisure, recreation and holidays	('000)	..	..	912	951	955
4.2	Business and professional	('000)	..	..	88	87	95
4.3	Other	('000)	..	..	89	89	101
	Accommodation						
5.1	Overnight stays in hotels and similar establishments	('000)	7,475	7,021	7,712	7,725	7,603
5.2	Guests in hotels and similar establishments	('000)	833	797	863	904	906
5.3	Overnight stays in all types of accommodation establishments	('000)	11,067	10,599	11,115	10,973	10,933
5.4	Average length of stay of non-resident tourists in all accommodation establishments	Nights	9.40	9.30	10.20	9.70	9.50
6.1	**Tourism expenditure in the country**	US$ Mn	704	757	869	953	923
6.2	"Travel" (*)	US$ Mn	561	614	722	770	754
6.3	"Passenger transport" (*)	US$ Mn	143	143	147	183	169
	DOMESTIC TOURISM						
	Accommodation						
7.1	Overnight stays in hotels and similar establishments	('000)	..	..	..	..	..
7.2	Guests in hotels and similar establishments	('000)	..	..	..	..	..
7.3	Overnight stays in all types of accommodation establishments	('000)	..	..	..	..	..
7.4	Average length of stay of resident tourists in all accommodation establishments	Nights	..	..	..	..	..
	OUTBOUND TOURISM						
8.1	**Departures**	('000)	179	157	174	203	201
8.2	**Tourism expenditure in other countries**	US$ Mn	204	180	238	292	308
8.3	"Travel" (*)	US$ Mn	180	154	215	256	268
8.4	"Passenger transport" (*)	US$ Mn	24	26	23	36	40
	TOURISM INDUSTRIES						
	Hotels and similar establishments						
9.1	Number of rooms	Units	..	..	..	..	..
9.2	Number of bed-places	Units	40,691	39,790	41,365	39,770	39,431
9.3	Occupancy rate	Percent	52.73	48.30	53.73	52.82	52.82
9.4	Average length of stay	Nights	9.00	8.80	9.00	9.50	8.40
	RELATED INDICATORS						
	Share of tourism expenditure (6.1) in:						
10.1	Gross Domestic Product (GDP)	Percent	18.2	18.2	17.9	17.9	16.6
10.2	Exports of goods	Percent	35.2	32.8	34.7	35.5	37.2
10.3	Exports of services	Percent	64.1	63.1	63.2	60.6	58.3

(*) Balance of Payments items: 6.1 to 6.3 correspond to the "Credit" side (and are receipts for the country) while 8.2 to 8.4 correspond to the "Debit" side (and are expenditures in other countries).

	Basic Indicators		Units	2001	2002	2003	2004	2005
	INBOUND TOURISM							
	Arrivals							
1.1	Visitors		('000)	..	..	..	..	..
1.2	Tourists (overnight visitors)		('000)	5.4	6.0	7.2	9.0	9.2
1.3	Same-day visitors		('000)	..	..	..	..	..
1.4	Cruise passengers		('000)	..	..	..	..	..
	Arrivals by region							
2.1	Africa		('000)	..	..	..	..	..
2.2	Americas		('000)	2.0	2.2	2.2	2.1	1.7
2.3	Europe		('000)	0.1	0.2	0.2	0.2	0.2
2.4	East Asia and the Pacific		('000)	3.1	3.4	4.4	4.5	5.6
2.5	South Asia		('000)	..	..	..	..	..
2.6	Middle East		('000)	..	..	..	..	..
	Arrivals by means of transport used							
3.1	Air		('000)	5.4	6.0	7.2	7.0	7.5
3.2	Rail		('000)	..	..	..	..	..
3.3	Road		('000)	..	..	..	..	..
3.4	Sea		('000)	..	..	..	2.0	1.7
	Arrivals by purpose of visit							
4.1	Leisure, recreation and holidays		('000)	1.5	1.4	1.4	2.7	2.7
4.2	Business and professional		('000)	1.9	2.2	2.2	3.0	3.1
4.3	Other		('000)	2.0	2.4	3.6	3.3	3.4
	Accommodation							
5.1	Overnight stays in hotels and similar establishments		('000)	..	..	..	..	..
5.2	Guests in hotels and similar establishments		('000)	..	..	..	..	..
5.3	Overnight stays in all types of accommodation establishments		('000)	30	37	40	38	41
5.4	Average length of stay of non-resident tourists in all accommodation establishments		Nights	5.57	6.09	5.61	4.17	4.50
6.1	**Tourism expenditure in the country**	(**)	US$ Mn	4	4	..	..	..
6.2	"Travel" (*)		US$ Mn	..	..	..	..	..
6.3	"Passenger transport" (*)		US$ Mn	..	..	..	..	..
	DOMESTIC TOURISM							
	Accommodation							
7.1	Overnight stays in hotels and similar establishments		('000)	..	..	..	..	..
7.2	Guests in hotels and similar establishments		('000)	..	..	..	..	..
7.3	Overnight stays in all types of accommodation establishments		('000)	..	..	..	..	..
7.4	Average length of stay of resident tourists in all accommodation establishments		Nights	..	..	..	..	..
	OUTBOUND TOURISM							
8.1	**Departures**		('000)	..	..	..	..	..
8.2	**Tourism expenditure in other countries**		US$ Mn	..	..	..	..	..
8.3	"Travel" (*)		US$ Mn	..	..	..	..	..
8.4	"Passenger transport" (*)		US$ Mn	..	..	..	..	..
	TOURISM INDUSTRIES							
	Hotels and similar establishments							
9.1	Number of rooms		Units	..	328	..	..	..
9.2	Number of bed-places		Units	..	..	..	..	..
9.3	Occupancy rate		Percent	..	..	..	..	..
9.4	Average length of stay		Nights	..	..	..	..	..
	RELATED INDICATORS							
	Share of tourism expenditure (6.1) in:							
10.1	Gross Domestic Product (GDP)		Percent	..	..	..	..	..
10.2	Exports of goods		Percent	..	..	..	..	..
10.3	Exports of services		Percent	..	..	..	..	..

(*) Balance of Payments items: 6.1 to 6.3 correspond to the "Credit" side (and are receipts for the country) while 8.2 to 8.4 correspond to the "Debit" side (and are expenditures in other countries).

(**) See Annex "Country notes".

MARTINIQUE

	Basic Indicators		Units	2001	2002	2003	2004	2005
	INBOUND TOURISM							
	Arrivals							
1.1	Visitors		('000)	663	654	722	630	577
1.2	Tourists (overnight visitors)		('000)	460	447	453	471	484
1.3	Same-day visitors		('000)	..	..	..	..	..
1.4	Cruise passengers		('000)	203	207	269	159	93
	Arrivals by region							
2.1	Africa		('000)	..	..	..	..	..
2.2	Americas		('000)	55	70	72	73	81
2.3	Europe		('000)	403	372	380	396	399
2.4	East Asia and the Pacific		('000)	..	..	..	..	..
2.5	South Asia		('000)	..	..	..	..	..
2.6	Middle East		('000)	..	..	..	..	..
	Arrivals by means of transport used							
3.1	Air		('000)	419	393	384	404	439
3.2	Rail		('000)	..	..	..	..	..
3.3	Road		('000)	..	..	..	..	..
3.4	Sea		('000)	41	54	70	67	45
	Arrivals by purpose of visit							
4.1	Leisure, recreation and holidays		('000)	367	390	384	393	374
4.2	Business and professional		('000)	66	44	53	61	79
4.3	Other		('000)	27	13	16	17	31
	Accommodation							
5.1	Overnight stays in hotels and similar establishments		('000)	2,030	1,991	1,693	1,705	1,924
5.2	Guests in hotels and similar establishments		('000)	234	198	187	192	216
5.3	Overnight stays in all types of accommodation establishments		('000)	5,556	6,022	6,136	6,770	6,496
5.4	Average length of stay of non-resident tourists in all accommodation establishments		Nights	12.10	13.50	13.50	14.40	13.40
6.1	**Tourism expenditure in the country**	(**)	US$ Mn	245	237	247	291	280
6.2	"Travel" (*)		US$ Mn	..	..	..	..	..
6.3	"Passenger transport" (*)		US$ Mn	..	..	..	..	..
	DOMESTIC TOURISM							
	Accommodation							
7.1	Overnight stays in hotels and similar establishments		('000)	..	..	..	..	..
7.2	Guests in hotels and similar establishments		('000)	..	..	..	..	..
7.3	Overnight stays in all types of accommodation establishments		('000)	..	..	..	..	..
7.4	Average length of stay of resident tourists in all accommodation establishments		Nights	..	..	..	..	..
	OUTBOUND TOURISM							
8.1	**Departures**		('000)	306	..	..	..	..
8.2	**Tourism expenditure in other countries**		US$ Mn	..	..	..	..	..
8.3	"Travel" (*)		US$ Mn	..	..	..	..	..
8.4	"Passenger transport" (*)		US$ Mn	..	..	..	..	..
	TOURISM INDUSTRIES							
	Hotels and similar establishments							
9.1	Number of rooms		Units	6,766	6,766	6,766	6,153	6,153
9.2	Number of bed-places		Units	14,566	14,566	14,566	13,548	13,548
9.3	Occupancy rate		Percent	42.60	42.70	53.60	51.80	57.30
9.4	Average length of stay		Nights	8.70	10.00	9.00	9.00	8.50
	RELATED INDICATORS							
	Share of tourism expenditure (6.1) in:							
10.1	Gross Domestic Product (GDP)		Percent	..	..	..	..	..
10.2	Exports of goods		Percent	..	..	..	..	..
10.3	Exports of services		Percent	..	..	..	..	..

(*) Balance of Payments items: 6.1 to 6.3 correspond to the "Credit" side (and are receipts for the country) while 8.2 to 8.4 correspond to the "Debit" side (and are expenditures in other countries).

(**) See Annex "Country notes".

	Basic Indicators	Units	2001	2002	2003	2004	2005
	INBOUND TOURISM						
	Arrivals						
1.1	Visitors	('000)	675	709	722	739	782
1.2	Tourists (overnight visitors)	('000)	660	682	702	719	761
1.3	Same-day visitors	('000)	9	9	11	11	11
1.4	Cruise passengers	('000)	6	18	9	9	9
	Arrivals by region						
2.1	Africa	('000)	168	172	174	175	185
2.2	Americas	('000)	8	7	8	8	9
2.3	Europe	('000)	438	452	466	477	503
2.4	East Asia and the Pacific	('000)	24	25	22	27	29
2.5	South Asia	('000)	21	23	27	27	31
2.6	Middle East	('000)	1	2	5	4	4
	Arrivals by means of transport used						
3.1	Air	('000)	650	668	690	708	748
3.2	Rail	('000)	..	..	..	..	..
3.3	Road	('000)	..	..	..	..	..
3.4	Sea	('000)	10	14	12	11	13
	Arrivals by purpose of visit						
4.1	Leisure, recreation and holidays	('000)	607	620	636	654	692
4.2	Business and professional	('000)	27	29	31	30	30
4.3	Other	('000)	41	60	55	55	59
	Accommodation						
5.1	Overnight stays in hotels and similar establishments	('000)	6,528	6,769	6,952	7,119	7,498
5.2	Guests in hotels and similar establishments	('000)	..	..	..	..	..
5.3	Overnight stays in all types of accommodation establishments	('000)	..	..	..	..	..
5.4	Average length of stay of non-resident tourists in all accommodation establishments	Nights	10.40	10.50	10.40	10.60	10.70
6.1	**Tourism expenditure in the country**	US$ Mn	820	829	960	1,156	1,189
6.2	"Travel" (*)	US$ Mn	623	612	697	856	871
6.3	"Passenger transport" (*)	US$ Mn	197	217	263	300	318
	DOMESTIC TOURISM						
	Accommodation						
7.1	Overnight stays in hotels and similar establishments	('000)	..	..	..	..	..
7.2	Guests in hotels and similar establishments	('000)	..	..	..	..	..
7.3	Overnight stays in all types of accommodation establishments	('000)	..	..	..	..	..
7.4	Average length of stay of resident tourists in all accommodation establishments	Nights	..	..	..	..	..
	OUTBOUND TOURISM						
8.1	**Departures**	('000)	161	162	161	180	183
8.2	**Tourism expenditure in other countries**	US$ Mn	216	224	236	277	295
8.3	"Travel" (*)	US$ Mn	198	204	216	255	275
8.4	"Passenger transport" (*)	US$ Mn	18	20	20	22	20
	TOURISM INDUSTRIES						
	Hotels and similar establishments						
9.1	Number of rooms	Units	9,024	9,623	9,647	10,640	10,497
9.2	Number of bed-places	Units	18,350	19,597	19,727	21,355	21,072
9.3	Occupancy rate	Percent	66.00	67.00	63.00	63.00	63.00
9.4	Average length of stay	Nights	..	..	..	..	..
	RELATED INDICATORS						
	Share of tourism expenditure (6.1) in:						
10.1	Gross Domestic Product (GDP)	Percent	18.1	18.2	18.3	19.1	18.4
10.2	Exports of goods	Percent	50.4	46.0	50.6	58.0	55.5
10.3	Exports of services	Percent	67.1	72.1	75.0	79.4	73.5

(*) Balance of Payments items: 6.1 to 6.3 correspond to the "Credit" side (and are receipts for the country) while 8.2 to 8.4 correspond to the "Debit" side (and are expenditures in other countries).

MEXICO

	Basic Indicators	Units	2001	2002	2003	2004	2005
	INBOUND TOURISM						
	Arrivals						
1.1	Visitors	('000)	100,718	100,153	92,330	99,250	103,146
1.2	Tourists (overnight visitors)	('000)	19,810	19,667	18,665	20,618	21,915
1.3	Same-day visitors	('000)	77,103	75,351	68,690	72,139	74,524
1.4	Cruise passengers	('000)	3,805	5,136	4,974	6,493	6,707
	Arrivals by region						
2.1	Africa	('000)	..	..	..	..	..
2.2	Americas	('000)	19,172	19,133	18,155	19,706	20,691
2.3	Europe	('000)	362	479	443	..	..
2.4	East Asia and the Pacific	('000)	..	..	..	..	..
2.5	South Asia	('000)	..	..	..	..	..
2.6	Middle East	('000)	..	..	..	..	..
	Arrivals by means of transport used						
3.1	Air	('000)	7,662	7,334	7,696	8,870	9,936
3.2	Rail	('000)	..	..	..	..	..
3.3	Road	('000)	12,148	12,333	10,969	11,748	11,979
3.4	Sea	('000)	..	..	..	..	..
	Arrivals by purpose of visit						
4.1	Leisure, recreation and holidays	('000)	6,070	5,754	6,105	7,035	7,697
4.2	Business and professional	('000)	609	632	539	586	786
4.3	Other	('000)	13,131	13,280	12,021	12,998	13,432
	Accommodation						
5.1	Overnight stays in hotels and similar establishments	('000)	29,665	25,291	26,011	30,227	33,623
5.2	Guests in hotels and similar establishments	('000)	9,410	7,869	8,556	9,972	10,691
5.3	Overnight stays in all types of accommodation establishments	('000)	..	..	..	..	..
5.4	Average length of stay of non-resident tourists in all accommodation establishments	Nights	10.20	10.28	10.32	10.14	9.93
6.1	**Tourism expenditure in the country**	US$ Mn	9,190	9,547	10,058	11,609	12,801
6.2	"Travel" (*)	US$ Mn	8,401	8,858	9,362	10,796	11,803
6.3	"Passenger transport" (*)	US$ Mn	789	689	696	813	998
	DOMESTIC TOURISM						
	Accommodation						
7.1	Overnight stays in hotels and similar establishments	('000)	57,475	57,174	58,715	64,355	64,607
7.2	Guests in hotels and similar establishments	('000)	29,618	29,939	31,128	34,454	34,547
7.3	Overnight stays in all types of accommodation establishments	('000)	..	..	..	..	..
7.4	Average length of stay of resident tourists in all accommodation establishments	Nights	..	..	..	..	..
	OUTBOUND TOURISM						
8.1	**Departures**	('000)	12,075	11,948	11,044	12,494	13,305
8.2	**Tourism expenditure in other countries**	US$ Mn	6,685	7,087	7,252	8,034	8,951
8.3	"Travel" (*)	US$ Mn	5,702	6,060	6,253	6,959	7,600
8.4	"Passenger transport" (*)	US$ Mn	983	1,027	999	1,075	1,351
	TOURISM INDUSTRIES						
	Hotels and similar establishments						
9.1	Number of rooms	Units	458,123	469,488	496,292	515,904	535,639
9.2	Number of bed-places	Units	916,246	938,976	992,584	1,031,808	1,071,278
9.3	Occupancy rate	Percent	52.83	49.65	48.28	51.38	52.03
9.4	Average length of stay	Nights	3.15	3.21	3.04	3.03	3.15
	RELATED INDICATORS						
	Share of tourism expenditure (6.1) in:						
10.1	Gross Domestic Product (GDP)	Percent	1.5	1.5	1.6	1.7	1.7
10.2	Exports of goods	Percent	5.8	5.9	6.1	6.2	6.0
10.3	Exports of services	Percent	72.4	74.9	79.7	82.6	79.3

(*) Balance of Payments items: 6.1 to 6.3 correspond to the "Credit" side (and are receipts for the country) while 8.2 to 8.4 correspond to the "Debit" side (and are expenditures in other countries).

MICRONESIA (FEDERATED STATES OF)

	Basic Indicators		Units	2001	2002	2003	2004	2005
	INBOUND TOURISM							
	Arrivals							
1.1	Visitors		('000)	..	..	..	..	..
1.2	Tourists (overnight visitors)		('000)	15.3	19.1	18.2	19.3	19.0
1.3	Same-day visitors		('000)	..	..	..	..	..
1.4	Cruise passengers		('000)	..	..	..	..	..
	Arrivals by region							
2.1	Africa		('000)	..	..	..	..	..
2.2	Americas		('000)	7.1	8.4	7.7	7.7	8.0
2.3	Europe		('000)	1.2	1.5	1.6	1.4	2.0
2.4	East Asia and the Pacific		('000)	6.9	9.0	8.9	10.0	8.9
2.5	South Asia		('000)	..	..	..	..	..
2.6	Middle East		('000)	..	..	..	..	..
	Arrivals by means of transport used							
3.1	Air		('000)	..	..	..	..	..
3.2	Rail		('000)	..	..	..	..	..
3.3	Road		('000)	..	..	..	..	..
3.4	Sea		('000)	..	..	..	..	..
	Arrivals by purpose of visit							
4.1	Leisure, recreation and holidays		('000)	11.8	14.1	13.0	13.1	13.4
4.2	Business and professional		('000)	2.7	3.7	3.8	4.4	4.3
4.3	Other		('000)	0.7	1.3	1.4	1.8	1.2
	Accommodation							
5.1	Overnight stays in hotels and similar establishments		('000)	..	..	..	..	..
5.2	Guests in hotels and similar establishments		('000)	..	..	..	..	..
5.3	Overnight stays in all types of accommodation establishments		('000)	..	..	..	..	..
5.4	Average length of stay of non-resident tourists in all accommodation establishments		Nights	..	..	..	..	..
6.1	**Tourism expenditure in the country**	(**)	US$ Mn	14.7	16.8	16.7	16.5	17.1
6.2	"Travel" (*)		US$ Mn	..	..	..	..	..
6.3	"Passenger transport" (*)		US$ Mn	..	..	..	..	..
	DOMESTIC TOURISM							
	Accommodation							
7.1	Overnight stays in hotels and similar establishments		('000)	..	..	..	..	..
7.2	Guests in hotels and similar establishments		('000)	..	..	..	..	..
7.3	Overnight stays in all types of accommodation establishments		('000)	..	..	..	..	..
7.4	Average length of stay of resident tourists in all accommodation establishments		Nights	..	..	..	..	..
	OUTBOUND TOURISM							
8.1	**Departures**		('000)	..	..	..	..	..
8.2	**Tourism expenditure in other countries**	(**)	US$ Mn	5.4	5.3	5.6	5.4	5.7
8.3	"Travel" (*)		US$ Mn	..	..	..	..	..
8.4	"Passenger transport" (*)		US$ Mn	..	..	..	..	..
	TOURISM INDUSTRIES							
	Hotels and similar establishments							
9.1	Number of rooms		Units	..	..	..	..	..
9.2	Number of bed-places		Units	..	..	..	..	..
9.3	Occupancy rate		Percent	..	..	..	..	..
9.4	Average length of stay		Nights	..	..	..	..	..
	RELATED INDICATORS							
	Share of tourism expenditure (6.1) in:							
10.1	Gross Domestic Product (GDP)		Percent	..	..	..	..	..
10.2	Exports of goods		Percent	..	..	..	..	..
10.3	Exports of services		Percent	..	..	..	..	..

(*) Balance of Payments items: 6.1 to 6.3 correspond to the "Credit" side (and are receipts for the country) while 8.2 to 8.4 correspond to the "Debit" side (and are expenditures in other countries).

(**) See Annex "Country notes".

MONACO

Basic Indicators		Units	2001	2002	2003	2004	2005
	INBOUND TOURISM						
	Arrivals						
1.1	Visitors	('000)	..	..	..	..	..
1.2	Tourists (overnight visitors)	('000)	270	263	235	250	286
1.3	Same-day visitors	('000)	..	..	..	..	..
1.4	Cruise passengers	('000)	72	56	80	125	133
	Arrivals by region						
2.1	Africa	('000)	2	2	2	2	3
2.2	Americas	('000)	37	32	24	25	29
2.3	Europe	('000)	207	205	187	190	214
2.4	East Asia and the Pacific	('000)	13	12	10	13	12
2.5	South Asia	('000)	..	..	..	..	..
2.6	Middle East	('000)	3	4	3	3	3
	Arrivals by means of transport used						
3.1	Air	('000)	169	169	151	168	196
3.2	Rail	('000)	..	..	..	..	..
3.3	Road	('000)	..	..	..	..	..
3.4	Sea	('000)	101	93	84	82	90
	Arrivals by purpose of visit						
4.1	Leisure, recreation and holidays	('000)	188	183	178	192	219
4.2	Business and professional	('000)	82	79	57	59	67
4.3	Other	('000)	..	..	..	..	..
	Accommodation						
5.1	Overnight stays in hotels and similar establishments	('000)	798	765	674	695	803
5.2	Guests in hotels and similar establishments	('000)	270	263	235	250	286
5.3	Overnight stays in all types of accommodation establishments	('000)	..	..	..	..	..
5.4	Average length of stay of non-resident tourists in all accommodation establishments	Nights	..	..	..	..	..
6.1	**Tourism expenditure in the country**	US$ Mn	..	..	..	..	..
6.2	"Travel" (*)	US$ Mn	..	..	..	..	..
6.3	"Passenger transport" (*)	US$ Mn	..	..	..	..	..
	DOMESTIC TOURISM						
	Accommodation						
7.1	Overnight stays in hotels and similar establishments	('000)	..	..	..	..	..
7.2	Guests in hotels and similar establishments	('000)	..	..	..	..	..
7.3	Overnight stays in all types of accommodation establishments	('000)	..	..	..	..	..
7.4	Average length of stay of resident tourists in all accommodation establishments	Nights	..	..	..	..	..
	OUTBOUND TOURISM						
8.1	**Departures**	('000)	..	..	..	..	..
8.2	**Tourism expenditure in other countries**	US$ Mn	..	..	..	..	..
8.3	"Travel" (*)	US$ Mn	..	..	..	..	..
8.4	"Passenger transport" (*)	US$ Mn	..	..	..	..	..
	TOURISM INDUSTRIES						
	Hotels and similar establishments						
9.1	Number of rooms	Units	2,174	2,150	2,174	2,249	2,649
9.2	Number of bed-places	Units	3,545	3,513	3,232	3,737	5,312
9.3	Occupancy rate	Percent	65.90	63.75	59.04	58.02	58.39
9.4	Average length of stay	Nights	2.96	2.91	2.87	2.78	2.81
	RELATED INDICATORS						
	Share of tourism expenditure (6.1) in:						
10.1	Gross Domestic Product (GDP)	Percent	..	..	..	..	..
10.2	Exports of goods	Percent	..	..	..	..	..
10.3	Exports of services	Percent	..	..	..	..	..

(*) Balance of Payments items: 6.1 to 6.3 correspond to the "Credit" side (and are receipts for the country) while 8.2 to 8.4 correspond to the "Debit" side (and are expenditures in other countries).

MONGOLIA

	Basic Indicators	Units	2001	2002	2003	2004	2005
	INBOUND TOURISM						
	Arrivals						
1.1	Visitors	('000)	192	235	205	305	345
1.2	Tourists (overnight visitors)	('000)	166	229	201	301	338
1.3	Same-day visitors	('000)	..	..	..	..	..
1.4	Cruise passengers	('000)	..	..	..	..	..
	Arrivals by region						
2.1	Africa	('000)	..	..	..	..	..
2.2	Americas	('000)	6	8	7	12	13
2.3	Europe	('000)	79	98	72	99	100
2.4	East Asia and the Pacific	('000)	79	122	121	188	223
2.5	South Asia	('000)	..	1	1	1	1
2.6	Middle East	('000)	..	..	..	..	..
	Arrivals by means of transport used						
3.1	Air	('000)	..	..	..	..	..
3.2	Rail	('000)	..	..	..	..	..
3.3	Road	('000)	..	..	..	..	..
3.4	Sea	('000)	..	..	..	..	..
	Arrivals by purpose of visit						
4.1	Leisure, recreation and holidays	('000)	32	51	21	64	65
4.2	Business and professional	('000)	24	28	39	73	86
4.3	Other	('000)	136	150	141	164	187
	Accommodation						
5.1	Overnight stays in hotels and similar establishments	('000)	..	..	..	..	..
5.2	Guests in hotels and similar establishments	('000)	..	..	..	..	..
5.3	Overnight stays in all types of accommodation establishments	('000)	..	..	..	..	..
5.4	Average length of stay of non-resident tourists in all accommodation establishments	Nights	..	..	..	..	..
6.1	**Tourism expenditure in the country**	US$ Mn	49	143	154	205	223
6.2	"Travel" (*)	US$ Mn	39	130	143	185	201
6.3	"Passenger transport" (*)	US$ Mn	10	13	11	20	22
	DOMESTIC TOURISM						
	Accommodation						
7.1	Overnight stays in hotels and similar establishments	('000)	..	..	..	..	..
7.2	Guests in hotels and similar establishments	('000)	..	..	..	..	..
7.3	Overnight stays in all types of accommodation establishments	('000)	..	..	..	..	..
7.4	Average length of stay of resident tourists in all accommodation establishments	Nights	..	..	..	..	..
	OUTBOUND TOURISM						
8.1	**Departures**	('000)	..	..	..	..	..
8.2	**Tourism expenditure in other countries**	US$ Mn	59	125	144	207	222
8.3	"Travel" (*)	US$ Mn	55	119	138	193	205
8.4	"Passenger transport" (*)	US$ Mn	4	6	6	14	17
	TOURISM INDUSTRIES						
	Hotels and similar establishments						
9.1	Number of rooms	Units	..	..	..	..	..
9.2	Number of bed-places	Units	..	..	..	..	..
9.3	Occupancy rate	Percent	..	..	..	..	..
9.4	Average length of stay	Nights	..	..	..	..	..
	RELATED INDICATORS						
	Share of tourism expenditure (6.1) in:						
10.1	Gross Domestic Product (GDP)	Percent	4.8	12.8	12.1	12.7	11.9
10.2	Exports of goods	Percent	9.4	27.3	24.6	23.5	25.0
10.3	Exports of services	Percent	43.0	77.7	74.0	60.7	63.5

(*) Balance of Payments items: 6.1 to 6.3 correspond to the "Credit" side (and are receipts for the country) while 8.2 to 8.4 correspond to the "Debit" side (and are expenditures in other countries).

MONTSERRAT

	Basic Indicators	Units	2001	2002	2003	2004	2005
	INBOUND TOURISM						
	Arrivals						
1.1	Visitors	('000)	15.6	15.0	13.6	15.2	13.1
1.2	Tourists (overnight visitors)	('000)	9.8	9.8	8.4	10.1	9.7
1.3	Same-day visitors	('000)	5.8	5.2	5.2	5.1	3.4
1.4	Cruise passengers	('000)	0.3	..	0.8	0.4	0.3
	Arrivals by region						
2.1	Africa	('000)	..	..	..	..	..
2.2	Americas	('000)	7.2	7.0	5.9	6.8	6.4
2.3	Europe	('000)	2.5	2.8	2.4	3.2	3.2
2.4	East Asia and the Pacific	('000)	..	..	..	..	..
2.5	South Asia	('000)	..	..	..	..	..
2.6	Middle East	('000)	..	..	..	..	..
	Arrivals by means of transport used						
3.1	Air	('000)	1.8	1.9	1.3	1.6	5.6
3.2	Rail	('000)	..	..	..	..	..
3.3	Road	('000)	..	..	..	..	..
3.4	Sea	('000)	8.0	7.9	7.1	8.5	4.1
	Arrivals by purpose of visit						
4.1	Leisure, recreation and holidays	('000)	4.1	4.1	4.2	4.9	3.6
4.2	Business and professional	('000)	1.8	1.5	1.4	1.8	1.9
4.3	Other	('000)	3.9	4.2	2.8	3.4	4.2
	Accommodation						
5.1	Overnight stays in hotels and similar establishments	('000)	..	..	..	..	..
5.2	Guests in hotels and similar establishments	('000)	2.0	2.0	1.4	1.9	2.5
5.3	Overnight stays in all types of accommodation establishments	('000)	..	..	..	..	..
5.4	Average length of stay of non-resident tourists in all accommodation establishments	Nights	..	..	..	..	..
6.1	**Tourism expenditure in the country**	US$ Mn	..	..	..	..	..
6.2	"Travel" (*)	US$ Mn	8	9	7	9	9
6.3	"Passenger transport" (*)	US$ Mn	..	..	..	..	..
	DOMESTIC TOURISM						
	Accommodation						
7.1	Overnight stays in hotels and similar establishments	('000)	..	..	..	..	..
7.2	Guests in hotels and similar establishments	('000)	..	..	..	..	..
7.3	Overnight stays in all types of accommodation establishments	('000)	..	..	..	..	..
7.4	Average length of stay of resident tourists in all accommodation establishments	Nights	..	..	..	..	..
	OUTBOUND TOURISM						
8.1	**Departures**	('000)	..	..	..	..	..
8.2	**Tourism expenditure in other countries**	US$ Mn	..	..	..	..	..
8.3	"Travel" (*)	US$ Mn	2	2	2	2	3
8.4	"Passenger transport" (*)	US$ Mn	..	..	..	..	..
	TOURISM INDUSTRIES						
	Hotels and similar establishments						
9.1	Number of rooms	Units	..	..	..	..	..
9.2	Number of bed-places	Units	..	..	..	..	..
9.3	Occupancy rate	Percent	..	..	..	..	..
9.4	Average length of stay	Nights	..	..	..	..	..
	RELATED INDICATORS						
	Share of tourism expenditure (6.1) in: (**)						
10.1	Gross Domestic Product (GDP)	Percent	..	..	..	..	..
10.2	Exports of goods	Percent	800.0	450.0	350.0	180.0	450.0
10.3	Exports of services	Percent	53.3	64.3	58.3	60.0	60.0

(*) Balance of Payments items: 6.1 to 6.3 correspond to the "Credit" side (and are receipts for the country) while 8.2 to 8.4 correspond to the "Debit" side (and are expenditures in other countries).

(**) See Annex "Country notes".

	Basic Indicators	Units	2001	2002	2003	2004	2005
	INBOUND TOURISM						
	Arrivals						
1.1	Visitors	('000)	4,596	4,709	5,021	5,732	6,077
1.2	Tourists (overnight visitors)	('000)	4,380	4,453	4,761	5,477	5,843
1.3	Same-day visitors	('000)	..	..	..	..	..
1.4	Cruise passengers	('000)	216	255	260	256	233
	Arrivals by region						
2.1	Africa	('000)	97	92	103	123	144
2.2	Americas	('000)	149	119	108	128	140
2.3	Europe	('000)	1,864	1,869	1,880	2,309	2,607
2.4	East Asia and the Pacific	('000)	43	44	42	49	52
2.5	South Asia	('000)	6	6	5	6	8
2.6	Middle East	('000)	85	86	79	84	91
	Arrivals by means of transport used						
3.1	Air	('000)	2,146	2,095	2,139	2,548	2,986
3.2	Rail	('000)	..	..	..	..	..
3.3	Road	('000)	597	703	741	728	818
3.4	Sea	('000)	1,637	1,655	1,881	2,201	2,040
	Arrivals by purpose of visit						
4.1	Leisure, recreation and holidays	('000)	2,387	2,427	2,595	2,985	3,185
4.2	Business and professional	('000)	293	298	319	367	392
4.3	Other	('000)	1,699	1,728	1,847	2,125	2,267
	Accommodation						
5.1	Overnight stays in hotels and similar establishments	('000)	10,293	8,866	8,515	10,307	12,259
5.2	Guests in hotels and similar establishments	('000)	3,083	2,633	2,446	2,874	3,470
5.3	Overnight stays in all types of accommodation establishments	('000)	..	..	..	..	..
5.4	Average length of stay of non-resident tourists in all accommodation establishments	Nights	..	..	..	..	..
6.1	**Tourism expenditure in the country**	US$ Mn	2,966	3,157	3,802	4,541	5,426
6.2	"Travel" (*)	US$ Mn	2,583	2,646	3,221	3,923	4,610
6.3	"Passenger transport" (*)	US$ Mn	383	511	581	618	816
	DOMESTIC TOURISM						
	Accommodation						
7.1	Overnight stays in hotels and similar establishments	('000)	2,402	2,455	2,658	2,858	2,956
7.2	Guests in hotels and similar establishments	('000)	1,117	1,173	1,250	1,331	1,400
7.3	Overnight stays in all types of accommodation establishments	('000)	..	..	..	..	..
7.4	Average length of stay of resident tourists in all accommodation establishments	Nights	..	..	..	..	..
	OUTBOUND TOURISM						
8.1	**Departures**	('000)	1,701	1,533	1,612	1,603	2,247
8.2	**Tourism expenditure in other countries**	US$ Mn	589	670	845	913	999
8.3	"Travel" (*)	US$ Mn	389	444	548	575	612
8.4	"Passenger transport" (*)	US$ Mn	200	226	297	338	387
	TOURISM INDUSTRIES						
	Hotels and similar establishments						
9.1	Number of rooms	Units	47,755	49,389	52,918	57,431	59,864
9.2	Number of bed-places	Units	97,001	102,097	109,615	119,248	124,270
9.3	Occupancy rate	Percent	48.00	42.00	39.00	43.00	47.00
9.4	Average length of stay	Nights	6.50	5.70	5.50	5.40	..
	RELATED INDICATORS						
	Share of tourism expenditure (6.1) in:						
10.1	Gross Domestic Product (GDP)	Percent	8.7	8.7	8.7	9.1	10.5
10.2	Exports of goods	Percent	41.5	40.3	43.3	45.8	50.8
10.3	Exports of services	Percent	73.6	72.4	69.4	67.7	67.0

(*) Balance of Payments items: 6.1 to 6.3 correspond to the "Credit" side (and are receipts for the country) while 8.2 to 8.4 correspond to the "Debit" side (and are expenditures in other countries).

MOZAMBIQUE

	Basic Indicators	Units	2001	2002	2003	2004	2005
	INBOUND TOURISM						
	Arrivals						
1.1	Visitors	('000)	404	943	726	711	954
1.2	Tourists (overnight visitors)	('000)	323	541	441	470	578
1.3	Same-day visitors	('000)	81	402	285	241	376
1.4	Cruise passengers	('000)	..	..	..	..	..
	Arrivals by region						
2.1	Africa	('000)	368	848	592	623	852
2.2	Americas	('000)	..	10	5	6	12
2.3	Europe	('000)	37	54	43	57	48
2.4	East Asia and the Pacific	('000)	..	6	..	..	8
2.5	South Asia	('000)	..	..	..	..	..
2.6	Middle East	('000)	..	..	..	..	..
	Arrivals by means of transport used						
3.1	Air	('000)	15	55	70	116	156
3.2	Rail	('000)	..	..	..	..	..
3.3	Road	('000)	389	888	656	595	798
3.4	Sea	('000)	..	..	..	..	..
	Arrivals by purpose of visit						
4.1	Leisure, recreation and holidays	('000)	115	222	141	131	175
4.2	Business and professional	('000)	144	210	187	254	275
4.3	Other	('000)	64	109	113	85	128
	Accommodation						
5.1	Overnight stays in hotels and similar establishments	('000)	274	259	..	408	389
5.2	Guests in hotels and similar establishments	('000)	116	119	..	165	172
5.3	Overnight stays in all types of accommodation establishments	('000)	..	..	..	..	..
5.4	Average length of stay of non-resident tourists in all accommodation establishments	Nights	..	..	..	..	..
6.1	**Tourism expenditure in the country**	US$ Mn	..	65	106	96	138
6.2	"Travel" (*)	US$ Mn	64	63	98	95	130
6.3	"Passenger transport" (*)	US$ Mn	..	2	8	1	8
	DOMESTIC TOURISM						
	Accommodation						
7.1	Overnight stays in hotels and similar establishments	('000)	242	243	..	297	317
7.2	Guests in hotels and similar establishments	('000)	137	130	..	158	167
7.3	Overnight stays in all types of accommodation establishments	('000)	..	..	..	..	..
7.4	Average length of stay of resident tourists in all accommodation establishments	Nights	..	..	..	..	..
	OUTBOUND TOURISM						
8.1	**Departures**	('000)	..	..	..	..	..
8.2	**Tourism expenditure in other countries**	US$ Mn	132	115	141	140	187
8.3	"Travel" (*)	US$ Mn	114	113	140	134	176
8.4	"Passenger transport" (*)	US$ Mn	18	2	1	6	11
	TOURISM INDUSTRIES						
	Hotels and similar establishments						
9.1	Number of rooms	Units	..	..	6,899	..	..
9.2	Number of bed-places	Units	11,790	12,292	13,601	13,807	14,827
9.3	Occupancy rate	Percent	20.90	19.00	13.90	..	..
9.4	Average length of stay	Nights	2.00	2.30	2.10	2.19	2.10
	RELATED INDICATORS						
	Share of tourism expenditure (6.1) in:						
10.1	Gross Domestic Product (GDP)	Percent	..	1.6	2.2	1.6	2.1
10.2	Exports of goods	Percent	..	8.0	10.2	6.4	7.9
10.3	Exports of services	Percent	..	19.2	34.9	37.5	40.4

(*) Balance of Payments items: 6.1 to 6.3 correspond to the "Credit" side (and are receipts for the country) while 8.2 to 8.4 correspond to the "Debit" side (and are expenditures in other countries).

	Basic Indicators	Units	2001	2002	2003	2004	2005
	INBOUND TOURISM						
	Arrivals						
1.1	Visitors	('000)	475	487	597	657	660
1.2	Tourists (overnight visitors)	('000)	205	217	206	242	232
1.3	Same-day visitors	('000)	267	268	388	413	426
1.4	Cruise passengers	('000)	3	2	3	2	2
	Arrivals by region						
2.1	Africa	('000)	..	..	..	..	..
2.2	Americas	('000)	17	18	16	20	21
2.3	Europe	('000)	57	65	60	65	68
2.4	East Asia and the Pacific	('000)	122	124	116	142	130
2.5	South Asia	('000)	7	7	12	12	11
2.6	Middle East	('000)	1	2	1	2	2
	Arrivals by means of transport used						
3.1	Air	('000)	202	215	203	240	230
3.2	Rail	('000)	..	..	..	..	..
3.3	Road	('000)	270	270	391	415	428
3.4	Sea	('000)	3	2	3	2	2
	Arrivals by purpose of visit						
4.1	Leisure, recreation and holidays	('000)	126	138	129	164	151
4.2	Business and professional	('000)	37	37	44	40	36
4.3	Other	('000)	312	312	423	453	473
	Accommodation						
5.1	Overnight stays in hotels and similar establishments	('000)	1,434	1,521	1,416	1,679	1,626
5.2	Guests in hotels and similar establishments	('000)	..	..	..	..	..
5.3	Overnight stays in all types of accommodation establishments	('000)	..	..	..	..	..
5.4	Average length of stay of non-resident tourists in all accommodation establishments	Nights	7.00	7.00	7.50	7.00	7.00
6.1	**Tourism expenditure in the country**	US$ Mn	132	136	70	98	..
6.2	"Travel" (*)	US$ Mn	109	120	56	84	..
6.3	"Passenger transport" (*)	US$ Mn	23	16	14	14	..
	DOMESTIC TOURISM						
	Accommodation						
7.1	Overnight stays in hotels and similar establishments	('000)	..	..	..	..	..
7.2	Guests in hotels and similar establishments	('000)	..	..	..	..	..
7.3	Overnight stays in all types of accommodation establishments	('000)	..	..	..	..	..
7.4	Average length of stay of resident tourists in all accommodation establishments	Nights	..	..	..	..	..
	OUTBOUND TOURISM						
8.1	**Departures**	('000)	..	..	..	..	..
8.2	**Tourism expenditure in other countries**	US$ Mn	32	34	36	32	..
8.3	"Travel" (*)	US$ Mn	27	29	32	29	..
8.4	"Passenger transport" (*)	US$ Mn	5	5	4	3	..
	TOURISM INDUSTRIES						
	Hotels and similar establishments						
9.1	Number of rooms	Units	15,752	15,848	17,039	18,985	19,040
9.2	Number of bed-places	Units	31,504	31,696	34,078	37,970	38,080
9.3	Occupancy rate	Percent	22.00	23.00	20.00	21.00	20.00
9.4	Average length of stay	Nights	4.00	4.00	4.00	4.00	4.00
	RELATED INDICATORS						
	Share of tourism expenditure (6.1) in:						
10.1	Gross Domestic Product (GDP)	Percent	..	..	..	..	..
10.2	Exports of goods	Percent	5.2	5.6	2.6	3.3	..
10.3	Exports of services	Percent	32.4	31.9	28.1	38.4	..

(*) Balance of Payments items: 6.1 to 6.3 correspond to the "Credit" side (and are receipts for the country) while 8.2 to 8.4 correspond to the "Debit" side (and are expenditures in other countries).

NAMIBIA

	Basic Indicators	Units	2001	2002	2003	2004	2005
	INBOUND TOURISM						
	Arrivals						
1.1	Visitors	('000)	861	948	917	986	972
1.2	Tourists (overnight visitors)	('000)	670	757	695	..	778
1.3	Same-day visitors	('000)	30	42	44	..	78
1.4	Cruise passengers	('000)	..	..	..	..	..
	Arrivals by region						
2.1	Africa	('000)	536	592	526	..	602
2.2	Americas	('000)	9	10	12	..	15
2.3	Europe	('000)	112	141	142	..	146
2.4	East Asia and the Pacific	('000)	..	3	4	..	5
2.5	South Asia	('000)	..	..	..	..	..
2.6	Middle East	('000)	..	..	..	..	..
	Arrivals by means of transport used						
3.1	Air	('000)	165	183	167	167	185
3.2	Rail	('000)	..	3	4	..	2
3.3	Road	('000)	505	571	516	..	587
3.4	Sea	('000)	..	..	4	..	3
	Arrivals by purpose of visit						
4.1	Leisure, recreation and holidays	('000)	323	430	299	..	322
4.2	Business and professional	('000)	150	53	98	..	101
4.3	Other	('000)	198	274	298	..	355
	Accommodation						
5.1	Overnight stays in hotels and similar establishments	('000)	430	595	299	..	606
5.2	Guests in hotels and similar establishments	('000)	236	317	149	..	426
5.3	Overnight stays in all types of accommodation establishments	('000)	800	1,006	424	..	1,409
5.4	Average length of stay of non-resident tourists in all accommodation establishments	Nights	17.90	18.90	17.20	17.17	..
6.1	**Tourism expenditure in the country**	US$ Mn	264	251	383	426	..
6.2	"Travel" (*)	US$ Mn	236	218	333	405	348
6.3	"Passenger transport" (*)	US$ Mn	28	33	50	21	..
	DOMESTIC TOURISM						
	Accommodation						
7.1	Overnight stays in hotels and similar establishments	('000)	254	269	82	..	..
7.2	Guests in hotels and similar establishments	('000)	134	150	49	..	..
7.3	Overnight stays in all types of accommodation establishments	('000)	584	445	123	..	..
7.4	Average length of stay of resident tourists in all accommodation establishments	Nights	..	..	..	..	..
	OUTBOUND TOURISM						
8.1	**Departures**	('000)	..	..	..	..	..
8.2	**Tourism expenditure in other countries**	US$ Mn	..	..	..	..	..
8.3	"Travel" (*)	US$ Mn	71	55	74	122	108
8.4	"Passenger transport" (*)	US$ Mn	..	..	..	..	..
	TOURISM INDUSTRIES						
	Hotels and similar establishments						
9.1	Number of rooms	Units	2,352	2,726	2,749	..	2,900
9.2	Number of bed-places	Units	4,913	5,674	6,091	..	7,240
9.3	Occupancy rate	Percent	49.80	59.10	43.30	..	39.00
9.4	Average length of stay	Nights	1.90	1.90	1.90	..	1.90
	RELATED INDICATORS						
	Share of tourism expenditure (6.1) in:						
10.1	Gross Domestic Product (GDP)	Percent	8.2	8.0	8.6	7.5	..
10.2	Exports of goods	Percent	23.0	23.4	30.3	23.3	..
10.3	Exports of services	Percent	89.8	88.7	91.2	88.4	..

(*) Balance of Payments items: 6.1 to 6.3 correspond to the "Credit" side (and are receipts for the country) while 8.2 to 8.4 correspond to the "Debit" side (and are expenditures in other countries).

NEPAL

	Basic Indicators	Units	2001	2002	2003	2004	2005
	INBOUND TOURISM						
	Arrivals						
1.1	Visitors	('000)	..	..	..	..	..
1.2	Tourists (overnight visitors)	('000)	361	275	338	385	375
1.3	Same-day visitors	('000)	..	..	..	..	..
1.4	Cruise passengers	('000)	..	..	..	..	..
	Arrivals by region						
2.1	Africa	('000)	2	1	2	1	1
2.2	Americas	('000)	43	25	25	30	26
2.3	Europe	('000)	142	96	111	131	112
2.4	East Asia and the Pacific	('000)	88	68	92	97	93
2.5	South Asia	('000)	86	84	108	125	139
2.6	Middle East	('000)	..	..	..	..	..
	Arrivals by means of transport used						
3.1	Air	('000)	299	218	275	297	277
3.2	Rail	('000)	..	..	..	..	..
3.3	Road	('000)	62	57	63	88	98
3.4	Sea	('000)	..	..	..	..	..
	Arrivals by purpose of visit						
4.1	Leisure, recreation and holidays	('000)	288	169	164	237	222
4.2	Business and professional	('000)	37	35	41	31	39
4.3	Other	('000)	36	71	133	117	115
	Accommodation						
5.1	Overnight stays in hotels and similar establishments	('000)	..	..	..	..	..
5.2	Guests in hotels and similar establishments	('000)	..	..	..	..	..
5.3	Overnight stays in all types of accommodation establishments	('000)	..	..	..	..	..
5.4	Average length of stay of non-resident tourists in all accommodation establishments	Nights	11.93	7.92	9.60	13.51	9.09
6.1	**Tourism expenditure in the country**	US$ Mn	191	135	233	260	160
6.2	"Travel" (*)	US$ Mn	144	104	200	230	131
6.3	"Passenger transport" (*)	US$ Mn	47	31	33	30	29
	DOMESTIC TOURISM						
	Accommodation						
7.1	Overnight stays in hotels and similar establishments	('000)	..	..	..	..	..
7.2	Guests in hotels and similar establishments	('000)	..	..	..	..	..
7.3	Overnight stays in all types of accommodation establishments	('000)	..	..	..	..	..
7.4	Average length of stay of resident tourists in all accommodation establishments	Nights	..	..	..	..	..
	OUTBOUND TOURISM						
8.1	**Departures**	('000)	200	238	258	286	373
8.2	**Tourism expenditure in other countries**	US$ Mn	128	108	119	205	221
8.3	"Travel" (*)	US$ Mn	80	69	81	154	163
8.4	"Passenger transport" (*)	US$ Mn	48	39	38	51	58
	TOURISM INDUSTRIES						
	Hotels and similar establishments						
9.1	Number of rooms	Units	18,880	19,667	20,063	20,624	20,801
9.2	Number of bed-places	Units	36,163	37,616	38,270	39,107	39,384
9.3	Occupancy rate	Percent	..	..	..	..	..
9.4	Average length of stay	Nights	..	..	..	..	..
	RELATED INDICATORS						
	Share of tourism expenditure (6.1) in:						
10.1	Gross Domestic Product (GDP)	Percent	3.4	2.5	4.0	3.9	2.2
10.2	Exports of goods	Percent	26.5	21.4	33.1	33.6	17.7
10.3	Exports of services	Percent	46.2	44.3	62.6	56.4	42.1

(*) Balance of Payments items: 6.1 to 6.3 correspond to the "Credit" side (and are receipts for the country) while 8.2 to 8.4 correspond to the "Debit" side (and are expenditures in other countries).

NETHERLANDS

	Basic Indicators	Units	2001	2002	2003	2004	2005
	INBOUND TOURISM						
	Arrivals						
1.1	Visitors	('000)	..	..	..	..	..
1.2	Tourists (overnight visitors)	('000)	9,500	9,595	9,181	9,646	10,012
1.3	Same-day visitors	('000)	..	..	..	..	..
1.4	Cruise passengers	('000)	..	..	..	..	..
	Arrivals by region						
2.1	Africa	('000)	141	173	131	117	101
2.2	Americas	('000)	1,203	1,100	996	1,131	1,222
2.3	Europe	('000)	7,479	7,592	7,432	7,644	7,940
2.4	East Asia and the Pacific	('000)	678	731	622	754	749
2.5	South Asia	('000)	..	..	..	..	..
2.6	Middle East	('000)	..	..	..	..	..
	Arrivals by means of transport used						
3.1	Air	('000)	..	..	..	..	..
3.2	Rail	('000)	..	..	..	..	..
3.3	Road	('000)	..	..	..	..	..
3.4	Sea	('000)	..	..	..	..	..
	Arrivals by purpose of visit						
4.1	Leisure, recreation and holidays	('000)	..	..	..	..	..
4.2	Business and professional	('000)	..	..	..	..	..
4.3	Other	('000)	..	..	..	..	..
	Accommodation						
5.1	Overnight stays in hotels and similar establishments	('000)	14,955	14,922	13,798	14,616	15,143
5.2	Guests in hotels and similar establishments	('000)	7,445	7,433	6,931	7,601	8,081
5.3	Overnight stays in all types of accommodation establishments	('000)	25,502	26,368	25,342	25,385	25,210
5.4	Average length of stay of non-resident tourists in all accommodation establishments	Nights	2.70	2.70	2.80	2.60	2.50
6.1	**Tourism expenditure in the country**	US$ Mn	11,147	11,745	..	..	..
6.2	"Travel" (*)	US$ Mn	6,708	7,710	9,164	10,311	10,383
6.3	"Passenger transport" (*)	US$ Mn	4,439	4,035	..	..	..
	DOMESTIC TOURISM						
	Accommodation						
7.1	Overnight stays in hotels and similar establishments	('000)	13,608	13,593	13,384	13,761	14,375
7.2	Guests in hotels and similar establishments	('000)	7,601	7,515	7,379	7,911	8,301
7.3	Overnight stays in all types of accommodation establishments	('000)	54,973	56,004	55,864	55,518	54,951
7.4	Average length of stay of resident tourists in all accommodation establishments	Nights	..	..	..	..	..
	OUTBOUND TOURISM						
8.1	**Departures**	('000)	14,214	16,758	16,463	17,173	17,086
8.2	**Tourism expenditure in other countries**	US$ Mn	13,061	14,201	..	..	..
8.3	"Travel" (*)	US$ Mn	11,994	12,976	14,593	16,346	16,082
8.4	"Passenger transport" (*)	US$ Mn	1,067	1,225	..	..	..
	TOURISM INDUSTRIES						
	Hotels and similar establishments						
9.1	Number of rooms	Units	..	86,247	88,146	93,047	94,364
9.2	Number of bed-places	Units	174,000	177,435	180,158	189,835	192,215
9.3	Occupancy rate	Percent	46.20	45.50	42.80	42.10	42.10
9.4	Average length of stay	Nights	1.90	1.90	1.90	1.80	1.80
	RELATED INDICATORS						
	Share of tourism expenditure (6.1) in:						
10.1	Gross Domestic Product (GDP)	Percent	2.9	2.8	..	..	..
10.2	Exports of goods	Percent	5.5	5.6	..	..	..
10.3	Exports of services	Percent	21.8	20.9	..	..	..

(*) Balance of Payments items: 6.1 to 6.3 correspond to the "Credit" side (and are receipts for the country) while 8.2 to 8.4 correspond to the "Debit" side (and are expenditures in other countries).

Basic Indicators		Units	2001	2002	2003	2004	2005
	INBOUND TOURISM						
	Arrivals						
1.1	Visitors	('000)	152	158	166	177	182
1.2	Tourists (overnight visitors)	('000)	101	104	102	100	101
1.3	Same-day visitors	('000)	1	..	..	..	..
1.4	Cruise passengers	('000)	51	54	64	77	81
	Arrivals by region						
2.1	Africa	('000)	1	1	..	1	1
2.2	Americas	('000)	2	2	2	2	2
2.3	Europe	('000)	28	33	32	30	30
2.4	East Asia and the Pacific	('000)	70	68	65	66	68
2.5	South Asia	('000)	..	..	..	..	..
2.6	Middle East	('000)	..	..	..	..	..
	Arrivals by means of transport used						
3.1	Air	('000)	100	102	101	99	101
3.2	Rail	('000)	..	..	..	..	..
3.3	Road	('000)	..	..	..	..	..
3.4	Sea	('000)	1	2	1	1	..
	Arrivals by purpose of visit						
4.1	Leisure, recreation and holidays	('000)	77	70	71	73	76
4.2	Business and professional	('000)	10	12	10	11	12
4.3	Other	('000)	14	22	21	16	13
	Accommodation						
5.1	Overnight stays in hotels and similar establishments	('000)	400	352	343	369	350
5.2	Guests in hotels and similar establishments	('000)	86	82	75	79	77
5.3	Overnight stays in all types of accommodation establishments	('000)	..	..	..	..	..
5.4	Average length of stay of non-resident tourists in all accommodation establishments	Nights	13.70	16.30	15.60	16.20	16.80
6.1	**Tourism expenditure in the country**	US$ Mn	..	..	..	..	..
6.2	"Travel" (*)	US$ Mn	94	156	196	241	253
6.3	"Passenger transport" (*)	US$ Mn	..	..	..	..	..
	DOMESTIC TOURISM						
	Accommodation						
7.1	Overnight stays in hotels and similar establishments	('000)	162	193	240	263	299
7.2	Guests in hotels and similar establishments	('000)	51	54	59	63	69
7.3	Overnight stays in all types of accommodation establishments	('000)	..	..	..	..	..
7.4	Average length of stay of resident tourists in all accommodation establishments	Nights	..	..	..	..	..
	OUTBOUND TOURISM						
8.1	**Departures**	('000)	68	72	78	89	96
8.2	**Tourism expenditure in other countries**	US$ Mn	..	..	..	..	..
8.3	"Travel" (*)	US$ Mn	..	104	128	167	171
8.4	"Passenger transport" (*)	US$ Mn	..	..	..	..	..
	TOURISM INDUSTRIES						
	Hotels and similar establishments						
9.1	Number of rooms	Units	2,051	2,140	2,149	2,295	2,244
9.2	Number of bed-places	Units	..	..	..	..	..
9.3	Occupancy rate	Percent	47.80	57.10	59.70	59.60	61.30
9.4	Average length of stay	Nights	4.10	4.00	4.40	4.50	4.40
	RELATED INDICATORS						
	Share of tourism expenditure (6.1) in: (**)						
10.1	Gross Domestic Product (GDP)	Percent	..	..	..	..	..
10.2	Exports of goods	Percent	..	33.8	25.0	23.9	23.2
10.3	Exports of services	Percent	..	44.7	45.7	49.3	52.3

(*) Balance of Payments items: 6.1 to 6.3 correspond to the "Credit" side (and are receipts for the country) while 8.2 to 8.4 correspond to the "Debit" side (and are expenditures in other countries).

(**) See Annex "Country notes".

NEW ZEALAND

	Basic Indicators	Units	2001	2002	2003	2004	2005
	INBOUND TOURISM						
	Arrivals						
1.1	Visitors	('000)	1,909	2,045	2,104	2,334	2,366
1.2	Tourists (overnight visitors)	('000)	..	..	..	..	..
1.3	Same-day visitors	('000)	..	..	..	..	..
1.4	Cruise passengers	('000)	9	19	18	9	13
	Arrivals by region						
2.1	Africa	('000)	21	21	19	19	20
2.2	Americas	('000)	240	261	266	276	276
2.3	Europe	('000)	387	423	461	489	521
2.4	East Asia and the Pacific	('000)	1,159	1,240	1,272	1,468	1,484
2.5	South Asia	('000)	15	19	17	18	20
2.6	Middle East	('000)	5	6	7	8	9
	Arrivals by means of transport used						
3.1	Air	('000)	1,897	2,022	2,083	2,322	2,349
3.2	Rail	('000)	..	..	..	..	..
3.3	Road	('000)	..	..	..	..	..
3.4	Sea	('000)	13	23	21	12	17
	Arrivals by purpose of visit						
4.1	Leisure, recreation and holidays	('000)	989	1,074	1,083	1,190	1,192
4.2	Business and professional	('000)	247	252	262	303	319
4.3	Other	('000)	673	719	759	841	855
	Accommodation						
5.1	Overnight stays in hotels and similar establishments	('000)	..	..	..	..	..
5.2	Guests in hotels and similar establishments	('000)	..	..	..	..	..
5.3	Overnight stays in all types of accommodation establishments	('000)	10,452	11,625	11,683	12,927	13,449
5.4	Average length of stay of non-resident tourists in all accommodation establishments	Nights	..	..	..	..	..
6.1	**Tourism expenditure in the country**	US$ Mn	..	..	..	..	..
6.2	"Travel" (*)	US$ Mn	2,350	3,077	4,030	4,771	4,984
6.3	"Passenger transport" (*)	US$ Mn	..	..	..	..	..
	DOMESTIC TOURISM						
	Accommodation						
7.1	Overnight stays in hotels and similar establishments	('000)	..	..	..	..	..
7.2	Guests in hotels and similar establishments	('000)	..	..	..	..	..
7.3	Overnight stays in all types of accommodation establishments	('000)	16,697	17,294	17,894	18,022	18,062
7.4	Average length of stay of resident tourists in all accommodation establishments	Nights	..	..	..	..	..
	OUTBOUND TOURISM						
8.1	**Departures**	('000)	1,287	1,293	1,374	1,733	1,872
8.2	**Tourism expenditure in other countries**	US$ Mn	..	..	..	..	..
8.3	"Travel" (*)	US$ Mn	1,255	1,386	1,649	2,217	2,657
8.4	"Passenger transport" (*)	US$ Mn	..	..	..	..	..
	TOURISM INDUSTRIES						
	Hotels and similar establishments						
9.1	Number of rooms	Units	19,389	19,841	20,072	20,482	21,498
9.2	Number of bed-places	Units	..	..	..	..	..
9.3	Occupancy rate	Percent	52.30	54.24	54.28	56.07	54.15
9.4	Average length of stay	Nights	1.78	1.82	1.82	1.80	1.80
	RELATED INDICATORS						
	Share of tourism expenditure (6.1) in: (**)						
10.1	Gross Domestic Product (GDP)	Percent	4.5	5.1	5.0	4.8	4.6
10.2	Exports of goods	Percent	16.9	21.2	24.0	23.3	22.7
10.3	Exports of services	Percent	52.8	57.8	59.9	59.7	58.6

(*) Balance of Payments items: 6.1 to 6.3 correspond to the "Credit" side (and are receipts for the country) while 8.2 to 8.4 correspond to the "Debit" side (and are expenditures in other countries).

(**) See Annex "Country notes".

Basic Indicators		Units	2001	2002	2003	2004	2005
	INBOUND TOURISM						
	Arrivals						
1.1	Visitors	('000)	584	579	646	735	804
1.2	Tourists (overnight visitors)	('000)	483	472	526	615	712
1.3	Same-day visitors	('000)	90	102	110	113	79
1.4	Cruise passengers	('000)	10	5	10	7	13
	Arrivals by region						
2.1	Africa	('000)	1	..	..	1	1
2.2	Americas	('000)	432	417	464	553	619
2.3	Europe	('000)	40	45	49	53	59
2.4	East Asia and the Pacific	('000)	9	9	11	8	11
2.5	South Asia	('000)	1	1	1	..	2
2.6	Middle East	('000)	..	..	..	..	..
	Arrivals by means of transport used						
3.1	Air	('000)	172	164	180	204	235
3.2	Rail	('000)	..	..	..	..	..
3.3	Road	('000)	294	291	324	397	451
3.4	Sea	('000)	17	17	21	13	26
	Arrivals by purpose of visit						
4.1	Leisure, recreation and holidays	('000)	175	200	182	361	504
4.2	Business and professional	('000)	298	261	322	176	138
4.3	Other	('000)	10	11	22	77	70
	Accommodation						
5.1	Overnight stays in hotels and similar establishments	('000)	290	340	319	441	446
5.2	Guests in hotels and similar establishments	('000)	91	100	148	207	209
5.3	Overnight stays in all types of accommodation establishments	('000)	339	423	412	527	529
5.4	Average length of stay of non-resident tourists in all accommodation establishments	Nights	3.00	3.30	2.30	2.20	2.20
6.1	**Tourism expenditure in the country**	US$ Mn	138	138	164	196	211
6.2	"Travel" (*)	US$ Mn	135	135	160	192	207
6.3	"Passenger transport" (*)	US$ Mn	3	3	4	4	4
	DOMESTIC TOURISM						
	Accommodation						
7.1	Overnight stays in hotels and similar establishments	('000)	106	101	102	118	124
7.2	Guests in hotels and similar establishments	('000)	65	73	74	61	64
7.3	Overnight stays in all types of accommodation establishments	('000)	191	169	241	220	223
7.4	Average length of stay of resident tourists in all accommodation establishments	Nights	2.10	1.70	2.00	1.90	1.90
	OUTBOUND TOURISM						
8.1	**Departures**	('000)	499	532	562	701	740
8.2	**Tourism expenditure in other countries**	US$ Mn	128	125	139	154	161
8.3	"Travel" (*)	US$ Mn	76	69	75	89	90
8.4	"Passenger transport" (*)	US$ Mn	52	56	64	65	71
	TOURISM INDUSTRIES						
	Hotels and similar establishments						
9.1	Number of rooms	Units	3,442	4,225	4,418	4,753	5,335
9.2	Number of bed-places	Units	6,006	7,134	7,669	7,896	9,036
9.3	Occupancy rate	Percent	..	..	..	..	..
9.4	Average length of stay	Nights	2.60	2.60	2.20	2.10	2.10
	RELATED INDICATORS						
	Share of tourism expenditure (6.1) in:						
10.1	Gross Domestic Product (GDP)	Percent	3.4	3.4	4.0	4.4	4.3
10.2	Exports of goods	Percent	15.4	15.0	15.6	14.4	13.6
10.3	Exports of services	Percent	61.9	61.1	63.6	68.5	68.3

(*) Balance of Payments items: 6.1 to 6.3 correspond to the "Credit" side (and are receipts for the country) while 8.2 to 8.4 correspond to the "Debit" side (and are expenditures in other countries).

NIGER

Basic Indicators		Units	2001	2002	2003	2004	2005
	INBOUND TOURISM						
	Arrivals						
1.1	Visitors	('000)	..	..	..	..	..
1.2	Tourists (overnight visitors)	('000)	52	39	55	57	63
1.3	Same-day visitors	('000)	..	..	..	..	..
1.4	Cruise passengers	('000)	..	..	..	..	..
	Arrivals by region						
2.1	Africa	('000)	35	26	37	38	38
2.2	Americas	('000)	2	2	2	3	3
2.3	Europe	('000)	14	10	14	14	18
2.4	East Asia and the Pacific	('000)	1	1	1	2	3
2.5	South Asia	('000)	..	..	..	..	..
2.6	Middle East	('000)	..	..	..	..	..
	Arrivals by means of transport used						
3.1	Air	('000)	51	39	50	54	58
3.2	Rail	('000)	..	..	..	..	..
3.3	Road	('000)	..	..	..	..	..
3.4	Sea	('000)	..	..	..	..	..
	Arrivals by purpose of visit						
4.1	Leisure, recreation and holidays	('000)	9	7	9	10	11
4.2	Business and professional	('000)	28	21	29	31	37
4.3	Other	('000)	16	11	16	16	15
	Accommodation						
5.1	Overnight stays in hotels and similar establishments	('000)	116	101	121	124	140
5.2	Guests in hotels and similar establishments	('000)	..	..	..	..	..
5.3	Overnight stays in all types of accommodation establishments	('000)	246	215	253	263	298
5.4	Average length of stay of non-resident tourists in all accommodation establishments	Nights	7.00	7.00	8.00	8.00	8.00
6.1	**Tourism expenditure in the country**	US$ Mn	..	..	29	32	..
6.2	"Travel" (*)	US$ Mn	30	20	28	31	34
6.3	"Passenger transport" (*)	US$ Mn	..	..	1	1	..
	DOMESTIC TOURISM						
	Accommodation						
7.1	Overnight stays in hotels and similar establishments	('000)	31	37	25	15	18
7.2	Guests in hotels and similar establishments	('000)	12	13	11	8	8
7.3	Overnight stays in all types of accommodation establishments	('000)	..	..	..	..	..
7.4	Average length of stay of resident tourists in all accommodation establishments	Nights	..	..	..	..	..
	OUTBOUND TOURISM						
8.1	**Departures**	('000)	..	..	..	..	..
8.2	**Tourism expenditure in other countries**	US$ Mn	33	29	39	42	55
8.3	"Travel" (*)	US$ Mn	26	17	22	22	32
8.4	"Passenger transport" (*)	US$ Mn	7	12	17	20	23
	TOURISM INDUSTRIES						
	Hotels and similar establishments						
9.1	Number of rooms	Units	1,304	1,420	1,472	1,741	1,873
9.2	Number of bed-places	Units	2,563	2,750	2,843	3,011	3,285
9.3	Occupancy rate	Percent	43.00	37.00	44.00	45.00	46.00
9.4	Average length of stay	Nights	5.00	5.00	7.00	7.00	7.00
	RELATED INDICATORS						
	Share of tourism expenditure (6.1) in:						
10.1	Gross Domestic Product (GDP)	Percent	..	..	1.1	1.0	..
10.2	Exports of goods	Percent	..	..	8.2	7.3	..
10.3	Exports of services	Percent	..	..	46.0	34.4	..

(*) Balance of Payments items: 6.1 to 6.3 correspond to the "Credit" side (and are receipts for the country) while 8.2 to 8.4 correspond to the "Debit" side (and are expenditures in other countries).

Basic Indicators		Units	2001	2002	2003	2004	2005
	INBOUND TOURISM						
	Arrivals						
1.1	Visitors	('000)	1,753	2,046	2,253	2,646	2,778
1.2	Tourists (overnight visitors)	('000)	850	887	924	962	1,010
1.3	Same-day visitors	('000)	..	..	..	..	..
1.4	Cruise passengers	('000)	..	..	..	..	..
	Arrivals by region						
2.1	Africa	('000)	1,235	1,451	1,554	1,825	1,916
2.2	Americas	('000)	68	80	94	111	117
2.3	Europe	('000)	270	317	373	438	460
2.4	East Asia and the Pacific	('000)	108	111	130	153	161
2.5	South Asia	('000)	36	45	53	62	65
2.6	Middle East	('000)	29	35	41	48	50
	Arrivals by means of transport used						
3.1	Air	('000)	1,646	1,924	2,116	2,493	2,618
3.2	Rail	('000)	..	..	..	..	..
3.3	Road	('000)	86	99	112	125	131
3.4	Sea	('000)	21	22	25	28	29
	Arrivals by purpose of visit						
4.1	Leisure, recreation and holidays	('000)	282	293	304	315	331
4.2	Business and professional	('000)	426	445	464	483	507
4.3	Other	('000)	142	149	156	164	172
	Accommodation						
5.1	Overnight stays in hotels and similar establishments	('000)	..	..	..	..	..
5.2	Guests in hotels and similar establishments	('000)	..	..	..	..	..
5.3	Overnight stays in all types of accommodation establishments	('000)	..	..	..	..	..
5.4	Average length of stay of non-resident tourists in all accommodation establishments	Nights	..	..	..	..	..
6.1	**Tourism expenditure in the country**	US$ Mn	168	256	58	49	46
6.2	"Travel" (*)	US$ Mn	91	139	30	21	18
6.3	"Passenger transport" (*)	US$ Mn	77	117	28	28	28
	DOMESTIC TOURISM						
	Accommodation						
7.1	Overnight stays in hotels and similar establishments	('000)	..	..	..	..	..
7.2	Guests in hotels and similar establishments	('000)	..	..	..	..	..
7.3	Overnight stays in all types of accommodation establishments	('000)	..	..	..	..	..
7.4	Average length of stay of resident tourists in all accommodation establishments	Nights	..	..	..	..	..
	OUTBOUND TOURISM						
8.1	**Departures**	('000)	..	..	..	..	..
8.2	**Tourism expenditure in other countries**	US$ Mn	858	910	2,076	1,469	1,385
8.3	"Travel" (*)	US$ Mn	831	881	1,795	1,161	1,109
8.4	"Passenger transport" (*)	US$ Mn	27	29	281	308	276
	TOURISM INDUSTRIES						
	Hotels and similar establishments						
9.1	Number of rooms	Units	..	..	..	..	..
9.2	Number of bed-places	Units	27,678	30,699	37,528	37,738	38,870
9.3	Occupancy rate	Percent	75.40	79.30	82.50	85.60	81.20
9.4	Average length of stay	Nights	..	..	..	..	..
	RELATED INDICATORS						
	Share of tourism expenditure (6.1) in:						
10.1	Gross Domestic Product (GDP)	Percent	0.4	0.5	0.1	0.1	0.0
10.2	Exports of goods	Percent	0.9	1.6	0.2	0.1	0.1
10.3	Exports of services	Percent	10.2	10.1	1.7	1.5	1.1

(*) Balance of Payments items: 6.1 to 6.3 correspond to the "Credit" side (and are receipts for the country) while 8.2 to 8.4 correspond to the "Debit" side (and are expenditures in other countries).

NIUE

Basic Indicators		Units	2001	2002	2003	2004	2005
	INBOUND TOURISM						
	Arrivals						
1.1	Visitors	('000)	..	..	..	..	..
1.2	Tourists (overnight visitors)	('000)	1.4	2.1	2.7	2.6	2.8
1.3	Same-day visitors	('000)	..	..	..	..	..
1.4	Cruise passengers	('000)	..	..	..	..	..
	Arrivals by region						
2.1	Africa	('000)	..	..	..	..	..
2.2	Americas	('000)	0.2	0.3	0.2	0.1	0.2
2.3	Europe	('000)	0.1	0.3	0.2	0.2	0.3
2.4	East Asia and the Pacific	('000)	1.1	1.4	2.2	2.2	2.3
2.5	South Asia	('000)	..	..	..	..	..
2.6	Middle East	('000)	..	..	..	..	..
	Arrivals by means of transport used						
3.1	Air	('000)	1.4	2.1	2.7	2.6	2.8
3.2	Rail	('000)	..	..	..	..	..
3.3	Road	('000)	..	..	..	..	..
3.4	Sea	('000)	..	..	..	..	..
	Arrivals by purpose of visit						
4.1	Leisure, recreation and holidays	('000)	0.8	1.2	1.4	0.7	1.2
4.2	Business and professional	('000)	0.3	0.4	0.4	0.8	0.7
4.3	Other	('000)	0.3	0.5	0.9	1.0	0.9
	Accommodation						
5.1	Overnight stays in hotels and similar establishments	('000)	..	..	..	..	..
5.2	Guests in hotels and similar establishments	('000)	..	..	..	..	..
5.3	Overnight stays in all types of accommodation establishments	('000)	..	..	..	..	..
5.4	Average length of stay of non-resident tourists in all accommodation establishments	Nights	..	..	..	..	..
6.1	**Tourism expenditure in the country**	US$ Mn	..	..	..	..	1.2
6.2	"Travel" (*)	US$ Mn	..	..	..	..	..
6.3	"Passenger transport" (*)	US$ Mn	..	..	..	..	..
	DOMESTIC TOURISM						
	Accommodation						
7.1	Overnight stays in hotels and similar establishments	('000)	..	..	..	..	..
7.2	Guests in hotels and similar establishments	('000)	..	..	..	..	..
7.3	Overnight stays in all types of accommodation establishments	('000)	..	..	..	..	..
7.4	Average length of stay of resident tourists in all accommodation establishments	Nights	..	..	..	..	..
	OUTBOUND TOURISM						
8.1	**Departures**	('000)	1.0	1.1	..	1.5	..
8.2	**Tourism expenditure in other countries**	US$ Mn	..	..	..	..	..
8.3	"Travel" (*)	US$ Mn	..	..	..	..	..
8.4	"Passenger transport" (*)	US$ Mn	..	..	..	..	..
	TOURISM INDUSTRIES						
	Hotels and similar establishments						
9.1	Number of rooms	Units	72	72	72	42	58
9.2	Number of bed-places	Units	139	139	139	52	110
9.3	Occupancy rate	Percent	..	..	..	..	..
9.4	Average length of stay	Nights	..	7.00	7.00	7.00	7.00
	RELATED INDICATORS						
	Share of tourism expenditure (6.1) in:						
10.1	Gross Domestic Product (GDP)	Percent	..	..	..	..	..
10.2	Exports of goods	Percent	..	..	..	..	..
10.3	Exports of services	Percent	..	..	..	..	..

(*) Balance of Payments items: 6.1 to 6.3 correspond to the "Credit" side (and are receipts for the country) while 8.2 to 8.4 correspond to the "Debit" side (and are expenditures in other countries).

	Basic Indicators	Units	2001	2002	2003	2004	2005
	INBOUND TOURISM						
	Arrivals						
1.1	Visitors	('000)	444	476	459	536	507
1.2	Tourists (overnight visitors)	('000)	438	466	452	525	498
1.3	Same-day visitors	('000)	..	..	..	..	..
1.4	Cruise passengers	('000)	6	10	7	11	9
	Arrivals by region						
2.1	Africa	('000)	..	..	..	..	..
2.2	Americas	('000)	35	36	35	37	38
2.3	Europe	('000)	1	1	..	1	1
2.4	East Asia and the Pacific	('000)	407	437	423	495	465
2.5	South Asia	('000)	..	..	..	..	..
2.6	Middle East	('000)	..	..	..	..	..
	Arrivals by means of transport used						
3.1	Air	('000)	438	466	452	525	498
3.2	Rail	('000)	..	..	..	..	..
3.3	Road	('000)	..	..	..	..	..
3.4	Sea	('000)	6	10	7	11	9
	Arrivals by purpose of visit						
4.1	Leisure, recreation and holidays	('000)	444	476	459	536	507
4.2	Business and professional	('000)	..	..	..	..	..
4.3	Other	('000)	..	..	..	..	..
	Accommodation						
5.1	Overnight stays in hotels and similar establishments	('000)	..	..	..	..	..
5.2	Guests in hotels and similar establishments	('000)	..	..	..	..	..
5.3	Overnight stays in all types of accommodation establishments	('000)	..	..	..	..	..
5.4	Average length of stay of non-resident tourists in all accommodation establishments	Nights	..	..	..	..	..
6.1	**Tourism expenditure in the country**	US$ Mn	..	..	..	..	..
6.2	"Travel" (*)	US$ Mn	..	..	..	..	..
6.3	"Passenger transport" (*)	US$ Mn	..	..	..	..	..
	DOMESTIC TOURISM						
	Accommodation						
7.1	Overnight stays in hotels and similar establishments	('000)	..	..	..	..	..
7.2	Guests in hotels and similar establishments	('000)	..	..	..	..	..
7.3	Overnight stays in all types of accommodation establishments	('000)	..	..	..	..	..
7.4	Average length of stay of resident tourists in all accommodation establishments	Nights	..	..	..	..	..
	OUTBOUND TOURISM						
8.1	**Departures**	('000)	..	..	..	..	..
8.2	**Tourism expenditure in other countries**	US$ Mn	..	..	..	..	..
8.3	"Travel" (*)	US$ Mn	..	..	..	..	..
8.4	"Passenger transport" (*)	US$ Mn	..	..	..	..	..
	TOURISM INDUSTRIES						
	Hotels and similar establishments						
9.1	Number of rooms	Units	4,521	4,419	4,231	4,192	4,122
9.2	Number of bed-places	Units	..	..	..	..	..
9.3	Occupancy rate	Percent	54.43	63.36	64.88	71.75	70.16
9.4	Average length of stay	Nights	..	..	..	..	..
	RELATED INDICATORS						
	Share of tourism expenditure (6.1) in:						
10.1	Gross Domestic Product (GDP)	Percent	..	..	..	..	..
10.2	Exports of goods	Percent	..	..	..	..	..
10.3	Exports of services	Percent	..	..	..	..	..

(*) Balance of Payments items: 6.1 to 6.3 correspond to the "Credit" side (and are receipts for the country) while 8.2 to 8.4 correspond to the "Debit" side (and are expenditures in other countries).

NORWAY

	Basic Indicators	Units	2001	2002	2003	2004	2005
	INBOUND TOURISM						
	Arrivals						
1.1	Visitors	('000)	5,115	5,247	5,446	6,035	6,557
1.2	Tourists (overnight visitors)	('000)	3,073	3,111	3,269	3,628	3,859
1.3	Same-day visitors	('000)	1,238	1,222	1,163	1,200	1,254
1.4	Cruise passengers	('000)	804	914	1,014	1,207	1,444
	Arrivals by region						
2.1	Africa	('000)	..	..	..	..	..
2.2	Americas	('000)	141	126	144	176	155
2.3	Europe	('000)	2,817	2,865	3,009	3,307	3,521
2.4	East Asia and the Pacific	('000)	..	35	35	35	41
2.5	South Asia	('000)	..	..	..	..	..
2.6	Middle East	('000)	..	..	..	..	..
	Arrivals by means of transport used						
3.1	Air	('000)	998	1,011	1,170	1,414	1,560
3.2	Rail	('000)	78	83	79	123	108
3.3	Road	('000)	1,342	1,327	1,322	1,398	1,488
3.4	Sea	('000)	655	690	698	694	703
	Arrivals by purpose of visit						
4.1	Leisure, recreation and holidays	('000)	2,297	2,373	2,520	2,780	2,946
4.2	Business and professional	('000)	776	738	749	848	913
4.3	Other	('000)	..	..	..	..	..
	Accommodation						
5.1	Overnight stays in hotels and similar establishments	('000)	4,815	4,706	4,375	4,596	4,761
5.2	Guests in hotels and similar establishments	('000)	2,686	2,561	2,439	2,556	2,656
5.3	Overnight stays in all types of accommodation establishments	('000)	7,322	7,275	6,956	7,442	7,651
5.4	Average length of stay of non-resident tourists in all accommodation establishments	Nights	..	..	..	..	..
6.1	**Tourism expenditure in the country**	US$ Mn	2,380	2,581	2,989	3,455	3,884
6.2	"Travel" (*)	US$ Mn	1,958	2,179	2,500	2,931	3,278
6.3	"Passenger transport" (*)	US$ Mn	422	402	489	524	606
	DOMESTIC TOURISM						
	Accommodation						
7.1	Overnight stays in hotels and similar establishments	('000)	11,599	11,482	11,262	11,764	12,349
7.2	Guests in hotels and similar establishments	('000)	7,173	7,029	6,998	7,319	7,736
7.3	Overnight stays in all types of accommodation establishments	('000)	17,010	17,109	16,853	17,832	18,628
7.4	Average length of stay of resident tourists in all accommodation establishments	Nights	..	..	..	..	..
	OUTBOUND TOURISM						
8.1	**Departures**	('000)	2,348	2,629	2,588	2,916	3,122
8.2	**Tourism expenditure in other countries**	US$ Mn	4,671	5,542	6,992	8,788	..
8.3	"Travel" (*)	US$ Mn	4,363	5,121	6,619	8,383	9,753
8.4	"Passenger transport" (*)	US$ Mn	308	421	373	405	..
	TOURISM INDUSTRIES						
	Hotels and similar establishments						
9.1	Number of rooms	Units	66,427	66,728	67,113	66,373	67,522
9.2	Number of bed-places	Units	143,802	143,635	143,799	141,096	143,568
9.3	Occupancy rate	Percent	37.00	36.30	35.50	37.00	38.10
9.4	Average length of stay	Nights	1.67	..	..	..	..
	RELATED INDICATORS						
	Share of tourism expenditure (6.1) in:						
10.1	Gross Domestic Product (GDP)	Percent	1.4	1.4	1.4	1.4	1.4
10.2	Exports of goods	Percent	4.0	4.3	4.4	4.2	3.7
10.3	Exports of services	Percent	13.5	13.8	14.2	13.5	13.5

(*) Balance of Payments items: 6.1 to 6.3 correspond to the "Credit" side (and are receipts for the country) while 8.2 to 8.4 correspond to the "Debit" side (and are expenditures in other countries).

	Basic Indicators	Units	2001	2002	2003	2004	2005
	INBOUND TOURISM						
	Arrivals						
1.1	Visitors	('000)	1,095	1,112	1,210	1,407	..
1.2	Tourists (overnight visitors)	('000)	829	817	1,039	1,195	..
1.3	Same-day visitors	('000)	266	295	171	212	..
1.4	Cruise passengers	('000)	..	..	..	..	..
	Arrivals by region						
2.1	Africa	('000)	20	17	19	28	18
2.2	Americas	('000)	49	36	36	40	34
2.3	Europe	('000)	197	197	164	281	337
2.4	East Asia and the Pacific	('000)	37	66	51	55	69
2.5	South Asia	('000)	77	85	102	131	127
2.6	Middle East	('000)	155	193	205	249	199
	Arrivals by means of transport used						
3.1	Air	('000)	..	..	..	..	..
3.2	Rail	('000)	..	..	..	..	..
3.3	Road	('000)	..	..	..	..	..
3.4	Sea	('000)	..	..	..	..	..
	Arrivals by purpose of visit						
4.1	Leisure, recreation and holidays	('000)	381	392	349	491	..
4.2	Business and professional	('000)	152	164	213	298	..
4.3	Other	('000)	562	556	648	618	..
	Accommodation						
5.1	Overnight stays in hotels and similar establishments	('000)	744	739	777	995	1,394
5.2	Guests in hotels and similar establishments	('000)	647	643	630	908	1,114
5.3	Overnight stays in all types of accommodation establishments	('000)	3,815	3,965	..	..	..
5.4	Average length of stay of non-resident tourists in all accommodation establishments	Nights	4.60	4.90	..	..	..
6.1	**Tourism expenditure in the country**	US$ Mn	539	539	546	604	679
6.2	"Travel" (*)	US$ Mn	385	393	385	414	481
6.3	"Passenger transport" (*)	US$ Mn	154	146	161	190	198
	DOMESTIC TOURISM						
	Accommodation						
7.1	Overnight stays in hotels and similar establishments	('000)	..	221	301	326	354
7.2	Guests in hotels and similar establishments	('000)	208	219	257	293	293
7.3	Overnight stays in all types of accommodation establishments	('000)	..	..	..	..	..
7.4	Average length of stay of resident tourists in all accommodation establishments	Nights	..	..	..	..	..
	OUTBOUND TOURISM						
8.1	**Departures**	('000)	..	2,060	..	..	..
8.2	**Tourism expenditure in other countries**	US$ Mn	703	702	752	796	838
8.3	"Travel" (*)	US$ Mn	518	530	578	616	643
8.4	"Passenger transport" (*)	US$ Mn	185	172	174	180	195
	TOURISM INDUSTRIES						
	Hotels and similar establishments						
9.1	Number of rooms	Units	5,729	6,078	6,462	6,980	7,247
9.2	Number of bed-places	Units	8,649	9,208	9,778	10,839	11,245
9.3	Occupancy rate	Percent	45.00	41.00	39.00	43.00	47.00
9.4	Average length of stay	Nights	..	..	..	..	..
	RELATED INDICATORS						
	Share of tourism expenditure (6.1) in:						
10.1	Gross Domestic Product (GDP)	Percent	2.7	2.7	2.5	2.5	..
10.2	Exports of goods	Percent	4.9	4.8	4.7	4.5	3.6
10.3	Exports of services	Percent	88.9	88.9	84.7	83.2	82.6

(*) Balance of Payments items: 6.1 to 6.3 correspond to the "Credit" side (and are receipts for the country) while 8.2 to 8.4 correspond to the "Debit" side (and are expenditures in other countries).

PAKISTAN

	Basic Indicators	Units	2001	2002	2003	2004	2005
	INBOUND TOURISM						
	Arrivals						
1.1	Visitors	('000)	..	..	..	..	..
1.2	Tourists (overnight visitors)	('000)	500	498	501	648	798
1.3	Same-day visitors	('000)	..	..	..	..	..
1.4	Cruise passengers	('000)	..	..	..	..	..
	Arrivals by region						
2.1	Africa	('000)	15	12	12	13	15
2.2	Americas	('000)	82	88	86	103	147
2.3	Europe	('000)	205	215	193	281	357
2.4	East Asia and the Pacific	('000)	43	44	44	60	84
2.5	South Asia	('000)	124	116	147	160	159
2.6	Middle East	('000)	30	22	20	28	32
	Arrivals by means of transport used						
3.1	Air	('000)	407	408	385	536	682
3.2	Rail	('000)	44	..	..	..	34
3.3	Road	('000)	49	90	116	112	82
3.4	Sea	('000)	..	..	..	..	..
	Arrivals by purpose of visit						
4.1	Leisure, recreation and holidays	('000)	77	76	77	99	122
4.2	Business and professional	('000)	127	127	127	165	203
4.3	Other	('000)	296	295	297	384	473
	Accommodation						
5.1	Overnight stays in hotels and similar establishments	('000)	1,583	1,096	1,577	2,773	..
5.2	Guests in hotels and similar establishments	('000)	1,503	1,005	1,448	2,353	..
5.3	Overnight stays in all types of accommodation establishments	('000)	..	..	..	..	..
5.4	Average length of stay of non-resident tourists in all accommodation establishments	Nights	24.00	24.00	24.00	24.00	24.00
6.1	**Tourism expenditure in the country**	US$ Mn	533	562	620	765	827
6.2	"Travel" (*)	US$ Mn	88	97	122	179	181
6.3	"Passenger transport" (*)	US$ Mn	445	465	498	586	646
	DOMESTIC TOURISM						
	Accommodation						
7.1	Overnight stays in hotels and similar establishments	('000)	10,747	11,084	12,379	12,892	..
7.2	Guests in hotels and similar establishments	('000)	7,772	8,565	9,863	9,590	..
7.3	Overnight stays in all types of accommodation establishments	('000)	..	..	..	..	..
7.4	Average length of stay of resident tourists in all accommodation establishments	Nights	..	..	..	..	..
	OUTBOUND TOURISM						
8.1	**Departures**	('000)	..	..	..	..	..
8.2	**Tourism expenditure in other countries**	US$ Mn	555	491	1,163	1,612	1,748
8.3	"Travel" (*) (**)	US$ Mn	252	255	925	1,268	1,275
8.4	"Passenger transport" (*)	US$ Mn	303	236	238	344	473
	TOURISM INDUSTRIES						
	Hotels and similar establishments						
9.1	Number of rooms	Units	35,522	35,883	36,451	37,391	38,183
9.2	Number of bed-places	Units	53,286	54,725	54,677	56,087	57,275
9.3	Occupancy rate	Percent	55.00	55.00	55.00	58.00	58.00
9.4	Average length of stay	Nights	1.31	1.27	1.23	1.28	1.28
	RELATED INDICATORS						
	Share of tourism expenditure (6.1) in:						
10.1	Gross Domestic Product (GDP)	Percent	0.7	0.8	0.8	0.8	0.7
10.2	Exports of goods	Percent	5.8	5.7	5.2	5.8	5.4
10.3	Exports of services	Percent	36.5	23.1	20.9	27.8	22.5

(*) Balance of Payments items: 6.1 to 6.3 correspond to the "Credit" side (and are receipts for the country) while 8.2 to 8.4 correspond to the "Debit" side (and are expenditures in other countries).

(**) See Annex "Country notes".

	Basic Indicators		Units	2001	2002	2003	2004	2005
	INBOUND TOURISM							
	Arrivals							
1.1	Visitors		('000)	..	..	..	..	..
1.2	Tourists (overnight visitors)		('000)	54	59	68	95	86
1.3	Same-day visitors		('000)	..	..	..	..	..
1.4	Cruise passengers		('000)	..	..	..	..	..
	Arrivals by region							
2.1	Africa		('000)	..	..	..	..	..
2.2	Americas		('000)	5	5	5	7	6
2.3	Europe		('000)	1	1	1	2	2
2.4	East Asia and the Pacific		('000)	46	52	61	84	76
2.5	South Asia		('000)	..	..	..	..	..
2.6	Middle East		('000)	..	..	..	..	..
	Arrivals by means of transport used							
3.1	Air		('000)	54	59	68	95	86
3.2	Rail		('000)	..	..	..	..	..
3.3	Road		('000)	..	..	..	..	..
3.4	Sea		('000)	..	..	..	..	..
	Arrivals by purpose of visit							
4.1	Leisure, recreation and holidays		('000)	46	50	60	83	76
4.2	Business and professional		('000)	3	3	3	4	4
4.3	Other		('000)	5	5	5	7	6
	Accommodation							
5.1	Overnight stays in hotels and similar establishments		('000)	..	..	..	..	..
5.2	Guests in hotels and similar establishments		('000)	..	..	..	..	..
5.3	Overnight stays in all types of accommodation establishments		('000)	..	..	..	..	..
5.4	Average length of stay of non-resident tourists in all accommodation establishments		Nights	..	..	..	..	..
6.1	**Tourism expenditure in the country**	(**)	US$ Mn	59	47	76	97	..
6.2	"Travel" (*)		US$ Mn	..	..	..	..	..
6.3	"Passenger transport" (*)		US$ Mn	..	..	..	..	..
	DOMESTIC TOURISM							
	Accommodation							
7.1	Overnight stays in hotels and similar establishments		('000)	..	..	..	..	..
7.2	Guests in hotels and similar establishments		('000)	..	..	..	..	..
7.3	Overnight stays in all types of accommodation establishments		('000)	..	..	..	..	..
7.4	Average length of stay of resident tourists in all accommodation establishments		Nights	..	..	..	..	..
	OUTBOUND TOURISM							
8.1	**Departures**		('000)	..	..	..	..	..
8.2	**Tourism expenditure in other countries**	(**)	US$ Mn	2	2	2	2	..
8.3	"Travel" (*)		US$ Mn	..	..	..	..	..
8.4	"Passenger transport" (*)		US$ Mn	..	..	..	..	..
	TOURISM INDUSTRIES							
	Hotels and similar establishments							
9.1	Number of rooms		Units	925	967	959	959	..
9.2	Number of bed-places		Units	..	..	..	..	..
9.3	Occupancy rate		Percent	..	..	..	..	..
9.4	Average length of stay		Nights	7.00	7.00	7.00	6.00	..
	RELATED INDICATORS							
	Share of tourism expenditure (6.1) in:							
10.1	Gross Domestic Product (GDP)		Percent	..	..	..	..	..
10.2	Exports of goods		Percent	..	..	..	..	..
10.3	Exports of services		Percent	..	..	..	..	..

(*) Balance of Payments items: 6.1 to 6.3 correspond to the "Credit" side (and are receipts for the country) while 8.2 to 8.4 correspond to the "Debit" side (and are expenditures in other countries).

(**) See Annex "Country notes".

PALESTINE

	Basic Indicators	Units	2001	2002	2003	2004	2005
	INBOUND TOURISM						
	Arrivals						
1.1	Visitors	('000)	..	..	..	..	..
1.2	Tourists (overnight visitors)	('000)	43	33	37	56	88
1.3	Same-day visitors	('000)	..	..	..	..	..
1.4	Cruise passengers	('000)	..	..	..	..	..
	Arrivals by region						
2.1	Africa	('000)	1	1	1	1	1
2.2	Americas	('000)	8	6	6	11	14
2.3	Europe	('000)	24	18	24	35	55
2.4	East Asia and the Pacific	('000)	10	6	5	8	16
2.5	South Asia	('000)	..	..	..	..	..
2.6	Middle East	('000)	1	1	1	1	2
	Arrivals by means of transport used						
3.1	Air	('000)	..	..	..	..	..
3.2	Rail	('000)	..	..	..	..	..
3.3	Road	('000)	..	..	..	..	..
3.4	Sea	('000)	..	..	..	..	..
	Arrivals by purpose of visit						
4.1	Leisure, recreation and holidays	('000)	..	..	..	..	..
4.2	Business and professional	('000)	..	..	..	..	..
4.3	Other	('000)	..	..	..	..	..
	Accommodation						
5.1	Overnight stays in hotels and similar establishments	('000)	132	103	113	164	251
5.2	Guests in hotels and similar establishments	('000)	43	33	37	56	88
5.3	Overnight stays in all types of accommodation establishments	('000)	217	204	239	..	..
5.4	Average length of stay of non-resident tourists in all accommodation establishments	Nights	3.20	3.30	3.20	..	..
6.1	**Tourism expenditure in the country**	US$ Mn	..	..	..	..	..
6.2	"Travel" (*)	US$ Mn	35	33	107	56	..
6.3	"Passenger transport" (*)	US$ Mn	..	..	..	..	..
	DOMESTIC TOURISM						
	Accommodation						
7.1	Overnight stays in hotels and similar establishments	('000)	53	66	86	104	99
7.2	Guests in hotels and similar establishments	('000)	17	18	26	44	44
7.3	Overnight stays in all types of accommodation establishments	('000)	..	..	..	..	..
7.4	Average length of stay of resident tourists in all accommodation establishments	Nights	3.00	3.70	3.30	2.40	2.30
	OUTBOUND TOURISM						
8.1	**Departures**	('000)	..	..	..	..	..
8.2	**Tourism expenditure in other countries**	US$ Mn	..	..	..	..	..
8.3	"Travel" (*)	US$ Mn	424	388	317	286	..
8.4	"Passenger transport" (*)	US$ Mn	..	..	..	..	..
	TOURISM INDUSTRIES						
	Hotels and similar establishments						
9.1	Number of rooms	Units	2,860	3,098	3,050	3,554	3,691
9.2	Number of bed-places	Units	6,240	6,473	6,620	7,575	7,923
9.3	Occupancy rate	Percent	9.20	10.10	11.70	13.50	15.50
9.4	Average length of stay	Nights	3.10	3.30	3.20	2.50	2.70
	RELATED INDICATORS						
	Share of tourism expenditure (6.1) in: (**)						
10.1	Gross Domestic Product (GDP)	Percent	0.9	1.0	3.1	..	..
10.2	Exports of goods	Percent	7.8	9.0	28.6	13.9	..
10.3	Exports of services	Percent	19.7	17.2	50.0	30.9	..

(*) Balance of Payments items: 6.1 to 6.3 correspond to the "Credit" side (and are receipts for the country) while 8.2 to 8.4 correspond to the "Debit" side (and are expenditures in other countries).

(**) See Annex "Country notes".

	Basic Indicators	Units	2001	2002	2003	2004	2005
	INBOUND TOURISM						
	Arrivals						
1.1	Visitors	('000)	737	800	897	1,004	1,070
1.2	Tourists (overnight visitors)	('000)	519	534	566	621	702
1.3	Same-day visitors	('000)	218	267	331	383	368
1.4	Cruise passengers	('000)	92	194	224	290	255
	Arrivals by region						
2.1	Africa	('000)	..	..	..	..	..
2.2	Americas	('000)	367	376	411	439	507
2.3	Europe	('000)	32	38	43	45	52
2.4	East Asia and the Pacific	('000)	11	12	14	14	16
2.5	South Asia	('000)	..	..	..	..	..
2.6	Middle East	('000)	..	..	..	..	..
	Arrivals by means of transport used						
3.1	Air	('000)	392	409	450	476	546
3.2	Rail	('000)	..	..	..	..	..
3.3	Road	('000)	71	73	65	71	81
3.4	Sea	('000)	13	15	10	23	21
	Arrivals by purpose of visit						
4.1	Leisure, recreation and holidays	('000)	214	230	246	260	299
4.2	Business and professional	('000)	142	141	164	174	199
4.3	Other	('000)	37	38	40	42	48
	Accommodation						
5.1	Overnight stays in hotels and similar establishments	('000)	1,055	1,028	1,059	1,165	1,453
5.2	Guests in hotels and similar establishments	('000)	..	..	..	..	..
5.3	Overnight stays in all types of accommodation establishments	('000)	..	..	..	..	..
5.4	Average length of stay of non-resident tourists in all accommodation establishments	Nights	10.60	10.40	10.50	9.43	10.40
6.1	**Tourism expenditure in the country**	US$ Mn	665	710	804	903	1,108
6.2	"Travel" (*)	US$ Mn	477	513	585	651	780
6.3	"Passenger transport" (*)	US$ Mn	188	197	219	252	328
	DOMESTIC TOURISM						
	Accommodation						
7.1	Overnight stays in hotels and similar establishments	('000)	..	..	..	..	..
7.2	Guests in hotels and similar establishments	('000)	..	..	..	..	..
7.3	Overnight stays in all types of accommodation establishments	('000)	..	..	..	..	..
7.4	Average length of stay of resident tourists in all accommodation establishments	Nights	..	..	..	..	..
	OUTBOUND TOURISM						
8.1	**Departures**	('000)	200	200	227	256	285
8.2	**Tourism expenditure in other countries**	US$ Mn	227	252	267	294	388
8.3	"Travel" (*)	US$ Mn	174	179	208	239	271
8.4	"Passenger transport" (*)	US$ Mn	53	73	59	55	117
	TOURISM INDUSTRIES						
	Hotels and similar establishments						
9.1	Number of rooms	Units	14,165	14,302	14,488	14,898	15,700
9.2	Number of bed-places	Units	27,985	27,981	28,434	29,523	31,400
9.3	Occupancy rate	Percent	37.23	37.97	44.34	44.07	48.63
9.4	Average length of stay	Nights	2.30	2.08	2.10	2.20	2.22
	RELATED INDICATORS						
	Share of tourism expenditure (6.1) in:						
10.1	Gross Domestic Product (GDP)	Percent	5.6	5.8	6.2	6.4	7.2
10.2	Exports of goods	Percent	11.1	13.4	15.9	14.9	15.4
10.3	Exports of services	Percent	33.4	31.2	32.0	33.0	35.3

(*) Balance of Payments items: 6.1 to 6.3 correspond to the "Credit" side (and are receipts for the country) while 8.2 to 8.4 correspond to the "Debit" side (and are expenditures in other countries).

PAPUA NEW GUINEA

Basic Indicators		Units	2001	2002	2003	2004	2005
	INBOUND TOURISM						
	Arrivals						
1.1	Visitors	('000)	..	..	..	..	..
1.2	Tourists (overnight visitors)	('000)	54	54	56	59	69
1.3	Same-day visitors	('000)	..	..	..	..	..
1.4	Cruise passengers	('000)	..	..	..	..	..
	Arrivals by region						
2.1	Africa	('000)	..	..	..	..	..
2.2	Americas	('000)	6	7	5	5	6
2.3	Europe	('000)	5	5	4	5	4
2.4	East Asia and the Pacific	('000)	40	39	46	48	58
2.5	South Asia	('000)	3	2	1	1	1
2.6	Middle East	('000)	..	..	..	..	..
	Arrivals by means of transport used						
3.1	Air	('000)	54	54	56	59	69
3.2	Rail	('000)	..	..	..	..	..
3.3	Road	('000)	..	..	..	..	..
3.4	Sea	('000)	..	..	..	..	..
	Arrivals by purpose of visit						
4.1	Leisure, recreation and holidays	('000)	14	15	15	17	18
4.2	Business and professional	('000)	34	33	35	37	45
4.3	Other	('000)	6	5	6	5	6
	Accommodation						
5.1	Overnight stays in hotels and similar establishments	('000)	..	..	..	..	..
5.2	Guests in hotels and similar establishments	('000)	..	..	..	..	..
5.3	Overnight stays in all types of accommodation establishments	('000)	..	..	..	..	..
5.4	Average length of stay of non-resident tourists in all accommodation establishments	Nights	9.10	..	..	..	..
6.1	**Tourism expenditure in the country**	US$ Mn	..	..	..	5.9	3.7
6.2	"Travel" (*)	US$ Mn	5.2	2.8	4.0	5.8	3.6
6.3	"Passenger transport" (*)	US$ Mn	..	..	..	0.1	0.1
	DOMESTIC TOURISM						
	Accommodation						
7.1	Overnight stays in hotels and similar establishments	('000)	..	..	..	..	..
7.2	Guests in hotels and similar establishments	('000)	..	..	..	..	..
7.3	Overnight stays in all types of accommodation establishments	('000)	..	..	..	..	..
7.4	Average length of stay of resident tourists in all accommodation establishments	Nights	..	..	..	..	..
	OUTBOUND TOURISM						
8.1	**Departures**	('000)	38	92	..	..	..
8.2	**Tourism expenditure in other countries**	US$ Mn	..	..	..	71.9	56.2
8.3	"Travel" (*)	US$ Mn	38.2	59.5	51.9	71.2	55.6
8.4	"Passenger transport" (*)	US$ Mn	..	..	..	0.7	0.6
	TOURISM INDUSTRIES						
	Hotels and similar establishments						
9.1	Number of rooms	Units	1,976	2,824	2,830	..	..
9.2	Number of bed-places	Units	2,859	4,234	4,306	..	..
9.3	Occupancy rate	Percent	..	..	..	..	..
9.4	Average length of stay	Nights	9.10	..	..	..	..
	RELATED INDICATORS						
	Share of tourism expenditure (6.1) in:						
10.1	Gross Domestic Product (GDP)	Percent	..	..	..	0.1	0.1
10.2	Exports of goods	Percent	..	..	..	0.2	0.1
10.3	Exports of services	Percent	..	..	..	2.9	1.2

(*) Balance of Payments items: 6.1 to 6.3 correspond to the "Credit" side (and are receipts for the country) while 8.2 to 8.4 correspond to the "Debit" side (and are expenditures in other countries).

	Basic Indicators	Units	2001	2002	2003	2004	2005
	INBOUND TOURISM						
	Arrivals						
1.1	Visitors	('000)	3,550	3,194	2,859	2,589	2,648
1.2	Tourists (overnight visitors)	('000)	279	250	268	309	341
1.3	Same-day visitors	('000)	3,271	2,944	2,591	2,280	2,307
1.4	Cruise passengers	('000)	..	..	..	..	..
	Arrivals by region						
2.1	Africa	('000)	..	..	..	..	..
2.2	Americas	('000)	260	232	248	284	312
2.3	Europe	('000)	15	14	15	20	23
2.4	East Asia and the Pacific	('000)	3	5	4	5	5
2.5	South Asia	('000)	..	..	..	..	..
2.6	Middle East	('000)	..	..	..	..	..
	Arrivals by means of transport used						
3.1	Air	('000)	77	68	68	85	99
3.2	Rail	('000)	..	..	..	..	..
3.3	Road	('000)	195	176	195	217	232
3.4	Sea	('000)	7	6	5	8	10
	Arrivals by purpose of visit						
4.1	Leisure, recreation and holidays	('000)	134	121	129	149	164
4.2	Business and professional	('000)	30	27	29	33	37
4.3	Other	('000)	114	102	110	127	140
	Accommodation						
5.1	Overnight stays in hotels and similar establishments	('000)	316	219	..	..	..
5.2	Guests in hotels and similar establishments	('000)	135	88	..	..	..
5.3	Overnight stays in all types of accommodation establishments	('000)	..	..	..	..	..
5.4	Average length of stay of non-resident tourists in all accommodation establishments	Nights	2.33	2.50	2.50	2.50	2.50
6.1	**Tourism expenditure in the country**	US$ Mn	91	76	81	87	96
6.2	"Travel" (*)	US$ Mn	69	62	64	70	76
6.3	"Passenger transport" (*)	US$ Mn	22	14	17	17	20
	DOMESTIC TOURISM						
	Accommodation						
7.1	Overnight stays in hotels and similar establishments	('000)	..	..	..	..	..
7.2	Guests in hotels and similar establishments	('000)	..	..	..	..	..
7.3	Overnight stays in all types of accommodation establishments	('000)	..	..	..	..	..
7.4	Average length of stay of resident tourists in all accommodation establishments	Nights	..	..	..	..	..
	OUTBOUND TOURISM						
8.1	**Departures**	('000)	157	141	153	170	188
8.2	**Tourism expenditure in other countries**	US$ Mn	130	118	115	121	129
8.3	"Travel" (*)	US$ Mn	72	65	67	71	79
8.4	"Passenger transport" (*)	US$ Mn	58	53	48	50	50
	TOURISM INDUSTRIES						
	Hotels and similar establishments						
9.1	Number of rooms	Units	4,866	4,800	4,816	4,899	5,058
9.2	Number of bed-places	Units	10,705	10,597	10,483	10,565	10,939
9.3	Occupancy rate	Percent	37.00	36.00	38.00	40.00	44.00
9.4	Average length of stay	Nights	2.33	2.50	2.50	2.50	2.50
	RELATED INDICATORS						
	Share of tourism expenditure (6.1) in:						
10.1	Gross Domestic Product (GDP)	Percent	1.3	1.4	1.3	1.2	1.2
10.2	Exports of goods	Percent	4.8	4.1	3.7	3.0	2.9
10.3	Exports of services	Percent	16.4	13.4	14.1	13.8	14.5

(*) Balance of Payments items: 6.1 to 6.3 correspond to the "Credit" side (and are receipts for the country) while 8.2 to 8.4 correspond to the "Debit" side (and are expenditures in other countries).

PERU

	Basic Indicators	Units	2001	2002	2003	2004	2005
	INBOUND TOURISM						
	Arrivals						
1.1	Visitors	('000)	..	..	..	..	..
1.2	Tourists (overnight visitors)	('000)	901	998	1,070	1,277	1,486
1.3	Same-day visitors	('000)	..	..	..	..	..
1.4	Cruise passengers	('000)	4	4	4	7	8
	Arrivals by region						
2.1	Africa	('000)	2	2	2	3	3
2.2	Americas	('000)	534	714	762	925	1,061
2.3	Europe	('000)	221	236	252	285	345
2.4	East Asia and the Pacific	('000)	38	44	50	62	74
2.5	South Asia	('000)	1	1	1	1	2
2.6	Middle East	('000)	..	..	..	..	..
	Arrivals by means of transport used						
3.1	Air	('000)	547	589	618	736	875
3.2	Rail	('000)	..	..	..	..	..
3.3	Road	('000)	347	402	445	533	604
3.4	Sea	('000)	6	7	7	7	8
	Arrivals by purpose of visit						
4.1	Leisure, recreation and holidays	('000)	818	906	971	1,159	1,349
4.2	Business and professional	('000)	33	37	39	47	55
4.3	Other	('000)	50	55	59	70	82
	Accommodation						
5.1	Overnight stays in hotels and similar establishments	('000)	2,788	2,802	3,789	4,409	4,827
5.2	Guests in hotels and similar establishments	('000)	1,446	1,434	2,003	2,318	2,589
5.3	Overnight stays in all types of accommodation establishments	('000)	..	..	..	..	..
5.4	Average length of stay of non-resident tourists in all accommodation establishments	Nights	10.90	10.80	10.20	10.80	10.60
6.1	**Tourism expenditure in the country**	US$ Mn	763	863	1,001	1,169	1,371
6.2	"Travel" (*)	US$ Mn	733	814	941	1,079	1,241
6.3	"Passenger transport" (*)	US$ Mn	30	49	60	90	130
	DOMESTIC TOURISM						
	Accommodation						
7.1	Overnight stays in hotels and similar establishments	('000)	12,273	13,643	14,801	14,975	15,958
7.2	Guests in hotels and similar establishments	('000)	9,545	10,529	12,060	12,171	12,882
7.3	Overnight stays in all types of accommodation establishments	('000)	..	..	..	..	..
7.4	Average length of stay of resident tourists in all accommodation establishments	Nights	..	..	..	..	..
	OUTBOUND TOURISM						
8.1	**Departures**	('000)	1,060	1,232	1,392	1,635	1,841
8.2	**Tourism expenditure in other countries**	US$ Mn	774	780	794	821	900
8.3	"Travel" (*)	US$ Mn	546	580	598	620	680
8.4	"Passenger transport" (*)	US$ Mn	228	200	196	201	220
	TOURISM INDUSTRIES						
	Hotels and similar establishments						
9.1	Number of rooms	Units	120,123	121,591	123,932	128,253	132,019
9.2	Number of bed-places	Units	204,263	209,918	216,116	224,007	230,683
9.3	Occupancy rate	Percent	25.35	24.44	24.08	24.26	25.20
9.4	Average length of stay	Nights	1.37	1.37	1.32	1.34	1.34
	RELATED INDICATORS						
	Share of tourism expenditure (6.1) in:						
10.1	Gross Domestic Product (GDP)	Percent	1.4	1.5	1.6	1.7	1.7
10.2	Exports of goods	Percent	10.9	11.2	11.0	9.3	7.9
10.3	Exports of services	Percent	52.4	56.4	59.1	61.1	62.9

(*) Balance of Payments items: 6.1 to 6.3 correspond to the "Credit" side (and are receipts for the country) while 8.2 to 8.4 correspond to the "Debit" side (and are expenditures in other countries).

Basic Indicators		Units	2001	2002	2003	2004	2005
	INBOUND TOURISM						
	Arrivals						
1.1	Visitors	('000)	..	..	..	..	..
1.2	Tourists (overnight visitors)	('000)	1,797	1,933	1,907	2,291	2,623
1.3	Same-day visitors	('000)	..	..	..	..	..
1.4	Cruise passengers	('000)	4	5	5	8	2
	Arrivals by region						
2.1	Africa	('000)	2	1	1	2	2
2.2	Americas	('000)	451	454	444	546	605
2.3	Europe	('000)	202	184	177	212	246
2.4	East Asia and the Pacific	('000)	986	1,154	1,129	1,359	1,565
2.5	South Asia	('000)	22	21	22	25	28
2.6	Middle East	('000)	16	19	17	21	25
	Arrivals by means of transport used						
3.1	Air	('000)	1,770	1,905	1,880	2,260	2,586
3.2	Rail	('000)	..	..	..	..	..
3.3	Road	('000)	..	..	..	..	..
3.4	Sea	('000)	27	28	27	31	37
	Arrivals by purpose of visit						
4.1	Leisure, recreation and holidays	('000)	734	833	815	1,020	1,174
4.2	Business and professional	('000)	330	336	308	344	366
4.3	Other	('000)	706	736	757	896	1,047
	Accommodation						
5.1	Overnight stays in hotels and similar establishments	('000)	11,784	11,878	12,212	12,503	12,842
5.2	Guests in hotels and similar establishments	('000)	1,396	758	742	836	..
5.3	Overnight stays in all types of accommodation establishments	('000)	..	..	..	..	..
5.4	Average length of stay of non-resident tourists in all accommodation establishments	Nights	9.53	9.12	9.17	9.11	..
6.1	**Tourism expenditure in the country**	US$ Mn	2,011	2,018	1,821	2,390	2,620
6.2	"Travel" (*)	US$ Mn	1,742	1,761	1,544	2,017	2,130
6.3	"Passenger transport" (*)	US$ Mn	269	257	277	373	490
	DOMESTIC TOURISM						
	Accommodation						
7.1	Overnight stays in hotels and similar establishments	('000)	..	..	..	..	..
7.2	Guests in hotels and similar establishments	('000)	..	..	..	..	..
7.3	Overnight stays in all types of accommodation establishments	('000)	..	..	..	..	..
7.4	Average length of stay of resident tourists in all accommodation establishments	Nights	..	..	..	..	..
	OUTBOUND TOURISM						
8.1	**Departures**	('000)	1,787	1,969	1,803	1,920	2,144
8.2	**Tourism expenditure in other countries**	US$ Mn	1,918	1,874	1,649	1,526	1,547
8.3	"Travel" (*)	US$ Mn	1,711	1,626	1,413	1,275	1,279
8.4	"Passenger transport" (*)	US$ Mn	207	248	236	251	268
	TOURISM INDUSTRIES						
	Hotels and similar establishments						
9.1	Number of rooms	Units	28,971	37,944	21,409	29,489	29,757
9.2	Number of bed-places	Units	57,942	75,958	42,818	57,978	59,514
9.3	Occupancy rate	Percent	55.85	59.92	60.10	68.15	71.95
9.4	Average length of stay	Nights	2.73	2.63	2.63	2.73	2.58
	RELATED INDICATORS						
	Share of tourism expenditure (6.1) in:						
10.1	Gross Domestic Product (GDP)	Percent	2.6	2.6	2.3	2.7	2.7
10.2	Exports of goods	Percent	6.4	5.9	5.2	6.2	6.5
10.3	Exports of services	Percent	65.5	58.9	53.7	59.1	58.7

(*) Balance of Payments items: 6.1 to 6.3 correspond to the "Credit" side (and are receipts for the country) while 8.2 to 8.4 correspond to the "Debit" side (and are expenditures in other countries).

POLAND

Basic Indicators		Units	2001	2002	2003	2004	2005
	INBOUND TOURISM						
	Arrivals						
1.1	Visitors	('000)	61,431	50,735	52,130	61,918	64,606
1.2	Tourists (overnight visitors)	('000)	15,000	13,980	13,720	14,290	15,200
1.3	Same-day visitors	('000)	46,431	36,755	38,410	47,628	49,406
1.4	Cruise passengers	('000)	..	..	..	..	..
	Arrivals by region						
2.1	Africa	('000)	9	9	10	11	13
2.2	Americas	('000)	307	272	294	345	439
2.3	Europe	('000)	60,982	50,315	51,691	61,386	63,927
2.4	East Asia and the Pacific	('000)	83	87	89	123	163
2.5	South Asia	('000)	9	9	9	12	13
2.6	Middle East	('000)	6	6	6	6	8
	Arrivals by means of transport used						
3.1	Air	('000)	1,174	1,126	1,182	1,539	2,004
3.2	Rail	('000)	2,436	1,921	1,879	1,854	1,606
3.3	Road	('000)	56,353	46,255	47,442	57,666	60,591
3.4	Sea	('000)	1,468	1,433	1,627	859	404
	Arrivals by purpose of visit						
4.1	Leisure, recreation and holidays	('000)	3,750	3,430	3,920	3,080	3,680
4.2	Business and professional	('000)	4,240	4,050	4,100	3,945	4,240
4.3	Other	('000)	7,010	6,500	5,700	7,265	7,280
	Accommodation						
5.1	Overnight stays in hotels and similar establishments	('000)	4,918	4,999	5,450	6,876	7,869
5.2	Guests in hotels and similar establishments	('000)	2,488	2,536	2,701	3,385	3,723
5.3	Overnight stays in all types of accommodation establishments	('000)	6,991	7,085	7,828	9,313	10,542
5.4	Average length of stay of non-resident tourists in all accommodation establishments	Nights	4.50	3.90	4.10	4.60	4.40
6.1	**Tourism expenditure in the country**	US$ Mn	5,121	4,971	4,733	6,499	7,127
6.2	"Travel" (*)	US$ Mn	4,646	4,314	4,069	5,833	6,274
6.3	"Passenger transport" (*)	US$ Mn	475	657	664	666	853
	DOMESTIC TOURISM						
	Accommodation						
7.1	Overnight stays in hotels and similar establishments	('000)	8,297	8,382	8,813	11,572	12,464
7.2	Guests in hotels and similar establishments	('000)	4,340	4,580	4,834	6,273	6,805
7.3	Overnight stays in all types of accommodation establishments	('000)	38,956	37,127	37,520	37,344	38,076
7.4	Average length of stay of resident tourists in all accommodation establishments	Nights	3.52	3.37	3.32	3.16	3.10
	OUTBOUND TOURISM						
8.1	**Departures**	('000)	53,122	45,043	38,730	37,226	40,841
8.2	**Tourism expenditure in other countries**	US$ Mn	3,594	3,364	3,002	4,157	4,686
8.3	"Travel" (*)	US$ Mn	3,495	3,202	2,801	3,841	4,341
8.4	"Passenger transport" (*)	US$ Mn	99	162	201	316	345
	TOURISM INDUSTRIES						
	Hotels and similar establishments						
9.1	Number of rooms	Units	60,658	65,658	68,588	83,007	84,865
9.2	Number of bed-places	Units	118,213	127,559	134,323	165,311	169,609
9.3	Occupancy rate	Percent	37.90	35.70	35.67	32.20	40.50
9.4	Average length of stay	Nights	1.94	1.88	1.89	1.91	1.93
	RELATED INDICATORS						
	Share of tourism expenditure (6.1) in:						
10.1	Gross Domestic Product (GDP)	Percent	2.7	2.5	2.2	2.6	2.4
10.2	Exports of goods	Percent	12.3	10.6	7.8	7.9	7.4
10.3	Exports of services	Percent	52.5	49.5	42.4	48.2	43.9

(*) Balance of Payments items: 6.1 to 6.3 correspond to the "Credit" side (and are receipts for the country) while 8.2 to 8.4 correspond to the "Debit" side (and are expenditures in other countries).

	Basic Indicators	Units	2001	2002	2003	2004	2005
	INBOUND TOURISM						
	Arrivals						
1.1	Visitors	('000)	28,150	27,194	27,532	..	..
1.2	Tourists (overnight visitors)	('000)	12,167	11,644	11,707	11,617	..
1.3	Same-day visitors	('000)	15,814	15,389	15,535	..	..
1.4	Cruise passengers	('000)	169	161	290	459	..
	Arrivals by region						
2.1	Africa	('000)	..	..	..	..	..
2.2	Americas	('000)	536	464	481	494	..
2.3	Europe	('000)	11,282	10,849	10,888	10,754	..
2.4	East Asia and the Pacific	('000)	40	44	40	44	..
2.5	South Asia	('000)	..	..	..	..	..
2.6	Middle East	('000)	..	..	..	..	..
	Arrivals by means of transport used						
3.1	Air	('000)	5,259	5,073	5,162	..	..
3.2	Rail	('000)	93	90	92	..	..
3.3	Road	('000)	22,609	21,845	21,961	..	..
3.4	Sea	('000)	188	187	317	..	..
	Arrivals by purpose of visit						
4.1	Leisure, recreation and holidays	('000)	..	..	..	..	..
4.2	Business and professional	('000)	..	..	..	..	..
4.3	Other	('000)	..	..	..	..	..
	Accommodation						
5.1	Overnight stays in hotels and similar establishments	('000)	23,578	23,018	22,714	22,421	23,391
5.2	Guests in hotels and similar establishments	('000)	4,934	4,945	4,824	5,092	5,261
5.3	Overnight stays in all types of accommodation establishments	('000)	25,229	24,574	24,369	23,922	24,906
5.4	Average length of stay of non-resident tourists in all accommodation establishments	Nights	6.70	4.70	4.60	4.34	4.39
6.1	**Tourism expenditure in the country**	US$ Mn	6,236	6,595	7,607	8,991	9,222
6.2	"Travel" (*)	US$ Mn	5,468	5,798	6,622	7,811	7,893
6.3	"Passenger transport" (*)	US$ Mn	768	797	985	1,180	1,329
	DOMESTIC TOURISM						
	Accommodation						
7.1	Overnight stays in hotels and similar establishments	('000)	9,985	10,336	10,404	10,901	11,370
7.2	Guests in hotels and similar establishments	('000)	4,459	4,674	4,714	4,957	5,153
7.3	Overnight stays in all types of accommodation establishments	('000)	16,111	16,382	16,457	16,364	17,599
7.4	Average length of stay of resident tourists in all accommodation establishments	Nights	..	..	..	..	..
	OUTBOUND TOURISM						
8.1	**Departures**	('000)	..	..	..	..	..
8.2	**Tourism expenditure in other countries**	US$ Mn	2,606	2,632	2,982	3,368	3,763
8.3	"Travel" (*)	US$ Mn	2,114	2,125	2,409	2,762	3,073
8.4	"Passenger transport" (*)	US$ Mn	492	507	573	606	690
	TOURISM INDUSTRIES						
	Hotels and similar establishments						
9.1	Number of rooms	Units	99,120	99,849	105,986	106,429	112,890
9.2	Number of bed-places	Units	228,665	224,054	238,759	238,391	256,099
9.3	Occupancy rate	Percent	41.70	39.30	38.00	38.60	37.20
9.4	Average length of stay	Nights	3.60	3.50	3.30	3.10	3.30
	RELATED INDICATORS						
	Share of tourism expenditure (6.1) in:						
10.1	Gross Domestic Product (GDP)	Percent	5.7	5.5	5.2	5.4	5.3
10.2	Exports of goods	Percent	25.5	25.4	23.7	24.2	24.2
10.3	Exports of services	Percent	66.5	63.7	61.6	60.6	61.1

(*) Balance of Payments items: 6.1 to 6.3 correspond to the "Credit" side (and are receipts for the country) while 8.2 to 8.4 correspond to the "Debit" side (and are expenditures in other countries).

PUERTO RICO

	Basic Indicators		Units	2001	2002	2003	2004	2005
	INBOUND TOURISM							
	Arrivals							
1.1	Visitors		('000)	4,908	4,364	4,402	4,889	5,073
1.2	Tourists (overnight visitors)		('000)	3,551	3,087	3,238	3,541	3,686
1.3	Same-day visitors		('000)	..	1	..	..	..
1.4	Cruise passengers		('000)	1,357	1,276	1,164	1,348	1,387
	Arrivals by region							
2.1	Africa		('000)	..	..	..	..	..
2.2	Americas		('000)	2,635	2,230	2,471	2,754	2,847
2.3	Europe		('000)	..	..	..	..	..
2.4	East Asia and the Pacific		('000)	..	..	..	..	..
2.5	South Asia		('000)	..	..	..	..	..
2.6	Middle East		('000)	..	..	..	..	..
	Arrivals by means of transport used							
3.1	Air		('000)	3,551	3,087	3,238	3,541	3,686
3.2	Rail		('000)	..	..	..	..	..
3.3	Road		('000)	..	..	..	..	..
3.4	Sea		('000)	1,357	1,276	1,164	1,348	1,387
	Arrivals by purpose of visit							
4.1	Leisure, recreation and holidays		('000)	..	..	..	..	..
4.2	Business and professional		('000)	..	..	..	..	..
4.3	Other		('000)	..	..	..	..	..
	Accommodation							
5.1	Overnight stays in hotels and similar establishments		('000)	2,628	2,505	2,718	2,835	2,928
5.2	Guests in hotels and similar establishments		('000)	1,250	1,204	1,305	1,371	1,440
5.3	Overnight stays in all types of accommodation establishments		('000)	..	..	..	..	..
5.4	Average length of stay of non-resident tourists in all accommodation establishments		Nights	2.50	2.50	2.60	2.60	2.60
6.1	**Tourism expenditure in the country**	(**)	US$ Mn	2,728	2,486	2,677	3,024	3,239
6.2	"Travel" (*)		US$ Mn	..	..	..	..	..
6.3	"Passenger transport" (*)		US$ Mn	..	..	..	..	..
	DOMESTIC TOURISM							
	Accommodation							
7.1	Overnight stays in hotels and similar establishments		('000)	..	..	..	..	..
7.2	Guests in hotels and similar establishments		('000)	586	617	660	638	658
7.3	Overnight stays in all types of accommodation establishments		('000)	..	..	..	..	..
7.4	Average length of stay of resident tourists in all accommodation establishments		Nights	..	..	..	..	..
	OUTBOUND TOURISM							
8.1	**Departures**		('000)	1,331	1,227	1,272	1,361	1,410
8.2	**Tourism expenditure in other countries**	(**)	US$ Mn	1,456	1,319	1,420	1,584	1,663
8.3	"Travel" (*)		US$ Mn	1,004	928	985	1,085	1,143
8.4	"Passenger transport" (*)		US$ Mn	452	391	435	499	520
	TOURISM INDUSTRIES							
	Hotels and similar establishments							
9.1	Number of rooms		Units	12,353	12,768	12,788	12,864	13,459
9.2	Number of bed-places		Units	..	..	..	..	..
9.3	Occupancy rate		Percent	66.70	61.80	64.90	68.90	67.70
9.4	Average length of stay		Nights	2.70	2.70	2.60	2.60	2.63
	RELATED INDICATORS							
	Share of tourism expenditure (6.1) in:							
10.1	Gross Domestic Product (GDP)		Percent	3.9	3.5	3.6	3.8	3.9
10.2	Exports of goods		Percent	5.6	5.0	4.8	5.1	5.4
10.3	Exports of services		Percent	42.6	40.0	42.2	44.2	40.1

(*) Balance of Payments items: 6.1 to 6.3 correspond to the "Credit" side (and are receipts for the country) while 8.2 to 8.4 correspond to the "Debit" side (and are expenditures in other countries).

(**) See Annex "Country notes".

	Basic Indicators		Units	2001	2002	2003	2004	2005
	INBOUND TOURISM							
	Arrivals							
1.1	Visitors		('000)	..	..	..	..	..
1.2	Tourists (overnight visitors)		('000)	376	587	557	732	913
1.3	Same-day visitors		('000)	..	..	..	..	..
1.4	Cruise passengers		('000)	..	..	..	..	..
	Arrivals by region							
2.1	Africa		('000)	..	..	..	..	..
2.2	Americas		('000)	..	..	..	..	..
2.3	Europe		('000)	56	103	87	196	233
2.4	East Asia and the Pacific		('000)	60	108	127	146	159
2.5	South Asia		('000)	..	..	..	..	..
2.6	Middle East		('000)	231	312	283	295	365
	Arrivals by means of transport used							
3.1	Air		('000)	..	..	..	..	..
3.2	Rail		('000)	..	..	..	..	..
3.3	Road		('000)	..	..	..	..	..
3.4	Sea		('000)	..	..	..	..	..
	Arrivals by purpose of visit							
4.1	Leisure, recreation and holidays		('000)	..	..	..	..	..
4.2	Business and professional		('000)	..	..	..	..	..
4.3	Other		('000)	..	..	..	..	..
	Accommodation							
5.1	Overnight stays in hotels and similar establishments		('000)	507	698	848	983	1,024
5.2	Guests in hotels and similar establishments		('000)	..	..	..	..	..
5.3	Overnight stays in all types of accommodation establishments		('000)	..	..	..	..	..
5.4	Average length of stay of non-resident tourists in all accommodation establishments		Nights	1.40	1.20	1.50	1.30	1.10
6.1	**Tourism expenditure in the country**		US$ Mn	..	..	..	..	..
6.2	"Travel" (*)	(**)	US$ Mn	272	285	369	498	760
6.3	"Passenger transport" (*)		US$ Mn	..	..	..	..	..
	DOMESTIC TOURISM							
	Accommodation							
7.1	Overnight stays in hotels and similar establishments		('000)	..	..	..	..	..
7.2	Guests in hotels and similar establishments		('000)	..	..	..	..	..
7.3	Overnight stays in all types of accommodation establishments		('000)	..	..	..	..	..
7.4	Average length of stay of resident tourists in all accommodation establishments		Nights	..	..	..	..	..
	OUTBOUND TOURISM							
8.1	**Departures**		('000)	..	..	..	..	..
8.2	**Tourism expenditure in other countries**		US$ Mn	..	..	..	..	..
8.3	"Travel" (*)	(**)	US$ Mn	366	423	471	691	1,759
8.4	"Passenger transport" (*)		US$ Mn	..	..	..	..	..
	TOURISM INDUSTRIES							
	Hotels and similar establishments							
9.1	Number of rooms		Units	2,422	3,225	3,858	3,792	4,180
9.2	Number of bed-places		Units	3,362	4,889	5,266	5,414	5,810
9.3	Occupancy rate		Percent	41.00	39.00	44.00	50.00	48.00
9.4	Average length of stay		Nights	..	..	..	..	..
	RELATED INDICATORS							
	Share of tourism expenditure (6.1) in:							
10.1	Gross Domestic Product (GDP)		Percent	..	..	..	..	..
10.2	Exports of goods		Percent	..	..	..	..	..
10.3	Exports of services		Percent	..	..	..	..	..

(*) Balance of Payments items: 6.1 to 6.3 correspond to the "Credit" side (and are receipts for the country) while 8.2 to 8.4 correspond to the "Debit" side (and are expenditures in other countries).

(**) See Annex "Country notes".

REPUBLIC OF MOLDOVA

	Basic Indicators	Units	2001	2002	2003	2004	2005
	INBOUND TOURISM						
	Arrivals						
1.1	Visitors	('000)	16	20	24	26	25
1.2	Tourists (overnight visitors)	('000)	16	18	21	24	23
1.3	Same-day visitors	('000)	0.2	2.0	3.0	2.0	2.0
1.4	Cruise passengers	('000)	..	..	..	..	..
	Arrivals by region						
2.1	Africa	('000)	..	..	..	..	..
2.2	Americas	('000)	1.1	1.8	2.6	2.6	3.2
2.3	Europe	('000)	14.0	17.6	20.2	22.7	21.2
2.4	East Asia and the Pacific	('000)	0.4	0.4	0.3	0.3	0.3
2.5	South Asia	('000)	..	..	..	..	..
2.6	Middle East	('000)	0.1	0.3	0.5	0.4	0.4
	Arrivals by means of transport used						
3.1	Air	('000)	..	..	..	..	..
3.2	Rail	('000)	..	..	..	..	..
3.3	Road	('000)	..	..	..	..	..
3.4	Sea	('000)	..	..	..	..	..
	Arrivals by purpose of visit						
4.1	Leisure, recreation and holidays	('000)	4.2	8.0	9.9	11.8	7.8
4.2	Business and professional	('000)	11.0	11.5	13.0	13.0	16.4
4.3	Other	('000)	0.5	0.6	0.7	1.2	0.9
	Accommodation						
5.1	Overnight stays in hotels and similar establishments	('000)	64	76	84	153	170
5.2	Guests in hotels and similar establishments	('000)	..	..	..	68	66
5.3	Overnight stays in all types of accommodation establishments	('000)	..	..	..	174	187
5.4	Average length of stay of non-resident tourists in all accommodation establishments	Nights	..	..	..	2.50	2.80
6.1	**Tourism expenditure in the country**	US$ Mn	58	72	83	134	163
6.2	"Travel" (*)	US$ Mn	39	50	58	113	128
6.3	"Passenger transport" (*)	US$ Mn	19	22	25	21	35
	DOMESTIC TOURISM						
	Accommodation						
7.1	Overnight stays in hotels and similar establishments	('000)	..	..	..	251	264
7.2	Guests in hotels and similar establishments	('000)	..	..	..	99	104
7.3	Overnight stays in all types of accommodation establishments	('000)	253	316	400	1,313	1,432
7.4	Average length of stay of resident tourists in all accommodation establishments	Nights	..	..	..	6.00	6.10
	OUTBOUND TOURISM						
8.1	**Departures**	('000)	30	52	67	68	57
8.2	**Tourism expenditure in other countries**	US$ Mn	90	109	124	157	197
8.3	"Travel" (*)	US$ Mn	75	95	105	135	167
8.4	"Passenger transport" (*)	US$ Mn	15	14	19	22	30
	TOURISM INDUSTRIES						
	Hotels and similar establishments						
9.1	Number of rooms	Units	2,905	2,806	2,565	2,576	2,475
9.2	Number of bed-places	Units	5,479	5,484	4,651	4,850	4,581
9.3	Occupancy rate	Percent	17.10	14.00	22.10	25.20	26.50
9.4	Average length of stay	Nights	..	..	..	2.40	2.60
	RELATED INDICATORS						
	Share of tourism expenditure (6.1) in:						
10.1	Gross Domestic Product (GDP)	Percent	3.9	4.3	4.2	5.2	5.6
10.2	Exports of goods	Percent	10.2	10.9	10.3	13.5	14.8
10.3	Exports of services	Percent	33.9	33.2	32.7	37.7	38.4

(*) Balance of Payments items: 6.1 to 6.3 correspond to the "Credit" side (and are receipts for the country) while 8.2 to 8.4 correspond to the "Debit" side (and are expenditures in other countries).

Basic Indicators		Units	2001	2002	2003	2004	2005
	INBOUND TOURISM						
	Arrivals						
1.1	Visitors	('000)	..	..	..	..	..
1.2	Tourists (overnight visitors)	('000)	424	426	432	430	409
1.3	Same-day visitors	('000)	..	..	..	..	..
1.4	Cruise passengers	('000)	..	..	..	..	..
	Arrivals by region						
2.1	Africa	('000)	..	..	..	..	..
2.2	Americas	('000)	..	..	..	..	..
2.3	Europe	('000)	347	357	367	370	344
2.4	East Asia and the Pacific	('000)	..	..	..	..	..
2.5	South Asia	('000)	..	..	..	..	..
2.6	Middle East	('000)	..	..	..	..	..
	Arrivals by means of transport used						
3.1	Air	('000)	419	421	427	426	404
3.2	Rail	('000)	..	..	..	..	..
3.3	Road	('000)	..	..	..	..	..
3.4	Sea	('000)	5	5	5	4	5
	Arrivals by purpose of visit						
4.1	Leisure, recreation and holidays	('000)	209	206	209	183	162
4.2	Business and professional	('000)	44	45	44	52	47
4.3	Other	('000)	171	175	179	195	200
	Accommodation						
5.1	Overnight stays in hotels and similar establishments	('000)	1,112	1,087	..	1,154	1,112
5.2	Guests in hotels and similar establishments	('000)	194	198	209	193	180
5.3	Overnight stays in all types of accommodation establishments	('000)	..	..	..	..	..
5.4	Average length of stay of non-resident tourists in all accommodation establishments	Nights	15.80	16.40	16.50	16.40	17.00
6.1	**Tourism expenditure in the country** (**)	US$ Mn	281	329	413	448	384
6.2	"Travel" (*)	US$ Mn	..	..	..	..	..
6.3	"Passenger transport" (*)	US$ Mn	..	..	..	..	..
	DOMESTIC TOURISM						
	Accommodation						
7.1	Overnight stays in hotels and similar establishments	('000)	..	..	..	..	..
7.2	Guests in hotels and similar establishments	('000)	..	..	..	..	..
7.3	Overnight stays in all types of accommodation establishments	('000)	..	..	..	..	..
7.4	Average length of stay of resident tourists in all accommodation establishments	Nights	..	..	..	..	..
	OUTBOUND TOURISM						
8.1	**Departures**	('000)	309	319	333	385	395
8.2	**Tourism expenditure in other countries**	US$ Mn	..	..	..	..	..
8.3	"Travel" (*)	US$ Mn	..	..	..	..	..
8.4	"Passenger transport" (*)	US$ Mn	..	..	..	..	..
	TOURISM INDUSTRIES						
	Hotels and similar establishments						
9.1	Number of rooms	Units	2,771	2,850	2,910	2,904	2,930
9.2	Number of bed-places	Units	5,542	5,700	5,820	5,808	5,860
9.3	Occupancy rate	Percent	63.60	64.00	..	58.30	60.03
9.4	Average length of stay	Nights	6.70	7.00	6.90	6.80	6.90
	RELATED INDICATORS						
	Share of tourism expenditure (6.1) in:						
10.1	Gross Domestic Product (GDP)	Percent	..	..	..	..	..
10.2	Exports of goods	Percent	..	..	..	..	..
10.3	Exports of services	Percent	..	..	..	..	..

(*) Balance of Payments items: 6.1 to 6.3 correspond to the "Credit" side (and are receipts for the country) while 8.2 to 8.4 correspond to the "Debit" side (and are expenditures in other countries).

(**) See Annex "Country notes".

ROMANIA

	Basic Indicators	Units	2001	2002	2003	2004	2005
	INBOUND TOURISM						
	Arrivals						
1.1	Visitors	('000)	4,938	4,794	5,595	6,600	5,839
1.2	Tourists (overnight visitors)	('000)	..	..	..	..	..
1.3	Same-day visitors	('000)	..	..	..	..	..
1.4	Cruise passengers	('000)	135	137	152	186	187
	Arrivals by region						
2.1	Africa	('000)	5	5	5	7	7
2.2	Americas	('000)	96	102	115	139	154
2.3	Europe	('000)	4,757	4,604	5,392	6,361	5,580
2.4	East Asia and the Pacific	('000)	36	42	42	49	57
2.5	South Asia	('000)	14	12	13	15	16
2.6	Middle East	('000)	28	27	27	28	24
	Arrivals by means of transport used						
3.1	Air	('000)	705	689	752	704	919
3.2	Rail	('000)	476	374	347	308	305
3.3	Road	('000)	3,621	3,594	4,343	5,401	4,429
3.4	Sea	('000)	135	137	152	186	187
	Arrivals by purpose of visit						
4.1	Leisure, recreation and holidays	('000)	..	..	..	..	..
4.2	Business and professional	('000)	..	..	..	..	..
4.3	Other	('000)	..	..	..	..	..
	Accommodation						
5.1	Overnight stays in hotels and similar establishments	('000)	2,301	2,471	2,688	3,211	3,377
5.2	Guests in hotels and similar establishments	('000)	895	982	1,086	1,332	1,407
5.3	Overnight stays in all types of accommodation establishments	('000)	2,391	2,534	2,766	3,333	3,464
5.4	Average length of stay of non-resident tourists in all accommodation establishments	Nights	2.61	2.50	2.50	2.50	2.40
6.1	**Tourism expenditure in the country**	US$ Mn	419	400	523	607	1,310
6.2	"Travel" (*)	US$ Mn	362	335	449	503	1,044
6.3	"Passenger transport" (*)	US$ Mn	57	65	74	104	266
	DOMESTIC TOURISM						
	Accommodation						
7.1	Overnight stays in hotels and similar establishments	('000)	14,071	13,369	13,867	13,980	14,094
7.2	Guests in hotels and similar establishments	('000)	3,575	3,505	3,636	3,963	4,139
7.3	Overnight stays in all types of accommodation establishments	('000)	15,731	14,743	15,079	15,168	14,909
7.4	Average length of stay of resident tourists in all accommodation establishments	Nights	4.00	3.80	3.80	3.50	3.40
	OUTBOUND TOURISM						
8.1	**Departures**	('000)	6,408	5,757	6,497	6,972	7,140
8.2	**Tourism expenditure in other countries**	US$ Mn	475	448	572	672	1,022
8.3	"Travel" (*)	US$ Mn	449	396	479	539	878
8.4	"Passenger transport" (*)	US$ Mn	26	52	93	133	144
	TOURISM INDUSTRIES						
	Hotels and similar establishments						
9.1	Number of rooms	Units	95,226	95,062	97,320	101,574	105,219
9.2	Number of bed-places	Units	199,320	197,320	201,636	207,810	216,499
9.3	Occupancy rate	Percent	38.40	34.00	34.60	36.70	33.40
9.4	Average length of stay	Nights	3.70	3.60	3.50	3.25	3.20
	RELATED INDICATORS						
	Share of tourism expenditure (6.1) in:						
10.1	Gross Domestic Product (GDP)	Percent	1.0	0.9	0.9	0.8	1.3
10.2	Exports of goods	Percent	3.7	2.9	3.0	2.6	4.7
10.3	Exports of services	Percent	20.6	17.0	17.3	16.8	26.5

(*) Balance of Payments items: 6.1 to 6.3 correspond to the "Credit" side (and are receipts for the country) while 8.2 to 8.4 correspond to the "Debit" side (and are expenditures in other countries).

	Basic Indicators	Units	2001	2002	2003	2004	2005
	INBOUND TOURISM						
	Arrivals						
1.1	Visitors	('000)	21,595	23,309	22,521	22,064	22,201
1.2	Tourists (overnight visitors)	('000)	19,457	21,279	20,443	19,892	19,940
1.3	Same-day visitors	('000)	489	524	485	547	498
1.4	Cruise passengers	('000)	175	153	213	280	333
	Arrivals by region						
2.1	Africa	('000)	34	31	29	29	27
2.2	Americas	('000)	306	343	421	477	457
2.3	Europe	('000)	19,704	21,097	20,237	19,607	19,691
2.4	East Asia and the Pacific	('000)	869	1,150	1,107	1,314	1,315
2.5	South Asia	('000)	48	58	59	63	68
2.6	Middle East	('000)	24	28	32	32	33
	Arrivals by means of transport used						
3.1	Air	('000)	2,496	3,140	3,475	4,090	4,135
3.2	Rail	('000)	8,125	8,086	7,676	7,277	6,899
3.3	Road	('000)	10,007	11,138	10,447	9,544	10,020
3.4	Sea	('000)	967	945	923	1,153	1,147
	Arrivals by purpose of visit						
4.1	Leisure, recreation and holidays	('000)	2,380	3,106	3,152	2,861	2,385
4.2	Business and professional	('000)	3,028	3,014	2,568	2,723	3,226
4.3	Other	('000)	16,187	17,189	16,801	16,480	16,588
	Accommodation						
5.1	Overnight stays in hotels and similar establishments	('000)	10,200	10,564	10,036	10,687	10,696
5.2	Guests in hotels and similar establishments	('000)	3,215	3,231	3,101	3,275	3,438
5.3	Overnight stays in all types of accommodation establishments	('000)	..	11,357	10,858	11,516	11,643
5.4	Average length of stay of non-resident tourists in all accommodation establishments	Nights	..	..	..	4.38	4.63
6.1	**Tourism expenditure in the country**	US$ Mn	4,726	5,429	5,879	6,958	7,402
6.2	"Travel" (*)	US$ Mn	3,572	4,168	4,502	5,226	5,466
6.3	"Passenger transport" (*)	US$ Mn	1,154	1,261	1,377	1,732	1,936
	DOMESTIC TOURISM						
	Accommodation						
7.1	Overnight stays in hotels and similar establishments	('000)	37,143	35,343	35,499	35,549	40,730
7.2	Guests in hotels and similar establishments	('000)	13,874	13,678	13,539	13,741	14,909
7.3	Overnight stays in all types of accommodation establishments	('000)	..	146,890	140,160	143,039	155,201
7.4	Average length of stay of resident tourists in all accommodation establishments	Nights	..	11.20	10.80	11.00	9.00
	OUTBOUND TOURISM						
8.1	**Departures**	('000)	18,030	20,428	20,572	24,507	28,416
8.2	**Tourism expenditure in other countries**	US$ Mn	9,760	11,713	13,427	16,527	18,795
8.3	"Travel" (*)	US$ Mn	9,285	11,284	12,880	15,730	17,804
8.4	"Passenger transport" (*)	US$ Mn	475	429	547	797	991
	TOURISM INDUSTRIES						
	Hotels and similar establishments						
9.1	Number of rooms	Units	179,300	178,300	177,200	178,600	199,010
9.2	Number of bed-places	Units	338,429	343,339	364,017	344,400	414,086
9.3	Occupancy rate	Percent	38.00	37.00	34.00	37.00	34.00
9.4	Average length of stay	Nights	..	..	..	5.00	4.81
	RELATED INDICATORS						
	Share of tourism expenditure (6.1) in:						
10.1	Gross Domestic Product (GDP)	Percent	1.5	1.6	1.4	1.2	1.0
10.2	Exports of goods	Percent	4.6	5.1	4.3	3.8	3.0
10.3	Exports of services	Percent	41.3	39.9	36.2	34.3	30.1

(*) Balance of Payments items: 6.1 to 6.3 correspond to the "Credit" side (and are receipts for the country) while 8.2 to 8.4 correspond to the "Debit" side (and are expenditures in other countries).

SABA

	Basic Indicators	Units	2001	2002	2003	2004	2005
	INBOUND TOURISM						
	Arrivals						
1.1	Visitors	('000)	23.9	21.5	20.5	23.2	24.9
1.2	Tourists (overnight visitors)	('000)	9.0	10.8	10.3	11.0	11.5
1.3	Same-day visitors	('000)	14.9	10.7	10.2	12.2	13.4
1.4	Cruise passengers	('000)	..	..	..	..	..
	Arrivals by region						
2.1	Africa	('000)	..	..	..	..	..
2.2	Americas	('000)	4.4	4.4	4.1	4.8	4.9
2.3	Europe	('000)	4.0	4.6	4.7	5.0	5.5
2.4	East Asia and the Pacific	('000)	..	..	..	..	..
2.5	South Asia	('000)	..	..	..	..	..
2.6	Middle East	('000)	..	..	..	..	..
	Arrivals by means of transport used						
3.1	Air	('000)	5.9	7.9	6.8	7.3	7.4
3.2	Rail	('000)	..	..	..	..	..
3.3	Road	('000)	..	..	..	..	..
3.4	Sea	('000)	3.1	2.9	3.5	3.7	4.1
	Arrivals by purpose of visit						
4.1	Leisure, recreation and holidays	('000)	..	..	..	..	..
4.2	Business and professional	('000)	..	..	..	..	..
4.3	Other	('000)	..	..	..	..	..
	Accommodation						
5.1	Overnight stays in hotels and similar establishments	('000)	..	..	..	..	..
5.2	Guests in hotels and similar establishments	('000)	..	..	..	..	..
5.3	Overnight stays in all types of accommodation establishments	('000)	..	..	..	..	..
5.4	Average length of stay of non-resident tourists in all accommodation establishments	Nights	..	..	..	..	..
6.1	**Tourism expenditure in the country**	US$ Mn	..	..	..	..	..
6.2	"Travel" (*)	US$ Mn	..	..	..	..	..
6.3	"Passenger transport" (*)	US$ Mn	..	..	..	..	..
	DOMESTIC TOURISM						
	Accommodation						
7.1	Overnight stays in hotels and similar establishments	('000)	..	..	..	..	..
7.2	Guests in hotels and similar establishments	('000)	..	..	..	..	..
7.3	Overnight stays in all types of accommodation establishments	('000)	..	..	..	..	..
7.4	Average length of stay of resident tourists in all accommodation establishments	Nights	..	..	..	..	..
	OUTBOUND TOURISM						
8.1	**Departures**	('000)	..	..	..	..	..
8.2	**Tourism expenditure in other countries**	US$ Mn	..	..	..	..	..
8.3	"Travel" (*)	US$ Mn	..	..	..	..	..
8.4	"Passenger transport" (*)	US$ Mn	..	..	..	..	..
	TOURISM INDUSTRIES						
	Hotels and similar establishments						
9.1	Number of rooms	Units	85	..	..	..	..
9.2	Number of bed-places	Units	..	..	..	..	..
9.3	Occupancy rate	Percent	..	..	..	..	..
9.4	Average length of stay	Nights	..	..	..	..	..
	RELATED INDICATORS						
	Share of tourism expenditure (6.1) in:						
10.1	Gross Domestic Product (GDP)	Percent	..	..	..	..	..
10.2	Exports of goods	Percent	..	..	..	..	..
10.3	Exports of services	Percent	..	..	..	..	..

(*) Balance of Payments items: 6.1 to 6.3 correspond to the "Credit" side (and are receipts for the country) while 8.2 to 8.4 correspond to the "Debit" side (and are expenditures in other countries).

SAINT EUSTATIUS

Basic Indicators		Units	2001	2002	2003	2004	2005
	INBOUND TOURISM						
	Arrivals						
1.1	Visitors	('000)	30	..	..	..	..
1.2	Tourists (overnight visitors)	('000)	9.7	9.8	10.5	11.1	10.4
1.3	Same-day visitors	('000)	..	..	..	..	..
1.4	Cruise passengers	('000)	..	..	..	..	..
	Arrivals by region						
2.1	Africa	('000)	..	..	..	..	..
2.2	Americas	('000)	3.4	3.4	3.5	3.7	3.5
2.3	Europe	('000)	4.5	4.6	5.3	5.5	5.4
2.4	East Asia and the Pacific	('000)	..	..	..	..	..
2.5	South Asia	('000)	..	..	..	..	..
2.6	Middle East	('000)	..	..	..	..	..
	Arrivals by means of transport used						
3.1	Air	('000)	20	..	..	..	..
3.2	Rail	('000)	..	..	..	..	..
3.3	Road	('000)	..	..	..	..	..
3.4	Sea	('000)	10	..	..	..	..
	Arrivals by purpose of visit						
4.1	Leisure, recreation and holidays	('000)	..	..	..	..	..
4.2	Business and professional	('000)	..	..	..	..	..
4.3	Other	('000)	..	..	..	..	..
	Accommodation						
5.1	Overnight stays in hotels and similar establishments	('000)	..	..	..	..	..
5.2	Guests in hotels and similar establishments	('000)	..	..	..	..	..
5.3	Overnight stays in all types of accommodation establishments	('000)	..	..	..	..	..
5.4	Average length of stay of non-resident tourists in all accommodation establishments	Nights	..	..	..	..	..
6.1	**Tourism expenditure in the country**	US$ Mn	..	..	..	..	..
6.2	"Travel" (*)	US$ Mn	..	..	..	..	..
6.3	"Passenger transport" (*)	US$ Mn	..	..	..	..	..
	DOMESTIC TOURISM						
	Accommodation						
7.1	Overnight stays in hotels and similar establishments	('000)	..	..	..	..	..
7.2	Guests in hotels and similar establishments	('000)	..	..	..	..	..
7.3	Overnight stays in all types of accommodation establishments	('000)	..	..	..	..	..
7.4	Average length of stay of resident tourists in all accommodation establishments	Nights	..	..	..	..	..
	OUTBOUND TOURISM						
8.1	**Departures**	('000)	..	..	..	..	..
8.2	**Tourism expenditure in other countries**	US$ Mn	..	..	..	..	..
8.3	"Travel" (*)	US$ Mn	..	..	..	..	..
8.4	"Passenger transport" (*)	US$ Mn	..	..	..	..	..
	TOURISM INDUSTRIES						
	Hotels and similar establishments						
9.1	Number of rooms	Units	89	..	..	..	..
9.2	Number of bed-places	Units	..	..	..	..	..
9.3	Occupancy rate	Percent	..	..	..	..	..
9.4	Average length of stay	Nights	..	..	..	..	..
	RELATED INDICATORS						
	Share of tourism expenditure (6.1) in:						
10.1	Gross Domestic Product (GDP)	Percent	..	..	..	..	..
10.2	Exports of goods	Percent	..	..	..	..	..
10.3	Exports of services	Percent	..	..	..	..	..

(*) Balance of Payments items: 6.1 to 6.3 correspond to the "Credit" side (and are receipts for the country) while 8.2 to 8.4 correspond to the "Debit" side (and are expenditures in other countries).

SAINT KITTS AND NEVIS

	Basic Indicators	Units	2001	2002	2003	2004	2005
	INBOUND TOURISM						
	Arrivals						
1.1	Visitors	('000)	334	239	244	377	344
1.2	Tourists (overnight visitors)	('000)	71	69	91	118	127
1.3	Same-day visitors	('000)	4	3	3	4	3
1.4	Cruise passengers	('000)	259	167	150	255	214
	Arrivals by region						
2.1	Africa	('000)	..	..	..	..	..
2.2	Americas	('000)	59	60	..	..	..
2.3	Europe	('000)	11	..	..	..	..
2.4	East Asia and the Pacific	('000)	..	..	..	..	..
2.5	South Asia	('000)	..	..	..	..	..
2.6	Middle East	('000)	..	..	..	..	..
	Arrivals by means of transport used						
3.1	Air	('000)	74	72	94	122	130
3.2	Rail	('000)	..	..	..	..	..
3.3	Road	('000)	..	..	..	..	..
3.4	Sea	('000)	259	167	150	255	214
	Arrivals by purpose of visit						
4.1	Leisure, recreation and holidays	('000)	63	..	..	..	..
4.2	Business and professional	('000)	7	..	..	..	..
4.3	Other	('000)	1	..	..	..	..
	Accommodation						
5.1	Overnight stays in hotels and similar establishments	('000)	..	..	..	..	..
5.2	Guests in hotels and similar establishments	('000)	..	..	..	..	..
5.3	Overnight stays in all types of accommodation establishments	('000)	..	..	..	..	..
5.4	Average length of stay of non-resident tourists in all accommodation establishments	Nights	..	..	..	..	..
6.1	**Tourism expenditure in the country**	US$ Mn	..	..	..	..	..
6.2	"Travel" (*)	US$ Mn	62	57	75	103	107
6.3	"Passenger transport" (*)	US$ Mn	..	..	..	..	..
	DOMESTIC TOURISM						
	Accommodation						
7.1	Overnight stays in hotels and similar establishments	('000)	..	..	..	..	..
7.2	Guests in hotels and similar establishments	('000)	..	..	..	..	..
7.3	Overnight stays in all types of accommodation establishments	('000)	..	..	..	..	..
7.4	Average length of stay of resident tourists in all accommodation establishments	Nights	..	..	..	..	..
	OUTBOUND TOURISM						
8.1	**Departures**	('000)	..	..	..	..	..
8.2	**Tourism expenditure in other countries**	US$ Mn	..	..	..	..	..
8.3	"Travel" (*)	US$ Mn	8	8	8	10	11
8.4	"Passenger transport" (*)	US$ Mn	..	..	..	..	..
	TOURISM INDUSTRIES						
	Hotels and similar establishments						
9.1	Number of rooms	Units	1,489	1,438	1,611	1,825	..
9.2	Number of bed-places	Units	2,246	2,182	2,361	2,682	..
9.3	Occupancy rate	Percent	..	..	..	..	..
9.4	Average length of stay	Nights	..	..	..	..	..
	RELATED INDICATORS						
	Share of tourism expenditure (6.1) in: (**)						
10.1	Gross Domestic Product (GDP)	Percent	18.0	16.1	20.3	25.9	23.6
10.2	Exports of goods	Percent	112.7	90.5	131.6	180.7	184.5
10.3	Exports of services	Percent	63.3	63.3	69.4	76.3	74.8

(*) Balance of Payments items: 6.1 to 6.3 correspond to the "Credit" side (and are receipts for the country) while 8.2 to 8.4 correspond to the "Debit" side (and are expenditures in other countries).

(**) See Annex "Country notes".

	Basic Indicators	Units	2001	2002	2003	2004	2005
	INBOUND TOURISM						
	Arrivals						
1.1	Visitors	('000)	747	648	683	791	720
1.2	Tourists (overnight visitors)	('000)	250	253	277	298	318
1.3	Same-day visitors	('000)	7	8	13	11	8
1.4	Cruise passengers	('000)	490	387	393	481	394
	Arrivals by region						
2.1	Africa	('000)	..	..	..	..	..
2.2	Americas	('000)	165	175	183	197	215
2.3	Europe	('000)	83	76	90	97	102
2.4	East Asia and the Pacific	('000)	..	..	..	..	..
2.5	South Asia	('000)	..	..	..	..	..
2.6	Middle East	('000)	..	..	..	..	..
	Arrivals by means of transport used						
3.1	Air	('000)	..	..	..	..	..
3.2	Rail	('000)	..	..	..	..	..
3.3	Road	('000)	..	..	..	..	..
3.4	Sea	('000)	..	..	..	..	..
	Arrivals by purpose of visit						
4.1	Leisure, recreation and holidays	('000)	..	..	243	268	292
4.2	Business and professional	('000)	..	..	13	12	16
4.3	Other	('000)	..	..	21	18	10
	Accommodation						
5.1	Overnight stays in hotels and similar establishments	('000)	..	..	..	..	..
5.2	Guests in hotels and similar establishments	('000)	..	230	245	263	285
5.3	Overnight stays in all types of accommodation establishments	('000)	..	..	..	..	..
5.4	Average length of stay of non-resident tourists in all accommodation establishments	Nights	..	..	..	..	..
6.1	**Tourism expenditure in the country**	US$ Mn	..	..	..	..	..
6.2	"Travel" (*)	US$ Mn	233	210	282	326	345
6.3	"Passenger transport" (*)	US$ Mn	..	..	..	..	..
	DOMESTIC TOURISM						
	Accommodation						
7.1	Overnight stays in hotels and similar establishments	('000)	..	..	..	..	..
7.2	Guests in hotels and similar establishments	('000)	..	..	..	..	..
7.3	Overnight stays in all types of accommodation establishments	('000)	..	..	..	..	..
7.4	Average length of stay of resident tourists in all accommodation establishments	Nights	..	..	..	..	..
	OUTBOUND TOURISM						
8.1	**Departures**	('000)	..	..	..	..	..
8.2	**Tourism expenditure in other countries**	US$ Mn	..	..	..	..	..
8.3	"Travel" (*)	US$ Mn	32	34	36	37	40
8.4	"Passenger transport" (*)	US$ Mn	..	..	..	..	..
	TOURISM INDUSTRIES						
	Hotels and similar establishments						
9.1	Number of rooms	Units	4,428	4,428	3,749	3,974	4,511
9.2	Number of bed-places	Units	8,236	8,236	6,748	7,153	8,120
9.3	Occupancy rate	Percent	57.00	56.10	62.70	64.80	64.80
9.4	Average length of stay	Nights	10.60	9.99	10.00	9.30	10.10
	RELATED INDICATORS						
	Share of tourism expenditure (6.1) in: (**)						
10.1	Gross Domestic Product (GDP)	Percent	35.6	31.5	40.6	42.7	41.8
10.2	Exports of goods	Percent	431.5	304.3	391.7	299.1	500.0
10.3	Exports of services	Percent	85.0	84.0	88.7	88.8	88.5

(*) Balance of Payments items: 6.1 to 6.3 correspond to the "Credit" side (and are receipts for the country) while 8.2 to 8.4 correspond to the "Debit" side (and are expenditures in other countries).

(**) See Annex "Country notes".

SAINT MAARTEN

Basic Indicators		Units	2001	2002	2003	2004	2005
	INBOUND TOURISM						
	Arrivals						
1.1	Visitors	('000)	1,271	1,436	1,600	1,823	1,950
1.2	Tourists (overnight visitors)	('000)	403	381	428	475	462
1.3	Same-day visitors	('000)	..	..	..	..	..
1.4	Cruise passengers	('000)	868	1,055	1,172	1,348	1,488
	Arrivals by region						
2.1	Africa	('000)	..	..	..	..	..
2.2	Americas	('000)	270	260	301	338	329
2.3	Europe	('000)	97	87	88	96	92
2.4	East Asia and the Pacific	('000)	..	..	..	..	..
2.5	South Asia	('000)	..	..	..	..	..
2.6	Middle East	('000)	..	..	..	..	..
	Arrivals by means of transport used						
3.1	Air	('000)	403	381	428	475	462
3.2	Rail	('000)	..	..	..	..	..
3.3	Road	('000)	..	..	..	..	..
3.4	Sea	('000)	868	1,055	1,172	1,348	1,488
	Arrivals by purpose of visit						
4.1	Leisure, recreation and holidays	('000)	..	..	..	..	..
4.2	Business and professional	('000)	..	..	..	..	..
4.3	Other	('000)	..	..	..	..	..
	Accommodation						
5.1	Overnight stays in hotels and similar establishments	('000)	..	..	..	..	..
5.2	Guests in hotels and similar establishments	('000)	..	..	..	..	..
5.3	Overnight stays in all types of accommodation establishments	('000)	..	..	..	..	..
5.4	Average length of stay of non-resident tourists in all accommodation establishments	Nights	..	..	..	..	..
6.1	**Tourism expenditure in the country**	US$ Mn	..	..	..	..	..
6.2	"Travel" (*)	US$ Mn	484	489	538	613	619
6.3	"Passenger transport" (*)	US$ Mn	..	..	..	..	..
	DOMESTIC TOURISM						
	Accommodation						
7.1	Overnight stays in hotels and similar establishments	('000)	..	..	..	..	..
7.2	Guests in hotels and similar establishments	('000)	..	..	..	..	..
7.3	Overnight stays in all types of accommodation establishments	('000)	..	..	..	..	..
7.4	Average length of stay of resident tourists in all accommodation establishments	Nights	..	..	..	..	..
	OUTBOUND TOURISM						
8.1	**Departures**	('000)	..	..	..	..	..
8.2	**Tourism expenditure in other countries**	US$ Mn	..	..	..	..	..
8.3	"Travel" (*)	US$ Mn	137	140	143	88	104
8.4	"Passenger transport" (*)	US$ Mn	..	..	..	..	..
	TOURISM INDUSTRIES						
	Hotels and similar establishments						
9.1	Number of rooms	Units	3,548	3,532	..	..	..
9.2	Number of bed-places	Units	..	6,358	..	..	..
9.3	Occupancy rate	Percent	52.00	56.70	56.20	..	..
9.4	Average length of stay	Nights	..	..	..	..	..
	RELATED INDICATORS						
	Share of tourism expenditure (6.1) in:						
10.1	Gross Domestic Product (GDP)	Percent	..	..	..	..	..
10.2	Exports of goods	Percent	..	..	..	..	..
10.3	Exports of services	Percent	..	..	..	..	..

(*) Balance of Payments items: 6.1 to 6.3 correspond to the "Credit" side (and are receipts for the country) while 8.2 to 8.4 correspond to the "Debit" side (and are expenditures in other countries).

SAINT VINCENT AND THE GRENADINES

Basic Indicators		Units	2001	2002	2003	2004	2005
	INBOUND TOURISM						
	Arrivals						
1.1	Visitors	('000)	254	247	242	262	258
1.2	Tourists (overnight visitors)	('000)	71	78	79	87	96
1.3	Same-day visitors	('000)	15	13	14	13	9
1.4	Cruise passengers	('000)	168	157	149	162	154
	Arrivals by region						
2.1	Africa	('000)	..	..	..	..	..
2.2	Americas	('000)	51	58	60	67	74
2.3	Europe	('000)	19	18	17	19	20
2.4	East Asia and the Pacific	('000)	..	..	..	..	..
2.5	South Asia	('000)	..	..	..	..	..
2.6	Middle East	('000)	..	..	..	..	..
	Arrivals by means of transport used						
3.1	Air	('000)	86	90	92	100	104
3.2	Rail	('000)	..	..	..	..	..
3.3	Road	('000)	..	..	..	..	..
3.4	Sea	('000)	168	157	149	162	154
	Arrivals by purpose of visit						
4.1	Leisure, recreation and holidays	('000)	..	61	63	63	68
4.2	Business and professional	('000)	..	13	14	17	21
4.3	Other	('000)	..	4	2	7	7
	Accommodation						
5.1	Overnight stays in hotels and similar establishments	('000)	..	..	..	..	..
5.2	Guests in hotels and similar establishments	('000)	34	28	26	28	31
5.3	Overnight stays in all types of accommodation establishments	('000)	..	..	..	..	..
5.4	Average length of stay of non-resident tourists in all accommodation establishments	Nights	..	11.90	7.20	12.50	..
6.1	**Tourism expenditure in the country**	US$ Mn	..	..	..	..	..
6.2	"Travel" (*)	US$ Mn	89	91	91	96	105
6.3	"Passenger transport" (*)	US$ Mn	..	..	..	..	..
	DOMESTIC TOURISM						
	Accommodation						
7.1	Overnight stays in hotels and similar establishments	('000)	..	..	..	..	..
7.2	Guests in hotels and similar establishments	('000)	..	..	..	..	..
7.3	Overnight stays in all types of accommodation establishments	('000)	..	..	..	..	..
7.4	Average length of stay of resident tourists in all accommodation establishments	Nights	..	..	..	..	..
	OUTBOUND TOURISM						
8.1	**Departures**	('000)	..	..	..	..	..
8.2	**Tourism expenditure in other countries**	US$ Mn	..	..	..	..	..
8.3	"Travel" (*)	US$ Mn	12	10	13	14	14
8.4	"Passenger transport" (*)	US$ Mn	..	..	..	..	..
	TOURISM INDUSTRIES						
	Hotels and similar establishments						
9.1	Number of rooms	Units	1,757	1,689	1,680	1,785	1,692
9.2	Number of bed-places	Units	3,514	3,378	3,360	3,570	3,384
9.3	Occupancy rate	Percent	..	..	..	..	..
9.4	Average length of stay	Nights	..	..	..	..	..
	RELATED INDICATORS						
	Share of tourism expenditure (6.1) in: (**)						
10.1	Gross Domestic Product (GDP)	Percent	25.7	24.9	23.9	23.8	24.5
10.2	Exports of goods	Percent	207.0	222.0	227.5	246.2	244.2
10.3	Exports of services	Percent	66.9	66.4	68.4	66.2	66.9

(*) Balance of Payments items: 6.1 to 6.3 correspond to the "Credit" side (and are receipts for the country) while 8.2 to 8.4 correspond to the "Debit" side (and are expenditures in other countries).

(**) See Annex "Country notes".

SAMOA

	Basic Indicators	Units	2001	2002	2003	2004	2005
	INBOUND TOURISM						
	Arrivals						
1.1	Visitors	('000)	..	..	..	..	..
1.2	Tourists (overnight visitors)	('000)	88	89	92	98	102
1.3	Same-day visitors	('000)	..	..	..	..	..
1.4	Cruise passengers	('000)	..	..	..	..	..
	Arrivals by region						
2.1	Africa	('000)	..	..	..	..	..
2.2	Americas	('000)	9	9	9	8	10
2.3	Europe	('000)	6	5	5	5	5
2.4	East Asia and the Pacific	('000)	73	75	78	85	87
2.5	South Asia	('000)	..	..	..	..	..
2.6	Middle East	('000)	..	..	..	..	..
	Arrivals by means of transport used						
3.1	Air	('000)	85	86	89	94	99
3.2	Rail	('000)	..	..	..	..	..
3.3	Road	('000)	..	..	..	..	..
3.4	Sea	('000)	3	3	3	4	3
	Arrivals by purpose of visit						
4.1	Leisure, recreation and holidays	('000)	29	29	30	30	34
4.2	Business and professional	('000)	11	10	10	11	10
4.3	Other	('000)	48	50	52	57	58
	Accommodation						
5.1	Overnight stays in hotels and similar establishments	('000)	..	..	..	..	..
5.2	Guests in hotels and similar establishments	('000)	..	..	..	..	..
5.3	Overnight stays in all types of accommodation establishments	('000)	..	..	..	..	..
5.4	Average length of stay of non-resident tourists in all accommodation establishments	Nights	..	..	..	..	..
6.1	**Tourism expenditure in the country**	US$ Mn	..	..	..	71	78
6.2	"Travel" (*)	US$ Mn	39	45	54	70	77
6.3	"Passenger transport" (*)	US$ Mn	..	..	..	1	1
	DOMESTIC TOURISM						
	Accommodation						
7.1	Overnight stays in hotels and similar establishments	('000)	..	..	..	..	..
7.2	Guests in hotels and similar establishments	('000)	..	..	..	..	..
7.3	Overnight stays in all types of accommodation establishments	('000)	..	..	..	..	..
7.4	Average length of stay of resident tourists in all accommodation establishments	Nights	..	..	..	..	..
	OUTBOUND TOURISM						
8.1	**Departures**	('000)	..	..	..	..	..
8.2	**Tourism expenditure in other countries**	US$ Mn	..	..	..	12	13
8.3	"Travel" (*)	US$ Mn	..	..	..	5	9
8.4	"Passenger transport" (*)	US$ Mn	..	..	..	7	4
	TOURISM INDUSTRIES						
	Hotels and similar establishments						
9.1	Number of rooms	Units	817	850	939	..	..
9.2	Number of bed-places	Units	1,920	1,945	2,131	..	..
9.3	Occupancy rate	Percent	..	..	..	..	..
9.4	Average length of stay	Nights	..	..	..	..	..
	RELATED INDICATORS						
	Share of tourism expenditure (6.1) in:						
10.1	Gross Domestic Product (GDP)	Percent	..	..	..	19.9	19.5
10.2	Exports of goods	Percent	..	..	..	591.7	650.0
10.3	Exports of services	Percent	..	..	..	74.7	69.6

(*) Balance of Payments items: 6.1 to 6.3 correspond to the "Credit" side (and are receipts for the country) while 8.2 to 8.4 correspond to the "Debit" side (and are expenditures in other countries).

	Basic Indicators	Units	2001	2002	2003	2004	2005
	INBOUND TOURISM						
	Arrivals						
1.1	Visitors	('000)	3,036	3,102	2,882	2,812	2,107
1.2	Tourists (overnight visitors)	('000)	49	46	41	42	50
1.3	Same-day visitors	('000)	..	..	..	..	2,057
1.4	Cruise passengers	('000)	..	..	..	..	..
	Arrivals by region						
2.1	Africa	('000)	..	..	..	..	..
2.2	Americas	('000)	..	..	..	..	17
2.3	Europe	('000)	..	..	..	..	2,035
2.4	East Asia and the Pacific	('000)	..	..	..	..	53
2.5	South Asia	('000)	..	..	..	..	..
2.6	Middle East	('000)	..	..	..	..	..
	Arrivals by means of transport used						
3.1	Air	('000)	..	..	..	..	..
3.2	Rail	('000)	..	..	..	..	..
3.3	Road	('000)	3,036	3,102	2,882	2,812	2,107
3.4	Sea	('000)	..	..	..	..	..
	Arrivals by purpose of visit						
4.1	Leisure, recreation and holidays	('000)	..	..	..	..	738
4.2	Business and professional	('000)	..	..	..	..	695
4.3	Other	('000)	..	..	..	..	674
	Accommodation						
5.1	Overnight stays in hotels and similar establishments	('000)	75	69	64	68	80
5.2	Guests in hotels and similar establishments	('000)	49	46	41	42	50
5.3	Overnight stays in all types of accommodation establishments	('000)	..	..	..	..	..
5.4	Average length of stay of non-resident tourists in all accommodation establishments	Nights	..	..	..	1.64	1.61
6.1	**Tourism expenditure in the country**	US$ Mn	..	..	..	..	..
6.2	"Travel" (*)	US$ Mn	..	..	..	..	..
6.3	"Passenger transport" (*)	US$ Mn	..	..	..	..	..
	DOMESTIC TOURISM						
	Accommodation						
7.1	Overnight stays in hotels and similar establishments	('000)	..	..	..	..	..
7.2	Guests in hotels and similar establishments	('000)	..	..	..	..	..
7.3	Overnight stays in all types of accommodation establishments	('000)	..	..	..	..	..
7.4	Average length of stay of resident tourists in all accommodation establishments	Nights	..	..	..	..	..
	OUTBOUND TOURISM						
8.1	**Departures**	('000)	..	..	..	..	..
8.2	**Tourism expenditure in other countries**	US$ Mn	..	..	..	..	..
8.3	"Travel" (*)	US$ Mn	..	..	..	..	..
8.4	"Passenger transport" (*)	US$ Mn	..	..	..	..	..
	TOURISM INDUSTRIES						
	Hotels and similar establishments						
9.1	Number of rooms	Units	486	500	683	685	718
9.2	Number of bed-places	Units	1,164	1,180	1,549	1,549	1,593
9.3	Occupancy rate	Percent	..	..	..	..	54.10
9.4	Average length of stay	Nights	1.53	1.51	1.57	1.63	1.61
	RELATED INDICATORS						
	Share of tourism expenditure (6.1) in:						
10.1	Gross Domestic Product (GDP)	Percent	..	..	..	..	..
10.2	Exports of goods	Percent	..	..	..	..	..
10.3	Exports of services	Percent	..	..	..	..	..

(*) Balance of Payments items: 6.1 to 6.3 correspond to the "Credit" side (and are receipts for the country) while 8.2 to 8.4 correspond to the "Debit" side (and are expenditures in other countries).

SAO TOME AND PRINCIPE

	Basic Indicators	Units	2001	2002	2003	2004	2005
	INBOUND TOURISM						
	Arrivals						
1.1	Visitors	('000)	7.7	..	..	..	..
1.2	Tourists (overnight visitors)	('000)	7.5	9.2	9.6	10.7	10.5
1.3	Same-day visitors	('000)	0.2	..	..	..	..
1.4	Cruise passengers	('000)	..	..	..	..	..
	Arrivals by region						
2.1	Africa	('000)	1.4	1.8	2.1	2.2	2.0
2.2	Americas	('000)	..	..	0.3	0.3	0.2
2.3	Europe	('000)	4.2	2.4	6.3	6.3	7.7
2.4	East Asia and the Pacific	('000)	..	..	..	..	..
2.5	South Asia	('000)	..	..	..	..	..
2.6	Middle East	('000)	..	..	..	..	..
	Arrivals by means of transport used						
3.1	Air	('000)	7.5	9.2	9.6	10.7	10.5
3.2	Rail	('000)	..	..	..	..	..
3.3	Road	('000)	..	..	..	..	..
3.4	Sea	('000)	..	..	..	..	..
	Arrivals by purpose of visit						
4.1	Leisure, recreation and holidays	('000)	3.2	..	..	..	9.0
4.2	Business and professional	('000)	0.6	..	..	..	1.0
4.3	Other	('000)	3.8	..	..	..	0.5
	Accommodation						
5.1	Overnight stays in hotels and similar establishments	('000)	..	..	..	..	..
5.2	Guests in hotels and similar establishments	('000)	..	..	..	..	..
5.3	Overnight stays in all types of accommodation establishments	('000)	..	..	..	..	..
5.4	Average length of stay of non-resident tourists in all accommodation establishments	Nights	..	..	..	..	..
6.1	**Tourism expenditure in the country**	US$ Mn	..	..	..	..	..
6.2	"Travel" (*)	US$ Mn	9.6	10.1	10.6	12.8	13.6
6.3	"Passenger transport" (*)	US$ Mn	..	..	..	..	..
	DOMESTIC TOURISM						
	Accommodation						
7.1	Overnight stays in hotels and similar establishments	('000)	..	..	..	..	..
7.2	Guests in hotels and similar establishments	('000)	..	..	..	..	..
7.3	Overnight stays in all types of accommodation establishments	('000)	..	..	..	..	..
7.4	Average length of stay of resident tourists in all accommodation establishments	Nights	..	..	..	..	..
	OUTBOUND TOURISM						
8.1	**Departures**	('000)	..	..	..	..	..
8.2	**Tourism expenditure in other countries**	US$ Mn	2.0	1.9	..	..	..
8.3	"Travel" (*)	US$ Mn	0.6	0.6	..	..	..
8.4	"Passenger transport" (*)	US$ Mn	1.4	1.3	..	..	..
	TOURISM INDUSTRIES						
	Hotels and similar establishments						
9.1	Number of rooms	Units	..	..	..	..	..
9.2	Number of bed-places	Units	..	..	..	..	..
9.3	Occupancy rate	Percent	..	..	..	..	..
9.4	Average length of stay	Nights	..	..	..	..	..
	RELATED INDICATORS						
	Share of tourism expenditure (6.1) in: (**)						
10.1	Gross Domestic Product (GDP)	Percent	20.0	18.7	17.7	22.5	23.9
10.2	Exports of goods	Percent	320.0	202.0	151.4	320.0	453.3
10.3	Exports of services	Percent	73.8	77.7	75.7	75.3	75.6

(*) Balance of Payments items: 6.1 to 6.3 correspond to the "Credit" side (and are receipts for the country) while 8.2 to 8.4 correspond to the "Debit" side (and are expenditures in other countries).

(**) See Annex "Country notes".

SAUDI ARABIA

	Basic Indicators		Units	2001	2002	2003	2004	2005
	INBOUND TOURISM							
	Arrivals							
1.1	Visitors		('000)	..	..	..	11,083	10,417
1.2	Tourists (overnight visitors)		('000)	6,727	7,511	7,332	8,599	8,037
1.3	Same-day visitors		('000)	..	..	..	2,484	2,380
1.4	Cruise passengers		('000)	..	..	..	..	..
	Arrivals by region							
2.1	Africa		('000)	535	607	525	675	436
2.2	Americas		('000)	47	52	46	53	70
2.3	Europe		('000)	305	339	334	424	340
2.4	East Asia and the Pacific		('000)	596	660	612	753	439
2.5	South Asia		('000)	1,371	1,619	1,869	1,933	1,142
2.6	Middle East		('000)	3,853	4,213	3,924	4,752	5,607
	Arrivals by means of transport used							
3.1	Air		('000)	..	..	..	4,194	4,287
3.2	Rail		('000)	..	..	..	..	..
3.3	Road		('000)	..	..	..	3,824	3,301
3.4	Sea		('000)	..	..	..	581	488
	Arrivals by purpose of visit							
4.1	Leisure, recreation and holidays		('000)	..	..	..	433	397
4.2	Business and professional		('000)	..	..	..	2,381	1,951
4.3	Other		('000)	..	..	..	5,785	5,689
	Accommodation							
5.1	Overnight stays in hotels and similar establishments		('000)	..	..	..	63,341	62,120
5.2	Guests in hotels and similar establishments		('000)	..	..	..	..	..
5.3	Overnight stays in all types of accommodation establishments		('000)	..	..	..	112,556	91,359
5.4	Average length of stay of non-resident tourists in all accommodation establishments		Nights	..	..	..	13.12	10.70
6.1	**Tourism expenditure in the country**	(**)	US$ Mn	..	..	3,418	6,486	5,181
6.2	"Travel" (*)		US$ Mn	..	..	..	..	..
6.3	"Passenger transport" (*)		US$ Mn	..	..	..	..	..
	DOMESTIC TOURISM							
	Accommodation							
7.1	Overnight stays in hotels and similar establishments		('000)	..	..	..	111,656	103,238
7.2	Guests in hotels and similar establishments		('000)	..	..	..	..	..
7.3	Overnight stays in all types of accommodation establishments		('000)	..	334,100	284,900	215,220	196,737
7.4	Average length of stay of resident tourists in all accommodation establishments		Nights	..	..	5.90	6.10	6.40
	OUTBOUND TOURISM							
8.1	**Departures**		('000)	..	7,896	4,104	4,235	5,009
8.2	**Tourism expenditure in other countries**	(**)	US$ Mn	..	7,370	4,165	5,038	4,764
8.3	"Travel" (*)		US$ Mn	..	..	..	..	..
8.4	"Passenger transport" (*)		US$ Mn	..	..	..	..	..
	TOURISM INDUSTRIES							
	Hotels and similar establishments							
9.1	Number of rooms		Units	81,197	81,197	81,197	96,144	104,093
9.2	Number of bed-places		Units	..	..	..	..	..
9.3	Occupancy rate		Percent	..	..	42.00	50.60	51.30
9.4	Average length of stay		Nights	..	..	2.70	2.27	2.23
	RELATED INDICATORS							
	Share of tourism expenditure (6.1) in:							
10.1	Gross Domestic Product (GDP)		Percent	..	..	..	..	..
10.2	Exports of goods		Percent	..	..	..	..	..
10.3	Exports of services		Percent	..	..	..	..	..

(*) Balance of Payments items: 6.1 to 6.3 correspond to the "Credit" side (and are receipts for the country) while 8.2 to 8.4 correspond to the "Debit" side (and are expenditures in other countries).

(**) See Annex "Country notes".

SENEGAL

	Basic Indicators	Units	2001	2002	2003	2004	2005
	INBOUND TOURISM						
	Arrivals						
1.1	Visitors	('000)	..	..	502	677	779
1.2	Tourists (overnight visitors)	('000)	396	427	495	667	769
1.3	Same-day visitors	('000)	..	..	..	..	..
1.4	Cruise passengers	('000)	13	7	7	10	9
	Arrivals by region						
2.1	Africa	('000)	78	86	86	209	265
2.2	Americas	('000)	11	10	10	25	26
2.3	Europe	('000)	301	323	252	349	393
2.4	East Asia and the Pacific	('000)	2	2	2	..	..
2.5	South Asia	('000)	..	..	..	..	..
2.6	Middle East	('000)	1	1	1	..	..
	Arrivals by means of transport used						
3.1	Air	('000)	..	..	..	523	564
3.2	Rail	('000)	..	..	..	..	..
3.3	Road	('000)	..	..	..	144	206
3.4	Sea	('000)	..	..	..	10	9
	Arrivals by purpose of visit						
4.1	Leisure, recreation and holidays	('000)	..	..	..	..	..
4.2	Business and professional	('000)	..	..	..	..	..
4.3	Other	('000)	..	..	..	..	..
	Accommodation						
5.1	Overnight stays in hotels and similar establishments	('000)	1,497	1,569	1,451	1,349	1,397
5.2	Guests in hotels and similar establishments	('000)	396	427	354	363	387
5.3	Overnight stays in all types of accommodation establishments	('000)	..	..	..	..	..
5.4	Average length of stay of non-resident tourists in all accommodation establishments	Nights	3.80	3.70	4.10	3.50	3.40
6.1	**Tourism expenditure in the country**	US$ Mn	175	210	269	287	..
6.2	"Travel" (*)	US$ Mn	174	190	209	212	..
6.3	"Passenger transport" (*)	US$ Mn	1	20	60	75	..
	DOMESTIC TOURISM						
	Accommodation						
7.1	Overnight stays in hotels and similar establishments	('000)	118	133	156	159	198
7.2	Guests in hotels and similar establishments	('000)	57	61	65	71	81
7.3	Overnight stays in all types of accommodation establishments	('000)	..	..	..	..	..
7.4	Average length of stay of resident tourists in all accommodation establishments	Nights	..	..	..	..	..
	OUTBOUND TOURISM						
8.1	**Departures**	('000)	..	..	..	..	..
8.2	**Tourism expenditure in other countries**	US$ Mn	112	112	129	138	..
8.3	"Travel" (*)	US$ Mn	43	43	55	57	..
8.4	"Passenger transport" (*)	US$ Mn	69	69	74	81	..
	TOURISM INDUSTRIES						
	Hotels and similar establishments						
9.1	Number of rooms	Units	9,589	9,905	10,268	10,884	15,842
9.2	Number of bed-places	Units	19,208	19,729	20,437	21,741	31,229
9.3	Occupancy rate	Percent	37.70	38.60	37.10	34.00	34.40
9.4	Average length of stay	Nights	3.80	3.70	4.10	3.70	3.60
	RELATED INDICATORS						
	Share of tourism expenditure (6.1) in:						
10.1	Gross Domestic Product (GDP)	Percent	3.8	4.2	4.2	3.8	..
10.2	Exports of goods	Percent	17.4	19.7	21.4	19.0	..
10.3	Exports of services	Percent	44.0	46.1	47.3	42.8	..

(*) Balance of Payments items: 6.1 to 6.3 correspond to the "Credit" side (and are receipts for the country) while 8.2 to 8.4 correspond to the "Debit" side (and are expenditures in other countries).

	Basic Indicators		Units	2001	2002	2003	2004	2005
	INBOUND TOURISM							
	Arrivals							
1.1	Visitors		('000)	..	..	..	..	..
1.2	Tourists (overnight visitors)		('000)	351	448	481	580	725
1.3	Same-day visitors		('000)	..	..	..	..	..
1.4	Cruise passengers		('000)	..	..	..	..	..
	Arrivals by region							
2.1	Africa		('000)	..	..	..	..	..
2.2	Americas		('000)	11	15	17	17	20
2.3	Europe		('000)	327	419	450	545	683
2.4	East Asia and the Pacific		('000)	3	3	4	6	7
2.5	South Asia		('000)	..	..	..	..	..
2.6	Middle East		('000)	..	..	..	..	..
	Arrivals by means of transport used							
3.1	Air		('000)	..	..	..	..	..
3.2	Rail		('000)	..	..	..	..	..
3.3	Road		('000)	..	..	..	..	..
3.4	Sea		('000)	..	..	..	..	..
	Arrivals by purpose of visit							
4.1	Leisure, recreation and holidays		('000)	..	..	..	..	..
4.2	Business and professional		('000)	..	..	..	..	..
4.3	Other		('000)	..	..	..	..	..
	Accommodation							
5.1	Overnight stays in hotels and similar establishments		('000)	1,047	1,404	1,425	1,715	1,966
5.2	Guests in hotels and similar establishments		('000)	313	408	435	524	624
5.3	Overnight stays in all types of accommodation establishments		('000)	1,281	1,650	1,707	2,075	2,575
5.4	Average length of stay of non-resident tourists in all accommodation establishments		Nights	..	..	..	..	..
6.1	**Tourism expenditure in the country**		US$ Mn	..	..	..	..	..
6.2	"Travel" (*)	(**)	US$ Mn	54	97	201	..	..
6.3	"Passenger transport" (*)		US$ Mn	..	..	..	..	..
	DOMESTIC TOURISM							
	Accommodation							
7.1	Overnight stays in hotels and similar establishments		('000)	5,297	5,118	4,650	4,915	4,707
7.2	Guests in hotels and similar establishments		('000)	1,531	1,543	1,353	1,377	1,347
7.3	Overnight stays in all types of accommodation establishments		('000)	9,926	9,246	8,953	9,129	9,136
7.4	Average length of stay of resident tourists in all accommodation establishments		Nights	4.30	4.00	4.20	4.40	4.38
	OUTBOUND TOURISM							
8.1	**Departures**		('000)	..	..	..	..	..
8.2	**Tourism expenditure in other countries**		US$ Mn	..	..	..	..	..
8.3	"Travel" (*)		US$ Mn	..	..	..	..	..
8.4	"Passenger transport" (*)		US$ Mn	..	..	..	..	..
	TOURISM INDUSTRIES							
	Hotels and similar establishments							
9.1	Number of rooms		Units	37,782	37,882	37,101	38,736	39,730
9.2	Number of bed-places		Units	79,558	79,532	77,509	83,025	85,723
9.3	Occupancy rate		Percent	21.80	22.50	21.50	21.90	21.33
9.4	Average length of stay		Nights	4.20	4.00	4.10	4.19	4.17
	RELATED INDICATORS							
	Share of tourism expenditure (6.1) in:							
10.1	Gross Domestic Product (GDP)		Percent	..	..	..	..	..
10.2	Exports of goods		Percent	..	..	..	..	..
10.3	Exports of services		Percent	..	..	..	..	..

(*) Balance of Payments items: 6.1 to 6.3 correspond to the "Credit" side (and are receipts for the country) while 8.2 to 8.4 correspond to the "Debit" side (and are expenditures in other countries).

(**) See Annex "Country notes".

SEYCHELLES

	Basic Indicators	Units	2001	2002	2003	2004	2005
	INBOUND TOURISM						
	Arrivals						
1.1	Visitors	('000)	138	135	127	126	135
1.2	Tourists (overnight visitors)	('000)	130	132	122	121	129
1.3	Same-day visitors	('000)	..	..	..	..	..
1.4	Cruise passengers	('000)	8	3	5	5	6
	Arrivals by region						
2.1	Africa	('000)	14	14	14	13	12
2.2	Americas	('000)	7	4	3	4	4
2.3	Europe	('000)	103	108	100	99	104
2.4	East Asia and the Pacific	('000)	3	3	2	2	3
2.5	South Asia	('000)	2	2	1	1	2
2.6	Middle East	('000)	1	2	2	2	4
	Arrivals by means of transport used						
3.1	Air	('000)	127	129	119	117	125
3.2	Rail	('000)	..	..	..	..	..
3.3	Road	('000)	..	..	..	..	..
3.4	Sea	('000)	3	3	3	4	4
	Arrivals by purpose of visit						
4.1	Leisure, recreation and holidays	('000)	116	117	110	108	116
4.2	Business and professional	('000)	6	7	6	7	7
4.3	Other	('000)	8	8	6	6	6
	Accommodation						
5.1	Overnight stays in hotels and similar establishments	('000)	913	883	825	798	..
5.2	Guests in hotels and similar establishments	('000)	..	..	..	..	..
5.3	Overnight stays in all types of accommodation establishments	('000)	..	..	..	..	..
5.4	Average length of stay of non-resident tourists in all accommodation establishments	Nights	10.40	10.10	10.10	10.00	9.70
6.1	**Tourism expenditure in the country**	US$ Mn	221	247	259	256	269
6.2	"Travel" (*)	US$ Mn	146	164	171	172	192
6.3	"Passenger transport" (*)	US$ Mn	75	83	88	84	77
	DOMESTIC TOURISM						
	Accommodation						
7.1	Overnight stays in hotels and similar establishments	('000)	12	14	8	10	..
7.2	Guests in hotels and similar establishments	('000)	..	..	..	..	..
7.3	Overnight stays in all types of accommodation establishments	('000)	..	..	..	..	..
7.4	Average length of stay of resident tourists in all accommodation establishments	Nights	..	..	..	..	..
	OUTBOUND TOURISM						
8.1	**Departures**	('000)	41	53	50	48	52
8.2	**Tourism expenditure in other countries**	US$ Mn	41	53	54	53	59
8.3	"Travel" (*)	US$ Mn	23	33	36	34	39
8.4	"Passenger transport" (*)	US$ Mn	18	20	18	19	20
	TOURISM INDUSTRIES						
	Hotels and similar establishments						
9.1	Number of rooms	Units	2,444	2,358	2,435	2,477	..
9.2	Number of bed-places	Units	4,940	4,780	4,930	5,030	4,920
9.3	Occupancy rate	Percent	52.00	51.00	51.00	44.00	46.00
9.4	Average length of stay	Nights	..	..	..	..	..
	RELATED INDICATORS						
	Share of tourism expenditure (6.1) in:						
10.1	Gross Domestic Product (GDP)	Percent	35.7	35.4	36.8	36.4	38.8
10.2	Exports of goods	Percent	102.3	104.2	90.6	85.0	75.6
10.3	Exports of services	Percent	75.2	78.9	78.5	78.3	73.1

(*) Balance of Payments items: 6.1 to 6.3 correspond to the "Credit" side (and are receipts for the country) while 8.2 to 8.4 correspond to the "Debit" side (and are expenditures in other countries).

	Basic Indicators	Units	2001	2002	2003	2004	2005
	INBOUND TOURISM						
	Arrivals						
1.1	Visitors	('000)	..	..	..	..	..
1.2	Tourists (overnight visitors)	('000)	24	28	38	44	40
1.3	Same-day visitors	('000)	..	..	..	..	..
1.4	Cruise passengers	('000)	..	..	..	..	..
	Arrivals by region						
2.1	Africa	('000)	11	13	23	24	22
2.2	Americas	('000)	3	4	5	5	5
2.3	Europe	('000)	6	7	6	9	10
2.4	East Asia and the Pacific	('000)	2	2	2	2	2
2.5	South Asia	('000)	..	..	..	..	..
2.6	Middle East	('000)	1	2	2	3	1
	Arrivals by means of transport used						
3.1	Air	('000)	24	28	38	44	40
3.2	Rail	('000)	..	..	..	..	..
3.3	Road	('000)	..	..	..	..	..
3.4	Sea	('000)	..	..	..	..	..
	Arrivals by purpose of visit						
4.1	Leisure, recreation and holidays	('000)	4	5	8	7	5
4.2	Business and professional	('000)	10	11	20	15	14
4.3	Other	('000)	10	12	9	22	21
	Accommodation						
5.1	Overnight stays in hotels and similar establishments	('000)	120	142	191	218	280
5.2	Guests in hotels and similar establishments	('000)	..	..	..	..	..
5.3	Overnight stays in all types of accommodation establishments	('000)	..	..	..	..	..
5.4	Average length of stay of non-resident tourists in all accommodation establishments	Nights	2.40	2.43	3.16	2.80	7.00
6.1	**Tourism expenditure in the country**	US$ Mn	..	..	..	..	..
6.2	"Travel" (*)	US$ Mn	14	38	60	58	64
6.3	"Passenger transport" (*)	US$ Mn	..	..	..	..	..
	DOMESTIC TOURISM						
	Accommodation						
7.1	Overnight stays in hotels and similar establishments	('000)	..	..	..	..	..
7.2	Guests in hotels and similar establishments	('000)	..	..	..	..	..
7.3	Overnight stays in all types of accommodation establishments	('000)	..	..	..	..	..
7.4	Average length of stay of resident tourists in all accommodation establishments	Nights	..	..	..	..	..
	OUTBOUND TOURISM						
8.1	**Departures**	('000)	20	27	13	28	63
8.2	**Tourism expenditure in other countries**	US$ Mn	42.2	39.1	37.8	30.3	33.6
8.3	"Travel" (*)	US$ Mn	42	39	37	30	32
8.4	"Passenger transport" (*)	US$ Mn	0.2	0.1	0.8	0.3	1.6
	TOURISM INDUSTRIES						
	Hotels and similar establishments						
9.1	Number of rooms	Units	739	869	1,457	1,622	2,012
9.2	Number of bed-places	Units	863	993	1,718	2,331	2,519
9.3	Occupancy rate	Percent	19.00	14.00	13.00	12.00	11.00
9.4	Average length of stay	Nights	5.00	5.00	5.00	5.00	7.00
	RELATED INDICATORS						
	Share of tourism expenditure (6.1) in: (**)						
10.1	Gross Domestic Product (GDP)	Percent	1.7	4.1	6.1	5.4	5.4
10.2	Exports of goods	Percent	48.3	63.3	54.1	37.7	34.6
10.3	Exports of services	Percent	26.9	100.0	90.9	95.1	82.1

(*) Balance of Payments items: 6.1 to 6.3 correspond to the "Credit" side (and are receipts for the country) while 8.2 to 8.4 correspond to the "Debit" side (and are expenditures in other countries).

(**) See Annex "Country notes".

SINGAPORE

	Basic Indicators	Units	2001	2002	2003	2004	2005
	INBOUND TOURISM						
	Arrivals						
1.1	Visitors	('000)	7,522	7,567	6,127	8,329	8,943
1.2	Tourists (overnight visitors)	('000)	5,857	5,855	4,703	6,553	7,080
1.3	Same-day visitors	('000)	1,665	1,712	1,424	1,776	1,863
1.4	Cruise passengers	('000)	..	..	..	..	..
	Arrivals by region						
2.1	Africa	('000)	81	70	56	71	79
2.2	Americas	('000)	434	416	315	422	470
2.3	Europe	('000)	1,124	1,112	885	1,081	1,136
2.4	East Asia and the Pacific	('000)	5,298	5,426	4,426	6,073	6,445
2.5	South Asia	('000)	508	490	415	626	751
2.6	Middle East	('000)	72	47	30	55	56
	Arrivals by means of transport used						
3.1	Air	('000)	5,404	5,394	4,232	5,728	6,267
3.2	Rail	('000)	..	..	..	..	..
3.3	Road	('000)	921	997	867	1,269	1,312
3.4	Sea	('000)	1,197	1,177	1,028	1,332	1,364
	Arrivals by purpose of visit						
4.1	Leisure, recreation and holidays	('000)	3,488	3,548	2,713	..	..
4.2	Business and professional	('000)	1,601	1,567	1,299	..	..
4.3	Other	('000)	2,434	2,452	2,115	..	..
	Accommodation						
5.1	Overnight stays in hotels and similar establishments	('000)	..	..	..	..	..
5.2	Guests in hotels and similar establishments	('000)	4,456	4,483	3,473	..	..
5.3	Overnight stays in all types of accommodation establishments	('000)	..	..	..	..	..
5.4	Average length of stay of non-resident tourists in all accommodation establishments	Nights	3.19	3.08	3.18	3.21	3.38
6.1	**Tourism expenditure in the country**	US$ Mn	..	..	..	..	..
6.2	"Travel" (*)	US$ Mn	4,619	4,428	3,783	5,224	5,736
6.3	"Passenger transport" (*)	US$ Mn	..	..	..	..	..
	DOMESTIC TOURISM						
	Accommodation						
7.1	Overnight stays in hotels and similar establishments	('000)	..	..	..	..	..
7.2	Guests in hotels and similar establishments	('000)	..	..	..	..	..
7.3	Overnight stays in all types of accommodation establishments	('000)	..	..	..	..	..
7.4	Average length of stay of resident tourists in all accommodation establishments	Nights	..	..	..	..	..
	OUTBOUND TOURISM						
8.1	**Departures**	('000)	4,363	4,399	4,221	5,165	5,159
8.2	**Tourism expenditure in other countries**	US$ Mn	..	..	..	..	..
8.3	"Travel" (*)	US$ Mn	6,621	8,157	7,991	9,585	9,853
8.4	"Passenger transport" (*)	US$ Mn	..	..	..	..	..
	TOURISM INDUSTRIES						
	Hotels and similar establishments						
9.1	Number of rooms	Units	35,674	35,989	35,930	36,765	36,861
9.2	Number of bed-places	Units	..	..	..	..	..
9.3	Occupancy rate	Percent	76.30	74.40	67.20	80.60	83.80
9.4	Average length of stay	Nights	2.70	2.62	2.70	..	..
	RELATED INDICATORS						
	Share of tourism expenditure (6.1) in: (**)						
10.1	Gross Domestic Product (GDP)	Percent	5.4	5.0	4.1	4.9	4.9
10.2	Exports of goods	Percent	3.4	3.1	2.3	2.6	2.5
10.3	Exports of services	Percent	16.8	15.0	10.4	11.2	11.2

(*) Balance of Payments items: 6.1 to 6.3 correspond to the "Credit" side (and are receipts for the country) while 8.2 to 8.4 correspond to the "Debit" side (and are expenditures in other countries).

(**) See Annex "Country notes".

Basic Indicators		Units	2001	2002	2003	2004	2005
	INBOUND TOURISM						
	Arrivals						
1.1	Visitors	('000)	27,761	26,450	24,985	26,415	29,396
1.2	Tourists (overnight visitors)	('000)	1,219	1,399	1,387	1,401	1,515
1.3	Same-day visitors	('000)	..	..	..	..	..
1.4	Cruise passengers	('000)	..	..	..	..	..
	Arrivals by region						
2.1	Africa	('000)	3	3	3	2	2
2.2	Americas	('000)	36	33	34	39	42
2.3	Europe	('000)	1,148	1,326	1,316	1,317	1,413
2.4	East Asia and the Pacific	('000)	30	34	32	42	56
2.5	South Asia	('000)	2	1	1	..	1
2.6	Middle East	('000)	..	..	..	..	..
	Arrivals by means of transport used						
3.1	Air	('000)	6	7	9	14	16
3.2	Rail	('000)	56	55	56	57	54
3.3	Road	('000)	11,800	11,566	11,407	12,535	13,807
3.4	Sea	('000)	3	3	3	4	3
	Arrivals by purpose of visit						
4.1	Leisure, recreation and holidays	('000)	..	..	..	..	..
4.2	Business and professional	('000)	..	..	..	..	..
4.3	Other	('000)	..	..	..	..	..
	Accommodation						
5.1	Overnight stays in hotels and similar establishments	('000)	3,550	4,050	3,989	3,820	4,055
5.2	Guests in hotels and similar establishments	('000)	1,033	1,154	1,151	1,188	1,307
5.3	Overnight stays in all types of accommodation establishments	('000)	4,378	5,043	4,964	4,675	4,872
5.4	Average length of stay of non-resident tourists in all accommodation establishments	Nights	3.60	3.60	3.60	3.30	3.20
6.1	**Tourism expenditure in the country**	US$ Mn	649	742	876	932	..
6.2	"Travel" (*)	US$ Mn	641	736	865	901	1,210
6.3	"Passenger transport" (*)	US$ Mn	8	6	11	31	..
	DOMESTIC TOURISM						
	Accommodation						
7.1	Overnight stays in hotels and similar establishments	('000)	3,837	4,917	4,789	4,148	3,978
7.2	Guests in hotels and similar establishments	('000)	1,460	1,591	1,530	1,439	1,495
7.3	Overnight stays in all types of accommodation establishments	('000)	6,942	7,263	7,095	6,074	5,861
7.4	Average length of stay of resident tourists in all accommodation establishments	Nights	3.60	3.50	3.60	3.30	3.10
	OUTBOUND TOURISM						
8.1	**Departures**	('000)	373	437	408	457	486
8.2	**Tourism expenditure in other countries**	US$ Mn	340	506	662	903	..
8.3	"Travel" (*)	US$ Mn	289	442	573	745	846
8.4	"Passenger transport" (*)	US$ Mn	51	64	89	158	..
	TOURISM INDUSTRIES						
	Hotels and similar establishments						
9.1	Number of rooms	Units	31,655	34,619	35,853	35,544	35,688
9.2	Number of bed-places	Units	82,156	87,554	90,773	90,004	90,093
9.3	Occupancy rate	Percent	33.20	40.00	38.70	34.70	35.00
9.4	Average length of stay	Nights	3.00	3.20	3.20	2.90	2.80
	RELATED INDICATORS						
	Share of tourism expenditure (6.1) in:						
10.1	Gross Domestic Product (GDP)	Percent	3.1	3.1	2.7	2.3	2.6
10.2	Exports of goods	Percent	5.1	5.1	4.0	3.4	3.8
10.3	Exports of services	Percent	26.1	26.4	26.6	25.0	27.5

(*) Balance of Payments items: 6.1 to 6.3 correspond to the "Credit" side (and are receipts for the country) while 8.2 to 8.4 correspond to the "Debit" side (and are expenditures in other countries).

SLOVENIA

	Basic Indicators	Units	2001	2002	2003	2004	2005
	INBOUND TOURISM						
	Arrivals						
1.1	Visitors	('000)	61,878	60,031	59,388	63,013	60,230
1.2	Tourists (overnight visitors)	('000)	1,219	1,302	1,373	1,499	1,555
1.3	Same-day visitors	('000)	..	..	..	..	..
1.4	Cruise passengers	('000)	..	..	..	..	..
	Arrivals by region						
2.1	Africa	('000)	3	4	4	6	2
2.2	Americas	('000)	33	36	36	46	48
2.3	Europe	('000)	1,160	1,236	1,308	1,411	1,453
2.4	East Asia and the Pacific	('000)	15	17	17	24	28
2.5	South Asia	('000)	4	4	4	6	5
2.6	Middle East	('000)	4	4	4	6	2
	Arrivals by means of transport used						
3.1	Air	('000)	226	241	264	288	298
3.2	Rail	('000)	23	25	41	45	47
3.3	Road	('000)	968	1,034	1,067	1,165	1,208
3.4	Sea	('000)	2	2	1	1	2
	Arrivals by purpose of visit						
4.1	Leisure, recreation and holidays	('000)	748	799	894	976	1,012
4.2	Business and professional	('000)	213	228	273	298	309
4.3	Other	('000)	258	275	206	225	233
	Accommodation						
5.1	Overnight stays in hotels and similar establishments	('000)	2,879	3,049	3,166	3,258	3,322
5.2	Guests in hotels and similar establishments	('000)	933	1,006	1,053	1,125	1,192
5.3	Overnight stays in all types of accommodation establishments	('000)	3,813	4,021	4,175	4,363	4,399
5.4	Average length of stay of non-resident tourists in all accommodation establishments	Nights	3.13	3.09	3.04	2.91	2.80
6.1	**Tourism expenditure in the country**	US$ Mn	1,059	1,152	1,427	1,726	1,894
6.2	"Travel" (*)	US$ Mn	1,001	1,086	1,342	1,625	1,795
6.3	"Passenger transport" (*)	US$ Mn	58	66	85	101	99
	DOMESTIC TOURISM						
	Accommodation						
7.1	Overnight stays in hotels and similar establishments	('000)	1,715	1,714	1,725	1,707	1,653
7.2	Guests in hotels and similar establishments	('000)	468	463	463	467	459
7.3	Overnight stays in all types of accommodation establishments	('000)	3,316	3,300	3,327	3,223	3,171
7.4	Average length of stay of resident tourists in all accommodation establishments	Nights	3.82	3.84	3.81	3.83	3.80
	OUTBOUND TOURISM						
8.1	**Departures**	('000)	2,055	2,127	2,114	2,800	..
8.2	**Tourism expenditure in other countries**	US$ Mn	560	647	806	937	1,019
8.3	"Travel" (*)	US$ Mn	528	608	753	868	950
8.4	"Passenger transport" (*)	US$ Mn	32	39	53	69	69
	TOURISM INDUSTRIES						
	Hotels and similar establishments						
9.1	Number of rooms	Units	14,970	15,056	15,534	15,785	15,811
9.2	Number of bed-places	Units	30,490	30,715	31,997	32,652	33,151
9.3	Occupancy rate	Percent	46.39	47.39	47.60	47.98	47.56
9.4	Average length of stay	Nights	3.28	3.24	3.23	3.12	3.20
	RELATED INDICATORS						
	Share of tourism expenditure (6.1) in:						
10.1	Gross Domestic Product (GDP)	Percent	5.4	5.2	5.1	5.3	5.6
10.2	Exports of goods	Percent	11.3	11.0	11.0	10.7	10.4
10.3	Exports of services	Percent	54.0	49.8	51.1	50.0	47.6

(*) Balance of Payments items: 6.1 to 6.3 correspond to the "Credit" side (and are receipts for the country) while 8.2 to 8.4 correspond to the "Debit" side (and are expenditures in other countries).

	Basic Indicators	Units	2001	2002	2003	2004	2005
	INBOUND TOURISM						
	Arrivals						
1.1	Visitors	('000)	..	..	..	..	..
1.2	Tourists (overnight visitors)	('000)	..	..	6.6	..	9.4
1.3	Same-day visitors	('000)	..	..	..	..	..
1.4	Cruise passengers	('000)	..	..	..	..	..
	Arrivals by region						
2.1	Africa	('000)	..	..	..	..	..
2.2	Americas	('000)	..	..	0.6	..	0.6
2.3	Europe	('000)	..	..	0.5	..	0.5
2.4	East Asia and the Pacific	('000)	..	..	5.4	..	8.1
2.5	South Asia	('000)	..	..	..	..	..
2.6	Middle East	('000)	..	..	..	..	..
	Arrivals by means of transport used						
3.1	Air	('000)	..	..	..	..	..
3.2	Rail	('000)	..	..	..	..	..
3.3	Road	('000)	..	..	..	..	..
3.4	Sea	('000)	..	..	..	..	..
	Arrivals by purpose of visit						
4.1	Leisure, recreation and holidays	('000)	..	..	..	..	..
4.2	Business and professional	('000)	..	..	..	..	..
4.3	Other	('000)	..	..	..	..	..
	Accommodation						
5.1	Overnight stays in hotels and similar establishments	('000)	..	..	..	..	..
5.2	Guests in hotels and similar establishments	('000)	..	..	..	..	..
5.3	Overnight stays in all types of accommodation establishments	('000)	..	..	..	..	..
5.4	Average length of stay of non-resident tourists in all accommodation establishments	Nights	..	..	..	..	..
6.1	**Tourism expenditure in the country**	US$ Mn	..	..	..	..	..
6.2	"Travel" (*)	US$ Mn	5	1	2	4	2
6.3	"Passenger transport" (*)	US$ Mn	..	..	..	..	..
	DOMESTIC TOURISM						
	Accommodation						
7.1	Overnight stays in hotels and similar establishments	('000)	..	..	..	..	..
7.2	Guests in hotels and similar establishments	('000)	..	..	..	..	..
7.3	Overnight stays in all types of accommodation establishments	('000)	..	..	..	..	..
7.4	Average length of stay of resident tourists in all accommodation establishments	Nights	..	..	..	..	..
	OUTBOUND TOURISM						
8.1	**Departures**	('000)	..	..	..	..	..
8.2	**Tourism expenditure in other countries**	US$ Mn	..	..	..	..	..
8.3	"Travel" (*)	US$ Mn	7	6	4	9	5
8.4	"Passenger transport" (*)	US$ Mn	..	..	..	..	..
	TOURISM INDUSTRIES						
	Hotels and similar establishments						
9.1	Number of rooms	Units	..	..	..	..	..
9.2	Number of bed-places	Units	..	..	..	..	..
9.3	Occupancy rate	Percent	..	..	..	..	..
9.4	Average length of stay	Nights	..	..	..	..	..
	RELATED INDICATORS						
	Share of tourism expenditure (6.1) in:						
10.1	Gross Domestic Product (GDP)	Percent	..	..	..	..	..
10.2	Exports of goods	Percent	..	..	..	..	..
10.3	Exports of services	Percent	..	..	..	..	..

(*) Balance of Payments items: 6.1 to 6.3 correspond to the "Credit" side (and are receipts for the country) while 8.2 to 8.4 correspond to the "Debit" side (and are expenditures in other countries).

SOUTH AFRICA

	Basic Indicators	Units	2001	2002	2003	2004	2005
	INBOUND TOURISM						
	Arrivals						
1.1	Visitors	('000)	5,908	6,550	6,640	6,815	7,518
1.2	Tourists (overnight visitors)	('000)	5,787	6,430	6,505	6,678	7,369
1.3	Same-day visitors	('000)	..	..	..	..	..
1.4	Cruise passengers	('000)	..	..	..	..	..
	Arrivals by region						
2.1	Africa	('000)	4,131	4,453	4,450	4,638	5,370
2.2	Americas	('000)	242	255	262	291	322
2.3	Europe	('000)	975	1,213	1,275	1,249	1,269
2.4	East Asia and the Pacific	('000)	194	229	225	239	239
2.5	South Asia	('000)	28	34	41	36	36
2.6	Middle East	('000)	13	15	15	16	17
	Arrivals by means of transport used						
3.1	Air	('000)	1,596	1,885	1,980	2,025	2,127
3.2	Rail	('000)	7	6	4	6	450
3.3	Road	('000)	4,288	4,640	4,651	4,781	4,938
3.4	Sea	('000)	17	18	5	3	3
	Arrivals by purpose of visit						
4.1	Leisure, recreation and holidays	('000)	4,962	5,596	5,853	6,081	6,812
4.2	Business and professional	('000)	556	540	406	361	335
4.3	Other	('000)	269	294	246	236	222
	Accommodation						
5.1	Overnight stays in hotels and similar establishments	('000)	..	..	..	..	..
5.2	Guests in hotels and similar establishments	('000)	..	..	..	..	..
5.3	Overnight stays in all types of accommodation establishments	('000)	..	..	..	..	..
5.4	Average length of stay of non-resident tourists in all accommodation establishments	Nights	..	..	..	..	..
6.1	**Tourism expenditure in the country**	US$ Mn	3,256	3,696	6,533	7,380	8,448
6.2	"Travel" (*)	US$ Mn	2,569	2,923	5,571	6,322	7,335
6.3	"Passenger transport" (*)	US$ Mn	687	773	962	1,058	1,113
	DOMESTIC TOURISM						
	Accommodation						
7.1	Overnight stays in hotels and similar establishments	('000)	..	..	..	..	..
7.2	Guests in hotels and similar establishments	('000)	..	..	..	..	..
7.3	Overnight stays in all types of accommodation establishments	('000)	..	..	..	..	..
7.4	Average length of stay of resident tourists in all accommodation establishments	Nights	..	..	..	..	..
	OUTBOUND TOURISM						
8.1	**Departures**	('000)	3,733	3,794	..	..	..
8.2	**Tourism expenditure in other countries**	US$ Mn	2,366	2,251	3,654	4,238	4,813
8.3	"Travel" (*)	US$ Mn	1,878	1,811	2,889	3,157	3,374
8.4	"Passenger transport" (*)	US$ Mn	488	440	765	1,081	1,439
	TOURISM INDUSTRIES						
	Hotels and similar establishments						
9.1	Number of rooms	Units	51,874	52,257	52,329	52,728	54,853
9.2	Number of bed-places	Units	108,906	110,133	110,479	..	..
9.3	Occupancy rate	Percent	52.72	56.90	57.70	60.00	60.48
9.4	Average length of stay	Nights	..	..	..	..	..
	RELATED INDICATORS						
	Share of tourism expenditure (6.1) in:						
10.1	Gross Domestic Product (GDP)	Percent	2.7	3.3	3.9	3.4	3.5
10.2	Exports of goods	Percent	10.5	11.6	16.9	15.3	15.5
10.3	Exports of services	Percent	70.0	79.1	82.6	81.9	82.5

(*) Balance of Payments items: 6.1 to 6.3 correspond to the "Credit" side (and are receipts for the country) while 8.2 to 8.4 correspond to the "Debit" side (and are expenditures in other countries).

	Basic Indicators	Units	2001	2002	2003	2004	2005
	INBOUND TOURISM						
	Arrivals						
1.1	Visitors	('000)	75,678	80,024	82,326	85,981	92,563
1.2	Tourists (overnight visitors)	('000)	50,094	52,327	50,854	52,430	55,914
1.3	Same-day visitors	('000)	25,585	27,697	31,472	33,551	36,649
1.4	Cruise passengers	('000)	..	..	..	..	..
	Arrivals by region						
2.1	Africa	('000)	..	..	..	..	..
2.2	Americas	('000)	2,174	2,080	1,894	2,079	2,233
2.3	Europe	('000)	46,827	49,304	47,835	49,239	52,190
2.4	East Asia and the Pacific	('000)	265	241	237	151	181
2.5	South Asia	('000)	..	..	..	..	..
2.6	Middle East	('000)	..	..	..	..	..
	Arrivals by means of transport used						
3.1	Air	('000)	35,331	34,947	36,923	38,524	40,730
3.2	Rail	('000)	457	458	292	298	290
3.3	Road	('000)	11,739	13,872	12,118	12,097	13,121
3.4	Sea	('000)	2,566	3,050	1,521	1,511	1,772
	Arrivals by purpose of visit						
4.1	Leisure, recreation and holidays	('000)	42,102	43,253	40,393	41,377	43,898
4.2	Business and professional	('000)	3,648	4,091	5,686	5,286	5,940
4.3	Other	('000)	4,343	4,983	4,775	5,767	6,075
	Accommodation						
5.1	Overnight stays in hotels and similar establishments	('000)	143,421	135,836	136,865	134,654	138,762
5.2	Guests in hotels and similar establishments	('000)	27,012	26,611	27,249	27,620	29,029
5.3	Overnight stays in all types of accommodation establishments	('000)	232,035	220,707	217,852	209,081	209,518
5.4	Average length of stay of non-resident tourists in all accommodation establishments	Nights	5.31	5.10	5.02	4.88	4.78
6.1	**Tourism expenditure in the country**	US$ Mn	33,829	35,468	43,863	49,996	52,960
6.2	"Travel" (*)	US$ Mn	30,550	31,880	39,634	45,067	47,681
6.3	"Passenger transport" (*)	US$ Mn	3,279	3,588	4,229	4,929	5,279
	DOMESTIC TOURISM						
	Accommodation						
7.1	Overnight stays in hotels and similar establishments	('000)	85,261	86,718	91,295	100,044	106,875
7.2	Guests in hotels and similar establishments	('000)	32,892	33,258	35,283	39,211	41,600
7.3	Overnight stays in all types of accommodation establishments	('000)	116,554	118,179	124,689	135,188	143,874
7.4	Average length of stay of resident tourists in all accommodation establishments	Nights	2.59	2.61	2.59	2.55	2.57
	OUTBOUND TOURISM						
8.1	**Departures**	('000)	4,139	3,871	4,094	5,121	10,508
8.2	**Tourism expenditure in other countries**	US$ Mn	8,466	9,366	11,330	14,864	18,440
8.3	"Travel" (*)	US$ Mn	6,529	7,295	9,071	12,153	15,046
8.4	"Passenger transport" (*)	US$ Mn	1,937	2,071	2,259	2,711	3,394
	TOURISM INDUSTRIES						
	Hotels and similar establishments						
9.1	Number of rooms	Units	685,668	713,481	740,890	766,952	797,354
9.2	Number of bed-places	Units	1,333,441	1,395,383	1,451,922	1,511,592	1,578,629
9.3	Occupancy rate	Percent	58.07	55.27	54.47	53.47	54.24
9.4	Average length of stay	Nights	3.82	3.72	3.65	3.51	3.48
	RELATED INDICATORS						
	Share of tourism expenditure (6.1) in:						
10.1	Gross Domestic Product (GDP)	Percent	5.6	5.2	5.0	4.8	4.7
10.2	Exports of goods	Percent	28.8	27.9	27.8	27.0	27.2
10.3	Exports of services	Percent	60.8	58.9	59.0	58.1	56.6

(*) Balance of Payments items: 6.1 to 6.3 correspond to the "Credit" side (and are receipts for the country) while 8.2 to 8.4 correspond to the "Debit" side (and are expenditures in other countries).

SRI LANKA

	Basic Indicators	Units	2001	2002	2003	2004	2005
	INBOUND TOURISM						
	Arrivals						
1.1	Visitors	('000)	397	457	583	681	669
1.2	Tourists (overnight visitors)	('000)	337	393	501	566	549
1.3	Same-day visitors	('000)	60	64	82	115	120
1.4	Cruise passengers	('000)	..	..	..	..	..
	Arrivals by region						
2.1	Africa	('000)	1	2	2	2	2
2.2	Americas	('000)	16	20	26	31	47
2.3	Europe	('000)	211	208	266	299	236
2.4	East Asia and the Pacific	('000)	49	66	84	91	101
2.5	South Asia	('000)	54	90	116	133	152
2.6	Middle East	('000)	6	6	7	10	10
	Arrivals by means of transport used						
3.1	Air	('000)	337	393	500	566	549
3.2	Rail	('000)	..	..	..	..	..
3.3	Road	('000)	..	..	..	..	..
3.4	Sea	('000)	0.2	..	0.2	0.2	0.3
	Arrivals by purpose of visit						
4.1	Leisure, recreation and holidays	('000)	301	336	404	443	382
4.2	Business and professional	('000)	23	42	56	74	105
4.3	Other	('000)	13	15	41	49	62
	Accommodation						
5.1	Overnight stays in hotels and similar establishments	('000)	2,876	3,180	4,184	4,744	3,249
5.2	Guests in hotels and similar establishments	('000)	..	..	..	..	..
5.3	Overnight stays in all types of accommodation establishments	('000)	3,342	3,989	5,093	5,742	4,754
5.4	Average length of stay of non-resident tourists in all accommodation establishments	Nights	9.90	10.10	10.20	10.10	8.70
6.1	**Tourism expenditure in the country**	US$ Mn	347	594	709	808	729
6.2	"Travel" (*)	US$ Mn	213	363	441	513	429
6.3	"Passenger transport" (*)	US$ Mn	134	231	268	295	300
	DOMESTIC TOURISM						
	Accommodation						
7.1	Overnight stays in hotels and similar establishments	('000)	1,063	1,243	1,327	1,381	1,292
7.2	Guests in hotels and similar establishments	('000)	..	..	..	..	..
7.3	Overnight stays in all types of accommodation establishments	('000)	..	..	..	..	..
7.4	Average length of stay of resident tourists in all accommodation establishments	Nights	..	..	..	..	..
	OUTBOUND TOURISM						
8.1	**Departures**	('000)	505	533	561	680	727
8.2	**Tourism expenditure in other countries**	US$ Mn	404	438	462	499	553
8.3	"Travel" (*)	US$ Mn	251	263	279	296	315
8.4	"Passenger transport" (*)	US$ Mn	153	175	183	203	238
	TOURISM INDUSTRIES						
	Hotels and similar establishments						
9.1	Number of rooms	Units	15,637	16,318	16,973	17,640	17,124
9.2	Number of bed-places	Units	29,074	30,218	31,331	32,578	31,277
9.3	Occupancy rate	Percent	42.10	43.10	53.20	59.30	45.40
9.4	Average length of stay	Nights	..	..	..	..	..
	RELATED INDICATORS						
	Share of tourism expenditure (6.1) in:						
10.1	Gross Domestic Product (GDP)	Percent	2.2	3.6	3.9	4.0	3.1
10.2	Exports of goods	Percent	7.2	12.6	13.8	14.0	11.5
10.3	Exports of services	Percent	25.6	46.8	50.2	52.9	47.3

(*) Balance of Payments items: 6.1 to 6.3 correspond to the "Credit" side (and are receipts for the country) while 8.2 to 8.4 correspond to the "Debit" side (and are expenditures in other countries).

Basic Indicators		Units	2001	2002	2003	2004	2005
	INBOUND TOURISM						
	Arrivals						
1.1	Visitors	('000)	..	..	..	..	..
1.2	Tourists (overnight visitors)	('000)	50	52	52	61	246
1.3	Same-day visitors	('000)	..	..	..	..	..
1.4	Cruise passengers	('000)	..	..	..	..	..
	Arrivals by region						
2.1	Africa	('000)	7	7	7	9	59
2.2	Americas	('000)	4	..	..	..	21
2.3	Europe	('000)	11	12	14	17	56
2.4	East Asia and the Pacific	('000)	10	13	14	17	109
2.5	South Asia	('000)	5	..	..	..	..
2.6	Middle East	('000)	13	..	..	..	..
	Arrivals by means of transport used						
3.1	Air	('000)	42	42	40	51	197
3.2	Rail	('000)	..	..	..	..	..
3.3	Road	('000)	3	3	3	3	12
3.4	Sea	('000)	5	7	8	8	37
	Arrivals by purpose of visit						
4.1	Leisure, recreation and holidays	('000)	35	..	..	..	13
4.2	Business and professional	('000)	10	..	..	..	61
4.3	Other	('000)	5	..	..	..	172
	Accommodation						
5.1	Overnight stays in hotels and similar establishments	('000)	..	..	..	..	..
5.2	Guests in hotels and similar establishments	('000)	..	..	..	..	..
5.3	Overnight stays in all types of accommodation establishments	('000)	..	..	..	..	..
5.4	Average length of stay of non-resident tourists in all accommodation establishments	Nights	..	..	..	..	..
6.1	**Tourism expenditure in the country** (**)	US$ Mn	..	..	..	..	..
6.2	"Travel" (*)	US$ Mn	3	108	18	21	89
6.3	"Passenger transport" (*)	US$ Mn	..	..	..	..	..
	DOMESTIC TOURISM						
	Accommodation						
7.1	Overnight stays in hotels and similar establishments	('000)	..	..	..	..	..
7.2	Guests in hotels and similar establishments	('000)	..	..	..	..	..
7.3	Overnight stays in all types of accommodation establishments	('000)	..	..	..	..	..
7.4	Average length of stay of resident tourists in all accommodation establishments	Nights	..	..	..	..	..
	OUTBOUND TOURISM						
8.1	**Departures**	('000)	..	..	..	..	..
8.2	**Tourism expenditure in other countries**	US$ Mn	..	..	..	..	..
8.3	"Travel" (*)	US$ Mn	74	91	119	176	668
8.4	"Passenger transport" (*)	US$ Mn	..	..	..	..	..
	TOURISM INDUSTRIES						
	Hotels and similar establishments						
9.1	Number of rooms	Units	..	..	..	4,200	4,200
9.2	Number of bed-places	Units	..	..	..	10,102	10,102
9.3	Occupancy rate	Percent	..	..	..	79.10	..
9.4	Average length of stay	Nights	..	..	..	8.00	8.00
	RELATED INDICATORS						
	Share of tourism expenditure (6.1) in: (**)						
10.1	Gross Domestic Product (GDP)	Percent	0.0	0.7	0.1	0.1	0.3
10.2	Exports of goods	Percent	0.2	5.5	0.7	0.6	1.8
10.3	Exports of services	Percent	20.0	81.8	50.0	47.7	78.1

(*) Balance of Payments items: 6.1 to 6.3 correspond to the "Credit" side (and are receipts for the country) while 8.2 to 8.4 correspond to the "Debit" side (and are expenditures in other countries).

(**) See Annex "Country notes".

SURINAME

	Basic Indicators	Units	2001	2002	2003	2004	2005
	INBOUND TOURISM						
	Arrivals						
1.1	Visitors	('000)	68	..	100	..	..
1.2	Tourists (overnight visitors)	('000)	54	60	82	138	160
1.3	Same-day visitors	('000)	..	..	..	..	..
1.4	Cruise passengers	('000)	14	..	17	..	..
	Arrivals by region						
2.1	Africa	('000)	..	..	..	..	..
2.2	Americas	('000)	3	4	7	45	56
2.3	Europe	('000)	49	54	74	87	95
2.4	East Asia and the Pacific	('000)	1	1	1	..	3
2.5	South Asia	('000)	..	..	..	..	..
2.6	Middle East	('000)	..	..	..	..	..
	Arrivals by means of transport used						
3.1	Air	('000)	54	60	82	75	122
3.2	Rail	('000)	..	..	..	..	..
3.3	Road	('000)	..	..	..	..	..
3.4	Sea	('000)	14	..	17	16	38
	Arrivals by purpose of visit						
4.1	Leisure, recreation and holidays	('000)	42	48	61	32	43
4.2	Business and professional	('000)	3	3	12	14	16
4.3	Other	('000)	9	9	9	91	101
	Accommodation						
5.1	Overnight stays in hotels and similar establishments	('000)	..	..	..	..	..
5.2	Guests in hotels and similar establishments	('000)	7	7	27	42	..
5.3	Overnight stays in all types of accommodation establishments	('000)	..	..	..	..	..
5.4	Average length of stay of non-resident tourists in all accommodation establishments	Nights	..	..	..	..	..
6.1	**Tourism expenditure in the country**	US$ Mn	26	17	18	52	96
6.2	"Travel" (*)	US$ Mn	14	3	4	17	45
6.3	"Passenger transport" (*)	US$ Mn	12	14	14	35	51
	DOMESTIC TOURISM						
	Accommodation						
7.1	Overnight stays in hotels and similar establishments	('000)	..	..	..	..	..
7.2	Guests in hotels and similar establishments	('000)	..	..	..	..	..
7.3	Overnight stays in all types of accommodation establishments	('000)	..	..	..	..	..
7.4	Average length of stay of resident tourists in all accommodation establishments	Nights	..	..	..	..	..
	OUTBOUND TOURISM						
8.1	**Departures**	('000)	..	..	..	..	..
8.2	**Tourism expenditure in other countries**	US$ Mn	62	54	68	85	94
8.3	"Travel" (*)	US$ Mn	23	10	6	14	17
8.4	"Passenger transport" (*)	US$ Mn	39	44	62	71	77
	TOURISM INDUSTRIES						
	Hotels and similar establishments						
9.1	Number of rooms	Units	1,640	2,014	2,160	4,271	4,575
9.2	Number of bed-places	Units	..	..	..	..	..
9.3	Occupancy rate	Percent	..	..	..	..	..
9.4	Average length of stay	Nights	..	..	..	..	..
	RELATED INDICATORS						
	Share of tourism expenditure (6.1) in:						
10.1	Gross Domestic Product (GDP)	Percent	3.4	1.8	1.8	4.5	7.2
10.2	Exports of goods	Percent	5.9	4.6	3.7	6.6	7.9
10.3	Exports of services	Percent	44.1	43.6	30.5	36.9	47.1

(*) Balance of Payments items: 6.1 to 6.3 correspond to the "Credit" side (and are receipts for the country) while 8.2 to 8.4 correspond to the "Debit" side (and are expenditures in other countries).

	Basic Indicators	Units	2001	2002	2003	2004	2005
	INBOUND TOURISM						
	Arrivals						
1.1	Visitors	('000)	1,312	1,371	1,543	..	1,182
1.2	Tourists (overnight visitors)	('000)	283	256	461	459	839
1.3	Same-day visitors	('000)	..	..	..	..	130
1.4	Cruise passengers	('000)	..	..	..	..	..
	Arrivals by region						
2.1	Africa	('000)	145	173	110	152	134
2.2	Americas	('000)	20	10	11	5	4
2.3	Europe	('000)	85	40	88	111	98
2.4	East Asia and the Pacific	('000)	6	5	2	3	3
2.5	South Asia	('000)	..	..	..	..	..
2.6	Middle East	('000)	..	..	..	..	..
	Arrivals by means of transport used						
3.1	Air	('000)	13	14	17	..	22
3.2	Rail	('000)	2	..	..	..	..
3.3	Road	('000)	1,297	1,357	1,526	..	1,160
3.4	Sea	('000)	..	..	..	..	..
	Arrivals by purpose of visit						
4.1	Leisure, recreation and holidays	('000)	150	125	170	168	705
4.2	Business and professional	('000)	93	109	122	121	168
4.3	Other	('000)	40	22	169	170	309
	Accommodation						
5.1	Overnight stays in hotels and similar establishments	('000)	..	..	..	..	..
5.2	Guests in hotels and similar establishments	('000)	283	256	219	352	312
5.3	Overnight stays in all types of accommodation establishments	('000)	..	..	..	..	..
5.4	Average length of stay of non-resident tourists in all accommodation establishments	Nights	1.00	0.83	1.00	0.83	1.25
6.1	**Tourism expenditure in the country**	US$ Mn	32.0	68.0	113.0	54.1	69.3
6.2	"Travel" (*)	US$ Mn	30	62	101	54	69
6.3	"Passenger transport" (*)	US$ Mn	2.0	6.0	12.0	0.1	0.3
	DOMESTIC TOURISM						
	Accommodation						
7.1	Overnight stays in hotels and similar establishments	('000)	50	76	136	..	39
7.2	Guests in hotels and similar establishments	('000)	..	..	..	..	..
7.3	Overnight stays in all types of accommodation establishments	('000)	..	..	..	..	..
7.4	Average length of stay of resident tourists in all accommodation establishments	Nights	..	..	..	..	..
	OUTBOUND TOURISM						
8.1	**Departures**	('000)	..	..	..	..	1,082
8.2	**Tourism expenditure in other countries**	US$ Mn	48	40	44	22	23
8.3	"Travel" (*)	US$ Mn	47	39	43	16	15
8.4	"Passenger transport" (*)	US$ Mn	1	1	1	6	8
	TOURISM INDUSTRIES						
	Hotels and similar establishments						
9.1	Number of rooms	Units	1,276	1,153	1,339	1,307	1,244
9.2	Number of bed-places	Units	2,585	2,283	2,436	2,490	2,377
9.3	Occupancy rate	Percent	42.00	33.30	33.60	..	38.64
9.4	Average length of stay	Nights	1.00	0.83	1.00	..	2.00
	RELATED INDICATORS						
	Share of tourism expenditure (6.1) in:						
10.1	Gross Domestic Product (GDP)	Percent	2.5	5.7	5.9	2.1	2.5
10.2	Exports of goods	Percent	3.1	6.6	6.9	3.1	3.8
10.3	Exports of services	Percent	28.1	66.7	44.3	11.7	24.6

(*) Balance of Payments items: 6.1 to 6.3 correspond to the "Credit" side (and are receipts for the country) while 8.2 to 8.4 correspond to the "Debit" side (and are expenditures in other countries).

SWEDEN

Basic Indicators		Units	2001	2002	2003	2004	2005
	INBOUND TOURISM						
	Arrivals						
1.1	Visitors	('000)	14,721	14,271	..	..	..
1.2	Tourists (overnight visitors)	('000)	7,431	7,458	7,627	..	..
1.3	Same-day visitors	('000)	7,290	6,813	..	..	..
1.4	Cruise passengers	('000)	..	..	..	..	..
	Arrivals by region						
2.1	Africa	('000)	37	42	46	..	..
2.2	Americas	('000)	546	413	467	..	..
2.3	Europe	('000)	6,437	6,656	6,696	..	..
2.4	East Asia and the Pacific	('000)	411	348	380	..	..
2.5	South Asia	('000)	..	..	..	..	..
2.6	Middle East	('000)	..	..	..	..	..
	Arrivals by means of transport used						
3.1	Air	('000)	3,083	2,700	..	..	..
3.2	Rail	('000)	579	485	..	..	..
3.3	Road	('000)	1,553	1,715	..	..	..
3.4	Sea	('000)	2,221	2,558	..	..	..
	Arrivals by purpose of visit						
4.1	Leisure, recreation and holidays	('000)	3,188	3,495	3,536	..	..
4.2	Business and professional	('000)	2,781	2,414	2,518	..	..
4.3	Other	('000)	1,463	1,548	1,573	..	..
	Accommodation						
5.1	Overnight stays in hotels and similar establishments	('000)	4,927	4,868	4,833	5,061	5,382
5.2	Guests in hotels and similar establishments	('000)	2,586	2,577	2,552	2,610	2,736
5.3	Overnight stays in all types of accommodation establishments	('000)	9,133	9,768	9,715	9,724	10,078
5.4	Average length of stay of non-resident tourists in all accommodation establishments	Nights	2.22	2.28	2.28	2.08	2.06
6.1	**Tourism expenditure in the country**	US$ Mn	5,200	5,671	6,548	7,649	8,584
6.2	"Travel" (*)	US$ Mn	4,253	4,710	5,304	6,163	7,361
6.3	"Passenger transport" (*)	US$ Mn	947	961	1,244	1,486	1,223
	DOMESTIC TOURISM						
	Accommodation						
7.1	Overnight stays in hotels and similar establishments	('000)	16,737	16,143	16,235	16,465	17,517
7.2	Guests in hotels and similar establishments	('000)	10,612	10,375	10,359	10,509	11,096
7.3	Overnight stays in all types of accommodation establishments	('000)	32,061	33,128	34,339	32,942	34,862
7.4	Average length of stay of resident tourists in all accommodation establishments	Nights	2.20	2.22	2.23	2.04	1.97
	OUTBOUND TOURISM						
8.1	**Departures**	('000)	10,741	12,888	12,649	13,967	12,598
8.2	**Tourism expenditure in other countries**	US$ Mn	7,916	8,221	9,375	10,984	11,847
8.3	"Travel" (*)	US$ Mn	6,921	7,301	8,296	10,130	10,776
8.4	"Passenger transport" (*)	US$ Mn	995	920	1,079	854	1,071
	TOURISM INDUSTRIES						
	Hotels and similar establishments						
9.1	Number of rooms	Units	99,267	95,125	96,372	98,888	100,155
9.2	Number of bed-places	Units	194,839	180,804	184,771	189,988	197,470
9.3	Occupancy rate	Percent	34.40	35.20	34.30	34.30	35.00
9.4	Average length of stay	Nights	..	..	..	..	..
	RELATED INDICATORS						
	Share of tourism expenditure (6.1) in:						
10.1	Gross Domestic Product (GDP)	Percent	2.4	2.3	2.2	2.2	2.4
10.2	Exports of goods	Percent	6.8	6.7	6.4	6.1	6.4
10.3	Exports of services	Percent	23.6	23.6	21.4	19.8	19.9

(*) Balance of Payments items: 6.1 to 6.3 correspond to the "Credit" side (and are receipts for the country) while 8.2 to 8.4 correspond to the "Debit" side (and are expenditures in other countries).

Basic Indicators		Units	2001	2002	2003	2004	2005
	INBOUND TOURISM						
	Arrivals						
1.1	Visitors	('000)	..	..	..	..	..
1.2	Tourists (overnight visitors)	('000)	7,455	6,868	6,530	..	7,229
1.3	Same-day visitors	('000)	..	..	..	..	..
1.4	Cruise passengers	('000)	..	..	..	..	..
	Arrivals by region						
2.1	Africa	('000)	79	74	73	..	78
2.2	Americas	('000)	1,027	871	757	..	830
2.3	Europe	('000)	5,277	4,906	4,821	..	5,305
2.4	East Asia and the Pacific	('000)	938	865	727	..	847
2.5	South Asia	('000)	72	80	85	..	93
2.6	Middle East	('000)	62	70	67	..	76
	Arrivals by means of transport used						
3.1	Air	('000)	..	..	..	..	..
3.2	Rail	('000)	..	..	..	..	..
3.3	Road	('000)	..	..	..	..	..
3.4	Sea	('000)	..	..	..	..	..
	Arrivals by purpose of visit						
4.1	Leisure, recreation and holidays	('000)	..	..	..	..	..
4.2	Business and professional	('000)	..	..	..	..	..
4.3	Other	('000)	..	..	..	..	..
	Accommodation						
5.1	Overnight stays in hotels and similar establishments	('000)	19,273	17,768	16,964	17,247	18,321
5.2	Guests in hotels and similar establishments	('000)	7,455	6,868	6,530	..	7,229
5.3	Overnight stays in all types of accommodation establishments	('000)	32,111	29,641	28,569	..	..
5.4	Average length of stay of non-resident tourists in all accommodation establishments	Nights	..	..	..	..	..
6.1	**Tourism expenditure in the country**	US$ Mn	10,013	9,742	11,048	12,351	12,961
6.2	"Travel" (*)	US$ Mn	7,505	7,885	9,169	10,542	11,063
6.3	"Passenger transport" (*)	US$ Mn	2,508	1,857	1,879	1,809	1,898
	DOMESTIC TOURISM						
	Accommodation						
7.1	Overnight stays in hotels and similar establishments	('000)	14,313	14,196	14,236	13,837	14,622
7.2	Guests in hotels and similar establishments	('000)	6,151	6,190	6,195	..	6,574
7.3	Overnight stays in all types of accommodation establishments	('000)	36,219	36,254	36,392	35,360	..
7.4	Average length of stay of resident tourists in all accommodation establishments	Nights	..	..	..	..	..
	OUTBOUND TOURISM						
8.1	**Departures**	('000)	11,554	11,427	..	..	..
8.2	**Tourism expenditure in other countries**	US$ Mn	8,179	8,347	9,194	10,599	11,060
8.3	"Travel" (*)	US$ Mn	6,235	6,674	7,463	8,779	9,262
8.4	"Passenger transport" (*)	US$ Mn	1,944	1,673	1,731	1,820	1,798
	TOURISM INDUSTRIES						
	Hotels and similar establishments						
9.1	Number of rooms	Units	140,644	139,943	139,969	..	127,410
9.2	Number of bed-places	Units	260,124	259,004	258,726	..	239,150
9.3	Occupancy rate	Percent	41.80	40.10	38.70	..	..
9.4	Average length of stay	Nights	2.60	2.40	2.50	..	..
	RELATED INDICATORS						
	Share of tourism expenditure (6.1) in:						
10.1	Gross Domestic Product (GDP)	Percent	4.0	3.5	3.4	3.5	3.5
10.2	Exports of goods	Percent	10.4	9.3	9.3	8.7	8.6
10.3	Exports of services	Percent	35.2	32.1	31.4	28.7	27.5

(*) Balance of Payments items: 6.1 to 6.3 correspond to the "Credit" side (and are receipts for the country) while 8.2 to 8.4 correspond to the "Debit" side (and are expenditures in other countries).

SYRIAN ARAB REPUBLIC

	Basic Indicators	Units	2001	2002	2003	2004	2005
	INBOUND TOURISM						
	Arrivals						
1.1	Visitors	('000)	3,327	4,273	4,388	6,154	5,838
1.2	Tourists (overnight visitors)	('000)	1,801	2,186	2,085	3,033	3,368
1.3	Same-day visitors	('000)	1,525	2,087	2,303	3,121	2,470
1.4	Cruise passengers	('000)	..	..	..	..	..
	Arrivals by region						
2.1	Africa	('000)	71	71	73	90	93
2.2	Americas	('000)	43	45	44	58	58
2.3	Europe	('000)	472	646	652	933	947
2.4	East Asia and the Pacific	('000)	23	28	26	37	35
2.5	South Asia	('000)	237	340	228	218	269
2.6	Middle East	('000)	2,425	3,094	3,325	4,761	4,370
	Arrivals by means of transport used						
3.1	Air	('000)	428	501	443	579	604
3.2	Rail	('000)	..	..	..	..	..
3.3	Road	('000)	2,951	3,766	3,941	5,566	5,219
3.4	Sea	('000)	10	6	5	8	15
	Arrivals by purpose of visit						
4.1	Leisure, recreation and holidays	('000)	2,333	2,361	2,426	3,401	3,227
4.2	Business and professional	('000)	300	398	408	573	543
4.3	Other	('000)	693	1,514	1,554	2,180	2,068
	Accommodation						
5.1	Overnight stays in hotels and similar establishments	('000)	1,888	1,941	5,775	7,995	8,803
5.2	Guests in hotels and similar establishments	('000)	878	847	863	1,232	1,380
5.3	Overnight stays in all types of accommodation establishments	('000)	..	..	20,700	27,930	30,948
5.4	Average length of stay of non-resident tourists in all accommodation establishments	Nights	3.00	10.40	10.40	10.00	9.18
6.1	**Tourism expenditure in the country**	US$ Mn	..	..	877	1,888	2,283
6.2	"Travel" (*)	US$ Mn	1,150	970	773	1,800	2,175
6.3	"Passenger transport" (*)	US$ Mn	..	..	104	88	108
	DOMESTIC TOURISM						
	Accommodation						
7.1	Overnight stays in hotels and similar establishments	('000)	1,068	1,053	1,052	981	964
7.2	Guests in hotels and similar establishments	('000)	696	688	679	661	649
7.3	Overnight stays in all types of accommodation establishments	('000)	..	..	..	..	..
7.4	Average length of stay of resident tourists in all accommodation establishments	Nights	..	..	..	..	..
	OUTBOUND TOURISM						
8.1	**Departures**	('000)	3,492	3,299	3,997	4,309	4,564
8.2	**Tourism expenditure in other countries**	US$ Mn	..	..	734	698	593
8.3	"Travel" (*)	US$ Mn	670	760	700	650	550
8.4	"Passenger transport" (*)	US$ Mn	..	..	34	48	43
	TOURISM INDUSTRIES						
	Hotels and similar establishments						
9.1	Number of rooms	Units	15,705	16,042	16,966	17,267	18,798
9.2	Number of bed-places	Units	34,537	35,253	38,928	39,985	43,262
9.3	Occupancy rate	Percent	25.00	..	..	60.00	64.00
9.4	Average length of stay	Nights	1.88	..	..	..	..
	RELATED INDICATORS						
	Share of tourism expenditure (6.1) in:						
10.1	Gross Domestic Product (GDP)	Percent	..	..	3.5	7.2	8.3
10.2	Exports of goods	Percent	..	..	13.4	34.2	33.2
10.3	Exports of services	Percent	..	..	58.1	65.1	67.4

(*) Balance of Payments items: 6.1 to 6.3 correspond to the "Credit" side (and are receipts for the country) while 8.2 to 8.4 correspond to the "Debit" side (and are expenditures in other countries).

TAIWAN (PROVINCE OF CHINA)

	Basic Indicators	Units	2001	2002	2003	2004	2005
	INBOUND TOURISM						
	Arrivals						
1.1	Visitors	('000)	2,831	2,978	2,248	2,950	3,378
1.2	Tourists (overnight visitors)	('000)	..	..	..	..	..
1.3	Same-day visitors	('000)	..	..	..	..	..
1.4	Cruise passengers	('000)	..	..	..	..	..
	Arrivals by region						
2.1	Africa	('000)	9	9	7	10	9
2.2	Americas	('000)	389	406	312	441	453
2.3	Europe	('000)	148	147	118	164	172
2.4	East Asia and the Pacific	('000)	1,718	1,762	1,349	1,782	2,131
2.5	South Asia	('000)	13	14	12	16	17
2.6	Middle East	('000)	9	10	8	13	13
	Arrivals by means of transport used						
3.1	Air	('000)	2,814	2,954	2,228	2,916	3,341
3.2	Rail	('000)	..	..	..	..	..
3.3	Road	('000)	..	..	..	..	..
3.4	Sea	('000)	17	24	20	35	37
	Arrivals by purpose of visit						
4.1	Leisure, recreation and holidays	('000)	1,022	1,029	695	1,032	1,382
4.2	Business and professional	('000)	915	933	779	1,001	1,033
4.3	Other	('000)	894	1,016	774	917	963
	Accommodation						
5.1	Overnight stays in hotels and similar establishments	('000)	..	..	..	..	..
5.2	Guests in hotels and similar establishments	('000)	..	..	..	..	..
5.3	Overnight stays in all types of accommodation establishments	('000)	16,987	16,856	14,461	18,838	20,593
5.4	Average length of stay of non-resident tourists in all accommodation establishments	Nights	7.37	7.54	7.97	7.61	7.10
6.1	**Tourism expenditure in the country**	US$ Mn	4,849	5,077	3,578	4,670	5,803
6.2	"Travel" (*)	US$ Mn	4,335	4,583	2,977	4,054	5,040
6.3	"Passenger transport" (*)	US$ Mn	514	494	601	616	763
	DOMESTIC TOURISM						
	Accommodation						
7.1	Overnight stays in hotels and similar establishments	('000)	..	..	..	..	..
7.2	Guests in hotels and similar establishments	('000)	..	..	..	..	..
7.3	Overnight stays in all types of accommodation establishments	('000)	..	..	..	..	..
7.4	Average length of stay of resident tourists in all accommodation establishments	Nights	..	..	..	..	..
	OUTBOUND TOURISM						
8.1	**Departures**	('000)	7,153	7,319	5,923	7,781	8,208
8.2	**Tourism expenditure in other countries**	US$ Mn	8,691	8,229	7,402	9,376	10,047
8.3	"Travel" (*)	US$ Mn	7,319	6,956	6,480	8,170	8,682
8.4	"Passenger transport" (*)	US$ Mn	1,372	1,273	922	1,206	1,365
	TOURISM INDUSTRIES						
	Hotels and similar establishments						
9.1	Number of rooms	Units	20,789	21,763	21,896	21,744	21,434
9.2	Number of bed-places	Units	..	..	..	..	..
9.3	Occupancy rate	Percent	61.62	61.30	56.43	65.59	72.00
9.4	Average length of stay	Nights	..	..	..	..	..
	RELATED INDICATORS						
	Share of tourism expenditure (6.1) in:						
10.1	Gross Domestic Product (GDP)	Percent	..	..	..	..	..
10.2	Exports of goods	Percent	4.0	3.8	2.4	2.6	2.9
10.3	Exports of services	Percent	24.4	23.5	15.4	18.1	22.4

(*) Balance of Payments items: 6.1 to 6.3 correspond to the "Credit" side (and are receipts for the country) while 8.2 to 8.4 correspond to the "Debit" side (and are expenditures in other countries).

THAILAND

	Basic Indicators	Units	2001	2002	2003	2004	2005
	INBOUND TOURISM						
	Arrivals						
1.1	Visitors	('000)	10,751	..	..	..	..
1.2	Tourists (overnight visitors)	('000)	10,133	10,873	10,082	11,737	11,567
1.3	Same-day visitors	('000)	618	..	..	..	..
1.4	Cruise passengers	('000)	..	..	..	..	..
	Arrivals by region						
2.1	Africa	('000)	91	89	67	83	73
2.2	Americas	('000)	604	640	577	693	740
2.3	Europe	('000)	2,396	2,550	2,321	2,706	2,779
2.4	East Asia and the Pacific	('000)	6,492	6,955	6,510	7,501	7,195
2.5	South Asia	('000)	350	414	411	495	552
2.6	Middle East	('000)	129	151	118	173	179
	Arrivals by means of transport used						
3.1	Air	('000)	8,456	8,955	8,164	9,803	9,544
3.2	Rail	('000)	..	..	..	..	..
3.3	Road	('000)	1,427	1,693	1,738	1,688	1,781
3.4	Sea	('000)	250	225	180	247	242
	Arrivals by purpose of visit						
4.1	Leisure, recreation and holidays	('000)	8,876	9,639	8,792	10,165	9,458
4.2	Business and professional	('000)	1,014	972	985	1,174	1,545
4.3	Other	('000)	171	188	227	312	514
	Accommodation						
5.1	Overnight stays in hotels and similar establishments	('000)	79,796	..	81,931	94,666	..
5.2	Guests in hotels and similar establishments	('000)	10,004	..	..	11,585	..
5.3	Overnight stays in all types of accommodation establishments	('000)	..	..	..	..	..
5.4	Average length of stay of non-resident tourists in all accommodation establishments	Nights	7.93	7.98	8.19	8.13	8.20
6.1	**Tourism expenditure in the country**	US$ Mn	9,380	10,388	10,456	13,054	12,629
6.2	"Travel" (*)	US$ Mn	7,076	7,901	7,856	10,043	10,104
6.3	"Passenger transport" (*)	US$ Mn	2,304	2,487	2,600	3,011	2,525
	DOMESTIC TOURISM						
	Accommodation						
7.1	Overnight stays in hotels and similar establishments	('000)	103,593	..	..	..	..
7.2	Guests in hotels and similar establishments	('000)	..	..	..	..	..
7.3	Overnight stays in all types of accommodation establishments	('000)	..	..	..	..	..
7.4	Average length of stay of resident tourists in all accommodation establishments	Nights	..	..	..	..	..
	OUTBOUND TOURISM						
8.1	**Departures**	('000)	2,011	2,250	2,152	2,709	3,047
8.2	**Tourism expenditure in other countries**	US$ Mn	3,334	3,888	3,539	5,343	5,790
8.3	"Travel" (*)	US$ Mn	2,924	3,303	2,921	4,514	4,995
8.4	"Passenger transport" (*)	US$ Mn	410	585	618	829	795
	TOURISM INDUSTRIES						
	Hotels and similar establishments						
9.1	Number of rooms	Units	320,565	335,421	348,094	357,922	..
9.2	Number of bed-places	Units	..	..	..	..	..
9.3	Occupancy rate	Percent	51.94	..	..	52.57	..
9.4	Average length of stay	Nights	2.25	..	..	..	..
	RELATED INDICATORS						
	Share of tourism expenditure (6.1) in:						
10.1	Gross Domestic Product (GDP)	Percent	8.1	8.2	7.3	8.1	7.2
10.2	Exports of goods	Percent	14.9	15.7	13.4	13.7	11.6
10.3	Exports of services	Percent	72.0	67.5	66.2	68.6	61.2

(*) Balance of Payments items: 6.1 to 6.3 correspond to the "Credit" side (and are receipts for the country) while 8.2 to 8.4 correspond to the "Debit" side (and are expenditures in other countries).

	Basic Indicators	Units	2001	2002	2003	2004	2005
	INBOUND TOURISM						
	Arrivals						
1.1	Visitors	('000)	1,730	2,079	2,183	2,594	3,246
1.2	Tourists (overnight visitors)	('000)	99	123	158	165	197
1.3	Same-day visitors	('000)	..	..	..	..	..
1.4	Cruise passengers	('000)	..	..	..	..	..
	Arrivals by region						
2.1	Africa	('000)	..	..	..	..	..
2.2	Americas	('000)	8	8	8	8	8
2.3	Europe	('000)	87	111	143	151	183
2.4	East Asia and the Pacific	('000)	1	2	2	2	3
2.5	South Asia	('000)	..	..	..	..	..
2.6	Middle East	('000)	..	..	..	..	..
	Arrivals by means of transport used						
3.1	Air	('000)	105	116	104	105	129
3.2	Rail	('000)	33	41	42	41	44
3.3	Road	('000)	1,592	1,922	2,036	2,448	3,073
3.4	Sea	('000)	..	..	..	..	..
	Arrivals by purpose of visit						
4.1	Leisure, recreation and holidays	('000)	..	..	..	..	..
4.2	Business and professional	('000)	..	..	..	..	..
4.3	Other	('000)	..	..	..	..	..
	Accommodation						
5.1	Overnight stays in hotels and similar establishments	('000)	197	249	321	329	391
5.2	Guests in hotels and similar establishments	('000)	92	115	149	154	181
5.3	Overnight stays in all types of accommodation establishments	('000)	213	275	346	361	443
5.4	Average length of stay of non-resident tourists in all accommodation establishments	Nights	2.20	2.20	2.20	2.20	2.30
6.1	**Tourism expenditure in the country**	US$ Mn	49	55	65	77	92
6.2	"Travel" (*)	US$ Mn	26	39	57	72	84
6.3	"Passenger transport" (*)	US$ Mn	23	16	8	5	8
	DOMESTIC TOURISM						
	Accommodation						
7.1	Overnight stays in hotels and similar establishments	('000)	266	366	347	289	275
7.2	Guests in hotels and similar establishments	('000)	119	154	146	128	128
7.3	Overnight stays in all types of accommodation establishments	('000)	1,042	1,576	1,661	1,505	1,527
7.4	Average length of stay of resident tourists in all accommodation establishments	Nights	4.40	4.90	5.10	5.00	4.90
	OUTBOUND TOURISM						
8.1	**Departures**	('000)	..	..	..	..	..
8.2	**Tourism expenditure in other countries**	US$ Mn	60	61	71	83	94
8.3	"Travel" (*)	US$ Mn	39	45	48	54	60
8.4	"Passenger transport" (*)	US$ Mn	21	16	23	29	34
	TOURISM INDUSTRIES						
	Hotels and similar establishments						
9.1	Number of rooms	Units	6,726	6,813	6,825	6,918	6,883
9.2	Number of bed-places	Units	16,342	16,488	16,297	16,479	16,407
9.3	Occupancy rate	Percent	7.80	10.20	11.20	10.30	11.10
9.4	Average length of stay	Nights	3.80	4.20	4.20	4.00	3.90
	RELATED INDICATORS						
	Share of tourism expenditure (6.1) in:						
10.1	Gross Domestic Product (GDP)	Percent	1.4	1.5	1.4	1.4	1.6
10.2	Exports of goods	Percent	4.2	4.9	4.8	4.6	4.5
10.3	Exports of services	Percent	20.0	21.7	19.9	18.9	19.5

(*) Balance of Payments items: 6.1 to 6.3 correspond to the "Credit" side (and are receipts for the country) while 8.2 to 8.4 correspond to the "Debit" side (and are expenditures in other countries).

TOGO

	Basic Indicators	Units	2001	2002	2003	2004	2005
	INBOUND TOURISM						
	Arrivals						
1.1	Visitors	('000)	..	..	..	..	..
1.2	Tourists (overnight visitors)	('000)	57	58	61	83	81
1.3	Same-day visitors	('000)	..	..	..	..	..
1.4	Cruise passengers	('000)	..	..	..	..	..
	Arrivals by region						
2.1	Africa	('000)	34	29	31	44	46
2.2	Americas	('000)	2	2	2	3	3
2.3	Europe	('000)	18	24	24	30	27
2.4	East Asia and the Pacific	('000)	1	1	1	3	3
2.5	South Asia	('000)	..	..	..	..	..
2.6	Middle East	('000)	2	2	1	3	2
	Arrivals by means of transport used						
3.1	Air	('000)	..	..	..	..	..
3.2	Rail	('000)	..	..	..	..	..
3.3	Road	('000)	..	..	..	..	..
3.4	Sea	('000)	..	..	..	..	..
	Arrivals by purpose of visit						
4.1	Leisure, recreation and holidays	('000)	..	..	..	..	..
4.2	Business and professional	('000)	..	..	..	..	..
4.3	Other	('000)	..	..	..	..	..
	Accommodation						
5.1	Overnight stays in hotels and similar establishments	('000)	121	117	136	183	157
5.2	Guests in hotels and similar establishments	('000)	57	58	61	83	81
5.3	Overnight stays in all types of accommodation establishments	('000)	..	..	..	..	..
5.4	Average length of stay of non-resident tourists in all accommodation establishments	Nights	..	..	..	..	..
6.1	**Tourism expenditure in the country**	US$ Mn	14	16	26	25	..
6.2	"Travel" (*)	US$ Mn	11	13	15	19	..
6.3	"Passenger transport" (*)	US$ Mn	3	3	11	6	..
	DOMESTIC TOURISM						
	Accommodation						
7.1	Overnight stays in hotels and similar establishments	('000)	36	20	18	29	25
7.2	Guests in hotels and similar establishments	('000)	..	..	10	14	12
7.3	Overnight stays in all types of accommodation establishments	('000)	..	..	..	..	..
7.4	Average length of stay of resident tourists in all accommodation establishments	Nights	..	..	..	..	..
	OUTBOUND TOURISM						
8.1	**Departures**	('000)	..	..	..	..	..
8.2	**Tourism expenditure in other countries**	US$ Mn	20	26	37	38	..
8.3	"Travel" (*)	US$ Mn	5	5	7	8	..
8.4	"Passenger transport" (*)	US$ Mn	15	21	30	30	..
	TOURISM INDUSTRIES						
	Hotels and similar establishments						
9.1	Number of rooms	Units	2,888	4,365	4,480	4,728	4,944
9.2	Number of bed-places	Units	4,244	6,546	6,720	7,216	7,636
9.3	Occupancy rate	Percent	14.50	13.70	10.70	10.11	9.30
9.4	Average length of stay	Nights	2.10	2.00	2.10	2.10	1.90
	RELATED INDICATORS						
	Share of tourism expenditure (6.1) in:						
10.1	Gross Domestic Product (GDP)	Percent	1.1	1.1	1.5	1.2	..
10.2	Exports of goods	Percent	3.9	3.8	4.3	4.2	..
10.3	Exports of services	Percent	19.4	17.8	27.4	16.7	..

(*) Balance of Payments items: 6.1 to 6.3 correspond to the "Credit" side (and are receipts for the country) while 8.2 to 8.4 correspond to the "Debit" side (and are expenditures in other countries).

Basic Indicators		Units	2001	2002	2003	2004	2005
	INBOUND TOURISM						
	Arrivals						
1.1	Visitors	('000)	38	45	51	51	..
1.2	Tourists (overnight visitors)	('000)	32	37	40	41	42
1.3	Same-day visitors	('000)	..	..	..	..	..
1.4	Cruise passengers	('000)	6	8	11	10	..
	Arrivals by region						
2.1	Africa	('000)	..	..	..	..	..
2.2	Americas	('000)	7	8	8	8	8
2.3	Europe	('000)	4	4	4	3	3
2.4	East Asia and the Pacific	('000)	21	24	28	29	30
2.5	South Asia	('000)	..	..	..	..	..
2.6	Middle East	('000)	..	..	..	..	..
	Arrivals by means of transport used						
3.1	Air	('000)	32	37	40	41	42
3.2	Rail	('000)	..	..	..	..	..
3.3	Road	('000)	..	..	..	..	..
3.4	Sea	('000)	6	8	11	10	..
	Arrivals by purpose of visit						
4.1	Leisure, recreation and holidays	('000)	14	16	16	..	..
4.2	Business and professional	('000)	6	1	3	..	..
4.3	Other	('000)	12	20	20	..	..
	Accommodation						
5.1	Overnight stays in hotels and similar establishments	('000)	..	..	..	..	..
5.2	Guests in hotels and similar establishments	('000)	..	..	..	..	..
5.3	Overnight stays in all types of accommodation establishments	('000)	..	..	..	..	..
5.4	Average length of stay of non-resident tourists in all accommodation establishments	Nights	..	..	..	..	..
6.1	**Tourism expenditure in the country**	US$ Mn	..	..	..	..	..
6.2	"Travel" (*) (**)	US$ Mn	7	8	14	15	11
6.3	"Passenger transport" (*)	US$ Mn	..	..	..	..	..
	DOMESTIC TOURISM						
	Accommodation						
7.1	Overnight stays in hotels and similar establishments	('000)	..	..	..	..	..
7.2	Guests in hotels and similar establishments	('000)	..	..	..	..	..
7.3	Overnight stays in all types of accommodation establishments	('000)	..	..	..	..	..
7.4	Average length of stay of resident tourists in all accommodation establishments	Nights	..	..	..	..	..
	OUTBOUND TOURISM						
8.1	**Departures**	('000)	..	..	..	..	..
8.2	**Tourism expenditure in other countries**	US$ Mn	..	..	..	..	..
8.3	"Travel" (*)	US$ Mn	3	3	..	..	..
8.4	"Passenger transport" (*)	US$ Mn	..	..	..	..	..
	TOURISM INDUSTRIES						
	Hotels and similar establishments						
9.1	Number of rooms	Units	..	..	..	..	..
9.2	Number of bed-places	Units	..	..	..	..	..
9.3	Occupancy rate	Percent	..	..	..	..	..
9.4	Average length of stay	Nights	..	..	..	..	..
	RELATED INDICATORS						
	Share of tourism expenditure (6.1) in: (**)						
10.1	Gross Domestic Product (GDP)	Percent	5.2	5.5	8.3	7.0	4.5
10.2	Exports of goods	Percent	100.0	44.4	..	..	..
10.3	Exports of services	Percent	35.0	34.8	..	..	..

(*) Balance of Payments items: 6.1 to 6.3 correspond to the "Credit" side (and are receipts for the country) while 8.2 to 8.4 correspond to the "Debit" side (and are expenditures in other countries).

(**) See Annex "Country notes".

TRINIDAD AND TOBAGO

	Basic Indicators	Units	2001	2002	2003	2004	2005
	INBOUND TOURISM						
	Arrivals						
1.1	Visitors	('000)	465	444	465	497	530
1.2	Tourists (overnight visitors)	('000)	383	384	409	443	463
1.3	Same-day visitors	('000)	..	..	..	..	..
1.4	Cruise passengers	('000)	82	60	56	54	67
	Arrivals by region						
2.1	Africa	('000)	1	1	1	1	1
2.2	Americas	('000)	286	308	324	347	365
2.3	Europe	('000)	89	71	79	90	91
2.4	East Asia and the Pacific	('000)	4	3	3	3	3
2.5	South Asia	('000)	1	1	1	1	2
2.6	Middle East	('000)	..	..	..	..	..
	Arrivals by means of transport used						
3.1	Air	('000)	383	384	409	443	463
3.2	Rail	('000)	..	..	..	..	..
3.3	Road	('000)	..	..	..	..	..
3.4	Sea	('000)	82	60	56	54	67
	Arrivals by purpose of visit						
4.1	Leisure, recreation and holidays	('000)	292	250	281	299	313
4.2	Business and professional	('000)	69	72	79	86	89
4.3	Other	('000)	22	62	49	58	61
	Accommodation						
5.1	Overnight stays in hotels and similar establishments	('000)	..	..	..	..	..
5.2	Guests in hotels and similar establishments	('000)	..	..	..	..	..
5.3	Overnight stays in all types of accommodation establishments	('000)	..	..	..	..	..
5.4	Average length of stay of non-resident tourists in all accommodation establishments	Nights	..	16.90	14.40	14.40	14.30
6.1	**Tourism expenditure in the country**	US$ Mn	361	402	437	568	661
6.2	"Travel" (*)	US$ Mn	201	242	249	341	453
6.3	"Passenger transport" (*)	US$ Mn	160	160	188	227	208
	DOMESTIC TOURISM						
	Accommodation						
7.1	Overnight stays in hotels and similar establishments	('000)	..	..	..	..	..
7.2	Guests in hotels and similar establishments	('000)	..	..	..	..	..
7.3	Overnight stays in all types of accommodation establishments	('000)	..	..	..	..	..
7.4	Average length of stay of resident tourists in all accommodation establishments	Nights	..	..	..	..	..
	OUTBOUND TOURISM						
8.1	**Departures**	('000)	..	..	..	..	..
8.2	**Tourism expenditure in other countries**	US$ Mn	172	208	143	141	288
8.3	"Travel" (*)	US$ Mn	151	186	107	96	222
8.4	"Passenger transport" (*)	US$ Mn	21	22	36	45	66
	TOURISM INDUSTRIES						
	Hotels and similar establishments						
9.1	Number of rooms	Units	4,493	4,387	5,378	6,007	5,929
9.2	Number of bed-places	Units	..	..	..	..	..
9.3	Occupancy rate	Percent	43.20	41.00	..	..	..
9.4	Average length of stay	Nights	..	..	..	..	..
	RELATED INDICATORS						
	Share of tourism expenditure (6.1) in:						
10.1	Gross Domestic Product (GDP)	Percent	4.1	4.4	4.1	4.6	4.5
10.2	Exports of goods	Percent	8.4	10.3	8.4	8.9	7.5
10.3	Exports of services	Percent	62.9	63.1	63.8	66.7	73.4

(*) Balance of Payments items: 6.1 to 6.3 correspond to the "Credit" side (and are receipts for the country) while 8.2 to 8.4 correspond to the "Debit" side (and are expenditures in other countries).

Basic Indicators		Units	2001	2002	2003	2004	2005
	INBOUND TOURISM						
	Arrivals						
1.1	Visitors	('000)	5,663	5,322	5,492	6,419	6,975
1.2	Tourists (overnight visitors)	('000)	5,387	5,064	5,114	5,998	6,378
1.3	Same-day visitors	('000)	..	..	..	..	..
1.4	Cruise passengers	('000)	276	258	378	421	597
	Arrivals by region						
2.1	Africa	('000)	676	786	872	985	993
2.2	Americas	('000)	28	22	23	30	35
2.3	Europe	('000)	3,610	2,919	2,840	3,482	3,869
2.4	East Asia and the Pacific	('000)	8	7	9	11	14
2.5	South Asia	('000)	..	..	..	..	..
2.6	Middle East	('000)	1,046	1,311	1,356	1,472	1,440
	Arrivals by means of transport used						
3.1	Air	('000)	3,761	3,066	2,992	3,664	4,053
3.2	Rail	('000)	..	..	..	..	..
3.3	Road	('000)	1,554	1,920	2,033	2,250	2,232
3.4	Sea	('000)	72	78	89	84	94
	Arrivals by purpose of visit						
4.1	Leisure, recreation and holidays	('000)	..	..	..	..	..
4.2	Business and professional	('000)	..	..	..	..	..
4.3	Other	('000)	..	..	..	..	..
	Accommodation						
5.1	Overnight stays in hotels and similar establishments	('000)	33,006	25,897	25,301	30,665	33,587
5.2	Guests in hotels and similar establishments	('000)	5,233	4,245	4,064	4,900	5,442
5.3	Overnight stays in all types of accommodation establishments	('000)	..	..	..	..	..
5.4	Average length of stay of non-resident tourists in all accommodation establishments	Nights	6.10	5.10	4.90	5.10	5.30
6.1	**Tourism expenditure in the country**	US$ Mn	2,061	1,832	1,935	2,432	2,782
6.2	"Travel" (*)	US$ Mn	1,751	1,524	1,583	1,970	2,124
6.3	"Passenger transport" (*)	US$ Mn	310	308	352	462	658
	DOMESTIC TOURISM						
	Accommodation						
7.1	Overnight stays in hotels and similar establishments	('000)	2,328	2,621	2,809	2,822	2,723
7.2	Guests in hotels and similar establishments	('000)	..	1,191	1,225	1,242	1,224
7.3	Overnight stays in all types of accommodation establishments	('000)	..	..	..	..	..
7.4	Average length of stay of resident tourists in all accommodation establishments	Nights	..	..	2.30	2.30	2.20
	OUTBOUND TOURISM						
8.1	**Departures**	('000)	1,669	1,939	2,274	2,312	2,241
8.2	**Tourism expenditure in other countries**	US$ Mn	322	303	355	427	443
8.3	"Travel" (*)	US$ Mn	273	260	300	340	365
8.4	"Passenger transport" (*)	US$ Mn	49	43	55	87	78
	TOURISM INDUSTRIES						
	Hotels and similar establishments						
9.1	Number of rooms	Units	102,800	107,159	111,009	113,076	114,919
9.2	Number of bed-places	Units	205,605	214,319	222,018	226,153	229,837
9.3	Occupancy rate	Percent	55.20	44.00	42.00	48.70	51.50
9.4	Average length of stay	Nights	6.30	6.10	6.20	6.30	6.20
	RELATED INDICATORS						
	Share of tourism expenditure (6.1) in:						
10.1	Gross Domestic Product (GDP)	Percent	10.3	8.7	7.7	8.6	9.7
10.2	Exports of goods	Percent	31.1	26.7	24.1	25.1	26.5
10.3	Exports of services	Percent	70.8	68.3	65.9	67.0	69.5

(*) Balance of Payments items: 6.1 to 6.3 correspond to the "Credit" side (and are receipts for the country) while 8.2 to 8.4 correspond to the "Debit" side (and are expenditures in other countries).

TURKEY

	Basic Indicators	Units	2001	2002	2003	2004	2005
	INBOUND TOURISM						
	Arrivals						
1.1	Visitors	('000)	11,619	13,256	14,030	17,517	21,125
1.2	Tourists (overnight visitors)	('000)	10,783	12,790	13,341	16,826	20,273
1.3	Same-day visitors	('000)	836	466	689	691	852
1.4	Cruise passengers	('000)	..	..	..	..	..
	Arrivals by region						
2.1	Africa	('000)	119	131	119	131	154
2.2	Americas	('000)	327	254	213	283	391
2.3	Europe	('000)	9,473	11,359	11,872	14,946	17,663
2.4	East Asia and the Pacific	('000)	247	281	242	288	422
2.5	South Asia	('000)	342	451	522	661	995
2.6	Middle East	('000)	263	304	359	498	626
	Arrivals by means of transport used						
3.1	Air	('000)	8,459	9,990	10,080	12,575	14,980
3.2	Rail	('000)	56	55	63	73	80
3.3	Road	('000)	1,966	2,465	2,894	3,717	4,745
3.4	Sea	('000)	1,138	745	992	1,152	1,320
	Arrivals by purpose of visit						
4.1	Leisure, recreation and holidays	('000)	8,375	10,049	10,512	13,310	15,769
4.2	Business and professional	('000)	1,243	1,381	1,543	1,897	1,972
4.3	Other	('000)	1,659	1,492	1,647	1,996	2,782
	Accommodation						
5.1	Overnight stays in hotels and similar establishments	('000)	36,307	43,225	40,819	49,614	55,996
5.2	Guests in hotels and similar establishments	('000)	8,769	9,859	8,983	10,962	12,937
5.3	Overnight stays in all types of accommodation establishments	('000)	36,368	43,312	40,866	49,728	56,108
5.4	Average length of stay of non-resident tourists in all accommodation establishments	Nights	4.14	4.39	4.54	4.53	4.33
6.1	**Tourism expenditure in the country**	US$ Mn	..	..	..	..	..
6.2	"Travel" (*)	US$ Mn	10,067	11,901	13,203	15,888	18,152
6.3	"Passenger transport" (*)	US$ Mn	..	..	..	..	..
	DOMESTIC TOURISM						
	Accommodation						
7.1	Overnight stays in hotels and similar establishments	('000)	14,147	15,152	16,199	18,341	18,807
7.2	Guests in hotels and similar establishments	('000)	7,741	7,908	8,423	9,720	10,454
7.3	Overnight stays in all types of accommodation establishments	('000)	14,178	15,202	16,234	18,357	18,819
7.4	Average length of stay of resident tourists in all accommodation establishments	Nights	1.83	1.92	1.93	1.89	1.80
	OUTBOUND TOURISM						
8.1	**Departures**	('000)	4,856	5,131	5,928	7,299	8,246
8.2	**Tourism expenditure in other countries**	US$ Mn	..	..	..	..	..
8.3	"Travel" (*)	US$ Mn	1,738	1,881	2,113	2,524	2,872
8.4	"Passenger transport" (*)	US$ Mn	..	..	..	..	..
	TOURISM INDUSTRIES						
	Hotels and similar establishments						
9.1	Number of rooms	Units	176,635	189,528	201,510	217,066	230,605
9.2	Number of bed-places	Units	366,605	393,718	418,177	452,424	481,704
9.3	Occupancy rate	Percent	46.67	48.69	46.90	50.07	52.38
9.4	Average length of stay	Nights	3.10	3.29	3.28	3.29	3.20
	RELATED INDICATORS						
	Share of tourism expenditure (6.1) in: (**)						
10.1	Gross Domestic Product (GDP)	Percent	6.9	6.5	5.5	5.2	5.0
10.2	Exports of goods	Percent	29.3	29.7	25.8	23.7	23.6
10.3	Exports of services	Percent	66.1	84.8	73.3	69.2	70.2

(*) Balance of Payments items: 6.1 to 6.3 correspond to the "Credit" side (and are receipts for the country) while 8.2 to 8.4 correspond to the "Debit" side (and are expenditures in other countries).

(**) See Annex "Country notes".

	Basic Indicators	Units	2001	2002	2003	2004	2005
	INBOUND TOURISM						
	Arrivals						
1.1	Visitors	('000)	..	..	..	..	..
1.2	Tourists (overnight visitors)	('000)	5.2	10.8	8.2	14.8	11.6
1.3	Same-day visitors	('000)	..	..	..	..	..
1.4	Cruise passengers	('000)	..	..	..	..	..
	Arrivals by region						
2.1	Africa	('000)	..	..	..	..	..
2.2	Americas	('000)	0.4	0.2	0.2	0.4	0.4
2.3	Europe	('000)	2.8	2.3	1.9	3.9	3.3
2.4	East Asia and the Pacific	('000)	0.7	0.5	0.5	1.1	0.8
2.5	South Asia	('000)	1.3	7.6	5.6	9.4	7.2
2.6	Middle East	('000)	..	..	..	..	..
	Arrivals by means of transport used						
3.1	Air	('000)	1.1	4.8	2.7	3.8	2.7
3.2	Rail	('000)	..	..	..	..	..
3.3	Road	('000)	4.1	6.0	5.5	11.0	8.9
3.4	Sea	('000)	..	..	..	..	..
	Arrivals by purpose of visit						
4.1	Leisure, recreation and holidays	('000)	1.3	5.0	1.2	2.9	9.0
4.2	Business and professional	('000)	..	..	0.6	1.4	1.3
4.3	Other	('000)	3.9	5.8	6.4	10.5	1.3
	Accommodation						
5.1	Overnight stays in hotels and similar establishments	('000)	..	..	..	..	..
5.2	Guests in hotels and similar establishments	('000)	..	..	..	..	..
5.3	Overnight stays in all types of accommodation establishments	('000)	..	..	..	..	..
5.4	Average length of stay of non-resident tourists in all accommodation establishments	Nights	6.00	6.00	6.00	6.00	6.00
6.1	**Tourism expenditure in the country**	US$ Mn	..	..	..	..	..
6.2	"Travel" (*)	US$ Mn	..	..	..	..	..
6.3	"Passenger transport" (*)	US$ Mn	..	..	..	..	..
	DOMESTIC TOURISM						
	Accommodation						
7.1	Overnight stays in hotels and similar establishments	('000)	..	..	..	..	..
7.2	Guests in hotels and similar establishments	('000)	..	..	..	..	..
7.3	Overnight stays in all types of accommodation establishments	('000)	..	..	..	..	..
7.4	Average length of stay of resident tourists in all accommodation establishments	Nights	..	..	..	..	..
	OUTBOUND TOURISM						
8.1	**Departures**	('000)	111	79	34	32	33
8.2	**Tourism expenditure in other countries**	US$ Mn	..	..	..	..	..
8.3	"Travel" (*)	US$ Mn	..	..	..	..	..
8.4	"Passenger transport" (*)	US$ Mn	..	..	..	..	..
	TOURISM INDUSTRIES						
	Hotels and similar establishments						
9.1	Number of rooms	Units	956	970	970	970	..
9.2	Number of bed-places	Units	1,661	1,675	1,675	1,675	..
9.3	Occupancy rate	Percent	6.00	12.00	10.00	19.00	..
9.4	Average length of stay	Nights	7.00	7.00	8.00	8.00	..
	RELATED INDICATORS						
	Share of tourism expenditure (6.1) in:						
10.1	Gross Domestic Product (GDP)	Percent	..	..	..	..	..
10.2	Exports of goods	Percent	..	..	..	..	..
10.3	Exports of services	Percent	..	..	..	..	..

(*) Balance of Payments items: 6.1 to 6.3 correspond to the "Credit" side (and are receipts for the country) while 8.2 to 8.4 correspond to the "Debit" side (and are expenditures in other countries).

TURKS AND CAICOS ISLANDS

Basic Indicators		Units	2001	2002	2003	2004	2005
	INBOUND TOURISM						
	Arrivals						
1.1	Visitors	('000)	..	..	..	..	..
1.2	Tourists (overnight visitors)	('000)	166	155	164	173	200
1.3	Same-day visitors	('000)	..	..	..	..	..
1.4	Cruise passengers	('000)	..	..	..	..	..
	Arrivals by region						
2.1	Africa	('000)	..	..	..	..	..
2.2	Americas	('000)	148	140	..	..	..
2.3	Europe	('000)	11	11	..	..	..
2.4	East Asia and the Pacific	('000)	..	..	..	..	..
2.5	South Asia	('000)	..	..	..	..	..
2.6	Middle East	('000)	..	..	..	..	..
	Arrivals by means of transport used						
3.1	Air	('000)	164	154	158	..	..
3.2	Rail	('000)	..	..	..	..	..
3.3	Road	('000)	..	..	..	..	..
3.4	Sea	('000)	1	3	..	..	..
	Arrivals by purpose of visit						
4.1	Leisure, recreation and holidays	('000)	74	90	96	..	..
4.2	Business and professional	('000)	65	47	59	..	..
4.3	Other	('000)	26	18	9	..	..
	Accommodation						
5.1	Overnight stays in hotels and similar establishments	('000)	..	..	..	..	..
5.2	Guests in hotels and similar establishments	('000)	..	..	..	..	..
5.3	Overnight stays in all types of accommodation establishments	('000)	1,239	1,172	..	..	..
5.4	Average length of stay of non-resident tourists in all accommodation establishments	Nights	7.70	7.80	..	..	..
6.1	**Tourism expenditure in the country** (**)	US$ Mn	311	292	..	..	..
6.2	"Travel" (*)	US$ Mn	..	..	..	..	..
6.3	"Passenger transport" (*)	US$ Mn	..	..	..	..	..
	DOMESTIC TOURISM						
	Accommodation						
7.1	Overnight stays in hotels and similar establishments	('000)	..	..	..	..	..
7.2	Guests in hotels and similar establishments	('000)	..	..	..	..	..
7.3	Overnight stays in all types of accommodation establishments	('000)	..	..	..	..	..
7.4	Average length of stay of resident tourists in all accommodation establishments	Nights	..	..	..	..	..
	OUTBOUND TOURISM						
8.1	**Departures**	('000)	..	..	..	..	..
8.2	**Tourism expenditure in other countries**	US$ Mn	..	..	..	..	..
8.3	"Travel" (*)	US$ Mn	..	..	..	..	..
8.4	"Passenger transport" (*)	US$ Mn	..	..	..	..	..
	TOURISM INDUSTRIES						
	Hotels and similar establishments						
9.1	Number of rooms	Units	2,210	2,370	2,473	..	..
9.2	Number of bed-places	Units	3,868	4,148	4,946	..	..
9.3	Occupancy rate	Percent	78.00	73.00	..	..	..
9.4	Average length of stay	Nights	..	..	..	..	..
	RELATED INDICATORS						
	Share of tourism expenditure (6.1) in:						
10.1	Gross Domestic Product (GDP)	Percent	..	..	..	..	..
10.2	Exports of goods	Percent	..	..	..	..	..
10.3	Exports of services	Percent	..	..	..	..	..

(*) Balance of Payments items: 6.1 to 6.3 correspond to the "Credit" side (and are receipts for the country) while 8.2 to 8.4 correspond to the "Debit" side (and are expenditures in other countries).

(**) See Annex "Country notes".

	Basic Indicators	Units	2001	2002	2003	2004	2005
	INBOUND TOURISM						
	Arrivals						
1.1	Visitors	('000)	..	..	..	..	..
1.2	Tourists (overnight visitors)	('000)	1.1	1.3	1.4	1.3	1.1
1.3	Same-day visitors	('000)	..	..	..	..	..
1.4	Cruise passengers	('000)	..	..	..	..	..
	Arrivals by region						
2.1	Africa	('000)	..	..	..	..	..
2.2	Americas	('000)	0.1	0.1	0.1	0.1	0.1
2.3	Europe	('000)	0.1	0.1	0.1	0.1	0.1
2.4	East Asia and the Pacific	('000)	0.9	1.1	1.1	1.0	0.8
2.5	South Asia	('000)	..	..	..	..	..
2.6	Middle East	('000)	..	..	..	..	..
	Arrivals by means of transport used						
3.1	Air	('000)	..	..	1.1	1.1	0.9
3.2	Rail	('000)	..	..	..	..	..
3.3	Road	('000)	..	..	..	..	..
3.4	Sea	('000)	..	..	0.3	0.2	0.2
	Arrivals by purpose of visit						
4.1	Leisure, recreation and holidays	('000)	0.1	0.2	0.2	0.2	0.2
4.2	Business and professional	('000)	0.5	0.3	0.3	0.9	0.6
4.3	Other	('000)	0.5	0.8	0.9	0.2	0.3
	Accommodation						
5.1	Overnight stays in hotels and similar establishments	('000)	..	..	..	..	..
5.2	Guests in hotels and similar establishments	('000)	..	..	..	..	..
5.3	Overnight stays in all types of accommodation establishments	('000)	..	..	..	..	..
5.4	Average length of stay of non-resident tourists in all accommodation establishments	Nights	..	..	..	..	..
6.1	**Tourism expenditure in the country**	US$ Mn	..	..	..	..	..
6.2	"Travel" (*)	US$ Mn	..	..	..	..	..
6.3	"Passenger transport" (*)	US$ Mn	..	..	..	..	..
	DOMESTIC TOURISM						
	Accommodation						
7.1	Overnight stays in hotels and similar establishments	('000)	..	..	..	..	..
7.2	Guests in hotels and similar establishments	('000)	..	..	..	..	..
7.3	Overnight stays in all types of accommodation establishments	('000)	..	..	..	..	..
7.4	Average length of stay of resident tourists in all accommodation establishments	Nights	..	..	..	..	..
	OUTBOUND TOURISM						
8.1	**Departures**	('000)	2.8	2.7	2.6	2.3	..
8.2	**Tourism expenditure in other countries**	US$ Mn	..	..	..	..	..
8.3	"Travel" (*)	US$ Mn	..	..	..	..	..
8.4	"Passenger transport" (*)	US$ Mn	..	..	..	..	..
	TOURISM INDUSTRIES						
	Hotels and similar establishments						
9.1	Number of rooms	Units	..	..	..	..	..
9.2	Number of bed-places	Units	..	..	..	..	..
9.3	Occupancy rate	Percent	..	..	..	..	..
9.4	Average length of stay	Nights	..	..	..	..	..
	RELATED INDICATORS						
	Share of tourism expenditure (6.1) in:						
10.1	Gross Domestic Product (GDP)	Percent	..	..	..	..	..
10.2	Exports of goods	Percent	..	..	..	..	..
10.3	Exports of services	Percent	..	..	..	..	..

(*) Balance of Payments items: 6.1 to 6.3 correspond to the "Credit" side (and are receipts for the country) while 8.2 to 8.4 correspond to the "Debit" side (and are expenditures in other countries).

UGANDA

	Basic Indicators	Units	2001	2002	2003	2004	2005
	INBOUND TOURISM						
	Arrivals						
1.1	Visitors	('000)	..	..	..	..	..
1.2	Tourists (overnight visitors)	('000)	205	254	305	512	468
1.3	Same-day visitors	('000)	..	..	..	..	..
1.4	Cruise passengers	('000)	..	..	..	..	..
	Arrivals by region						
2.1	Africa	('000)	150	192	233	406	337
2.2	Americas	('000)	13	15	16	23	29
2.3	Europe	('000)	30	34	39	49	62
2.4	East Asia and the Pacific	('000)	5	4	5	8	10
2.5	South Asia	('000)	5	6	8	12	14
2.6	Middle East	('000)	2	2	2	3	3
	Arrivals by means of transport used						
3.1	Air	('000)	80	86	97	131	172
3.2	Rail	('000)	..	..	..	..	..
3.3	Road	('000)	125	168	208	381	296
3.4	Sea	('000)	..	..	..	..	..
	Arrivals by purpose of visit						
4.1	Leisure, recreation and holidays	('000)	45	69	76	86	9
4.2	Business and professional	('000)	53	59	67	81	31
4.3	Other	('000)	107	126	162	345	428
	Accommodation						
5.1	Overnight stays in hotels and similar establishments	('000)	..	..	..	..	..
5.2	Guests in hotels and similar establishments	('000)	..	..	..	..	..
5.3	Overnight stays in all types of accommodation establishments	('000)	820	1,016	..	..	..
5.4	Average length of stay of non-resident tourists in all accommodation establishments	Nights	..	..	..	..	..
6.1	**Tourism expenditure in the country**	US$ Mn	187	195	185	257	357
6.2	"Travel" (*)	US$ Mn	165	172	184	256	355
6.3	"Passenger transport" (*)	US$ Mn	22	23	1	1	2
	DOMESTIC TOURISM						
	Accommodation						
7.1	Overnight stays in hotels and similar establishments	('000)	..	..	..	..	..
7.2	Guests in hotels and similar establishments	('000)	..	..	..	..	..
7.3	Overnight stays in all types of accommodation establishments	('000)	..	..	..	..	..
7.4	Average length of stay of resident tourists in all accommodation establishments	Nights	..	..	..	..	..
	OUTBOUND TOURISM						
8.1	**Departures**	('000)	152	184	189	231	189
8.2	**Tourism expenditure in other countries**	US$ Mn	..	..	..	136	137
8.3	"Travel" (*)	US$ Mn	..	..	..	133	133
8.4	"Passenger transport" (*)	US$ Mn	..	..	..	3	4
	TOURISM INDUSTRIES						
	Hotels and similar establishments						
9.1	Number of rooms	Units	17,837	19,385	..	..	..
9.2	Number of bed-places	Units	27,113	29,295	..	..	..
9.3	Occupancy rate	Percent	..	..	..	..	..
9.4	Average length of stay	Nights	..	..	..	..	..
	RELATED INDICATORS						
	Share of tourism expenditure (6.1) in:						
10.1	Gross Domestic Product (GDP)	Percent	3.3	3.3	3.0	3.8	4.1
10.2	Exports of goods	Percent	39.3	40.5	32.9	36.2	41.3
10.3	Exports of services	Percent	86.2	86.7	69.5	71.8	74.7

(*) Balance of Payments items: 6.1 to 6.3 correspond to the "Credit" side (and are receipts for the country) while 8.2 to 8.4 correspond to the "Debit" side (and are expenditures in other countries).

UKRAINE

Basic Indicators			Units	2001	2002	2003	2004	2005
	INBOUND TOURISM							
	Arrivals							
1.1	Visitors		('000)	11,877	12,793	15,161	..	..
1.2	Tourists (overnight visitors)		('000)	9,174	10,517	12,514	15,629	..
1.3	Same-day visitors		('000)	2,645	2,215	2,556	..	..
1.4	Cruise passengers		('000)	58	61	91	..	..
	Arrivals by region							
2.1	Africa		('000)	5	5	12	..	..
2.2	Americas		('000)	64	53	83	..	..
2.3	Europe		('000)	9,061	10,409	12,345	..	..
2.4	East Asia and the Pacific		('000)	17	22	26	..	..
2.5	South Asia		('000)	7	10	14	..	..
2.6	Middle East		('000)	13	15	19	..	..
	Arrivals by means of transport used							
3.1	Air		('000)	605	665	675	..	..
3.2	Rail		('000)	7,138	7,684	7,230	..	..
3.3	Road		('000)	3,844	4,137	4,309	..	..
3.4	Sea		('000)	290	307	300	..	..
	Arrivals by purpose of visit							
4.1	Leisure, recreation and holidays		('000)	574	613	728	..	..
4.2	Business and professional		('000)	1,655	1,786	2,122	..	..
4.3	Other		('000)	9,647	10,393	12,310	..	..
	Accommodation							
5.1	Overnight stays in hotels and similar establishments		('000)	1,070	1,453	1,420	..	..
5.2	Guests in hotels and similar establishments		('000)	..	..	..	..	..
5.3	Overnight stays in all types of accommodation establishments		('000)	5,177	4,757	4,479	..	..
5.4	Average length of stay of non-resident tourists in all accommodation establishments		Nights	4.80	5.00	4.80	..	..
6.1	**Tourism expenditure in the country**	(**)	US$ Mn	759	1,001	1,204	2,931	3,542
6.2	"Travel" (*)		US$ Mn	573	788	935	2,560	3,125
6.3	"Passenger transport" (*)		US$ Mn	186	213	269	371	417
	DOMESTIC TOURISM							
	Accommodation							
7.1	Overnight stays in hotels and similar establishments		('000)	8,299	8,398	8,411	..	..
7.2	Guests in hotels and similar establishments		('000)	..	..	..	..	..
7.3	Overnight stays in all types of accommodation establishments		('000)	40,129	38,951	38,100	..	..
7.4	Average length of stay of resident tourists in all accommodation establishments		Nights	..	..	..	..	..
	OUTBOUND TOURISM							
8.1	**Departures**		('000)	14,849	14,729	14,795	15,488	..
8.2	**Tourism expenditure in other countries**	(**)	US$ Mn	676	794	953	2,660	3,078
8.3	"Travel" (*)		US$ Mn	566	657	789	2,463	2,805
8.4	"Passenger transport" (*)		US$ Mn	110	137	164	197	273
	TOURISM INDUSTRIES							
	Hotels and similar establishments							
9.1	Number of rooms		Units	43,487	35,139	32,572	..	..
9.2	Number of bed-places		Units	100,677	90,289	86,243	..	..
9.3	Occupancy rate		Percent	25.00	26.00	30.00	..	..
9.4	Average length of stay		Nights	2.60	2.60	2.60	..	..
	RELATED INDICATORS							
	Share of tourism expenditure (6.1) in:							
10.1	Gross Domestic Product (GDP)		Percent	2.0	2.4	2.4	4.5	4.3
10.2	Exports of goods		Percent	4.4	5.4	5.1	8.8	10.1
10.3	Exports of services		Percent	19.0	21.4	23.1	37.3	37.9

(*) Balance of Payments items: 6.1 to 6.3 correspond to the "Credit" side (and are receipts for the country) while 8.2 to 8.4 correspond to the "Debit" side (and are expenditures in other countries).

(**) See Annex "Country notes".

UNITED ARAB EMIRATES

	Basic Indicators		Units	2001	2002	2003	2004	2005
	INBOUND TOURISM							
	Arrivals							
1.1	Visitors		('000)	..	..	..	..	..
1.2	Tourists (overnight visitors)		('000)	4,134	5,445	5,871	..	..
1.3	Same-day visitors		('000)	..	..	..	..	..
1.4	Cruise passengers		('000)	..	..	..	..	..
	Arrivals by region							
2.1	Africa		('000)	218	311	307	..	..
2.2	Americas		('000)	150	239	272	..	..
2.3	Europe		('000)	1,115	1,468	1,585	..	..
2.4	East Asia and the Pacific		('000)	285	395	428	..	..
2.5	South Asia		('000)	590	807	922	..	..
2.6	Middle East		('000)	1,221	1,557	1,583	..	..
	Arrivals by means of transport used							
3.1	Air		('000)	..	..	..	..	..
3.2	Rail		('000)	..	..	..	..	..
3.3	Road		('000)	..	..	..	..	..
3.4	Sea		('000)	..	..	..	..	..
	Arrivals by purpose of visit							
4.1	Leisure, recreation and holidays		('000)	..	..	..	..	..
4.2	Business and professional		('000)	..	..	..	..	..
4.3	Other		('000)	..	..	..	..	..
	Accommodation							
5.1	Overnight stays in hotels and similar establishments		('000)	10,126	12,360	14,192	..	..
5.2	Guests in hotels and similar establishments		('000)	4,134	5,445	5,871	..	..
5.3	Overnight stays in all types of accommodation establishments		('000)	..	..	..	..	..
5.4	Average length of stay of non-resident tourists in all accommodation establishments		Nights	..	..	..	..	..
6.1	**Tourism expenditure in the country**	(**)	US$ Mn	1,200	1,332	1,439	1,594	2,200
6.2	"Travel" (*)		US$ Mn	..	..	..	..	..
6.3	"Passenger transport" (*)		US$ Mn	..	..	..	..	..
	DOMESTIC TOURISM							
	Accommodation							
7.1	Overnight stays in hotels and similar establishments		('000)	..	..	..	..	..
7.2	Guests in hotels and similar establishments		('000)	..	..	..	..	..
7.3	Overnight stays in all types of accommodation establishments		('000)	..	..	..	..	..
7.4	Average length of stay of resident tourists in all accommodation establishments		Nights	..	..	..	..	..
	OUTBOUND TOURISM							
8.1	**Departures**		('000)	..	..	..	..	..
8.2	**Tourism expenditure in other countries**	(**)	US$ Mn	3,321	3,654	3,959	4,475	5,300
8.3	"Travel" (*)		US$ Mn	..	..	..	..	..
8.4	"Passenger transport" (*)		US$ Mn	..	..	..	..	..
	TOURISM INDUSTRIES							
	Hotels and similar establishments							
9.1	Number of rooms		Units	31,786	34,536	38,402	..	..
9.2	Number of bed-places		Units	51,951	56,142	60,572	..	..
9.3	Occupancy rate		Percent	60.10	67.20	68.00	..	..
9.4	Average length of stay		Nights	..	..	..	..	..
	RELATED INDICATORS							
	Share of tourism expenditure (6.1) in:							
10.1	Gross Domestic Product (GDP)		Percent	..	..	..	..	..
10.2	Exports of goods		Percent	..	..	..	..	..
10.3	Exports of services		Percent	..	..	..	..	..

(*) Balance of Payments items: 6.1 to 6.3 correspond to the "Credit" side (and are receipts for the country) while 8.2 to 8.4 correspond to the "Debit" side (and are expenditures in other countries).

(**) See Annex "Country notes".

	Basic Indicators		Units	2001	2002	2003	2004	2005
	INBOUND TOURISM							
	Arrivals							
1.1	Visitors		('000)	22,835	24,180	24,715	27,755	29,971
1.2	Tourists (overnight visitors)		('000)	..	..	..	..	..
1.3	Same-day visitors		('000)	1,853	1,873	1,928	2,077	1,995
1.4	Cruise passengers		('000)	..	..	..	..	..
	Arrivals by region							
2.1	Africa		('000)	630	631	569	639	654
2.2	Americas		('000)	4,582	4,619	4,326	4,692	4,597
2.3	Europe		('000)	15,059	16,409	17,371	19,582	21,742
2.4	East Asia and the Pacific		('000)	1,834	1,854	1,809	2,086	2,190
2.5	South Asia		('000)	326	308	294	371	407
2.6	Middle East		('000)	402	360	346	384	380
	Arrivals by means of transport used							
3.1	Air		('000)	16,054	17,098	17,635	20,002	22,023
3.2	Rail		('000)	2,779	2,677	2,711	2,983	3,252
3.3	Road		('000)	..	..	..	..	..
3.4	Sea		('000)	4,002	4,405	4,369	4,770	4,697
	Arrivals by purpose of visit							
4.1	Leisure, recreation and holidays		('000)	7,585	7,735	7,973	9,275	9,693
4.2	Business and professional		('000)	7,387	7,840	7,590	8,055	8,820
4.3	Other		('000)	7,862	8,605	9,152	10,425	11,459
	Accommodation							
5.1	Overnight stays in hotels and similar establishments		('000)	49,781	48,377	49,003	53,789	58,909
5.2	Guests in hotels and similar establishments		('000)	17,019	14,176	14,397	13,172	..
5.3	Overnight stays in all types of accommodation establishments		('000)	189,516	199,285	203,432	227,406	247,587
5.4	Average length of stay of non-resident tourists in all accommodation establishments		Nights	8.30	8.20	8.20	8.20	8.30
6.1	**Tourism expenditure in the country**	(**)	US$ Mn	26,137	27,819	30,736	37,166	39,573
6.2	"Travel" (*)		US$ Mn	18,864	20,549	22,668	28,202	30,577
6.3	"Passenger transport" (*)		US$ Mn	7,273	7,270	8,068	8,964	8,996
	DOMESTIC TOURISM							
	Accommodation							
7.1	Overnight stays in hotels and similar establishments		('000)	134,420	130,560	118,480	106,510	117,926
7.2	Guests in hotels and similar establishments		('000)	54,960	57,680	52,020	48,100	52,611
7.3	Overnight stays in all types of accommodation establishments		('000)	529,600	531,940	490,540	408,950	442,300
7.4	Average length of stay of resident tourists in all accommodation establishments		Nights	..	..	..	..	..
	OUTBOUND TOURISM							
8.1	**Departures**		('000)	58,281	59,377	61,424	64,194	66,494
8.2	**Tourism expenditure in other countries**	(**)	US$ Mn	46,411	51,125	58,627	69,463	73,786
8.3	"Travel" (*)		US$ Mn	37,931	41,744	47,853	56,444	59,593
8.4	"Passenger transport" (*)		US$ Mn	8,480	9,381	10,774	13,019	14,193
	TOURISM INDUSTRIES							
	Hotels and similar establishments							
9.1	Number of rooms		Units	..	..	..	..	..
9.2	Number of bed-places		Units	1,130,000	1,188,000	1,062,000	1,223,000	1,062,000
9.3	Occupancy rate		Percent	42.00	44.00	44.00	45.00	44.00
9.4	Average length of stay		Nights	..	..	..	..	..
	RELATED INDICATORS							
	Share of tourism expenditure (6.1) in:							
10.1	Gross Domestic Product (GDP)		Percent	1.8	1.8	1.7	1.7	1.8
10.2	Exports of goods		Percent	9.6	9.9	10.0	10.6	10.3
10.3	Exports of services		Percent	21.6	20.6	19.4	18.8	19.6

(*) Balance of Payments items: 6.1 to 6.3 correspond to the "Credit" side (and are receipts for the country) while 8.2 to 8.4 correspond to the "Debit" side (and are expenditures in other countries).

(**) See Annex "Country notes".

UNITED REPUBLIC OF TANZANIA

	Basic Indicators	Units	2001	2002	2003	2004	2005
	INBOUND TOURISM						
	Arrivals						
1.1	Visitors	('000)	525	575	576	583	613
1.2	Tourists (overnight visitors)	('000)	501	550	552	566	590
1.3	Same-day visitors	('000)	24	25	24	17	23
1.4	Cruise passengers	('000)	..	..	..	..	..
	Arrivals by region						
2.1	Africa	('000)	213	250	268	256	276
2.2	Americas	('000)	46	59	50	53	62
2.3	Europe	('000)	162	192	191	222	220
2.4	East Asia and the Pacific	('000)	47	30	27	23	25
2.5	South Asia	('000)	28	28	27	17	20
2.6	Middle East	('000)	30	17	14	12	11
	Arrivals by means of transport used						
3.1	Air	('000)	315	316	320	257	331
3.2	Rail	('000)	16	25	16	5	6
3.3	Road	('000)	173	214	215	297	266
3.4	Sea	('000)	21	20	25	24	10
	Arrivals by purpose of visit						
4.1	Leisure, recreation and holidays	('000)	341	358	337	429	467
4.2	Business and professional	('000)	152	115	133	83	85
4.3	Other	('000)	32	102	106	71	61
	Accommodation						
5.1	Overnight stays in hotels and similar establishments	('000)	..	..	..	..	..
5.2	Guests in hotels and similar establishments	('000)	..	..	..	..	..
5.3	Overnight stays in all types of accommodation establishments	('000)	2,632	4,459	5,500	5,525	6,130
5.4	Average length of stay of non-resident tourists in all accommodation establishments	Nights	..	..	..	..	..
6.1	**Tourism expenditure in the country**	US$ Mn	626	639	654	762	836
6.2	"Travel" (*)	US$ Mn	615	635	647	746	824
6.3	"Passenger transport" (*)	US$ Mn	11	4	7	16	12
	DOMESTIC TOURISM						
	Accommodation						
7.1	Overnight stays in hotels and similar establishments	('000)	..	..	..	..	..
7.2	Guests in hotels and similar establishments	('000)	..	..	..	..	..
7.3	Overnight stays in all types of accommodation establishments	('000)	2,917	3,971	4,100	4,100	4,500
7.4	Average length of stay of resident tourists in all accommodation establishments	Nights	..	..	..	..	..
	OUTBOUND TOURISM						
8.1	**Departures**	('000)	..	..	..	..	..
8.2	**Tourism expenditure in other countries**	US$ Mn	363	362	375	470	577
8.3	"Travel" (*)	US$ Mn	327	338	353	445	554
8.4	"Passenger transport" (*)	US$ Mn	36	24	22	25	23
	TOURISM INDUSTRIES						
	Hotels and similar establishments						
9.1	Number of rooms	Units	10,325	25,300	30,600	30,840	31,365
9.2	Number of bed-places	Units	18,284	45,500	55,500	55,932	56,562
9.3	Occupancy rate	Percent	58.60	51.00	47.00	47.00	48.00
9.4	Average length of stay	Nights	8.00	10.00	10.00	11.00	12.00
	RELATED INDICATORS						
	Share of tourism expenditure (6.1) in:						
10.1	Gross Domestic Product (GDP)	Percent	6.6	6.5	6.4	6.7	6.9
10.2	Exports of goods	Percent	73.6	65.2	53.8	51.7	50.2
10.3	Exports of services	Percent	68.4	69.5	69.0	68.2	68.2

(*) Balance of Payments items: 6.1 to 6.3 correspond to the "Credit" side (and are receipts for the country) while 8.2 to 8.4 correspond to the "Debit" side (and are expenditures in other countries).

	Basic Indicators		Units	2001	2002	2003	2004	2005
	INBOUND TOURISM							
	Arrivals							
1.1	Visitors		('000)	..	..	..	..	..
1.2	Tourists (overnight visitors)		('000)	46,907	43,581	41,218	46,086	49,206
1.3	Same-day visitors		('000)	..	..	..	..	..
1.4	Cruise passengers		('000)	..	..	..	..	..
	Arrivals by region							
2.1	Africa		('000)	287	241	236	240	252
2.2	Americas		('000)	29,578	28,036	26,368	29,196	31,178
2.3	Europe		('000)	9,907	8,964	8,982	10,056	10,702
2.4	East Asia and the Pacific		('000)	6,535	5,889	5,192	6,087	6,518
2.5	South Asia		('000)	363	324	330	370	411
2.6	Middle East		('000)	237	127	110	137	144
	Arrivals by means of transport used							
3.1	Air		('000)	27,381	24,185	23,076	25,824	27,685
3.2	Rail		('000)	..	..	..	..	..
3.3	Road		('000)	19,076	18,954	17,759	19,844	21,105
3.4	Sea		('000)	450	386	376	418	419
	Arrivals by purpose of visit							
4.1	Leisure, recreation and holidays		('000)	7,991	8,182	8,094	9,592	10,232
4.2	Business and professional		('000)	5,364	5,792	5,011	5,202	5,637
4.3	Other		('000)	4,766	5,142	4,921	5,528	5,810
	Accommodation							
5.1	Overnight stays in hotels and similar establishments		('000)	..	..	..	..	..
5.2	Guests in hotels and similar establishments		('000)	13,934	14,911	13,898	16,034	16,975
5.3	Overnight stays in all types of accommodation establishments		('000)	..	..	..	..	..
5.4	Average length of stay of non-resident tourists in all accommodation establishments		Nights	..	..	..	..	..
6.1	**Tourism expenditure in the country**		US$ Mn	106,705	101,798	98,998	112,941	122,944
6.2	"Travel" (*)	(**)	US$ Mn	88,779	84,752	83,305	94,090	102,014
6.3	"Passenger transport" (*)		US$ Mn	17,926	17,046	15,693	18,851	20,930
	DOMESTIC TOURISM							
	Accommodation							
7.1	Overnight stays in hotels and similar establishments		('000)	..	..	..	..	..
7.2	Guests in hotels and similar establishments		('000)	..	..	..	..	..
7.3	Overnight stays in all types of accommodation establishments		('000)	..	..	..	..	..
7.4	Average length of stay of resident tourists in all accommodation establishments		Nights	..	..	..	..	..
	OUTBOUND TOURISM							
8.1	**Departures**		('000)	59,433	58,065	56,250	61,809	63,503
8.2	**Tourism expenditure in other countries**		US$ Mn	85,453	81,707	81,889	93,386	99,624
8.3	"Travel" (*)	(**)	US$ Mn	62,820	61,738	60,932	69,663	73,558
8.4	"Passenger transport" (*)		US$ Mn	22,633	19,969	20,957	23,723	26,066
	TOURISM INDUSTRIES							
	Hotels and similar establishments							
9.1	Number of rooms		Units	4,200,000	4,397,534	4,415,696	4,411,908	4,402,466
9.2	Number of bed-places		Units	..	..	..	..	..
9.3	Occupancy rate		Percent	60.10	59.10	61.10	61.30	63.10
9.4	Average length of stay		Nights	..	..	..	..	..
	RELATED INDICATORS							
	Share of tourism expenditure (6.1) in:							
10.1	Gross Domestic Product (GDP)		Percent	1.1	1.0	0.9	1.0	1.0
10.2	Exports of goods		Percent	14.8	14.8	13.8	13.9	13.7
10.3	Exports of services		Percent	37.7	35.3	33.1	33.1	32.6

(*) Balance of Payments items: 6.1 to 6.3 correspond to the "Credit" side (and are receipts for the country) while 8.2 to 8.4 correspond to the "Debit" side (and are expenditures in other countries).

(**) See Annex "Country notes".

UNITED STATES VIRGIN ISLANDS

Basic Indicators		Units	2001	2002	2003	2004	2005
	INBOUND TOURISM						
	Arrivals						
1.1	Visitors	('000)	2,497	2,337	2,395	2,620	2,605
1.2	Tourists (overnight visitors)	('000)	527	520	538	544	575
1.3	Same-day visitors	('000)	79	78	83	111	118
1.4	Cruise passengers	('000)	1,891	1,739	1,774	1,965	1,912
	Arrivals by region						
2.1	Africa	('000)	..	1	..	..	..
2.2	Americas	('000)	541	494	531	561	561
2.3	Europe	('000)	9	6	8	16	19
2.4	East Asia and the Pacific	('000)	..	..	..	..	..
2.5	South Asia	('000)	..	..	..	..	..
2.6	Middle East	('000)	..	..	..	..	..
	Arrivals by means of transport used						
3.1	Air	('000)	606	598	621	655	693
3.2	Rail	('000)	..	..	..	..	..
3.3	Road	('000)	..	..	..	..	..
3.4	Sea	('000)	1,891	1,739	1,774	1,965	1,912
	Arrivals by purpose of visit						
4.1	Leisure, recreation and holidays	('000)	..	..	..	..	..
4.2	Business and professional	('000)	..	..	..	..	..
4.3	Other	('000)	..	..	..	..	..
	Accommodation						
5.1	Overnight stays in hotels and similar establishments	('000)	..	..	..	..	..
5.2	Guests in hotels and similar establishments	('000)	597	586	623	604	610
5.3	Overnight stays in all types of accommodation establishments	('000)	1,040	1,057	1,052	1,096	1,095
5.4	Average length of stay of non-resident tourists in all accommodation establishments	Nights	..	..	..	..	..
6.1	**Tourism expenditure in the country** (**)	US$ Mn	1,234	1,195	1,257	1,356	1,493
6.2	"Travel" (*)	US$ Mn	..	..	..	..	..
6.3	"Passenger transport" (*)	US$ Mn	..	..	..	..	..
	DOMESTIC TOURISM						
	Accommodation						
7.1	Overnight stays in hotels and similar establishments	('000)	..	..	..	..	..
7.2	Guests in hotels and similar establishments	('000)	52	65	68	69	80
7.3	Overnight stays in all types of accommodation establishments	('000)	..	..	..	..	..
7.4	Average length of stay of resident tourists in all accommodation establishments	Nights	..	..	..	..	..
	OUTBOUND TOURISM						
8.1	**Departures**	('000)	..	..	..	..	..
8.2	**Tourism expenditure in other countries**	US$ Mn	..	..	..	..	..
8.3	"Travel" (*)	US$ Mn	..	..	..	..	..
8.4	"Passenger transport" (*)	US$ Mn	..	..	..	..	..
	TOURISM INDUSTRIES						
	Hotels and similar establishments						
9.1	Number of rooms	Units	5,053	5,138	5,045	4,959	4,762
9.2	Number of bed-places	Units	..	..	..	..	..
9.3	Occupancy rate	Percent	56.20	56.60	57.20	61.30	63.80
9.4	Average length of stay	Nights	4.50	4.70	4.30	4.30	4.30
	RELATED INDICATORS						
	Share of tourism expenditure (6.1) in:						
10.1	Gross Domestic Product (GDP)	Percent	..	..	..	..	..
10.2	Exports of goods	Percent	..	..	..	..	..
10.3	Exports of services	Percent	..	..	..	..	..

(*) Balance of Payments items: 6.1 to 6.3 correspond to the "Credit" side (and are receipts for the country) while 8.2 to 8.4 correspond to the "Debit" side (and are expenditures in other countries).

(**) See Annex "Country notes".

URUGUAY

Basic Indicators		Units	2001	2002	2003	2004	2005
	INBOUND TOURISM						
	Arrivals						
1.1	Visitors	('000)	2,136	1,354	1,508	1,871	1,917
1.2	Tourists (overnight visitors)	('000)	1,892	1,258	1,420	1,756	1,808
1.3	Same-day visitors	('000)	245	95	88	115	109
1.4	Cruise passengers	('000)	64	..	..	..	..
	Arrivals by region						
2.1	Africa	('000)	..	..	..	..	..
2.2	Americas	('000)	1,708	1,031	1,160	1,458	1,498
2.3	Europe	('000)	70	56	73	97	120
2.4	East Asia and the Pacific	('000)	6	6	6	7	12
2.5	South Asia	('000)	..	..	..	..	..
2.6	Middle East	('000)	..	..	..	..	..
	Arrivals by means of transport used						
3.1	Air	('000)	332	299	314	380	406
3.2	Rail	('000)	..	..	..	..	..
3.3	Road	('000)	1,064	586	649	801	819
3.4	Sea	('000)	741	469	537	691	692
	Arrivals by purpose of visit						
4.1	Leisure, recreation and holidays	('000)	1,285	783	948	1,230	1,249
4.2	Business and professional	('000)	120	94	91	128	137
4.3	Other	('000)	731	477	469	513	531
	Accommodation						
5.1	Overnight stays in hotels and similar establishments	('000)	2,304	1,486	1,903	2,673	2,620
5.2	Guests in hotels and similar establishments	('000)	546	322	411	557	608
5.3	Overnight stays in all types of accommodation establishments	('000)	2,992	2,927	3,531	2,938	2,925
5.4	Average length of stay of non-resident tourists in all accommodation establishments	Nights	6.60	7.40	7.10	6.35	4.51
6.1	**Tourism expenditure in the country**	US$ Mn	700	409	419	591	690
6.2	"Travel" (*)	US$ Mn	611	351	345	494	594
6.3	"Passenger transport" (*)	US$ Mn	89	58	74	97	96
	DOMESTIC TOURISM						
	Accommodation						
7.1	Overnight stays in hotels and similar establishments	('000)	..	..	..	..	..
7.2	Guests in hotels and similar establishments	('000)	..	..	..	..	..
7.3	Overnight stays in all types of accommodation establishments	('000)	..	..	..	..	..
7.4	Average length of stay of resident tourists in all accommodation establishments	Nights	..	..	..	..	..
	OUTBOUND TOURISM						
8.1	**Departures**	('000)	531	530	495	569	658
8.2	**Tourism expenditure in other countries**	US$ Mn	333	243	236	267	328
8.3	"Travel" (*)	US$ Mn	252	178	169	194	252
8.4	"Passenger transport" (*)	US$ Mn	81	65	67	73	76
	TOURISM INDUSTRIES						
	Hotels and similar establishments						
9.1	Number of rooms	Units	18,057	18,060	18,160	19,151	14,729
9.2	Number of bed-places	Units	41,451	41,559	41,759	43,726	26,222
9.3	Occupancy rate	Percent	..	..	..	..	..
9.4	Average length of stay	Nights	4.26	4.40	4.60	4.78	4.31
	RELATED INDICATORS						
	Share of tourism expenditure (6.1) in:						
10.1	Gross Domestic Product (GDP)	Percent	3.8	3.3	3.7	4.5	4.1
10.2	Exports of goods	Percent	32.7	21.3	18.4	18.8	18.4
10.3	Exports of services	Percent	62.3	54.2	52.2	51.3	51.9

(*) Balance of Payments items: 6.1 to 6.3 correspond to the "Credit" side (and are receipts for the country) while 8.2 to 8.4 correspond to the "Debit" side (and are expenditures in other countries).

UZBEKISTAN

	Basic Indicators		Units	2001	2002	2003	2004	2005
	INBOUND TOURISM							
	Arrivals							
1.1	Visitors		('000)	..	..	..	..	..
1.2	Tourists (overnight visitors)		('000)	345	332	231	262	..
1.3	Same-day visitors		('000)	..	..	..	..	..
1.4	Cruise passengers		('000)	..	..	..	..	..
	Arrivals by region							
2.1	Africa		('000)	1	1	1	1	..
2.2	Americas		('000)	10	4	2	12	..
2.3	Europe		('000)	109	100	51	69	..
2.4	East Asia and the Pacific		('000)	193	195	145	140	..
2.5	South Asia		('000)	8	8	8	10	..
2.6	Middle East		('000)	24	24	24	30	..
	Arrivals by means of transport used							
3.1	Air		('000)	323	296	220	235	..
3.2	Rail		('000)	21	15	10	25	..
3.3	Road		('000)	1	1	1	2	..
3.4	Sea		('000)	..	..	..	..	..
	Arrivals by purpose of visit							
4.1	Leisure, recreation and holidays		('000)	45	43	21	34	..
4.2	Business and professional		('000)	76	73	22	37	..
4.3	Other		('000)	224	215	188	190	..
	Accommodation							
5.1	Overnight stays in hotels and similar establishments		('000)	699	672	457	487	..
5.2	Guests in hotels and similar establishments		('000)	..	..	..	..	..
5.3	Overnight stays in all types of accommodation establishments		('000)	1,082	1,069	935	964	..
5.4	Average length of stay of non-resident tourists in all accommodation establishments		Nights	3.10	3.10	3.10	3.70	..
6.1	**Tourism expenditure in the country**	(**)	US$ Mn	72	68	48	57	..
6.2	"Travel" (*)		US$ Mn	22	22	24	28	..
6.3	"Passenger transport" (*)		US$ Mn	50	46	24	29	..
	DOMESTIC TOURISM							
	Accommodation							
7.1	Overnight stays in hotels and similar establishments		('000)	612	588	484	667	..
7.2	Guests in hotels and similar establishments		('000)	..	..	..	..	..
7.3	Overnight stays in all types of accommodation establishments		('000)	1,557	1,497	1,255	1,438	..
7.4	Average length of stay of resident tourists in all accommodation establishments		Nights	..	..	..	..	..
	OUTBOUND TOURISM							
8.1	**Departures**		('000)	183	264	400	455	..
8.2	**Tourism expenditure in other countries**		US$ Mn	..	..	..	..	..
8.3	"Travel" (*)		US$ Mn	..	..	..	..	..
8.4	"Passenger transport" (*)		US$ Mn	..	..	..	..	..
	TOURISM INDUSTRIES							
	Hotels and similar establishments							
9.1	Number of rooms		Units	7,332	7,332	7,332	7,332	..
9.2	Number of bed-places		Units	15,670	15,670	15,670	15,670	..
9.3	Occupancy rate		Percent	35.00	35.20	31.00	31.00	..
9.4	Average length of stay		Nights	3.10	3.10	3.10	3.70	..
	RELATED INDICATORS							
	Share of tourism expenditure (6.1) in:							
10.1	Gross Domestic Product (GDP)		Percent	0.6	0.7	0.5	0.5	..
10.2	Exports of goods		Percent	..	..	..	..	..
10.3	Exports of services		Percent	..	..	..	..	..

(*) Balance of Payments items: 6.1 to 6.3 correspond to the "Credit" side (and are receipts for the country) while 8.2 to 8.4 correspond to the "Debit" side (and are expenditures in other countries).

(**) See Annex "Country notes".

Basic Indicators		Units	2001	2002	2003	2004	2005
	INBOUND TOURISM						
	Arrivals						
1.1	Visitors	('000)	106	98	102	99	126
1.2	Tourists (overnight visitors)	('000)	53	49	50	61	62
1.3	Same-day visitors	('000)	..	..	..	..	..
1.4	Cruise passengers	('000)	53	49	52	38	64
	Arrivals by region						
2.1	Africa	('000)	..	..	..	..	..
2.2	Americas	('000)	1	1	2	2	2
2.3	Europe	('000)	3	3	3	3	3
2.4	East Asia and the Pacific	('000)	48	44	45	55	56
2.5	South Asia	('000)	..	..	..	..	..
2.6	Middle East	('000)	..	..	..	..	..
	Arrivals by means of transport used						
3.1	Air	('000)	53	49	50	61	62
3.2	Rail	('000)	..	..	..	..	..
3.3	Road	('000)	..	..	..	..	..
3.4	Sea	('000)	53	49	52	38	64
	Arrivals by purpose of visit						
4.1	Leisure, recreation and holidays	('000)	42	39	39	47	48
4.2	Business and professional	('000)	6	6	7	8	8
4.3	Other	('000)	5	4	4	6	6
	Accommodation						
5.1	Overnight stays in hotels and similar establishments	('000)	372	334	316	352	..
5.2	Guests in hotels and similar establishments	('000)	194	172	158	179	..
5.3	Overnight stays in all types of accommodation establishments	('000)	..	..	..	..	..
5.4	Average length of stay of non-resident tourists in all accommodation establishments	Nights	8.30	8.90	9.50	9.10	..
6.1	**Tourism expenditure in the country**	US$ Mn	58	62	71	82	93
6.2	"Travel" (*)	US$ Mn	46	44	52	64	74
6.3	"Passenger transport" (*)	US$ Mn	12	18	19	18	19
	DOMESTIC TOURISM						
	Accommodation						
7.1	Overnight stays in hotels and similar establishments	('000)	..	..	..	..	..
7.2	Guests in hotels and similar establishments	('000)	..	..	..	..	..
7.3	Overnight stays in all types of accommodation establishments	('000)	..	..	..	..	..
7.4	Average length of stay of resident tourists in all accommodation establishments	Nights	..	..	..	..	..
	OUTBOUND TOURISM						
8.1	**Departures**	('000)	12	12	13	13	14
8.2	**Tourism expenditure in other countries**	US$ Mn	..	11	14	15	13
8.3	"Travel" (*)	US$ Mn	8	9	12	13	11
8.4	"Passenger transport" (*)	US$ Mn	..	2	2	2	2
	TOURISM INDUSTRIES						
	Hotels and similar establishments						
9.1	Number of rooms	Units	1,044	993	895	874	..
9.2	Number of bed-places	Units	2,737	2,662	2,370	6,193	..
9.3	Occupancy rate	Percent	49.80	44.20	46.50	51.90	..
9.4	Average length of stay	Nights	8.30	8.90	9.50	9.10	..
	RELATED INDICATORS						
	Share of tourism expenditure (6.1) in:						
10.1	Gross Domestic Product (GDP)	Percent	24.7	26.4	25.7	25.9	27.3
10.2	Exports of goods	Percent	290.0	310.0	263.0	215.8	244.7
10.3	Exports of services	Percent	48.7	73.8	71.7	73.2	72.7

(*) Balance of Payments items: 6.1 to 6.3 correspond to the "Credit" side (and are receipts for the country) while 8.2 to 8.4 correspond to the "Debit" side (and are expenditures in other countries).

VENEZUELA

	Basic Indicators	Units	2001	2002	2003	2004	2005
	INBOUND TOURISM						
	Arrivals						
1.1	Visitors	('000)	792	590	435	618	841
1.2	Tourists (overnight visitors)	('000)	584	432	337	486	706
1.3	Same-day visitors	('000)	208	158	98	..	..
1.4	Cruise passengers	('000)	..	..	..	132	135
	Arrivals by region						
2.1	Africa	('000)	1	1	..	1	1
2.2	Americas	('000)	280	185	154	218	308
2.3	Europe	('000)	291	237	175	258	383
2.4	East Asia and the Pacific	('000)	7	4	3	4	6
2.5	South Asia	('000)	..	..	..	..	..
2.6	Middle East	('000)	1	..	..	..	1
	Arrivals by means of transport used						
3.1	Air	('000)	578	409	335	484	704
3.2	Rail	('000)	..	..	..	..	..
3.3	Road	('000)	3	21	..	..	..
3.4	Sea	('000)	3	2	2	2	2
	Arrivals by purpose of visit						
4.1	Leisure, recreation and holidays	('000)	167	124	82	167	173
4.2	Business and professional	('000)	322	230	169	185	273
4.3	Other	('000)	95	78	86	135	260
	Accommodation						
5.1	Overnight stays in hotels and similar establishments	('000)	4,050	4,694	4,023	..	..
5.2	Guests in hotels and similar establishments	('000)	..	..	..	300	435
5.3	Overnight stays in all types of accommodation establishments	('000)	10,512	9,126	9,819	..	..
5.4	Average length of stay of non-resident tourists in all accommodation establishments	Nights	13.00	15.00	15.30	15.61	16.65
6.1	**Tourism expenditure in the country**	US$ Mn	677	484	378	531	713
6.2	"Travel" (*)	US$ Mn	615	434	331	477	641
6.3	"Passenger transport" (*)	US$ Mn	62	50	47	54	72
	DOMESTIC TOURISM						
	Accommodation						
7.1	Overnight stays in hotels and similar establishments	('000)	..	..	..	..	..
7.2	Guests in hotels and similar establishments	('000)	..	..	..	..	..
7.3	Overnight stays in all types of accommodation establishments	('000)	..	..	..	..	..
7.4	Average length of stay of resident tourists in all accommodation establishments	Nights	..	..	..	4.04	4.38
	OUTBOUND TOURISM						
8.1	**Departures**	('000)	933	881	832	816	1,067
8.2	**Tourism expenditure in other countries**	US$ Mn	1,718	1,546	1,311	1,603	1,837
8.3	"Travel" (*)	US$ Mn	1,108	981	859	1,076	1,281
8.4	"Passenger transport" (*)	US$ Mn	610	565	452	527	556
	TOURISM INDUSTRIES						
	Hotels and similar establishments						
9.1	Number of rooms	Units	78,212	80,022	82,366	84,607	68,819
9.2	Number of bed-places	Units	169,910	174,447	180,556	187,753	157,112
9.3	Occupancy rate	Percent	..	..	..	55.94	..
9.4	Average length of stay	Nights	7.00	..	..	..	..
	RELATED INDICATORS						
	Share of tourism expenditure (6.1) in:						
10.1	Gross Domestic Product (GDP)	Percent	0.6	0.5	0.5	0.5	0.5
10.2	Exports of goods	Percent	2.5	1.8	1.4	1.4	1.3
10.3	Exports of services	Percent	49.2	47.8	43.1	48.4	53.4

(*) Balance of Payments items: 6.1 to 6.3 correspond to the "Credit" side (and are receipts for the country) while 8.2 to 8.4 correspond to the "Debit" side (and are expenditures in other countries).

	Basic Indicators		Units	2001	2002	2003	2004	2005
	INBOUND TOURISM							
	Arrivals							
1.1	Visitors		('000)	2,330	2,628	2,429	2,928	3,468
1.2	Tourists (overnight visitors)		('000)	1,599	..	..	..	..
1.3	Same-day visitors		('000)	446	..	..	..	..
1.4	Cruise passengers		('000)	285	309	241	263	..
	Arrivals by region							
2.1	Africa		('000)	2	..	..	..	..
2.2	Americas		('000)	269	304	259	326	397
2.3	Europe		('000)	315	343	294	355	426
2.4	East Asia and the Pacific		('000)	1,489	1,695	1,670	2,008	2,365
2.5	South Asia		('000)	8	..	..	..	..
2.6	Middle East		('000)	..	..	..	..	..
	Arrivals by means of transport used							
3.1	Air		('000)	1,294	1,540	1,395	1,822	..
3.2	Rail		('000)	..	..	..	..	..
3.3	Road		('000)	751	779	793	843	..
3.4	Sea		('000)	285	309	241	263	..
	Arrivals by purpose of visit							
4.1	Leisure, recreation and holidays		('000)	1,225	1,460	1,239	1,584	2,042
4.2	Business and professional		('000)	395	446	468	522	493
4.3	Other		('000)	710	722	722	822	933
	Accommodation							
5.1	Overnight stays in hotels and similar establishments		('000)	6,873	..	..	..	..
5.2	Guests in hotels and similar establishments		('000)	..	..	..	..	..
5.3	Overnight stays in all types of accommodation establishments		('000)	..	..	..	..	..
5.4	Average length of stay of non-resident tourists in all accommodation establishments		Nights	6.00	..	..	..	..
6.1	**Tourism expenditure in the country**	(**)	US$ Mn	..	..	1,400	1,700	1,880
6.2	"Travel" (*)		US$ Mn	..	..	..	..	..
6.3	"Passenger transport" (*)		US$ Mn	..	..	..	..	..
	DOMESTIC TOURISM							
	Accommodation							
7.1	Overnight stays in hotels and similar establishments		('000)	18,640	..	..	..	..
7.2	Guests in hotels and similar establishments		('000)	..	..	..	..	..
7.3	Overnight stays in all types of accommodation establishments		('000)	..	..	..	..	..
7.4	Average length of stay of resident tourists in all accommodation establishments		Nights	..	..	..	..	..
	OUTBOUND TOURISM							
8.1	**Departures**		('000)	..	..	..	..	..
8.2	**Tourism expenditure in other countries**		US$ Mn	..	..	..	..	..
8.3	"Travel" (*)		US$ Mn	..	..	..	..	..
8.4	"Passenger transport" (*)		US$ Mn	..	..	..	..	..
	TOURISM INDUSTRIES							
	Hotels and similar establishments							
9.1	Number of rooms		Units	74,000	..	..	..	..
9.2	Number of bed-places		Units	133,940	..	..	..	..
9.3	Occupancy rate		Percent	52.00	..	..	..	..
9.4	Average length of stay		Nights	2.50	..	..	..	..
	RELATED INDICATORS							
	Share of tourism expenditure (6.1) in:							
10.1	Gross Domestic Product (GDP)		Percent	..	..	..	..	..
10.2	Exports of goods		Percent	..	..	..	..	..
10.3	Exports of services		Percent	..	..	..	..	..

(*) Balance of Payments items: 6.1 to 6.3 correspond to the "Credit" side (and are receipts for the country) while 8.2 to 8.4 correspond to the "Debit" side (and are expenditures in other countries).

(**) See Annex "Country notes".

YEMEN

Basic Indicators		Units	2001	2002	2003	2004	2005
	INBOUND TOURISM						
	Arrivals						
1.1	Visitors	('000)	..	..	..	..	..
1.2	Tourists (overnight visitors)	('000)	76	98	155	274	336
1.3	Same-day visitors	('000)	..	..	..	..	..
1.4	Cruise passengers	('000)	..	..	..	..	..
	Arrivals by region						
2.1	Africa	('000)	5	3	9	11	13
2.2	Americas	('000)	3	4	13	18	18
2.3	Europe	('000)	27	16	13	29	26
2.4	East Asia and the Pacific	('000)	6	11	17	41	39
2.5	South Asia	('000)	..	..	..	..	..
2.6	Middle East	('000)	35	63	103	176	240
	Arrivals by means of transport used						
3.1	Air	('000)	..	..	..	..	..
3.2	Rail	('000)	..	..	..	..	..
3.3	Road	('000)	..	..	..	..	..
3.4	Sea	('000)	..	..	..	..	..
	Arrivals by purpose of visit						
4.1	Leisure, recreation and holidays	('000)	..	..	..	..	..
4.2	Business and professional	('000)	..	..	..	..	..
4.3	Other	('000)	..	..	..	..	..
	Accommodation						
5.1	Overnight stays in hotels and similar establishments	('000)	224	588	928	1,642	2,017
5.2	Guests in hotels and similar establishments	('000)	76	98	155	274	336
5.3	Overnight stays in all types of accommodation establishments	('000)	..	..	..	..	..
5.4	Average length of stay of non-resident tourists in all accommodation establishments	Nights	2.97	6.00	6.00	6.00	6.00
6.1	**Tourism expenditure in the country**	US$ Mn	..	..	..	..	..
6.2	"Travel" (*)	US$ Mn	38	38	139	139	181
6.3	"Passenger transport" (*)	US$ Mn	..	..	..	..	..
	DOMESTIC TOURISM						
	Accommodation						
7.1	Overnight stays in hotels and similar establishments	('000)	1,237	1,289	3,359	..	4,172
7.2	Guests in hotels and similar establishments	('000)	530	692	597	..	..
7.3	Overnight stays in all types of accommodation establishments	('000)	..	..	..	..	..
7.4	Average length of stay of resident tourists in all accommodation establishments	Nights	..	..	..	..	..
	OUTBOUND TOURISM						
8.1	**Departures**	('000)	..	..	..	..	..
8.2	**Tourism expenditure in other countries**	US$ Mn	136	135	134	183	224
8.3	"Travel" (*)	US$ Mn	79	78	77	126	167
8.4	"Passenger transport" (*)	US$ Mn	57	57	57	57	57
	TOURISM INDUSTRIES						
	Hotels and similar establishments						
9.1	Number of rooms	Units	13,151	13,301	13,280	12,890	15,265
9.2	Number of bed-places	Units	30,342	31,269	33,816	30,142	34,844
9.3	Occupancy rate	Percent	..	..	..	..	..
9.4	Average length of stay	Nights	..	..	..	..	..
	RELATED INDICATORS						
	Share of tourism expenditure (6.1) in: (**)						
10.1	Gross Domestic Product (GDP)	Percent	0.4	0.4	1.2	1.1	1.3
10.2	Exports of goods	Percent	1.1	1.0	3.5	3.0	2.8
10.3	Exports of services	Percent	22.9	22.9	43.7	37.6	48.7

(*) Balance of Payments items: 6.1 to 6.3 correspond to the "Credit" side (and are receipts for the country) while 8.2 to 8.4 correspond to the "Debit" side (and are expenditures in other countries).

(**) See Annex "Country notes".

Basic Indicators			Units	2001	2002	2003	2004	2005
	INBOUND TOURISM							
	Arrivals							
1.1	Visitors		('000)	..	..	..	..	..
1.2	Tourists (overnight visitors)		('000)	492	565	413	515	669
1.3	Same-day visitors		('000)	..	..	..	..	..
1.4	Cruise passengers		('000)	..	..	..	..	..
	Arrivals by region							
2.1	Africa		('000)	317	364	298	367	461
2.2	Americas		('000)	30	34	23	29	38
2.3	Europe		('000)	113	130	71	92	122
2.4	East Asia and the Pacific		('000)	30	34	17	23	39
2.5	South Asia		('000)	3	3	3	4	9
2.6	Middle East		('000)	..	..	..	..	..
	Arrivals by means of transport used							
3.1	Air		('000)	62	71	104	137	164
3.2	Rail		('000)	..	..	..	..	..
3.3	Road		('000)	430	494	309	378	504
3.4	Sea		('000)	..	..	..	..	..
	Arrivals by purpose of visit							
4.1	Leisure, recreation and holidays		('000)	147	152	144	195	206
4.2	Business and professional		('000)	201	248	156	160	253
4.3	Other		('000)	144	165	113	160	210
	Accommodation							
5.1	Overnight stays in hotels and similar establishments		('000)	..	..	..	..	..
5.2	Guests in hotels and similar establishments		('000)	..	..	..	..	..
5.3	Overnight stays in all types of accommodation establishments		('000)	..	..	..	..	..
5.4	Average length of stay of non-resident tourists in all accommodation establishments		Nights	9.00	8.00	6.00	6.00	6.00
6.1	**Tourism expenditure in the country**	(**)	US$ Mn	117	134	149	161	164
6.2	"Travel" (*)		US$ Mn	..	..	..	..	..
6.3	"Passenger transport" (*)		US$ Mn	..	..	..	..	..
	DOMESTIC TOURISM							
	Accommodation							
7.1	Overnight stays in hotels and similar establishments		('000)	185	217	241	267	289
7.2	Guests in hotels and similar establishments		('000)	..	..	..	..	..
7.3	Overnight stays in all types of accommodation establishments		('000)	..	..	..	..	..
7.4	Average length of stay of resident tourists in all accommodation establishments		Nights	..	..	..	..	..
	OUTBOUND TOURISM							
8.1	**Departures**		('000)	..	..	..	..	..
8.2	**Tourism expenditure in other countries**		US$ Mn	..	..	..	..	..
8.3	"Travel" (*)	(**)	US$ Mn	57	67	77	89	94
8.4	"Passenger transport" (*)		US$ Mn	..	..	..	..	..
	TOURISM INDUSTRIES							
	Hotels and similar establishments							
9.1	Number of rooms		Units	4,822	5,060	5,202	5,360	5,521
9.2	Number of bed-places		Units	8,136	8,601	8,774	9,115	9,417
9.3	Occupancy rate		Percent	51.10	50.40	53.20	55.20	57.20
9.4	Average length of stay		Nights	..	..	..	..	..
	RELATED INDICATORS							
	Share of tourism expenditure (6.1) in:							
10.1	Gross Domestic Product (GDP)		Percent	..	..	..	..	..
10.2	Exports of goods		Percent	..	..	..	..	..
10.3	Exports of services		Percent	..	..	..	..	..

(*) Balance of Payments items: 6.1 to 6.3 correspond to the "Credit" side (and are receipts for the country) while 8.2 to 8.4 correspond to the "Debit" side (and are expenditures in other countries).

(**) See Annex "Country notes".

ZIMBABWE

	Basic Indicators		Units	2001	2002	2003	2004	2005
	INBOUND TOURISM							
	Arrivals							
1.1	Visitors		('000)	2,217	2,041	2,256	1,854	1,559
1.2	Tourists (overnight visitors)		('000)	2,068	..	..	..	..
1.3	Same-day visitors		('000)	149	..	..	..	..
1.4	Cruise passengers		('000)	..	..	..	..	..
	Arrivals by region							
2.1	Africa		('000)	1,737	1,760	1,942	1,523	1,356
2.2	Americas		('000)	112	65	61	75	44
2.3	Europe		('000)	265	150	170	156	113
2.4	East Asia and the Pacific		('000)	103	66	68	90	39
2.5	South Asia		('000)	..	..	12	6	5
2.6	Middle East		('000)	..	..	2	4	2
	Arrivals by means of transport used							
3.1	Air		('000)	452	340	340	330	327
3.2	Rail		('000)	..	..	..	..	..
3.3	Road		('000)	2,311	1,738	2,016	1,524	1,231
3.4	Sea		('000)	..	..	..	..	..
	Arrivals by purpose of visit							
4.1	Leisure, recreation and holidays		('000)	1,781	..	..	964	970
4.2	Business and professional		('000)	436	..	..	593	265
4.3	Other		('000)	..	..	..	297	323
	Accommodation							
5.1	Overnight stays in hotels and similar establishments		('000)	..	..	..	..	..
5.2	Guests in hotels and similar establishments		('000)	..	..	..	..	..
5.3	Overnight stays in all types of accommodation establishments		('000)	..	..	..	..	..
5.4	Average length of stay of non-resident tourists in all accommodation establishments		Nights	..	..	3.00	4.00	3.00
6.1	**Tourism expenditure in the country**	(**)	US$ Mn	81	76	61	194	99
6.2	"Travel" (*)		US$ Mn	..	..	..	..	..
6.3	"Passenger transport" (*)		US$ Mn	..	..	..	..	..
	DOMESTIC TOURISM							
	Accommodation							
7.1	Overnight stays in hotels and similar establishments		('000)	..	..	..	..	..
7.2	Guests in hotels and similar establishments		('000)	..	..	..	..	..
7.3	Overnight stays in all types of accommodation establishments		('000)	..	..	..	..	..
7.4	Average length of stay of resident tourists in all accommodation establishments		Nights	..	..	..	..	..
	OUTBOUND TOURISM							
8.1	**Departures**		('000)	..	..	..	..	..
8.2	**Tourism expenditure in other countries**		US$ Mn	..	..	..	..	..
8.3	"Travel" (*)		US$ Mn	..	..	..	..	..
8.4	"Passenger transport" (*)		US$ Mn	..	..	..	..	..
	TOURISM INDUSTRIES							
	Hotels and similar establishments							
9.1	Number of rooms		Units	5,590	5,766	5,766	5,766	5,657
9.2	Number of bed-places		Units	11,723	12,053	12,053	12,053	11,282
9.3	Occupancy rate		Percent	31.00	36.00	38.50	30.00	34.00
9.4	Average length of stay		Nights	..	3.00	3.00	4.00	3.00
	RELATED INDICATORS							
	Share of tourism expenditure (6.1) in:							
10.1	Gross Domestic Product (GDP)		Percent	..	..	..	..	..
10.2	Exports of goods		Percent	..	..	..	..	..
10.3	Exports of services		Percent	..	..	..	..	..

(*) Balance of Payments items: 6.1 to 6.3 correspond to the "Credit" side (and are receipts for the country) while 8.2 to 8.4 correspond to the "Debit" side (and are expenditures in other countries).

(**) See Annex "Country notes".

Annexes

- Basic references
- Country notes
- IMF notes

INBOUND TOURISM

Arrivals

When a person visits the same country several times a year, each visit by the same person is counted as a separate arrival. If a person visits several countries during the course of a single trip, his/her arrival in each country is recorded separately. Consequently, arrivals are not necessarily equal to the number of different persons travelling.

Arrivals data correspond to *international visitors* to the economic territory of the country of reference and include both tourists and same-day non-resident visitors.

Data may be obtained from different sources: border statistics derived from administrative records (police, immigration, traffic counts, and other types of controls), border surveys and registrations at accommodation establishments.

Arrivals by region

The aggregate of basic indicators (2.1) to (2.6) does not always correspond to the total of the basic indicators (1.1) or (1.2), due to the exclusion by some countries of "nationals residing abroad" and of "arrivals from other countries of the world".

Accommodation

Overnight stays refers to the number of nights spent by non-resident tourists in accommodation establishments (*guests*). If one person travels to a country and spends five nights there, that makes five tourist overnight stays (or person-nights).

Average length of stay refers to the average number of nights spent by non-resident guests in the country.

Expenditure

Expenditure associated with tourism activity of visitors has been traditionally identified with the travel item of the Balance of Payments (BOP): in the case of inbound tourism, those expenditures associated with non-resident visitors are registered as "credits" in the BOP and refers to "travel receipts".

The new conceptual framework approved by the United Nations Statistical Commission in relation to the measurement of tourism macroeconomic activity (the so-called Tourism Satellite Account) considers that "tourism industries and products" includes transport of passengers. Consequently, a better estimate of tourism-related expenditures by resident and non-resident visitors in an international scenario would be, in terms of the BOP, the value of the travel item plus that of the passenger transport item.

Nevertheless, users should be aware that BOP estimates include, in addition to expenditures associated with visitors, those related to other types of individuals.

The data published should allow international comparability and therefore correspond to those published by the International Monetary Fund (IMF) (and provided by the Central Banks); in the case of a significant difference with data provided to UNWTO by National Tourism Administrations (NTAs), the NTAs data will be given separately in Annex "Country notes".

DOMESTIC TOURISM

Indicators are the same as for Accommodation in Inbound Tourism but referred to resident tourists.

OUTBOUND TOURISM

Departures data correspond to tourists and same-day resident visitors outside the economic territory of the country of reference. As in the case of arrivals, departures are not necessarily equal to the number of different persons travelling.

Indicators on expenditure are equivalent to those for Inbound Tourism but registered as "debits" in the BOP's *travel* and *passenger transport* items.

The data published are also provided by IMF and the same previous warning is applicable.

TOURISM INDUSTRIES

Hotels and similar establishments

The number of *rooms* and *bed-places* refers to the capacity in hotels and similar establishments for providing temporary accommodation to visitors.

Occupancy rate refers to the relationship between available capacity and the extent to which it is used. This rate may refer either to use of rooms or of beds. Occupancy rate is based on the number of overnight stays of both resident and non-resident tourists.

Average length of stay refers to both resident and non-resident overnight stays.

For additional references, visit
http://www.unwto.org/statistics/basic_references/index-en.htm

ALBANIA

(1.1,2.2-4.3) Visitors and other travellers; (1.2,5.2,7.2) Arrivals in hotels only; (4.3) Transit.
Sources: (1.1-5.4,7.1-7.4,9.1-9.4) Institute of Statistics - INSTAT; (6.1-6.3,8.2-8.4) International Monetary Fund.

ALGERIA

(1.1,3.1-3.4) Including nationals residing abroad:

2001	705,187
2002	736,915
2003	861,373
2004	865,157
2005	1,001,884

(2.1-2.6,4.1,4.2) Excluding nationals residing abroad; (6.1,8.2) The expenditure figures are those provided by the country to UNWTO, which do not appear in the International Monetary Fund data used in the preparation of this edition of the Compendium.
Sources: "Ministère du Tourisme" and "Office National des Statistiques".

AMERICAN SAMOA

(1.2,2.4,4.1-4.3) Including Western Samoa; (4.3) Visit friends, relatives.
Source: American Samoa Government - Department of Commerce - Statistics Division.

ANDORRA

Source: "Ministerio de Turismo y Medio Ambiente".

ANGOLA

(5.1,5.2,7.1,7.2) Hotels only.
Sources: (1.2-7.3,9.1-9.4) (6.2/2001) "Ministério de Hotelaria e Turismo - Gabinete de Estudos, Planeamento e Estatística"; (6.2/2002-2005) (6.3,8.2-8.4) International Monetary Fund.

ANGUILLA

(1.1,3.1-4.2) Arrivals of non-resident visitors at national borders; (1.2,2.2-2.3) Arrivals of non-resident tourists at national borders; excluding nationals residing abroad; (9.1) Hotels, guest houses, apartments/villas; (9.3) Rooms; January-May; (10.2,10.3) This section includes only the "travel" item because the "passenger transport" item was not included in the data provided by the International Monetary Fund for the preparation of this edition of the Compendium.
Sources: (1.1-5.4,9.1,9.3) Statistical Department - Ministry of Finance; (6.2,8.3) International Monetary Fund.

ANTIGUA AND BARBUDA

(1.1) Excluding yacht passenger arrivals; (2.2,2.3,3.1) Air arrivals; excluding nationals residing abroad; (10.1-10.3) This section includes only the "travel" item because the "passenger transport" item was not included in the data provided by the International Monetary Fund for the preparation of this edition of the Compendium.
Sources: (1.1-2.3) Eastern Caribbean Central Bank; (6.2,8.3) International Monetary Fund.

ARGENTINA

Starting 2004, as a result of the importance of the "Survey on International Tourism", the estimates of the series of the "Travel" item of the Balance of Payments were modified. For this reason, the data are not rigorously comparable with those of previous years.
Note 2004-2005: Provisional data.
Sources: (1.2-5.4,7.1,7.2,8.1,9.1-9.3) "Dirección de Estudios de Mercado y Estadística - Secretaría de Turismo de la Nación"; (6.1-6.3,8.2-8.4) International Monetary Fund.

ARMENIA

Sources: (1.2-5.4,7.3,8.1,9.2-9.4) Tourism Department - Ministry of Trade and Economic Development; (6.1-6.3,8.2-8.4) International Monetary Fund.

ARUBA

(1.2,2.2-4.3) Arrivals of non-resident tourists at national borders; (5.4) Non-resident tourists staying in hotels and similar establishments; (9.3) Rooms.
Sources: (1.1-5.4,9.1-9.3) Aruba Tourism Authority; (6.1-6.3,8.2-8.4) International Monetary Fund.

AUSTRALIA

(1.1) Excluding nationals residing abroad and crew members; (1.2,1.3) Arrivals by air; (2.1-4.3) Arrivals of non-resident visitors at national borders; (5.1,7.1) The estimates include hotels, resorts, motels and motor inns; guest houses and B&Bs; and backpackers / hostels; (5.3,7.3) The estimates include all forms of commercial accommodation; (9.1-9.3) Hotels, motels, guests houses and serviced apartments with 15 rooms or more; (9.3) Rooms; (9.4) Inbound tourism in commercial accommodation.
Sources: (1.1-5.4,7.1-7.4,8.1,9.1-9.4) Australian Bureau of Statistics; (6.1-6.3,8.2-8.4) International Monetary Fund.

AUSTRIA

(1.2-2.6) Non-resident tourists staying in all types of accommodation establishments; (5.1,5.2,7.1,7.2) Including holiday villages; (5.3,7.3) Excluding private accommodation; (8.1/2003) More than 4 overnight stays; (9.1) Hotels only; (9.2) Hotels and holiday villages; (9.3) Based on summer season; (9.4) Average length of stay in hotels and similar establishments; including holiday villages.
Sources: (1.2-5.4,7.1-7.4,8.1,9.1-9.4) Department for Tourism and Historic Objects - Federal Ministry of Economics and Labour; (6.1-6.3,8.2-8.4) International Monetary Fund.

AZERBAIJAN

Sources: (1.2-5.2,7.1,7.2,8.1,9.1,9.2) Ministry of Culture and Tourism; (6.1-6.3,8.2-8.4) International Monetary Fund.

BAHAMAS

(1.2,2.1-2.6,4.1-4.3) Arrivals of non-resident tourists at national borders; (5.2) Arrivals in hotels only; (9.1,9.2) Hotels, apartments, cottages and villas - Licensed properties only; (9.3) Rooms.
Sources: (1.1-5.4,9.1-9.4) Bahamas Ministry of Tourism; (6.1-6.3,8.2-8.4) International Monetary Fund.

BAHRAIN

(1.1,2.1-4.3) Arrivals of non-resident visitors at national borders; excluding nationals residing abroad; (3.1) Arrivals at Bahrain International Airport; (3.3) Arrivals through King Fahad Causeway; (3.4) Arrivals at Mina Salman Port; (5.1,9.1,9.2) Classified hotels only.
Sources: (1.1-5.4,9.1-9.3) Tourism Affairs - Ministry of Information; (6.1-6.3,8.2-8.4) International Monetary Fund.

BANGLADESH

Sources: (1.2-5.4,8.1,9.1-9.3) Bangladesh Parjatan Corporation; (6.1-6.3,8.2-8.4) International Monetary Fund.

BARBADOS

(1.2,2.1-4.3) Arrivals of non-resident tourists at national borders; (9.1,9.2) Hotels, apartment hotels, apartments and cottages, guest houses; (9.3) Rooms.
Sources: (1.1-5.4,9.1-9.4) Barbados Tourism Authority; (6.1-6.3,8.2-8.4) International Monetary Fund.

BELARUS

(1.2,2.2-2.4) Organized tourism.
Sources: (1.2,2.2-2.4,8.1) Ministry of Statistics and Analysis; (6.1-6.3,8.2-8.4) International Monetary Fund.

BELGIUM

(1.2,2.1-2.6,4.1-4.3) Non-resident tourists staying in all types of accommodation establishments; (5.1,5.2,7.1,7.2) Hotels only; (9.1,9.2) Hotels and holiday villages.
Sources: (1.2-5.3,7.1-7.3,8.1,9.1,9.2) (6.1-6.3,8.2-8.4/2001) "Institut National de Statistique"; (6.1-6.3,8.2-8.4/2002-2005) International Monetary Fund.

BELIZE

(1.3) In transit and border permits; (2.2-4.2) Arrivals of non-resident tourists at national borders; (10.1-10.3) This section includes only the "travel" item because the "passenger transport" item was not included in the data provided by the International Monetary Fund for the preparation of this edition of the Compendium.
Sources: (1.1-5.4,7.3,9.1-9.4) Belize Tourist Board; (6.2,8.2-8.4) International Monetary Fund.

BENIN

(1.2-4.3) Arrivals of non-resident tourists at national borders; (1.1-5.3/2003-2005) Estimates.
Sources: (1.1-5.4,7.1) "Direction du tourisme et de l'hôtellerie - Ministère de la culture, de l'artisanat et du tourisme"; (6.1-6.3,8.2-8.4) International Monetary Fund.

BERMUDA

(1.1) Excluding nationals residing abroad; (1.2,2.2-2.4,4.1-4.3) Air arrivals; (5.3) Including overnight stays at private houses; (6.1,8.2) The expenditure figures are those provided by the country to UNWTO, which do not appear in the International Monetary Fund data used in the preparation of this edition of the Compendium; (9.3) Rooms.
Source: Bermuda Department of Tourism.

BHUTAN

(6.1) The expenditure figures are those provided by the country to UNWTO, which do not appear in the International Monetary Fund data used in the preparation of this edition of the Compendium.
Source: Department of Tourism - Royal Government of Bhutan.

BOLIVIA

(1.2) Arrivals of non-resident tourists at national borders; (2.1-2.4) Non-resident tourists staying in hotels and similar establishments; (3.4) Arrivals by lake; (4.1-4.3) Data based on surveys; (5.1-5.4,7.1-7.4,9.1,9.2) Department capitals only; (9.3) Bed-places (hotels); (9.4) Days, hotels and similar establishments, inbound tourism.
Note 2003-2005: Provisional data.
Sources: (1.2-5.4,7.1-7.4,8.1,9.1-9.4) "Viceministerio de Turismo - Ministerio de Producción y Microempresa"; (6.1-6.3,8.2-8.4) International Monetary Fund.

BONAIRE

Sources: (1.1-5.4,9.1-9.4) Tourism Corporation of Bonaire (TCB); (6.2,8.3) Central Bank of the Netherlands Antilles.

BOSNIA AND HERZEGOVINA

(1.2,2.2-2.4) Non-resident tourists staying in all types of accommodation establishments; (2.5,2.6) Less than 500 arrivals; (9.1,9.2) Excluding the Republic Srpska.
Sources: (1.2-5.3,7.3,9.1,9.2) Agency for Statistics of Bosnia and Herzegovina; (6.1-6.3,8.2-8.4) International Monetary Fund.

BOTSWANA

Sources: (1.1-5.2,7.1,9.1-9.4) Department of Tourism - Ministry of Environment, Wildlife and Tourism; (6.1-6.3,8.2-8.4) International Monetary Fund.

BRAZIL

(3.4) Including arrivals by river; (5.4) Days; (6.1) The country provides UNWTO with aggregate expenditure figures that differ significantly from the International Monetary Fund data used in the preparation of this edition of the Compendium (data based on the sample survey conducted by EMBRATUR). The country figures are as follows:
2001: 3,701
2002: 3,120
2003: 3,386
2004: 3,676
2005: 4,849
Note 2005: Estimates.
Sources: (1.2-5.4,8.1) "Instituto Brasileiro de Turismo (EMBRATUR)"; (6.1-6.3,8.2-8.4) International Monetary Fund.

BRITISH VIRGIN ISLANDS

(1.1-9.4/2004/2005) Estimates; (6.1) The expenditure figures are those provided by the country to UNWTO, which do not appear in the International Monetary Fund data used in the preparation of this edition of the Compendium; (9.3) Rooms.
Source: The Development Planning Unit - Ministry of Finance.

BRUNEI DARUSSALAM

Source: Tourism Development Division - Ministry of Industry and Primary Resources.

BULGARIA

(1.1,1.2) Excluding children without own passports; (1.3) Transit visitors; (3.4) Sea and inland waterways; (5.1,5.3,5.4,7.1,7.3,9.2-9.4) Covers mainly former Stateowned and Public Sector in accommodation. Considerable part of the private sector (more than 70% in 1998) is not included in the data; (9.2) Hotels only; (9.3) Bed-places in hotels.
Sources: (1.1-4.3,5.1,5.3,5.4,7.1,7.3,8.1,9.2-9.4) "Tourism Policy" Directorate - State Agency for Tourism; (5.2,7.2) EUROSTAT (New Cronos); (6.1-6.3,8.2-8.4) International Monetary Fund.

BURKINA FASO

(1.2,2.1-2.6,5.2) Non-resident tourists staying in hotels and similar establishments; (4.1-4.3) Including domestic tourism; (6.1) The country provides UNWTO with aggregate expenditure figures that differ significantly from the International Monetary Fund data used in the preparation of this edition of the Compendium. The country figures are as follows:
2001: 35
2002: 39
2003: 48
2004: 57
2005: 53
(9.3) Rooms.
Sources: (1.2-5.4,7.1,7.2,9.3) "Service de l'analyse statistique et de la Coopération touristique - Ministère de la Culture, des Arts et du Tourisme"; (6.1-6.3,8.2-8.4) International Monetary Fund.

BURUNDI

(1.2-4.3) Arrivals of non-resident tourists at national borders; including nationals residing abroad; (3.4) Arrivals by lake.
Sources: (1.2-5.1,8.1,9.1,9.2) "Office National du Tourisme"; (6.1-6.3,8.2-8.4) International Monetary Fund.

CAMBODIA

(1.2) International tourist arrivals by all means of transport; (2.2-2.5/2001) Arrivals by air; (2.2-2.5,3.1-3.4/2004/2005) Excluding arrivals in the Phreah Vihear Province: 2004: 67,843; 2005: 88,615; (3.3/2001/2002) Arrivals by land and boat; (3.4) Arrivals by boat; (4.1-4.3/2001/2002) Arrivals by air; (4.1/2001/2002) Including arrivals at Siem Reap Airport by direct-flights: 2001: 133,688; 2002: 202,791; (4.1-4.3/2005) Excluding arrivals in the Phreah Vihear Province: 88,615; (5.4) Days.
Sources: (1.2-5.4,8.1,9.1-9.3) Ministry of Tourism; (6.1-6.3,8.2-8.4) International Monetary Fund.

CAMEROON

(1.2,2.1-2.6,5.2) Non-resident tourists staying in hotels and similar establishments.
Sources: (1.2-5.2,7.1,7.2,9.1,9.2) "Ministère du Tourisme"; (6.1-6.3,8.2-8.4) International Monetary Fund.

CANADA

(1.1,1.3) Data based on customs counts and adjusted using questionnaire surveys; (1.2,2.1-4.3) Arrivals of non-resident tourists at national borders; (4.2) Including convention; (8.1) Person-trips (one or more nights); Note 2005: Provisional data.
Note: Different types of methodological changes that affect the estimates for 2001 for expenditures and characteristics of International Tourists to Canada, have been introduced in 2002. Therefore, Statistics Canada advises not to compare the estimates for 2001 with the years prior because of these methodological changes for the non-count estimates (one of the reasons average length of stay numbers are not provided).
Sources: (1.1-4.3,5.3,7.1,7.3,8.1) Canadian Tourism Commission; (6.1-6.3,8.2-8.4) International Monetary Fund.

CAPE VERDE

(1.2,2.1-2.3) Non-resident tourists staying in hotels and similar establishments.
Sources: (1.2,2.1-2.3,5.1,5.2,7.1,7.2,9.1-9.4) "Instituto Nacional de Estatística"; (6.1-6.3,8.2-8.4) International Monetary Fund.

CAYMAN ISLANDS

(1.2,2.2-2.4,4.1-4.3) Arrivals by air; (5.4,9.4) Days; (6.1) The expenditure figures are those provided by the country to UNWTO, which do not appear in the International Monetary Fund data used in the preparation of this edition of the Compendium. Including expenditure by cruise passengers; (9.1,9.2) Hotels and apartments; (9.3) Hotels (rooms).
Source: Cayman Islands Department of Tourism.

CENTRAL AFRICAN REPUBLIC

(1.2,2.1-2.6,4.1-4.3) Arrivals by air to Bangui only.
Sources: (1.2-5.4,7.1-7.4,8.1,9.1-9.4) (6.1,8.2/2003/2004) "Ministère du Développement du Tourisme et de l'Artisanat"; (6.1,8.2/2001/2002) "Banque des Etats de l'Afrique Centrale (B.E.A.C.)".

CHAD

(1.2,2.1-2.6,5.2) Non-resident tourists staying in hotels and similar establishments; (9.3) Rooms.
Sources: (1.1-5.4,7.1,8.1,9.1-9.4) "Direction des Études et de la Programmation - Ministère du Développement Touristique"; (6.1,8.2) "Banque des Etats de l'Afrique Centrale (B.E.A.C.)".

CHILE

(5.1,5.2,7.1,7.2) Figures for 2005 are not comparable with those of previous years due to a revision of the National Census of Tourism Accommodation Establishments.
Sources: (1.2-5.4,7.1,7.2,8.1,9.1-9.4) "Servicio Nacional de Turismo - SERNATUR"; (6.1-6.3,8.2-8.4) International Monetary Fund.

CHINA

(1.1,2.1-2.6,3.1-3.4) Including ethnic Chinese arriving from "Hong Kong, China", "Macao, China", "Taiwan (Province of China)" and overseas Chinese, of which most same-day visitors are from "Hong Kong, China" and "Macao, China"; (4.1-4.3) Excluding ethnic Chinese arriving from "Hong Kong, China", "Macao, China", "Taiwan (Province of China)" and overseas Chinese; (7.1,9.1,9.2) Only refer to the star-rated hotels; (8.1) Including air crew members and other servicemen; (9.3) Rooms; (9.4) Inbound tourism only.
Sources: (1.1-5.4,7.1,8.1,9.1-9.4) National Tourism Administration; (6.1-6.3,8.2-8.4) International Monetary Fund.

COLOMBIA

(1.1,2.1-2.6,3.1-3.4,4.1-4.3) Arrivals of non-resident visitors at national borders. Excluding cruise passengers; (9.3) Rooms.
Note 2005: Provisional data.
Sources: (1.1-4.3,8.1) "Dirección de Extranjería - Departamento Administrativo de Seguridad (DAS)"; (6.1-6.3,8.2-8.4) International Monetary Fund; (9.1-9.3) "Dirección de Turismo - Ministerio de Comercio, Industria y Turismo, Asociación Hotelera de Colombia (COTELCO)".

COMOROS

(1.2,2.1,2.3,4.1-4.3) Air arrivals; (6.1) The expenditure figures are those provided by the country to UNWTO, which do not appear in the International Monetary Fund data used in the preparation of this edition of the Compendium.
Source: "Direction Nationale de la Promotion du Tourisme et de l'Hôtellerie - Ministère du Transport, Tourisme, Postes et Télécommunications".

CONGO

(1.2-2.3,5.2) Non-resident tourists staying in hotels and similar establishments; (9.3) Rooms.
Sources: (1.2-5.2,7.1,7.2,9.1-9.4) "Direction Générale du Tourisme et de l'Hôtellerie - Ministère de la Culture, des Arts et du Tourisme"; (6.1-6.3,8.2-8.4) International Monetary Fund.

COOK ISLANDS

(1.2,2.2-2.4,4.1-4.3) Air and sea arrivals; (6.1) The expenditure figures are those provided by the country to UNWTO, which do not appear in the International Monetary Fund data used in the preparation of this edition of the Compendium; (9.3) Rooms.
Source: Cook Islands Tourism Corporation and Cook Islands Statistics Office.

COSTA RICA

(4.1) Pleasure trips and visits to relatives; (5.4) In the central area of the country; (9.3) "Five category" establishments in San José Metropolitan Area (survey).
Sources: (1.1-5.4,8.1,9.1,9.3) "Instituto Costarricense de Turismo"; (6.1-6.3,8.2-8.4) International Monetary Fund.

CROATIA

(1.2,2.2-2.4) Non-resident tourists staying in all types of accommodation establishments; including arrivals in ports of nautical tourism; (3.1-3.4) Arrivals of non-resident visitors at national borders; (3.4/2004) Since 2004 a new methodology and new coverage have been applied and data are not comparable to previous years; (5.3,7.3) Including nights in ports of nautical tourism; (9.4) Internal tourism (domestic and inbound) in all accommodation facilities (including ports of nautical tourism).
Sources: (1.1-5.4,7.1-7.4,9.1-9.4) Central Bureau of Statistics; (6.1-6.3,8.2-8.4) International Monetary Fund.

CUBA

(1.1,2.1-2.6) Arrivals of non-resident visitors at national borders; (1.2,4.1-4.3) Air arrivals; (1.3) Including cruise passengers; (5.1,7.1,9.1,9.2) Hotels, motels & apart-hotels; (5.3,7.3) Hotels, motels, apart-hotels, camping/caravaning and other; (6.1) The expenditure figures are those provided by the country to UNWTO, which do not appear in the International Monetary Fund data used in the preparation of this edition of the Compendium; (8.1) Including only tours authorized by the "Instituto de Turismo"; (9.3) Rooms.
Source: "Oficina Nacional de Estadísticas".

CURAÇAO

(1.2,1.3,2.2,2.3,3.1,4.1-4.3) Arrivals by air; (3.4) Cruise ship arrivals; (4.1-4.3) Differences in overall totals due to incompletion of items on the E/D card by visitors; (6.1) The expenditure figures are those provided by the country to UNWTO, which do not appear in the International Monetary Fund data used in the preparation of this edition of the Compendium; (9.1) Hotels, guest houses, apartments; (9.3) Rooms.
Source: Curaçao Tourist Board.

CYPRUS

(1.2,2.1-2.6) Arrivals of non-resident tourists at national borders; (1.3) Including transit & cruise passengers; (3.4) Including transit passengers; (5.4) Data extracted from the Tourist Expenditure (Departures) Survey and concerns stay in any type of accommodation; (9.3) Bed-places; (9.4) From 2000 onwards, average length of stay calculations are based on guest nights and arrivals at hotels and similar establishments.
Sources: (1.1-5.4,7.1-7.4,8.1,9.1-9.4) Cyprus Tourism Organization; (6.1-6.3,8.2-8.4) International Monetary Fund.

CZECH REPUBLIC

(1.2,2.1-2.4) Non-resident tourists staying in all types of accommodation establishments.
Sources: (1.2-5.4,7.1-7.4,9.1-9.4) Department of Conception and International Cooperation in Tourism - Ministry for Regional Development; (6.1-6.3,8.2-8.4) International Monetary Fund.

DEMOCRATIC REPUBLIC OF THE CONGO

(1.2,2.1-2.4,4.1-4.3/2002-2004) Arrivals by air only; (9.1) Registered hotels.
Note 2005: Provisional data.
Source: "Office National du Tourisme".

DENMARK

(1.2,2.2-2.4,5.1-5.3,7.1-7.3) New coverage from 2000; (1.2,2.2-2.4) Non-resident tourists staying in all types of accommodation establishments; (1.2-5.3,7.1-7.3,8.1) New methodology from 2004; (5.2,7.2) Hotels only; (9.1-9.3) Only hotels and holiday dwellings with 40 beds or more; (9.3) Bed-places; (10.1-10.3) This section includes only the "travel" item because the "passenger transport" item was not included in the data provided by the International Monetary Fund for the preparation of this edition of the Compendium.
Sources: (1.2-5.4,7.1-7.4,8.1,9.1-9.3) Statistics Denmark; (6.2,8.3) International Monetary Fund.

DJIBOUTI

(1.2) Non-resident tourists staying in hotels; (9.3) Rooms.
Sources: (1.2,5.1,5.2,9.1-9.3) "Office national du tourisme"; (6.2,8.3) "Banque centrale".

DOMINICA

(1.2,2.2,2.3,4.1-4.3) Arrivals of non-resident tourists at national borders; (3.1,3.4) Arrivals of non-resident visitors at national borders; excluding cruise ships; (5.4) Days; (10.1-10.3) This section includes only the "travel" item because the "passenger transport" item was not included in the data provided by the International Monetary Fund for the preparation of this edition of the Compendium.
Sources: (1.1-5.4,9.1) Central Statistical Office - Ministry of Finance; (6.2,8.3) International Monetary Fund.

DOMINICAN REPUBLIC

(1.2) Arrivals by air only; including nationals residing abroad; (1.4) All arrivals by sea; (2.2-2.4) Arrivals by air; excluding nationals residing abroad; (2.2-2.4/2001-2004) (4.1-4.3/2001/2002) Excluding the passengers at Herrera airport; (4.1-4.3) Arrivals by air only; including nationals residing abroad; (9.1,9.2) Hotels; (9.3) Rooms; (10.1-10.3) This section includes only the "travel" item because the "passenger transport" item was not included in the data provided by the International Monetary Fund for the preparation of this edition of the Compendium.
Note 2005: Provisional data.
Sources: (1.1-5.4,8.1,9.1-9.4) "Secretaría de Estado de Turismo"; (6.2,8.2-8.4) International Monetary Fund.

ECUADOR

(1.1) Excluding nationals residing abroad; (1.1-3.4,8.1/2005) Provisional data.
Sources: (1.1-3.4,8.1,9.1,9.2) "Ministerio de Turismo"; (6.1-6.3,8.2-8.4) International Monetary Fund.

EGYPT

(1.1,2.1-3.4) Arrivals of non-resident visitors at national borders; (4.1-4.3) Arrivals of non-resident tourists at national borders; (7.1) Hotels only. Main regions only, namely: Cairo, Giza, South Sinai, Red Sea, Luxor, Aswan, Alexandria; (8.1) Travel for tourism and non-tourism purposes (more than 50% for work purpose); (9.3) Rooms.
Sources: (1.1-5.4,7.1-7.4,8.1,9.1-9.4) Ministry of Tourism; (6.1-6.3,8.2-8.4) International Monetary Fund.

EL SALVADOR

(1.2,2.1-4.3) Arrivals of non-resident tourists at national borders; (6.1) The country provides UNWTO with aggregate expenditure figures that differ significantly from the International Monetary Fund data used in the preparation of this edition of the Compendium. The country figures are as follows (US$ million):
2001: 235
2002: 342
2003: 373
2004: 425
2005: 644
This tourism expenditure is obtained based on research carried out jointly with the Central Reserve Bank of El Salvador and the Salvadorian Tourism Corporation aimed at identifying the basic profile of an international tourist visiting El Salvador.
(9.3) Bed-places.
Sources: (1.1-5.4,8.1,9.1-9.4) "Corporación Salvadoreña de Turismo (CORSATUR) - Ministerio de Turismo"; (6.1-6.3,8.2-8.4) International Monetary Fund.

ERITREA

(1.1) Including nationals residing abroad; (2.1-2.6) Excluding nationals residing abroad; (5.1,7.1) Only hotels and similar establishments in the three major towns: Asmara, Karen and Massawa; (6.1) The expenditure figures used were the ones provided by the country to UNWTO, as this data series is more complete than that provided by the International Monetary Fund (IMF) for the preparation of this Compendium; (9.1,9.2/2001-2004) Only major towns of Eritrea; (9.1,9.2/2005) All hotels and similar establishments in Eritrea; (10.1-10.3) It was not possible to complete this section because the "travel" and "passenger transport" items were not included in the data provided by the International Monetary Fund for the preparation of this edition of the Compendium.
Source: Ministry of Tourism.

ESTONIA

(1.1,3.1-4.3) Arrivals of non-resident visitors at national borders; (1.1-1.3,3.1-4.3,8.1/2004) Starting from 2004, border statistics are not collected any more; (1.2/2004/2005) Calculated on the basis of accommodation statistics and "Foreign Visitor Survey" carried out by the Statistical Office of Estonia; (2.1-2.4) Non-resident tourists staying in all types of accommodation establishments; (4.3) Shopping, transit, visiting friends; (9.1-9.4) Including the data of health resorts providing accommodation service.
Sources: (1.1-5.4,7.3,7.4,8.1,9.1-9.4) Estonian Tourist Board / Enterprise Estonia; (6.1-6.3,8.2-8.4) International Monetary Fund; (7.1,7.2) EUROSTAT (New Cronos).

ETHIOPIA

(1.2) Arrivals through all ports of entry; including nationals residing abroad; (2.1-2.6,3.1-3.3) Arrivals through all ports of entry; (4.1-4.3/2001) Arrivals to Bole airport only; (4.1-4.3/2002-2005) Arrivals through all ports of entry; (9.1,9.2/2001) Including all government and private hotels; (9.1,9.2/2002/2003/2005) Excluding unclassified hotels; (9.3) Bed-places; (9.4) Ethiopian Fiscal Year.
Sources: (1.2-5.4,9.1-9.4) Ethiopian Tourism Commission; (6.1-6.3,8.2-8.4) International Monetary Fund.

FIJI

(1.2,2.2-4.3) Arrivals of non-resident tourists at national borders; excluding nationals residing abroad; (5.4) Days; (6.1-6.3,8.2-8.4) The expenditure figures are those provided by the country to UNWTO, which do not appear in the International Monetary Fund data used in the preparation of this edition of the Compendium; (9.3) Rooms.
Source: Fiji Islands Bureau of Statistics.

FINLAND

(1.1,2.1-4.3) Arrivals of non-resident visitors at national borders. Border Survey; (1.2) Arrivals of non-resident tourists at national borders; (5.1-5.3,7.1-7.3) Due to a change in the methodology, data for 2004 are not comparable to previous years; (8.1) Overnight trips abroad, including cruises abroad with overnight on board only.
Sources: (1.1-5.4,7.1-7.4,8.1,9.1-9.4) Tourism Statistics - Statistics Finland; (6.1-6.3,8.2-8.4) International Monetary Fund.

FRANCE

(1.2,2.1-2.6,5.3) Estimates based on the 1996 survey at national borders. Data revised from 1996; (2.4) Including South Asia; (3.1-4.3) Estimates; (5.1,5.2,7.1,7.2,9.1-9.3) Hotels only; (5.3,7.3) All types of accommodation; (5.4) Inbound average length of stay; (7.3) Revised and back-extrapolated series; (9.3) Net room occupancy rate; (10.1-10.3) This section includes only the "travel" item because the "passenger transport" item was not included in the data provided by the International Monetary Fund for the preparation of this edition of the Compendium.
2005: Provisional data.
Sources: (1.2-5.4,7.1-7.4,8.1,9.1-9.4) "Bureau des études, des statistiques et des comptes économiques - Direction du Tourisme"; (6.2,8.3) International Monetary Fund.

FRENCH GUIANA

(1.2,6.1/2005) 2005 survey at Cayenne-Rochambeau airport on departure.
Sources: "Comité du Tourisme de la Guyane" and "INSEE Guyane".

FRENCH POLYNESIA

(1.2,2.2-4.3) Arrivals of non-resident tourists at national borders; excluding nationals residing abroad; (5.2) Hotels only; (5.4,9.4) Days; (9.1,9.2) Hotels only; at 31st December of each year; (9.3) Rooms in hotels.
Sources: (1.2-5.4,9.1-9.4) "Service du Tourisme"; (6.1-6.3,8.2-8.4) International Monetary Fund.

GABON

(1.2,2.1-2.6,3.1) Arrivals of non-resident tourists at Libreville airport.
Sources: (1.1-5.1,8.1,9.1,9.3) "Centre Gabonais de Promotion Touristique (GABONTOUR)"; (6.1-6.3,8.2-8.4) International Monetary Fund.

GAMBIA

(1.2,2.1-2.3,3.1,4.1) Charter tourists only; (1.1-4.1/2005) Provisional data.
Sources: (1.1-4.1,8.1,9.1,9.4) Gambia Tourism Authority; (6.1-6.3,8.2-8.4) International Monetary Fund.

GEORGIA

(4.1-4.3) Arrivals in hotels only.
Sources: (1.2-4.3,5.3,8.1,9.1-9.3) Department of Tourism and Resorts - Ministry of Economic Development; (5.2,7.2) State Department for Statistics - Ministry of Economic Development; (6.1-6.3,8.2-8.4) International Monetary Fund.

GERMANY

(1.2,2.1-2.6) Non-resident tourists staying in all types of accommodation establishments; (9.3) Bed-places; (9.4) Inbound tourism in hotels and similar establishments.
Sources: (1.2-5.3,7.1-7.3,8.1,9.1-9.4) "Statistiches Bundesamt"; (6.1-6.3,8.2-8.4) International Monetary Fund.

GHANA

(1.2) Including nationals residing abroad; (2.1-2.6) Excluding nationals residing abroad.
Sources: (1.2-4.3,9.1-9.3) Ghana Tourist Board and Ministry of Tourism and Modernisation of the Capital City; (6.1-6.3,8.2-8.4) International Monetary Fund.

GREECE

(1.1,3.1-3.4) Arrivals of non-resident visitors at national borders; (1.2,2.1-2.6) Arrivals of non-resident tourists at national borders; information based on administrative data; (3.4) Including cruise passengers.
Sources: (1.1-5.4,7.1-7.4,9.3) National Statistical Service; (6.1-6.3,8.2-8.4) International Monetary Fund; (9.1,9.2) Hellenic Chamber of Hotels.

GRENADA

(1.2,2.2-4.3) Arrivals of non-resident tourists at national borders; (9.1,9.2) Hotels, cottages/apartments and guest houses; (9.3) Rooms; (10.1-10.3) This section includes only the "travel" item because the "passenger transport" item was not included in the data provided by the International Monetary Fund for the preparation of this edition of the Compendium.
Sources: (1.1-5.4,9.1-9.4) Grenada Board of Tourism; (6.2,8.3) International Monetary Fund.

GUADELOUPE

(1.2) Arrivals by air; excluding the north islands (Saint Martin and Saint Barthelemy); (1.2/2001) Non-resident tourists staying in all types of accommodation establishments; (1.2/2003/2004) Non-resident tourists staying in hotels only; (1.2,2.3,3.1/2005) Data based on a survey conducted at Guadeloupe airport; (5.2) Hotels only; (9.1) Hotels; (9.3) Rooms.
Source: "Comité du Tourisme des Îles de la Guadeloupe".

GUAM

(1.2) Air and sea arrivals; (2.2-2.4) Air arrivals only; (4.1-4.3) Civilian air arrivals only; (9.1) Rooms available.
Source: Guam Visitors Bureau.

GUATEMALA

(8.2) The country provides UNWTO with aggregate expenditure figures that differ significantly from the International Monetary Fund data. The country figures are as follows:
2001: 407
2002: 517
2003: 601
2004: 735
2005: 754
Sources: (1.2-3.4,8.1,9.1-9.3) "Instituto Guatemalteco de Turismo - INGUAT"; (6.1-6.3,8.2-8.4) International Monetary Fund.

GUINEA

(1.2,2.1-2.6,4.1-4.3/2003/2005) Arrivals by air at Conakry airport; (5.2) Hotels only; (6.2) The expenditure figures used were the ones provided by the country to UNWTO, as this data series is more complete than that provided by the International Monetary Fund (IMF) for the preparation of this Compendium.
Note 2005: Provisional data.
Sources: (1.2-5.4,6.2,9.1-9.4) "Division Observatoire du Tourisme - Ministère du Tourisme, de l'Hôtellerie et de l'Artisanat"; (6.3,8.2-8.4) International Monetary Fund.

GUINEA BISSAU

(1.2,2.1-2.6,4.1-4.3) Arrivals by air; (2.1-2.6,4.1-4.3/2005) Arrivals at "Osvaldo Vieira" Airport.
Sources: (1.2-4.3) "Ministério do Turismo e do Ordenamento do Território"; (6.1-6.3,8.2-8.4) International Monetary Fund.

GUYANA

(1.2,2.2,2.3,3.1/2002-2005) Arrivals to Timehri airport only.
Sources: (1.2-3.1) Guyana Tourism Authority; (6.1-6.3,8.2-8.4) International Monetary Fund.

HAITI

(10.1-10.3) This section includes only the "travel" item because the "passenger transport" item was not included in the data provided by the International Monetary Fund for the preparation of this edition of the Compendium.
Sources: (1.1-3.4) "Ministère du Tourisme"; (6.2,8.2-8.4) International Monetary Fund.

HONDURAS

(1.2,2.1-4.3) Arrivals of non-resident tourists at national borders.
Sources: (1.1-5.4,8.1,9.1-9.4) "Instituto Hondureño de Turismo" (6.1-6.3,8.2-8.4) International Monetary Fund.

HONG KONG, CHINA

(6.1-6.3) The expenditure figures used were the ones provided by the country to UNWTO, as this data series is more complete than that provided by the International Monetary Fund (IMF) for the preparation of this Compendium (Source: HKTB Visitors Survey); (8.1) Excluding Hong Kong residents to Macao and Mainland China; (9.1) Hotels (high/medium tariffs) and hostels/ guest houses; (9.3) Rooms.
Sources: (1.1-8.1,9.1,9.3) Hong Kong Tourism Board; (8.3) Census and Statistics Department.

HUNGARY

(1.1/2001-2003) (3.1-3.4) Departures of non-resident visitors; (1.1-1.4,4.1-4.3/2004) New series; (2.1-2.4) Non-resident tourists staying in all types of accommodation establishments; (3.4) By river; (9.3) Rooms, July-June.
Sources: (1.1-5.4,7.1-7.4,8.1,9.1-9.4) Hungarian Central statistical Office; (6.1-6.3,8.2-8.4) International Monetary Fund.

ICELAND

(1.2,2.1-2.4) Non-resident tourists staying in all types of accommodation establishments; (3.1,3.4) Arrivals of non-resident tourists at the Icelandic borders.
Note: Due to the introduction of Schengen in March 2001, the data collection on arrivals and departures at the Icelandic borders was changed. From 2002 this data collection is done by the Icelandic Tourist Board.
Sources: (1.2-2.4,5.1-5.4,7.1-7.4,9.1-9.4) "Hagstofa Íslands Statistics Iceland"; (3.1,3.4) Icelandic Tourist Board; (6.1-6.3,8.2-8.4) International Monetary Fund.

INDIA

(1.2,2.1-4.3) Arrivals of non-resident tourists at national borders; excluding nationals residing abroad; (4.1) Including other purposes; (8.1) Departures of nationals only, irrespective of purpose; (9.1,9.2) In classified hotels; (9.3) Rooms.
Sources: (1.1-4.3,8.1,9.1-9.3) Market Research Division - Government of India; (6.1-6.3,8.2-8.4) International Monetary Fund.

INDONESIA

(5.2,7.2,7.4,9.3) Classified hotels only; (9.1,9.2) All forms of commercial accommodation; (9.3) Rooms.
Sources: (1.2-5.4,7.1-7.4,8.1,9.1-9.3) Ministry of Culture and Tourism and BPS Statistics Indonesia; (6.1-6.3,8.2-8.4) International Monetary Fund.

IRAN, ISLAMIC REPUBLIC OF

(3.3) Including rail; (5.2,7.2) Hotels only; (9.1,9.2) Hotels only, 21 March-20 March; (9.3) Estimates (Bed-places).
Sources: (1.2-5.4,7.1-7.4,8.1,9.1-9.4) Iran Cultural Heritage and Tourism Organization (ICHTO); (6.1-6.3,8.2-8.4) Central Bank of Islamic Republic of Iran.

IRELAND

(1.2,2.3,3.3,4.1-4.3,5.4) Including tourists from North Ireland; (3.3) Including rail; (8.1) Including same-day visitors; (9.1) Excluding hostels; (9.3) Rooms, hotels only.
Sources: (1.2-5.4,7.1-7.4,8.1,9.1-9.3) Fáilte Ireland; (6.1-6.3,8.2-8.4) International Monetary Fund.

ISRAEL

(1.1) Arrivals of non-resident visitors at national borders; excluding nationals residing abroad; (1.2,2.1-4.3) Arrivals of non-resident tourists at national borders; excluding nationals residing abroad; (3.3) Including tourists' reentry after a visit of up to 7 days in Sinai; (3.4) Including US Navy personnel on courtesy visits; (4.3) Including visit friends and relatives and pilgrimage; (5.1) Tourist hotels and aparthotels; (6.2) Including the expenditures of foreign workers in Israel (US$ Million):
2001: 1,097
2002: 1,125
2003: 997
2004: 905
2005: 929
(9.3) Bed-occupancy in hotels and similar establishments open; (9.4) Inbound tourism in tourist hotels.
Sources: (1.1-5.4,7.1-7.3,8.1,9.1-9.4) Ministry of Tourism; (6.1-6.3,8.2-8.4) International Monetary Fund.

ITALY

(1.1,3.1-4.3) Arrivals of non-resident visitors at national borders; excluding seasonal and border workers; (1.1-4.3,8.1) Border survey of the "Ufficio Italiano dei Cambi"; (1.2,2.1-2.6) Arrivals of non-resident tourists at national borders; excluding seasonal and border workers; (1.3) Including cruise passengers; (5.1,5.2) Hotels only; (8.1) Number of resident tourists (overnight visitors) abroad; (9.3) Bed-places.
Sources: (1.1-4.3,8.1) "Ufficio Italiano dei Cambi"; (5.1-5.4,7.1-7.4,9.1-9.4) "Statistiche sul Turismo - Istituto Nazionale di Statistica (ISTAT)"; (6.1-6.3,8.2-8.4) International Monetary Fund.

JAMAICA

(1.2,2.1-4.3) Arrivals of non-resident tourists by air; including nationals residing abroad; E/D cards; (5.3) Data obtained by multiplying the average length of stay by number of stopovers of each country of origin; (5.4) Intended length of stay; (9.3) Rooms; (9.4) Hotel nights only.
Sources: (1.1-5.4,9.1-9.4) Jamaica Tourist Board; (6.1-6.3,8.2-8.4) International Monetary Fund.

JAPAN

(1.2,2.1-2.6,4.1-4.3) Arrivals of non-resident tourists at national borders; excluding nationals residing abroad; (3.1,3.4) Arrivals of non-resident visitors at national borders; including foreign residents in Japan; (5.4) Days; (6.2/2003) The calculation method has been changed since January 2003; (9.1) Government registered and unregistered hotels and "ryokans" (inns); (9.3) Occupancy rate of major government registered hotels (rooms).

Sources: (1.2-5.4,7.1,8.1,9.1,9.3) Japan National Tourist Organization; (6.1-6.3,8.2-8.4) International Monetary Fund.

JORDAN

(1.1-1.3) Including nationals residing abroad; (2.1-2.6) Arrivals of non-resident tourists at national borders; excluding nationals residing abroad; (3.1-3.4) Arrivals of resident and non resident visitors; (5.4) For organized tours only; (9.3) Rooms.
Sources: (1.1-5.4,7.1-7.4,8.1,9.1-9.4) Ministry of Tourism and Antiquities; (6.1-6.3,8.2-8.4) International Monetary Fund.

KAZAKHSTAN

(2.1-2.6,3.1-4.3) Arrivals of non-resident visitors at national borders.
Sources: (1.1-5.4,7.1,8.1,9.1-9.3) Agency of Statistics of the Republic of Kazakhstan; (6.1-6.3,8.2-8.4) International Monetary Fund.

KENYA

(1.1,2.1-4.3) Arrivals of non-resident visitors from all border entry points; excluding nationals residing abroad; (9.3) Bed-places; (9.4) Days.
Sources: (1.1-5.4,7.1,7.4,9.1-9.4) Kenya Tourist Board; (6.1-6.3,8.2-8.4) International Monetary Fund.

KIRIBATI

(1.2,2.2-2.4,3.1) Air arrivals. 2001-2003: Tarawa and Christmas Island. 2004/2005: Tarawa only; (4.1-4.3) Air arrivals. 2001: Tarawa and Christmas Island. 2002-2005: Tarawa only; (6.1) The expenditure figures are those provided by the country to UNWTO, which do not appear in the International Monetary Fund data used in the preparation of this edition of the Compendium.
Source: Ministry of Communication, Transport and Tourism Development.

KOREA, REPUBLIC OF

(1.1) Including nationals residing abroad and crew members; (2.1-2.6) Excluding nationals residing abroad; (3.1,3.4) Excluding overseas Koreans and crew members; (8.2) The country provides UNWTO with aggregate expenditure figures that differ significantly from the International Monetary Fund data used in the preparation of this edition of the Compendium (excluding expenses of students studying overseas). The country figures are as follows:
2001: 6,547
2002: 9,038
2003: 8,248
2004: 9,856
(9.1) Hotels only; (9.3) Rooms.
Sources: (1.1-5.4,8.1,9.1,9.3) Ministry of Culture and Tourism; (6.1-6.3,8.2-8.4) International Monetary Fund.

KUWAIT

(1.1,2.1-2.6,3.1-3.4) Arrivals of non-resident visitors at national borders; (1.2,4.1-4.3) Non-resident tourists staying in hotels and similar establishments.
Sources: (1.1-5.4,8.1,9.1,9.2) Ministry of Planning; (6.1-6.3,8.2-8.4) International Monetary Fund.

KYRGYZSTAN

(1.2,2.2-2.5,8.1/2003-2005) New data source: Department of Customs Control.
Sources: (1.1-5.2,7.1,7.2,8.1,9.1,9.2) National Statistical Committee; (6.1-6.3,8.2-8.4) International Monetary Fund.

LAO PEOPLE'S DEMOCRATIC REPUBLIC

(1.2) Arrivals of non-resident tourists at national borders; (2.2-2.5,3.1,3.3,4.1-4.3) Arrivals of non-resident visitors at national borders; (5.4) Days; (10.1-10.3) This section includes only the "travel" item because the "passenger transport" item was not included in the data provided by the International Monetary Fund for the preparation of this edition of the Compendium.
Sources: (1.1-5.4,9.1-9.3) (6.2/2002-2005) National Tourism Authority; (6.2,8.3/2001) International Monetary Fund.

LATVIA

(1.1,3.1-3.4) Arrivals of non-resident visitors at national border. Data by State Border Guard. (1.2-1.4,2.2-2.5,4.1-4.3) Non-resident departures. Survey of persons crossing the state border; (1.3) Including cruise passengers; (4.3) Including visit friends and relatives and health treatment; (5.3,7.3) Overnight stays in all collective accommodation establishments; (5.4) Average length of stay of overnight non-resident visitors; survey of persons crossing the state border; (8.1) Data by State Border Guard; (9.3) Bed-places.
Sources: (1.1-5.4,7.1-7.4,8.1,9.1-9.4) Transport and Tourism Statistics Section - Central Statistical Bureau; (6.1-6.3,8.2-8.4) International Monetary Fund.

LEBANON

(1.2) Excluding Syrian nationals; (6.1/2001) The expenditure figures are those provided by the country to UNWTO, which do not appear in the International Monetary Fund data used in the preparation of this edition of the Compendium. Due to lack of data on international tourism receipts concerning statistics on inbound tourism, the Department of "Internet and Statistics Service of the Ministry of Tourism" considers that a tourist spends an average of US$ 1,000.
Sources: "Ministère du Tourisme"; (6.1-6.3,8.2-8.4/2002-2005) International Monetary Fund.

LESOTHO

(1.1,2.1-4.3) Arrivals of non-resident visitors at national borders; (1.1-4.3/2004/2005) Estimates; (10.1-10.3) This section includes only the "travel" item because the "passenger transport" item was not included in the data provided by the International Monetary Fund for the preparation of this edition of the Compendium.
Sources: (1.1-4.3,9.1,9.3) Lesotho Tourism Development Corporation; (6.2,8.2-8.4) International Monetary Fund.

LIBYAN ARAB JAMAHIRIYA

(1.1,2.1-2.6) Including all travellers (visitors and other travellers not defined as visitors by UNWTO); (3.1-3.4) Arrivals of non-resident visitors at national borders; (4.1-4.3) Arrivals of non-resident tourists at national borders.
Note 2001-2004: Preliminary data.
Sources: (1.1-5.4,7.3,9.1-9.3) General People's Committee for Tourism; (6.1-6.3,8.2-8.4) International Monetary Fund.

LIECHTENSTEIN

(1.2,2.2-2.4) Non-resident tourists staying in hotels and similar establishments; (9.3) Bed-places.
Source: "Liechtenstein Tourismus".

LITHUANIA

(2.1-2.4) Non-resident tourists staying in all types of accommodation establishments; (3.1-3.4,4.1-4.3) Arrivals of non-resident tourists at national borders; (5.1,5.2,7.1,7.2,9.1-9.4) Hotels only; (9.3) Rooms.
Sources: (1.1-5.4,7.1-7.4,8.1,9.1-9.4) Lithuanian State Department of Tourism; (6.1-6.3,8.2-8.4) International Monetary Fund.

LUXEMBOURG

(1.2,2.2,2.3) Non-resident tourists staying in all types of accommodation establishments; including youth hostels, tourist private accommodation and others; (5.1,7.1) Nights in hotels, inns and guest houses; (5.3,7.3) Including tourist private accommodation and others; (9.3) Rooms.
Sources: (1.2-5.4,7.1-7.4,8.1,9.1-9.4) "Office National du Tourisme"; (6.1-6.3,8.2-8.4) International Monetary Fund.

MACAO, CHINA

(1.1,2.1-4.3) Arrivals of non-resident visitors at national borders; (1.1-1.3,2.4,3.1-3.4) Including ethnic Chinese arriving from "Hong Kong, China"; (1.2,1.3) Estimates; (3.1) Including entrees by helicopter; (6.1) The expenditure figures used were the ones provided by the country to UNWTO, as this data series is more complete than that provided by the International Monetary Fund (IMF) for the preparation of this Compendium. Including gambling receipts; (8.1) Package tours; (9.1,9.2) Hotels, guest houses and pousadas (inns); (9.3) Rooms; (10.1-10.3) It was not possible to complete this section because the "travel" and "passenger transport" items were not included in the data provided by the International Monetary Fund for the preparation of this edition of the Compendium.
Source: Macau Government Tourist Office.

MADAGASCAR

(1.2,2.1-2.4,3.1,4.1-4.3) Arrivals of non-resident tourists by air; (9.3) Rooms.
Sources: (1.2-5.4,9.1-9.4) "Ministère de la Culture et du Tourisme"; (6.1-6.3,8.2-8.4) International Monetary Fund; (8.1) "Police des frontières".

MALAWI

(1.2-4.3) Departures; (5.3/2004) Provisional data; (9.3) Bed-places.
Sources: (1.2-5.4,9.1-9.4) Ministry of Information and Tourism; (6.1-6.3,8.2-8.4/2001) International Monetary Fund; (6.1-6.3,8.2-8.4/2002-2005) Reserve Bank of Malawi.

MALAYSIA

(1.2,2.1-2.6) Arrivals of non-resident tourists at national borders; including Singapore residents crossing the frontier by road through Johore Causeway; (3.1-3.4,4.1-4.3) Peninsular Malaysia only; (8.1) Outgoing Peninsular Malaysians, including departures via Johore Causeway by road; (9.1) Hotels with 10 rooms and above; (9.3) Rooms.
Sources: (1.1-5.2,7.2,8.1,9.1,9.3) Tourism Malaysia; (6.1-6.3,8.2-8.4) International Monetary Fund.

MALDIVES

(1.2,2.1-2.6) Air arrivals; (5.1,9.1-9.4) Tourist resorts and hotels; (9.4) Days; (10.1-10.3) This section includes only the “travel” item because the “passenger transport” item was not included in the data provided by the International Monetary Fund for the preparation of this edition of the Compendium.
Sources: (1.2-5.1,8.1,9.1-9.4) Ministry of Tourism; (6.2,8.2-8.4) International Monetary Fund.

MALI

(1.2) Arrivals by air; (2.1-2.6) Non-resident tourists staying in hotels and similar establishments; (9.3) Rooms.
Sources: (1.2-5.4,7.1-7.4,9.1-9.4) "Office malien du tourisme et de l'hôtellerie (O.MA.T.HO)"; (6.1-6.3,8.2-8.4) International Monetary Fund.

MALTA

(1.2,2.1-2.6,3.1,3.4/2001-2003) Arrivals of non-resident tourists at national borders; (1.2,2.2-2.6,3.1,3.4/2004/2005) Departures by air and by sea; (4.1-4.3,5.1-5.3/2003-2005) Tourist departures by air; (8.1/2002-2005) By air only; (9.3) Bed-places.
Sources: (1.1-5.4,8.1,9.2-9.4) Malta Tourism Authority and National Statistics Office; (6.1-6.3,8.2-8.4) International Monetary Fund.

MARSHALL ISLANDS

(1.2,2.2-2.4,4.1-4.3/2001-2003) Air arrivals; (1.2,2.2-2.4,4.1-4.3/2004/2005) Air and sea arrivals; (6.1) The expenditure figures are those provided by the country to UNWTO, which do not appear in the International Monetary Fund data used in the preparation of this edition of the Compendium.
Source: Marshall Islands Visitors Authority.

MARTINIQUE

(1.2,2.2,2.3,4.1-4.3) Arrivals of non-resident tourists at national borders; (6.1) The expenditure figures are those provided by the country to UNWTO, which do not appear in the International Monetary Fund data used in the preparation of this edition of the Compendium; (9.1) Hotels and holiday villages (Club Méditerranée); (9.3) Rooms in hotels and similar establishments.
Source: "Comité Martiniquais du Tourisme".

MAURITIUS

(1.2,2.1-3.4) Arrivals of non-resident tourists at national borders; (4.1-4.3) Arrivals of non-resident visitors at national borders; (5.4) Large hotels; (9.3) Rooms.
Note 2005: Provisional data.
Sources: (1.1-5.4,8.1,9.1-9.3) Ministry of Tourism and Leisure; (6.1-6.3,8.2-8.4) International Monetary Fund.

MEXICO

(1.2,2.2-4.3) Arrivals of non-resident tourists at national borders; including nationals residing abroad; (1.3) Including visitors of the US border zone with a length of stay under 24 hours; (2.2/2004/2005) United States and Canada only; (3.3) Including rail; (5.1) Selected tourism resorts; (5.2,7.2) Hotels only; (9.3) Rooms; (9.4) Foreign tourism only.
2005: Preliminary data.
Sources: (1.1-5.4,7.1,7.2,8.1,9.1-9.4) "Secretaría de Turismo de México (SECTUR)"; (6.1-6.3,8.2-8.4) International Monetary Fund.

MICRONESIA (FEDERATED STATES OF)

(1.2,2.2-2.4,4.1-4.3) Arrivals in the States of Kosrae, Chuuk, Pohnpei and Yap; excluding FSM citizens; (6.1,8.2) The expenditure figures are those provided by the country to UNWTO, which do not appear in the International Monetary Fund data used in the preparation of this edition of the Compendium. Fiscal years (October 1 to September 30).
Source: Department of Economic Affairs.

MONACO

(1.2,2.1-4.2) Non-resident tourists staying in hotels and similar establishments.
Source: "Direction du Tourisme et des Congrès".

MONGOLIA

(1.2,2.2-2.4) (4.1-4.3/2002-2005) Arrivals of non-resident tourists at national borders. Excluding diplomats and foreign residents in Mongolia; (4.1-4.3/2001) Arrivals of non-resident visitors at national borders.
Sources: (1.1-4.3) (6.1-6.3,8.2-8.4/2005) Tourism Policy and Coordination Department - Ministry of Road Transport and Tourism; (6.1-6.3,8.2-8.4/2001-2004) International Monetary Fund.

MONTSERRAT

(10.2,10.3) This section includes only the "travel" item because the "passenger transport" item was not included in the data provided by the International Monetary Fund for the preparation of this edition of the Compendium.
Sources: (1.1-5.2) Statistics Department Montserrat; (6.2,8.3) International Monetary Fund.

MOROCCO

(1.2,3.1-4.3) Arrivals of non-resident tourists at national borders; including nationals residing abroad; (2.1-2.6) Arrivals of non-resident tourists at national borders; excluding nationals residing abroad; (5.1,5.2,7.1,7.2,9.1-9.3) Classified hotels, holiday villages and tourist residences; (9.3) Rooms; (9.4) Foreign tourists.
Sources: (1.1-5.2,7.1,7.2,8.1,9.1-9.4) "Ministère du tourisme"; (6.1-6.3,8.2-8.4) International Monetary Fund.

MOZAMBIQUE

Sources: (1.1-4.3,9.1-9.4) Ministry of Tourism; (5.1,5.2,7.1,7.2) "Instituto Nacional de Estatística"; (6.1-6.3,8.2-8.4) International Monetary Fund.

MYANMAR

(1.2,2.2-2.6) Including tourist arrivals through border entry points to Yangon; (4.1-4.3) Arrivals of non-resident visitors at national borders; (5.1,9.4) State-run hotels and similar establishments only; (9.1,9.2) State-run hotels and private registered guest houses; (9.3) Rooms.
Sources: (1.1-5.4,9.1-9.4) Ministry of Hotels and Tourism; (6.1-6.3,8.2-8.4) International Monetary Fund.

NAMIBIA

(2.1-4.3) Arrivals of non-resident tourists at national borders; (2.2) United States only; (2.4) Australia only; (9.3) Bed-places.
Sources: (1.1-5.4,7.1-7.3,9.1-9.4) Ministry of Environment and Tourism; (6.1-6.3,8.3) International Monetary Fund.

NEPAL

(1.2) Including arrivals from India; (3.3) Land; (9.1,9.2) Hotels in Kathmandu and in the interior of the country.
Sources: (1.2-5.4,8.1,9.1,9.2) Nepal Tourism Board; (6.1-6.3,8.2-8.4) International Monetary Fund.

NETHERLANDS

(1.2-2.4) Non-resident tourists staying in all types of accommodation establishments; (5.1,7.1) Hotels and boarding houses; (8.1) Holiday departures of nationals; (8.1/2002) New survey; (9.2) Hotels; (9.3) Bed-places; (9.4) All types of accommodation establishments.
Sources: (1.2-5.4,7.1-7.3,8.1,9.1-9.4) Statistics Netherlands; (6.1-6.3,8.2-8.4) International Monetary Fund.

NEW CALEDONIA

(1.2,2.1-4.3) Including nationals residing abroad; (4.1) Holidays and visit relatives; (4.2) Business only; (5.1,5.2,7.1,7.2) Hotels in Noumea only; (8.1) Returning residents; (9.3) Rooms in Noumea; (9.4) Days, hotels in Noumea; (10.2,10.3) This section includes only the "travel" item because the "passenger transport" item was not included in the data provided by the International Monetary Fund for the preparation of this edition of the Compendium.
Sources: (1.1-5.4,7.1,7.2,8.1,9.1-9.4) (6.2/2001) "Institut de la Statistique et des Études Économiques (ISEE)"; (6.2,8.3/2002-2005) International Monetary Fund.

NEW ZEALAND

(1.1,3.1-4.3) Arrivals of non-resident visitors at national borders; including nationals residing abroad; (2.1-2.6) Arrivals of non-resident visitors at national borders; excluding nationals residing abroad; (5.3,7.3) Estimated from total guest nights in commercial accommodation establishments with an annual turnover at least NZ$30,000, based on average percentage of international and domestic guests in Jan, Apr, Jul and Oct; (8.1) Short-term departures of NZ residents (calendar year); (9.1) Refer to "staying units" capacity in hotels, motels and hosted guest houses; (10.1-10.3) This section includes only the "travel" item because the "passenger transport" item was not included in the data provided by the International Monetary Fund for the preparation of this edition of the Compendium.
Sources: (1.1-5.3,7.3,8.1,9.1-9.4) Ministry of Tourism; (6.2,8.3) International Monetary Fund.

NICARAGUA

(1.2,2.1-4.3) Arrivals of non-resident tourists at national borders; (1.2/2001-2004) (2.1-2.5) Excluding nationals residing abroad; (1.2/2005) Including nationals residing abroad; (5.1-5.4,7.1-7.4,9.4/2005) Preliminary data; (5.1,7.1) Main accommodation establishments in the country (7); (5.3,7.3) Total number of establishments in the country; (9.1,9.2) Hotels and similar establishments classified in higher categories; (9.4) All types of accommodation establishments, inbound tourism.

Sources: (1.1-5.4,7.1-7.4,8.1,9.1-9.4) "Instituto Nicaragüense de Turismo (INTUR)"; (6.1-6.3,8.2-8.4) International Monetary Fund.

NIGER

(5.4) Days.
Sources: (1.2-5.4,7.1,7.2,9.1-9.4) (6.2,8.2-8.4/2005) "Ministère du Tourisme et de l'Artisanat"; (6.1-6.3,8.2-8.4/2001-2004) International Monetary Fund.

NIGERIA

(1.1,2.1-2.6,3.1-3.4) Arrivals of non-resident visitors at national borders; (1.2,4.1-4.3) Arrivals of non-resident tourists at national borders.
Sources: (1.1-4.3,9.2,9.3) Nigerian Tourism Development Corporation; (6.1-6.3,8.2-8.4) International Monetary Fund.

NIUE

(1.2) Arrivals by air; including Niueans residing usually in New Zealand; (8.1) Returning residents.
Source: Statistics Niue.

NORTHERN MARIANA ISLANDS

(1.1,2.2-2.4) Arrivals of non-resident visitors at national borders; (1.2) Arrivals by air; (2.2) Including Guam; (9.1) Covers 68 per cent of the total hotel room inventory.
Source: Marianas Visitors Authority.

NORWAY

(1.1-4.2) Figures are based on "The Guest survey" carried out by "Institute of Transport Economics"; (2.2-4.2) Arrivals of non-resident tourists at national borders; (2.2) United States only; (2.4) Japan only; (5.1) Nights in registered establishments; (5.1,9.1,9.2) Figures for hotels and similar establishments relate to establishments with 20 or more beds the whole year; (8.1) Holiday trips; (9.3) Bed-places.
Sources: (1.1-5.3,7.1-7.3,8.1,9.1-9.4) Statistics Norway and Institute of Transport Economics; (6.1-6.3,8.2-8.4) International Monetary Fund.

OMAN

(1.1-1.3,4.1-4.3,5.3,5.4) Inbound Tourism Survey; (2.1-2.6) Non-resident tourists staying in hotels and similar establishments; (4.1-4.3) Arrivals of non-resident visitors at national borders; (8.1) Outbound Tourism Survey; including same-day visitors; (9.3) Rooms.
Sources: (1.1-1.3,4.1-4.3,5.3,5.4,8.1) Ministry of National Economy and Ministry of Commerce and Industry; (2.1-2.6,5.1,5.2,7.1,7.2,9.1-9.3) Directorate General of Tourism - Ministry of Tourism; (6.1-6.3,8.2-8.4) International Monetary Fund.

PAKISTAN

(5.4) Days; (8.3) The country provides UNWTO with aggregate expenditure figures that differ significantly from the International Monetary Fund data used in the preparation of this edition of the Compendium. The country figures are as follows:
2001: 255
2002: 179
2003: 880
2004: 1,319
2005: 1,277
Sources: (1.2-5.4,7.1,7.2,9.1-9.4) Pakistan Tourism Development Corporation - Ministry of Tourism; (6.1-6.3,8.2-8.4) International Monetary Fund.

PALAU

(1.2-4.3) Air arrivals (Palau International Airport); (6.1,8.2) The expenditure figures are those provided by the country to UNWTO, which do not appear in the International Monetary Fund data used in the preparation of this edition of the Compendium.
Source: Office of Planning and Statistics, Bureau of Budget and Planning - Ministry of Finance.

PALESTINE

(1.2,2.1-2.6) Non-resident tourists staying in hotels; (5.1,5.2,7.1,7.2) Hotels only; (10.1-10.3) This section includes only the "travel" item because the "passenger transport" item was not included in the data provided by the International Monetary Fund for the preparation of this edition of the Compendium.
Sources: (1.2-5.2,7.1-7.4,9.1-9.4) Palestinian Central Bureau of Statistics; (6.2,8.3) International Monetary Fund; (6.2,8.3,10-1-10.3) West Bank and Gaza.

PANAMA

(1.1) Arrivals of non-resident visitors, Tocúmen International Airport (TIA), Paso Canoa frontier (PCF), the ports of Cristóbal and Balboa (PCB) and IPAT statistics; (2.2-2.4) Arrivals of non-resident visitors, TIA and IPAT statistics; (3.1-3.4) Arrivals of non-resident tourists, TIA, PCF, PCB and IPAT statistics; excluding arrivals to other ports of entry (non specified) (000)= 2001:42; 2002:35; 2003:40; 2004:51; 2005:54; (4.1-4.3) Arrivals of non-resident tourists, TIA and IPAT statistics; (5.1) Hotels in Panama City and IPAT statistics; (9.1,9.2) Rooms/bed-places recorded for international tourism; (9.3) Rooms.
2004-2005: Preliminary data.
Sources: (1.1-5.4,8.1,9.1-9.4) "Instituto Panameño de Turismo"; (6.1-6.3,8.2-8.4) International Monetary Fund.

PAPUA NEW GUINEA

Sources: (1.2-5.4,8.1,9.1-9.4) Papua New Guinea Tourism Promotion Authority; (6.1-6.3,8.2-8.4) International Monetary Fund.

PARAGUAY

(1.1-3.4,8.1) E/D cards in the "Silvio Petirossi" airport and passenger counts at the national border crossings - National Police and SENATUR; (1.2,2.1-4.3) Excluding nationals residing abroad and crew members; (3.4) River; (9.3) Bed-places.
Sources: (1.1-5.4,8.1,9.1-9.4) "Secretaría Nacional de Turismo - SENATUR"; (6.1-6.3,8.2-8.4) International Monetary Fund.

PERU

(1.2) Including overnight cruise passengers; (1.2,2.1-2.5) From 2002, new estimated series including tourists with identity document other than a passport; (1.4) Overnight cruise passengers; (3.4) Includes the arrivals by river and lake; (5.1,5.2,5.4,7.1,7.2,9.1-9.4/2003-2005) Preliminary estimates.
Sources: (1.1-5.4,7.1,7.2,8.1,9.1-9.4) "Ministerio de Comercio Exterior y Turismo (MINCETUR) - Vice Ministerio de Turismo"; (6.1-6.3,8.2-8.4) International Monetary Fund.

PHILIPPINES

(1.2,3.1-4.3) Arrivals of non-resident tourists at national borders; including nationals residing abroad; (2.1-2.6) Arrivals of non-resident tourists at national borders; excluding nationals residing abroad; (4.1-4.3) Air arrivals; (8.1) Including overseas contract workers; (9.1,9.2) Classified hotels only; (9.3,9.4) Classified hotels in Metro Manila.
Sources: (1.2-5.4,8.1,9.1-9.4) Department of Tourism; (6.1-6.3,8.2-8.4) International Monetary Fund.

POLAND

(1.1,2.1-3.4) Arrivals of non-resident visitors at national borders; (4.1-4.3) Arrivals of non-resident tourists at national borders, based on surveys by the Institute of Tourism; (5.4) Both collective and private accommodation establishments, based on surveys by the Institute of Tourism; (8.1) Outbound trips registered at frontiers; (9.3) Rooms.
Sources: (1.1-5.4,7.1-7.3,8.1,9.1-9.4) Institute of Tourism; (6.1-6.3,8.2-8.4) International Monetary Fund.

PORTUGAL

(1.1,3.1-3.4) Arrivals of non-resident visitors at national borders; (1.1,1.3,3.1-3.4/2004) Due to a change in the methodology, data are not available from 2004; (1.2,2.2-2.4) Arrivals of non-resident tourists at national borders; excluding nationals residing abroad; including arrivals from abroad in Madeira and Azores; (1.2,1.4,2.2-2.4/2005) Due to a change in the methodology, data are not available from 2005; (1.4) Including transit sea passengers; (5.3) Including nights in accommodation establishments in Madeira and Azores; (9.1,9.3) Hotels, motels, inns, boarding houses & "pousadas" (July-June); (9.3) Bed-places (classified hotels); (9.4) All types of accommodation establishments.
Sources: (1.1-5.4,7.1-7.3,9.1-9.4) "Direcçao-Geral do Turismo (DGT)"; (6.1-6.3,8.2-8.4) International Monetary Fund.

PUERTO RICO

(1.2) Arrivals of non-resident tourists by air; (2.2) United States Virgin Islands and the United States only; (5.1,5.4) Including residents and non-residents; (6.1,8.2-8.4) The expenditure figures are those provided by the country to UNWTO, which do not appear in the International Monetary Fund data used in the preparation of this edition of the Compendium; (9.1) Rooms classified by the "Compañía de Turismo" of Puerto Rico; (9.3) Rooms; including rooms occupied by residents of Puerto Rico.
Data: Fiscal years (July-June).
Source: (1.2-3.4,6.1,8.1,8.2-8.4,10.1-10.3) "Junta de Planificación de Puerto Rico"; (5.1,5.2,5.4,7.2,9.1,9.3,9.4) "Compañía de Turismo de Puerto Rico".

QATAR

(1.2,2.3-2.6,5.1,5.4,9.1-9.3) Hotels only; (6.2,8.3) The expenditure figures are those provided by the country to UNWTO, which do not appear in the International Monetary Fund data used in the preparation of this edition of the Compendium; (9.3) Bed-places.
Sources: (1.2-5.4,9.1-9.3) The Planning Council - Statistics Department; (6.2,8.3) Qatar Central Bank.

REPUBLIC OF MOLDOVA

(1.1-4.3,8.1) (5.1,7.3/2001-2003) Visitors who enjoyed the services of the economic agents officially registered under tourism activity and accommodation.
Note: Excluding the left side of the river Nistru and the municipality of Bender.
Sources: (1.1-5.4,7.1-7.4,8.1,9.1-9.4) National Bureau of Statistics; (6.1-6.3,8.2-8.4) International Monetary Fund.

REUNION

(5.4) Days; (6.1) The expenditure figures are those provided by the country to UNWTO, which do not appear in the International Monetary Fund data used in the preparation of this edition of the Compendium.
Sources: "Institut National de la Statistique et des Études Économique - INSEE" and "Comité du Tourisme de la Réunion".

ROMANIA

Sources: (1.1-5.4,7.1-7.4,8.1,9.1-9.4) National Authority for Tourism - Ministry of Transports, Constructions and Tourism; (6.1-6.3,8.2-8.4) International Monetary Fund.

RUSSIAN FEDERATION

(1.1,2.1-4.3) Arrivals of non-resident visitors at national borders; (9.1,9.2) Accommodation in hotels and other tourist establishments.
Sources: (1.1-5.4,7.1-7.4,8.1,9.1-9.4) Russian Federal Agency for Tourism; (6.1-6.3,8.2-8.4) International Monetary Fund.

SABA

(1.3) Mainly from St. Maarten.
Sources: Saba Tourist Bureau, Caribbean Tourism Organization and Central Bank of the Netherlands Antilles.

SAINT EUSTATIUS

(1.1) Air and sea arrivals; including nationals residing abroad; (1.2,2.2,2.3) Arrivals of non-resident tourists at national borders; excluding Netherlands Antillean residents.
Source: Central Bank of the Netherlands Antilles.

SAINT KITTS AND NEVIS

(1.2,2.2,2.3) Arrivals of non-resident tourists by air; (1.4,3.4) Yacht and cruise ship arrivals; (10.1-10.3) This section includes only the "travel" item because the "passenger transport" item was not included in the data provided by the International Monetary Fund for the preparation of this edition of the Compendium.
Sources: (1.1-3.4,9.1,9.2) Ministry of Finance, Planning and Development; (6.2,8.3) International Monetary Fund.

SAINT LUCIA

(1.1) Excluding yacht passenger arrivals; (1.2,2.2-4.3) Arrivals of non-resident tourists at national borders; excluding nationals residing abroad; (9.3) Rooms; (10.1-10.3) This section includes only the "travel" item because the "passenger transport" item was not included in the data provided by the International Monetary Fund for the preparation of this edition of the Compendium.
Note 2005: Provisional data.
Sources: (1.1-5.2,9.1-9.4) Saint Lucia Tourist Board; (6.2,8.3) International Monetary Fund.

SAINT MAARTEN

(1.2,2.2,2.3) By air; including arrivals to Saint Maarten (the French side of the island); (3.1) Arrivals at Juliana Airport (including visitors destined to Saint Maarten, French side); (6.2,8.3) Including the estimates for Saba and Saint Eustatius; (9.1,9.2) Hotels, guest houses and apartments.
Sources: (1.1-3.4,9.1-9.3) St. Maarten Tourist Bureau; (6.2,8.3) Central Bank of the Netherlands Antilles.

SAINT VINCENT AND THE GRENADINES

(1.2,2.2-2.3,4.1-4.3) Arrivals of non-resident tourists by air; (3.4) Including cruise ship and yacht passengers; (9.1) Hotels, apartments, cottages, villas and guest houses; (10.1-10.3) This section includes only the "travel" item because the "passenger transport" item was not included in the data provided by the International Monetary Fund for the preparation of this edition of the Compendium.
Sources: (1.1-5.4,9.1,9.2) Ministry of Tourism and Culture; (6.2,8.3) International Monetary Fund.

SAMOA

Sources: (1.2-4.3,9.1,9.2) (6.2/2001-2003) Samoa Tourism Authority and Statistical Services Division (Ministry of Finance); (6.1-6.3,8.2-8.4/2004/2005) International Monetary Fund.

SAN MARINO

(1.1) Including Italian visitors; (1.2) Non-resident tourists staying in hotels and similar establishments; including Italian tourists; (9.1,9.2) Hotels only.
Note: New methodology from 2005.
Source: "Ufficio di Stato per il Turismo".

SAO TOME AND PRINCIPE

(10.1-10.3) This section includes only the "travel" item because the "passenger transport" item was not included in the data provided by the International Monetary Fund for the preparation of this edition of the Compendium.
Sources: (1.1-4.3) "Direcçao do Turismo e Hotelaria"; (6.2,8.2-8.4/2001/2001) International Monetary Fund; (6.2/2003-2005) "Banco Central".

SAUDI ARABIA

(6.1,8.2) The expenditure figures are those provided by the country to UNWTO, which do not appear in the International Monetary Fund data used in the preparation of this edition of the Compendium.
Source: The Supreme Commission for Tourism.

SENEGAL

(1.2/2001/2002) (2.1-2.6/2001-2003) Non-resident tourists staying in hotels and similar establishments; (1.2/2003-2005) (2.1-2.3/2004/2005) Arrivals of non-resident tourists at national borders; (5.1,5.2,7.1,7.2,9.1,9.2) Hotels and holiday villages; (9.3) Bed-places.
Sources: (1.1-5.4,7.1,7.2,9.1-9.4) "Ministère du Tourisme et des Transports Aériens"; (6.1-6.3,8.2-8.4) International Monetary Fund.

SERBIA AND MONTENEGRO

(1.2,2.2-2.4) Non-resident tourists staying in all types of accommodation establishments; including rented private rooms, houses and flats; (6.2) The expenditure figures are those provided by the country to UNWTO, which do not appear in the International Monetary Fund data used in the preparation of this edition of the Compendium. Starting 1997 data are presented according to the IMF's Fifth issue of instructions on balance of payments; (9.1,9.2) As of 31st August of each year; (9.2,9.3) Permanent bed-places.
Source: Statistical Office of Serbia and Montenegro.

SEYCHELLES

(1.2,2.1-4.3) Arrivals of non-resident tourists at national borders; (5.4) Nights based on departures; (9.1,9.2) Hotels and guest houses; (9.3) Bed-places.
Sources: (1.1-5.4,7.1,8.1,9.1-9.3) Ministry of Information Technology and Communication; (6.1-6.3,8.2-8.4) International Monetary Fund.

SIERRA LEONE

(1.2,2.1-2.6,4.1-4.3) Arrivals by air; (9.1,9.2) Hotels only; (10.1-10.3) This section includes only the "travel" item because the "passenger transport" item was not included in the data provided by the International Monetary Fund for the preparation of this edition of the Compendium.
Sources: (1.2-5.4,8.1,9.1-9.4) National Tourist Board; (6.2,8.2-8.4) International Monetary Fund.

SINGAPORE

(1.1) Excluding arrivals of Malaysian citizens by land; including same-day visitors; (4.1-4.3,5.2/2004) Starting from April 2004, fields such as purpose of visit, accommodation, frequency of trip and travel arrangement have been removed from the disembarkation/ embarkation card. Data not available; (5.4,9.4) Days; (9.1) Hotels (gazetted and non-gazetted); (9.3) Rooms; classified hotels only; (10.1-10.3) This section includes only the "travel" item because the "passenger transport" item was not included in the data provided by the International Monetary Fund for the preparation of this edition of the Compendium.
Sources: (1.1-5.4,8.1,9.1-9.4) Singapore Tourism Board; (6.2,8.3) International Monetary Fund.

SLOVAKIA

(1.1) Including the border with the Czech Republic; (1.2,2.1-2.5) Non-resident tourists staying in all types of accommodation establishments; (5.4,9.4) Inbound tourism in all types of tourism accommodation establishments; (8.1) Tourism organized through Slovak travel agencies.
Sources: (1.1-5.4,7.1-7.4,8.1,9.1-9.4) (6.1-6.3,8.2-8.4/2001/2004) Department of Tourism - Ministry of Economy; (6.1-6.3,8.2-8.4/2002/2003) International Monetary Fund.

SLOVENIA

(1.1) Including all categories of travellers irrespective of purpose of visit; (1.2,2.1-2.6) Non-resident tourists staying in all types of accommodation establishments; (2.1,2.5,2.6) Estimates; (3.1-3.4,4.1-4.3) Non-resident tourists staying in all types of accommodation establishments; data from 3 yearly survey on foreign tourists in Slovenia in Summer; (8.1) Quarterly survey on travels of domestic population.
Sources: (1.1-5.4,7.1-7.4,8.1,9.1-9.4) Statistical Office - Information Society and Tourism Statistics; (6.1-6.3,8.2-8.4) International Monetary Fund.

SOLOMON ISLANDS

(1.2,2.2-2.4/2005) Without 1st quarter.
Sources: (1.2,2.2-2.4) Solomon Islands National Statistics Office; (6.2,8.3) Central Bank of Solomon Islands.

SOUTH AFRICA

(1.1,3.1-3.4) Excluding nationals residing abroad. Including arrivals by purpose of holiday, business, study, work, transit, border traffic and contract workers; (1.2,2.1-2.6,4.1-4.3) Arrivals of non-resident tourists at national borders; excluding arrivals by work and contract workers; (9.3) Rooms (hotels).
Sources: (1.1-4.3,8.1,9.1-9.3) Statistics South Africa and South African Tourism; (6.1-6.3,8.2-8.4) International Monetary Fund.

SPAIN

(1.1) Arrivals of non-resident visitors at national borders; including nationals residing abroad; (2.2-4.3) Arrivals of non-resident tourists at national borders; including nationals residing abroad; (2.4) Japan only; (5.1,7.1) Nights in hotels and "hostales" (accommodation establishments providing limited services); (5.3,7.3) Nights in hotels, "hostales", camping sites, tourism apartments and rural dwellings; (5.4,7.4,9.1-9.4) Hotels and "hostales" only; (8.1) Since 2005 a new methodology has been applied and data are not comparable to previous years; (9.3) Bed-places.
Sources: (1.1-4.3,8.1) "Instituto de Estudios Turísticos"; (5.1-5.4,7.1-7.4,9.1-9.4) "Instituto Nacional de Estadística"; (6.1-6.3,8.2-8.4) International Monetary Fund.

SRI LANKA

(1.2,2.1-4.3) Arrivals of non-resident tourists at national borders; excluding nationals residing abroad; (9.1,9.2) Hotels, motels, inns, guest houses and apart-hotels; (9.3) Rooms.
Sources: (1.1-5.4,7.1,8.1,9.1-9.3) Sri Lanka Tourist Board; (6.1-6.3,8.2-8.4) International Monetary Fund.

SUDAN

(1.2-4.3/2005) Arrivals of non-resident tourists at national borders; including nationals residing abroad; (6.1) The country provides UNWTO with aggregate expenditure figures that differ significantly from the International Monetary Fund data used in the preparation of this edition of the Compendium. The country figures are as follows:
2001: 60
2002: 62
2003: 63
2004: 68
2005: 316
(10.1-10.3) This section includes only the "travel" item because the "passenger transport" item was not included in the data provided by the International Monetary Fund for the preparation of this edition of the Compendium.
Sources: (1.2-4.3,9.1-9.4) Ministry of Tourism and Wildlife; (6.2,8.3) International Monetary Fund.

SURINAME

(1.2,2.2-2.4,4.1-4.3,5.2/2001-2003) (3.1) (5.2/2004) Arrivals at Zanderij Airport; (1.2,2.2-2.4,4.1-4.3/2004/2005) Arrivals at Zanderij Airport, Zorg en Hoop Airport, Albina and Nickerie; (1.4/2001-2003) (3.4) Arrivals via Nw. Nickerie Harbour.
Sources: (1.1-1.4,2.2-2.4,4.1-4.3,5.2/2001-2003) (3.1,3.4/2001-2004) General Bureau of Statistics (ABS); (1.2,2.2-2.4,4.1-4.3,5.2/2004/2005) (3.1,3.4/2005) (9.1) Suriname Tourism Foundation; (6.1-6.3,8.2-8.4) International Monetary Fund.

SWAZILAND

(1.2,4.1-4.3/2001/2002) Arrivals in hotels only; (2.1-2.4,5.2) Arrivals in hotels only; (9.3) Bed-places.

Sources: (1.1-5.4,7.1,8.1,9.1-9.4) Swaziland Tourism Authority and Ministry of Tourism, Environment and Communications; (6.1-6.3,8.2-8.4) International Monetary Fund.

SWEDEN

(1.1-4.3) Data according to IBIS-Survey (Incoming Visitors to Sweden) during the years 2001 to 2003, (no data collected before 2001 or after 2003). Source: Swedish Tourist Authority and Statistics Sweden; (1.2,2.1-4.3) Arrivals of non-resident tourists at national borders; (3.2) Data includes rail and others; (5.1,7.1,9.1,9.2) Hotels only; (9.3) Bed-places.
Sources: (1.1-5.3,7.1-7.3,8.1,9.1-9.3) NUTEK - The Swedish Agency for Economic and Regional Growth; (6.1-6.3,8.2-8.4) International Monetary Fund.

SWITZERLAND

(1.2,2.1-2.6,5.1,5.2,7.1,7.2,9.1,9.2/2001-2004) Hotels, motels and inns; (1.2,2.1-2.6,5.1,5.2,7.1,7.2,9.1,9.2/2005) Hotels and health establishments; (9.3) Net occupancy rates (bed-places available); (9.4) Non-resident tourists staying in hotels and similar establishments (foreign tourists).
Sources: (1.2-5.3,7.1-7.3,8.1,9.1-9.4) Swiss Federal Statistical Office; (6.1-6.3,8.2-8.4) International Monetary Fund.

SYRIAN ARAB REPUBLIC

(1.1,2.1-4.3) Arrivals of non-resident visitors at national borders; excluding arrivals of nationals residing abroad; (9.3) Rooms.
Sources: (1.1-5.4,7.1,7.2,8.1,9.1-9.4) Ministry of Tourism - Data source: the survey of the incoming tourism in 2002 and 2004; (6.1-6.3,8.2-8.4) International Monetary Fund.

TAIWAN (PROVINCE OF CHINA)

(1.1) Including nationals residing abroad; (2.1-2.6) Excluding nationals residing abroad.
Sources: (1.1-5.4,8.1,9.1,9.3) Planning Division Tourism Bureau - Ministry of Transportation and Communication; (6.1-6.3,8.2-8.4) International Monetary Fund.

THAILAND

(1.2,3.1-3.4) Including arrivals of nationals residing abroad; (2.1-2.6,4.1-4.3) Excluding arrivals of nationals residing abroad; (3.3) Including rail; (5.4) Days; (9.3) In main tourist destinations only.
Sources: (1.1-5.4,7.1,8.1,9.1-9.4) Tourism Authority of Thailand (TAT); (6.1-6.3,8.2-8.4) International Monetary Fund.

THE FORMER YUGOSLAV REPUBLIC OF MACEDONIA

(1.2,2.2-2.4) Non-resident tourists staying in all types of accommodation establishments; (3.1-3.3) Arrivals of non-resident visitors at national borders; (9.4) Average length of stay in all accommodation establishments.
Sources: (1.1-5.4,7.1-7.4,9.1-9.4) State Statistical Office; (6.1-6.3,8.2-8.4) International Monetary Fund.

TOGO

(1.2) Non-resident tourists staying in hotels and similar establishments; (9.3) Rooms.
Sources: (1.2-5.2,7.1,7.2,9.1-9.4) "Ministère du Tourisme, de l'Artisanat et des Loisirs"; (6.1-6.3,8.2-8.4) International Monetary Fund.

TONGA

(1.2,2.2-2.4,4.1-4.3) Arrivals by air; (6.2) The expenditure figures used were the ones provided by the country to UNWTO, as this data series is more complete than that provided by the International Monetary Fund (IMF); (10.1-10.3) This section includes only the “travel” item because the “passenger transport” item was not included in the data provided by the International Monetary Fund for the preparation of this edition of the Compendium.
Sources: (1.1-4.3) Tonga Visitors Bureau; (6.2) National Reserve Bank of Tonga; (8.3) International Monetary Fund.

TRINIDAD AND TOBAGO

(1.2,2.1-2.5,4.1-4.3) Arrivals by air; (4.1) Including visit friends and relatives.
Sources: (1.1-5.4,9.1,9.3) (6.1-6.3,8.2-8.4/2005) Central Statistical Office - Ministry of Planning and Development; (6.1-6.3,8.2-8.4/2001-2004) International Monetary Fund.

TUNISIA

(1.2,2.1-3.4) Arrivals of non-resident tourists at national borders; excluding nationals residing abroad; (9.1,9.2) Classified and unclassified hotels, boarding houses and holiday villages; (9.3) Bed-places.
Sources: (1.1-5.4,7.1,8.1,9.1-9.4) "Ministère du Tourisme - Office National du Tourisme" and "Institut National de la Statistique"; (6.1-6.3,8.2-8.4) International Monetary Fund.

TURKEY

(1.1,3.1-3.4) Arrivals of non-resident visitors at national borders; (1.3) Sea arrivals (excluding one land border from 1989); (2.1-2.6) Arrivals of non-resident tourists at national borders; (3.4) Including cruise passengers; (4.1-4.3) Departures of non-resident visitors; (5.3) Survey in accommodation establishments licensed by Ministry of Tourism; (5.3,7.3) Including camping sites; (6.2) Including expenditure of the nationals residing abroad; (9.3,9.4) Classified hotels; excluding camping sites; (9.3) Bed-places; (10.1-10.3) This section includes only the "travel" item because the "passenger transport" item was not included in the data provided by the International Monetary Fund for the preparation of this edition of the Compendium.
Sources: (1.1-3.4,5.1-5.4,7.1-7.4,8.1,9.1-9.4) (6.2/2001/2002) Ministry of Culture and Tourism; (4.1-4.3) Departing Visitors Survey - Turkish Statistical Institute (TURKSTAT); (6.2/2003-2005) (8.3) International Monetary Fund.

TURKMENISTAN

Source: State Committee for Tourism and Sport.

TURKS AND CAICOS ISLANDS

(6.1) The expenditure figures are those provided by the country to UNWTO, which do not appear in the International Monetary Fund data used in the preparation of this edition of the Compendium.
Source: Turks and Caicos Tourist Board.

TUVALU

Source: Central Statistics Division - Ministry of Finance, Economic Planning and Industry.

UGANDA

Sources: (1.2-5.3,8.1,9.1,9.2) Ministry of Tourism, Trade an Industry and Uganda Bureau of Statistics; (6.1-6.3,8.2-8.4) International Monetary Fund.

UKRAINE

(2.1-2.6) Arrivals of non-resident tourists at national borders; (3.1-3.4/2001/2002) Arrivals of non-resident visitors at national borders; (3.1-3.4/2003) Arrivals of non-resident tourists at national borders; (4.1-4.3) Arrivals of non-resident visitors at national borders; (6.1,8.2) The country provides UNWTO with aggregate expenditure figures that differ significantly from the International Monetary Fund data used in the preparation of this edition of the Compendium. The country figures are as follows:

	6.1	8.2
2001:	3,957	512
2002:	4,523	497
2003:	5,341	492

Sources: (1.1-5.4,7.1,7.3,8.1,9.1-9.4) State Tourism Administration; (6.1-6.3,8.2-8.4) International Monetary Fund.

UNITED ARAB EMIRATES

(1.2) Arrivals in hotels only. Including domestic tourism and nationals residing abroad; (2.1-2.6) Arrivals in hotels only. Excluding domestic tourism and nationals residing abroad; (5.1) Nights in hotels only. Including domestic tourism and nationals residing abroad; (6.1,8.2) The expenditure figures are those provided by the country to UNWTO, which do not appear in the International Monetary Fund data used in the preparation of this edition of the Compendium; (9.1,9.2) Hotels only; (9.3) Rooms rented.
Source: Ministry of Economy and Planning - Planning Sector.

UNITED KINGDOM

(3.2) Tunnel; (5.4) Days; (6.1,8.2) The country provides UNWTO with aggregate expenditure figures that differ significantly from the International Monetary Fund data used in the preparation of this edition of the Compendium. The country figures are as follows:

	6.1	8.2
2001:	16,276	36,467
2002:	17,591	40,409
2003:	19,356	46,614
2004:	23,847	55,434

(9.3) Bed-places (England only).
Sources: (1.1-4.3,5.3,5.4,7.3,8.1,9.3) VisitBritain; (5.1,5.2,7.1,7.2,9.2) EUROSTAT (New Cronos); (6.1-6.3,8.2-8.4) International Monetary Fund.

UNITED REPUBLIC OF TANZANIA

Sources: (1.1-5.3,7.3,9.1-9.4) Tourism Division - Ministry of Natural Resources and Tourism and National Bureau of Statistics; (6.1-6.3,8.2-8.4) International Monetary Fund.

UNITED STATES

(1.2,2.2) Including Mexicans staying one or more nights in the US; (3.1-3.4) Preliminary estimates; (3.3) Including a very small percentage (0.2%) of travelers for whom transportation mode is not known; (4.1-4.3) Main trip purpose; (4.1-4.3,5.2) Overseas only; excluding Mexico (data are not available); (6.2,8.3) The country provides UNWTO with expenditure figures that differ significantly from the International Monetary Fund data used in the preparation of this edition of the Compendium. The country figures are as follows:

	6.2	8.3
2001:	71,893	60,200
2002:	66,605	58,715
2003:	64,348	57,444
2004:	74,547	65,750
2005:	81,680	69,175

(8.1) Including Americans staying one or more nights in Mexico.
Sources: (1.2-3.4,8.1) Office of Travel and Tourism Industries; (6.1-6.3,8.2-8.4) International Monetary Fund; (9.1,9.3) American Hotel & Lodging Association (AHLA).

UNITED STATES VIRGIN ISLANDS

(2.1-2.4) Non-resident tourists staying in hotels and similar establishments; (3.1) Visitor air arrivals; excluding resident arrivals and inter-island traffic but including same-day visitors; (3.4) Cruise passengers; (5.3) Including domestic tourist nights (about 40% of total); (6.1) The expenditure figures are those provided by the country to UNWTO, which do not appear in the International Monetary Fund data used in the preparation of this edition of the Compendium; (9.1,9.3) Hotel units and condominium or villa units; (9.3) Rooms.
2005: Provisional data.
Source: Bureau of Economic Research.

URUGUAY

(1.1,4.1-4.3) Including nationals residing abroad; (2.2-3.4) Excluding nationals residing abroad; (3.3) Including rail; (5.4) Days; (9.1,9.2/2005) Excluding unclassified hotels.
Sources: (1.1-5.4,8.1,9.1-9.4) "Ministerio de Turismo y Deporte"; (6.1-6.3,8.2-8.4) International Monetary Fund.

UZBEKISTAN

(6.1-6.3) The expenditure figures are those provided by the country to UNWTO, which do not appear in the International Monetary Fund data used in the preparation of this edition of the Compendium.
Source: National Company "Uzbektourism".

VANUATU

(5.4) Days; (9.3) Rooms.
Sources: (1.1-5.4,8.1,9.1-9.4) Vanuatu National Statistics Office; (6.1-6.3,8.2-8.4) International Monetary Fund.

VENEZUELA

(1.2,2.1-4.3) Arrivals of non-resident tourists at national borders; (9.1,9.2) Hotels and Paradores/Pousadas; (9.1,9.2/2005) Hotels only.
Sources: (1.1-5.4,8.1,9.1-9.4) "Ministerio de Turismo"; (6.1-6.3,8.2-8.4) International Monetary Fund.

VIET NAM

(1.1) Including nationals residing abroad; (1.4,3.4) Including cruise and sea passengers; (2.1-4.3) Arrivals of non-resident visitors at national borders; (6.1) The expenditure figures are those provided by the country to UNWTO, which do not appear in the International Monetary Fund data used in the preparation of this edition of the Compendium.
Source: Viet Nam National Administration of Tourism.

YEMEN

(1.2,2.1-2.6,5.2) Non-resident tourists staying in hotels and similar establishments; (10.1-10.3) This section includes only the "travel" item because the "passenger transport" item was not included in the data provided by the International Monetary Fund for the preparation of this edition of the Compendium.
Sources: (1.2-5.4,7.1,7.2,9.1,9.2) Ministry of Culture and Tourism - Yemen Tourism Promotion Board; (6.2,8.2-8.4) International Monetary Fund.

ZAMBIA

(5.4) Days; (6.1,8.3) The expenditure figures used were the ones provided by the country to UNWTO, as this data series is more complete than that provided by the International Monetary Fund (IMF) for the preparation of this Compendium; (9.3) Rooms.
Note 2001-2002: Provisional data.
Source: Ministry of Tourism, Environment and Natural Resources.

ZIMBABWE

(2.1-2.4,3.1-3.3,4.1,4.2) Arrivals of non-resident visitors at national borders; (3.1,3.3/2001-2003) Including persons in transit; (6.1) The expenditure figures are those provided by the country to UNWTO, which do not appear in the International Monetary Fund data used in the preparation of this edition of the Compendium; (9.1,9.2) Graded hotels only; (9.3) Bed-places.
Source: Zimbabwe Tourism Authority - ZTA.

AFRIQUE DU SUD

(1.1,3.1-3.4) À l'exclusion des nationaux résidant à l'étranger. Y compris les arrivées par motif de vacances, affaires, études, travail, transit, trafic frontalier et travailleurs contractuels; (1.2,2.1-2.6,4.1-4.3) Arrivées de touristes non résidents aux frontières nationales; à l'exclusion des arrivées par travail et les travailleurs contractuels; (9.3) Chambres (hôtels).
Sources: (1.1-4.3,8.1,9.1-9.3) "Statistics South Africa" et "South African Tourism"; (6.1-6.3,8.2-8.4) Fonds monétaire international.

ALBANIE

(1.1,2.2-4.3) Visiteurs et autres voyageurs; (1.2,5.2,7.2) Arrivées dans les hôtels seulement; (4.3) Transit.
Sources: (1.1-5.4,7.1-7.4,9.1-9.4) "Institute of Statistics - INSTAT"; (6.1-6.3,8.2-8.4) Fonds monétaire international.

ALGERIE

(1.1,3.1-3.4) Y compris les nationaux résidant à l'étranger:

2001	705.187
2002	736.915
2003	861.373
2004	865.157
2005	1.001.884

(2.1-2.6,4.1,4.2) À l'exclusion des nationaux résidant à l'étranger; (6.1,8.2) Les chiffres de dépense sont ceux que le pays a fournis à l'OMT mais ils ne figurent pas dans les données du Fonds monétaire international qui ont servi à la préparation de la présente édition du Compendium.
Sources: Ministère du Tourisme et Office National des Statistiques.

ALLEMAGNE

(1.2,2.1-2.6) Touristes non résidents dans tous types d'établissements d'hébergement; (9.3) Places-lit; (9.4) Tourisme récepteur, hôtels et établissements assimilés.
Sources: (1.2-5.3,7.1-7.3,8.1,9.1-9.4) "Statistiches Bundesamt"; (6.1-6.3,8.2-8.4) Fonds monétaire international.

ANDORRE

Source: "Ministerio de Turismo y Medio Ambiente".

ANGOLA

(5.1,5.2,7.1,7.2) Hôtels uniquement.
Sources: (1.2-7.3,9.1-9.4) (6.2/2001) "Ministério de Hotelaria e Turismo - Gabinete de Estudos, Planeamento e Estatística"; (6.2/2002-2005) (6.3,8.2-8.4) Fonds monétaire international.

ANGUILLA

(1.1,3.1-4.2) Arrivées de visiteurs non résidents aux frontières nationales; (1.2,2.2-2.3) Arrivées de touristes non résidents aux frontières nationales; à l'exclusion des nationaux résidant à l'étranger; (9.1) Hôtels, pensions de famille, appartements/ villas; (9.3) Chambres; janvier-mai; (10.2,10.3) Cette section comprend uniquement le poste « voyages » parce que le poste « transport de passagers » ne figure pas dans les données du Fonds monétaire international qui ont servi à la préparation de la présente édition du Compendium.
Sources: (1.1-5.4,9.1,9.3) "Statistical Department - Ministry of Finance"; (6.2,8.3) Fonds monétaire international.

ANTIGUA-ET-BARBUDA

(1.1) À l'exclusion des arrivées de passagers en yacht; (2.2,2.3,3.1) Arrivées par voie aérienne; á l'exclusion des nationaux résidant à l'étranger; (10.1-10.3) Cette section comprend uniquement le poste « voyages » parce que le poste « transport de passagers » ne figure pas dans les données du Fonds monétaire international qui ont servi à la préparation de la présente édition du Compendium.
Sources: (1.1-2.3) "Eastern Caribbean Central Bank"; (6.2,8.3) Fonds monétaire international.

ARABIE SAOUDITE

(6.1,8.2) Les chiffres de dépense sont ceux que le pays a fournis à l'OMT mais ils ne figurent pas dans les données du Fonds monétaire international qui ont servi à la préparation de la présente édition du Compendium.
Source: "The Supreme Commission for Tourism".

ARGENTINE

À partir de 2004, vu l'importance de l'« Enquête sur le tourisme international », des modifications ont été apportées aux estimations de la série du poste « Voyages » de la balance des paiements. C'est la raison pour laquelle les données ne sont pas rigoureusement comparables avec celles des années précédentes.
Note 2004-2005: Données provisoires.
Sources: (1.2-5.4,7.1,7.2,8.1,9.1-9.3) "Dirección de Estudios de Mercado y Estadística - Secretaría de Turismo de la Nación"; (6.1-6.3,8.2-8.4) Fonds monétaire international.

ARMENIE

Sources: (1.2-5.4,7.3,8.1,9.2-9.4) "Tourism Department - Ministry of Trade and Economic Development"; (6.1-6.3,8.2-8.4) Fonds monétaire international.

ARUBA

(1.2,2.2-4.3) Arrivées de touristes non résidents aux frontières nationales; (5.4) Touristes non résidents dans les hôtels et établissements assimilés; (9.3) Chambres.
Sources: (1.1-5.4,9.1-9.3) "Aruba Tourism Authority"; (6.1-6.3,8.2-8.4) Fonds monétaire international.

AUSTRALIE

(1.1) À l'exclusion des nationaux résidant à l'étranger et membres des équipages; (1.2,1.3) Arrivées par voie aérienne; (2.1-4.3) Arrivées de visiteurs non résidents aux frontières nationales; (5.1,7.1) Les estimations comprennent les hôtels, les complexes hôteliers et les motels; les pensions de famille et les chambres d'hôte, ainsi que les gîtes d'étape et les auberges; (5.3,7.3) Les estimations comprennent toutes les formes d'hébergement commercial; (9.1-9.3) Hôtels, motels, pensions de famille et appartements avec services hôteliers avec 15 chambres ou plus; (9.3) Chambres; (9.4) Tourisme récepteur dans l'hébergement commercial.
Sources: (1.1-5.4,7.1-7.4,8.1,9.1-9.4) "Australian Bureau of Statistics"; (6.1-6.3,8.2-8.4) Fonds monétaire international.

AUTRICHE

(1.2-2.6) Touristes non résidents dans tous types d'établissements d'hébergement; (5.1,5.2,7.1,7.2) Villages de vacances compris; (5.3,7.3) À l'exclusion de l'hébergement privé; (8.1/2003) Plus de 4 nuitées; (9.1) Uniquement hôtels; (9.2) Hôtels et villages de vacances; (9.3) Sur la base de la saison d'été; (9.4) Durée moyenne du séjour dans les hôtels et établissements assimilés; villages de vacances compris.
Sources: (1.2-5.4,7.1-7.4,8.1,9.1-9.4) "Department for Tourism and Historic Objects - Federal Ministry of Economics and Labour"; (6.1-6.3,8.2-8.4) Fonds monétaire international.

AZERBAIDJAN

Sources: (1.2-5.2,7.1,7.2,8.1,9.1,9.2) "Ministry of Culture and Tourism"; (6.1-6.3,8.2-8.4) Fonds monétaire international.

BAHAMAS

(1.2,2.1-2.6,4.1-4.3) Arrivées de touristes non résidents aux frontières nationales; (5.2) Arrivées dans les hôtels seulement; (9.1,9.2) Hôtels, appartements, bungalows et villas - Etablissements homologués uniquement; (9.3) Chambres.
Sources: (1.1-5.4,9.1-9.4) "Bahamas Ministry of Tourism"; (6.1-6.3,8.2-8.4) Fonds monétaire international.

BAHREIN

(1.1,2.1-4.3) Arrivées de visiteurs non résidents aux frontières nationales; à l'exclusion des nationaux résidant à l'étranger; (3.1) Arrivées à l'aéroport international de Bahreïn; (3.3) Arrivées à travers le "King Fahad Causeway"; (3.4) Arrivées au port Mina Salman; (5.1,9.1,9.2) Hôtels homologués seulement.
Sources: (1.1-5.4,9.1-9.3) "Tourism Affairs - Ministry of Information"; (6.1-6.3,8.2-8.4) Fonds monétaire international.

BANGLADESH

Sources: (1.2-5.4,8.1,9.1-9.3) "Bangladesh Parjatan Corporation"; (6.1-6.3,8.2-8.4) Fonds monétaire international.

BARBADE

(1.2,2.1-4.3) Arrivées de touristes non résidents aux frontières nationales; (9.1,9.2) Hôtels, hôtels-appartements, appartements et bungalows, pensions de famille; (9.3) Chambres.
Sources: (1.1-5.4,9.1-9.4) "Barbados Tourism Authority"; (6.1-6.3,8.2-8.4) Fonds monétaire international.

BELARUS

(1.2,2.2-2.4) Tourisme organisé.
Sources: (1.2,2.2-2.4,8.1) "Ministry of Statistics and Analysis"; (6.1-6.3,8.2-8.4) Fonds monétaire international.

BELGIQUE

(1.2,2.1-2.6,4.1-4.3) Touristes non résidents dans tous types d'établissements d'hébergement; (5.1,5.2,7.1,7.2) Hôtels uniquement; (9.1,9.2) Hôtels et villages de vacances.
Sources: (1.2-5.3,7.1-7.3,8.1,9.1,9.2) (6.1-6.3,8.2-8.4/2001) Institut National de Statistique; (6.1-6.3,8.2-8.4/2002-2005) Fonds monétaire international.

BELIZE

(1.3) Passagers en transit et passages aux frontières; (2.2-4.2) Arrivées de touristes non résidents aux frontières nationales; (10.1-10.3) Cette section comprend uniquement le poste « voyages » parce que le poste « transport de passagers » ne figure pas dans les données du Fonds monétaire international qui ont servi à la préparation de la présente édition du Compendium.
Sources: (1.1-5.4,7.3,9.1-9.4) "Belize Tourist Board"; (6.2,8.2-8.4) Fonds monétaire international.

BENIN

(1.2-4.3) Arrivées de touristes non résidents aux frontières nationales; (1.1-5.3/2003-2005) Estimations.
Sources: (1.1-5.4,7.1) Direction du tourisme et de l'hôtellerie - Ministère de la culture, de l'artisanat et du tourisme; (6.1-6.3,8.2-8.4) Fonds monétaire international.

BERMUDES

(1.1) À l'exclusion des nationaux résidant à l'étranger; (1.2,2.2-2.4,4.1-4.3) Arrivées par voie aérienne; (5.3) Y compris les nuitées dans les résidences particulières; (6.1,8.2) Les chiffres de dépense sont ceux que le pays a fournis à l'OMT mais ils ne figurent pas dans les données du Fonds monétaire international qui ont servi à la préparation de la présente édition du Compendium; (9.3) Chambres.
Source: "Bermuda Department of Tourism".

BHOUTAN

(6.1) Les chiffres de dépense sont ceux que le pays a fournis à l'OMT mais ils ne figurent pas dans les données du Fonds monétaire international qui ont servi à la préparation de la présente édition du Compendium.
Source: "Department of Tourism - Royal Government of Bhutan".

BOLIVIE

(1.2) Arrivées de touristes non résidents aux frontières nationales; (2.1-2.4) Touristes non résidents dans les hôtels et établissements assimilés; (3.4) Arrivées par voie lacustre; (4.1-4.3) Données tirées d'enquêtes; (5.1-5.4,7.1-7.4,9.1,9.2) Capitales de département seulement; (9.3) Places-lit (hôtels); (9.4) Jours, hôtels et établissements assimilés, tourisme récepteur.
Note 2003-2005: Données provisoires.
Sources: (1.2-5.4,7.1-7.4,8.1,9.1-9.4) "Viceministerio de Turismo - Ministerio de Producción y Microempresa"; (6.1-6.3,8.2-8.4) Fonds monétaire international.

BONAIRE

Sources: (1.1-5.4,9.1-9.4) "Tourism Corporation of Bonaire (TCB)"; (6.2,8.3) "Central Bank of the Netherlands Antilles".

BOSNIE-HERZEGOVINE

(1.2,2.2-2.4) Touristes non résidents dans tous types d'établissements d'hébergement; (2.5,2.6) Moins de 500 arrivées; (9.1,9.2) À l'exclusion de la République Srpska.
Sources: (1.2-5.3,7.3,9.1,9.2) "Agency for Statistics of Bosnia and Herzegovina"; (6.1-6.3,8.2-8.4) Fonds monétaire international.

BOTSWANA

Sources: (1.1-5.2,7.1,9.1-9.4) "Department of Tourism - Ministry of Environment, Wildlife and Tourism"; (6.1-6.3,8.2-8.4) Fonds monétaire international.

BRESIL

(3.4) Y compris les arrivées par voie fluviale; (5.4) Jours; (6.1) Pour la dépense, le pays fournit à l'OMT des niveaux d'agrégation qui diffèrent de façon significative des données du Fonds monétaire international utilisées pour la préparation de la présente édition du Compendium (données tirées de l'enquête par sondage réalisée par EMBRATUR). Les données du pays sont les suivantes :
2001: 3.701
2002: 3.120
2003: 3.386
2004: 3.676
2005: 4.849
Note 2005: Estimations.
Sources: (1.2-5.4,8.1) "Instituto Brasileiro de Turismo (EMBRATUR)"; (6.1-6.3,8.2-8.4) Fonds monétaire international.

BRUNEI DARUSSALAM

Source: "Tourism Development Division - Ministry of Industry and Primary Resources".

BULGARIE

(1.1,1.2) À l'exclusion d'enfants sans passeports personnels; (1.3) Visiteurs en transit; (3.4) Mer et voies d'eau intérieures; (5.1,5.3,5.4,7.1,7.3,9.2-9.4) Couvre principalement l'ancien hébergement du secteur public et celui propriété de l'Etat. Une partie considérable du secteur privé (plus de 70 pour cent en 1998) n'est pas inclus dans ces données; (9.2) Hôtels uniquement; (9.3) Places-lit dans les hôtels.
Sources: (1.1-4.3,5.1,5.3,5.4,7.1,7.3,8.1,9.2-9.4) ""Tourism Policy" Directorate - State Agency for Tourism"; (5.2,7.2) "EUROSTAT (New Cronos)"; (6.1-6.3,8.2-8.4) Fonds monétaire international.

BURKINA FASO

(1.2,2.1-2.6,5.2) Touristes non résidents dans les hôtels et établissements assimilés; (4.1-4.3) Y compris le tourisme interne; (6.1) Pour la dépense, le pays fournit à l'OMT des niveaux d'agrégation qui diffèrent de façon significative des données du Fonds monétaire international utilisées pour la préparation de la présente édition du Compendium. Les données du pays sont les suivantes :
2001: 35
2002: 39
2003: 48
2004: 57
2005: 53
(9.3) Chambres.
Sources: (1.2-5.4,7.1,7.2,9.3) Service de l'analyse statistique et de la Coopération touristique - Ministère de la Culture, des Arts et du Tourisme; (6.1-6.3,8.2-8.4) Fonds monétaire international.

BURUNDI

(1.2-4.3) Arrivées de touristes non résidents aux frontières nationales; y compris les nationaux résidant à l'étranger; (3.4) Arrivées par voie lacustre.
Sources: (1.2-5.1,8.1,9.1,9.2) Office National du Tourisme; (6.1-6.3,8.2-8.4) Fonds monétaire international.

CAMBODGE

(1.2) Arrivées de touristes internationaux par tous moyens de transport; (2.2-2.5/2001) Arrivées par voie aérienne; (2.2-2.5,3.1-3.4/2004/2005) À l'exclusion des arrivées dans la région "Phreah Vihear": 2004: 67.843; 2005: 88.615; (3.3/2001/2002) Arrivées par terre ou par navire; (3.4) Arrivées par navire; (4.1-4.3/2001/2002) Arrivées par voie aérienne; (4.1/2001/2002) Y compris les arrivées à l'aéroport de Siem Reap en vols directs: 2001: 133.688; 2002: 202.791; (4.1-4.3/2005) À l'exclusion des arrivées dans la région "Phreah Vihear": 88.615; (5.4) Jours.
Sources: (1.2-5.4,8.1,9.1-9.3) "Ministry of Tourism"; (6.1-6.3,8.2-8.4) Fonds monétaire international.

CAMEROUN

(1.2,2.1-2.6,5.2) Touristes non résidents dans les hôtels et établissements assimilés.
Sources: (1.2-5.2,7.1,7.2,9.1,9.2) Ministère du Tourisme; (6.1-6.3,8.2-8.4) Fonds monétaire international.

CANADA

(1.1,1.3) Données élaborées à partir des inventaires douaniers et ajustées en fonction des résultats d'enquêtes; (1.2,2.1-4.3) Arrivées de touristes non résidents aux frontières nationales; (4.2) Y compris congrès; (8.1) Voyages- personnes (une/plusieurs nuits); Note 2005: Données provisoires.
Note: En 2002, il a été adopté différents types de changements méthodologiques qui ont eu des effets sur les estimations des dépenses et des caractéristiques des touristes internationaux ayant visité le Canada en 2001. Pour 2001, Statistique Canada

conseille par conséquent de ne pas comparer les estimations ne reposant pas sur des comptages aux données des années précédentes (c'est une des raisons pour lesquelles les données de durée moyenne du séjour ne sont pas fournies).
Sources: (1.1-4.3,5.3,7.1,7.3,8.1) "Canadian Tourism Commission"; (6.1-6.3,8.2-8.4) Fonds monétaire international.

CAP-VERT

(1.2,2.1-2.3) Touristes non résidents dans les hôtels et établissements assimilés.
Sources: (1.2,2.1-2.3,5.1,5.2,7.1,7.2,9.1-9.4) "Instituto Nacional de Estatística"; (6.1-6.3,8.2-8.4) Fonds monétaire international.

CHILI

(5.1,5.2,7.1,7.2) Les chiffres de 2005 ne sont pas comparables à ceux des années précédentes en raison de la mise à jour du recensement national des établissements d'hébergement touristique.
Sources: (1.2-5.4,7.1,7.2,8.1,9.1-9.4) "Servicio Nacional de Turismo - SERNATUR"; (6.1-6.3,8.2-8.4) Fonds monétaire international.

CHINE

(1.1,2.1-2.6,3.1-3.4) Y compris les arrivées de personnes d'origine ethnique chinoise en provenance de "Hong-Kong, Chine", "Macao, Chine", "Taïwan (Province de Chine)" et chinois de l'étranger, la plupart visiteurs de la journée (excursionnistes) en provenance de "Hong-Kong, Chine" et de "Macao, Chine"; (4.1-4.3) À l'exclusion des arrivées de personnes d'origine chinoise de souche en provenance de "Hong-Kong, Chine", "Macao, Chine", "Taïwan (Province de Chine)" et chinois de l'étranger; (7.1,9.1,9.2) Ne concernent que les hôtels classés par étoiles; (8.1) Y compris les membres des équipages et autres membres des forces armées; (9.3) Chambres; (9.4) Tourisme récepteur uniquement.
Sources: (1.1-5.4,7.1,8.1,9.1-9.4) "National Tourism Administration"; (6.1-6.3,8.2-8.4) Fonds monétaire international.

CHYPRE

(1.2,2.1-2.6) Arrivées de touristes non résidents aux frontières nationales; (1.3) Y compris les passagers en croisière/transit; (3.4) Y compris les passagers en croisière; (5.4) Ces données extraites de l'enquête sur les dépenses des touristes (départs), concernent les séjours dans tous les types d'hébergement; (9.3) Places-lit; (9.4) À partir de 2000, la durée moyenne du séjour est calculée sur la base des nuitées et des arrivées de clients dans les hôtels et établissements assimilés.
Sources: (1.1-5.4,7.1-7.4,8.1,9.1-9.4) "Cyprus Tourism Organization"; (6.1-6.3,8.2-8.4) Fonds monétaire international.

COLOMBIE

(1.1,2.1-2.6,3.1-3.4,4.1-4.3) Arrivées de visiteurs non résidents aux frontières nationales. À l'exclusion des passagers en croisière; (9.3) Chambres.
Note 2005: Données provisoires.
Sources: (1.1-4.3,8.1) "Dirección de Extranjería - Departamento Administrativo de Seguridad (DAS)"; (6.1-6.3,8.2-8.4) Fonds monétaire international; (9.1-9.3) "Dirección de Turismo - Ministerio de Comercio, Industria y Turismo, Asociación Hotelera de Colombia (COTELCO)".

COMORES

(1.2,2.1,2.3,4.1-4.3) Arrivées par voie aérienne; (6.1) Les chiffres de dépense sont ceux que le pays a fournis à l'OMT mais ils ne figurent pas dans les données du Fonds monétaire international qui ont servi à la préparation de la présente édition du Compendium.
Source: Direction Nationale de la Promotion du Tourisme et de l'Hôtellerie - Ministère du Transport, Tourisme, Postes et Télécommunications.

CONGO

(1.2-2.3,5.2) Touristes non résidents dans les hôtels et établissements assimilés; (9.3) Chambres.
Sources: (1.2-5.2,7.1,7.2,9.1-9.4) Direction Générale du Tourisme et de l'Hôtellerie - Ministère de la Culture, des Arts et du Tourisme; (6.1-6.3,8.2-8.4) Fonds monétaire international.

COREE, REPUBLIQUE DE

(1.1) Y compris les nationaux résidant à l'étranger et membres des équipages; (2.1-2.6) À l'exclusion des nationaux résidant à l'étranger; (3.1,3.4) À l'exclusion des nationaux résidant à l'étranger et membres des équipages; (8.2) Pour la dépense, le pays fournit à l'OMT des niveaux d'agrégation qui diffèrent de façon significative des données du Fonds monétaire international utilisées pour la préparation de la présente édition du Compendium (à l'exclusion des dépenses des étudiants qui font des études à l'étranger). Les données du pays sont les suivantes :
2001: 6.547
2002: 9.038
2003: 8.248
2004: 9.856
(9.1) Hôtels seulement; (9.3) Chambres.

Sources: (1.1-5.4,8.1,9.1,9.3) "Ministry of Culture and Tourism"; (6.1-6.3,8.2-8.4) Fonds monétaire international.

COSTA RICA

(4.1) Voyages d'agrément et visites aux parents; (5.4) Dans la zone centrale du pays; (9.3) Etablissements de catégorie "5 étoiles" dans la zone métropolitaine de San José (enquête).
Sources: (1.1-5.4,8.1,9.1,9.3) "Instituto Costarricense de Turismo"; (6.1-6.3,8.2-8.4) Fonds monétaire international.

CROATIE

(1.2,2.2-2.4) Touristes non résidents dans tous types d'établissements d'hébergement; y compris les arrivées dans des ports à tourisme nautique; (3.1-3.4) Arrivées de visiteurs non résidents aux frontières nationales; (3.4/2004) Depuis 2004, une nouvelle méthodologie et une nouvelle couverture ont été appliquées. L'information n'est donc pas comparable à celle des années précédentes; (5.3,7.3) Y compris les nuitées dans des ports à tourisme nautique; (9.4) Tourisme intérieur (interne et récepteur) dans l'ensemble des moyens d'hébergement (y compris les ports à tourisme nautique).
Sources: (1.1-5.4,7.1-7.4,9.1-9.4) "Central Bureau of Statistics"; (6.1-6.3,8.2-8.4) Fonds monétaire international.

CUBA

(1.1,2.1-2.6) Arrivées de visiteurs non résidents aux frontières nationales; (1.2,4.1-4.3) Arrivées par voie aérienne; (1.3) Y compris les passagers en croisière; (5.1,7.1,9.1,9.2) Hôtels, motels et apart-hôtels; (5.3,7.3) Hôtels, motels, apart-hôtels, terrains de camping/caravaning et autres; (6.1) Les chiffres de dépense sont ceux que le pays a fournis à l'OMT mais ils ne figurent pas dans les données du Fonds monétaire international qui ont servi à la préparation de la présente édition du Compendium; (8.1) Comprend seulement circuits contrôlés par l'Instituto de Turismo; (9.3) Chambres.
Source: "Oficina Nacional de Estadísticas".

CURAÇAO

(1.2,1.3,2.2,2.3,3.1,4.1-4.3) Arrivées par voie aérienne; (3.4) Arrivées de passagers en croisière; (4.1-4.3) Les différences entre les totaux globaux sont dues au caractère incomplet des cartes d'embarquement et de débarquement remplies par les visiteurs; (6.1) Les chiffres de dépense sont ceux que le pays a fournis à l'OMT mais ils ne figurent pas dans les données du Fonds monétaire international qui ont servi à la préparation de la présente édition du Compendium; (9.1) Hôtels, pensions de famille, appartements; (9.3) Chambres.
Source: "Curaçao Tourist Board".

DANEMARK

(1.2-2.2-2.4,5.1-5.3,7.1-7.3) Nouvelle couverture depuis 2000; (1.2,2.2-2.4) Touristes non résidents dans tous types d'établissements d'hébergement; (1.2-5.3,7.1-7.3,8.1) Nouvelle méthodologie à partir de 2004; (5.2,7.2) Hôtels uniquement; (9.1-9.3) Hôtels et logements pour vacances avec 40 lits et plus seulement; (9.3) Places-lit; (10.1-10.3) Cette section comprend uniquement le poste « voyages » parce que le poste « transport de passagers » ne figure pas dans les données du Fonds monétaire international qui ont servi à la préparation de la présente édition du Compendium.
Sources: (1.2-5.4,7.1-7.4,8.1,9.1-9.3) "Statistics Denmark"; (6.2,8.3) Fonds monétaire international.

DJIBOUTI

(1.2-2.3,5.2) Touristes non résidents dans les hôtels; (9.3) Chambres.
Sources: (1.2,5.1,5.2,9.1-9.3) Office national du tourisme; (6.2,8.3) Banque centrale.

DOMINIQUE

(1.2,2.2,2.3,4.1-4.3) Arrivées de touristes non résidents aux frontières nationales; (3.1,3.4) Arrivées de visiteurs non résidents aux frontières nationales; à l'exclusion des passagers en croisière; (5.4) Jours; (10.1-10.3) Cette section comprend uniquement le poste « voyages » parce que le poste « transport de passagers » ne figure pas dans les données du Fonds monétaire international qui ont servi à la préparation de la présente édition du Compendium.
Sources: (1.1-5.4,9.1) "Central Statistical Office - Ministry of Finance"; (6.2,8.3) Fonds monétaire international.

EGYPTE

(1.1,2.1-3.4) Arrivées de visiteurs non résidents aux frontières nationales; (4.1-4.3) Arrivées de touristes non résidents aux frontières nationales; (7.1) Hôtels seulement dans les principales régions: le Caire, Giza, le Sud du Sinaï, la Mer Rouge, Luxor, Aswan, Alexandrie; (8.1) Voyages à des fins de tourisme et de non-tourisme (plus de 50 % des départs ont lieu pour des motifs de travail); (9.3) Chambres.
Sources: (1.1-5.4,7.1-7.4,8.1,9.1-9.4) "Ministry of Tourism"; (6.1-6.3,8.2-8.4) Fonds monétaire international.

EL SALVADOR

(1.2,2.1-4.3) Arrivées de touristes non résidents aux frontières nationales; (6.1) Pour la dépense, le pays fournit à l'OMT des niveaux d'agrégation qui diffèrent de façon significative des données du Fonds monétaire international utilisées pour la préparation de la présente édition du Compendium. Les données du pays sont les suivantes (millions $E.U.) :
2001: 235
2002: 342
2003: 373
2004: 425
2005: 644
Cette dépense touristique est obtenue à partir d'études communes menées avec le "Banco Central de Reserva" d'El Salvador et la "Corporación Salvadoreña de Turismo" pour préciser le profil de base du touriste international qui visite ce pays.
(9.3) Places-lit.
Sources: (1.1-5.4,8.1,9.1-9.4) "Corporación Salvadoreña de Turismo (CORSATUR) - Ministerio de Turismo"; (6.1-6.3,8.2-8.4) Fonds monétaire international.

EMIRATS ARABES UNIS

(1.2) Arrivées dans les hôtels seulement. Y compris le tourisme interne et les nationaux résidant à l'étranger; (2.1-2.6) Arrivées dans les hôtels seulement. À l'exclusion du tourisme interne et des nationaux résidant à l'étranger; (5.1) Nuitées dans les hôtels seulement. Y compris le tourisme interne et les nationaux résidant à l'étranger; (6.1,8.2) Les chiffres de dépense sont ceux que le pays a fournis à l'OMT mais ils ne figurent pas dans les données du Fonds monétaire international qui ont servi à la préparation de la présente édition du Compendium; (9.1,9.2) Hôtels seulement; (9.3) Chambres louées.
Source: "Ministry of Economy and Planning - Planning Sector".

EQUATEUR

(1.1) À l'exclusion des nationaux résidant à l'étranger; (1.1-3.4,8.1/2005) Données provisoires.
Sources: (1.1-3.4,8.1,9.1,9.2) "Ministerio de Turismo"; (6.1-6.3,8.2-8.4) Fonds monétaire international.

ERYTHREE

(1.1) Y compris les nationaux résidant à l'étranger; (2.1-2.6) À l'exclusion des nationaux résidant à l'étranger; (5.1,7.1) Uniquement hôtels et établissements assimilés dans les trois villes principales: Asmara, Karen et Massawa; (6.1) Les données de dépense sont celles que le pays a fournies à l'OMT car il s'agit d'une série plus complète que celle obtenue du Fonds monétaire international (FMI) pour la préparation de la présente édition du Compendium; (9.1,9.2/2001-2004) Uniquement dans les villes principales d'Erythrée; (9.1,9.2/2005) Tous les hôtels et établissements assimilés en Erythrée; (10.1-10.3) Cette section n'a pas pu être remplie parce que les postes « voyages » et « transport de passagers » ne figurent pas dans les données du Fonds monétaire international qui ont servi à la préparation de la présente édition du Compendium.
Source: "Ministry of Tourism".

ESPAGNE

(1.1) Arrivées de visiteurs non résidents aux frontières nationales; y compris les nationaux résidant à l'étranger; (2.2-4.3) Arrivées de touristes non résidents aux frontières nationales; y compris les nationaux résidant à l'étranger; (2.4) Japon seulement; (5.1,7.1) Nuitées dans les hôtels et les "hostales" (établissements d'hébergement offrant des services limités); (5.3,7.3) Nuitées dans les hôtels, "hostales", terrains de camping, appartements touristiques et logements ruraux; (5.4,7.4,9.1-9.4) Hôtels et "hostales" seulement; (8.1) Nouvelle méthodoligie à partir de 2005. L'information n'est donc pas comparable à celle des années précédentes; (9.3) Places-lit.
Sources: (1.1-4.3,8.1) "Instituto de Estudios Turísticos"; (5.1-5.4,7.1-7.4,9.1-9.4) "Instituto Nacional de Estadística"; (6.1-6.3,8.2-8.4) Fonds monétaire international.

ESTONIE

(1.1,3.1-4.3) Arrivées de visiteurs non résidents aux frontières nationales; (1.1-1.3,3.1-4.3,8.1/2004) À partir de 2004, les statistiques de frontière ne sont plus collectées; (1.2/2004/2005) Calculé sur la base des statistiques d'hébergement et de la "Foreign Visitor Survey" menée par la "Statistical Office of Estonia"; (2.1-2.4) Touristes non résidents dans tous types d'établissements d'hébergement; (4.3) Achats, transit, visites à des amis; (9.1-9.4) Y compris les données des stations thermales et climatiques assurant l'hébergement.
Sources: (1.1-5.4,7.3,7.4,8.1,9.1-9.4) "Estonian Tourist Board / Enterprise Estonia"; (6.1-6.3,8.2-8.4) Fonds monétaire international; (7.1,7.2) "EUROSTAT (New Cronos)".

ETATS-UNIS

(1.2,2.2) Y compris les Mexicains passant une nuit ou plus aux Etats-Unis; (3.1-3.4) Estimations préliminaires; (3.3) Y compris un très petit pourcentage (0.2%) de voyageurs dont on ne connaît pas le mode de transport utilisé; (4.1-4.3) Motif principal de voyage; (4.1-4.3,5.2) Outre-mer uniquement; à l'exclusion du Mexique (les données ne sont pas disponibles); (6.2,8.3) Pour la dépense, le pays fournit à l'OMT des données qui diffèrent de façon significative des données du Fonds monétaire international utilisées pour la préparation de la présente édition du Compendium. Les données du pays sont les suivantes :

	6.2	8.3
2001:	71.893	60.200
2002:	66.605	58.715
2003:	64.348	57.444
2004:	74.547	65.750
2005:	81.680	69.175

(8.1) Y compris les Américains passant une nuit ou plus au Mexique.
Sources: (1.2-3.4,8.1) "Office of Travel and Tourism Industries"; (6.1-6.3,8.2-8.4) Fonds monétaire international; (9.1,9.3) "American Hotel & Lodging Association (AHLA)".

ETHIOPIE

(1.2) Arrivées à travers tous les ports d'entrée; y compris les nationaux résidant à l'étranger; (2.1-2.6,3.1-3.3) Arrivées à travers tous les ports d'entrée; (4.1-4.3/2001) Arrivées à l'aéroport de Bole seulement; (4.1-4.3/2002-2005) Arrivées à travers tous les ports d'entrée; (9.1,9.2/2001) Y compris les hôtels privés et de l'état; (9.1,9.2/2002/2003/2005) À l'exclusion des hôtels non-homologués; (9.3) Places-lit; (9.4) Années fiscales éthiopiennes.
Sources: (1.2-5.4,9.1-9.4) "Ethiopian Tourism Commission"; (6.1-6.3,8.2-8.4) Fonds monétaire international.

EX-REPUBLIQUE YOUGOSLAVE DE MACEDOINE

(1.2,2.2-2.4) Touristes non résidents dans tous types d'établissements d'hébergement; (3.1-3.3) Arrivées de visiteurs non résidents aux frontières nationales; (9.4) Durée moyenne du séjour dans tous les établissements d'hébergement.
Sources: (1.1-5.4,7.1-7.4,9.1-9.4) "State Statistical Office"; (6.1-6.3,8.2-8.4) Fonds monétaire international.

FEDERATION DE RUSSIE

(1.1,2.1-4.3) Arrivées de visiteurs non résidents aux frontières nationales; (9.1,9.2) Hébergement dans les hôtels et autres établissements touristiques.
Sources: (1.1-5.4,7.1-7.4,8.1,9.1-9.4) "Russian Federal Agency for Tourism"; (6.1-6.3,8.2-8.4) Fonds monétaire international.

FIDJI

(1.2,2.2-4.3) Arrivées de touristes non résidents aux frontières nationales; à l'exclusion des nationaux résidant à l'étranger; (5.4) Jours; (6.1-6.3,8.2-8.4) Les chiffres de dépense sont ceux que le pays a fournis à l'OMT mais ils ne figurent pas dans les données du Fonds monétaire international qui ont servi à la préparation de la présente édition du Compendium; (9.3) Chambres.
Source: "Fiji Islands Bureau of Statistics".

FINLANDE

(1.1,2.1-4.3) Arrivées de visiteurs non résidents aux frontières nationales. Enquête aux frontières; (1.2) Arrivées de touristes non résidents aux frontières nationales; (5.1-5.3,7.1-7.3) Dû à un changement dans la méthodologie, l'information n'est pas comparable à celle des années précédentes; (8.1) Voyages à l'étranger, croisières avec nuitées à bord comprises.
Sources: (1.1-5.4,7.1-7.4,8.1,9.1-9.4) "Tourism Statistics - Statistics Finland"; (6.1-6.3,8.2-8.4) Fonds monétaire international.

FRANCE

(1.2,2.1-2.6,5.3) Estimation à partir de l'enquête aux frontières 1996. Données révisées depuis 1996; (2.4) Y compris Asie du Sud; (3.1-4.3) Estimation; (5.1,5.2,7.1,7.2,9.1-9.3) Hôtels uniquement; (5.3,7.3) Tous modes d'hébergement; (5.4) Durée moyenne du séjour récepteur; (7.3) Série révisée et rétropolée; (9.3) Taux net des chambres; (10.1-10.3) Cette section comprend uniquement le poste « voyages » parce que le poste « transport de passagers » ne figure pas dans les données du Fonds monétaire international qui ont servi à la préparation de la présente édition du Compendium.
2005: Données provisoires.
Sources: (1.2-5.4,7.1-7.4,8.1,9.1-9.4) Bureau des études, des statistiques et des comptes économiques - Direction du Tourisme; (6.2,8.3) Fonds monétaire international.

GABON

(1.2,2.1-2.6,3.1) Arrivées de touristes non résidents à l'aéroport de Libreville.
Sources: (1.1-5.1,8.1,9.1,9.3) Centre Gabonais de Promotion Touristique (GABONTOUR); (6.1-6.3,8.2-8.4) Fonds monétaire international.

GAMBIE

(1.2,2.1-2.3,3.1,4.1) Arrivées en vols à la demande seulement; (1.1-4.1/2005) Données provisoires.
Sources: (1.1-4.1,8.1,9.1,9.4) "Gambia Tourism Authority"; (6.1-6.3,8.2-8.4) Fonds monétaire international.

GEORGIE

(4.1-4.3) Arrivées dans les hôtels seulement.
Sources: (1.2-4.3,5.3,8.1,9.1-9.3) "Department of Tourism and Resorts - Ministry of Economic Development"; (5.2,7.2) "State Department for Statistics - Ministry of Economic Development"; (6.1-6.3,8.2-8.4) Fonds monétaire international.

GHANA

(1.2) Y compris les nationaux résidant à l'étranger; (2.1-2.6) À l'exclusion des nationaux résidant à l'étranger.
Sources: (1.2-4.3,9.1-9.3) "Ghana Tourist Board" et "Ministry of Tourism and Modernisation of the Capital City"; (6.1-6.3,8.2-8.4) Fonds monétaire international.

GRECE

(1.1,3.1-3.4) Arrivées de visiteurs non résidents aux frontières nationales; (1.2,2.1-2.6) Arrivées de touristes non résidents aux frontières nationales; information tirée de données administratives; (3.4) Y compris les passagers en croisière.
Sources: (1.1-5.4,7.1-7.4,9.3) "National Statistical Service"; (6.1-6.3,8.2-8.4) Fonds monétaire international; (9.1,9.2) "Hellenic Chamber of Hotels".

GRENADE

(1.2,2.2-4.3) Arrivées de touristes non résidents aux frontières nationales; (9.1,9.2) Hôtels, bungalows/ appartements et pensions de famille; (9.3) Chambres; (10.1-10.3) Cette section comprend uniquement le poste « voyages » parce que le poste « transport de passagers » ne figure pas dans les données du Fonds monétaire international qui ont servi à la préparation de la présente édition du Compendium.
Sources: (1.1-5.4,9.1-9.4) "Grenada Board of Tourism"; (6.2,8.3) Fonds monétaire international.

GUADELOUPE

(1.2) Arrivées par voie aérienne; À l'exclusion des îles du nord (Saint Martin et Saint Barthélemy); (1.2/2001) Touristes non résidents dans tous types d'établissements d'hébergement; (1.2/2003/2004) Touristes non résidents dans les hôtels seulement; (1.2,2.3,3.1/2005) Données tirées d'une enquête réalisée à l'aéroport de Guadeloupe; (5.2) Hôtels seulement; (9.1) Hôtels; (9.3) Chambres.
Source: Comité du Tourisme des Îles de la Guadeloupe.

GUAM

(1.2) Arrivées par voies aérienne et maritime; (2.2-2.4) Arrivées par voie aérienne uniquement; (4.1-4.3) Uniquement arrivées de civils par voie aérienne; (9.1) Chambres disponibles.
Source: "Guam Visitors Bureau".

GUATEMALA

(8.2) Pour la dépense, le pays fournit à l'OMT des niveaux d'agrégation qui diffèrent de façon significative des données du Fonds monétaire international. Les données du pays sont les suivantes :
2001: 407
2002: 517
2003: 601
2004: 735
2005: 754
Sources: (1.2-3.4,8.1,9.1-9.3) "Instituto Guatemalteco de Turismo - INGUAT"; (6.1-6.3,8.2-8.4) Fonds monétaire international.

GUINEE

(1.2,2.1-2.6,4.1-4.3/2003/2005) Arrivées par voie aérienne à l'aéroport de Conakry; (5.2) Hôtels seulement; (6.2) Les données de dépense sont celles que le pays a fournies à l'OMT car il s'agit d'une série plus complète que celle obtenue du Fonds monétaire international (FMI) pour la préparation de la présente édition du Compendium.
Note 2005: Données provisoires.
Sources: (1.2-5.4,6.2,9.1-9.4) Division Observatoire du Tourisme - Ministère du Tourisme, de l'Hôtellerie et de l'Artisanat; (6.3,8.2-8.4) Fonds monétaire international.

GUINEE-BISSAU

(1.2,2.1-2.6,4.1-4.3) Arrivées par voie aérienne; (2.1-2.6,4.1-4.3/2005) Arrivées à l'aéroport "Osvaldo Vieira".
Sources: (1.2-4.3) "Ministério do Turismo e do Ordenamento do Território"; (6.1-6.3,8.2-8.4) Fonds monétaire international.

GUYANE

(1.2,2.2,2.3,3.1/2002-2005) Arrivées à l'aéroport de Timehri seulement.

Sources: (1.2-3.1) "Guyana Tourism Authority"; (6.1-6.3,8.2-8.4) Fonds monétaire international.

GUYANE FRANÇAISE

(1.2,6.1/2005) Enquête 2005 au départ de l'aéroport de Cayenne-Rochambeau.
Sources: Comité du Tourisme de la Guyane et INSEE Guyane.

HAITI

(10.1-10.3) Cette section comprend uniquement le poste « voyages » parce que le poste « transport de passagers » ne figure pas dans les données du Fonds monétaire international qui ont servi à la préparation de la présente édition du Compendium.
Sources: (1.1-3.4) Ministère du Tourisme; (6.2,8.2-8.4) Fonds monétaire international.

HONDURAS

(1.2,2.1-4.3) Arrivées de touristes non résidents aux frontières nationales.
Sources: (1.1-5.4,8.1,9.1-9.4) "Instituto Hondureño de Turismo" (6.1-6.3,8.2-8.4) Fonds monétaire international.

HONG-KONG, CHINE

(6.1-6.3) Les données de dépense sont celles que le pays a fournies à l'OMT car il s'agit d'une série plus complète que celle obtenue du Fonds monétaire international (FMI) pour la préparation de la présente édition du Compendium. (Source: "HKTB Visitors Survey"); (8.1) À l'exclusion des résidents de Hong-Kong voyageant à Macao et Chine; (9.1) Hôtels (tarifs élevés/moyens) et auberges/ pensions de famille; (9.3) Chambres.
Sources: (1.1-8.1,9.1,9.3) "Hong Kong Tourism Board"; (8.3) "Census and Statistics Department".

HUNGARY

(1.1/2001-2003) (3.1-3.4) Départs de visiteurs non résidents; (1.1-1.4,4.1-4.3/2004) Nouvelle série; (2.1-2.4) Touristes non résidents dans tous types d'établissements d'hébergement; (3.4) Voie fluviale; (9.3) Chambres, juillet-juin.
Sources: (1.1-5.4,7.1-7.4,8.1,9.1-9.4) "Hungarian Central statistical Office"; (6.1-6.3,8.2-8.4) Fonds monétaire international.

ILES CAIMANES

(1.2,2.2-2.4,4.1-4.3) Arrivées par voie aérienne; (5.4,9.4) Jours; (6.1) Les chiffres de dépense sont ceux que le pays a fournis à l'OMT mais ils ne figurent pas dans les données du Fonds monétaire international qui ont servi à la préparation de la présente édition du Compendium. Y compris les dépenses des passagers en croisière; (9.1,9.2) Hôtels et appartements; (9.3) Hôtels (chambres).
Source: "Cayman Islands Department of Tourism".

ILES COOK

(1.2,2.2-2.4,4.1-4.3) Arrivées par voies aérienne et maritime; (6.1) Les chiffres de dépense sont ceux que le pays a fournis à l'OMT mais ils ne figurent pas dans les données du Fonds monétaire international qui ont servi à la préparation de la présente édition du Compendium; (9.3) Chambres.
Source: "Cook Islands Tourism Corporation" et "Cook Islands Statistics Office".

ILES MARIANNES SEPTENTRIONALES

(1.1,2.2-2.4) Arrivées de visiteurs non résidents aux frontières nationales; (1.2) Arrivées par voie aérienne; (2.2) Y compris Guam; (9.1) Couvre 68 pour cent du nombre total de chambres recensées.
Source: "Marianas Visitors Authority".

ILES MARSHALL

(1.2,2.2-2.4,4.1-4.3/2001-2003) Arrivées par voie aérienne; (1.2,2.2-2.4,4.1-4.3/2004/2005) Arrivées par voies aérienne et maritime; (6.1) Les chiffres de dépense sont ceux que le pays a fournis à l'OMT mais ils ne figurent pas dans les données du Fonds monétaire international qui ont servi à la préparation de la présente édition du Compendium.
Source: "Marshall Islands Visitors Authority".

ILES SALOMON

(1.2,2.2-2.4/2005) À l'exclusion du 1er trimestre.
Sources: (1.2,2.2-2.4) "Solomon Islands National Statistics Office"; (6.2,8.3) "Central Bank of Solomon Islands".

ILES TURQUES ET CAIQUES

(6.1) Les chiffres de dépense sont ceux que le pays a fournis à l'OMT mais ils ne figurent pas dans les données du Fonds monétaire international qui ont servi à la préparation de la présente édition du Compendium.
Source: "Turks and Caicos Tourist Board".

ILES VIERGES AMERICAINES

(2.1-2.4) Touristes non résidents dans les hôtels et établissements assimilés; (3.1) Arrivées de visiteurs par voie aérienne; à l'exclusion des arrivées de résidents et le trafic entre les îles, mais compris les visiteurs de la journée (excursionnistes); (3.4) Passagers en croisière; (5.3) Y compris celles de touristes nationaux (environ 40 pour cent de l'ensemble); (6.1) Les chiffres de dépense sont ceux que le pays a fournis à l'OMT mais ils ne figurent pas dans les données du Fonds monétaire international qui ont servi à la préparation de la présente édition du Compendium; (9.1,9.3) Hôtels et condominiums ou villas; (9.3) Chambres.
2005: Données provisoires.
Source: "Bureau of Economic Research".

ILES VIERGES BRITANNIQUES

(1.1-9.4/2004/2005) Estimations; (6.1) Les chiffres de dépense sont ceux que le pays a fournis à l'OMT mais ils ne figurent pas dans les données du Fonds monétaire international qui ont servi à la préparation de la présente édition du Compendium; (9.3) Chambres.
Source: "The Development Planning Unit - Ministry of Finance".

INDE

(1.2,2.1-4.3) Arrivées de touristes non résidents aux frontières nationales; à l'exclusion des nationaux résidant à l'étranger; (4.1) Y compris autres motifs; (8.1) Départs de nationaux seulement, pour tous motifs de visite; (9.1,9.2) Hôtels homologués; (9.3) Chambres.
Sources: (1.1-4.3,8.1,9.1-9.3) "Market Research Division - Government of India"; (6.1-6.3,8.2-8.4) Fonds monétaire international.

INDONESIE

(5.2,7.2,7.4,9.3) Hôtels homologués seulement; (9.1,9.2) Toutes formes d'hébergement commercial; (9.3) Chambres.
Sources: (1.2-5.4,7.1-7.4,8.1,9.1-9.3) "Ministry of Culture and Tourism" et "BPS Statistics Indonesia"; (6.1-6.3,8.2-8.4) Fonds monétaire international.

IRAN, REPUBLIQUE ISLAMIQUE D'

(3.3) Y compris chemin de fer; (5.2,7.2) Hôtels seulement; (9.1,9.2) Hôtels seulement, 21 mars - 20 mars; (9.3) Estimations (Places-lit).
Sources: (1.2-5.4,7.1-7.4,8.1,9.1-9.4) "Iran Cultural Heritage and Tourism Organization (ICHTO)"; (6.1-6.3,8.2-8.4) "Central Bank of Islamic Republic of Iran".

IRLANDE

(1.2,2.3,3.3,4.1-4.3,5.4) Y compris les touristes en provenance de l'Irlande du Nord; (3.3) Y compris chemin de fer; (8.1) Y compris les visiteurs de la journée (excursionnistes); (9.1) À l'exclusion des hôtelleries; (9.3) Chambres, hôtels seulement.
Sources: (1.2-5.4,7.1-7.4,8.1,9.1-9.3) "Fáilte Ireland"; (6.1-6.3,8.2-8.4) Fonds monétaire international.

ISLANDE

(1.2,2.1-2.4) Touristes non résidents dans tous types d'établissements d'hébergement; (3.1,3.4) Arrivées de touristes non résidents aux postes-frontières islandais.
Note: Suite à l'application des accords de Schengen à partir de mars 2001, la collecte des données sur les arrivées et les départs aux postes-frontières islandais a subi des changements. Depuis 2002, le "Icelandic Tourist Board" est chargé de la collecte de ces données.
Sources: (1.2-2.4,5.1-5.4,7.1-7.4,9.1-9.4) "Hagstofa Íslands Statistics Iceland"; (3.1,3.4) "Icelandic Tourist Board"; (6.1-6.3,8.2-8.4) Fonds monétaire international.

ISRAEL

(1.1) Arrivées de visiteurs non résidents aux frontières nationales; à l'exclusion des nationaux résidant à l'étranger; (1.2,2.1-4.3) Arrivées de touristes non résidents aux frontières nationales; à l'exclusion des nationaux résidant à l'étranger; (3.3) Y compris nouvelles entrées de touristes après une visite au Sinaï d'un maximum de 7 jours; (3.4) Y compris les membres de la marine des Etats-Unis en visite de courtoisie; (4.3) Y compris visites à des parents et amis et pèlerinages; (5.1) Hôtels de touristes et aparthôtels; (6.2) Y compris les dépenses des travailleurs étrangers en Israël (Mn $E.U.):
2001: 1.097

2002: 1.125
2003: 997
2004: 905
2005: 929
(9.3) Taux d'occupation/lits dans hôtels et établissements assimilés ouverts; (9.4) Tourisme récepteur dans hôtels touristiques.
Sources: (1.1-5.4,7.1-7.3,8.1,9.1-9.4) "Ministry of Tourism"; (6.1-6.3,8.2-8.4) Fonds monétaire international.

ITALIE

(1.1,3.1-4.3) Arrivées de visiteurs non résidents aux frontières nationales; à l'exclusion des travailleurs saisonniers et frontaliers; (1.1-4.3,8.1) Enquête aux frontières de l'"Ufficio Italiano dei Cambi"; (1.2,2.1-2.6) Arrivées de touristes non résidents aux frontières nationales; à l'exclusion des travailleurs saisonniers et frontaliers; (1.3) Y compris les passagers en croisière; (5.1,5.2) Hôtels seulement; (8.1) Nombre de touristes résidents (visiteurs qui passent la nuit) voyageant à l'étranger; (9.3) Places-lit.
Sources: (1.1-4.3,8.1) "Ufficio Italiano dei Cambi"; (5.1-5.4,7.1-7.4,9.1-9.4) "Statistiche sul Turismo - Istituto Nazionale di Statistica (ISTAT)"; (6.1-6.3,8.2-8.4) Fonds monétaire international.

JAMAHIRIYA ARABE LIBYENNE

(1.1,2.1-2.6) Y compris tous voyageurs (visiteurs et autres voyageurs non définis comme visiteurs par l'OMT); (3.1-3.4) Arrivées de visiteurs non résidents aux frontières nationales; (4.1-4.3) Arrivées de touristes non résidents aux frontières nationales.
Note 2001-2004: Données préliminaires.
Sources: "General People's Committee for Tourism"; (6.1-6.3,8.2-8.4) Fonds monétaire international.

JAMAIQUE

(1.2,2.1-4.3) Arrivées de touristes non résidents par voie aérienne; y compris les nationaux résidant à l'étranger; cartes E/D; (5.3) Données obtenues en multipliant la durée moyenne du séjour par le nombre d'escales dans chacun des pays d'origine; (5.4) Durée de séjour prévue; (9.3) Chambres; (9.4) Nuitées dans les hôtels seulement.
Sources: (1.1-5.4,9.1-9.4) "Jamaica Tourist Board"; (6.1-6.3,8.2-8.4) Fonds monétaire international.

JAPON

(1.2,2.1-2.6,4.1-4.3) Arrivées de touristes non résidents aux frontières nationales; à l'exclusion des nationaux résidant à l'étranger; (3.1,3.4) Arrivées de visiteurs non résidents aux frontières nationales; y compris les résidents étrangers au Japon; (5.4) Jours; (6.2/2003) La méthode de calcul a changé depuis janvier 2003; (9.1) Hôtels homologués et non homologués, ainsi que "ryokans" (auberges); (9.3) Taux d'occupation des principaux hôtels gouvernementaux homologués (chambres).
Sources: (1.2-5.4,7.1,8.1,9.1,9.3) "Japan National Tourist Organization"; (6.1-6.3,8.2-8.4) Fonds monétaire international.

JORDANIE

(1.1-1.3) Y compris les nationaux résidant à l'étranger; (2.1-2.6) Arrivées de touristes non résidents aux frontières nationales; à l'exclusion des nationaux résidant à l'étranger; (3.1-3.4) Arrivées de visiteurs résidents et non résidents; (5.4) Circuits organisés seulement; (9.3) Chambres.
Sources: (1.1-5.4,7.1-7.4,8.1,9.1-9.4) "Ministry of Tourism and Antiquities"; (6.1-6.3,8.2-8.4) Fonds monétaire international.

KAZAKHSTAN

(2.1-2.6,3.1-4.3) Arrivées de visiteurs non résidents aux frontières nationales.
Sources: (1.1-5.4,7.1,8.1,9.1-9.3) "Agency of Statistics of the Republic of Kazakhstan"; (6.1-6.3,8.2-8.4) Fonds monétaire international.

KENYA

(1.1,2.1-4.3) Arrivées de visiteurs non résidents à travers tous les postes frontière; à l'exclusion des nationaux résidant à l'étranger; (9.3) Places-lit; (9.4) Jours.
Sources: (1.1-5.4,7.1,7.4,9.1-9.4) "Kenya Tourist Board"; (6.1-6.3,8.2-8.4) Fonds monétaire international.

KIRGHIZISTAN

(1.2,2.2-2.5,8.1/2003-2005) Nouvelle source d'information: Département du Contrôle douanier.
Sources: (1.1-5.2,7.1,7.2,8.1,9.1,9.2) "National Statistical Committee"; (6.1-6.3,8.2-8.4) Fonds monétaire international.

KIRIBATI

(1.2,2.2-2.4,3.1) Arrivées par voie aérienne. 2001-2003: Tarawa et Ile Christmas. 2004/2005: Tarawa uniquement; (4.1-4.3) Arrivées par voie aérienne. 2001: Tarawa et Ile Christmas. 2002-2005: Tarawa uniquement; (6.1) Les chiffres de dépense sont ceux que le pays a fournis à l'OMT mais ils ne figurent pas dans les données du Fonds monétaire international qui ont servi à la préparation de la présente édition du Compendium.
Source: "Ministry of Communication, Transport and Tourism Development".

KOWEIT

(1.1,2.1-2.6,3.1-3.4) Arrivées de visiteurs non résidents aux frontières nationales; (1.2,4.1-4.3) Touristes non résidents dans les hôtels et établissements assimilés.
Sources: (1.1-5.4,8.1,9.1,9.2) "Ministry of Planning"; (6.1-6.3,8.2-8.4) Fonds monétaire international.

LESOTHO

(1.1,2.1-4.3) Arrivées de visiteurs non résidents aux frontières nationales; (1.1-4.3/2004/2005) Estimations; (10.1-10.3) Cette section comprend uniquement le poste « voyages » parce que le poste « transport de passagers » ne figure pas dans les données du Fonds monétaire international qui ont servi à la préparation de la présente édition du Compendium.
Sources: (1.1-4.3,9.1,9.3) "Lesotho Tourism Development Corporation"; (6.2,8.2-8.4) Fonds monétaire international.

LETTONIE

(1.1,3.1-3.4) Arrivées de visiteurs non résidents aux frontières nationales. Données provenant de la Police d'Etat aux frontières; (1.2-1.4,2.2-2.5,4.1-4.3) Départs des non-résidents. Enquête auprès des personnes qui traversent les frontières du pays; (1.3) Y compris les passagers en croisière; (4.3) Y compris les visites à des parents et amis et traitement médical; (5.3,7.3) Nuitées dans tous les établissements d'hébergement collectif; (5.4) Durée moyenne du séjour des visiteurs non résidents passant une ou plusieurs nuits; enquête auprès des personnes qui traversent les frontières du pays; (8.1) Données provenant de la Police d'Etat aux frontières; (9.3) Places-lit.
Sources: (1.1-5.4,7.1-7.4,8.1,9.1-9.4) "Transport and Tourism Statistics Section - Central Statistical Bureau"; (6.1-6.3,8.2-8.4) Fonds monétaire international.

LIBAN

(1.2) À l'exclusion des ressortissants syriens; (6.1/2001) Les chiffres de dépense sont ceux que le pays a fournis à l'OMT mais ils ne figurent pas dans les données du Fonds monétaire international qui ont servi à la préparation de la présente édition du Compendium. Du fait d'un manque de données sur les recettes du tourisme international concernant les statistiques sur le tourisme récepteur, le Département "Internet et Service Statistique du Ministère du Tourisme" considère qu'un touriste dépense en moyenne 1.000$EU.
Sources: Ministère du Tourisme; (6.1-6.3,8.2-8.4/2002-2005) Fonds monétaire international.

LIECHTENSTEIN

(1.2,2.2-2.4) Touristes non résidents dans les hôtels et établissements assimilés; (9.3) Places-lit.
Source: "Liechtenstein Tourismus".

LITUANIE

(2.1-2.4) Touristes non résidents dans tous types d'établissements d'hébergement; (3.1-3.4,4.1-4.3) Arrivées de touristes non résidents aux frontières nationales; (5.1,5.2,7.1,7.2,9.1-9.4) Hôtels seulement; (9.3) Chambres.
Sources: (1.1-5.4,7.1-7.4,8.1,9.1-9.4) "Lithuanian State Department of Tourism"; (6.1-6.3,8.2-8.4) Fonds monétaire international.

LUXEMBOURG

(1.2,2.2,2.3) Touristes non résidents dans tous types d'établissements d'hébergement; y compris auberges de jeunesse, hébergement touristique privé et autres; (5.1,7.1) Nuitées dans hôtels, auberges et pensions de famille; (5.3,7.3) Y compris l'hébergement touristique privé et autres; (9.3) Chambres.
Sources: (1.2-5.4,7.1-7.4,8.1,9.1-9.4) Office National du Tourisme; (6.1-6.3,8.2-8.4) Fonds monétaire international.

MACAO, CHINE

(1.1,2.1-4.3) Arrivées de visiteurs non résidents aux frontières nationales; (1.1-1.3,2.4,3.1-3.4) Y compris chinois de souche provenant de "Hong-Kong, Chine"; (1.2,1.3) Estimations; (3.1) Y compris les arrivées en hélicoptère; (6.1) Les données de dépense sont celles que le pays a fournies à l'OMT car il s'agit d'une série plus complète que celle obtenue du Fonds monétaire international (FMI) pour la préparation de la présente édition du Compendium. Y compris les recettes en provenance du jeu; (8.1) Circuits organisés; (9.1,9.2) Hôtels, pensions de famille et "pousadas" (auberges); (9.3) Chambres; (10.1-10.3) Cette section n'a pas pu être remplie parce que les postes « voyages » et « transport de passagers » ne figurent pas dans les données du Fonds monétaire international qui ont servi à la préparation de la présente édition du Compendium.
Source: "Macau Government Tourist Office".

MADAGASCAR

(1.2,2.1-2.4,3.1,4.1-4.3) Arrivées de touristes non résidents par voie aérienne; (9.3) Chambres.
Sources: (1.2-5.4,9.1-9.4) Ministère de la Culture et du Tourisme; (6.1-6.3,8.2-8.4) Fonds monétaire international; (8.1) Police des frontières.

MALAISIE

(1.2,2.1-2.6) Arrivées de touristes non résidents aux frontières nationales; y compris les résidents de Singapour qui traversent la frontière par le Johore Causeway; (3.1-3.4,4.1-4.3) Péninsule de Malaisie seulement; (8.1) Déplacement des Malaisiens péninsulaires; y compris les départs par voie terrestre utilisant le Johore Causeway; (9.1) Hôtels avec 10 chambres et plus; (9.3) Chambres.
Sources: (1.1-5.2,7.2,8.1,9.1,9.3) "Tourism Malaysia"; (6.1-6.3,8.2-8.4) Fonds monétaire international.

MALAWI

(1.2-4.3) Départs; (5.3/2004) Donnée provisoire; (9.3) Places-lit.
Sources: (1.2-5.4,9.1-9.4) "Ministry of Information and Tourism"; (6.1-6.3,8.2-8.4/2001) Fonds monétaire international; (6.1-6.3,8.2-8.4/2002-2005) "Reserve Bank of Malawi".

MALDIVES

(1.2,2.1-2.6) Arrivées par voie aérienne; (5.1,9.1-9.4) Centres touristiques et hôtels; (9.4) Jours; (10.1-10.3) Cette section comprend uniquement le poste « voyages » parce que le poste « transport de passagers » ne figure pas dans les données du Fonds monétaire international qui ont servi à la préparation de la présente édition du Compendium.
Sources: (1.2-5.1,8.1,9.1-9.4) "Ministry of Tourism"; (6.2,8.2-8.4) Fonds monétaire international.

MALI

(1.2) Arrivées par voie aérienne; (2.1-2.6) Touristes non résidents dans les hôtels et établissements assimilés; (9.3) Chambres.
Sources: (1.2-5.4,7.1-7.4,9.1-9.4) Office malien du tourisme et de l'hôtellerie (O.MA.T.HO); (6.1-6.3,8.2-8.4) Fonds monétaire international.

MALTE

(1.2,2.1-2.6,3.1,3.4/2001-2003) Arrivées de touristes non résidents aux frontières nationales; (1.2,2.2-2.6,3.1,3.4/2004/2005) Départs par voies aérienne et maritime; (4.1-4.3,5.1-5.3/2003-2005) Départs de touristes par voie aérienne; (8.1/2002-2005) Par voie aérienne uniquement; (9.3) Places-lit.
Sources: (1.1-5.4,8.1,9.2-9.4) "Malta Tourism Authority" et "National Statistics Office"; (6.1-6.3,8.2-8.4) Fonds monétaire international.

MAROC

(1.2,3.1-4.3) Arrivées de touristes non résidents aux frontières nationales; y compris les nationaux résidant à l'étranger; (2.1-2.6) Arrivées de touristes non résidents aux frontières nationales; à l'exclusion des nationaux résidant à l'étranger; (5.1,5.2,7.1,7.2,9.1-9.3) Hôtels homologués, villages de vacances et résidences touristiques; (9.3) Chambres; (9.4) Touristes étrangers.
Sources: (1.1-5.2,7.1,7.2,8.1,9.1-9.4) Ministère du tourisme; (6.1-6.3,8.2-8.4) Fonds monétaire international.

MARTINIQUE

(1.2,2.2,2.3,4.1-4.3) Arrivées de touristes non résidents aux frontières nationales; (6.1) Les chiffres de dépense sont ceux que le pays a fournis à l'OMT mais ils ne figurent pas dans les données du Fonds monétaire international qui ont servi à la préparation de la présente édition du Compendium; (9.1) Hôtels et villages de vacances (Club Méditerranée); (9.3) Chambres dans les hôtels et établissements assimilés.
Source: Comité Martiniquais du Tourisme.

MAURICE

(1.2,2.1-3.4) Arrivées de touristes non résidents aux frontières nationales; (4.1-4.3) Arrivées de visiteurs non résidents aux frontières nationales; (5.4) Grands hôtels; (9.3) Chambres.
Note 2005: Données provisoires.
Sources: (1.1-5.4,8.1,9.1-9.3) "Ministry of Tourism and Leisure"; (6.1-6.3,8.2-8.4) Fonds monétaire international.

MEXIQUE

(1.2,2.2-4.3) Arrivées de touristes non résidents aux frontières nationales; y compris les nationaux résidant à l'étranger; (1.3) Y compris les visiteurs de la frange frontalière avec les Etats Unis avec séjour inférieur à 24 h; (2.2/2004/2005) États-Unis et Canada uniquement; (3.3) Y compris chemin de fer; (5.1) Sélection de centres touristiques; (5.2,7.2) Hôtels seulement; (9.3) Chambres; (9.4) Tourisme étranger seulement.
2005: Données préliminaires.
Sources: (1.1-5.4,7.1,7.2,8.1,9.1-9.4) "Secretaría de Turismo de México (SECTUR)"; (6.1-6.3,8.2-8.4) Fonds monétaire international.

MICRONESIE (ETATS FEDERES DE)

(1.2,2.2-2.4,4.1-4.3) Arrivées dans les États de Kosrae, Chuuk, Pohnpei et Yap; à l'exclusion des citoyens de EFM; (6.1,8.2) Les chiffres de dépense sont ceux que le pays a fournis à l'OMT mais ils ne figurent pas dans les données du Fonds monétaire international qui ont servi à la préparation de la présente édition du Compendium. Années fiscales (1 octobre - 30 septembre).
Source: "Department of Economic Affairs".

MONACO

(1.2,2.1-4.2) Touristes non résidents dans les hôtels et établissements assimilés.
Source: Direction du Tourisme et des Congrès.

MONGOLIE

(1.2,2.2-2.4) (4.1-4.3/2002-2005) Arrivées de touristes non résidents aux frontières nationales. Sont exclus les diplomates et les étrangers qui résident en Mongolie; (4.1-4.3/2001) Arrivées de visiteurs non résidents aux frontières nationales.
Sources: (1.1-4.3) (6.1-6.3,8.2-8.4/2005) "Tourism Policy and Coordination Department - Ministry of Road Transport and Tourism"; (6.1-6.3,8.2-8.4/2001-2004) Fonds monétaire international.

MONTSERRAT

(10.2,10.3) Cette section comprend uniquement le poste « voyages » parce que le poste « transport de passagers » ne figure pas dans les données du Fonds monétaire international qui ont servi à la préparation de la présente édition du Compendium.
Sources: (1.1-5.2) "Statistics Department Montserrat"; (6.2,8.3) Fonds monétaire international.

MOZAMBIQUE

Sources: (1.1-4.3,9.1-9.4) "Ministry of Tourism"; (5.1,5.2,7.1,7.2) "Instituto Nacional de Estatística"; (6.1-6.3,8.2-8.4) Fonds monétaire international.

MYANMAR

(1.2,2.2-2.6) Comprenant les arrivées de touristes aux postes-frontières de Yangon; (4.1-4.3) Arrivées de visiteurs non résidents aux frontières nationales; (5.1,9.4) Hôtels et établissements assimilés gérés uniquement par l'Etat; (9.1,9.2) Hôtels gérés par l'Etat et pensions de famille privées homologuées; (9.3) Chambres.
Sources: (1.1-5.4,9.1-9.4) "Ministry of Hotels and Tourism"; (6.1-6.3,8.2-8.4) Fonds monétaire international.

NAMIBIE

(2.1-4.3) Arrivées de touristes non résidents aux frontières nationales; (2.2) Etats-Unis uniquement; (2.4) Australie uniquement; (9.3) Places-lit.
Sources: (1.1-5.4,7.1-7.3,9.1-9.4) "Ministry of Environment and Tourism"; (6.1-6.3,8.3) Fonds monétaire international.

NEPAL

(1.2) Y compris les arrivées en provenance de l'Inde; (3.3) Voie terrestre; (9.1,9.2) Hôtels à Katmandou et à l'intérieur du pays.
Sources: (1.2-5.4,8.1,9.1,9.2) "Nepal Tourism Board"; (6.1-6.3,8.2-8.4) Fonds monétaire international.

NICARAGUA

(1.2,2.1-4.3) Arrivées de touristes non résidents aux frontières nationales; (1.2/2001-2004) (2.1-2.5) Nationaux résidant à l'étranger exclus; (1.2/2005) Nationaux résidant à l'étranger compris; (5.1-5.4,7.1-7.4,9.4/2005) Données préliminaires; (5.1,7.1) Principaux établissements d'hébergement dans l'ensemble du pays (7); (5.3,7.3) Total de établissements dans l'ensemble du pays; (9.1,9.2) Hôtels et établissements assimilés classés en catégories supérieures; (9.4) Tous types d'établissements d'hébergement, tourisme récepteur.
Sources: (1.1-5.4,7.1-7.4,8.1,9.1-9.4) "Instituto Nicaragüense de Turismo (INTUR)"; (6.1-6.3,8.2-8.4) Fonds monétaire international.

NIGER

(5.4) Jours.
Sources: (1.2-5.4,7.1,7.2,9.1-9.4) (6.2,8.2-8.4/2005) Ministère du Tourisme et de l'Artisanat; (6.1-6.3,8.2-8.4/2001-2004) Fonds monétaire international.

NIGERIA

(1.1,2.1-2.6,3.1-3.4) Arrivées de visiteurs non résidents aux frontières nationales; (1.2,4.1-4.3) Arrivées de touristes non résidents aux frontières nationales.

Sources: (1.1-4.3,9.2,9.3) "Nigerian Tourism Development Corporation"; (6.1-6.3,8.2-8.4) Fonds monétaire international.

NIOUE

(1.2) Arrivées par voie aérienne; y compris les nationaux résidant normalement en Nouvelle-Zélande; (8.1) Retours des résidents.
Source: "Statistics Niue".

NORVEGE

(1.1-4.2) Les chiffres se fondent sur "l'enquête auprès de la clientèle" de l'Institut d'économie des transports; (2.2-4.2) Arrivées de touristes non résidents aux frontières nationales; (2.2) Etats-Unis seulement; (2.4) Japon seulement; (5.1) Nuitées dans les établissements classés; (5.1,9.1,9.2) Les chiffres des hôtels et établissements assimilés se réfèrent aux établissements de 20 places-lit et plus tout au long de l'année; (8.1) Voyages pour vacances; (9.3) Places-lit.
Sources: (1.1-5.3,7.1-7.3,8.1,9.1-9.4) "Statistics Norway" et "Institute of Transport Economics"; (6.1-6.3,8.2-8.4) Fonds monétaire international.

NOUVELLE-CALEDONIE

(1.2,2.1-4.3) Y compris les nationaux résidant à l'étranger; (4.1) Vacances et visites à des parents; (4.2) Affaires uniquement; (5.1,5.2,7.1,7.2) Hôtels de Nouméa uniquement; (8.1) Retours des résidents; (9.3) Chambres à Nouméa; (9.4) Jours, hôtels de Nouméa; (10.2,10.3) Cette section comprend uniquement le poste « voyages » parce que le poste « transport de passagers » ne figure pas dans les données du Fonds monétaire international qui ont servi à la préparation de la présente édition du Compendium.
Sources: (1.1-5.4,7.1,7.2,8.1,9.1-9.4) (6.2/2001) Institut de la Statistique et des Études Économiques (ISEE); (6.2,8.3/2002-2005) Fonds monétaire international.

NOUVELLE-ZELANDE

(1.1,3.1-4.3) Arrivées de visiteurs non résidents aux frontières nationales; nationaux résidant à l'étranger compris; (2.1-2.6) Arrivées de visiteurs non résidents aux frontières nationales, nationaux résidant à l'étranger exclus; (5.3,7.3) Estimation à partir du total des nuitées de clients des établissements d'hébergement commerciaux ayant un chiffre d'affaires annuel d'au moins NZ$30.000, sur la base du pourcentage moyen de clients du tourisme international et du tourisme interne en jan, avr, juil et oct; (8.1) Départs pour peu de temps de résidents de NZ (année civile); (9.1) Il s'agit de la capacité des « unités de séjour » des hôtels, motels et pensions de famille; (10.1-10.3) Cette section comprend uniquement le poste « voyages » parce que le poste « transport de passagers » ne figure pas dans les données du Fonds monétaire international qui ont servi à la préparation de la présente édition du Compendium.
Sources: (1.1-5.3,7.3,8.1,9.1-9.4) "Ministry of Tourism"; (6.2,8.3) Fonds monétaire international.

OMAN

(1.1-1.3,4.1-4.3,5.3,5.4) Enquête du tourisme récepteur; (2.1-2.6) Touristes non résidents dans les hôtels et établissements assimilés; (4.1-4.3) Arrivées de visiteurs non résidents aux frontières nationales; (8.1) Enquête du tourisme émetteur; y compris les visiteurs de la journée (excursionnistes); (9.3) Chambres.
Sources: (1.1-1.3,4.1-4.3,5.3,5.4,8.1) "Ministry of National Economy and Ministry of Commerce and Industry"; (2.1-2.6,5.1,5.2,7.1,7.2,9.1-9.3) "Directorate General of Tourism - Ministry of Tourism"; (6.1-6.3,8.2-8.4) Fonds monétaire international.

OUGANDA

Sources: (1.2-5.3,8.1,9.1,9.2) "Ministry of Tourism, Trade an Industry" et "Uganda Bureau of Statistics"; (6.1-6.3,8.2-8.4) Fonds monétaire international.

OUZBEKISTAN

(6.1-6.3) Les chiffres de dépense sont ceux que le pays a fournis à l'OMT mais ils ne figurent pas dans les données du Fonds monétaire international qui ont servi à la préparation de la présente édition du Compendium.
Source: "National Company "Uzbektourism".

PAKISTAN

(5.4) Jours; (8.3) Pour la dépense, le pays fournit à l'OMT des niveaux d'agrégation qui diffèrent de façon significative des données du Fonds monétaire international utilisées pour la préparation de la présente édition du Compendium. Les données du pays sont les suivantes :
2001: 255
2002: 179
2003: 880
2004: 1.319
2005: 1.277

Sources: (1.2-5.4,7.1,7.2,9.1-9.4) "Pakistan Tourism Development Corporation - Ministry of Tourism"; (6.1-6.3,8.2-8.4) Fonds monétaire international.

PALAOS

(1.2-4.3) Arrivées par voie aérienne (aéroport international de Palau); (6.1,8.2) Les chiffres de dépense sont ceux que le pays a fournis à l'OMT mais ils ne figurent pas dans les données du Fonds monétaire international qui ont servi à la préparation de la présente édition du Compendium.
Source: "Office of Planning and Statistics, Bureau of Budget and Planning - Ministry of Finance".

PALESTINE

(1.2,2.1-2.6) Touristes non résidents dans les hôtels; (5.1,5.2,7.1,7.2) Hôtels seulement; (10.1-10.3) Cette section comprend uniquement le poste « voyages » parce que le poste « transport de passagers » ne figure pas dans les données du Fonds monétaire international qui ont servi à la préparation de la présente édition du Compendium.
Sources: (1.2-5.2,7.1-7.4,9.1-9.4) "Palestinian Central Bureau of Statistics"; (6.2,8.3) Fonds monétaire international; (6.2,8.3,10.1-10.3) Cisjordanie et Gaza.

PANAMA

(1.1) Arrivées de visiteurs non résidents, aéroport international de Tocúmen (AIT), frontière de Paso Canoa (FPC), ports de Cristóbal et Balboa (PCB) et statistiques IPAT; (2.2-2.4) Arrivées de visiteurs non résidents, AIT et statistiques IPAT; (3.1-3.4) Arrivées de touristes non résidents, AIT, FPC, PCB et statistiques IPAT; à l'exclusion des arrivées à d'autres ports d'entrées (non spécifiés) (000)= 2001:42; 2002:35; 2003:40; 2004:51; 2005:54; (4.1-4.3) Arrivées de touristes non résidents, AIT et statistiques IPAT; (5.1) Hôtels de Panama-City et statistiques IPAT; (9.1,9.2) Chambres/places-lit recensées pour le tourisme international; (9.3) Chambres.
2004-2005: Données préliminaires.
Sources: (1.1-5.4,8.1,9.1-9.4) "Instituto Panameño de Turismo"; (6.1-6.3,8.2-8.4) Fonds monétaire international.

POPOUASIE-NOUVELLE-GUINEE

Sources: (1.2-5.4,8.1,9.1-9.4) "Papua New Guinea Tourism Promotion Authority"; (6.1-6.3,8.2-8.4) Fonds monétaire international.

PARAGUAY

(1.1-3.4,8.1) Cartes d'embarquement et de débarquement à l'aéroport Silvio Petirossi et comptages des passagers lors du franchissement des frontières nationales – Police nationale et SENATUR; (1.2,2.1-4.3) À l'exclusion des nationaux résidant à l'étranger et membres des équipages; (3.4) Voie fluviale; (9.3) Places-lit.
Sources: (1.1-5.4,8.1,9.1-9.4) "Secretaría Nacional de Turismo - SENATUR"; (6.1-6.3,8.2-8.4) Fonds monétaire international.

PAYS-BAS

(1.2-2.4) Touristes non résidents dans tous types d'établissements d'hébergement; (5.1,7.1) Hôtels et pensions; (8.1) Départs en vacances des ressortissants nationaux; (8.1/2002) Nouvelle enquête; (9.2) Hôtels; (9.3) Places-lit; (9.4) Tous types d'établissements d'hébergement.
Sources: (1.2-5.4,7.1-7.3,8.1,9.1-9.4) "Statistics Netherlands"; (6.1-6.3,8.2-8.4) Fonds monétaire international.

PEROU

(1.2) Y compris les passagers en croisière qui passent la nuit; (1.2,2.1-2.5) À partir de 2002, nouvelle série estimée comprenant les touristes avec une pièce d'identité autre qu'un passeport ; (1.4) Passagers en croisière qui passent la nuit; (3.4) Comprend les arrivées par voie fluviale et lacustre; (5.1,5.2,5.4,7.1,7.2,9.1-9.4/2003-2005) Estimations préliminaires.
Sources: (1.1-5.4,7.1,7.2,8.1,9.1-9.4) "Ministerio de Comercio Exterior y Turismo (MINCETUR) - Vice Ministerio de Turismo"; (6.1-6.3,8.2-8.4) Fonds monétaire international.

PHILIPPINES

(1.2,3.1-4.3) Arrivées de touristes non résidents aux frontières nationales; y compris les nationaux résidant à l'étranger; (2.1-2.6) Arrivées de touristes non résidents aux frontières nationales; à l'exclusion des nationaux résidant à l'étranger; (4.1-4.3) Arrivées par voie aérienne; (8.1) Y compris les travailleurs sous contrat en provenance d'outre-mer; (9.1,9.2) Hôtels homologués seulement; (9.3,9.4) Hôtels homologués dans la région de Manille seulement.
Sources: (1.2-5.4,8.1,9.1-9.4) "Department of Tourism"; (6.1-6.3,8.2-8.4) Fonds monétaire international.

POLOGNE

(1.1,2.1-3.4) Arrivées de visiteurs non résidents aux frontières nationales; (4.1-4.3) Arrivées de touristes non résidents aux frontières nationales, d'après les enquêtes de l'Institut du tourisme; (5.4) Établissements d'hébergement collectif et privé, d'après les enquêtes de l'Institut du tourisme; (8.1) Voyages du tourisme émetteur enregistrés aux frontières; (9.3) Chambres.

Sources: (1.1-5.4,7.1-7.3,8.1,9.1-9.4) "Institute of Tourism"; (6.1-6.3,8.2-8.4) Fonds monétaire international.

POLYNESIE FRANÇAISE

(1.2,2.2-4.3) Arrivées de touristes non résidents aux frontières nationales; à l'exclusion des nationaux résidant à l'étranger; (5.2) Hôtels seulement; (5.4,9.4) Jours; (9.1,9.2) Hôtels seulement; au 31 décembre de chaque année; (9.3) Chambres dans hôtels.
Sources: (1.2-5.4,9.1-9.4) Service du Tourisme; (6.1-6.3,8.2-8.4) Fonds monétaire international.

PORTO RICO

(1.2) Arrivées de touristes non résidents par voie aérienne; (2.2) Iles Vierges Américaines et Etats-Unis seulement; (5.1,5.4) Y compris résidents et non résidents; (6.1,8.2-8.4) Les chiffres de dépense sont ceux que le pays a fournis à l'OMT mais ils ne figurent pas dans les données du Fonds monétaire international qui ont servi à la préparation de la présente édition du Compendium; (9.1) Chambres classées par la "Compañía de Turismo" de Porto Rico; (9.3) Chambres; y compris les chambres occupées par des résidents de Porto Rico.
Données: Années fiscales (juillet-juin).
Sources: (1.2-3.4,6.1,8.1,8.2-8.4,10.1-10.3) "Junta de Planificación de Puerto Rico"; (5.1,5.2,5.4,7.2,9.1,9.3,9.4) "Compañía de Turismo de Puerto Rico".

PORTUGAL

(1.1,3.1-3.4) Arrivées de visiteurs non résidents aux frontières nationales; (1.1,1.3,3.1-3.4/2004) La méthodologie a été modifiée et pour cela, à partir de 2004 les données ne sont pas disponibles; (1.2,2.2-2.4) Arrivées de touristes non résidents aux frontières nationales; à l'exclusion des nationaux résidant à l'étranger; y compris les arrivées à Madère et Açores; (1.2,1.4,2.2-2.4/2005) La méthodologie a été modifiée et pour cela, à partir de 2005 les données ne sont pas disponibles; (1.4) Y compris les passagers par voie maritime en transit; (5.3) Y compris les nuitées dans des établissements d'hébergement à Madère et Açores; (9.1,9.2) Hôtels, motels, auberges, pensions, "pousadas" (juillet-juin); (9.3) Places-lit (hôtels homologués); (9.4) Tous types d'établissements d'hébergement.
Sources: (1.1-5.4,7.1-7.3,9.1-9.4) "Direcçao-Geral do Turismo (DGT)"; (6.1-6.3,8.2-8.4) Fonds monétaire international.

QATAR

(1.2,2.3-2.6,5.1,5.4,9.1-9.3) Hôtels seulement; (6.2,8.3) Les chiffres de dépense sont ceux que le pays a fournis à l'OMT mais ils ne figurent pas dans les données du Fonds monétaire international qui ont servi à la préparation de la présente édition du Compendium; (9.3) Places-lit.
Sources: (1.2-5.4,9.1-9.3) "The Planning Council - Statistics Department"; (6.2,8.3) "Qatar Central Bank".

REPUBLIQUE ARABE SYRIENNE

(1.1,2.1-4.3) Arrivées de visiteurs non résidents aux frontières nationales; à l'exclusion des arrivées des nationaux résidant à l'étranger; (9.3) Chambres.
Sources: (1.1-5.4,7.1,7.2,8.1,9.1-9.4) "Ministry of Tourism" - Source des données: enquête du tourisme récepteur en 2002 et 2004; (6.1-6.3,8.2-8.4) Fonds monétaire international.

REPUBLIQUE CENTRAFRICAINE

(1.2,2.1-2.6,4.1-4.3) Arrivées par voie aérienne à Bangui uniquement.
Sources: (1.2-5.4,7.1-7.4,8.1,9.1-9.4) (6.1,8.2/2003/2004) Ministère du Développement du Tourisme et de l'Artisanat; (6.1,8.2/2001/2002) Banque des Etats de l'Afrique Centrale (B.E.A.C.).

REPUBLIQUE DE MOLDOVA

(1.1-4.3,8.1) (5.1,7.3/2001-2003) Visiteurs qui ont bénéficié des services des agents économiques officiellement enregistrés avec le type d'activité tourisme et des unités d'hébergement qui leur appartiennent.
Note: À l'exception de la rive gauche de la rivière Nistru et de la municipalité de Bender.
Sources: (1.1-5.4,7.1-7.4,8.1,9.1-9.4) "National Bureau of Statistics"; (6.1-6.3,8.2-8.4) Fonds monétaire international.

REPUBLIQUE DEMOCRATIQUE DU CONGO

(1.2,2.1-2.4,4.1-4.3/2002-2004) Arrivées par voie aérienne uniquement; (9.1) Hôtels homologués.
Note 2005: Données provisoires.
Source: Office National du Tourisme.

REPUBLIQUE DEMOCRATIQUE POPULAIRE LAO

(1.2) Arrivées de touristes non résidents aux frontières nationales; (2.2-2.5,3.1,3.3,4.1-4.3) Arrivées de visiteurs non résidents aux frontières nationales; (5.4) Jours; (10.1-10.3) Cette section comprend uniquement le poste « voyages » parce que le poste « transport de passagers » ne figure pas dans les données du Fonds monétaire international qui ont servi à la préparation de la présente édition du Compendium.

Sources: (1.1-5.4,9.1-9.3) (6.2/2002-2005) "National Tourism Authority"; (6.2,8.3/2001) Fonds monétaire international.

REPUBLIQUE DOMINICAINE

(1.2) Arrivées par voie aérienne uniquement; y compris les nationaux résidant à l'étranger; (1.4) Toutes les arrivées par voie maritime; (2.2-2.4) Arrivées par voie aérienne; à l'exclusion des nationaux résidant à l'étranger; (2.2-2.4/2001-2004) (4.1-4.3/2001/2002) À l'exclusion des passagers de l'aéroport de Herrera; (4.1-4.3) Arrivées par voie aérienne uniquement; y compris les nationaux résidant à l'étranger; (9.1,9.2) Hôtels; (9.3) Chambres; (10.1-10.3) Cette section comprend uniquement le poste « voyages » parce que le poste « transport de passagers » ne figure pas dans les données du Fonds monétaire international qui ont servi à la préparation de la présente édition du Compendium.
Note 2005: Données provisoires.
Sources: (1.1-5.4,8.1,9.1-9.4) "Secretaría de Estado de Turismo"; (6.2,8.2-8.4) Fonds monétaire international.

REPUBLIQUE TCHEQUE

(1.2,2.1-2.4) Touristes non résidents dans tous types d'établissements d'hébergement.
Sources: (1.2-5.4,7.1-7.4,9.1-9.4) "Department of Conception and International Cooperation in Tourism - Ministry for Regional Development"; (6.1-6.3,8.2-8.4) Fonds monétaire international.

REPUBLIQUE-UNIE DE TANZANIE

Sources: (1.1-5.3,7.3,9.1-9.4) "Tourism Division - Ministry of Natural Resources and Tourism" et "National Bureau of Statistics"; (6.1-6.3,8.2-8.4) Fonds monétaire international.

REUNION

(5.4) Jours; (6.1) Les chiffres de dépense sont ceux que le pays a fournis à l'OMT mais ils ne figurent pas dans les données du Fonds monétaire international qui ont servi à la préparation de la présente édition du Compendium.
Sources: Institut National de la Statistique et des Études Économique - INSEE et Comité du Tourisme de la Réunion.

ROUMANIE

Sources: (1.1-5.4,7.1-7.4,8.1,9.1-9.4) "National Authority for Tourism - Ministry of Transports, Constructions and Tourism"; (6.1-6.3,8.2-8.4) Fonds monétaire international.

ROYAUME-UNI

(3.2) Tunnel; (5.4) Jours; (6.1,8.2) Pour la dépense, le pays fournit à l'OMT des niveaux d'agrégation qui diffèrent de façon significative des données du Fonds monétaire international utilisées pour la préparation de la présente édition du Compendium. Les données du pays sont les suivantes :

	6.1	8.2
2001:	16.276	36.467
2002:	17.591	40.409
2003:	19.356	46.614
2004:	23.847	55.434

(9.3) Places-lit (Angleterre seulement).
Sources: (1.1-4.3,5.3,5.4,7.3,8.1,9.3) "VisitBritain"; (5.1,5.2,7.1,7.2,9.2) "EUROSTAT (New Cronos)"; (6.1-6.3,8.2-8.4) Fonds monétaire international.

SABA

(1.3) Principalement de St. Martin.
Sources: "Saba Tourist Bureau", "Caribbean Tourism Organization" et "Central Bank of the Netherlands Antilles".

SAINT-EUSTACHE

(1.1) Arrivées par voies aérienne et maritime; y compris les nationaux résidant à l'étranger; (1.2,2.2,2.3) Arrivées de touristes non résidents aux frontières nationales; à l'exclusion des résidents des Antilles Néerlandaises.
Source: "Central Bank of the Netherlands Antilles".

SAINT-KITTS-ET-NEVIS

(1.2,2.2,2.3) Arrivées de touristes non résidents par voie aérienne; (1.4,3.4) Arrivées en yacht et en bateau de croisière; (10.1-10.3) Cette section comprend uniquement le poste « voyages » parce que le poste « transport de passagers » ne figure pas dans les données du Fonds monétaire international qui ont servi à la préparation de la présente édition du Compendium.
Sources: (1.1-3.4,9.1,9.2) "Ministry of Finance, Planning and Development"; (6.2,8.3) Fonds monétaire international.

SAINT-MARIN

(1.1) Y compris les visiteurs Italiens; (1.2) Touristes non résidents dans les hôtels et établissements assimilés; y compris les touristes Italiens; (9.1,9.2) Hôtels seulement.
Note: Nouvelle méthodologie à partir de 2005.
Source: "Ufficio di Stato per il Turismo".

SAINT-MARTIN

(1.2,2.2,2.3) Par voie aérienne; y compris les arrivées à Saint-Martin (côté français de l'île); (3.1) Arrivées à l'aéroport "Juliana" (y compris les visiteurs à destination de Saint-Martin (côté français); (6.2,8.3) Y compris estimations pour Saba et Saint-Eustache; (9.1,9.2) Hôtels, pensions de famille et appartements.
Sources: (1.1-3.4,9.1-9.3) "St. Maarten Tourist Bureau"; (6.2,8.3) "Central Bank of the Netherlands Antilles".

SAINT-VINCENT-ET-LES-GRENADINES

(1.2,2.2-2.3,4.1-4.3) Arrivées de touristes non résidents par voie aérienne; (3.4) Y compris les passagers en croisière et en yacht; (9.1) Hôtels, appartements, bungalows, villas et pensions de famille; (10.1-10.3) Cette section comprend uniquement le poste « voyages » parce que le poste « transport de passagers » ne figure pas dans les données du Fonds monétaire international qui ont servi à la préparation de la présente édition du Compendium.
Sources: (1.1-5.4,9.1,9.2) "Ministry of Tourism and Culture"; (6.2,8.3) Fonds monétaire international.

SAINTE-LUCIE

(1.1) À l'exclusion des arrivées de passagers en yacht; (1.2,2.2-4.3) Arrivées de touristes non résidents aux frontières nationales; à l'exclusion des nationaux résidant à l'étranger; (9.3) Chambres; (10.1-10.3) Cette section comprend uniquement le poste « voyages » parce que le poste « transport de passagers » ne figure pas dans les données du Fonds monétaire international qui ont servi à la préparation de la présente édition du Compendium.
Note 2005: Données provisoires.
Sources: (1.1-5.2,9.1-9.4) "Saint Lucia Tourist Board"; (6.2,8.3) Fonds monétaire international.

SAMOA

Sources: (1.2-4.3,9.1,9.2) (6.2/2001-2003) "Samoa Tourism Authority" et "Statistical Services Division (Ministry of Finance)"; (6.1-6.3,8.2-8.4/2004/2005) Fonds monétaire international.

SAMOA AMERICAINES

(1.2,2.4,4.1-4.3) Y compris le Samoa occidental; (4.3) Visites à des parents, amis.
Source: "American Samoa Government - Department of Commerce - Statistics Division".

SAO TOME-ET-PRINCIPE

(10.1-10.3) Cette section comprend uniquement le poste « voyages » parce que le poste « transport de passagers » ne figure pas dans les données du Fonds monétaire international qui ont servi à la préparation de la présente édition du Compendium.
Sources: (1.1-4.3) "Direcçao do Turismo e Hotelaria"; (6.2,8.2-8.4/2001/2002) Fonds monétaire international; (6.2/2003-2005) "Banco Central".

SENEGAL

(1.2/2001/2002) (2.1-2.6/2001-2003) Touristes non résidents dans les hôtels et établissements assimilés; (1.2/2003-2005) (2.1-2.3/2004/2005) Arrivées de touristes non résidents aux frontières nationales; (5.1,5.2,7.1,7.2,9.1,9.2) Hôtels et villages de vacances; (9.3) Places-lit.
Sources: (1.1-5.4,7.1,7.2,9.1-9.4) Ministère du Tourisme et des Transports Aériens; (6.1-6.3,8.2-8.4) Fonds monétaire international.

SERBIE-ET-MONTENEGRO

(1.2,2.2-2.4) Touristes non résidents dans tous types d'établissements d'hébergement; y compris chambres, maisons et appartements loués du secteur privé; (6.2) Les chiffres de dépense sont ceux que le pays a fournis à l'OMT mais ils ne figurent pas dans les données du Fonds monétaire international qui ont servi à la préparation de la présente édition du Compendium. À partir de 1997, les données sont présentées conformément aux instructions du 5e manuel de la balance des paiements du FMI; (9.1,9.2) Au 31 août de chaque année; (9.2,9.3) Places-lit permanentes.
Source: "Statistical Office of Serbia and Montenegro".

SEYCHELLES

(1.2,2.1-4.3) Arrivées de touristes non résidents aux frontières nationales; (5.4) Chiffres des nuitées élaborés à partir des départs; (9.1,9.2) Hôtels et pensions de famille; (9.3) Places-lit.

Sources: (1.1-5.4,7.1,8.1,9.1-9.3) "Ministry of Information Technology and Communication"; (6.1-6.3,8.2-8.4) Fonds monétaire international.

SIERRA LEONE

(1.2,2.1-2.6,4.1-4.3) Arrivées par voie aérienne; (9.1,9.2) Hôtels seulement; (10.1-10.3) Cette section comprend uniquement le poste « voyages » parce que le poste « transport de passagers » ne figure pas dans les données du Fonds monétaire international qui ont servi à la préparation de la présente édition du Compendium.
Sources: (1.2-5.4,8.1,9.1-9.4) "National Tourist Board"; (6.2,8.2-8.4) Fonds monétaire international.

SINGAPOUR

(1.1) À l'exclusion des arrivées de Malaisiens par voie terrestre; y compris les visiteurs de la journée (excursionnistes); (4.1-4.3,5.2/2004) Depuis avril 2004, certains champs comme motif de la visite, hébergement, fréquence des visites et préparatifs de voyage ont été supprimés de la carte d'embarquement/débarquement. Données non disponibles; (5.4,9.4) Jours; (9.1) Hôtels (homologués et non-homologués); (9.3) Chambres; hôtels homologués seulement; (10.1-10.3) Cette section comprend uniquement le poste « voyages » parce que le poste « transport de passagers » ne figure pas dans les données du Fonds monétaire international qui ont servi à la préparation de la présente édition du Compendium.
Sources: (1.1-5.4,8.1,9.1-9.4) "Singapore Tourism Board"; (6.2,8.3) Fonds monétaire international.

SLOVAQUIE

(1.1) Y compris les arrivées en provenance de la République Tchèque; (1.2,2.1-2.5) Touristes non résidents dans tous types d'établissements d'hébergement; (5.4,9.4) Tourisme récepteur dans tous types d'établissements d'hébergement touristique; (8.1) Tourisme organisé à travers l'agence de voyages slovaque.
Sources: (1.1-5.4,7.1-7.4,8.1,9.1-9.4) (6.1-6.3,8.2-8.4/2001/2004) "Department of Tourism - Ministry of Economy"; (6.1-6.3,8.2-8.4/2002/2003) Fonds monétaire international.

SLOVENIE

(1.1) Y compris toutes les catégories de voyageurs, quel que soit le motif de la visite; (1.2,2.1-2.6) Touristes non résidents dans tous types d'établissements d'hébergement; (2.1,2.5,2.6) Estimations; (3.1-3.4,4.1-4.3) Touristes non résidents dans tous types d'établissements d'hébergement; données provenant de l'enquête (été) auprès des touristes étrangers en Slovénie portant sur 3 années; (8.1) Enquête trimestrielle des voyages de la population résidente.
Sources: (1.1-5.4,7.1-7.4,8.1,9.1-9.4) "Statistical Office - Information Society and Tourism Statistics"; (6.1-6.3,8.2-8.4) Fonds monétaire international.

SOUDAN

(1.2-4.3/2005) Arrivées de touristes non résidents aux frontières nationales; y compris les nationaux résidant à l'étranger; (6.1) Pour la dépense, le pays fournit à l'OMT des niveaux d'agrégation qui diffèrent de façon significative des données du Fonds monétaire international utilisées pour la préparation de la présente édition du Compendium. Les données du pays sont les suivantes :
2001: 60
2002: 62
2003: 63
2004: 68
2005: 316
(10.1-10.3) Cette section comprend uniquement le poste « voyages » parce que le poste « transport de passagers » ne figure pas dans les données du Fonds monétaire international qui ont servi à la préparation de la présente édition du Compendium.
Sources: (1.2-4.3,9.1-9.4) "Ministry of Tourism and Wildlife"; (6.2,8.3) Fonds monétaire international.

SRI LANKA

(1.2,2.1-4.3) Arrivées de touristes non résidents aux frontières nationales; à l'exclusion des nationaux résidant à l'étranger; (9.1,9.2) Hôtels, motels, auberges, pensions de famille et apart-hôtels; (9.3) Chambres.
Sources: (1.1-5.4,7.1,8.1,9.1-9.3) "Sri Lanka Tourist Board"; (6.1-6.3,8.2-8.4) Fonds monétaire international.

SUEDE

(1.1-4.3) Données reposant sur l'enquête IBIS (auprès des visiteurs du tourisme récepteur) portant sur les années 2001 à 2003 (aucune donnée n'a été collectée avant 2001 ni après 2003). Source: "Swedish Tourist Authority" et "Statistics Sweden"; (1.2,2.1-4.3) Arrivées de touristes non résidents aux frontières nationales; (3.2) Transport ferroviaire et autres modes de transport compris; (5.1,7.1,9.1,9.2) Hôtels seulement; (9.3) Places-lit.
Sources: (1.1-5.3,7.1-7.3,8.1,9.1-9.3) "NUTEK - The Swedish Agency for Economic and Regional Growth"; (6.1-6.3,8.2-8.4) Fonds monétaire international.

SUISSE

(1.2,2.1-2.6,5.1,5.2,7.1,7.2,9.1,9.2/2001-2004) Hôtels, motels et auberges; (1.2,2.1-2.6,5.1,5.2,7.1,7.2,9.1,9.2/2005) Hôtels et établissements de cure; (9.3) Taux d'occupation nets (places-lit disponibles); (9.4) Touristes non résidents dans les hôtels et établissements assimilés (touristes étrangers).
Sources: (1.2-5.3,7.1-7.3,8.1,9.1-9.4) "Swiss Federal Statistical Office"; (6.1-6.3,8.2-8.4) Fonds monétaire international.

SURINAME

(1.2,2.2-2.4,4.1-4.3,5.2/2001-2003) (3.1) (5.2/2004) Arrivées à l'aéroport de Zanderij; (1.2,2.2-2.4,4.1-4.3/2004/2005) Arrivées à l'aéroport de Zanderij, aéroport Zorg en Hoop, Albina et Nickerie; (1.4/2001-2003) (3.4) Arrivées au port Nw. Nickerie.
Sources: (1.1-1.4,2.2-2.4,4.1-4.3,5.2/2001-2003) (3.1,3.4/2001-2004) "General Bureau of Statistics (ABS)"; (1.2,2.2-2.4,4.1-4.3,5.2/2004/2005) (3.1,3.4/2005) (9.1) "Suriname Tourism Foundation"; (6.1-6.3,8.2-8.4) Fonds monétaire international.

SWAZILAND

(1.2,4.1-4.3/2001/2002) Arrivées dans les hôtels seulement; (2.1-2.4,5.2) Arrivées dans les hôtels seulement; (9.3) Places-lit.
Sources: (1.1-5.4,7.1,8.1,9.1-9.4) "Swaziland Tourism Authority" et "Ministry of Tourism, Environment and Communications"; (6.1-6.3,8.2-8.4) Fonds monétaire international.

TAIWAN (PROVINCE DE CHINE)

(1.1) Y compris les nationaux résidant à l'étranger; (2.1-2.6) À l'exclusion des nationaux résidant à l'étranger.
Sources: (1.1-5.4,8.1,9.1,9.3) "Planning Division Tourism Bureau - Ministry of Transportation and Communication"; (6.1-6.3,8.2-8.4) Fonds monétaire international.

TCHAD

(1.2,2.1-2.6,5.2) Touristes non résidents dans les hôtels et établissements assimilés; (9.3) Chambres.
Sources: (1.1-5.4,7.1,8.1,9.1-9.4) Direction des Études et de la Programmation - Ministère du Développement Touristique; (6.1,8.2) Banque des Etats de l'Afrique Centrale (B.E.A.C.).

THAILANDE

(1.2,3.1-3.4) Y compris les arrivées des nationaux résidant à l'étranger; (2.1-2.6,4.1-4.3) À l'exclusion des arrivées des nationaux résidant à l'étranger; (3.3) Y compris chemin de fer; (5.4) Jours; (9.3) Dans les principales destinations touristiques seulement.
Sources: (1.1-5.4,7.1,8.1,9.1-9.4) "Tourism Authority of Thailand (TAT)"; (6.1-6.3,8.2-8.4) Fonds monétaire international.

TOGO

(1.2) Touristes non résidents dans les hôtels et établissements assimilés; (9.3) Chambres.
Sources: (1.2-5.2,7.1,7.2,9.1-9.4) Ministère du Tourisme, de l'Artisanat et des Loisirs; (6.1-6.3,8.2-8.4) Fonds monétaire international.

TONGA

(1.2,2.2-2.4,4.1-4.3) Arrivées par voie aérienne; (6.2) Les données de dépense sont celles que le pays a fournies à l'OMT car il s'agit d'une série plus complète que celle obtenue du Fonds monétaire international (FMI); (10.1-10.3) Cette section comprend uniquement le poste « voyages » parce que le poste « transport de passagers » ne figure pas dans les données du Fonds monétaire international qui ont servi à la préparation de la présente édition du Compendium.
Sources: (1.1-4.3) "Tonga Visitors Bureau"; (6.2) "National Reserve Bank of Tonga"; (8.3) Fonds monétaire international.

TRINITE-ET-TOBAGO

(1.2,2.1-2.5,4.1-4.3) Arrivées par voie aérienne; (4.1) Y compris les visites à des parents et amis.
Sources: (1.1-5.4,9.1,9.3) (6.1-6.3,8.2-8.4/2005) "Central Statistical Office - Ministry of Planning and Development"; (6.1-6.3,8.2-8.4/2001-2004) Fonds monétaire international.

TUNISIE

(1.2,2.1-3.4) Arrivées de touristes non résidents aux frontières nationales; à l'exclusion des nationaux résidant à l'étranger; (9.1,9.2) Hôtels homologués et non-homologués, pensions et villages de vacances; (9.3) Places-lit.
Sources: (1.1-5.4,7.1,8.1,9.1-9.4) Ministère du Tourisme - Office National du Tourisme et Institut National de la Statistique; (6.1-6.3,8.2-8.4) Fonds monétaire international.

TURQUIE

(1.1,3.1-3.4) Arrivées de visiteurs non résidents aux frontières nationales; (1.3) Arrivées par mer (à l'exclusion d'une frontière terrestre depuis 1989); (2.1-2.6) Arrivées de touristes non résidents aux frontières nationales; (3.4) Y compris les passagers en croisière; (4.1-4.3) Départs de visiteurs non résidents; (5.3) Enquête auprès des établissements d'hébergement homologués par le Ministère du Tourisme; (5.3,7.3) Y compris les terrains de camping; (6.2) Y compris les dépenses des nationaux résidant à l'étranger; (9.3,9.4) Hôtels homologués; à l'exclusion des terrains de camping; (9.3) Places-lit; (10.1-10.3) Cette section comprend uniquement le poste « voyages » parce que le poste « transport de passagers » ne figure pas dans les données du Fonds monétaire international qui ont servi à la préparation de la présente édition du Compendium.
Sources: (1.1-3.4,5.1-5.4,7.1-7.4,8.1,9.1-9.4) (6.2/2001/2002) "Ministry of Culture and Tourism"; (4.1-4.3) "Departing Visitors Survey - Turkish Statistical Institute (TURKSTAT)"; (6.2/2003-2005) (8.3) Fonds monétaire international.

TURKMENISTAN

Source: "State Committee for Tourism and Sport".

TUVALU

Source: "Central Statistics Division - Ministry of Finance, Economic Planning and Industry".

UKRAINE

(2.1-2.6) Arrivées de touristes non résidents aux frontières nationales; (3.1-3.4/2001/2002) Arrivées de visiteurs non résidents aux frontières nationales; (3.1-3.4/2003) Arrivées de touristes non résidents aux frontières nationales; (4.1-4.3) Arrivées de visiteurs non résidents aux frontières nationales; (6.1,8.2) Pour la dépense, le pays fournit à l'OMT des niveaux d'agrégation qui diffèrent de façon significative des données du Fonds monétaire international utilisées pour la préparation de la présente édition du Compendium. Les données du pays sont les suivantes :

	6.1	8.2
2001:	3.957	512
2002:	4.523	497
2003:	5.341	492

Sources: (1.1-5.4,7.1,7.3,8.1,9.1-9.4) "State Tourism Administration"; (6.1-6.3,8.2-8.4) Fonds monétaire international.

URUGUAY

(1.1,4.1-4.3) Y compris les nationaux résidant à l'étranger; (2.2-3.4) À l'exclusion des nationaux résidant à l'étranger; (3.3) Y compris chemin de fer; (5.4) Jours; (9.1,9.2/2005) À l'exclusion des hôtels non-homologués.
Sources: (1.1-5.4,8.1,9.1-9.4) "Ministerio de Turismo y Deporte"; (6.1-6.3,8.2-8.4) Fonds monétaire international.

VANUATU

(5.4) Jours; (9.3) Chambres.
Sources: (1.1-5.4,8.1,9.1-9.4) "Vanuatu National Statistics Office"; (6.1-6.3,8.2-8.4) Fonds monétaire international.

VENEZUELA

(1.2,2.1-4.3) Arrivées de touristes non résidents aux frontières nationales; (9.1,9.2) Hôtels et Parador/"Pousadas"; (9.1,9.2/2005) Hôtels uniquement.
Sources: (1.1-5.4,8.1,9.1-9.4) "Ministerio de Turismo"; (6.1-6.3,8.2-8.4) Fonds monétaire international.

VIET-NAM

(1.1) Y compris les nationaux résidant à l'étranger; (1.4,3.4) Y compris les arrivées de passagers en croisière et par voie maritime; (2.1-4.3) Arrivées de visiteurs non résidents aux frontières nationales; (6.1) Les chiffres de dépense sont ceux que le pays a fournis à l'OMT mais ils ne figurent pas dans les données du Fonds monétaire international qui ont servi à la préparation de la présente édition du Compendium.
Source: "Viet Nam National Administration of Tourism".

YEMEN

(1.2,2.1-2.6,5.2) Touristes non résidents dans les hôtels et établissements assimilés; (10.1-10.3) Cette section comprend uniquement le poste « voyages » parce que le poste « transport de passagers » ne figure pas dans les données du Fonds monétaire international qui ont servi à la préparation de la présente édition du Compendium.
Sources: (1.2-5.4,7.1,7.2,9.1,9.2) "Ministry of Culture and Tourism - Yemen Tourism Promotion Board"; (6.2,8.2-8.4) Fonds monétaire international.

ZAMBIE

(5.4) Jours; (6.1,8.3) Les données de dépense sont celles que le pays a fournies à l'OMT car il s'agit d'une série plus complète que celle obtenue du Fonds monétaire international (FMI) pour la préparation de la présente édition du Compendium; (9.3) Chambres.
Note 2001-2002: Données provisoires.
Source: "Ministry of Tourism, Environment and Natural Resources".

ZIMBABWE

(2.1-2.4,3.1-3.3,4.1,4.2) Arrivées de visiteurs non résidents aux frontières nationales; (3.1,3.3/2001-2003) Y compris les personnes en transit; (6.1) Les chiffres de dépense sont ceux que le pays a fournis à l'OMT mais ils ne figurent pas dans les données du Fonds monétaire international qui ont servi à la préparation de la présente édition du Compendium; (9.1,9.2) Hôtels classés uniquement; (9.3) Places-lit.
Source: "Zimbabwe Tourism Authority - ZTA".

ALBANIA

(1.1,2.2-4.3) Visitantes y otros viajeros; (1.2,5.2,7.2) Llegadas en hoteles únicamente; (4.3) Tránsito.
Fuentes: (1.1-5.4,7.1-7.4,9.1-9.4) "Institute of Statistics - INSTAT"; (6.1-6.3,8.2-8.4) Fondo Monetario Internacional.

ALEMANIA

(1.2,2.1-2.6) Turistas no residentes alojados en todo tipo de establecimientos de alojamiento; (9.3) Plazas-cama; (9.4) Turismo receptor, hoteles y establecimientos asimilados.
Fuentes: (1.2-5.3,7.1-7.3,8.1,9.1-9.4) "Statistiches Bundesamt"; (6.1-6.3,8.2-8.4) Fondo Monetario Internacional.

ANDORRA

Fuente: Ministerio de Turismo y Medio Ambiente.

ANGOLA

(5.1,5.2,7.1,7.2) Hoteles únicamente.
Fuentes: (1.2-7.3,9.1-9.4) (6.2/2001) "Ministério de Hotelaria e Turismo - Gabinete de Estudos, Planeamento e Estatística"; (6.2/2002-2005) (6.3,8.2-8.4) Fondo Monetario Internacional.

ANGUILA

(1.1,3.1-4.2) Llegadas de visitantes no residentes en las fronteras nacionales; (1.2,2.2-2.3) Llegadas de turistas no residentes en las fronteras nacionales; excluidos los nacionales residentes en el extranjero; (9.1) Hoteles, casas de huéspedes y apartamentos/ villas; (9.3) Habitaciones; enero-mayo; (10.2,10.3) Este apartado incluye únicamente la partida "viajes" debido a que la partida "transporte de pasajeros" no figura en los datos del Fondo Monetario Internacional utilizados para la preparación de esta edición del Compendio.
Fuentes: (1.1-5.4,9.1,9.3) "Statistical Department - Ministry of Finance"; (6.2,8.3) Fondo Monetario Internacional.

ANTIGUA Y BARBUDA

(1.1) Excluidas las llegadas de pasajeros en yate; (2.2,2.3,3.1) Llegadas por vía aérea; excluidos los nacionales residentes en el extranjero; (10.1-10.3) Este apartado incluye únicamente la partida "viajes" debido a que la partida "transporte de pasajeros" no figura en los datos del Fondo Monetario Internacional utilizados para la preparación de esta edición del Compendio.
Fuentes: (1.1-2.3) "Eastern Caribbean Central Bank"; (6.2,8.3) Fondo Monetario Internacional.

ARABIA SAUDITA

(6.1,8.2) Las cifras de gasto corresponden a las facilitadas por el país a la OMT y que, sin embargo, no figuran en los datos del Fondo Monetario Internacional utilizados para la preparación de esta edición del Compendio.
Fuente: "The Supreme Commission for Tourism".

ARGELIA

(1.1,3.1-3.4) Incluidos los nacionales residentes en el extranjero:

2001	705.187
2002	736.915
2003	861.373
2004	865.157
2005	1.001.884

(2.1-2.6,4.1,4.2) Excluidos los nacionales residentes en el extranjero; (6.1,8.2) Las cifras de gasto corresponden a las facilitadas por el país a la OMT y que, sin embargo, no figuran en los datos del Fondo Monetario Internacional utilizados para la preparación de esta edición del Compendio.
Fuentes: "Ministère du Tourisme" y "Office National des Statistiques".

ARGENTINA

A partir del año 2004, como resultado de la importancia de la "Encuesta de Turismo Internacional" se modificaron las estimaciones de la serie de la cuenta "Viajes" de la Balanza de Pagos. Por este motivo, los datos no son rigurosamente comparables con los años anteriores.
Nota 2004-2005: Datos provisionales.
Fuentes: (1.2-5.4,7.1,7.2,8.1,9.1-9.3) Dirección de Estudios de Mercado y Estadística - Secretaría de Turismo de la Nación; (6.1-6.3,8.2-8.4) Fondo Monetario Internacional.

ARMENIA

Fuentes: (1.2-5.4,7.3,8.1,9.2-9.4) "Tourism Department - Ministry of Trade and Economic Development"; (6.1-6.3,8.2-8.4) Fondo Monetario Internacional.

ARUBA

(1.2,2.2-4.3) Llegadas de turistas no residentes en las fronteras nacionales; (5.4) Turistas no residentes alojados en hoteles y establecimientos asimilados; (9.3) Habitaciones.
Fuentes: (1.1-5.4,9.1-9.3) "Aruba Tourism Authority"; (6.1-6.3,8.2-8.4) Fondo Monetario Internacional.

AUSTRALIA

(1.1) Excluidos los nacionales residentes en el extranjero y miembros de tripulaciones; (1.2,1.3) Llegadas por vía aérea; (2.1-4.3) Llegadas de visitantes no residentes en las fronteras nacionales; (5.1,7.1) Las estimaciones incluyen hoteles, complejos turísticos, moteles y hoteles de carretera, casas de huéspedes y pensiones, y albergues para mochileros; (5.3,7.3) Las estimaciones comprenden todo tipo de alojamiento comercial; (9.1-9.3) Hoteles, moteles, casas de huéspedes y apartamentos de servicio hotelero con 15 habitaciones o más; (9.3) Habitaciones; (9.4) Turismo receptor en alojamientos comerciales.
Fuentes: (1.1-5.4,7.1-7.4,8.1,9.1-9.4) "Australian Bureau of Statistics"; (6.1-6.3,8.2-8.4) Fondo Monetario Internacional.

AUSTRIA

(1.2-2.6) Turistas no residentes alojados en hoteles y establecimientos asimilados; (5.1,5.2,7.1,7.2) Incluidos los complejos vacacionales; (5.3,7.3) Excluido el alojamiento privado; (8.1/2003) Más de 4 pernoctaciones; (9.1) Sólo hoteles; (9.2) Hoteles y complejos vacacionales; (9.3) Basado en la temporada de verano; (9.4) Duración media de la estancia en hoteles y establecimientos asimilados; incluidos los complejos vacacionales.
Fuentes: (1.2-5.4,7.1-7.4,8.1,9.1-9.4) "Department for Tourism and Historic Objects - Federal Ministry of Economics and Labour"; (6.1-6.3,8.2-8.4) Fondo Monetario Internacional.

AZERBAIYAN

Fuentes: (1.2-5.2,7.1,7.2,8.1,9.1,9.2) "Ministry of Culture and Tourism"; (6.1-6.3,8.2-8.4) Fondo Monetario Internacional.

BAHAMAS

(1.2,2.1-2.6,4.1-4.3) Llegadas de turistas no residentes en las fronteras nacionales; (5.2) Llegadas en hoteles únicamente; (9.1,9.2) Hoteles, apartamentos, bungalows y villas - Establecimientos homologados únicamente; (9.3) Habitaciones.
Fuentes: (1.1-5.4,9.1-9.4) "Bahamas Ministry of Tourism"; (6.1-6.3,8.2-8.4) Fondo Monetario Internacional.

BAHREIN

(1.1,2.1-4.3) Llegadas de visitantes no residentes en las fronteras nacionales; excluidos los nacionales residentes en el extranjero; (3.1) Llegadas al aeropuerto internacional de Bahrein; (3.3) Llegadas a través del "King Fahad Causeway"; (3.4) Llegadas al puerto Mina Salman; (5.1,9.1,9.2) Únicamente hoteles clasificados.
Fuentes: (1.1-5.4,9.1-9.3) "Tourism Affairs - Ministry of Information"; (6.1-6.3,8.2-8.4) Fondo Monetario Internacional.

BANGLADESH

Fuentes: (1.2-5.4,8.1,9.1-9.3) "Bangladesh Parjatan Corporation"; (6.1-6.3,8.2-8.4) Fondo Monetario Internacional.

BARBADOS

(1.2,2.1-4.3) Llegadas de turistas no residentes en las fronteras nacionales; (9.1,9.2) Hoteles, hoteles-apartamento, apartamentos y bungalows, casas de huéspedes; (9.3) Habitaciones.
Fuentes: (1.1-5.4,9.1-9.4) "Barbados Tourism Authority"; (6.1-6.3,8.2-8.4) Fondo Monetario Internacional.

BELARUS

(1.2,2.2-2.4) Turismo organizado.
Fuentes: (1.2,2.2-2.4,8.1) "Ministry of Statistics and Analysis"; (6.1-6.3,8.2-8.4) Fondo Monetario Internacional.

BELGICA

(1.2,2.1-2.6,4.1-4.3) Turistas no residentes alojados en todo tipo de establecimientos de alojamiento; (5.1,5.2,7.1,7.2) Hoteles únicamente; (9.1,9.2) Hoteles y poblados de vacaciones.
Fuentes: (1.2-5.3,7.1-7.3,8.1,9.1,9.2) (6.1-6.3,8.2-8.4/2001) "Institut National de Statistique"; (6.1-6.3,8.2-8.4/2002-2005) Fondo Monetario Internacional.

BELICE

(1.3) Pasajeros en tránsito y cruces de frontera; (2.2-4.2) Llegadas de turistas no residentes en las fronteras nacionales; (10.1-10.3) Este apartado incluye únicamente la partida "viajes" debido a que la partida "transporte de pasajeros" no figura en los datos del Fondo Monetario Internacional utilizados para la preparación de esta edición del Compendio.

Fuentes: (1.1-5.4,7.3,9.1-9.4) "Belize Tourist Board"; (6.2,8.2-8.4) Fondo Monetario Internacional.

BENIN

(1.2-4.3) Llegadas de turistas no residentes en las fronteras nacionales; (1.1-5.3/2003-2005) Estimaciones.
Fuentes: (1.1-5.4,7.1) "Direction du tourisme et de l'hôtellerie - Ministère de la culture, de l'artisanat et du tourisme"; (6.1-6.3,8.2-8.4) Fondo Monetario Internacional.

BERMUDA

(1.1) Excluidos los nacionales residentes en el extranjero; (1.2,2.2-2.4,4.1-4.3) Llegadas por vía aérea; (5.3) Incluidas las pernoctaciones en casas particulares; (6.1,8.2) Las cifras de gasto corresponden a las facilitadas por el país a la OMT y que, sin embargo, no figuran en los datos del Fondo Monetario Internacional utilizados para la preparación de esta edición del Compendio; (9.3) Habitaciones.
Fuente: "Bermuda Department of Tourism".

BHUTAN

(6.1) Las cifras de gasto corresponden a las facilitadas por el país a la OMT y que, sin embargo, no figuran en los datos del Fondo Monetario Internacional utilizados para la preparación de esta edición del Compendio.
Fuente: "Department of Tourism - Royal Government of Bhutan".

BOLIVIA

(1.2) Llegadas de turistas no residentes en las fronteras nacionales; (2.1-2.4) Turistas no residentes alojados en hoteles y establecimientos asimilados; (3.4) Llegadas por vía lacustre; (4.1-4.3) Datos procedentes de encuestas; (5.1-5.,7.1-7.4,9.1,9.2) Capitales de departamento únicamente; (9.3) Plazas-cama (hoteles); (9.4) Días, hoteles y establecimientos asimilados, turismo receptor.
Nota 2003-2005: Datos preliminares.
Fuentes: (1.2-5.4,7.1-7.4,8.1,9.1-9.4) Viceministerio de Turismo - Ministerio de Producción y Microempresa; (6.1-6.3,8.2-8.4) Fondo Monetario Internacional.

BONAIRE

Fuentes: (1.1-5.4,9.1-9.4) "Tourism Corporation of Bonaire (TCB)"; (6.2,8.3) "Central Bank of the Netherlands Antilles".

BOSNIA Y HERZEGOVINA

(1.2,2.2-2.4) Turistas no residentes alojados en todo tipo de establecimientos de alojamiento; (2.5,2.6) Menos de 500 llegadas; (9.1,9.2) Excluida la República Srpska.
Fuentes: (1.2-5.3,7.3,9.1,9.2) "Agency for Statistics of Bosnia and Herzegovina"; (6.1-6.3,8.2-8.4) Fondo Monetario Internacional.

BOTSWANA

Fuentes: (1.1-5.2,7.1,9.1-9.4) "Department of Tourism - Ministry of Environment, Wildlife and Tourism"; (6.1-6.3,8.2-8.4) Fondo Monetario Internacional.

BRASIL

(3.4) Incluidas las llegadas por vía fluvial; (5.4) Días; (6.1) El país facilita a la OMT niveles agregados de gasto que son significativamente diferentes a los datos del Fondo Monetario Internacional utilizados para la preparación de esta edición del Compendio (datos obtenidos en la encuesta por muestreo realizada por EMBRATUR). Los datos del país son:
2001: 3.701
2002: 3.120
2003: 3.386
2004: 3.676
2005: 4.849
Nota 2005: Estimaciones.
Fuentes: (1.2-5.4,8.1) "Instituto Brasileiro de Turismo (EMBRATUR)"; (6.1-6.3,8.2-8.4) Fondo Monetario Internacional.

BRUNEI DARUSSALAM

Fuente: "Tourism Development Division - Ministry of Industry and Primary Resources".

BULGARIA

(1.1,1.2) Se excluye a los niños sin pasaporte propio; (1.3) Visitantes en tránsito; (3.4) Mar y ríos del interior del país; (5.1,5.3,5.4,7.1,7.3,9.2-9.4) Cubre prácticamente el antiguo alojamiento del sector público y de propiedad del Estado. Una parte considerable del sector privado (más del 70 por ciento en 1998) no está incluido en los datos; (9.2) Hoteles únicamente; (9.3) Plazas-cama en los hoteles.
Fuentes: (1.1-4.3,5.1,5.3,5.4,7.1,7.3,8.1,9.2-9.4) ""Tourism Policy" Directorate - State Agency for Tourism"; (5.2,7.2) "EUROSTAT (New Cronos)"; (6.1-6.3,8.2-8.4) Fondo Monetario Internacional.

BURKINA FASO

(1.2,2.1-2.6,5.2) Turistas no residentes alojados en hoteles y establecimientos asimilados; (4.1-4.3) Incluido el turismo interno; (6.1) El país facilita a la OMT niveles agregados de gasto que son significativamente diferentes a los datos del Fondo Monetario Internacional utilizados para la preparación de esta edición del Compendio. Los datos del país son:
2001: 35
2002: 39
2003: 48
2004: 57
2005: 53
(9.3) Habitaciones.
Fuentes: (1.2-5.4,7.1,7.2,9.3) "Service de l'analyse statistique et de la Coopération touristique - Ministère de la Culture, des Arts et du Tourisme"; (6.1-6.3,8.2-8.4) Fondo Monetario Internacional.

BURUNDI

(1.2-4.3) Llegadas de turistas no residentes en las fronteras nacionales; incluidos los nacionales residentes en el extranjero; (3.4) Llegadas por vía lacustre.
Fuentes: (1.2-5.1,8.1,9.1,9.2) "Office National du Tourisme"; (6.1-6.3,8.2-8.4) Fondo Monetario Internacional.

CABO VERDE

(1.2,2.1-2.3) Turistas no residentes alojados en hoteles y establecimientos asimilados.
Fuentes: (1.2,2.1-2.3,5.1,5.2,7.1,7.2,9.1-9.4) "Instituto Nacional de Estatística"; (6.1-6.3,8.2-8.4) Fondo Monetario Internacional.

CAMBOYA

(1.2) Llegadas de turistas internacionales por todo el conjunto de medios de transporte; (2.2-2.5/2001) Llegadas por vía aérea; /2.2-2.5,3.1-3.4/2004/2005) Excluidas las llegadas a la provincia "Phreah Vihear": 2004: 67.843; 2005: 88.615; (3.3/2001/2002) Llegadas por tierra y barco; (3.4) Llegadas por barco; (4.1-4.3/2001/2002) Llegadas por vía aérea; (4.1/2001/2002) Incluidas las llegadas al aeropuerto de Siem Reap en vuelos directos: 2001: 133.688; 2002: 202.791; (4.1-4.3/2005) Excluidas las llegadas a la provincia "Phreah Vihear": 88.615; (5.4) Días.
Fuentes: (1.2-5.4,8.1,9.1-9.3) "Ministry of Tourism"; (6.1-6.3,8.2-8.4) Fondo Monetario Internacional.

CAMERUN

(1.2,2.1-2.6,5.2) Turistas no residentes alojados en hoteles y establecimientos asimilados.
Fuentes: (1.2-5.2,7.1,7.2,9.1,9.2) "Ministère du Tourisme"; (6.1-6.3,8.2-8.4) Fondo Monetario Internacional.

CANADA

(1.1,1.3) Datos basados en la contabilidad aduanera, ajustándola en función de los resultados de las encuestas; (1.2,2.1-4.3) Llegadas de turistas no residentes en las fronteras nacionales; (4.2) Incluye congresos; (8.1) Viajes-persona (una/varias noches); Nota 2005: Datos provisionales.
Nota: En 2002 se introdujeron diferentes tipos de cambios metodológicos que afectan a las estimaciones de 2001 para los gastos y las características de los turistas internacionales que visitaron Canadá. El organismo "Statistics Canada" aconseja, por lo tanto, no comparar las estimaciones para 2001 con las de los años anteriores debido a dichos cambios metodológicos para las estimaciones no contabilizables (una de las razones de que no se aporten datos de duración media de la estancia).
Fuentes: (1.1-4.3,5.3,7.1,7.3,8.1) "Canadian Tourism Commission"; (6.1-6.3,8.2-8.4) Fondo Monetario Internacional.

CHAD

(1.2,2.1-2.6,5.2) Turistas no residentes alojados en hoteles y establecimientos asimilados; (9.3) Habitaciones.
Fuentes: (1.1-5.4,7.1,8.1,9.1-9.4) "Direction des Études et de la Programmation - Ministère du Développement Touristique"; (6.1,8.2) "Banque des Etats de l'Afrique Centrale (B.E.A.C.)".

CHILE

(5.1,5.2,7.1,7.2) Las cifras de 2005 no son comparables con años anteriores debido a una actualización del Censo con cobertura nacional de Establecimientos de Alojamiento Turístico.

Fuentes: (1.2-5.4,7.1,7.2,8.1,9.1-9.4) Servicio Nacional de Turismo - SERNATUR; (6.1-6.3,8.2-8.4) Fondo Monetario Internacional.

CHINA

(1.1,2.1-2.6,3.1-3.4) Incluidas las llegadas de personas de origen étnico chino procedentes de "Hong Kong, China", "Macao, China", "Taiwán (Provincia de China)" y de ultramar, la mayor parte de excursionistas proceden de "Hong Kong, China" y "Macao, China"; (4.1-4.3) Excluidas las llegadas de turistas de origen étnico chino procedentes de "Hong Kong, China", "Macao, China", "Taiwán (Provincia de China)" y de ultramar; (7.1,9.1,9.2) Referido sólo a los hoteles clasificados con estrellas; (8.1) Incluidos los miembros de las tripulaciones y otros miembros de las fuerzas armadas; (9.3) Habitaciones; (9.4) Turismo receptor.
Fuentes: (1.1-5.4,7.1,8.1,9.1-9.4) "National Tourism Administration"; (6.1-6.3,8.2-8.4) Fondo Monetario Internacional.

CHIPRE

(1.2,2.1-2.6) Llegadas de turistas no residentes en las fronteras nacionales; (1.3) Incluidos los pasajeros en crucero y en tránsito; (3.4) Incluidos los pasajeros en crucero; (5.4) Datos extraídos de la encuesta de gastos turísticos (salidas) referidos a la estancia y al tipo de alojamiento; (9.3) Plazas-cama; (9.4) A partir de 2000, los cálculos de la duración media de las estancias se basan en las pernoctaciones y en las llegadas a hoteles y establecimientos asimilados.
Fuentes: (1.1-5.4,7.1-7.4,8.1,9.1-9.4) "Cyprus Tourism Organization"; (6.1-6.3,8.2-8.4) Fondo Monetario Internacional.

COLOMBIA

(1.1,2.1-2.6,3.1-3.4,4.1-4.3) Llegadas de visitantes no residentes en las fronteras nacionales. Excluidos los pasajeros en crucero; (9.3) Habitaciones.
Nota 2005: Datos provisionales.
Fuentes: (1.1-4.3,8.1) Dirección de Extranjería - Departamento Administrativo de Seguridad (DAS); (6.1-6.3,8.2-8.4) Fondo Monetario Internacional; (9.1-9.3) Dirección de Turismo - Ministerio de Comercio, Industria y Turismo, Asociación Hotelera de Colombia (COTELCO).

COMORAS

(1.2,2.1,2.3,4.1-4.3) Llegadas por vía aérea; (6.1) Las cifras de gasto corresponden a las facilitadas por el país a la OMT y que, sin embargo, no figuran en los datos del Fondo Monetario Internacional utilizados para la preparación de esta edición del Compendio.
Fuente: "Direction Nationale de la Promotion du Tourisme et de l'Hôtellerie - Ministère du Transport, Tourisme, Postes et Télécommunications".

CONGO

(1.2-2.3,5.2) Turistas no residentes alojados en hoteles y establecimientos asimilados; (9.3) Habitaciones.
Fuentes: (1.2-5.2,7.1,7.2,9.1-9.4) "Direction Générale du Tourisme et de l'Hôtellerie - Ministère de la Culture, des Arts et du Tourisme"; (6.1-6.3,8.2-8.4) Fondo Monetario Internacional.

COREA, REPUBLICA DE

(1.1) Incluidos los nacionales residentes en el extranjero y miembros de las tripulaciones; (2.1-2.6) Excluidos los nacionales residentes en el extranjero; (3.1,3.4) Excluidos los nacionales residentes en el extranjero y miembros de las tripulaciones; (8.2) El país facilita a la OMT niveles agregados de gasto que son significativamente diferentes a los datos del Fondo Monetario Internacional utilizados para la preparación de esta edición del Compendio (excluidos los gastos de los estudiantes que realizan sus estudios fuera del país). Los datos del país son:
2001: 6.547
2002: 9.038
2003: 8.248
2004: 9.856
(9.1) Hoteles únicamente; (9.3) Habitaciones.
Fuentes: (1.1-5.4,8.1,9.1,9.3) "Ministry of Culture and Tourism"; (6.1-6.3,8.2-8.4) Fondo Monetario Internacional.

COSTA RICA

(4.1) Viajes de placer y visita a familiares; (5.4) En la zona central del país; (9.3) En establecimientos de "cinco categorías" en el Gran Área Metropolitana de San José (estudio por muestreo).
Fuentes: (1.1-5.4,8.1,9.1,9.3) Instituto Costarricense de Turismo; (6.1-6.3,8.2-8.4) Fondo Monetario Internacional.

CROACIA

(1.2,2.2-2.4) Turistas no residentes alojados en todo tipo de establecimientos de alojamiento; incluidas las llegadas a los puertos de turismo náutico; (3.1-3.4) Llegadas de visitantes no residentes en las fronteras nacionales; (3.4/2004) Desde 2004 se aplicó una nueva metodología y cobertura y por lo tanto la información no es comparable con años anteriores; (5.3,7.3)

Incluidas las pernoctaciones en puertos de turismo náutico; (9.4) Turismo interior (interno y receptor) en todos los medios de alojamiento (incluidos los puertos de turismo náutico).
Fuentes: (1.1-5.4,7.1-7.4,9.1-9.4) "Central Bureau of Statistics"; (6.1-6.3,8.2-8.4) Fondo Monetario Internacional.

CUBA

(1.1,2.1-2.6) Llegadas de visitantes no residentes en las fronteras nacionales; (1.2,4.1-4.3) Llegadas por vía aérea; (1.3) Incluidos los pasajeros en crucero; (5.1,7.1,9.1,9.2) Hoteles, moteles y aparthoteles; (5.3,7.3) Hoteles, moteles, aparthoteles, terrenos de camping/caravaning y otros; (6.1) Las cifras de gasto corresponden a las facilitadas por el país a la OMT y que, sin embargo, no figuran en los datos del Fondo Monetario Internacional utilizados para la preparación de esta edición del Compendio; (8.1) Comprende sólo giras controladas por el Instituto del Turismo; (9.3) Habitaciones.
Fuente: Oficina Nacional de Estadísticas.

CURAÇAO

(1.2,1.3,2.2,2.3,3.1,4.1-4.3) Llegadas por vía aérea; (3.4) Llegadas de pasajeros en crucero; (4.1-4.3) Diferencias en los totales globales debido a la falta de datos completos en las tarjetas de embarque y desembarque de los visitantes; (6.1) Las cifras de gasto corresponden a las facilitadas por el país a la OMT y que, sin embargo, no figuran en los datos del Fondo Monetario Internacional utilizados para la preparación de esta edición del Compendio; (9.1) Hoteles, casas de huéspedes y apartamentos; (9.3) Habitaciones.
Fuente: "Curaçao Tourist Board".

DINAMARCA

(1.2,2.2-2.4,5.1-5.3,7.1-7.3) Nueva cobertura desde 2000; (1.2,2.2-2.4) Turistas no residentes alojados en todo tipo de establecimientos de alojamiento; (1.2-5.3,7.1-7.3,8.1) Nueva metodología a partir de 2004; (5.2,7.2) Hoteles únicamente; (9.1-9.3) Únicamente hoteles y alojamientos de vacaciones con 40 camas o más; (9.3) Plazas-cama; (10.1-10.3) Este apartado incluye únicamente la partida "viajes" debido a que la partida "transporte de pasajeros" no figura en los datos del Fondo Monetario Internacional utilizados para la preparación de esta edición del Compendio.
Fuentes: (1.2-5.4,7.1-7.4,8.1,9.1-9.3) "Statistics Denmark"; (6.2,8.3) Fondo Monetario Internacional.

DJIBOUTI

(1.2) Turistas no residentes alojados en hoteles; (9.3) Habitaciones.
Fuentes: (1.2,5.1,5.2,9.1-9.3) "Office national du tourisme"; (6.2,8.3) "Banque centrale".

DOMINICA

(1.2,2.2,2.3,4.1-4.3) Llegadas de turistas no residentes en las fronteras nacionales; (3.1,3.4) Llegadas de visitantes no residentes en las fronteras nacionales; excluidos los pasajeros en crucero; (5.4) Días; (10.1-10.3) Este apartado incluye únicamente la partida "viajes" debido a que la partida "transporte de pasajeros" no figura en los datos del Fondo Monetario Internacional utilizados para la preparación de esta edición del Compendio.
Fuentes: (1.1-5.4,9.1) "Central Statistical Office - Ministry of Finance"; (6.2,8.3) Fondo Monetario Internacional.

ECUADOR

(1.1) Excluidos los nacionales residentes en el extranjero; (1.1-3.4,8.1/2005) Datos provisionales.
Fuentes: (1.1-3.4,8.1,9.1,9.2) Ministerio de Turismo; (6.1-6.3,8.2-8.4) Fondo Monetario Internacional.

EGIPTO

(1.1,2.1-3.4) Llegadas de visitantes no residentes en las fronteras nacionales; (4.1-4.3) Llegadas de turistas no residentes en las fronteras nacionales; (7.1) Hoteles únicamente en las principales regiones: Cairo, Giza, Sur del Sinaí, Mar Rojo, Luxor, Aswan, Alejandría; (8.1) Viajes por turismo y no-turismo (más del 50% por motivo de trabajo); (9.3) Habitaciones.
Fuentes: (1.1-5.4,7.1-7.4,8.1,9.1-9.4) "Ministry of Tourism"; (6.1-6.3,8.2-8.4) Fondo Monetario Internacional.

EL SALVADOR

(1.2,2.1-4.3) Llegadas de turistas no residentes en las fronteras nacionales; (6.1) El país facilita a la OMT niveles agregados de gasto que son significativamente diferentes a los datos del Fondo Monetario Internacional utilizados para la preparación de esta edición del Compendio. Los datos del país son (millones $EE.UU.):
2001: 235
2002: 342
2003: 373
2004: 425
2005: 644
Dicho gasto turístico es obtenido en base a investigaciones conjuntas con el Banco Central de Reserva de El Salvador y la Corporación Salvadoreña de Turismo para la identificación de un Perfil Básico de Turista internacional que visita El Salvador.
(9.3) Plazas-cama.

Fuentes: (1.1-5.4,8.1,9.1-9.4) Corporación Salvadoreña de Turismo (CORSATUR) - Ministerio de Turismo; (6.1-6.3,8.2-8.4) Fondo Monetario Internacional.

EMIRATOS ARABES UNIDOS

(1.2) Llegadas en los hoteles únicamente. Incluido el turismo interno y los nacionales residentes en el extranjero; (2.1-2.6) Llegadas en los hoteles únicamente. Excluido el turismo interno y los nacionales residentes en el extranjero; (5.1) Pernoctaciones en los hoteles únicamente. Incluido el turismo interno y los nacionales residentes en el extranjero; (6.1,8.2) Las cifras de gasto corresponden a las facilitadas por el país a la OMT y que, sin embargo, no figuran en los datos del Fondo Monetario Internacional utilizados para la preparación de esta edición del Compendio; (9.1,9.2) Hoteles únicamente; (9.3) Habitaciones alquiladas.
Fuente: "Ministry of Economy and Planning - Planning Sector".

ERITREA

(1.1) Incluidos los nacionales residentes en el extranjero; (2.1-2.6) Excluidos los nacionales residentes en el extranjero; (5.1,7.1) Únicamente hoteles y establecimientos asimilados en las tres principales ciudades: Asmara, Karen y Massawa; (6.1) Los datos de gastos corresponden a los facilitados por el país a la OMT, por tratarse de una serie más completa que la facilitada por el Fondo Monetario Internacional (FMI) para la preparación de esta edición del Compendio; (9.1,9.2/2001-2004) Únicamente en las principales ciudades de Eritrea: (9.1,9.2/2005) Todos los hoteles y establecimientos asimilados en Eritrea; (10.1-10.3) Este apartado no se ha podido completar debido a que las partidas “viajes” y “transporte de pasajeros” no figuran en los datos del Fondo Monetario Internacional utilizados para la preparación de esta edición del Compendio.
Fuente: "Ministry of Tourism".

ESLOVAQUIA

(1.1) Incluida la frontera con la República Checa; (1.2,2.1-2.5) Turistas no residentes alojados en todo tipo de establecimientos de alojamiento; (5.4,9.4) Turismo receptor en todo tipo de establecimientos de alojamiento turístico; (8.1) Turismo organizado a través de la Agencia de viajes eslovaca.
Fuentes: (1.1-5.4,7.1-7.4,8.1,9.1-9.4) (6.1-6.3,8.2-8.4/2001/2004) "Department of Tourism - Ministry of Economy"; (6.1-6.3,8.2-8.4/2002/2003) Fondo Monetario Internacional.

ESLOVENIA

(1.1) Incluidas todas las categorías de viajeros por cualquier motivo de visita; (1.2,2.1-2.6) Turistas no residentes alojados en todo tipo de establecimientos de alojamiento; (2.1,2.5,2.6) Estimaciones; (3.1-3.4,4.1-4.3) Turistas no residentes alojados en todo tipo de establecimientos de alojamiento; datos procedentes de la encuesta sobre 3 años realizada en verano entre los turistas extranjeros llegados a Eslovenia; (8.1) Encuesta trimestral de los viajes de la población residente.
Fuentes: (1.1-5.4,7.1-7.4,8.1,9.1-9.4) "Statistical Office - Information Society and Tourism Statistics"; (6.1-6.3,8.2-8.4) Fondo Monetario Internacional.

ESPAÑA

(1.1) Llegadas de visitantes no residentes en las fronteras nacionales; incluidos los nacionales residentes en el extranjero; (2.2-4.3) Llegadas de turistas no residentes en las fronteras nacionales; incluidos los nacionales residentes en el extranjero; (2.4) Japón únicamente; (5.1,7.1) Pernoctaciones en hoteles y hostales; (5.3,7.3) Pernoctaciones en hoteles, hostales, terrenos de camping, apartamentos turísticos y alojamientos/casas rurales; (5.4,7.4,9.1-9.4) Hoteles y hostales únicamente; (8.1) Desde 2005 se aplicó una nueva metodología y por lo tanto la información no es comparable con años anteriores; (9.3) Plazas-cama.
Fuentes: (1.1-4.3,8.1) Instituto de Estudios Turísticos; (5.1-5.4,7.1-7.4,9.1-9.4) Instituto Nacional de Estadística; (6.1-6.3,8.2-8.4) Fondo Monetario Internacional.

ESTADOS UNIDOS

(1.2,2.2) Incluidos los mexicanos que pasan una noche o más en EE.UU.; (3.1-3.4) Estimaciones preliminares; (3.3) Incluye un muy pequeño porcentaje (0.2%) de viajeros cuyo modo de transporte no se conoce; (4.1-4.3) Principal motivo del viaje; (4.1-4.3,5.2) Ultramar únicamente; excluido México (los datos no están disponibles); (6.2,8.3) El país facilita a la OMT datos de gasto que son significativamente diferentes a los datos del Fondo Monetario Internacional utilizados para la preparación de esta edición del Compendio. Los datos del país son:

	6.2	8.3
2001:	71.893	60.200
2002:	66.605	58.715
2003:	64.348	57.444
2004:	74.547	65.750
2005:	81.680	69.175

(8.1) Incluidos los americanos que pasan una o varias noches en México.
Fuentes: (1.2-3.4,8.1) "Office of Travel and Tourism Industries"; (6.1-6.3,8.2-8.4) Fondo Monetario Internacional; (9.1,9.3) "American Hotel & Lodging Association (AHLA)".

ESTONIA

(1.1,3.1-4.3) Llegadas de visitantes no residentes en las fronteras nacionales; (1.1-1.3,3.1-4.3,8.1/2004) A partir de 2004 no se recopilan las estadísticas de fronteras; (1.2/2004/2005) Calculado en base a las estadísticas de alojamiento y a la "Foreign Visitor Survey" realizada por la "Statistical Office of Estonia"; (2.1-2.4) Turistas no residentes alojados en todo tipo de establecimientos de alojamiento; (4.3) Compras, tránsito, visitas a los amigos; (9.1-9.4) Se incluyen los datos de complejos de salud que ofrecen un servicio de alojamiento.
Fuentes: (1.1-5.4,7.3,7.4,8.1,9.1-9.4) "Estonian Tourist Board / Enterprise Estonia"; (6.1-6.3,8.2-8.4) Fondo Monetario Internacional; (7.1,7.2) "EUROSTAT (New Cronos)".

ETIOPIA

(1.2) Llegadas a todos los puestos fronterizos; incluidos los nacionales residentes en el extranjero; (2.1-2.6,3.1-3.3) Llegadas a todos los puestos fronterizos; (4.1-4.3/2001) Llegadas al aeropuerto de Bole únicamente; (4.1-4.3/2002-2005) Llegadas a todos los puestos fronterizos; (9.1,9.2/2001) Incluidos los hoteles privados y estatales; (9.1,9.2/2002/2003/2005) Excluidos los hoteles sin homologar; (9.3) Plazas-cama; (9.4) Años fiscales etíopes.
Fuentes: (1.2-5.4,9.1-9.4) "Ethiopian Tourism Commission"; (6.1-6.3,8.2-8.4) Fondo Monetario Internacional.

EX REPUBLICA YUGOSLAVA DE MACEDONIA

(1.2,2.2-2.4) Turistas no residentes alojados en todo tipo de establecimientos de alojamiento; (3.1-3.3) Llegadas de visitantes no residentes en las fronteras nacionales; (9.4) Duración media de la estancia en todos los establecimientos de alojamiento.
Fuentes: (1.1-5.4,7.1-7.4,9.1-9.4) "State Statistical Office"; (6.1-6.3,8.2-8.4) Fondo Monetario Internacional.

FEDERACION DE RUSIA

(1.1,2.1-4.3) Llegadas de visitantes no residentes en las fronteras nacionales; (9.1,9.2) Alojamiento en hoteles y en otros establecimientos de carácter turístico.
Fuentes: (1.1-5.4,7.1-7.4,8.1,9.1-9.4) "Russian Federal Agency for Tourism"; (6.1-6.3,8.2-8.4) Fondo Monetario Internacional.

FIJI

(1.2,2.2-4.3) Llegadas de turistas no residentes en las fronteras nacionales; excluidos los nacionales residentes en el extranjero; (5.4) Días; (6.1-6.3,8.2-8.4) Las cifras de gasto corresponden a las facilitadas por el país a la OMT y que, sin embargo, no figuran en los datos del Fondo Monetario Internacional utilizados para la preparación de esta edición del Compendio; (9.3) Habitaciones.
Fuente: "Fiji Islands Bureau of Statistics".

FILIPINAS

(1.2,3.1-4.3) Llegadas de turistas no residentes en las fronteras nacionales; incluidos los nacionales residentes en el extranjero; (2.1-2.6) Llegadas de turistas no residentes en las fronteras nacionales; excluidos los nacionales residentes en el extranjero; (4.1-4.3) Llegadas por vía aérea; (8.1) Incluidos los trabajadores con contrato procedentes de ultramar; (9.1,9.2) Hoteles homologados únicamente; (9.3,9.4) Hoteles homologados en Metro Manila.
Fuentes: (1.2-5.4,8.1,9.1-9.4) "Department of Tourism"; (6.1-6.3,8.2-8.4) Fondo Monetario Internacional.

FINLANDIA

(1.1,2.1-4.3) Llegadas de visitantes no residentes en las fronteras nacionales. Encuesta en las fronteras; (1.2) Llegadas de turistas no residentes en las fronteras nacionales; (5.1-5.3,7.1-7.3) Debido a un cambio en la metodología, la información de 2004 no es comparable con años anteriores; (8.1) Viajes al extranjero, incluidos los cruceros con pernoctaciones a bordo.
Fuentes: (1.1-5.4,7.1-7.4,8.1,9.1-9.4) "Tourism Statistics - Statistics Finland"; (6.1-6.3,8.2-8.4) Fondo Monetario Internacional.

FRANCIA

(1.2,2.1-2.6,5.3) Estimación basada en la encuesta en fronteras de 1996. Datos revisados desde 1996; (2.4) Incluye Asia Meridional; (3.1-4.3) Estimaciones; (5.1,5.2,7.1,7.2,9.1-9.3) Hoteles únicamente; (5.3,7.3) Todo tipo de alojamiento; (5.4) Duración media de la estancia del turismo receptor; (7.3) Serie revisada y extrapolada retroactivamente; (9.3) Tasa neta de ocupación de las habitaciones; (10.1-10.3) Este apartado incluye únicamente la partida "viajes" debido a que la partida "transporte de pasajeros" no figura en los datos del Fondo Monetario Internacional utilizados para la preparación de esta edición del Compendio.
2005: Datos provisionales.
Fuentes: (1.2-5.4,7.1-7.4,8.1,9.1-9.4) "Bureau des études, des statistiques et des comptes économiques - Direction du Tourisme"; (6.2,8.3) Fondo Monetario Internacional.

GABON

(1.2,2.1-2.6,3.1) Llegadas de turistas no residentes al aeropuerto de Libreville.

Fuentes: (1.1-5.1,8.1,9.1,9.3) "Centre Gabonais de Promotion Touristique (GABONTOUR)"; (6.1-6.3,8.2-8.4) Fondo Monetario Internacional.

GAMBIA

(1.2,2.1-2.3,3.1,4.1) Llegadas en vuelos fletados únicamente; (1.1-4.1/2005) Datos provisionales.
Fuentes: (1.1-4.1,8.1,9.1,9.4) "Gambia Tourism Authority"; (6.1-6.3,8.2-8.4) Fondo Monetario Internacional.

GEORGIA

(4.1-4.3) Llegadas en hoteles únicamente.
Fuentes: (1.2-4.3,5.3,8.1,9.1-9.3) "Department of Tourism and Resorts - Ministry of Economic Development"; (5.2,7.2) "State Department for Statistics - Ministry of Economic Development"; (6.1-6.3,8.2-8.4) Fondo Monetario Internacional.

GHANA

(1.2) Incluidos los nacionales residentes en el extranjero; (2.1-2.6) Excluidos los nacionales residentes en el extranjero.
Fuentes: (1.2-4.3,9.1-9.3) "Ghana Tourist Board" y "Ministry of Tourism and Modernisation of the Capital City"; (6.1-6.3,8.2-8.4) Fondo Monetario Internacional.

GRANADA

(1.2,2.2-4.3) Llegadas de turistas no residentes en las fronteras nacionales; (9.1,9.2) Hoteles, bungalows/ apartamentos y casas de huéspedes; (9.3) Habitaciones; (10.1-10.3) Este apartado incluye únicamente la partida "viajes" debido a que la partida "transporte de pasajeros" no figura en los datos del Fondo Monetario Internacional utilizados para la preparación de esta edición del Compendio.
Fuentes: (1.1-5.4,9.1-9.4) "Grenada Board of Tourism"; (6.2,8.3) Fondo Monetario Internacional.

GRECIA

(1.1,3.1-3.4) Llegadas de visitantes no residentes en las fronteras nacionales; (1.2,2.1-2.6) Llegadas de turistas no residentes en las fronteras nacionales; información procedente de datos administrativos; (3.4) Incluidos los pasajeros en crucero.
Fuentes: (1.1-5.4,7.1-7.4,9.3) "National Statistical Service"; (6.1-6.3,8.2-8.4) Fondo Monetario Internacional; (9.1,9.2) "Hellenic Chamber of Hotels".

GUADALUPE

(1.2) Llegadas por vía aérea; excluidas las islas del norte (San Martín y San Barthelemy); (1.2/2001) Turistas no residentes alojados en todo tipo de establecimientos de alojamiento; (1.2/2003/2004) Turistas no residentes alojados en hoteles únicamente; (1.2,2.3,3.1/2005) Datos obtenidos en una encuesta realizada en el aeropuerto de Guadalupe; (5.2) Hoteles únicamente; (9.1) Hoteles; (9.3) Habitaciones.
Fuente: "Comité du Tourisme des Îles de la Guadeloupe".

GUAM

(1.2) Llegadas por vías aérea y marítima; (2.2-2.4) Llegadas por vía aérea únicamente; (4.1-4.3) Llegadas de civiles por vía aérea únicamente; (9.1) Habitaciones disponibles.
Fuente: "Guam Visitors Bureau".

GUATEMALA

(8.2) El país facilita a la OMT niveles agregados de gasto que son significativamente diferentes a los datos del Fondo Monetario Internacional. Los datos del país son:
2001: 407
2002: 517
2003: 601
2004: 735
2005: 754
Fuentes: (1.2-3.4,8.1,9.1-9.3) Instituto Guatemalteco de Turismo - INGUAT; (6.1-6.3,8.2-8.4) Fondo Monetario Internacional.

GUINEA

(1.2,2.1-2.6,4.1-4.3/2003/2005) Llegadas por vía aérea al aeropuerto de Conakry; (5.2) Hoteles únicamente; (6.2) Los datos de gastos corresponden a los facilitados por el país a la OMT, por tratarse de una serie más completa que la facilitada por el Fondo Monetario Internacional (FMI) para la preparación de esta edición del Compendio.
Nota 2005: Datos provisionales..
Fuentes: (1.2-5.4,6.2,9.1-9.4) "Division Observatoire du Tourisme - Ministère du Tourisme, de l'Hôtellerie et de l'Artisanat"; (6.3,8.2-8.4) Fondo Monetario Internacional.

GUINEA-BISSAU

(1.2,2.1-2.6,4.1-4.3) Llegadas por vía aérea; (2.1-2.6,4.1-4.3/2005) Llegadas al aeropuerto "Osvaldo Vieira".
Fuentes: (1.2-4.3) "Ministério do Turismo e do Ordenamento do Território"; (6.1-6.3,8.2-8.4) Fondo Monetario Internacional.

GUYANA

(1.2,2.2,2.3,3.1/2002-2005) Llegadas al aeropuerto de Timehri únicamente.
Fuentes: (1.2-3.1) "Guyana Tourism Authority"; (6.1-6.3,8.2-8.4) Fondo Monetario Internacional.

GUYANA FRANCESA

(1.2,6.1/2005) Encuesta 2005 en el aeropuerto de Cayenne-Rochambeau a la salida.
Fuentes: "Comité du Tourisme de la Guyane" e "INSEE Guyane".

HAITI

(10.1-10.3) Este apartado incluye únicamente la partida “viajes” debido a que la partida “transporte de pasajeros” no figura en los datos del Fondo Monetario Internacional utilizados para la preparación de esta edición del Compendio.
Fuentes: (1.1-3.4) "Ministère du Tourisme"; (6.2,8.2-8.4) Fondo Monetario Internacional.

HONDURAS

(1.2,2.1-4.3) Llegadas de turistas no residentes en las fronteras nacionales.
Fuentes: (1.1-5.4,8.1,9.1-9.4) Instituto Hondureño de Turismo; (6.1-6.3,8.2-8.4) Fondo Monetario Internacional.

HONG KONG, CHINA

(6.1-6.3) Las datos de gastos corresponden a los facilitados por el país a la OMT, por tratarse de una serie más completa que la facilitada por el Fondo Monetario Internacional (FMI) para la preparación de esta edición del Compendio. (Fuente: "HKTB Visitors Survey"); (8.1) Excluidos los residentes de Hong Kong viajando a Macao y China; (9.1) Hoteles (tarifas altas/medias) y albergues/ casas huéspedes; (9.3) Habitaciones.
Fuentes: (1.1-8.1,9.1,9.3) "Hong Kong Tourism Board"; (8.3) "Census and Statistics Department".

HUNGRIA

(1.1/2001-2003) (3.1-3.4) Salidas de visitantes no residentes; (1.1-1.4,4.1-4.3/2004) Nueva serie; (2.1-2.4) Turistas no residentes alojados en todo tipo de establecimientos de alojamiento; (3.4) Por vía fluvial; (9.3) Habitaciones, Julio-Junio.
Fuentes: (1.1-5.4,7.1-7.4,8.1,9.1-9.4) "Hungarian Central statistical Office"; (6.1-6.3,8.2-8.4) Fondo Monetario Internacional.

INDIA

(1.2,2.1-4.3) Llegadas de turistas no residentes en las fronteras nacionales: excluidos los nacionales residentes en el extranjero; (4.1) Incluye otros motivos; (8.1) Salidas de nacionales del país únicamente, por cualquier motivo de visita; (9.1,9.2) En hoteles homologados; (9.3) Habitaciones.
Fuentes: (1.1-4.3,8.1,9.1-9.3) "Market Research Division - Government of India"; (6.1-6.3,8.2-8.4) Fondo Monetario Internacional.

INDONESIA

(5.2,7.2,7.4,9.3) Únicamente hoteles clasificados; (9.1,9.2) Conjunto de los medios comerciales de alojamiento; (9.3) Habitaciones.
Fuentes: (1.2-5.4,7.1-7.4,8.1,9.1-9.3) "Ministry of Culture and Tourism" y "BPS Statistics Indonesia"; (6.1-6.3,8.2-8.4) Fondo Monetario Internacional.

IRAN, REPUBLICA ISLAMICA DEL

(3.3) Incluye ferrocarril; (5.2,7.2) Hoteles únicamente; (9.1,9.2) Hoteles únicamente, 21 de Marzo-20 de Marzo; (9.3) Estimaciones (plazas-cama).
Fuentes: (1.2-5.4,7.1-7.4,8.1,9.1-9.4) "Iran Cultural Heritage and Tourism Organization (ICHTO)"; (6.1-6.3,8.2-8.4) "Central Bank of Islamic Republic of Iran".

IRLANDA

(1.2,2.3,3.3,4.1-4.3,5.4) Incluidos los turistas procedentes de Irlanda del Norte; (3.3) Incluye ferrocarril; (8.1) Incluidos los visitantes del día (excursionistas); (9.1) Excluidos los hostales; (9.3) Habitaciones, hoteles únicamente.
Fuentes: (1.2-5.4,7.1-7.4,8.1,9.1-9.3) "Fáilte Ireland"; (6.1-6.3,8.2-8.4) Fondo Monetario Internacional.

ISLANDIA

(1.2,2.1-2.4) Turistas no residentes alojados en todo tipo de establecimientos de alojamiento; (3.1,3.4) Llegadas de turistas no residentes a las fronteras islandesas.
Nota: Debido a la introducción del Schengen en marzo de 2001, la recopilación de datos sobre entradas y salidas en las fronteras islandesas sufrió cambios. A partir de 2002 la recopilación de estos datos es realizada por "Icelandic Tourist Board".
Fuentes: (1.2-2.4,5.1-5.4,7.1-7.4,9.1-9.4) "Hagstofa Íslands Statistics Iceland"; (3.1,3.4) "Icelandic Tourist Board"; (6.1-6.3,8.2-8.4) Fondo Monetario Internacional.

ISLAS CAIMAN

(1.2,2.2-2.4,4.1-4.3) Llegadas por vía aérea; (5.4,9.4) Días; (6.1) Las cifras de gasto corresponden a las facilitadas por el país a la OMT y que, sin embargo, no figuran en los datos del Fondo Monetario Internacional utilizados para la preparación de esta edición del Compendio. Incluidos los gastos de los pasajeros en crucero; (9.1,9.2) Hoteles y apartamentos; (9.3) Hoteles (habitaciones).
Fuente: "Cayman Islands Department of Tourism".

ISLAS COOK

(1.2,2.2-2.4,4.1-4.3) Llegadas por vías aérea y marítima; (6.1) Las cifras de gasto corresponden a las facilitadas por el país a la OMT y que, sin embargo, no figuran en los datos del Fondo Monetario Internacional utilizados para la preparación de esta edición del Compendio; (9.3) Habitaciones.
Fuente: "Cook Islands Tourism Corporation" y "Cook Islands Statistics Office".

ISLAS MARIANAS SEPTENTRIONALES

(1.1,2.2-2.4) Llegadas de visitantes no residentes en las fronteras nacionales; (1.2) Llegadas por vía aérea; (2.2) Incluye Guam; (9.1) Cubre el 68 por ciento del total de habitaciones censadas.
Fuente: "Marianas Visitors Authority".

ISLAS MARSHALL

(1.2,2.2-2.4,4.1-4.3/2001-2003) Llegadas por vía aérea; (1.2,2.2-2.4,4.1-4.3/2004/2005) Llegadas por vías aérea y marítima; (6.1) Las cifras de gasto corresponden a las facilitadas por el país a la OMT y que, sin embargo, no figuran en los datos del Fondo Monetario Internacional utilizados para la preparación de esta edición del Compendio.
Fuente: "Marshall Islands Visitors Authority".

ISLAS SALOMON

(1.2,2.2-2.4/2005) Excluido el 1er trimestre.
Fuentes: (1.2,2.2-2.4) "Solomon Islands National Statistics Office"; (6.2,8.3) "Central Bank of Solomon Islands".

ISLAS TURCAS Y CAICOS

(6.1) Las cifras de gasto corresponden a las facilitadas por el país a la OMT y que, sin embargo, no figuran en los datos del Fondo Monetario Internacional utilizados para la preparación de esta edición del Compendio.
Fuente: "Turks and Caicos Tourist Board".

ISLAS VIRGENES AMERICANAS

(2.1-2.4) Turistas no residentes alojados en hoteles y establecimientos asimilados; (3.1) Llegadas de visitantes por vía aérea; excluidas las llegadas de residentes y el tráfico entre las islas pero incluidos los excursionistas; (3.4) Pasajeros en crucero; (5.3) Incluido el turismo interno (cerca del 40% del total); (6.1) Las cifras de gasto corresponden a las facilitadas por el país a la OMT y que, sin embargo, no figuran en los datos del Fondo Monetario Internacional utilizados para la preparación de esta edición del Compendio; (9.1,9.3) Hoteles y condominios o villas; (9.3) Habitaciones.
2005: Datos provisionales.
Fuente: "Bureau of Economic Research".

ISLAS VIRGENES BRITANICAS

(1.1-9.4/2004/2005) Estimaciones; (6.1) Las cifras de gasto corresponden a las facilitadas por el país a la OMT y que, sin embargo, no figuran en los datos del Fondo Monetario Internacional utilizados para la preparación de esta edición del Compendio; (9.3) Habitaciones.
Fuente: "The Development Planning Unit - Ministry of Finance".

ISRAEL

(1.1) Llegadas de visitantes no residentes en las fronteras nacionales; excluidos los nacionales residentes en el extranjero; (1.2,2.1-4.3) Llegadas de turistas no residentes en las fronteras nacionales; excluidos los nacionales residentes en el

extranjero; (3.3) Incluidas las nuevas entradas tras una visita de hasta 7 días en el Sinaí; (3.4) Incluido el personal de la flota de EE.UU. en visita de cortesía; (4.3) Incluidas las visitas a familiares y amigos y peregrinaciones; (5.1) Hoteles turísticos y apart-hoteles; (6.2) Incluidos los gastos de los trabajadores extranjeros en Israel (Millones de $EE.UU.):
2001: 1.097
2002: 1.125
2003: 997
2004: 905
2005: 929
(9.3) Tasa de ocupación/camas en hoteles y establecimientos asimilados abiertos; (9.4) Turismo receptor en hoteles turísticos.
Fuentes: (1.1-5.4,7.1-7.3,8.1,9.1-9.4) "Ministry of Tourism"; (6.1-6.3,8.2-8.4) Fondo Monetario Internacional.

ITALIA

(1.1,3.1-4.3) Llegadas de visitantes no residentes en las fronteras nacionales; excluidos los trabajadores estacionales o fronterizos; (1.1-4.3,8.1) Encuesta en fronteras del "Ufficio Italiano dei Cambi"; (1.2,2.1-2.6) Llegadas de turistas no residentes en las fronteras nacionales; excluidos los trabajadores estacionales o fronterizos; (1.3) Incluidos los pasajeros en crucero; (5.1,5.2) Hoteles únicamente; (8.1) Número de turistas residentes (visitantes que pernoctan) que viajan al extranjero; (9.3) Plazas-cama.
Fuentes: (1.1-4.3,8.1) "Ufficio Italiano dei Cambi"; (5.1-5.4,7.1-7.4,9.1-9.4) "Statistiche sul Turismo - Istituto Nazionale di Statistica (ISTAT)"; (6.1-6.3,8.2-8.4) Fondo Monetario Internacional.

JAMAHIRIYA ARABE LIBIA

(1.1,2.1-2.6) Incluidos todos los viajeros (visitantes y otros viajeros no definidos como viajeros por la OMT); (3.1-3.4) Llegadas de visitantes no residentes en las fronteras nacionales; (4.1-4.3) Llegadas de turistas no residentes en las fronteras nacionales.
Nota 2001-200: Datos preliminares.
Fuente: "General People's Committee for Tourism"; (6.1-6.3,8.2-8.4) Fondo Monetario Internacional.

JAMAICA

(1.2,2.1-4.3) Llegadas por vía aérea de turistas no residentes; incluidos los nacionales residentes en el extranjero; tarjetas E/D; (5.3) Datos obtenidos multiplicando la duración media de la estancia por el número de escalas en cada uno de los países de origen; (5.4) Duración de estancia prevista; (9.3) Habitaciones; (9.4) Pernoctaciones en los hoteles únicamente.
Fuentes: (1.1-5.4,9.1-9.4) "Jamaica Tourist Board"; (6.1-6.3,8.2-8.4) Fondo Monetario Internacional.

JAPON

(1.2,2.1-2.6,4.1-4.3) Llegadas de turistas no residentes en las fronteras nacionales; excluidos los nacionales residentes en el extranjero; (3.1,3.4) Llegadas de visitantes no residentes en las fronteras nacionales; incluidos los residentes extranjeros en Japón; (5.4) Días; (6.2/2003) El método de cálculo ha sido cambiado desde enero de 2003; (9.1) Hoteles homologados y no homologados así como "ryokans" (posadas); (9.3) Tasa de ocupación de los principales hoteles gubernamentales homologados (habitaciones).
Fuentes: (1.2-5.4,7.1,8.1,9.1,9.3) "Japan National Tourist Organization"; (6.1-6.3,8.2-8.4) Fondo Monetario Internacional.

JORDANIA

(1.1-1.3) Incluidos los nacionales residentes en el extranjero; (2.1-2.6) Llegadas de turistas no residentes en las fronteras nacionales; excluidos los nacionales residentes en el extranjero; (3.1-3.4) Llegadas de visitantes residentes y no residentes; (5.4) Para visitas organizadas únicamente; (9.3) Habitaciones.
Fuentes: (1.1-5.4,7.1-7.4,8.1,9.1-9.4) "Ministry of Tourism and Antiquities"; (6.1-6.3,8.2-8.4) Fondo Monetario Internacional.

KAZAJSTAN

(2.1-2.6,3.1-4.3) Llegadas de visitantes no residentes en las fronteras nacionales.
Fuentes: (1.1-5.,7.1,8.1,9.1-9.3) "Agency of Statistics of the Republic of Kazakhstan"; (6.1-6.3,8.2-8.4) Fondo Monetario Internacional.

KENYA

(1.1,2.1-4.3) Llegadas de visitantes no residentes a través de todos los puestos fronterizos; excluidos los nacionales residentes en el extranjero; (9.3) Plazas-cama; (9.4) Días.
Fuentes: (1.1-5.4,7.1,7.4,9.1-9.4) "Kenya Tourist Board"; (6.1-6.3,8.2-8.4) Fondo Monetario Internacional.

KIRGUISTAN

(1.2,2.2-2.5,8.1/2003-2005) Nueva fuente de información: Departamento de Control Aduanero.
Fuentes: (1.1-5.2,7.1,7.2,8.1,9.1,9.2) "National Statistical Committee"; (6.1-6.3,8.2-8.4) Fondo Monetario Internacional.

KIRIBATI

(1.2,2.2-2.4,3.1) Llegadas por vía aérea. 2001-2003: Tarawa e Isla Christmas. 2004/2005: Tarawa únicamente; (4.1-4.3) Llegadas por vía aérea. 2001: Tarawa e Isla Christmas. 2002-2005: Tarawa únicamente; (6.1) Las cifras de gasto corresponden a las facilitadas por el país a la OMT y que, sin embargo, no figuran en los datos del Fondo Monetario Internacional utilizados para la preparación de esta edición del Compendio.
Fuente: "Ministry of Communication, Transport and Tourism Development".

KUWAIT

(1.1,2.1-2.6,3.1-3.4) Llegadas de visitantes no residentes en las fronteras nacionales; (1.2,4.1-4.3) Turistas no residentes alojados en hoteles y establecimientos asimilados.
Fuentes: (1.1-5.4,8.1,9.1,9.2) "Ministry of Planning"; (6.1-6.3,8.2-8.4) Fondo Monetario Internacional.

LESOTHO

(1.1,2.1-4.3) Llegadas de visitantes no residentes en las fronteras nacionales; (1.1-4.3/2004/2005) Estimaciones; (10.1-10.3) Este apartado incluye únicamente la partida "viajes" debido a que la partida "transporte de pasajeros" no figura en los datos del Fondo Monetario Internacional utilizados para la preparación de esta edición del Compendio.
Fuentes: (1.1-4.3,9.1,9.3) "Lesotho Tourism Development Corporation"; (6.2,8.2-8.4) Fondo Monetario Internacional.

LETONIA

(1.1,3.1-3.4) Llegadas de visitantes no residentes en las fronteras nacionales. Datos procedentes de la Policía Estatal de Fronteras; (1.2-1.4,2.2-2.5,4.1-4.3) Salidas de no residentes. Encuesta realizada en los puestos fronterizos del país; (1.3) Incluidos los pasajeros en crucero; (4.3) Incluidas las visitas a parientes y amigos y tratamientos de salud; (5.3,5,4) Pernoctaciones en todos los establecimientos de alojamiento colectivo; (5.4) Duración media de la estancia de visitantes no residentes que pernoctan; encuesta realizada en los puestos fronterizos del país; (8.1) Datos procedentes de la Policía Estatal de Fronteras; (9.3) Plazas-cama.
Fuentes: (1.1-5.4,7.1-7.4,8.1,9.1-9.4) "Transport and Tourism Statistics Section - Central Statistical Bureau"; (6.1-6.3,8.2-8.4) Fondo Monetario Internacional.

LIBANO

(1.2) Excluidos los nacionales de Siria; (6.1/2001) Las cifras de gasto corresponden a las facilitadas por el país a la OMT y que, sin embargo, no figuran en los datos del Fondo Monetario Internacional utilizados para la preparación de esta edición del Compendio. Por falta de datos sobre ingresos por turismo internacional relativo a estadísticas del turismo receptor, el Departamento "Internet y Servicio Estadístico del Ministerio de Turismo" considera que un turista gasta una media de 1.000 $EEUU.
Fuentes: "Ministère du Tourisme"; (6.1-6.3,8.2-8.4/2002-2005) Fondo Monetario Internacional.

LIECHTENSTEIN

(1.2,2.2-2.4) Turistas no residentes alojados en hoteles y establecimientos asimilados; (9.3) Plazas-cama.
Fuente: "Liechtenstein Tourismus".

LITUANIA

(2.1-2.4) Turistas no residentes alojados en todo tipo de establecimientos de alojamiento; (3.1-3.4,4.1-4.3) Llegadas de turistas no residentes en las fronteras nacionales; (5.1,5.2,7.1,7.2,9.1-9.4) Hoteles únicamente; (9.3) Habitaciones.
Fuentes: (1.1-5.4,7.1-7.4,8.1,9.1-9.4) "Lithuanian State Department of Tourism"; (6.1-6.3,8.2-8.4) Fondo Monetario Internacional.

LUXEMBURGO

(1.2,2.2,2.3) Turistas no residentes alojados en todo tipo de establecimientos de alojamiento; incluye albergues de juventud, alojamientos turísticos privados y otros; (5.1,7.1) Pernoctaciones en hoteles, albergues y casas de huéspedes; (5.3,7.3) Incluidos los alojamientos turísticos privados y otros; (9.3) Habitaciones.
Fuentes: (1.2-5.4,7.1-7.4,8.1,9.1-9.4) "Office National du Tourisme"; (6.1-6.3,8.2-8.4) Fondo Monetario Internacional.

MACAO, CHINA

(1.1,2.1-4.3) Llegadas de visitantes no residentes en las fronteras nacionales; (1.1-1.3,2.4,3.1-3.4) Incluidas las personas de origen étnico chino procedentes de "Hong Kong, China"; (1.2,1.3) Estimaciones; (3.1) Incluidas las llegadas en helicóptero; (6.1) Los datos de gastos corresponden a los facilitados por el país a la OMT, por tratarse de una serie más completa que la facilitada por el Fondo Monetario Internacional (FMI) para la preparación de esta edición del Compendio. Incluidos los ingresos procedentes del juego; (8.1) Viajes organizados; (9.1,9.2) Hoteles, casas de huéspedes y "pousadas"; (9.3) Habitaciones; (10.1-10.3) Este apartado no se ha podido completar debido a que las partidas "viajes" y "transporte de pasajeros" no figuran en los datos del Fondo Monetario Internacional utilizados para la preparación de esta edición del Compendio.

Fuente: "Macau Government Tourist Office".

MADAGASCAR

(1.2,2.1-2.4,3.1,4.1-4.3) Llegadas de turistas no residentes por vía aérea; (9.3) Habitaciones.
Fuentes: (1.2-5.4,9.1-9.4) "Ministère de la Culture et du Tourisme"; (6.1-6.3,8.2-8.4) Fondo Monetario Internacional; (8.1) "Police des frontières".

MALASIA

(1.2,2.1-2.6) Llegadas de turistas no residentes en las fronteras nacionales; incluidos los residentes de Singapur que cruzan la frontera por la Johore Causeway; (3.1-3.4,4.1-4.3) Península de Malasia únicamente; (8.1) Salidas de malasios peninsulares, incluidas las salidas por carretera a través de la frontera Johore Causeway; (9.1) Hoteles con 10 habitaciones y más; (9.3) Habitaciones.
Fuentes: (1.1-5.2,7.2,8.1,9.1,9.3) "Tourism Malaysia"; (6.1-6.3,8.2-8.4) Fondo Monetario Internacional.

MALAWI

(1.2-4.3) Salidas; (5.3/2004) Dato provisional; (9.3) Plazas-cama.
Fuentes: (1.2-5.4,9.1-9.4) "Ministry of Information and Tourism"; (6.1-6.3,8.2-8.4/2001) Fondo Monetario Internacional; (6.1-6.3,8.2-8.4/2002-2005) "Reserve Bank of Malawi".

MALDIVAS

(1.2,2.1-2.6) Llegadas por vía aérea; (5.1,9.1-9.4) Centros turísticos y hoteles; (9.4) Días; (10.1-10.3) Este apartado incluye únicamente la partida "viajes" debido a que la partida "transporte de pasajeros" no figura en los datos del Fondo Monetario Internacional utilizados para la preparación de esta edición del Compendio.
Fuentes: (1.2-5.1,8.1,9.1-9.4) "Ministry of Tourism"; (6.2,8.2-8.4) Fondo Monetario Internacional.

MALI

(1.2) Llegadas por vía aérea; (2.1-2.6) Turistas no residentes alojados en hoteles y establecimientos asimilados; (9.3) Habitaciones.
Fuentes: (1.2-5.4,7.1-7.4,9.1-9.4) "Office malien du tourisme et de l'hôtellerie (O.MA.T.HO)"; (6.1-6.3,8.2-8.4) Fondo Monetario Internacional.

MALTA

(1.2,2.1-2.6,3.1,3.4/2001-2003) Llegadas de turistas no residentes en las fronteras nacionales; (1.2,2.2-2.6,3.1,3.4/2004/2005) Salidas de turistas por vías aérea y marítima; (4.1-4.3,5.1-5.3/2003-2005) Salidas de turistas por vía aérea; (8.1/2002-2005) Por vía aérea únicamente; (9.3) Plazas-cama.
Fuentes: (1.1-5.4,8.1,9.2-9.4) "Malta Tourism Authority" y "National Statistics Office"; (6.1-6.3,8.2-8.4) Fondo Monetario Internacional.

MARRUECOS

(1.2,3.1-4.3) Llegadas de turistas no residentes en las fronteras nacionales; incluidos los nacionales residentes en el extranjero; (2.1-2.6) Llegadas de turistas no residentes en las fronteras nacionales; excluidos los nacionales residentes en el extranjero; (5.1,5.2,7.1,7.2,9.1-9.3) Hoteles homologados, ciudades de vacaciones y residencias turísticas; (9.3) Habitaciones; (9.4) Turistas extranjeros.
Fuentes: (1.1-5.2,7.1,7.2,8.1,9.1-9.4) "Ministère du tourisme"; (6.1-6.3,8.2-8.4) Fondo Monetario Internacional.

MARTINICA

(1.2,2.2,2.3,4.1-4.3) Llegadas de turistas no residentes en las fronteras nacionales; (6.1) Las cifras de gasto corresponden a las facilitadas por el país a la OMT y que, sin embargo, no figuran en los datos del Fondo Monetario Internacional utilizados para la preparación de esta edición del Compendio; (9.1) Hoteles y ciudades de vacaciones ("Club Méditerranée"); (9.3) Habitaciones en hoteles y establecimientos asimilados.
Fuente: "Comité Martiniquais du Tourisme".

MAURICIO

(1.2,2.1-3.4) Llegadas de turistas no residentes en las fronteras nacionales; (4.1-4.3) Llegadas de visitantes no residentes en las fronteras nacionales; (5.4) Grandes hoteles; (9.3) Habitaciones.
Nota 2005: Datos provisionales.
Fuentes: (1.1-5.4,8.1,9.1-9.3) "Ministry of Tourism and Leisure"; (6.1-6.3,8.2-8.4) Fondo Monetario Internacional.

MEXICO

(1.2,2.2-4.3) Llegadas de turistas no residentes en las fronteras nacionales; incluidos los nacionales residentes en el extranjero; (1.3) Incluidos los visitantes de la franja fronteriza con EE.UU. y estancia inferior a 24h; (2.2/2004/2005) Estados Unidos y Canadá únicamente; (3.3) Incluye ferrocarril; (5.1) Centros turísticos seleccionados; (5.2,7.2) Hoteles únicamente; (9.3) Habitaciones; (9.4) Turismo extranjero únicamente.
2005: Datos preliminares.
Fuentes: (1.1-5.4,7.1,7.2,8.1,9.1-9.4) Secretaría de Turismo de México (SECTUR); (6.1-6.3,8.2-8.4) Fondo Monetario Internacional.

MICRONESIA (ESTADOS FEDERADOS DE)

(1.2,2.2-2.4,4.1-4.3) Llegadas en los Estados de Kosrae, Chuuk, Pohnpei y Yap; excluidos los ciudadanos de EFM; (6.1,8.2) Las cifras de gasto corresponden a las facilitadas por el país a la OMT y que, sin embargo, no figuran en los datos del Fondo Monetario Internacional utilizados para la preparación de esta edición del Compendio. Años fiscales (1 octubre - 30 septiembre).
Fuente: "Department of Economic Affairs".

MONACO

(1.2,2.1-4.2) Turistas no residentes alojados en hoteles y establecimientos asimilados.
Fuente: "Direction du Tourisme et des Congrès".

MONGOLIA

(1.2,2.2-2.4) (4.1-4.3/2002-2005) Llegadas de turistas no residentes en las fronteras nacionales. Excluidos los diplomáticos y extranjeros residentes en Mongolia; (4.1-4.3/2001) Llegadas de visitantes no residentes en las fronteras nacionales.
Fuentes: (1.1-4.3) (6.1-6.3,8.2-8.4/2005) "Tourism Policy and Coordination Department - Ministry of Road Transport and Tourism"; (6.1-6.3,8.2-8.4/2001-2004) Fondo Monetario Internacional.

MONTSERRAT

(10.2,10.3) Este apartado incluye únicamente la partida "viajes" debido a que la partida "transporte de pasajeros" no figura en los datos del Fondo Monetario Internacional utilizados para la preparación de esta edición del Compendio.
Fuentes: (1.1-5.2) "Statistics Department Montserrat"; (6.2,8.3) Fondo Monetario Internacional.

MOZAMBIQUE

Fuentes: (1.1-4.3,9.1-9.4) "Ministry of Tourism"; (5.1,5.2,7.1,7.2) "Instituto Nacional de Estatística"; (6.1-6.3,8.2-8.4) Fondo Monetario Internacional.

MYANMAR

(1.2,2.2-2.6) Incluidas las llegadas de turistas a través de los puntos de entrada fronterizos a Yangon; (4.1-4.3) Llegadas de visitantes no residentes en las fronteras nacionales; (5.1,9.4) Hoteles y establecimientos asimilados administrados por el Estado únicamente; (9.1,9.2) Hoteles administrados por el Estado y casas de huéspedes privadas homologadas; (9.3) Habitaciones.
Fuentes: (1.1-5.4,9.1-9.4) "Ministry of Hotels and Tourism"; (6.1-6.3,8.2-8.4) Fondo Monetario Internacional.

NAMIBIA

(2.1-4.3) Llegadas de turistas no residentes en las fronteras nacionales; (2.2) Estados Unidos únicamente; (2.4) Australia únicamente; (9.3) Plazas-camas.
Fuentes: (1.1-5.4,7.1-7.3,9.1-9.4) "Ministry of Environment and Tourism"; (6.1-6.3,8.3) Fondo Monetario Internacional.

NEPAL

(1.2) Incluidas las llegadas procedentes de la India; (3.3) Vía terrestre; (9.1,9.2) Hoteles en Katmandú y en el interior del país.
Fuentes: (1.2-5.4,8.1,9.1,9.2) "Nepal Tourism Board"; (6.1-6.3,8.2-8.4) Fondo Monetario Internacional.

NICARAGUA

(1.2,2.1-4.3) Llegadas de turistas no residentes en las fronteras nacionales; (1.2/2001-2004) (2.1-2.5) Excluidos los nacionales residentes en el extranjero; (1.2/2005) Incluidos los nacionales residentes en el extranjero; (5.1-5.4,7.1-7.4,9.4/2005) Datos preliminares; (5.1,7.1) Principales establecimientos de alojamiento del país (7); (5.3,7.3) Total de establecimientos del país; (9.1,9.2) Hoteles y establecimientos asimilados ubicados en categorías superiores; (9.4) Todo tipo de establecimientos de alojamiento, turismo receptor.
Fuentes: (1.1-5.4,7.1-7.4,8.1,9.1-9.4) Instituto Nicaragüense de Turismo (INTUR); (6.1-6.3,8.2-8.4) Fondo Monetario Internacional.

NIGER

(5.4) Días.
Fuentes: (1.2-5.4,7.1,7.2,9.1-9.4) (6.2,8.2-8.4/2005) "Ministère du Tourisme et de l'Artisanat"; (6.1-6.3,8.2-8.4/2001-2004) Fondo Monetario Internacional.

NIGERIA

(1.1,2.1-2.6,3.1-3.4) Llegadas de visitantes no residentes en las fronteras nacionales; (1.2,4.1-4.3) Llegadas de turistas no residentes en las fronteras nacionales.
Fuentes: (1.1-4.3,9.2,9.3) "Nigerian Tourism Development Corporation"; (6.1-6.3,8.2-8.4) Fondo Monetario Internacional.

NIUE

(1.2) Llegadas por vía aérea, incluidos los nacionales de Niue que residen normalmente en Nueva Zelandia; (8.1) Residentes que regresan.
Fuente: "Statistics Niue".

NORUEGA

(1.1-4.2) Las cifras se basan en "The Guest survey", un estudio realizado por el "Institute of Transport Economics"; (2.2-4.2) Llegadas de turistas no residentes en las fronteras nacionales; (2.2) Estados Unidos únicamente; (2.4) Japón únicamente; (5.1) Pernoctaciones en establecimientos homologados; (5.1,9.1,9.2) Las cifras para hoteles y establecimientos asimilados se refieren a establecimientos con 20 camas o más durante todo el año; (8.1) Viajes por vacaciones; (9.3) Plazas-cama.
Fuentes: (1.1-5.3,7.1-7.3,8.1,9.1-9.4) "Statistics Norway" e "Institute of Transport Economics"; (6.1-6.3,8.2-8.4) Fondo Monetario Internacional.

NUEVA CALEDONIA

(1.2,2.1-4.3) Incluidos los nacionales residentes en el extranjero; (4.1) Vacaciones y visitas a parientes; (4.2) Negocios únicamente; (5.1,5.2,7.1,7.2) Hoteles en Noumea únicamente; (8.1) Residentes que regresan; (9.3) Habitaciones en Noumea; (9.4) Días, hoteles en Noumea; (10.2,10.3) Este apartado incluye únicamente la partida "viajes" debido a que la partida "transporte de pasajeros" no figura en los datos del Fondo Monetario Internacional utilizados para la preparación de esta edición del Compendio.
Fuentes: (1.1-5.4,7.1,7.2,8.1,9.1-9.4) (6.2/2001) "Institut de la Statistique et des Études Économiques (ISEE)"; (6.2,8.3/2002-2005) Fondo Monetario Internacional.

NUEVA ZELANDIA

(1.1,3.1-4.3) Llegadas de visitantes no residentes en las fronteras nacionales; incluidos los nacionales residentes en el extranjero; (2.1-2.6) Llegadas de visitantes no residentes en las fronteras nacionales; excluidos los nacionales residentes en el extranjero; (5.3,7.3) Estimación a partir del número total de pernoctaciones en establecimientos comerciales hoteleros con un volumen de negocio anual de al menos 30.000 dólares neozelandeses, y basada en el porcentaje medio de huéspedes internacionales e internos en enero, abril, julio y octubre; (8.1) Salidas de residentes de NZ de corta duración (año civil); (9.1) Referencia a la capacidad de "unidades de estancia" en hoteles, moteles y casas de huéspedes; (10.1-10.3) Este apartado incluye únicamente la partida "viajes" debido a que la partida "transporte de pasajeros" no figura en los datos del Fondo Monetario Internacional utilizados para la preparación de esta edición del Compendio.
Fuentes: (1.1-5.3,7.3,8.1,9.1-9.4) "Ministry of Tourism"; (6.2,8.3) Fondo Monetario Internacional.

OMAN

(1.1-1.3,4.1-4.3,5.3,5.4) Encuesta de turismo receptor; (2.1-2.6) Turistas no residentes alojados en hoteles y establecimientos asimilados; (4.1-4.3) Llegadas de visitantes no residentes en las fronteras nacionales; (8.1) Encuesta de turismo emisor; incluidos los visitantes del día (excursionistas); (9.3) Habitaciones.
Fuentes: (1.1-1.3,4.1-4.3,5.3,5.4,8.1) "Ministry of National Economy and Ministry of Commerce and Industry"; (2.1-2.6,5.1,5.2,7.1,7.2,9.1-9.3) "Directorate General of Tourism - Ministry of Tourism"; (6.1-6.3,8.2-8.4) Fondo Monetario Internacional.

PAISES BAJOS

(1.2-2.4) Turistas no residentes alojados en todo tipo de establecimientos de alojamiento; (5.1,7.1) Hoteles y pensiones; (8.1) Salidas de nacionales por vacaciones; (8.1/2002) Nueva encuesta; (9.2) Hoteles; (9.3) Plazas-cama; (9.4) Todo tipo de establecimientos de alojamiento.
Fuentes: (1.2-5.4,7.1-7.3,8.1,9.1-9.4) "Statistics Netherlands"; (6.1-6.3,8.2-8.4) Fondo Monetario Internacional.

PAKISTAN

(5.4) Días; (8.3) El país facilita a la OMT niveles agregados de gasto que son significativamente diferentes a los datos del Fondo Monetario Internacional utilizados para la preparación de esta edición del Compendio. Los datos del país son:

2001: 255
2002: 179
2003: 880
2004: 1.319
2005: 1.277
Fuentes: (1.2-5.4,7.1,7.2,9.1-9.4) "Pakistan Tourism Development Corporation - Ministry of Tourism"; (6.1-6.3,8.2-8.4) Fondo Monetario Internacional.

PALAU

(1.2-4.3) Llegadas por vía aérea (aeropuerto internacional de Palau); (6.1,8.2) Las cifras de gasto corresponden a las facilitadas por el país a la OMT y que, sin embargo, no figuran en los datos del Fondo Monetario Internacional utilizados para la preparación de esta edición del Compendio.
Fuente: "Office of Planning and Statistics, Bureau of Budget and Planning - Ministry of Finance".

PALESTINA

(1.2,2.1-2.6) Turistas no residentes alojados en hotels; (5.1,5.2,7.1,7.2) Hoteles únicamente; (10.1-10.3) Este apartado incluye únicamente la partida "viajes" debido a que la partida "transporte de pasajeros" no figura en los datos del Fondo Monetario Internacional utilizados para la preparación de esta edición del Compendio.
Fuentes: (1.2-5.2,7.1-7.4,9.1-9.4) "Palestinian Central Bureau of Statistics"; (6.2,8.3) Fondo Monetario Internacional; (6.2,8.3,10.1-10.3) Cisjordania y Gaza.

PANAMA

(1.1) Llegadas de visitantes no residentes: Aeropuerto Internacional Tocúmen (AIT), frontera de Paso Canoa (FPC), puertos de Cristóbal y Balboa (PCB) y estadísticas IPAT; (2.2-2.4) Llegadas de visitantes no residentes, AIT y estadísticas IPAT; (3.1-3.4) Llegadas de turistas no residentes, AIT, FPC, PCB y estadísticas IPAT; excluidas las llegadas a otros puertos de entrada (sin especificar) (000)= 2001:42; 2002:35; 2003:40; 2004:51; 2005:54 (4.1-4.3) Llegadas de turistas no residentes, AIT y estadísticas IPAT; (5.1) Hoteles de la Ciudad de Panamá y estadísticas IPAT; (9.1,9.2) Habitaciones/ plazas cama inventariadas para turismo internacional; (9.3) Habitaciones.
2004-2005: Datos preliminares.
Fuentes: (1.1-5.4,8.1,9.1-9.4) Instituto Panameño de Turismo; (6.1-6.3,8.2-8.4) Fondo Monetario Internacional.

PAPUA NUEVA GUINEA

Fuentes: (1.2-5.4,8.1,9.1-9.4) "Papua New Guinea Tourism Promotion Authority"; (6.1-6.3,8.2-8.4) Fondo Monetario Internacional.

PARAGUAY

(1.1-3.4,8.1) Tarjetas E/D en el aeropuerto Silvio Petirossi y planillas de pasajeros en los puestos terrestres - Policía Nacional y SENATUR; (1.2,2.1-4.3) Excluidos los nacionales residentes en el extranjero y miembros de tripulación; (3.4) Vía fluvial; (9.3) Plazas-cama.
Fuentes: (1.1-5.4,8.1,9.1-9.4) Secretaría Nacional de Turismo - SENATUR; (6.1-6.3,8.2-8.4) Fondo Monetario Internacional.

PERU

(1.2) Incluye a los pasajeros en crucero que pernoctan; (1.2,2.1-2.5) A partir de 2002, nueva serie estimada incluyendo a los turistas con un documento de identidad diferente al pasaporte; (1.4) Pasajeros en crucero que pernoctan; (3.4) Incluye las llegadas por vía fluvial y lacustre; (5.1,5.2,5.4,7.1,7.2,9.1-9.4/2003-2005) Estimaciones preliminares.
Fuentes: (1.1-5.4,7.1,7.2,8.1,9.1-9.4) Ministerio de Comercio Exterior y Turismo (MINCETUR) - Vice Ministerio de Turismo; (6.1-6.3,8.2-8.4) Fondo Monetario Internacional.

POLINESIA FRANCESA

(1.2,2.2-4.3) Llegadas de turistas no residentes en las fronteras nacionales; excluidos los nacionales residentes en el extranjero; (5.2) Hoteles únicamente; (5.4,9.4) Días; (9.1,9.2) Hoteles únicamente; al 31 de diciembre de cada año; (9.3) Habitaciones en hoteles.
Fuentes: (1.2-5.4,9.1-9.4) "Service du Tourisme"; (6.1-6.3,8.2-8.4) Fondo Monetario Internacional.

POLONIA

(1.1,2.1-3.4) Llegadas de visitantes no residentes en las fronteras nacionales; (4.1-4.3) Llegadas de turistas no residentes en las fronteras nacionales, según encuestas del Instituto de Turismo; (5.4) Establecimientos de alojamiento colectivo y privado, según encuestas del Instituto de Turismo; (8.1) Viajes de turismo emisor registrados en las fronteras; (9.3) Habitaciones.
Fuentes: (1.1-5.4,7.1-7.3,8.1,9.1-9.4) "Institute of Tourism"; (6.1-6.3,8.2-8.4) Fondo Monetario Internacional.

PORTUGAL

(1.1,3.1-3.4) Llegadas de visitantes no residentes en las fronteras nacionales; (1.1,1.3,3.1-3.4/2004) Debido a un cambio de metodología, a partir de 2004 los datos no están disponibles; (1.2,2.2-2.4) Llegadas de turistas no residentes en las fronteras nacionales; excluidos los nacionales residentes en el extranjero; incluidas las llegadas procedentes del extranjero a Madeira y Azores; (1.2,1.4,2.2-2.4/2005) Debido a un cambio de metodología, a partir de 2005 los datos no están disponibles; (1.4) Incluidos los pasajeros por mar en tránsito; (5.3) Incluidas las pernoctaciones en alojamientos de Madeira y Azores; (9.1,9.2) Hoteles, moteles, albergues, pensiones y "pousadas" (julio-junio); (9.3) Plazas-cama (hoteles homologados); (9.4) Todo tipo de establecimientos de alojamiento.
Fuentes: (1.1-5.4,7.1-7.3,9.1-9.4) "Direcçao-Geral do Turismo (DGT)"; (6.1-6.3,8.2-8.4) Fondo Monetario Internacional.

PUERTO RICO

(1.2) Llegadas de turistas no residentes por vía aérea; (2.2) Únicamente Islas Vírgenes Americanas y Estados Unidos; (5.1,5.4) Incluye residentes y no residentes; (6.1,8.2-8.4) Las cifras de gasto corresponden a las facilitadas por el país a la OMT y que, sin embargo, no figuran en los datos del Fondo Monetario Internacional utilizados para la preparación de esta edición del Compendio; (9.1) Habitaciones endosadas por la Compañía de Turismo de Puerto Rico; (9.3) Habitaciones; incluidas las habitaciones ocupadas por residentes de Puerto Rico.
Datos: Años fiscales (julio-junio).
Fuentes: (1.2-3.4,6.1,8.1,8.2-8.4,10.1-10.3) Junta de Planificación de Puerto Rico; (5.1,5.2,5.4,7.2,9.1,9.3,9.4) Compañía de Turismo de Puerto Rico.

QATAR

(1.2,2.3-2.6,5.1,5.4,9.1-9.3) Hoteles únicamente; (6.2,8.3) Las cifras de gasto corresponden a las facilitadas por el país a la OMT y que, sin embargo, no figuran en los datos del Fondo Monetario Internacional utilizados para la preparación de esta edición del Compendio; (9.3) Plazas-cama.
Fuentes: (1.2-5.4,9.1-9.3) "The Planning Council - Statistics Department"; (6.2,8.3) "Qatar Central Bank".

REINO UNIDO

(3.2) Túnel; (5.4) Días; (6.1,8.2) El país facilita a la OMT niveles agregados de gasto que son significativamente diferentes a los datos del Fondo Monetario Internacional utilizados para la preparación de esta edición del Compendio. Los datos del país son:

	6.1	8.2
2001:	16.276	36.467
2002:	17.591	40.409
2003:	19.356	46.614
2004:	23.847	55.434

(9.3) Plazas-cama (Inglaterra únicamente).
Fuentes: (1.1-4.3,5.3,5.4,7.3,8.1,9.3) "VisitBritain"; (5.1,5.2,7.1,7.2,9.2) "EUROSTAT (New Cronos)"; (6.1-6.3,8.2-8.4) Fondo Monetario Internacional.

REPUBLICA ARABE SIRIA

(1.1,2.1-4.3) Llegadas de visitantes no residentes en las fronteras nacionales; excluidas las llegadas de nacionales residentes en el extranjero; (9.3) Habitaciones.
Fuentes: (1.1-5.4,7.1,7.2,8.1,9.1-9.4) "Ministry of Tourism" - Fuente de los datos: encuesta del turismo receptor en 2002 y 2004; (6.1-6.3,8.2-8.4) Fondo Monetario Internacional.

REPUBLICA CENTROAFRICANA

(1.2,2.1-2.6,4.1-4.3) Llegadas por vía aérea a Bangui únicamente.
Fuentes: (1.2-5.4,7.1-7.4,8.1,9.1-9.4) (6.1,8.2/2003/2004) "Ministère du Développement du Tourisme et de l'Artisanat"; (6.1,8.2/2001/2002) "Banque des Etats de l'Afrique Centrale (B.E.A.C.)".

REPUBLICA CHECA

(1.2,2.1-2.4) Turistas no residentes alojados en todo tipo de establecimientos de alojamiento.
Fuentes: (1.2-5.4,7.1-7.4,9.1-9.4) "Department of Conception and International Cooperation in Tourism - Ministry for Regional Development"; (6.1-6.3,8.2-8.4) Fondo Monetario Internacional.

REPUBLICA DE MOLDOVA

(1.1-4.3,8.1) (5.1,7.3/2001-2003) Visitantes que se beneficiaron de los servicios de los agentes económicos registrados oficialmente en la actividad turística y en el alojamiento.
Nota: Excluido el margen izquierdo del río Nistru y la municipalidad de Bender.
Fuentes: (1.1-5.4,7.1-7.4,8.1,9.1-9.4) "National Bureau of Statistics"; (6.1-6.3,8.2-8.4) Fondo Monetario Internacional.

REPUBLICA DEMOCRATICA DEL CONGO

(1.2,2.1-2.4,4.1-4.3/2002-2004) Llegadas por vía aérea únicamente; (9.1) Hoteles homologados.
Nota 2005: Datos provisionales.
Source: "Office National du Tourisme".

REPUBLICA DEMOCRATICA POPULAR LAO

(1.2) Llegadas de turistas no residentes en las fronteras nacionales; (2.2-2.5,3.1,3.3,4.1-4.3) Llegadas de visitantes no residentes en las fronteras nacionales; (5.4) Días; (10.1-10.3) Este apartado incluye únicamente la partida "viajes" debido a que la partida "transporte de pasajeros" no figura en los datos del Fondo Monetario Internacional utilizados para la preparación de esta edición del Compendio.
Fuentes: (1.1-5.4,9.1-9.3) (6.2/2002-2005) "National Tourism Authority"; (6.2,8.3/2001) Fondo Monetario Internacional.

REPUBLICA DOMINICANA

(1.2) Llegadas por vía aérea únicamente; incluidos los nacionales residentes en el extranjero; (1.4) Todas las llegadas por mar; (2.2-2.4) Llegadas por vía aérea; excluidos los nacionales residentes en el extranjero; (2.2-2.4/2001-2004) (4.1-4.3/2001/2002) Excluidos los pasajeros del aeropuerto de Herrera; (4.1-4.3) Llegadas por vía aérea únicamente; incluidos los nacionales residentes en el extranjero; (9.1,9.2) Hoteles; (9.3) Habitaciones; (10.1-10.3) Este apartado incluye únicamente la partida "viajes" debido a que la partida "transporte de pasajeros" no figura en los datos del Fondo Monetario Internacional utilizados para la preparación de esta edición del Compendio.
Nota 2005: Datos provisionales.
Fuentes: (1.1-5.4,8.1,9.1-9.4) Secretaría de Estado de Turismo; (6.2,8.2-8.4) Fondo Monetario Internacional.

REPUBLICA UNIDA DE TANZANIA

Fuentes: (1.1-5.3,7.3,9.1-9.4) "Tourism Division - Ministry of Natural Resources and Tourism" y "National Bureau of Statistics"; (6.1-6.3,8.2-8.4) Fondo Monetario Internacional.

REUNION

(5.4) Días; (6.1) Las cifras de gasto corresponden a las facilitadas por el país a la OMT y que, sin embargo, no figuran en los datos del Fondo Monetario Internacional utilizados para la preparación de esta edición del Compendio.
Fuentes: "Institut National de la Statistique et des Études Économique - INSEE" y "Comité du Tourisme de la Réunion".

RUMANIA

Fuentes: (1.1-5.4,7.1-7.4,8.1,9.1-9.4) "National Authority for Tourism - Ministry of Transports, Constructions and Tourism"; (6.1-6.3,8.2-8.4) Fondo Monetario Internacional.

SABA

(1.3) Principalmente desde San Martín.
Fuentes: "Saba Tourist Bureau", "Caribbean Tourism Organization" y "Central Bank of the Netherlands Antilles".

SAINT KITTS Y NEVIS

(1.2,2.2,2.3) Llegadas de turistas no residentes por vía aérea; (1.4,3.4) Llegadas en yates y cruceros; (10.1-10.3) Este apartado incluye únicamente la partida "viajes" debido a que la partida "transporte de pasajeros" no figura en los datos del Fondo Monetario Internacional utilizados para la preparación de esta edición del Compendio.
Fuentes: (1.1-3.4,9.1,9.2) "Ministry of Finance, Planning and Development"; (6.2,8.3) Fondo Monetario Internacional.

SAMOA

Fuentes: (1.2-4.3,9.1,9.2) (6.2/2001-2003) "Samoa Tourism Authority" y "Statistical Services Division (Ministry of Finance)"; (6.1-6.3,8.2-8.4/2004/2005) Fondo Monetario Internacional.

SAMOA AMERICANA

(1.2,2.4,4.1-4.3) Incluye Samoa Occidental; (4.3) Visitas a parientes, amigos.
Fuente: "American Samoa Government - Department of Commerce - Statistics Division".

SAN EUSTAQUIO

(1.1) Llegadas por vías aérea y marítima; incluidos los nacionales residentes en el extranjero; (1.2,2.2,2.3) Llegadas de turistas no residentes en las fronteras nacionales; excluidos los residentes de las Antillas Neerlandesas.
Fuente: "Central Bank of the Netherlands Antilles".

SAN MARINO

(1.1) Incluidos los visitantes italianos; (1.2) Turistas no residentes alojados en hoteles y establecimientos asimilados; incluidos los turistas italianos; (9.1,9.2) Hoteles únicamente.
Nota: Nueva metodología a partir de 2005.
Fuente: "Ufficio di Stato per il Turismo".

SAN MARTIN

(1.2,2.2,2.3) Por vía aérea; incluidas las llegadas a San Martín (parte francesa de la isla); (3.1) Llegadas al aeropuerto "Juliana" (incluidos los visitantes con destino a San Martín (parte francesa); (6.2,8.3) Incluidas las estimaciones para Saba y San Eustaquio; (9.1,9.2) Hoteles, casas de huéspedes y apartamentos.
Fuentes: (1.1-3.4,9.1-9.3) "St. Maarten Tourist Bureau"; (6.2,8.3) "Central Bank of the Netherlands Antilles".

SAN VICENTE Y LAS GRANADINAS

(1.2,2.2-2.3,4.1-4.3) Llegadas de turistas no residentes por vía aérea; (3.4) Incluidos los pasajeros en crucero y en yate; (9.1) Hoteles, apartamentos, bungalows, villas y casas de huéspedes; (10.1-10.3) Este apartado incluye únicamente la partida "viajes" debido a que la partida "transporte de pasajeros" no figura en los datos del Fondo Monetario Internacional utilizados para la preparación de esta edición del Compendio.
Fuentes: (1.1-5.4,9.1,9.2) "Ministry of Tourism and Culture"; (6.2,8.3) Fondo Monetario Internacional.

SANTA LUCIA

(1.1) Excluidas las llegadas de pasajeros en yate; (1.1,2.2-4.3) Llegadas de turistas no residentes en las fronteras nacionales; excluidos los nacionales residentes en el extranjero; (9.3) Habitaciones; (10.1-10.3) Este apartado incluye únicamente la partida "viajes" debido a que la partida "transporte de pasajeros" no figura en los datos del Fondo Monetario Internacional utilizados para la preparación de esta edición del Compendio.
Nota 2005: Datos provisionales.
Fuentes: (1.1-5.2,9.1-9.4) "Saint Lucia Tourist Board"; (6.2,8.3) Fondo Monetario Internacional.

SANTO TOME Y PRINCIPE

(10.1-10.3) Este apartado incluye únicamente la partida "viajes" debido a que la partida "transporte de pasajeros" no figura en los datos del Fondo Monetario Internacional utilizados para la preparación de esta edición del Compendio.
Fuentes: (1.1-4.3) "Direcçao do Turismo e Hotelaria"; (6.2,8.2-8.4/2001/2002) Fondo Monetario Internacional; (6.2/2003-2005) Banco Central.

SENEGAL

(1.2/2001/2002) (2.1-2.6/2001-2003) Turistas no residentes alojados en hoteles y establecimientos asimilados; (1.2/2003-2005) (2.1-2.3/2004/2005) Llegadas de turistas no residentes en las fronteras nacionales; (5.1,5.2,7.1,7.2,9.1,9.2) Hoteles y ciudades de vacaciones; (9.3) Plazas-cama.
Fuentes: (1.1-5.4,7.1,7.2,9.1-9.4) "Ministère du Tourisme et des Transports Aériens"; (6.1-6.3,8.2-8.4) Fondo Monetario Internacional.

SERBIA Y MONTENEGRO

(1.2,2.2-2.4) Turistas no residentes alojados en todo tipo de establecimientos de alojamiento; incluye habitaciones, casas y apartamentos alquilados del sector privado; (6.2) Las cifras de gasto corresponden a las facilitadas por el país a la OMT y que, sin embargo, no figuran en los datos del Fondo Monetario Internacional utilizados para la preparación de esta edición del Compendio. A partir de 1997, los datos se presentan de acuerdo con la quinta edición de las instrucciones sobre balanzas de pagos del FMI; (9.1,9.2) Al 31 de agosto de cada año; (9.2,9.3) Plazas-cama permanentes.
Fuente: "Statistical Office of Serbia and Montenegro".

SEYCHELLES

(1.2,2.1-4.3) Llegadas de turistas no residentes en las fronteras nacionales; (5.4) Pernoctaciones basadas en las salidas; (9.1,9.2) Hoteles y casas de huéspedes; (9.3) Plazas-cama.
Fuentes: (1.1-5.4,7.1,8.1,9.1-9.3) "Ministry of Information Technology and Communication"; (6.1-6.3,8.2-8.4) Fondo Monetario Internacional.

SIERRA LEONA

(1.2,2.1-2.6,4.1-4.3) Llegadas por vía aérea; (9.1,9.2) Hoteles únicamente; (10.1-10.3) Este apartado incluye únicamente la partida "viajes" debido a que la partida "transporte de pasajeros" no figura en los datos del Fondo Monetario Internacional utilizados para la preparación de esta edición del Compendio.
Fuentes: (1.2-5.4,8.1,9.1-9.4) "National Tourist Board"; (6.2,8.2-8.4) Fondo Monetario Internacional.

SINGAPUR

(1.1) Excluidas las llegadas de ciudadanos malasios por vía terrestre; incluidos visitantes del día (excursionistas); (4.1-4.3,5.2/2004) Desde el mes de abril de 2004, se han suprimido de la tarjeta de embarque/ desembarque los campos de motivo de la visita, alojamiento, frecuencia del desplazamiento y disposiciones de viaje. Datos no disponibles; (5.4,9.4) Días; (9.1) Hoteles (homologados y no homologados); (9.3) Habitaciones; hoteles homologados únicamente; (10.1-10.3) Este apartado incluye únicamente la partida “viajes” debido a que la partida “transporte de pasajeros” no figura en los datos del Fondo Monetario Internacional utilizados para la preparación de esta edición del Compendio.
Fuentes: (1.1-5.4,8.1,9.1-9.4) "Singapore Tourism Board"; (6.2,8.3) Fondo Monetario Internacional.

SRI LANKA

(1.2,2.1-4.3) Llegadas de turistas no residentes en las fronteras nacionales; excluidos los nacionales residentes en el extranjero; (9.1,9.2) Hoteles, moteles, albergues, casas de huéspedes y aparthoteles; (9.3) Habitaciones.
Fuentes: (1.1-5.4,7.1,8.1,9.1-9.3) "Sri Lanka Tourist Board"; (6.1-6.3,8.2-8.4) Fondo Monetario Internacional.

SUDAFRICA

(1.1,3.1-3.4) Excluidos los nacionales residentes en el extranjero. Incluidas las llegadas por motivo de vacaciones, negocios, estudios, trabajo, tránsito, tráfico fronterizo y trabajadores con contrato; (1.2,2.1-2.6,4.1-4.3) Llegadas de turistas no residentes en las fronteras nacionales; excluidas las llegadas por trabajo y los trabajadores con contrato; (9.3) Habitaciones (hoteles).
Fuentes: (1.1-4.3,8.1,9.1-9.3) "Statistics South Africa" y "South African Tourism"; (6.1-6.3,8.2-8.4) Fondo Monetario Internacional.

SUDAN

(1.2-4.3/2005) Llegadas de turistas no residentes en las fronteras nacionales; incluidos los nacionales residentes en el extranjero; (6.1) El país facilita a la OMT niveles agregados de gasto que son significativamente diferentes a los datos del Fondo Monetario Internacional utilizados para la preparación de esta edición del Compendio. Los datos del país son:
2001: 60
2002: 62
2003: 63
2004: 68
2005: 316
(10.1-10.3) Este apartado incluye únicamente la partida “viajes” debido a que la partida “transporte de pasajeros” no figura en los datos del Fondo Monetario Internacional utilizados para la preparación de esta edición del Compendio.
Fuentes: (1.2-4.3,9.1-9.4) "Ministry of Tourism and Wildlife"; (6.2,8.3) Fondo Monetario Internacional.

SUECIA

(1.1-4.3) Datos según la encuesta IBIS (visitantes llegados a Suecia) durante los años 2001 a 2003, (no se han recopilado datos anteriores a 2001 ni posteriores a 2003). Fuente: Autoridad de Turismo de Suecia y Estadísticas de Suecia; (1.2,2.1-4.3) Llegadas de turistas no residentes en las fronteras nacionales; (3.2) Los datos incluyen ferrocarril y otros medios de transporte; (5.1,7.1,9.1,9.2) Hoteles únicamente; (9.3) Plazas-cama.
Fuentes: (1.1-5.3,7.1-7.3,8.1,9.1-9.3) "NUTEK - The Swedish Agency for Economic and Regional Growth"; (6.1-6.3,8.2-8.4) Fondo Monetario Internacional.

SUIZA

(1.2,2.1-2.6,5.1,5.2,7.1,7.2,9.1,9.2/2001-2004) Hoteles, moteles y posadas; (1.2,2.1-2.6,5.1,5.2,7.1,7.2,9.1,9.2/2005) Hoteles y establecimientos de cura; (9.3) Tasa neta de ocupación (plazas-cama disponibles); (9.4) Turistas no residentes alojados en hoteles y establecimientos asimilados (turistas extranjeros).
Fuentes: (1.2-5.3,7.1-7.3,8.1,9.1-9.4) "Swiss Federal Statistical Office"; (6.1-6.3,8.2-8.4) Fondo Monetario Internacional.

SURINAME

(1.2,2.2-2.4,4.1-4.3,5.2/2001-2003) (3.1) (5.2/2004) Llegadas al aeropuerto de Zanderij; (1.2,2.2-2.4,4.1-4.3/2004/2005) Llegadas al aeropuerto de Zanderij, aeropuerto Zorg en Hoop, Albina y Nickerie; (1.4/2001-2003) (3.4) Llegadas al puerto Nw. Nickerie.
Fuentes: (1.1-1.4,2.2-2.4,4.1-4.3,5.2/2001-2003) (3.1,3.4/2001-2004) “General Bureau of Statistics (ABS)”; (1.2,2.2-2.4,4.1-4.3,5.2/2004/2005) (3.1,3.4/2005) (9.1) “Suriname Tourism Foundation”; (6.1-6.3,8.2-8.4) Fondo Monetario Internacional.

SWAZILANDIA

(1.2,4.1-4.3/2001/2002) Llegadas en los hoteles únicamente; (2.1-2.4,5.2) Llegadas en los hoteles únicamente; (9.3) Plazas-cama.
Fuentes: (1.1-5.4,7.1,8.1,9.1-9.4) "Swaziland Tourism Authority" y "Ministry of Tourism, Environment and Communications"; (6.1-6.3,8.2-8.4) Fondo Monetario Internacional.

TAILANDIA

(1.2,3.1-3.4) Incluidas las llegadas de nacionales residentes en el extranjero; (2.1-2.6,4.1-4.3) Excluidas las llegadas de nacionales residentes en el extranjero; (3.3) Incluye ferrocarril; (5.4) Días; (9.3) En los principales destinos turísticos únicamente.
Fuentes: (1.1-5.4,7.1,8.1,9.1-9.4) "Tourism Authority of Thailand (TAT)"; (6.1-6.3,8.2-8.4) Fondo Monetario Internacional.

TAIWAN (PROVINCIA DE CHINA)

(1.1) Incluidos los nacionales residentes en el extranjero; (2.1-2.6) Excluidos los nacionales residentes en el extranjero.
Fuentes: "(1.1-5.4,8.1,9.1,9.3) "Planning Division Tourism Bureau - Ministry of Transportation and Communication"; (6.1-6.3,8.2-8.4) Fondo Monetario Internacional.

TOGO

(1.2) Turistas no residentes alojados en hoteles y establecimientos asimilados; (9.3) Habitaciones.
Fuentes: (1.2-5.2,7.1,7.2,9.1-9.4) "Ministère du Tourisme, de l'Artisanat et des Loisirs"; (6.1-6.3,8.2-8.4) Fondo Monetario Internacional.

TONGA

(1.2,2.2-2.4,4.1-4.3) Llegadas por vía aérea; (6.2) Los datos de gastos corresponden a los facilitados por el país a la OMT, por tratarse de una serie más completa que la facilitada por el Fondo Monetario Internacional (FMI); (10.1-10.3) Este apartado incluye únicamente la partida "viajes" debido a que la partida "transporte de pasajeros" no figura en los datos del Fondo Monetario Internacional utilizados para la preparación de esta edición del Compendio.
Fuentes: (1.1-4.3) "Tonga Visitors Bureau"; (6.2) "National Reserve Bank of Tonga"; (8.3) Fondo Monetario Internacional.

TRINIDAD Y TABAGO

(1.2,2.1-2.5,4.1-4.3) Llegadas por vía aérea; (4.1) Incluidas las visitas a familiares y amigos.
Fuentes: (1.1-5.4,9.1,9.3) (6.1-6.3,8.2-8.4/2005) "Central Statistical Office - Ministry of Planning and Development"; (6.1-6.3,8.2-8.4/2001-2004) Fondo Monetario Internacional.

TUNEZ

(1.2,2.1-3.4) Llegadas de turistas no residentes en las fronteras nacionales; excluidos los nacionales residentes en el extranjero; (9.1,9.2) Hoteles homologados y no homologados, pensiones y ciudades de vacaciones; (9.3) Plazas-cama.
Fuentes: (1.1-5.4,7.1,8.1,9.1-9.4) "Ministère du Tourisme - Office National du Tourisme" e "Institut National de la Statistique"; (6.1-6.3,8.2-8.4) Fondo Monetario Internacional.

TURKMENISTAN

Fuente: "State Committee for Tourism and Sport".

TURQUIA

(1.1,3.1-3.4) Llegadas de visitantes no residentes en las fronteras nacionales; (1.3) Llegadas por mar (excluida una frontera terrestre desde 1989); (2.1-2.6) Llegadas de turistas no residentes en las fronteras nacionales; (3.4) Incluidos los pasajeros en crucero; (4.1-4.3) Salidas de visitantes no residentes; (5.3) Encuesta en establecimientos de alojamiento homologados por el Ministerio de Turismo; (5.3,7.3) Incluidos los terrenos de camping; (6.2) Incluidos los gastos de los nacionales residentes en el extranjero; (9.3,9.4) Hoteles homologados, excluidos los terrenos de camping; (9.3) Plazas-cama; (10.1-10.3) Este apartado incluye únicamente la partida "viajes" debido a que la partida "transporte de pasajeros" no figura en los datos del Fondo Monetario Internacional utilizados para la preparación de esta edición del Compendio.
Fuentes: (1.1-3.4,5.1-5.4,7.1-7.4,8.1,9.1-9.4) (6.2/2001/2002) "Ministry of Culture and Tourism"; (4.1-4.3) "Departing Visitors Survey - Turkish Statistical Institute (TURKSTAT)"; (6.2/2003-2005) (8.3) Fondo Monetario Internacional.

TUVALU

Fuente: "Central Statistics Division - Ministry of Finance, Economic Planning and Industry".

UCRANIA

(2.1-2.6) Llegadas de turistas no residentes en las fronteras nacionales; (3.1-3.4/2001/2002) Llegadas de visitantes no residentes en las fronteras nacionales; (3.1-3.4/2003) Llegadas de turistas no residentes en las fronteras nacionales; (4.1-4.3) Llegadas de visitantes no residentes en las fronteras nacionales; (6.1,8.2) El país facilita a la OMT niveles agregados de gasto que son significativamente diferentes a los datos del Fondo Monetario Internacional utilizados para la preparación de esta edición del Compendio. Los datos del país son:

	6.1	8.2
2001:	3.957	512

2002:	4.523	497
2003:	5.341	492

Fuentes: (1.1-5.4,7.1,7.3,8.1,9.1-9.4) "State Tourism Administration"; (6.1-6.3,8.2-8.4) Fondo Monetario Internacional.

UGANDA

Fuentes: (1.2-5.3,8.1,9.1,9.2) "Ministry of Tourism, Trade an Industry" y "Uganda Bureau of Statistics"; (6.1-6.3,8.2-8.4) Fondo Monetario Internacional.

URUGUAY

(1.1,4.1-4.3) Incluidos los nacionales residentes en el extranjero; (2.2-3.4) Excluidos los nacionales residentes en el extranjero; (3.3) Incluye ferrocarril; (5.4) Días; (9.1,9.2/2005) Excluidos los hoteles sin homologar.
Fuentes: (1.1-5.4,8.1,9.1-9.4) Ministerio de Turismo y Deporte; (6.1-6.3,8.2-8.4) Fondo Monetario Internacional.

UZBEKISTAN

(6.1-6.3) Las cifras de gasto corresponden a las facilitadas por el país a la OMT y que, sin embargo, no figuran en los datos del Fondo Monetario Internacional utilizados para la preparación de esta edición del Compendio.
Fuente: "National Company "Uzbektourism".

VANUATU

(5.4) Días; (7.1) Habitaciones.
Fuentes: (1.1-5.4,8.1,9.1-9.4) "Vanuatu National Statistics Office"; (6.1-6.3,8.2-8.4) Fondo Monetario Internacional.

VENEZUELA

(1.2,2.1-4.3) Llegadas de turistas no residentes en las fronteras nacionales; (9.1,9.2) Hotels y Paradores/"Pousadas"; (9.1,9.2/2005) Hoteles únicamente.
Fuentes: (1.1-5.4,8.1,9.1-9.4) Ministerio de Turismo; (6.1-6.3,8.2-8.4) Fondo Monetario Internacional.

VIET NAM

(1.1) Incluidos los nacionales residentes en el extranjero; (1.4,3.4) Incluidas las llegadas de pasajeros en crucero y por vía marítima; (2.1-4.3) Llegadas de visitantes no residentes en las fronteras nacionales; (6.1) Las cifras de gasto corresponden a las facilitadas por el país a la OMT y que, sin embargo, no figuran en los datos del Fondo Monetario Internacional utilizados para la preparación de esta edición del Compendio.
Fuente: "Viet Nam National Administration of Tourism".

YEMEN

(1.2,2.1-2.6,5.2) Turistas no residentes alojados en hoteles y establecimientos asimilados; (10.1-10.3) Este apartado incluye únicamente la partida "viajes" debido a que la partida "transporte de pasajeros" no figura en los datos del Fondo Monetario Internacional utilizados para la preparación de esta edición del Compendio.
Fuentes: (1.2-5.4,7.1,7.2,9.1,9.2) "Ministry of Culture and Tourism - Yemen Tourism Promotion Board"; (6.2,8.2-8.4) Fondo Monetario Internacional.

ZAMBIA

(5.4) Días; (6.1,8.3) Las datos de gastos corresponden a los facilitados por el país a la OMT, por tratarse de una serie más completa que la facilitada por el Fondo Monetario Internacional (FMI) para la preparación de esta edición del Compendio; (9.3) Habitaciones.
Nota 2001-2002: Datos provisionales.
Fuente: "Ministry of Tourism, Environment and Natural Resources".

ZIMBABWE

(2.1-2.4,3.1-3.3,4.1,4.2) Llegadas de visitantes no residentes en las fronteras nacionales; (3.1,3.3/2001-2003) Incluidas las personas en tránsito; (6.1) Las cifras de gasto corresponden a las facilitadas por el país a la OMT y que, sin embargo, no figuran en los datos del Fondo Monetario Internacional utilizados para la preparación de esta edición del Compendio; (9.1,9.2) Sólo hoteles clasificados; (9.3) Plazas-cama.
Fuente: "Zimbabwe Tourism Authority - ZTA".

ALBANIA

Transportation

Passenger. Bank reports are used to obtain data for sea, air, and other kinds of transport.

Travel

Credits and debits for the travel category (business and personal) are compiled by combining results from the travel survey (conducted by BOA and INSTAT three times a year) with data on arrivals and departures of Albanians and foreign travelers from the Ministry of Internal Affairs. The travel survey is used for the estimation of average duration of stay and average daily expenditures per traveler.

ANGOLA

Services

This category covers the following components: transportation, travel, insurance, royalties and license fees, and government services not included elsewhere. The information is obtained primarily from surveys and from the NBA, who conducted the official operations and the expenditures of Angolan embassies and consulates abroad, as well as from the Ministry of Fisheries on fishing licenses.

ANGUILLA

See East Caribbean.

ANTIGUA AND BARBUDA

See East Caribbean.

ARGENTINA

Transportation

INDEC compiles statistics on transportation. Data on passenger fares, on-board services, and excess baggage charges are obtained from surveys of the sea, air, and road passenger transport companies operating in Argentina. Data include both the international operations of resident carriers (credit) and the domestic operations of nonresident carriers (debit).

Travel

This item is calculated on the basis of the estimated number of passengers entering and departing Argentina, the number of days they stay, and the estimated average expenditure per person. To improve the estimates for this account, INDEC conducted surveys at main border crossings in 1996. (For more details, see *Estimación de la Cuenta Viajes del Balance de Pagos*–May 1999.)

ARMENIA

Transportation

In addition to the estimates made for the transportation of imported goods referred to above, additional data are obtained from other sources, such as surveys of transportation companies. These surveys collect information on both freight and passenger fares. The estimates are derived from the statistical survey on services conducted in 1999.

Travel

Data on travel are collected from surveys carried out by the NSS. To estimate the total amount of receipts and payments related to travel, the BPD collects data on the number of foreign arrivals and resident departures, the countries of origin and destination, length of stays, and cost of transportation, hotel, meals, and incidental costs. These estimates include expenditures in Armenia by nonresidents and by Armenians in foreign countries on short-term work assignments (that is, for periods of less than one year). The estimates are derived from the statistical survey on services conducted in 1999. Government ministries and agencies also provide data on expenditures on business trips abroad.

ARUBA

Transportation

The item comprises harbor dues and fees, freight, and passenger fares.

Travel

This item includes receipts from transactions in foreign currency, travelers' checks, and credit cards, as well as goods carried out of Aruba by tourists and paid for in foreign currency, travelers' checks, or credit cards. However, because of the difficulty in obtaining a breakdown for the expenses of resident credit card holders, their local expenses are also included. Steps will be taken to adjust the data on travel for these expenses. The item also includes payments related to medical treatments abroad and expenditures of students abroad.

AUSTRALIA

Transportation

Passenger. Data cover passenger services provided by sea and air. The main source of data is the quarterly ABS Survey of International Trade in Services (SITS). From the September quarter 1994 onward, for confidentiality reasons, the credit series also includes all non-freight earnings of resident transport operators and the expenses in Australia of nonresident transport operators. For confidentiality reasons, before the September quarter 1997, the debit series includes cruise fares. From the September quarter 1997 onward, these cruise fares are included in travel debits.

Travel

The ABS derives travel credits largely from data collected in the International Visitor Survey conducted by the Bureau of Tourism Research. ABS uses these data in conjunction with results from its monthly overseas arrivals and departures statistics, which it compiles from information collected by the Department of Immigration and Multicultural and Indigenous Affairs from arriving and departing international travelers.

Travel credits also include the receipts by domestic airlines from international airlines for the on-carriage, in Australia, of foreign visitors who have purchased tickets abroad. The source is the ABS SITS. Also included is the estimated expenditure of foreign military personnel on rest and recreation in Australia.

ABS compiles information on students' expenditure in Australia from student numbers and their associated fees, provided by the Department of Education, Science and Training, and estimated average expenditures on other goods and services sourced from a survey of foreign students.

Benchmark estimates for travel debits are compiled from a periodic household survey of returning Australian travelers. The survey provides a dissection of the average expenditure per travelers by purpose of travel (business and personal), by income earned abroad and cash taken abroad. Between these surveys, the bureau compiles estimates using data from the SITS, which covers businesses providing travel finance and outbound travel and collects data on prepaid tours, credit card usage, and traveler's checks issued. As with travel credits, the ABS uses these data in conjunction with results from its monthly overseas arrivals and departures statistics.

AUSTRIA

Transportation

This item covers freight revenues and expenditures, as well as international passenger transport and auxiliary services.

Travel

Travel now excludes international passenger transport. Monthly, quarterly and annual figures contain payments, including credit cards, Eurocheques, and travelers' checks, reported by banks. The respective clearing houses report gross debits and credits. For the services item of the current account, an external source is used in addition to the data taken from the ITRS reporting system. Statistics Austria is conducting a survey on behalf of the OeNB to gather data on the travel expenditure of Austrians abroad. The results are mainly used to derive the overall value of the debit side of the travel item, to determine the amount of goods bought by travelers abroad, and to determine the purposes of their visits.

AZERBAIJAN

Transportation

This category covers freight and passenger transportation, and port services for all modes of transport. Data on passenger fares and port service charges are based mainly on information collected by the SSC from marine shipping, airline, railway, and road transport companies. The credit entries for freight consist mostly of transit fees for the transit traffic from neighboring countries.

Travel

Data for the travel component are estimated by combining the SCC data on the number of foreign visitors entering Azerbaijan and Azerbaijan residents traveling abroad with data collected from the commercial banks on the average per capita expenditures of travelers.

BAHAMAS

Transportation

The data on freight and passenger services cover all modes of transport and port services. CBOB obtains entries for transportation services from surveys of both foreign and resident shipping and airline companies.

Travel

CBOB compiles travel credit entries using the Ministry of Tourism's tourist expenditure estimates, which are in turn based on exit surveys of foreign visitors (cruise and stopovers) conducted by the Ministry of Tourism. Estimates are compiled by taking the product of the number of foreign visitors and an estimate of an average expenditure per visit. CBOB compiles travel debit entries using exchange control records.

BAHRAIN

Transportation

In this category, debits for freight are estimated at 9 percent of the c.i.f. imports obtained from the CIO. Credit entries for transportation services are derived from information provided by Gulf Air for tickets sold by its offices outside Bahrain and payments received by port and airport authorities against services provided to foreign ships and airlines.

Travel

Credits. Tourists and business travelers coming via air and sea and 10 percent of Saudi tourists coming to Bahrain via the causeway are assumed to stay in hotels and other apartments. FSD obtains data from MOF on gross output (revenue) of hotels (covering room rent and other revenue) and restaurants (sales). All rental revenue of hotels is assumed to be earned from nonresidents, while assumptions are made on the proportion of other revenue of hotels and sales of restaurants ascribable to nonresidents.

Using these estimates and data on the number of persons staying in hotels, obtained from the Tourism Directorate, FSD derives estimates of per capita expenditure. A lower estimate of per capita expenditure is applied to the number of tourists not staying in hotels. In addition, FSD makes an allowance for miscellaneous expenditures (e.g., taxi fares, purchases of souvenirs, etc.). Ninety percent of Saudis arriving via the causeway are considered day travelers and assumed to spend about BD 40 per person.

Debits. Bahrainis crossing the causeway are assumed to spend, on average, BD 30 per person. In addition, FSD makes an allowance for the overseas training costs of Bahraini officials. The directorate also uses survey reports on bank transactions, covering records on foreign currency notes and traveler's checks sold to residents (e.g., tourists, businessmen, students studying abroad).

BANGLADESH

Transportation

Transportation covers those services performed by residents in one economy for those of another, by all modes of transportation that are involved with carriage of passengers, movement of goods (freight), charter of carriers with crew, and other related supporting and auxiliary services.

Travel

The Statistics Department collects data on travel transactions through the banks. It records as credits the receipts from foreign visitors, and as debits the residents' expenditures abroad.

BARBADOS

Transportation

CBB derives the credit entries for freight from enterprise surveys. The debit entries for freight are estimated as 10 percent of imports c.i.f. and are assumed to represent services provided by nonresident carriers. The debit entries for passenger services, which represent sea and air fares paid by Barbadians to nonresident carriers, are estimated from survey forms returned by nonresident carriers. The credit entries cover receipts of domestic carriers for similar services. The port and airport authorities provide data on other transport services.

Travel

CBB obtains these estimates from BSS estimates. The BSS obtains values representing travelers' expenditures from information derived from surveys of travelers on the length of stay and type of accommodation. The compilers apply estimated average daily expenditures to the number of visitors recorded. For the debit entries, the CBB compilers supplement the data with exchange record information.

The credit entries on business travel include expenditures by foreign seasonal workers in Barbados, and the debit entries include expenditures abroad by resident seasonal workers. The Ministry of Labor provides these data.

In the case of personal travel, compilers classify the data by purpose of travel into health, education, and other. Compilers base credit estimates for students and health-related travelers on a survey of colleges and hospitals; they base debit entries on exchange record data.

BELARUS

Transportation

The main sources of information for freight and transport services are the ITRS and the MSA surveys of transport companies.

Travel

The main sources of data are (1) the MSA surveys of hotels and tourist companies, (2) the Frontier Troops State Committee for information on the number of foreign visitors and residents of the Republic of Belarus who enter and leave the country, and (3) other official sources of information such as the Ministry of Finance and the State Customs Committee.

The NBB estimates travel services on the basis of estimated average per diem expenditures, the number of residents traveling abroad and nonresidents traveling in the Republic of Belarus, and the estimated duration of their stay. The Frontier Troops State Committee provides data on the number of travelers, country of origin (for inward travelers), country of destination (for outward travelers), and types of travel (private, business, tourism, transit, etc.).

Travel debits include the estimated value of vehicles imported by resident individuals of the Republic of Belarus for noncommercial use. The SCC registers the number of vehicles and provides data on the aggregate value of vehicles brought into the country by natural persons.

BELGIUM

Transportation

Source data distinguish the means of transportation (sea, air, and other transport) and provide, within each category, a breakdown into passenger, freight, and other transport services. A further breakdown of transportation by five supplementary types is available.

Travel

Sources include data related to the use of credit cards. Some adjustments are made to consider the impact of border workers.

BELIZE

Transportation

Since Belize has no international shipping lines or international airline, credit entries contain only revenues collected from foreign carriers. The CBB collects these data from annual surveys of the International Airport and Port Authorities. It calculates the freight debit as 8 percent (derived from the survey of customs declaration forms) of the c.i.f. value of merchandise imports as reported by the CSO. It subtracts the value of banana and papaya boxes from the import numbers before the calculation of freight charges. No attempt is made to disaggregate freight services by air and land since the use of these types of transportation for imports is minimal.

The credit information represents revenues from foreign shipping companies to the port for services and to domestic agents for commission payments and other services rendered. The CBB deducts from these inflows and outflows the money sent to the shipping agencies to pay the nonresident crew of foreign vessels.

The debit entry for air transport–passenger consists only of payments for air tickets sold by airline agents. The ticket sales from branch offices of foreign airlines in Belize are not recorded here, since the branch offices are treated as resident companies, so remittances abroad are recorded under profits in income.

Travel

For travel credits, the CBB derives information by estimating expenditures of five main categories of nonresidents—seasonal and border workers, business, students, cruise ship passengers, and stay-over tourists. It estimates expenditures by seasonal and border workers in the country at 69 percent of the income earned by border and seasonal workers. This percentage was derived from a 2004 survey of nonresident workers. No information is collected on residents working temporarily abroad.

In 2005, CBB replaced estimates of tourist expenditure, previously based on the 2000 Visitor Expenditure and Motivational Survey (VEMS), with actual inflows reported in the commercial banks' foreign exchange purchases report under line item "Tourist Related Purchases." The change was necessary because purchases of foreign exchange from tourist establishments by commercial banks significantly exceeded tourist expenditure estimates obtained using the 2000 VEMS results. The inflows data are cleaned out to add/remove misclassified transactions. An upward adjustment of 5 percent is made to reflect tourism inflows not captured in the banking system.

Based on previous estimates, approximately 97 percent of total inflows accounted for personal, nonbusiness expenditures, while the balance of 3 percent is considered to be expenditure by business travelers. Expenditure by business and official visitors is obtained by taking the cleaned out "Tourist Related Purchases" data from the commercial banks' foreign exchange purchase report and multiplying it by 3 percent. The debit reflects expenditure on business travel by the public service (as recorded in the Overseas Expenditure of the Public Service database) and the public (as recorded in the database of all outflows of foreign currency from the banking system).

For expenditures by foreign students, CBB obtains the data from the annual BOP survey of educational establishments and the commercial banks reported inflows to educational institutions not covered by the annual BOP survey. The total obtained is assumed to represent 90 percent of foreign student coverage, so the number is adjusted accordingly.

Before 2005, CBB obtained its estimate of national tourism expenditures using stay-over tourist arrival numbers from the Immigration Department, cruise ship arrival numbers from the Belize Tourism Board, and estimates of average daily expenditure and average length of stay derived from the visitor expenditure survey.

Owing to the large numbers of people who move daily between Belize and Guatemala and between Belize and Mexico, it is necessary to adjust downward the number of arrivals through these two land borders. Certain ratios, developed during the expenditure surveys, are used to estimate the actual numbers of stay-over visitors. These ratios removed people traveling in-transit, adjusted for tourists who traveled for a short day trip to a neighboring country and were recorded as entering the country twice (called multiple-entry tourist), and removed seasonal/border workers and students that are accounted for elsewhere. At the international airport, citizens who reside abroad but travel to Belize using their Belizean passports are added, while in-transit visitors are excluded.

Travel debits consist of the total number of residents traveling through the international airport and multiplying this number by an average expenditure of BZ$1,795 per person. This number is checked by comparing the outflows on vacation travel and outbound credit card payments recorded by the commercial banks. Only part of the credit card outflows is attributed to travel, since businesses use credit cards to pay for imports.

BENIN

Transportation

This item covers freight and insurance relating to international shipping, other passenger transportation services (regardless of the mode of transport used), and port services. BCEAO estimates transportation services based on data gathered from the Joint Benin-Niger Railways and Transportation Organization, port authorities, shipowners and shipping agents, foreign airlines, and the Air Navigation Safety Agency.

Travel

BCEAO derives credit entries from surveys of hotels and travel agencies conducted by the Tourism and Hotel Business Directorate. Estimates are calculated based on the number of visitors, the number of overnight stays, and the estimated average expenditure by tourists.

Debit entries are drawn from data on pilgrimages provided by the Islamic Union of Benin, data on mission expenditures of government officials provided by the General Directorate of the Budget and Equipment, and an estimate of the holiday expenditures of technical assistants and other nonresidents.

These credit and debit entries are supplemented with the amounts obtained from the breakdown, by economic type, of exchanges of BCEAO banknotes between West African Economic and Monetary Union (WAEMU) member countries.

BOLIVIA

Transportation

This account covers freight and passenger services for all modes of transport. The BCB obtains transportation services data from surveys it conducts for this purpose.

Travel

Since 2000, this information is obtained through an annual survey conducted by the INE. This is in accordance with an agreement signed by the BCB, the Vice Ministry of Tourism, the National Service of Migration, and the INE. Travel transactions are broken down between business and personal travel.

BOSNIA AND HERZEGOVINA

Transportation

CBBH calculates the value of freight transportation services on the basis of the estimated difference between the value of imported goods at c.i.f. and f.o.b. values. Out of this amount, a part related to the services provided by nonresident carriers is estimated. The compilers derive passenger transportation services from Sarajevo airport statistics on air traffic of local and foreign carriers and from CBBH research on transport of nonresidents by bus.

Travel

CBBH estimates business trips according to its research on transactions of nonresident experts and staff of foreign embassies, as well as international civil and military organizations in BH.

For private travel, CBBH derives the estimates from data on foreign tourists from statistical institutes in BH, and data of other countries on BH tourists abroad, with estimates for unregistered inflows and outflows from tourism.

BOTSWANA

Transportation

Transportation services cover air, road, and rail transport for freight, passenger, and courier services. Annual surveys of transport companies (both private and parastatals) provide much of these data, but the surveys are supplemented by data captured from exchange control forms.

Travel

In the past, travel estimates were based on amounts reported on Forms A and S in the banks' exchange reporting system. These estimates were considered likely to be understated, particularly on the credit side, because of the incidence of pre-paid travel settled offshore and the likelihood that expenditure by nonresident visitors while in Botswana will not be classified to the travel item.

To improve the estimates on the credit side, a methodology was established using arrival statistics and the results of a Department of Tourism Visitor Survey. Arrival statistics are compiled by the TSU from migration cards, which classify noncitizen visitors according to their reasons for entering Botswana (tourism, business, seeking work, in transit, etc.). The Visitor Survey, which was first conducted for the 1998 year and is now being repeated approximately every two years, provides useful measures of lengths of stay and average expenditure in various categories of visitor. Estimates are made using information on the average length of stay and expenditure data for each category of visitor applied to the appropriate arrivals data.

The BOB derives data on travel by Botswana government officials from the MFDP's Cash Flow Unit.

On the debit side, the coverage of the item has been improved by the addition of a number of categories of expenditure that were not previously measured. These include:

- student expenditure abroad (derived from Ministry of Education disbursements);
- expenditure abroad by resident air travelers (estimated from air departures and assumptions about length of stay and average expenditure); and
- similar expenditure abroad by resident land travelers (estimated from purchases of foreign exchange for travel reported on Form A, less the amount estimated for air travelers).

BRAZIL

Transportation

The BCB uses data provided directly by Brazilian seagoing shipping companies and the National Waterways Transportation Agency, supplemented by exchange settlement data. Staff monitor separately the operations involving air, sea, and other (river/land) modes of transportation.

The source of data on passenger transport is the exchange settlement system. For charters, the BCB derives data from exchange settlements and the National Waterways Transportation Agency, which along with companies also supplies data on freight and cross-trade. Data on other transportation services are either reported by companies or based on exchange settlements.

Travel

The BCB uses exchange settlement data to compile this account. The data cover revenues and expenditures regarding sales and purchases by means of international credit cards, currency transactions between travelers and authorized exchange operators, and receipts and payments between domestic and foreign travel operators.

BULGARIA

Transportation

Passenger. Credit and debit entries are based on BNB estimates.

Travel

The BNB compiles estimates using a data model that combines data on numbers of travelers to and from Bulgaria with estimates of per capita expenditure to calculate the total credit and debit entries.

BURUNDI

Transportation

For passenger services, BRB compiles data on the basis of a survey of air carriers conducted by BRB's Financial Operations Department. The data are drawn exclusively from receipts from these companies and are recorded in the settlement statement.

Travel

BRB derives the entries for travel from a survey of hotels, foreign tourist spending in Burundi, and spending abroad by residents (BRB statement of exchange transactions).

CAMBODIA

Transportation

The NBC makes separate estimates for air and sea transportation services:

For *air* transportation services, it estimates freight on imports carried by nonresident airlines by applying an average freight rate per ton to the quantity of imports. The same methodology is used to estimate details of freight on exports carried by the resident airline.

For estimates of passenger airfares paid by residents to nonresident airlines, the NBC combines information on the number of passengers, collected from the Ministry of the Interior, on the numbers of resident and nonresident arrivals and departures, an average weighted airfare, and passenger loadings by the different airlines serving Phnom Penh. Passenger fares paid by nonresidents to the resident airline are estimated in the same manner.

Other air transportation services are estimated from information provided by the resident airline for expenditure in foreign ports and from information provided by the Civil Aviation Authority for expenditure in Cambodia by nonresident airlines.

For *sea* transport, the NBC estimates freight on imports carried by nonresident carriers by deducting freight on air imports from the estimate of freight on total imports and applying to the result the share of nonresident shipping. Freight on exports carried by resident carriers is estimated by multiplying an average freight rate for exported goods by the proportion of the tonnage of exports estimated to be carried by residents. For estimated passenger fares for sea transport, the NBC uses ITRS data.

Other sea transportation services are estimated from information provided by resident shipping agents and port authorities.

For 2003 onwards, NBC also uses ITRS data to estimate other transport: freight, passenger fares, and other transportation services.

Travel

For travel credits, NBC makes separate estimates for expenditures by gamblers, tourists, business travelers, and the expatriate staff of international agencies. For example, for tourists and business travelers, NBC combines data on the number of arrivals with data on the length of stay and the average pattern of expenditure, collected from the NBC International Visitors Survey 2005, Ministry of Tourism, and travel agents. For short-term employees of international organizations in Cambodia and employees of aid agencies, NBC bases estimates on the number of such staff and the pattern of expenditure.

Travel debits include estimates based on numbers of departures of residents, obtained from the Ministry of Interior and Ministry of Tourism data, their estimated length of stay abroad, and their pattern of expenditure, from the NBC Returned Cambodian Travelers' Survey 2005. The distinction between business and personal travel is not attempted.

CAMEROON

Services

The balance of payments staff prepare the data on the various types of services using the settlement balance obtained from bank forms—reports prepared by commercial banks concerning the transactions of their customers. To supplement the information in the settlement balance, staff use the data obtained, on the one hand, from questionnaires sent to consignees and to airline and insurance companies and, on the other hand, from the annual reports of reporting entities.

CANADA

Transportation

For *passenger* transport, BOPD relies on monthly administrative data, combined with estimates of average passenger fares from a quarterly sample survey of expenditure characteristics by the Culture, Tourism, and Center for Education Statistics Division (CTCES) of Statistics Canada. Included with passenger transport is coverage of cruise fares, which international standards define as travel.

Travel

The CTCES Division compiles the basic Canadian travel statistics. CTCES derives these statistics from a combination of census data and sample counts of travelers crossing the border, coupled with sample surveys used to collect specific information from travelers, including their expenditures and main purpose of visit. Beginning with the reference year 2000, a new air exit survey introduced on-site interviews for foreign travelers at eight key Canadian airports.

Travel is subdivided into travel for business reasons and travel for personal reasons: *Business* travel covers expenditures by cross-border workers, but insufficient data bar their identification as such in the Canadian statistics. Also, as a result of data limitations, cruise fares as noted above are recorded under transportation services rather than travel. As part of the business travel item, the CTCES calculates estimates of spending by crews (of airplanes, ships, boats, trains, and trucks).

For *personal* travel, data for health-related travel consist of foreign spending for hospital services in Canada. CTCES records these data from the annual hospital survey of the Canadian Institute for Health Information, projecting data for recent years where survey results are not yet available. With the 1995 reference year, CTCES introduced estimates for physician services linked to U.S. data on the payments side. Also starting in 1995, access to U.S. sources has enabled a fuller estimate covering payments, beyond provincial health plans, at major medical centers and university hospitals located in the United States.

On the receipt side of the education series, CTCES produces the estimates by combining the time series on the number of students with average tuition rates and adding estimates of other expenditure. For expenditures of Canadian students in the United States, the data have been supplied by the U.S. BEA from 1981 onward and were linked with balance of payments data for prior years. CTCES updates the data on student expenditures overseas to incorporate volume and expenditure estimates.

CAPE VERDE

Transportation

Staff derive the data on passenger and other transportation services from the exchange record and surveys of the national airline, fuel suppliers, and port and airport authorities.

Travel

Entries in the travel category include tourism, business travel, students, civil servants, and other travelers. Staff collect data from the exchange record.

CHILE

Transportation

Passenger. Credit and debit entries for passenger services are estimated on the basis of information obtained from quarterly forms provided by resident carriers (i.e., shipping companies and airlines) and by representatives of nonresident transport companies. The CBC supplements the data with information from annual surveys of resident carriers, a benchmark survey of other carriers, and data on vehicles crossing the border. Before complete information is obtained from the forms and surveys, preliminary estimates are made.

Travel

Both credit and debit entries are estimated by combining monthly data provided by immigration authorities on the number of foreign visitors and Chilean travelers who enter and exit the country, with data on average expenditures and length of stay obtained from surveys, which cover tourism by both incoming and outgoing travelers. The surveys are undertaken in accordance with an agreement between the CBC and the National Tourism Service, a government agency.

CHINA

Transportation

Until 1995, the SAFE obtained credit entries for transportation (shipment) and port services from the Ministry of Communications (MOC) and Ministry of Railways, among other sources. Beginning in 1996, the SAFE derives credit entries from the ITRS. Debit entries are drawn from import statistics compiled by Customs and from information derived from the ITRS.

Travel

The compilers obtain data on travel credits from the National Tourism Administration (NTA). The NTA collects the data through sample surveys conducted by the National Bureau of Statistics. Travel debits are calculated using data from the Immigration Administration Department of the Ministry of Public Security and relevant receipts of main international travel destinations (countries or areas) outside China.

COLOMBIA

Transportation

BR compiles credit and debit entries for passenger services and other transportation on the basis of data supplied by national and foreign airlines. It compiles freight credit entries on the basis of data supplied by national airlines and shipping companies, and it bases freight debit entries on data supplied by DIAN for imports of goods.

Travel

The travel component measures nonborder travel (via airports) and cross-border travel (through land-border crossing points). The data for nonborder travel are estimated on the basis of information on international passenger movements provided by the Civil Aviation authorities and the Administrative Department of Security. Data for cross-border travel are derived from quarterly surveys conducted at five land-border crossing points.

CONGO

Transportation

BEAC values shipping costs either directly, based on the reports of enterprises, the postal administration, and banks, or, if this is not available, by assuming that shipping costs are 18 percent of the c.i.f. value of imports. Other transportation entries include services rendered by carriers, mainly for the international transportation of passengers, and goods and services purchased by carriers and consumed in the course of their business.

Travel

Credit entries include expenditure in the Republic of Congo by foreign travelers, and debit entries include current expenditure by residents traveling abroad, regardless of the nature of the travel. The postal administration (SOPECO) and banks report the amounts for both types of entries; the banks report transactions in foreign banknotes, travelers' checks, transfers of travel agencies, tourists transiting the Republic of Congo, etc.

BEAC also collects the information by means of questionnaires sent to the United Nations and its affiliated agencies, the Congolese Public Treasury, and embassies (for scholarships paid directly abroad). It supplements these figures by an estimate of flows of BEAC and franc zone currency notes and an estimate of expenditure by technical assistants during their leave abroad.

COSTA RICA

Transportation

CBCR obtains data on freight, passenger, and other transportation services, as well as on other international transactions by air, land, and sea transportation companies, from information reported in the questionnaires it sends to such companies.

Travel

CBCR bases estimates on data the ICT reports on the number of foreigners visiting Costa Rica and residents traveling abroad. It also uses data from ICT sample surveys on per capita spending and average length-of-stay. The Directorate General of Migration and Foreign Travel provides the ICT with monthly data on the number of nonresident travelers entering Costa Rica and the number of residents leaving. The ICT undertakes surveys quarterly to derive the average amount spent and the average stay.

CÔTE D'IVOIRE

Transportation

The data on passenger services are collected from the national airline, Air Ivoire, and the offices of nonresident airlines. The figures for port services are collected from ports and from transit and consignment companies.

Travel

Credit entries are obtained primarily from statistics on arrivals of foreign tourists and hotel occupancy provided by the Ministry of Tourism and Crafts (formerly High Commission for Tourism). A direct survey of hotels is also conducted. Debit entries are based on estimates and mainly cover expenditure of non-Ivoirien residents while out of the country. These figures are derived from the income of nonnationals working in the private sector, the wages of technical assistants and non-Ivoirien staff of international organizations with offices in Côte d'Ivoire, and the length of the leave of such persons. Figures on government missions are obtained from the Payroll Directorate. The expenditure of Ivoirien students abroad is primarily taken from surveys of donors for foreign scholarships and of the Ministry of Higher Education for scholarships granted by the Ivoirien government.

CROATIA

Transportation

This category covers the international transportation of passengers, goods, and other transportation services.

From 1993–98, the data sources were the ITRS and questionnaires that CNB received from enterprises engaged in the international transportation of goods and passengers. Expenditures on transportation services also included 1) part of the differences between c.i.f. and f.o.b. imports, pertaining to services provided by nonresidents, and 2) estimates of the operating costs of Croatian transportation companies in international transportation.

As of the first quarter 1999, the CNB compiles revenues and expenditures from transportation services on the basis of data from the new CNB survey on international transportation services, with two exceptions: First, revenues and expenditures from road transport are still compiled from ITRS data, and second, data on c.i.f./f.o.b. adjustments for nonresident carriers are obtained from the questionnaires on transportation costs related to imports of goods, classified by modes of transportation and residency. From the first quarter of 1999, a breakdown by mode of transportation is available.

Travel

The travel component shows income from services rendered to foreign travelers and tourists, as well as expenditures incurred by domestic travelers and tourists abroad. From the second half of 1998, the CNB started carrying out the survey on the consumption by foreign travelers in Croatia and domestic travelers abroad. Since early 1999, the CNB data compilers have combined the results of this survey (stratified sample) with the Ministry of the Interior data on the total number of foreign and domestic travelers, along with the data on distribution of foreign travelers by countries contained in the CBS report on tourism for compiling the travel component.

CYPRUS

Transportation

This category covers freight and passenger services provided by sea and air transport operators. CBC derives debit entries for freight services from the estimates made to convert imports from a c.i.f. to an f.o.b. basis (i.e., freight and insurance are assumed to equal 8 percent of imports c.i.f.).

Concerning passenger transport, banks report the data through the settlements system. With respect to credits, CBC cross-checks the figures with data obtained from a limited survey of major resident passenger transport operators. The staff supplement settlement data for supporting, auxiliary, and other transport services with data from the financial statements or reports of international business companies engaged in such activities.

Travel

For travel credits for tourism, the central bank obtains data from CYSTAT, which conducts a monthly frontier survey on tourist expenditure in Cyprus. To obtain geographical allocation for travel credits, the CBC combines per person expenditure derived from the survey with the number of tourist arrivals, as given by the frontier survey of incoming travelers, which CYSTAT also conducts. With regard to education-related revenue, CBC conducts an annual survey among those colleges that provide educational services to nonresidents and compares the survey results with data reported by banks under the settlements system.

For travel debits, CBC obtains the value from the settlements system. Reported data include foreign exchange allowances issued to resident travelers for tourism purposes, foreign exchange issued for education, private medical spending abroad, payments by resident travel agents, and foreign exchange outflows through credit or debit cards.

CZECH REPUBLIC

Transportation

For receipts and expenditures related to air transport of goods and passengers, the CNB collects data directly from transportation companies. For other kinds of transport, the data are based on the commercial banks' records. Starting from 2001, data are available on the division into freight, passenger, and other transport.

Since 2006, a new survey-based data collection system (through the CZSO) is used for compiling data on transport services.

Travel

For 1993–98, the travel item was compiled using data the CZSO provided on the number of travelers; the CZSO obtained the information from police on the arrivals of foreign visitors and on the trips of Czech residents abroad. For average expenditures by foreigners during their stay in the Czech Republic and of Czech tourists during their trips abroad, the CNB based estimates on regular inquiries at selected border crossings. The estimates were also based on information from the banking sector on purchases of Czech currency by nonresidents and foreign currency by residents, on the use of credit and payment cards, and on the receipts and expenditures of hotels and travel agencies.

Since 1999, the banking statistics, complemented by the CZSO survey of travelers at accommodation establishments, have been the main source of information used to compile the travel item. From 1998 onwards, CNB has supplemented the travel data with data on personal expenditures on goods and services by foreigners in the Czech Republic and Czechs employed abroad for less than one year. Starting from 2001, the CNB produces data showing the split between business and personal travel.

DENMARK

Services

Statistics Denmark conducts a combined monthly (covering approximately 400 enterprises) and quarterly (covering approximately 1,200 enterprises) sample survey on trade in services and transfers. The sample has been drawn on the basis of the settlement system, using partly a cut-off method (monthly reporters) and partly a stratified sample method (quarterly reporters).

In the future, the sample will be considered fixed, but an update of the sample will be made each year to secure representativeness, that is, to replace enterprises that can no longer be a part of the sample. This update will be made on the basis of sources including the VAT (value added tax) Register, merchandise trade statistics, and the General Business Register. The survey incorporates a full breakdown by countries.

The import of travel is primarily based on a separate survey on personal and business travel.

The export of travel is based partly on accommodation statistics combined with a survey on overnight travelers' spending in Denmark and partly on different border surveys covering travelers on same-day visits.

The rest of the travel item is based on the general survey of trade in services.

Monthly data on services are estimated from information from the monthly reporters to the survey of trade in services and from extrapolations for the quarterly reporters, and by adding estimates for the travel item.

DOMINICA

See East Caribbean.

DOMINICAN REPUBLIC

Transportation

The BCRD's International Department compiles and classifies credit and debit entries by mode of transportation (sea, air, and land) and category of transportation (freight, passenger, and other transportation services). For freight services obtained by importers, compiling staff base entries on data recorded in customs declarations. For freight obtained from nonresidents, they derive the value from estimates for freight services provided by residents. For passenger transportation, they base data on the quarterly surveys of resident shipping and airline companies. They also collect data on port services from the port authorities.

Travel

The International Department staff derive estimates by combining data on numbers of travelers with estimates of the average stay and expenditure of nonresident and resident travelers. The department obtains the number of travelers from the BCRD's daily records of arrivals and departures of travelers at national airports. Staff cross-check the data with data from the National Statistics Office and the Secretariat of State for Tourism. Data from the National Migration Office are not used because of the delay in their availability. Staff obtain average stay and expenditure estimates from quarterly surveys undertaken by the BCRD's National Accounts Department.

EAST CARIBBEAN

Transportation

The estimates for passenger services cover receipts and payments for the transportation of passengers. The ECCB obtains the data from an annual balance of payments survey of airline companies and agencies, carried out by the CSOs and the ECCB.

Travel

On the credit side, this item covers total expenditures by visitors to countries in the East Caribbean region. The ECCB derives the figures by combining data on the number of visitors and their average length of stay (obtained from the immigration departments of member countries), with an estimate of the average daily expenditure per category of visitor. The latter component is obtained through benchmark surveys of visitor expenditures, conducted periodically and adjusted annually for inflation.

Estimates of travel debits are obtained from commercial banking statistics on sales of foreign exchange for travel purposes, as well as official sources providing data on student maintenance overseas and on travel to attend international conferences.

ECUADOR

Transportation

For credits and debits on sea transport, CBE uses its quarterly and annual surveys of shipping companies operating in Ecuador. To supplement that data, it uses information on passengers and cargo from the Merchant Marine and Coastal Administration (*Dirección de la Marina Mercante y del Litoral*, DIMERC)—the government regulatory authority for maritime traffic in Ecuador.

For air transport, CBE compiles data through monthly surveys of domestic and foreign air carriers, supplemented by information supplied by the Civil Aviation Administration (*Dirección General de Aviación Civil*, DAC). CBE also obtains data from its merchandise trade database, containing information about f.o.b. and c.i.f. goods imports.

Travel

The National Migration and Aliens Office (*Dirección Nacional de Migración y Extranjería*) supplies data on inbound and outbound tourism, obtained through nationwide surveys based on type of visa and place of entry/exit (ports and airports). Only nonimmigrant visas are considered for balance of payments purposes. These sources are supplemented by surveys of hotels, travel agencies, etc.

For travel expenditures, CBE estimates data from information derived from surveys on travelers and hotels on the length of stay and type of accommodation. CBE applies the estimated average daily expenditure to the number of visitors recorded. It also makes inquiries directly at accredited embassies and consulates in Ecuador.

EGYPT

Transportation

The credit entries for transportation cover amounts received by Egyptian shipping and airline companies for freight and passenger services. Other transportation covers receipts of Suez Canal dues and receipts of the Suez Mediterranean oil pipeline for transporting foreign companies' oil through pipeline services.

The debit entries for transportation cover amounts transferred to foreign shipping and airline companies for freight and passenger services, as well as payments for freight on imports estimated from the c.i.f. value of imports (10 percent). The entries also include payments made for maintenance and repair of Egyptian ships and aircraft at foreign ports and airports.

Travel

Compilers base the credit entries for travel on the number of nights spent by tourists in Egypt (data from the Ministry of Tourism) and the average expenditure per night (estimates from the CBE based on a survey conducted by the Ministry of Tourism). Separate details are not available for business and personal travel.

The debit entries for travel cover expenditures of government officials and private employees traveling abroad, pilgrimage, expenditures of students studying abroad, training, technical and educational missions, and expenditures abroad for medical care.

EL SALVADOR

Transportation

The item includes *freight* and all modes of *passenger* transportation, including rental of transportation equipment with crew. For freight transportation, CRB derives the credit data from surveys of enterprises operating in this field. It obtains debit data from customs forms, after deducting freight transportation carried out by resident enterprises.

For *other* forms of transportation, the credit data correspond to expenditure in the country by nonresident carriers, and CRB obtains these data by means of surveys of these enterprises, supplemented with information from the Autonomous Executive Port Commission (CEPA). The debit data record expenditure abroad by resident enterprises.

For *land* and *air* transportation, CRB obtains the data from various resident and nonresident enterprises surveyed.

Travel

Credit and debt entries are based on travel surveys, conducted by a private enterprise, which, in turn, are based on the number of foreign visitors to the country and average stay and expenditure obtained from the travel survey.

ESTONIA

Transportation

The transportation services item is compiled mainly on the basis of the transportation companies survey and data from the ITRS. Information on resident passenger services rendered by nonresident companies is obtained mainly from the SSO. BOPD conducts the transportation survey each quarter with nearly 400 local transport companies that provide international freight and passenger services. Most of these companies are involved in road transport, followed in importance by sea transport, air transport, and rail transport.

Travel

The main sources of information for travel services are the travel border survey conducted by the Market Research Institute and SSO, in cooperation with the Eesti Pank and the Estonian Tourist Board, and border statistics (provided by the Board of Border Guard). These sources provide data on sales and purchases of travel packages, as well as on the number of foreign tourists visiting Estonia and the length of their stay. The same sources provide information on the number of Estonian residents visiting foreign countries and the length of their stay. Relying on results of sample surveys, BOPD compiles cost-per-day estimates of such visits. As a result, the total amount of travel receipts and payments can be calculated.

The credit (receipts) entry for travel also includes 50 percent of the wages and salaries earned by nonresidents who have worked in Estonia for less than one year. Health-related and educational expenditures made by medical patients and students are treated as travel services.

ETHIOPIA

Transportation

The NBE obtains data from transportation companies. A survey form prepared by the NBE's Balance of Payments Division is sent to these companies and compiled quarterly by the staff of the division. Data on freight debits are estimated as 9.24 percent of imports c.i.f., which is 8.95 percent for freight and 0.29 percent for transit fees on imports.

Travel

The FESMD provides data on travel receipts, while travel payment data reflecting payments made by residents to nonresident transport companies are obtained both from FESMD and Ethiopian Airlines (EAL).

FIJI

Transportation

Data are derived largely from the FBS balance of payments survey covering resident and nonresident airlines, ports, and airports. Fiji's only resident airline, Air Pacific, operating on international routes reports its passenger fare earnings from nonresidents, and ports and airport agencies provide aviation fees and charges, port dues, pilotage, and stevedoring. Foreign airlines provide figures on passenger fares earned from residents.

Travel

The credit entries are derived from estimates of tourist expenditures and the per diem information, obtained from the International Visitor Survey (IVS), conducted by the Ministry of Tourism and Civil Aviation. Until the IVS results become available, estimates of tourist expenditure per diem for the current reference period are derived by inflating the per diem derived from the last IVS results by an index (referred to as the tourism expenditure index [TEI]). This index is calculated using the results from a quarterly survey of hotels (TEI survey) conducted by FBS. Travel debits are sourced entirely from the OET system.

FINLAND

Transportation

This category covers freight and passenger services by all modes of transport and port services. For sea transport, the BOF derives data from a quarterly survey of shipping companies; the survey seeks information on freight earnings from foreign traffic, passenger transport, and port expenditures abroad. For the estimates of freight that are deducted from imports in the trade statistics on the debit side (the cif-fob adjustment), the BOF derives the data from a survey conducted by the National Board of Customs.

For air transport and railway traffic, the BOF obtains data from Finnair, the National Board of Aviation, and the State Railways, respectively.

Travel

From 1999 onward, the data are based on border interviews and other tourism statistics conducted and compiled by Statistics Finland. Until 1998, data were derived from settlements reported by domestic banks; they included purchases of foreign currency by residents at home and abroad and sales of Finnish markkas to nonresidents in Finland and abroad. In addition, an estimate of foreign exchange transactions by Finnish residents abroad was added to travel income and expenditure. Other sources of information on travel included the use of travelers' checks and credit cards.

FRANCE

Transportation

The data are broken down by sea, air, and other transport and when significant, passenger and merchandise transportation services. The latter comprise an estimate of the portion of costs of transportation included in merchandise payments.

Travel

Data on travel are derived from (1) payments by credit card and (2) two surveys on inward and outward travel. Since 2003, a distinction is made between business and other travel.

GABON

Transportation

Credit entries for freight refer to receipts from nonresidents by the resident carrier, Société Nationale de Transports Maritimes (Sonatram). Debit entries for freight represent shipment costs, which compilers estimate on the basis of a central bank survey of large importers. The entries for passenger services cover earnings of air, sea, and land carriers.

Travel

Entries cover expenditures in Gabon by foreign travelers (credit) and expenditures of Gabonese residents traveling abroad (debit) for all purposes (tourism, business, study, holiday, medical care, official missions, etc.) and by any means of payment (banknotes, checks, credit transfers, money orders, etc.).

GAMBIA

Transportation

Data for transportation services are derived from returns provided by the Gambia ports authority and Civil Aviation Authority. Credit entries comprise services provided to nonresidents through the Trans-Gambia and the Banjul-Barra ferries, airport fees, landing and parking fees, and port services. Debit entries cover freight services acquired by importers estimated to be 12.4 percent of the value of imports c.i.f., remittances for air tickets and port services, and foreign expenditure of the above-mentioned enterprises.

Travel

In calculating travel credit, a model based approach is used. The CBG's Economic Research Department uses data provided by the Gambia Tourism Authority (GTA). The estimated average out-of-pocket expenditure is equivalent to 500 dalasis per tourist multiplied by tourist arrivals to obtain total tourists expenditure. This is added to income from hotel beds and arrival and departure fees. Travel debits are derived from data supplied by parastatals and government departments on staff travel and education-related expenditures.

GEORGIA

Transportation

In addition to the estimates of freight mentioned above, the main data sources are information from the Georgian Railways Limited and the ports and airports of Georgia. The BOPS also uses as data sources the indirect estimates based on information obtained from the Department of Border Defense, regarding the means of transport and numbers of persons entering and leaving the country.

Travel

The BOPS compiles travel data on the basis of information from the regular household survey. Additional information on business travel is collected from government organizations (ministries, departments, the NBG, etc.), as well as from the banking sector.

The BOPS also uses, as data sources, the indirect estimates based on (1) information obtained from the Department of Border Defense regarding the numbers of persons entering and leaving the country, (2) expenses abroad of those persons engaged in export-import operations in goods, and (3) expenses of those working abroad for less than one year.

GERMANY

Transportation

The ITRS provides data on passenger services and some basic information on freight services, broken down by modes of transport. For freight, reported data are not in all cases sufficiently detailed and need to be supplemented by estimates. These estimates are based on ratios, dating back to 1992, of freight services to the value of imports and exports of goods, broken down by mode of transport and by country. The ratios were derived from very detailed information that used to be available from foreign trade statistics before the introduction of the Intrastat system in 1993 and have remained constant since then.

Travel

For travel expenditures, a household sample survey was introduced in 2001 to cover for the loss of information on banknote transactions resulting from the introduction of the euro. Formerly, most travel transactions were estimated on the basis of the following: bank reports on the purchase and sale of foreign currency (banknotes, travelers' checks) by residents and of domestic currency by nonresidents, reports on bank transfers by travelers and travel agencies, as well as credit and debit card transactions of residents abroad and of nonresidents in Germany.

The sample survey is conducted by a private institute on behalf of the Bundesbank on a continuous basis. Since the results are only available with a time lag of five to six months after the reference quarter, preliminary figures are based on ARIMA-based estimates and are cross-checked with developments in monthly credit/debit card transactions.

The credit side of the travel account is compiled from ITRS reports and supplemented by partner country data and other secondary data sources, including the accommodation statistics of the FSO.

The purchase of goods and services by border workers is included under travel, but their income is excluded from travel. A breakdown between business travel and personal travel is available for the debit side.

GHANA

Transportation

This category covers freight and passenger services by air, land, and sea transport, as well as services rendered and acquired at the ports. BOG's International Finance Office therefore estimates entries for transportation services from information provided by the port authorities, airlines, and shipping companies, both local and foreign. Entries for freight debits are estimated based on merchandise imported into the country within a given period. Freight for non-oil imports are estimated using 9 percent (covering both freight and insurance) of f.o.b value of the imports. In the future, the BOG will source estimates for freight directly from the trade reporting system. For oil imports, the office collects information on freight on imported oil from TOR, VRA, and AMOC, using 2.4 percent of the f.o.b value of imports. It estimates freight credits based on information provided by transportation companies.

Travel

From March 2005 onward, the Ghana Tourist Board (the regulatory and monitoring governmental agency for tourism), in collaboration with the Ghana Immigration Service, introduced a new survey methodology to improve the data coverage of the actual expenditures abroad of returning Ghanian residents and the anticipated expenditures of nonresidents in Ghana. The processed data would be more useful in improving balance of payments data on travel.

GREECE

Transportation

BoG compiles the transportation items on the basis of settlements, supplemented with estimates derived from the conversion of imports from c.i.f. to f.o.b. Data are broken down by means of transport (sea, air, rail, and other means) as well as by transportation category (freight and passengers). The main category is sea transport-cross trading activity.

Travel

Prior to 2002, BoG compiled travel data on the basis of settlements. The introduction of the euro called for methodological changes in the compilation of travel data for balance of payments purposes. On a pilot basis in May 2002, BoG started a monthly frontier travel survey aimed at estimating travel expenditure and, since January 2003, has conducted the survey on a permanent basis.

GRENADA

See East Caribbean.

GUATEMALA

Transportation

The BOG sources debit entries for freight from customs declarations. The source of the data for passenger services and other transportation services is the foreign exchange statistics.

Travel

The BOG compiles the credit and debit entries by combining the data on tourists arrivals and departures (provided by the Migration Directorate) with the following: estimates of their average daily expenditures and their average length of stay (provided by the Guatemalan Institute of Tourism, for credits) and information on the amounts carried by travelers (from the foreign exchange statistics, for debits). The foreign exchange statistics also provide information on business travel, travel for medical treatment, study abroad, and official travel.

GUINEA

Transportation

The central bank asks banks and mining companies to perform their own surveys to estimate freight and insurance for imports they have reported on a c.i.f. or cost & freight basis. Otherwise, the central bank makes the estimates.

Travel

The central bank uses this category to record over-the-counter exchange transactions conducted through the banking system, as well as mission expenses of civil servants and staff of the semipublic mining companies. When the travel purpose is not clear, the compilers list the amounts under *personal travel.*

GUINEA-BISSAU

Transportation

This category covers freight and passenger services on all modes of transport, as well as port services.

Travel

Credit entries are derived from surveys of commercial banks and hotels concerning the expenditure of foreign visitors. Debit entries are derived from the records of banks and ministries.

GUYANA

Transportation

The account covers freight and passenger services for all modes of transport. The BOG conducts surveys to obtain these data.

Travel

Credit entries include all receipts from transactions in foreign currency at cambios, travelers' checks that are cashed in, and goods purchased by tourists while in Guyana. Debit entries comprise mainly purchases of travelers' checks, payments for medical treatment abroad, and other expenditures for students abroad.

HAITI

Transportation

Data on transportation services are estimated on the basis of information provided by the port and airport authorities and on the basis of annual surveys carried out at Haitian and foreign airlines and at shipping agencies. The debit entry for freight on imports includes insurance and is estimated at 7 percent of imports, c.i.f.

Travel

The Secretariat of State for Tourism gathers monthly statistics on the number of tourists in Haiti. Estimated income from travel is distributed under separate headings for tourists arriving by air, ship, and road, respectively. For those arriving by air, the number of tourists recorded during the period in question is multiplied by the average duration of their stay and by their estimated daily expenditures. Data coming from the airport authority related to the number of travelers are also used by the IED. For those arriving by ship and spending a maximum of 24 hours in Haiti (excursionists), the number is multiplied by an estimate of the sum spent on the day in question. The number of tourists crossing the border is obtained from data of the central bank's Tax Operations Division on tolls paid at counters. Travel debits are estimated based on the number of Haitians leaving the country.

HONDURAS

Transportation

This category covers freight and passenger services by all modes of transport, plus port services. The Economic Research Department derives the credit entries for transportation services from information provided by airport and seaport authorities and annual surveys of Honduran airline and shipping companies. It obtains debit entries for freight from information on freight and insurance reported in customs declaration forms, received monthly. The Economic Research Department obtains debit entries for passenger transportation by a survey of foreign airlines.

Travel

The department bases credit and debit entries for travel on surveys conducted by the Tourism Institute and the General Department of Migratory Policy. Estimates are compiled by combining the number of foreign visitors with estimates of average expenditures.

HONG KONG, CHINA

Services

The C&SD collects data on trade in services primarily from the *Annual Survey of Imports and Exports of Services* (*ASIES*), supplemented by results from other annual or quarterly surveys and administrative data sources. Data from administrative sources include those from the Hong Kong Tourism Board, the Immigration Department, and the Treasury. The value of financial intermediation services is indirectly measured using the "reference rate" method. Services data for 2005 presented in this *Yearbook* contain only the net balance and total credits and debits. A full breakdown of 11 service items will be compiled when the *ASIES* results for 2005 become available.

HUNGARY

Transportation

The primary data source (reports of monetary institutions) provides a breakdown by transportation category (passenger, freight, and other) but does not distinguish the means of transportation (sea, air, or other). In addition to the primary information sources, which record transportation services on separate accounts, an adjustment (related to the change in the terms of delivery of goods) relies on the data derived from the external trade statistics.

Transportation services are adjusted with a value equal to the adjustment in the terms of delivery of goods, but with the opposite sign. The estimation of the terms of delivery correction and its allocation between debits and credits for transportation services are based on bills of clearance. The HCSO carries out the estimation and allocation, and the MNB uses the data obtained.

Travel

Since 2004, the travel item of balance of payments is compiled from results of border surveys. Based on the survey results, the ITRS-based time series on travel have been revised going back to 2000. Up to 2003, settlement data (reports by the MNB, commercial banks, exchange offices, and companies holding accounts abroad) were used for compiling travel services.

Up to 2003, travel-related flows reported by banks and exchange offices were corrected with the following:

- The balance of cash transactions affecting households' foreign exchange (FX) accounts held at resident banks, as well as the balance of forint/foreign currency exchange transactions carried out at banks, were recorded under travel. As of 2003, relying on a direct survey of account holders (2000) and natural indicators, the MNB estimated separately the breakdown by various components (travel, income, current transfers, real estate investment) of the credit and debit entries for these cash transactions. It recorded the transaction values obtained under the appropriate items in the balance of payments. Simultaneously with the methodological switch, it had revised the time series going back to 1995.

- MNB primarily classifies as travel the foreign exchange bought by exchange offices from residents. Therefore, as of 1998, travel receipts included the excess of foreign currency purchased by exchange offices from residents over a "benchmark" value (of a similar item in 1997 for the period between 1998 and 2000, and from 2001, an amount equalling 5 percent of travel expenditures in the previous month). Before 1998, MNB treated these transactions as re-exchange of foreign exchange previously bought for travel purposes by residents and recorded them as correction entries to travel debit.

ICELAND

Transportation

The entries for transportation, freight, passenger, and port services are based on surveys of the main Icelandic airlines and shipping companies and estimates of other companies' data, based on bank reports on foreign exchange transactions.

Travel

Hospital, educational, and other travel services are estimated from the foreign exchange transactions reported by banks and payment card companies. Iceland is not able to distinguish between business and personal travel services from prevailing data sources.

INDIA

Transportation

This category covers all modes of transport and port services; RBI bases the data mainly on the receipts and payments reported by the banks in respect of transportation items. In addition to the foreign exchange transactions records, a source is the survey of unclassified receipts. These sources are supplemented by information collected from major airline and shipping companies in respect of payments from foreign accounts. The RBI also uses a benchmark Survey of Freight and Insurance on Exports to estimate freight receipts on account of exports.

Travel

For travel, the RBI obtains data from foreign exchange transactions records, supplemented by information from the surveys of unclassified receipts. The estimates of travel receipts also use the information on foreign tourist arrivals and expenditure, received from the Ministry of Tourism, as a cross-check of the foreign exchange transactions and survey data.

INDONESIA

Transportation

This category covers freight, passenger, and other by all modes of transport. Entries for the value of freight debits are mainly estimated on the basis of information on freight furnished in customs declaration forms.

For passenger service credits and freight credits, the BI collects data from ITRS. Data on passenger transportation debits are estimated based on a survey of travelers and average air fares derived from a survey of travel agencies.

Other transportation includes foreign exchange receipts for use of seaport and airport facilities. The seaport and airport authorities report these data.

Travel

For travel credits and debits, BI derives entries from census and surveys conducted by the Ministry of Tourism and the Central Bureau of Statistics. Estimates are made by combining the number of foreign visitors and the number of Indonesian travelers abroad with estimation of their average expenditures. It should be noted that part of the travel debit item is accounted for by *hajj* pilgrimages.

IRAN, ISLAMIC REPUBLIC OF

Services

The entries for transactions in services cover passenger services, freight and insurance, travel, and other public and private services—most of which are derived from the foreign exchange records of the banking system and from reports on receipts and payments provided by banks. The largest debit items are freight, other business services, and insurance, whereas the largest credit items are government and other business services.

Freight and insurance services are estimated based on the information on transportation undertaken by residents, which the central bank obtains from the foreign exchange records of the banking system. The CBI uses reports from the major land transportation companies to compare and adjust this figure. This item also includes an adjustment on the basis of statistics supplied by maritime transportation companies.

The central bank obtains data for other services items from the foreign exchange records of the banking system, which are recorded on a cash basis. Other services items include travel (university students and patients), other transport services (transportation companies), public services (including membership fees paid to international organizations), commissions, financial services, and cultural services (purchase of books and articles from abroad). The CBI uses statistics released by the Iran Touring and Tourism Organization (prepared for the World Tourism Organization) and a household budget questionnaire to derive the travel entries.

IRELAND

Transportation

Because merchandise imports have been valued on an f.o.b. basis since 1998, the freight element of the c.i.f. to f.o.b. adjustment on merchandise imports is now split and included under the transportation and insurance service headings. Apart from this, the CSO collects data primarily by means of quarterly inquiries to resident airline and shipping companies.

Passenger fares paid by residents of Ireland to foreign transport companies generally cannot be distinguished and are instead included in the travel (debit) item. Disbursements in Irish ports and airports by foreign carriers, time charters, and other receipts from abroad by Irish carriers are included in the air and sea transport items. These data are collected from administrative sources.

Travel

Data are based on estimates of the number of travelers and their per capita expenditures, provided internally by the Tourism and Travel Section of the CSO. These estimates of the number of travelers cover those traveling by public carriers (based on information supplied by sea, air, and land transport companies operating in international traffic) and those traveling privately by road across the Northern Ireland border. Expenditures by Irish residents abroad and by foreign visitors to Ireland are estimated from sample surveys of travelers conducted by the CSO. See also information given under *Transportation* above.

ISRAEL

Transportation

The major sources for freight and transportation are Israeli companies that operate ships and aircraft on international routes, foreign shipping and aviation companies that operate in Israel, the Ports Authority in Israel, ship and aircraft repair companies, companies that supply food and bunker oil to ships and aircraft, and the Civil Aviation Service of the Ministry of Transport. Transactions include receipts resulting from the transport of cargo by foreign carriers that are temporarily leased by Israeli companies. The data also include receipts and payments by ships owned by Israeli subsidiaries under a foreign flag (convenience flag), operated by Israeli agents only.

Some reports of Israeli shipping and aviation companies include a detailed breakdown of expenditures according to type of currency and not according to the location of the expenditures—in Israel or abroad. The item of *other expenditures* in these reports, which includes information from other sources, is corrected or adjusted (such as the purchase of tickets for travel abroad by Israelis in foreign currency, or the purchase in Israel of bunker oil in foreign currency). Beginning in 1971, repairs of Israeli ships and aircraft performed abroad by foreign insurance agents have been included in expenditures of Israeli shipping and aviation companies. At the same time, these expenditures have been recorded as income from insurance claims in the insurance item. Until 1971, this listing, as well as that included in the insurance item, was a net figure.

Travel

Credit entries are estimated using a semiannual survey of foreign tourists, conducted by the Ministry of Tourism and under the supervision of the Central Bureau of Statistics (CBS). The survey provides the average expenditure per tourist during each half year, while the total expenditure of foreign tourists is estimated according to the average expenditure and the total number of tourists leaving Israel each quarter. (This latter figure is obtained from the statistics of the Demography Department in the CBS.)

Debits are estimated on the basis of a quarterly updated survey conducted by the CBS for the year 1997 regarding the average expenditure per tourist and on current data on departures abroad of Israel residents published by the CBS.

ITALY

Transportation

Passenger transport items were estimated on the basis of the sample survey of transport enterprises and the UIC sample survey of international tourism (for data on the number of passengers). Starting from 2002, both passengers' transport costs and number of passengers are derived from the survey on international tourism.

Travel

Up to 1989, the data were compiled from transfers related to international trips for tourism, business, health, and education purposes and from credit card transactions. A monthly sample survey of travelers, introduced in 1996 and covering about 60 border points, has now become the main source of data for travel services. The survey provides a detailed breakdown by purpose of the travel, according to the supplementary items indicated in *BPM5*. Historical data for 1990–95 have been revised and adjusted in a linear manner with the results of the survey.

JAMAICA

Transportation

This category covers freight and passenger services by all types of transportation. The Port and Airport Authorities of Jamaica provide data for port services. The BOJ also derives data from annual surveys of the national airlines, foreign airlines, and shipping companies. It obtains information on passenger services from surveys of national airlines and foreign airlines. Data for freight are estimated at 15 percent of non-oil imports (c.i.f.) and 3 percent of oil imports (c.i.f.).

Travel

Compilers derive travel credits from expenditure surveys carried out by the Jamaica Tourist Board. Credit data also come from immigration statistics on the number of visitors and their average length of stay. Travel debits are compiled from banking records and from data supplied by the Ministry of Labor.

JAPAN

Transportation

Regarding payments for transportation services, the data compilers obtain the data mainly from the reports submitted by international shipping and airline companies, as well as the Payments Reports. This item includes the value of freight, deducted from the value of imports in the trade statistics. Distinctions between subitems, such as *sea transportation* and *air transportation*, depend on types of transportation methods.

Travel

The main sources of data, used to estimate the amount of the goods and services acquired from an economy by travelers, are survey results on expenditures of foreign travelers in Japan and Japanese overseas travelers. The data on per capita expenditure of these travelers are estimated by utilizing such travelers' numbers, released by the Japan National Tourist Organization.

Other expenditures, not covered by this survey, are estimated by utilizing data from other sources. For example, data on the expenditures of long-term international students are estimated by using data published by government agencies. In addition, data on large amounts of medical expenses are obtained from the Payments Reports. The distinction between business and personal travel is made by detailed information of the survey results and other sources.

JORDAN

Transportation

For credit and debit entries for transportation services (freight and passenger), CBJ derives data from information provided by Aqaba Port Authority and by airline shipping and land companies, respectively. The compilers record entries for freight credits on the basis of data on freight and other transportation extracted from ITRS forms. The breakdown between "passengers" and "other transportation" is estimated based on available information and indicators from the main transportation companies. Entries for freight debits are estimated at 9 percent of c.i.f. imports.

Travel

CBJ bases entries for travel on the number of departures and arrivals, provided by the Ministry of Tourism and Antiquities in cooperation with the Ministry of Interior, and on the results of tourism surveys, conducted by the DOS. These surveys provide information on the average expenditure of foreign tourists coming into Jordan and resident tourists traveling abroad, and on the average duration of stay. The compilers use data on the number of Jordanians studying abroad—sourced from the Ministry of Higher Education—to estimate education expenditures abroad, and they include these estimates in the travel debits.

KAZAKHSTAN

Transportation

This category covers all modes of transport and port services. NBK bases the data for passenger fares and port charges mainly on reports it collects from marine shipping, airline, railway, and road companies. Freight includes the data reported by cargo enterprises and estimated transportation of goods carried from/to the frontier countries and the rest of the countries. Freight estimates for frontier countries and for the rest of the countries are based on the yearly survey and used for the data beginning in 2000.

Travel

NBK estimates data on travel on the basis of estimated average expenditures, number of residents traveling abroad and nonresidents traveling in Kazakhstan, and the estimated duration of their stay. Information on travelers by country of origin or destination and type of travel is also available.

KENYA

Transportation

This category covers passenger fares, freight services by all modes of transport, and port services. The credit entries are derived from information obtained from Kenya Railways (KR), sea transport, air road, inland waterway (Lake Victoria) and pipeline transport firms. Data on passenger fares, port services, and leases are obtained from Kenya Airways (KA), the Kenya Airport Authority (KAA), Nairobi Airport Services (NAS), bus companies, and Kenya Ports Authority (KPA). Port services include services to shipping lines.

Travel

Data are obtained from CBK returns on invisible transactions. Plans are underway to conduct a sample survey of departing visitors, to which regular monthly data on travel receipts from the foreign exchange record of the CBK can be benchmarked.

KOREA, REPUBLIC OF

Transportation

For transportation services, the BOK derives entries from the KFX and from surveys of resident airlines and shipping companies. The KFX data provide a breakdown by transportation category (i.e., passenger transportation, freight, or other transportation).

Travel

The KFX data include both nonresidents' sales of foreign currency in Korea and residents' purchases of foreign currency in Korea. The KFX also covers the use of traveler's checks and credit cards. Business and personal travel will be distinguished from 2006.

KUWAIT

Transportation

The Kuwait Airways Corporation provides information on passenger tickets. For the freight component, CBK calculates estimates as a percentage of imports. The CBK's estimates for shipping services on imports allocate 95 percent of estimated freight services and 80 percent of estimated insurance services as balance of payments flows to foreign carriers and providers. For credit entries, CBK compiles estimates for services provided to nonresidents from reports provided by the Kuwait Oil Tankers Company and other shipping companies.

For the *other transportation* item, CBK compiles estimates of expenses abroad on the basis of data provided by the Kuwait Airways Corporation and Kuwaiti shipping companies. On the credit side, CBK compiles estimates from questionnaires and reports provided by the Kuwait Airways Corporation, Kuwaiti shipping companies, the Kuwait Ports Authority (for port dues), and the General Directorate of Civil Aviation (for airport dues). These estimates include transport and storage services provided to the international coalition forces stationed in Kuwait and Iraq from 2003 onwards.

Travel

The central bank compiles estimates of travel debits on the basis of questionnaires answered by travel agencies, surveys it prepares (the last of which took place during the period March-September 2000), and reports submitted by government agencies on expenses paid for education, conferences, trainees, medical treatment, and official missions abroad. For credit entries, the CBK calculates estimates based on the number of nonresident visitors to Kuwait and their average expenditures. The Immigration Department provides a figure on the number of nonresident visitors.

KYRGYZSTAN

Transportation

The NSC collects data from domestic airlines, railway, and road transportation companies. NBKR supplements these data with information it collects from enterprises and ITRS. It derives freight on imports provided by nonresidents from the estimated freight included in the c.i.f. value of imports and adjusted to exclude transportation provided by resident carriers.

Travel

The NSC assesses travel services on the basis of the estimated average per diem expenditures, number of residents traveling abroad and nonresidents traveling in the Kyrgyz Republic, and the estimated duration of their stay. The SCI provides data on the number of travelers, country of origin (for foreign travelers), country of destination (for domestic travelers), and types of travel (private, business, etc.).

LAO PEOPLE'S DEMOCRATIC REPUBLIC

Transportation

This item covers overflights, freight, and passengers. The BOL's Operation Department provides data on overflights, and the remaining elements are based on BOL staff estimates.

Travel

Credit entries are derived from information in surveys conducted by the National Tourism Authority of Lao PDR., including estimates of the number of visitors, the number of overnight stays, and the estimated average expenditure. Debit entries are derived from data from the Receipts and Payments reporting system provided by the Foreign Currency Department of BOL.

LATVIA

Transportation

For credit entries for passenger transportation by air, reporting agents declare total amounts received for the international carriage of passengers in the quarterly survey on transportation and intermediary services. The compilers use the data on the monthly number of residents and nonresidents crossing the state border, broken down by mode of transportation, for calculating the proportion of nonresidents in total border crossings. They use this ratio to determine the nonresident part of the international carriage of passengers broken down by mode of transportation. Debit entries are obtained by calculation, using 1) data on the number of departing passengers by airlines, submitted by the Riga international airport, 2) CSB data on the monthly number of residents and nonresidents crossing the state border by air, and 3) information on the average prices of airline tickets.

Travel

Compilers derive the data on travel from the CSB aggregated data on persons entering and leaving the country. Travelers are polled at border control points four times a year to obtain information about nonresident spending in Latvia and resident spending abroad. Using mathematical methods, the compilers calculate the average spending of a traveler and, thereafter, obtain travelers' total spending. The number of travelers is available from the State Border Guard of the Republic of Latvia, which registers persons entering and leaving the country.

For personal travel credit entries, compilers estimate expenditures of students, using the number of foreign students in Latvia, submitted by the Ministry of Education and universities. For debit entries, compilers use the information submitted by foreign embassies in Latvia on the number of Latvia's students and average expenditures by country.

LEBANON

Transportation

Only public sector operations are recorded before 2003. Using the information obtained from the ITRS, as of 2003, ESS also includes data on private sector transactions (banks, the nonbank financial sector, and the private sector, comprising households and private companies). This section also comprises freight transactions, estimated by applying a 7.5 percent average rate on the value of imports c.i.f. The obtained figure is subdivided among the sea, air, and other transport sections according to the weights obtained from the records of goods by the different ports of entry.

Travel

ESS bases estimates on the General Directorate of General Security data on arriving and departing travelers through all borders and on an evaluation of the average spending per individual. It also derives statistics from basic circular #1564, dated October 3, 1997, decision # 6754. (This circular was replaced by circular #63, dated June 10, 1999, decision #7299, amended for the last time with intermediary circular #24, dated August 26, 2002, decision #8216, related to ATMs and credit cards.) ESS adds these statistics to the data with the aim of improving the estimate of tourist expenditures and revenues. This circular covers all transactions done via automated teller machines (ATMs), as well as debit and credit cards, to keep track of nonresident expenditures in Lebanon and resident expenditures abroad. As of 2003, data from the ITRS have been added, giving this item a wider statistical coverage.

LESOTHO

Transportation

For passenger services/air travel, the CBL obtains data through a continuous survey covering travel agencies in Lesotho. For port services, it obtains data from the Department of Civil Aviation.

Travel

For expenditure by foreign visitors to Lesotho, the CBL obtains data from the Lesotho Tourism Development Corporation (LTDC), which phased out the Lesotho Tourist Board. Data on expenditure by Lesotho residents on trips abroad are obtained from foreign exchange declaration forms. Data on expenditure by government-funded Basotho students studying abroad are obtained from the National Manpower Development Secretariat. Data on expenditure by private-funded Basotho students studying abroad are obtained from the exchange control records.

The National University of Lesotho and the Center for Accounting Studies provide data on foreign students studying in Lesotho. The Lesotho Agricultural College and the Lesotho College of Education (formerly the National Teachers Training College) also provide information on fees and living expenditures by foreign students.

LIBYAN ARAB REPUBLIC

Transportation

The item includes passenger and freight services. CBL derives the data mainly from commercial bank records.

Travel

CBL obtains data on travel (for tourism, education, and medical expense) credits and debits from its records and commercial banks.

LITHUANIA

Transportation

This category includes cargo and passenger transportation services using all means of transportation, including seaport and airport services. The primary data source is the quarterly survey of the cross-border transactions of nonbank entities with nonresidents, conducted by SL. The quarterly survey is supplemented by a comprehensive annual survey of small road transport operators, covering their quarterly and annual transactions. Approximately 1,000 enterprises provide the data.

Travel

Travel services include all goods and services acquired by travelers in foreign countries. (A person living in a country in which he/she is not a resident for less than one year is considered a traveler.) Services for international passenger transportation (i.e., the transportation of passengers between countries) are not included in the travel item. Such services belong to the category of passenger transportation services.

Data on travel services are calculated on the basis of (1) the monthly data on the number of incoming and outgoing foreigners from non-Schengen countries, provided by the State Border Guard Service at the Ministry of the Interior; (2) the Department of Tourism's annual selective research on incoming foreigners and their average expenditure and length of stay; (3) the SL selective research on Lithuanian travelers and their average expenditure and length of stay; and (4) the data of quarterly surveys of enterprises providing accommodation services (hotels, health spa, etc.) and of enterprises involved in sales of touring packages.

LUXEMBOURG

Travel

The main sources are surveys, other statistics, and administrative data. Personal expenditures on goods and services by nonresident cross-border workers are recorded under business travel.

MACAO, CHINA

Transportation

The data on passenger, freight, and other transportation are obtained from statistics of various activity surveys and national accounts. Because the current survey system does not differentiate the value of this service among different modes of transportation, no breakdown on the type of transportation is available.

Travel

Credit entries for travel are mainly derived from national account statistics that include travelers' expenditures on gaming, accommodation, and other expenses, utilizing data of the Visitor Expenditure Survey, Hotel Survey, and administrative records on hotel and gaming receipts. Gaming expenditures of nonresidents are estimated based on an assumed rate applied to the total gaming receipts on administrative records. Travelers' expenditures on accommodation are estimated from the number of room nights sold and the average room rates, whereas expenditures on other areas are estimated by using the number of visitor arrivals, per capita spending of visitors, and other tourism data. The split between business and personal travel is based on purpose of visit reported by interviewed visitors.

Entries for business travel (debit) are mainly derived from the enterprise surveys and activity surveys, whereas those for personal travel (debit) are principally extracted from national account statistics that are mainly estimated from the Household Budget Survey and other statistics.

MALAWI

Transportation

The main subcomponents of transport are passenger, freight, and landing fees. Credits on passenger and freight transportation relate mostly to air transport, collected from the sole domestic airline operator, Air Malawi. Debits are derived from the adjustment of imports c.i.f. to f.o.b. by applying a 15 percent fixed factor for freight and insurance, which is fully attributed to air freight. In the medium term, the 15 percent will be split between freight and insurance so that the latter can be classified under insurance services in accordance with *BPM5*. Statistics on landing fees are obtained from the Civil Aviation Department for the credit side, and from Air Malawi for the debit side.

Travel

Data on travel debits are obtained from the exchange control records through forms that are completed for purchases and sales of foreign currency from authorized dealers. Credits are compiled on the basis of exit cards completed by tourists returning abroad to their original economies. The data tend to underestimate credits on travel.

MALAYSIA

Transportation

This category covers freight and passenger services by all modes of transport and port services. For transportation services, DSM derives entries from information provided by airport and seaport authorities, and annual surveys of Malaysian airline and shipping companies and foreign airline companies in Malaysia.

Travel

For travel credits, the DSM derives entries from expenditure surveys of foreign visitors carried out by the Malaysia Tourism Promotion Board. Estimates are compiled by combining the number of foreign visitors with estimates of average expenditures.

For travel debits, the DSM derives entries from the BNM records, supplemented with information provided by the Pilgrimage Fund Board and other ministries and agencies.

MALDIVES

Transportation

This category covers transportation of passengers, freight, and other items. Data on passenger services and on port services are obtained from MACL, Maldives Ports Authority, and Maldives National Shipping Limited (MNSL). Information on freight related to imports is derived from customs declarations, assuming (based on a survey of customs records) that 10.8 percent of imports c.i.f. is freight. Freight is reported on an aggregate basis, because data on air and sea freight are not available separately. At present, freight is reported on an aggregated basis.

Travel

Travel credits (receipts) are estimates by MMA based on data obtained from MOTC regarding tourist arrivals, tourist bednights, and room rates in resorts and hotels. Estimates are adjusted for seasonality. Travel receipts are calculated in three parts: receipts by tour operators, purchases at resorts, and expenditure outside of resorts.

Receipts by tour operators are calculated by multiplying bed nights by an estimated average daily expenditure. The other two items are aimed at covering the cost of incidentals, souvenirs, and similar—that is, any expenditure other than what is spent on the tour package. Purchases at resorts are calculated on the basis of a per diem estimate, while estimates of expenditure outside of resorts are based on numbers of arrivals.

Estimates of travel debits are obtained from various sources. Business travel covers expenditures relating to government travel and travel for tourism fairs, data for which are obtained from the foreign exchange records maintained by MMA and the MOTC, respectively. For personal travel, the health-related expenditure component is also obtained from the foreign exchange records of MMA and includes social security releases made for medical treatment.

Estimates of expenditure on education-related travel are obtained from the Ministry of Higher Education, Employment, and Social Security (MHES), which provides information on expenses associated with scholarships under the Education and Training project. The estimates for other travel are derived as the sum of total expenditure on hajj travel (obtained from hajj tour organizers and relevant government authorities) and the residual between the estimate of total expenditures by Maldivian travelers and travel under the other categories.

MALI

Transportation

Data on passenger services are collected from national and foreign airlines.

Travel

The amounts posted as credits to this account are determined from the results of surveys of the Tourism Commissioner's Office and of hotels concerning arrivals of foreign tourists and hotel occupancy.

The debits posted are mainly expenditure by non-Malian residents on leave. This expenditure is estimated on the basis of the income of expatriates working in the private sector, compensation of technical assistance personnel and non-Malian permanent staff in international organizations, as well as the length of leave of these groups of persons.

However, the figures pertaining to government missions are sourced from the National Directorate of the Treasury and Public Accounting. Expenditure by Malian students abroad is estimated from scholarships. Data on these scholarships, whether foreign or granted by the Malian government, are basically collected from the Ministry of Higher Secondary Education and Scientific Research.

MALTA

Transportation

The source for passenger transportation, separated by mode of transport, is the monthly survey of airline and shipping companies.

Travel

Gross earnings from tourism are being derived from the frontier surveys, TOURSTAT, and CRUISTAT. Data have been revised back to 1995 for comparability. Gross expenditure by residents traveling abroad is derived from information provided by the Tourism unit within the NSO. This is replacing the previous source, emanating from foreign currency transactions that banking institutions and other authorized dealers reported to the CBM on a monthly basis.

MAURITIUS

Transportation

The main data sources are the survey of airline and shipping companies (quarterly since 1999; half-yearly prior to then) and the CSO. Transportation credits measure receipts by domestic carriers from passenger fares, freight on exports and on shipments between other countries, and other port disbursements. Transportation debits measure payments made to nonresident carriers for passenger fares, freight on imports, and other port disbursements.

Travel

Travel credits are estimated from purchases by banks of foreign exchange from tourists, business travelers, hotels, cash dealers, and traders. Travel debit estimates are derived from the banking records of banks.

MEXICO

Transportation

For passenger fares, the central bank estimates the entries from information provided by the resident airlines on their total earnings on international transportation. It supplements these estimates with information from migration statistics on the number of residents and nonresidents traveling by air and from travel surveys on expenditures on ticket purchases by travelers.

Travel

The Bank of Mexico bases credit entries on the immigration authorities' reports on the number of nonresidents visiting Mexico and on its own sample surveys on travelers' average expenditure. It obtains the debit entries using a similar procedure.

Travel is broken down into tourists and excursionists (one-day visitors). Tourists are defined as those who have spent at least one night in the host country and as those who, having not spent at least one night in the host country, have visited it beyond the border area; excursionists are defined as those who have not spent the night in the host country. No distinction is made between business and personal travel.

MONGOLIA

Transportation

Mongolian Railways and Mongolian Airlines (MIAT) report information for the credit and debit entries for passenger fares and other distributive and auxiliary services. From imports c.i.f. to an f.o.b. conversion, 10.4 percent of the total import data are estimated to add to the debit side of transportation. The port services credit entries are derived from the report of Mongolia's Civil Aviation Authority, and the debit entries, from MIAT. The credit entries for port services represent payments by foreign airlines for the use of facilities at the airport in Ulaanbaatar.

Travel

Up to 1996, the credit and debit entries for travel were derived from the foreign exchange record. From 1997 onward, travel is estimated on the basis of information on the number of travelers combined with an estimate of the average duration of stay and an estimate of the per capita expenditures. Data on the number of travelers are complied by the Frontier Guards Administration of Mongolia, while the average number of nights per visit and the average daily expenditure are estimated and provided by the National Tourism Agency.

MONTSERRAT

See East Caribbean.

MOROCCO

Transportation

This item records, on both the credit and debit sides, payments relating to the transportation of goods and passengers, broken down by means of transportation: sea, air, and other.

Travel

Travel credits correspond to receipts from abroad received by tourism sector operators (travel agencies, hotels, clubs, tourist transportation, etc.). Receipts include encashment of travelers' checks and international credit card payments, as well as foreign currency banknotes exchanged via the banking system by tourists during their stay in Morocco. These credits also include part of the foreign currency banknotes exchanged by Moroccans residing abroad that are used to cover their board and lodging in Morocco.

Debit entries cover the various allocations of foreign banknotes to residents when they travel for purposes of tourism, business, education, medical care, training and missions, or pilgrimages. Debits also cover bank or postal transfers made to cover expenses incurred during this travel.

MOZAMBIQUE

Transportation

Data on transportation services are compiled from reports presented by the authorized foreign exchange banks and from the balance of payments surveys. Since 1995, specific surveys of selected transportation companies (railways, national airlines, and shipping) have been introduced. Very recently, owing to the process of improving the collection of transportation data by the Balance of Payment Service of the BM, the response rate of the surveys has improved substantively.

Travel

Data on travel credits and travel debits are based on reports presented by the authorized foreign exchange banks, exchange bureaus, and the country's main tourism authorities. A specific survey has been introduced in various hotels in the country. However, the response rate is low.

MYANMAR

Transportation

This item includes freight and passenger services for all modes of transport and port services. The source is the ITRS.

Travel

In compiling the travel item, the CBM uses the ITRS source, supplemented with estimates derived from data from the Immigration and Population Department for the number of tourists and from the Ministry of Hotels and Tourism for total travel expenditure.

NAMIBIA

Transportation

This component is estimated from the external trade data. In 1995, a specific survey was instituted, but the response rate has been very low, owing to a lack of cooperation from the reporting units (i.e., the national airlines, railways, and road transport operators) and the lack of awareness of the importance of balance of payments statistics among the respondents. However, the RD is in the process of improving the collection of these data.

Travel

Data on travel credits and debits are estimated on the basis of the Exit Survey 2002 contracted by the Ministry of Environment and Tourism because of the absence of comprehensive data. Estimates of data on travelers arriving in and departing from Namibia are made on the basis of various sources, such as the Ministry of Home Affairs, national airlines, and various hotels in the country.

NEPAL

Transportation

This category includes freight and passenger services by all modes of transport. The data are collected from commercial banks, the NRB, Indian airlines having offices in Nepal, and domestic airlines for three main categories, namely, freight, passenger services, and other transportation. The main credit items are the foreign exchange earnings of local airlines on passenger services and enterprises engaged in land transport. Debits reflect mainly freight charges, passenger services, and payments made to the foreign transport companies.

Travel

Data on travel are collected from the ITRS and the NRB's Foreign Exchange Management Department. This item includes, as credits, the receipts from foreign visitors in the form of cash, travelers' checks, drafts, etc. and the foreign exchange earnings from nonresidents of local hotels, travel agencies, and certain service agencies.

The item includes, as debits, the residents' expenditures abroad for business and personal travel, education expenses, medical treatment, and passport facilities (foreign exchange facilities provided to Nepalese passport holders going abroad).

NETHERLANDS

Services

As of the second quarter of 2003, Statistics Netherlands has been producing quarterly data on international trade in services. To that end, it adopted a new quarterly survey. In 2005 the reporting population for this survey comprised a sample of about 2,200 reporting agents (approximately 7 percent of the total population). A small number of large entities directly reports. In addition, Statistics Netherlands surveys a larger number of small and medium enterprises with less detail. The results are grossed up to a national level.

NEW ZEALAND

Transportation

The main types of transportation services data collected are for the carriage of goods (freight) and passengers. Also included under transportation services are charters of carriers, tugboat services, airport and harbor fees, and goods consumed by carriers in the course of their operations, including bunkering and provisioning. These data are provided from quarterly and annual surveys of resident airlines and shipping companies, nonresident airlines (through their New Zealand offices), and New Zealand agents acting for nonresident ship operators.

Travel

Data on the expenditure of overseas tourists in New Zealand are derived from an international visitors' survey, conducted by a marketing company for the Ministry of Tourism. In January 2003, the sampling of the International Visitor Survey changed to become "flight based." Flight-based sampling is a nonrandom method of sampling, allowing the specific targeting of passengers with certain characteristics that need to be represented in the sample of international visitors. Data on the characteristics of passengers is generated from the departure cards of passengers on the same flights in the previous year.

Where it is known that the sample needs to interview people with specific characteristics, interviewers approach passengers near the departure gate of flights known to carry passengers with these characteristics. The sample is selected from departing visitors at New Zealand's three largest international airports—Auckland, Wellington, and Christchurch. Estimates are also made for expenditure on education and health-related travel by nonresidents. The estimates for education-related travel are derived from a Survey of English Language Providers and Ministry of Education data. Health expenditure is derived from Crown Health Entity data.

Information on the expenditure of New Zealand residents traveling overseas is derived from a model that uses information obtained from a sample survey of returned New Zealand travelers (SORT). SORT, a two-year sample survey, began in the September 2002 quarter and ran until the quarter ended June 30, 2004.

NICARAGUA

Transportation

For air passenger services, it bases the data on an annual enterprise survey. Data on other transport include services reported by the National Ports Enterprise.

Travel

To estimate credit and debit entries, BCN combines information provided by the Directorate General of Migration and Aliens (on the number of nonresident and resident travelers and the average stay) with information derived from the annual survey undertaken by the Institute of Tourism (on the travelers' expenditures) plus the BCN's External Programming Department's estimates.

NIGERIA

Transportation

This category of services covers all modes of transportation plus port services. In the non-oil sector, credit entries reflect receipts from freight, passenger services, and port services provided by Nigeria to nonresidents. RSD obtains the data from bank returns made to the TED. Debit entries cover freight charges accruable to foreign carriers; these are estimated by adjusting the derived freight value for local components. Currently, freight cost is estimated at 10 percent of the c.i.f. value of imports.

Travel

For non-oil sector travel data (private), RSD obtains data from authorized dealers' returns to the TED but not broken down into the relevant components. Thus, the item does not provide separately the data on personal and business travel. The FOD cash flow statement captures foreign exchange disbursements on official travel. The oil sector travel item is estimated to move in tandem with the level of crude oil production activities.

NORWAY

Transportation

The estimation of receipts from the provision of maritime freight and passenger services of nonresidents is based partly on the ocean transport survey compiled by SN and partly on the ITRS. The latter source has less detailed information, but it is available at an earlier point of time; therefore, it is used as the basis for the preliminary balance of payments statistics.

Travel

Through 1991, entries for travel were based entirely upon data supplied by NCB on the sale of local currency in exchange for foreign currency, supplemented with data from credit card companies. From 1992, these sources have been supplemented with separate estimates based on tourist statistics (i.e., accommodation statistics, passenger transport statistics).

OMAN

Transportation

Data on transportation credits reflect the value of services provided to nonresidents at Omani ports.

Travel

Travel credit estimates are based on the number of foreign tourist arrivals as provided by the immigration authorities, multiplied by the average expenditure per tourist as estimated through a comprehensive survey.

Travel debits represent the estimated expenditure of students studying abroad, Omani pilgrims abroad, and health treatment received by Omani nationals abroad. Debits include estimates of expenditure by Omani residents abroad. In 2003, there was a change in the methodology to compile statistics on travel data to take into account the findings of a new tourism survey.

PAKISTAN

Transportation

This component covers all modes of transport and port services. SBP bases the data on a survey of foreign shipping companies and airlines, and the reporting of Pakistani shipping companies and airlines for the freight, passenger, and other components.

Travel

For both business and personal travel, SBP collects data through receipts and payments of the banking sector, plus the inward and outward remittances on travel through the exchange companies operating in Pakistan.

Further, through a survey of the respective companies, it collects the travel expenses of the crew of foreign shipping companies and airlines while on stay in Pakistan and the travel expenses of the crew of local shipping companies and airlines while on stay abroad.

PALESTINE (WEST BANK/GAZA)

Transportation

This item consists of the transportation costs of passengers and goods, as well as auxiliary services, such as storage, cargo handling, etc. The data are obtained from economic surveys conducted by the PCBS. The data also include an estimate for the freight element of the c.i.f./f.o.b. adjustment to the foreign trade statistics, namely, 8 percent of the c.i.f. value of imports.

Travel

The main sources used to compile the data on travel credits and debits are economic surveys, a hotel survey, the Palestinian expenditure and consumption survey (PECS), a labor force survey, and data from the Ministry of Islamic Affairs, the Ministry of Health, and the Ministry of High Education. These surveys and administrative records cover (for the debit data) all travel transactions of residents abroad, such as students abroad, medication costs abroad, part of the wages of Palestinian border workers in Israel, the expenditure of pilgrims (visitors to the holy city of Micah), etc.

The credit data cover nonresidents coming to the Palestinian Territories, such as tourists, foreign employees of consulates, representatives, international organizations, and those visiting relatives, etc.

PANAMA

Transportation

DSC derives information on freight on imports from customs declarations. It obtains data on passenger services from surveys of national airlines and agents of foreign airlines. For port services, it obtains data from agents of foreign air and shipping lines, national airlines, container terminals ports, and the Panama Canal Authority (for tolls and other services to Canal users).

Travel

DSC bases data on sample surveys it conducts in conjunction with the Panamanian Tourism Institute, on the expenditures of foreign visitors in Panama and of Panamanian residents on their trips abroad, and on information derived from migration statistics on the number of travelers.

PAPUA NEW GUINEA

Transportation

Transportation services include receipts and payments from freight, port handling, or other transportation-related services on traded goods.

Travel

Travel data cover passenger services by all modes of transport and port services related to the transportation of passengers. They include tickets, hotel rooms, airport taxes, and other travel expenses and receipts. Education-related expenditures are shown as a separate component of travel and include all tutorial fees and remittances or receipts associated with education at all levels.

PARAGUAY

Transportation

The main sources for freight data are shipment documents and surveys of land, air, and inland waterway transportation companies. Other sources to compile this item include the report on soya exports of the Paraguayan Chamber of Cereals and Oleaginous Products Exporters, regional reports prepared by the Ministry of Public Works, and the report on goods exported via inland waterways from the State Merchant Marine. The CBP obtains data to compile passenger services from the Capital Police, which reports the number of passengers entering and leaving the country using different carriers (air or land), multiplied by the ticket prices collected in surveys of local tourism operators.

Travel

Concerning inward tourism, the CBP obtains data monthly from the Directorate General of Tourism on the number of excursionists (mainly related to cross-border shopping) and tourists (who stay in the country for more than 24 hours). The central bank multiplies these data by an estimated daily expenditure based on UN estimates.

For outward tourism, the Capital Police provide data on the number of Paraguayan nationals leaving the country and, for air travel, their points of departure and destination. To calculate expenditure, the CBP uses a UN schedule of expenditure together with estimates based on interviews with tourism agents on cross-border shopping.

PERU

Transportation

CRBP bases the credit and debit entries on its quarterly survey of international transport companies and agents. It surveys all national companies and foreign airlines. Transactions of foreign shipping companies are reported by their agents or representatives in Peru.

The survey provides data on freight charges, sale of passenger fares, and supporting and auxiliary services by mode of transport (air, sea, and other transport). Compilers also use the import freight charges recorded in customs declaration forms after they adjust the data to subtract freight services provided by resident enterprises.

Travel

Data are estimated on the basis of tourism surveys (inward and outward) that the CRBP and PROMPERU conduct at the Jorge Chavez International Airport, the Santa Rosa post on the Chilean border, and the Yunguyo post on the Bolivian border. These surveys provide estimates on the average expenditure of nonresident travelers in Peru and resident travelers abroad.

The number of international travelers is provided by the Directorate General of Migration and Naturalization, an agency of the Ministry of the Interior. Data include travelers that cross the border and spend more than a night abroad and same-day visitors abroad (outward tourism) or in Peru (inward tourism). Debit entries also include the contra-entry of scholarships recorded as current transfers.

PHILIPPINES

Transportation

Transportation refers largely to data on merchandise freight, sourced from the foreign trade statistics. For other components of transportation services, the ITRS and the CAB company reports, obtained from the CBTS, provide the data.

Travel

For travel receipts, DES bases estimates on the Visitors Sample Survey (VSS), conducted by DOT. The VSS provides information on the average expenditure of foreign tourists and the average length of stay in the Philippines. For tourist-related travel expenditure abroad by residents, DES bases data on the ITRS.

Beginning with the 1999 report, travel credits include expenditure in the Philippines of nonresident OFWs during home visits. Travel debits include expenditures of resident OFWs in the host countries.

POLAND

Transportation

Data provided by the banking system on payments and by the surveys on enterprises for transportation services include services broken down by type (sea, air, railway, and other). These data are broken down by passenger transportation, freight, and other forms. Data received from the c.i.f./f.o.b. adjustment of the goods item are also included in freight transportation services. The value of these services is compiled as a fixed rate of the value of goods imports in the foreign trade statistics.

Travel

The travel item is compiled using data of the Institute of Tourism, which come from border surveys. The NBP receives data on expenditure of travellers': foreigners in Poland and Poles abroad.

When compiling monthly data, NBP makes estimates using information of the Border Guard (on numbers of arrivals and departures) and payments data (including settlements on travel items recorded in the banking system and also purchases and sales of foreign banknotes).

PORTUGAL

Transportation

BdP bases transportation data on the settlement statistics, supplemented with the estimates (see above) used to convert c.i.f. to f.o.b. valued goods. Data distinguish the means of transportation (sea, air, rail, or other transport) and provide a breakdown by transportation category (passenger, freight, or other transportation).

Travel

Travel data are based on settlements (e.g., bank transfers, cash, travelers' checks, debit and credit cards, and other means of settlement), on information provided by travel agencies, and on estimates produced by the BdP based on real indicators and prices of tourist activity (tourism statistics provided by the INE).

REPUBLIC OF MOLDOVA

Transportation

Besides the estimates made for transportation payments related to imported goods, referred to above, additional data are obtained from other sources. The main sources are the ITRS and the NBS data on transportation services, collected from companies providing transport services, such as motor transport. The Railways Office provides data on the use of railway services.

Travel

For travel, BPD compiles data using information provided by the NBS, the banking system, institutions that provide travel, and hotel services. Compilers also calculate estimates of expenditures abroad by persons engaged in the export/import of goods, by business travelers, and by workers residing abroad for less than one year. Estimates of students' travel expenditures are made from data provided by the Ministry of Education and Youth and Sports.

ROMANIA

Transportation

For export freight services, national compilers use banking records as the main source. For the credit side of the transportation balance, data are recorded on the basis of banks' customers declarations.

Travel

Data are based on information obtained from the banks, on an individual basis (transaction-by-transaction data collected from bank customers). Data are supplemented by additional data based on the transactions of the exchange offices, compiled by the SD.

Estimates are made of the amounts of foreign exchange that residents use when traveling abroad. For the foreign exchange transactions of nonresidents made through bureaus of exchange (credits), compilers derive data as the difference between the amounts of foreign exchange sold and purchased by nonresidents in the reporting period.

RUSSIAN FEDERATION

Services

The BR derives the data on transportation, royalties and license fees, and operational leases from enterprise surveys conducted by Rosstat.

Compilers estimate travel services via a model, using data on the number of border crossings classified by purpose of travel, average time of stay, and average expenditure per trip. The model uses data obtained from Rosstat surveys, the Federal Frontier Service of Russia, the Minfin of Russia, the Federal Migration Service of the Ministry of Internal Affairs, and sampling observations of offers by hotels and travel agencies conducted by the BR. Also used are partner country and mass media data. Besides, the BR estimates the number of cars imported for personal use—the costs of such cars being recorded under the travel debit item.

The BR obtains the data on all other services mainly from the ITRS. BR also uses, supplementary to ITRS, the information from the Minfin of Russia, local governments, and international organizations, for calculating financial services. It also uses data from the Minfin of Russia and other ministries for compiling government services.

RWANDA

Transportation

Passenger. Transportation services include the (1) transportation of nonresident passengers by the national airlines and road-transport companies and (2) transportation of resident passengers by foreign airlines.

Travel

The NBR derives credit entries from surveys conducted at hotels, guesthouses, and the Rwanda Office of Tourism and National Parks and from the exchange records. The amounts entered as debits are also drawn from the exchange records, supplemented with information from the ministries of National Education, Foreign Affairs and Cooperation, and the Interior's Immigration and Emigration Service. These data were not gathered for the period 1994–2000, and the balance of payments for each subsequent year has been compiled on the basis of estimates. Beginning in 2001, data from surveys have been used to compile this item.

SAINT KITTS AND NEVIS

See East Caribbean.

SAINT LUCIA

See East Caribbean.

SAINT VINCENT AND THE GRENADINES

See East Caribbean.

SAMOA

Transportation

Entries for transportation services are derived from the ticket system (mainly for data on services transactions of foreign shipping companies, the local shipping company, and the local airline) and from a monthly survey of all foreign airlines. Because imports are valued c.i.f., freight and insurance debits are not included in the services account to avoid double counting. This figure is shown as a memorandum item in the services and income account table of the CBS's *Quarterly Bulletin*.

Travel

Monthly entries for travel credits are estimated on the basis of tourist arrivals and the average tourist expenditure derived from the Western Samoa Visitor Survey conducted in 1990 and subsequently adjusted for price changes using the consumer price index. (Travel credits captured in the ticket system are replaced by the above entries.)

SAUDI ARABIA

Transportation

This item covers all air, marine, and land transport services and includes passenger, freight, and other services. The SAMA obtains data on air, marine, and land transport from the Saudi Arabian Airlines, the Presidency of Civil Aviation, the General Ports Authority, and the Saudi Land Transportation Company. Data on freight are estimated.

Travel

Foreign visitors are mainly pilgrims and Umrah performers year-round—especially those who visit Saudi Arabia around the months of Dhul-Hijjah and Ramadan each year. Expenditures are estimated on the basis of data that SAMA receives from the Ministry of Interior on actual numbers of pilgrims and other visitors. The SAMA obtains data on travel by residents of Saudi Arabia abroad from the commercial banks, which record the purpose for sales of foreign exchange.

SENEGAL

Transportation

This item covers freight, passenger services, and port services. Freight costs are estimated at 10 percent of c.i.f. imports, after adjustments. Information on passenger transportation is obtained from airline companies.

Travel

Credit entries are taken from surveys of hotels, tourist sites, etc. by the Ministry of Tourism. Estimates are based on the number of foreign visitors, their estimated average expenditure, and their average length of stay. Debit entries are obtained from statements of tourist allocations (including pilgrimage operations) granted by banks, plus data collected from airport authorities.

SEYCHELLES

Transportation

This item consists mainly of revenue from passenger services, port services, and freight. Passenger services represent air transportation only; data are obtained from Air Seychelles and agents of foreign airlines based in Seychelles.

Travel

Until 1991, revenue from travel was based on commercial bank records and a tourism expenditure survey carried out by NSB. Since 1992, however, the emergence of a parallel market for foreign exchange has reduced the coverage of commercial bank records, and total revenues from 1992 to 1995 are based on the NSB survey, although commercial bank receipts are also shown as part of overall revenue.

For foreign travel, bank records remain the source of data. In June 2001, with the introduction of exchange control regulations, these records have increased in importance.

SIERRA LEONE

Transportation

This category covers freight and passenger services for all modes of transport and port services. BSL derives data for transport services from an annual survey of airline and shipping companies that operate in Sierra Leone.

Travel

BSL compiles estimates of travel credits by combining data on tourist arrivals with estimates of their average expenditures, both of which are provided by the Sierra Leone Tourist Board. The BSL obtains information on government travel from banking records.

SINGAPORE

Transportation

Transportation covers freight, passenger, and port services. The credit entries for freight cover freight earnings of local shipping lines and airlines. Data are obtained from the TIS. The debit entries cover payments to nonresidents for freight services provided. The total cost of freight on imports is estimated by applying freight factors to the value of imports (c.i.f.). These factors are obtained from a survey of importers. Data on passenger and port services are obtained from the TIS and accounts of harbor and airport authorities.

Travel

The main source of information on expenditure by visitors who come in by air and sea is the Survey of Overseas Visitors to Singapore conducted by the Singapore Tourism Board. Estimates are also made for the expenditure of visitors coming to Singapore by road and rail. Entries for travel debits are derived from the number of returning Singapore residents and the estimated average expenditure per person.

SLOVAKIA

Transportation

This category covers all modes of transportation, including transit and passenger services. Data on transportation are generally obtained from the "monthly report on foreign exchange income and payments" and the "monthly report on receipts and payments for the account of nonresidents." Several items, including pipeline transit, are reported directly by individual respondents (such as pipeline operators).

SLOVENIA

Transportation

Transportation services are broken down by categories of transport (including rail and road) and services. The main source for recording transportation services is the ITRS.

Travel

The ITRS sources used in compiling the incoming travel item include (1) health- and education-related services, (2) payments made by nonresidents to Slovene tourist agencies, (3) expenditures in tolars of nonresidents, (4) money spent in casinos by nonresidents, (5) data on sales of goods to nonresidents in duty-free shops and consignment warehouses, (6) transactions with credit cards, and (7) the sales of tolars to nonresidents abroad.

The most important source—the sales of tolars to nonresidents in Slovenia—is estimated. The estimates are based on the number of nights spent by foreign travelers, the number of tourist arrivals/border crossings (from tourism statistics, compiled by the Statistical Office), and on the real effective exchange rate for the Slovene tolar.

Travel abroad consists of business and personal travel. The main source of the data is the ITRS, supplemented by adjustments to better reflect personal travel and the consumption by residents abroad. The estimates are based on the number of border crossings and average consumption. Average consumption is estimated using information from a 1993 survey of households.

SOLOMON ISLANDS

Transportation

Included here are passenger and freight services. Data are derived mainly from FET records.

Travel

Data on travel credits and debits are compiled from FET records. The disaggregation into business and personal travel is estimated from 1998.

SOUTH AFRICA

Transportation

This category covers freight and passenger services; information is obtained from the SARS, transport operators, and other organizations involved in these transactions.

Travel

Estimates are based on statistics compiled by Statistics South Africa, regarding the number of foreign tourists visiting South Africa and the number of South African tourists traveling abroad. Data are taken from periodic surveys conducted by the South African Tourism Board and from questionnaires completed during buying and selling of foreign exchange.

SPAIN

Travel

The data collection system does not allow for a breakdown by purpose of travel (business or personal). In 2005, a new estimation system was implemented for the credits (from 2000 data onwards). The new method combines the information provided by a border-spending survey with data on overnight stays in hotels and apartments and price indicators. Data for the period 1995–99 have been revised.

SRI LANKA

Transportation

This category covers all modes of transport and port services, divided into subcategories of passenger fares, freight, other (port and other) earnings and expenditure, and other related transactions.

The main source of data is the International Transactions Reporting System (ITRS) of commercial banks, which records values of transactions by purpose and currency of each transaction. In addition, for port-related services and passenger fares, CBSL obtains data from relevant institutions, using a sample survey to check the consistency of data recorded by the ITRS.

Travel

This category includes receipts and payments on official, business, medical, and educational travel. The ITRS is the main source of data. Necessary adjustments to receipts on travel are made, based on SLTB data on the number of tourist arrivals, their average duration of stay, and their average daily expenditure.

SUDAN

Transportation

Freight and passenger services. This category covers all modes of transport and port services. The BOS, the Ministry of Energy and Mining, commercial banks, and Sudan Customs are the main sources of data for freight and passenger services.

Travel

Sources are the reports of the commercial banks, hotels, and the foreign exchange bureaus; the reports include purchases of foreign currencies by residents at home and abroad and sales of Sudanese dinars to nonresidents in Sudan and abroad. The use of travelers' checks and credit cards is another source of information on travel.

SURINAME

Transportation

CBS derives transportation information from the ITRS, which provides a breakdown (i.e., sea transport, air transport, and other transportation). Adjustments are made with data received from the national airline company.

Travel

For the travel component, CBS derives data from the ITRS. Adjustments are made to include data provided by the national carrier.

SWAZILAND

Transportation

Data for transportation services are derived from the surveys of transport companies and their agencies, and supplemented by the ITRS.

Travel

These data are compiled from surveys of hotels, curio/gift shops, car hire services, travel agents, and educational institutions, which the BOP-IEO collects in conjunction with the DEO. The ITRS provides a substantial supplement to this set of statistics.

SWEDEN

Transportation

Transportation data are based on a survey compiled by Statistics Sweden.

Travel

Three sources are used: (1) reports from banks and currency dealers on sales and purchases to/from the public of banknotes and travelers' checks; the report also covers banks' sales and purchases of Swedish banknotes vis-à-vis foreign banks; (2) reports on transactions made with credit cards; the estimation is made on gross flows of Swedish banknotes exchanged abroad by travelers from Sweden and resold to the public by foreign banks; and (3) quarterly surveys covering, for example, travel agencies. A recurrent supplementary household survey serves as a basis for estimation of a split between tourism and business travel; it also supplies information for geographical breakdown estimates.

SWITZERLAND

Transportation

The data cover passenger transportation and transport services for goods exported and imported, for goods traffic through Switzerland on behalf of nonresidents, and for supporting services provided in connection with air and rail travel. The modes of transport include rail, air, sea, and transport by the Rhine fleet. The data sources are the annual and quarterly surveys carried out by the SNB.

Travel

The data cover business and personal travel, stays at health resorts and hospitals, travel related to studies, same-day travel, and transit travel, as well as adjustments for small volumes in cross-border traffic, duty-free shops, and consumption expenditure by cross-border commuters and holders of short-term residence permits. The data sources are surveys carried out by the Federal Statistical Office (FSO) and the SNB.

SYRIAN ARAB REPUBLIC

Transportation

For passenger services, CBS derives the data from information provided by the Syrian airline company (for credits) and foreign airlines (for debits). It cross-checks these data with information obtained from the foreign exchange records.

Travel

The compilers estimate travel credits using the information on the number of arriving foreign travelers, their nationality, the class of hotel, and standard expenditure samples obtained from an annual survey conducted by the Ministry of Tourism.

Compilers obtain travel debits from a similar survey, which determines typical expenditures of Syrian residents traveling abroad. The travel debits also include goods purchased abroad by Syrian travelers and recorded by Customs.

THAILAND

Transportation

For passenger services, BOT derives estimates from the ITRS and reports from Thai Airways International. For other transportation, entries are derived from the ITRS.

Travel

For travel credits, BOT compiles entries by combining the number of foreign visitors and their average length of stay, obtained from the Tourism Authority of Thailand (TAT), with adjusted estimates of average expenditures per person per day. The estimates are adjusted annually before 1999, and quarterly since, and the average expenditures per capita are based on expenditure surveys of foreign visitors carried out by the TAT.

Since 1992, BOT travel receipts have been adjusted upward by approximately 5 percent from the TAT baseline figures. This is to reflect the difference in the coverage and concepts used by the two institutions (i.e., the TAT defines the length of stay as between one and ninety days, whereas the BOT's definition is up to one year to conform with *BPM5*).

For travel debits, the central bank derives entries from foreign exchange records and quarterly surveys of Thai travelers carried out by the TAT.

THE FORMER YUGOSLAV REPUBLIC OF MACEDONIA

Transportation

The NBRM obtains data on transportation from the ITRS, allowing disaggregation by type of transportation (air, sea, rail, and road) and by category of services (freight, passenger, and other). An adjustment is made to freight debits based on the c.i.f./f.o.b. factor, and an adjustment is made to freight credits based on the difference between the statistical and the invoice value of exports.

Travel

The source of the data is the ITRS.

TOGO

Transportation

Other transportation services. Compilers record data here relating to port services and passenger services, excluding freight. Staff make entries on the basis of questionnaires sent to the port, airlines and shipping companies, domestic carriers, transit and consignment companies, etc. The data also include ticket issues, leased transportation, fueling, etc.

Travel

This component covers tourism transactions and expenditure on business travel and pilgrimages. It also covers the expenditure of Togolese students abroad. The sources of these data are the hotels, Ministry of Tourism, Directorates of Finance and of

Scholarships and Training Courses, organizations dealing with pilgrimages to the holy places, university and regional schools, etc.

TRINIDAD AND TOBAGO

Transportation

Subsumed under this category are passenger services, port services, and the provision of freight services by the national airline. Passenger fares (credit) relate to the passenger fares and excess baggage receipts accruing from nonresidents. Passenger fares (debit) pertain to similar payments by residents to foreign-owned carriers, as reported in the airline surveys. The national airline also supplies information on the value of freight services it provides to nonresidents (credit).

Travel

Compilers derive the estimates of travel credits from expenditure surveys conducted by the Central Statistical Office and from tourist arrival and departure information from the same source. Also included are estimates of expenditures by foreign students enrolled at the University of the West Indies. For travel debits, the compilers source the data from banking records.

TUNISIA

Transportation

Data are collected using periodic surveys of airlines and shipping lines operating in Tunisia, in addition to the bank settlement statements.

Travel

Operations not subject to a settlement in connection with studies and internships are obtained from surveys of the pertinent government agencies and organizations.

TURKEY

Transportation

CBRT also obtains data for passenger fares, excess baggage, and other transportation receipts and expenditures from the banks' foreign exchange records, showing them under *passenger* and *other transportation* respectively.

Travel

CBRT bases travel data on sample surveys conducted by TURKSTAT in cooperation with the Ministry of Culture and Tourism and the CBRT. These surveys cover the expenditure per capita of foreign visitors and citizens living abroad and of residents on their trips abroad. Estimates are then computed by multiplying the number of foreign visitors, citizens living abroad, and residents traveling abroad by the related average expenditure, obtained from surveys. In the surveys, business and personal travel are identified separately.

UGANDA

Transportation

This category is intended to cover all modes of transport. Passenger transportation is reported for air and road. Air passenger debits are reported with effect from January 2006 and are derived as the product of (1) the monthly number resident travelers departing from Entebbe Airport by destination provided by UBOS and (2) the average return air fare for respective destination. The average airfare is computed as the average for all airlines that fly out of Entebbe to the respective destination. No credits are reported since there is no operational resident owned airline.

Road passenger credits and debits have been revised back based on a similar methodology. In the past they have been estimated by growing a survey estimate obtained in 1995 using GDP growth. However, these data have been revised backwards for credits by multiplying the number of nonresident travelers (both arrivals and departures) through Malaba, Busia, and other border posts by the average transport fare quoted by different bus companies and the share of resident buses to the total number of buses that ply the respective route.

In the case of debits for transportation by road, passenger debits have been obtained by multiplying the number of resident travelers (both arrivals and departures) through Malaba, Busia, and other border posts by the average transport fare quoted by different bus companies and the share of nonresident owned buses to the total number of buses that ply the respective route. The average route fare is computed as the average for all buses plying the respective destination. Debit entries are the freight and auxiliary service amounts obtained after adjusting imports from c.i.f. values to f.o.b. values.

Travel

Travel (credit) estimates are projected forward from results of a survey conducted in 1993–94 for the years up to 1999. These estimates were derived from data on the number of travelers (recorded in immigration forms) with estimates for the average length of stay and the daily expenditures of foreign travelers. Figures for 1999–2002 are based on results from a survey conducted by the Ministry of Trade Tourism and Industry (MTTI) in 2001, while figures for 2003 onwards are based on results from a survey conducted by the Ministry of Trade Tourism and Industry (MTTI) in 2003 and data on travel (arrivals of nonresidents) provided by UBOS compiled from data provided by the Immigration Department.

Total travel credits are then computed as a product of the weighted average expenditure by the inward travelers computed by the MTTI and the number of travelers per quarter. The total expenditure figures have been increased to take account of expenditures by travelers who arrive through other border posts not considered by UBOS. There are currently no travel debits up to 2003, but estimates for 2004 onwards are obtained from the product of average expenditure of Ugandan residents returning from abroad obtained through surveys conducted by BOU and data from UBOS on the number of travelers.

In addition, a distinction is made between official and personal travel, based on the immigration statistics provided by UBOS. In the case of travel credits a further breakdown of personal travel into education and other personal is estimated from 2003 onwards based on surveys of nonresident students in Ugandan education institutions. The survey, however, covers a sample of secondary and tertiary institutions and omits primary education institutions, most of which provide free education under the government Universal Primary Education (UPE) for residents.

UKRAINE

Transportation

For freight and passenger services, the main sources of data are banking reports and the SSC survey of transportation companies. However, coverage is incomplete, and it is necessary to estimate missing information, especially for the debit entries. These estimates for freight are used in the conversion of data on c.i.f. imports from Customs to an f.o.b. basis.

Travel

Up to 2004, entries for this item were obtained by combining information derived from an SCSU quarterly survey on the basis of reports supplied by hotels and tour companies, and banks' reports on the purchase/sale of foreign currency and travelers' checks. Starting from 2004 the estimation of exports/imports of travel services is based on quarterly data on the number of nonresidents and Ukrainians crossing the border (classified by country and purpose of travel), average length of stay, and average expenditure per trip.

Data on the number of travelers are obtained from Ukraine's State Border Administration. Sources of data for estimating average length of stay and average expenditure per trip are the Cabinet of Ministers' regulations on the reimbursement of expenditures on business trips, SCSU survey data, data from the State Service on Tourism and Resorts of Ukraine's Ministry of Culture and Tourism, the Internet, and the mass media.

UNITED KINGDOM

Transportation

Estimates of passenger fares paid to nonresident operators are derived from the ONS International Passenger Survey.

Travel

This item covers goods and services provided to UK residents during trips of less than one year in foreign countries (and provided to nonresidents during similar trips to the UK), net of any purchases made with money earned or provided locally.

The estimates are based primarily on the IPS, which seeks information on expenditure from samples of foreign visitors leaving the UK and of UK residents returning from abroad. The survey distinguishes several purposes of visits, which are then aggregated as either business or personal.

For package tourists, estimates of the transport elements are deducted from the reported total package costs. Estimates of expenditure by UK residents on personal imports of cars are derived from the data received by HM Revenue and Customs.

UNITED REPUBLIC OF TANZANIA

Transportation

The main entry under transportation relates to freight transactions.

Travel

For travel debits, the compilers obtain data from commercial banks' exchange records and from bureaus of exchange.

For travel credits, the Ministry of Tourism and Natural Resources, in collaboration with the BoT, the National Bureau of Statistics, the Immigration Department, and the Zanzibar Commission for Tourism, conducts a tourism sector exit survey to obtain data.

UNITED STATES

Transportation

For passenger services, BEA bases estimates on data on numbers of travelers (provided by the Department of Homeland Security (DHS)) and estimates of average passenger fares (developed from a travel survey administered by the U.S. Department of Commerce (DOC)).

Travel

BEA prepares travel estimates (except for transactions with Canada and Mexico) by combining data on numbers of travelers, provided by the DHS, with estimates of average expenditures, obtained from a DOC survey of travelers. BEA derives estimates of travel transactions between the U.S. and Canada and between the U.S. and Mexico from data prepared by Statistics Canada and the Bank of Mexico.

URUGUAY

Transportation

DPF derives data for passenger fares from the annual survey of resident land, sea, and air transport companies and agents of foreign companies. It also conducts a survey of the main carriers on a quarterly basis.

Travel

For both travel credits and debits, the Ministry of Tourism compiles estimates on the basis of sample surveys of both inward and outward tourism, supplemented with data the National Migration Directorate provides on the number of travelers.

VANUATU

Transportation

This category covers freight and passenger services by all modes of transport (i.e., sea and air) and port services. Entries for transportation services are derived from information provided by airport and seaport authorities, Air Vanuatu, and stevedoring companies.

Travel

Entries for travel credits are derived from information on the number of foreign visitors, their average daily expenditures, and their average length of stay. The expenditure estimates are based on the 2005 Visitor's Survey conducted by National Statistics Office through the collaboration of the Reserve Bank of Vanuatu, the National Tourism Office, and the Tourism Council of the South Pacific and are rated forward, using CPI movements. Data on the number of visitors are obtained quarterly from migration statistics published by the Statistics Office.

Entries for travel debits are derived from an average expenditure figure provided by the Department of Finance and the residents' departure numbers from the Statistics Office. Also included is 70 percent of the value of training scholarships (the contra-entry is included in *current transfers, general government*).

VENEZUELA

Transportation

The item also includes payments for passenger transport on nonresident airlines and payments for port and airport services that the public oil industry and private airline companies make, estimated through surveys and indicators of volume of aircraft that the principal airport of the country reports.

Travel

The CBV measures credits and debits through a sample survey the INE and CBV carry out every quarter in the principal airport of the country. Compilers obtain data on average daily spending in U.S. dollars by category of traveler and reason for visit, average number of nights spent, and other indicators that allow an evaluation of the general profile of the traveler. These sample data are extrapolated by the total number of foreign visitors reported by the airports.

In addition, this category includes expenses for scholarships and missions that the public petroleum sector and nonpetroleum public sector incur abroad. The CBV validates the estimate through indicators of the activity, interviews for opinions in the principal hotels and travel agencies of the country, as well as reports and specialized.

YEMEN

Transportation

Data on debit entries for freight are estimated at 10 percent of the c.i.f. value of imports. Credit and debit entries for air transportation are derived from an airline survey. BOPD records the data it collects from airport authorities as credit entries under other air transportation, while it records data it collects from seaport authorities as credit entries under other sea transportation.

Travel

The Ministry of Tourism collects data from the immigration authorities on the number of foreign tourist arrivals. Number of tourist nights is estimated through a comprehensive survey to estimate the travel receipts. The BOPD reflects the data obtained from the Ministry of Tourism in the balance of payments statistics. Travel debits are estimated from the CBY records and the monthly international transactions reporting survey (ITRS) of commercial banks for students studying abroad, Yemeni pilgrims, and health treatments of Yemeni nationals abroad.

ZAMBIA

Transportation

Credit data comprise freight services only, which are estimated as 5.5 percent of the c.i.f value of nontraditional exports, plus data on inland freight reported by the mining companies on their metal exports.

Debits comprise estimates for freight, passenger, and other transport services. Freight debits are estimated as 10 percent of the c.i.f value of imports. Data on passenger transport and other transport services are estimated based on historical data. The BoZ plans to launch two enterprise surveys that would form the basis of compiling estimates of passenger and other transport services. These would consist of a quarterly survey of resident transportation companies and a survey of agents of nonresident airlines, primarily designed to capture data on passenger transportation.

Travel

Prior to June 1999, the BoZ compiled data on travel credits from reports the Zambia National Tourist Board (ZNTB) submitted. In June 1999 the Ministry of Tourism took over from ZNTB the task of conducting surveys of enterprises involved in providing travel services. The BoZ, collaborating with the Ministry of Tourism, has designed quarterly survey forms to capture, primarily, tourism revenues from hotels and companies involved in tours, car hire, and air charters. The first survey was launched in October of 2000 but has not been undertaken consistently, owing to a lack of funding and staff shortages.

Travel debits are estimated based on data on government employees' travel allowances and on government and quasi-government employees studying abroad. However, the BoZ is establishing reporting arrangements with the Ministry of Finance, the Ministry of Education, and the Cabinet Office for data on official expenditure on travel for purposes of education, medical, and training. In the past, this information was captured from the banks and the exchange bureau reporting system on purchases and sale of foreign exchange. However, the liberalization of the foreign exchange market in Zambia resulted in incomplete coverage. That is, banks are no longer obliged to report all their foreign exchange transactions, and ordinary customers are not legally required to declare the purpose of the foreign currency that they purchase from banks and bureaus of exchange.